FROM REVOLUTION TO ETHICS

From Revolution to Ethics

May 1968 and Contemporary French Thought

JULIAN BOURG

Second Edition

McGill-Queen's University Press
Montreal & Kingston • London • Chicago

ISBN 978-0-7735-5045-2 (paper)
ISBN 978-0-7735-5246-3 (ePDF)
ISBN 978-0-7735-5247-0 (EPUB)

Legal deposit fourth quarter 2017
Bibliothèque nationale du Québec

First edition 2007

Printed in Canada on acid-free paper that is 100% ancient forest free (100% post-consumer recycled), processed chlorine free

Funded by the Government of Canada | Financé par le gouvernement du Canada

Canada Council for the Arts | Conseil des arts du Canada

We acknowledge the support of the Canada Council for the Arts, which last year invested $153 million to bring the arts to Canadians throughout the country.

Nous remercions le Conseil des arts du Canada de son soutien. L'an dernier, le Conseil a investi 153 millions de dollars pour mettre de l'art dans la vie des Canadiennes et des Canadiens de tout le pays.

Library and Archives Canada Cataloguing in Publication

Bourg, Julian, 1969–
From revolution to ethics : May 1968 and contemporary French thought / Julian Bourg. Second edition.

Includes bibliographical references and index.
Issued in print and electronic formats.
ISBN 978-0-7735-5045-2 (paper). – ISBN 978-0-7735-5246-3 (ePDF).–
ISBN 978-0-7735-5247-0 (ePUB)

1. Social change – France – History – 20th century. 2. Social ethics – France – History – 20th century. 3. France – Moral conditions – History – 20th century. 4. France – Intellectual life – 20th century. 5. Philosophy, French – 20th century. 6. Postmodernism – France. 7. Feminism – France – History – 20th century. 8. General Strike, France, 1968. 9. Riots – France – Paris. I. Title.

DC420.B68 2017 306.094409'045 C2017-906097-X
C2017-906098-8

Typeset by Jay Tee Graphics Ltd. in Sabon 10/13

Contents

Acknowledgments vii

Abbreviations x

Preface to the Second Edition: 1968 at Fifty xi

Introduction 3

1 Cobblestone Beaches: Normative Contradictions of the May Revolt 19

PART ONE: THE SABRE AND THE KEYHOLE: FRENCH MAOISM, VIOLENCE, AND PRISONER DIGNITY

2 A Press Conference 45

3 Violence and the Gauche prolétarienne 51

4 The President's Man and the State's Thumb 61

5 Popular Justice and Incarcerated Leftists 68

6 The Groupe d'information sur les prisons 79

7 These Modern Bastilles 96

PART TWO: SPINOZA ON PROZAC: FROM INSTITUTIONAL PSYCHOTHERAPY TO THE PHILOSOPHY OF DESIRE

8 Anti-Psychiatry and the Philosophy of Desire 105

9 *Anti-Oedipus*: Redux and Reception, Ethics and Origins 112

10 Institutional Psychotherapy and the La Borde Psychiatric Clinic 125

11 Félix Guattari's Devolution 138

12 Gilles Deleuze's Spinozist Ethics 144

13 Schizophrenia and Fascism 159

14 Craziness Is a Dead End 174

PART THREE: "YOUR SEXUAL REVOLUTION IS NOT OURS": FRENCH FEMINIST "MORALISM" AND THE LIMITS OF DESIRE

15 Gender and '68: Tensions from the Start 179

16 Guy Hocquenghem's Dark Encounter with Feminism 187

17 Feminism, Law, Rape, and Leftist Male Reaction 193

18 Boy Trouble: French Pedophiliac Discourse of the 1970s 204

19 Desire Has Its Limits 219

PART FOUR: WHEN ALL BETS ARE OFF: ETHICAL JANSENISM AND THE NEW PHILOSOPHERS

20 The Main Event 227

21 Between the Union of the Left and Jansenism 247

22 Maurice Clavel 261

23 The Angel in the World 276

24 The Dialectic by the Side of the Road 289

25 John Locke Was Not French, or The Varieties of Ethical Experience 302

Conclusion 334

Notes 349

Bibliography 409

Index 449

Acknowledgments

I owe my deepest gratitude to my family – mom, dad, Jonathan, Kristen, and Steve – and my teachers – Susanna Barrows, the late Amos Funkenstein, Mary Gluck, Carla Hesse, Martin Jay, Randolph Starn, and the late Bernard Williams.

Colleagues and students at Washington University in St Louis, Bryn Mawr College, and Bucknell University helped move the manuscript along in a variety of ways. Among many, I would like to mention John Bowen, Howard Brick, David Ciepley, David Del Testa, John Enyeart, Ignacio Gallup-Diaz, John Hunter, Gerald Izenberg, Martin Jacobs, Madhavi Kale, John Kirkland, Kalala Ngalamulume, Linda Nicholson, Leslie Patrick, Michael Payne, Gary Steiner, Ann Tlusty, Sharon Ullman, Martha Verbrugee, Richard Waller, and Steven Zwicker. For interventions, I thank MQUP's anonymous readers, James Bernauer, Richard J. Bernstein, Gary Genosko, Adam Gopnik, Lynn Hunt, Stanley Hoffmann, Gene Irschick, Edward McGushin, Jeffrey Mehlman, Peter Sahlins, Jerrold Seigel, and Richard Wolin. I am indebted to the editors and staff at McGill-Queen's University Press, especially John Zucchi, Jonathan Crago, and Joan McGilvray.

In France I was fortunate to speak with a number of people who generously offered their memories and analyses of May 1968 and the 1970s. Hervé Hamon, Liane Mozère, Françoise Picq, and Jean-François Sabouret were repeatedly generous with their time and resources. I was also able to speak with Miguel Abensour, Cathy Bernheim, André Burguière, Monique Canto-Sperber, Jacques Capedevielle, Roland Castro, Christophe Charle, Jean Daniel, Régis Debray, Daniel Defert, Gil Delannoi, Vincent Descombes, Anne Dollé, Jean-Paul Dollé, François Dosse, Geneviève Fraisse, Marcel Gauchet, Gisèle Halimi, Marc Hatzfeld, Christian Jambet,

Jean Lacouture, Claude Lefort, Jacques Le Goff, Jean-Pierre Le Goff, Emmanuel Le Roy Ladurie, Bruno Latour, Michael Löwy, Robert Maggiori, Gilles Martinet, Jean-Luc Nancy, Pierre Nora, Michelle Perrot, Jean-Claude Polack, Roger-Pol Droit, Christophe Prochasson, Danielle Rancière, Jacques Rancière, René Remond, Nadja Ringart, Pierre Rosanvallon, Pierre Schapira, René Schérer, the late Laurent Schwartz, Paul Thibaud, Olivier Todd, Alain Touraine, the late Pierre Vidal-Naquet, and Michel Winock. Robert Misrahi responded to questions by mail. I thank them all for their *chaleur.*

As well as being indebted to the libraries at the institutions mentioned above, I owe a great deal to the Bibliothèque de documentation internationale contemporaine (University of Paris-X), the Bibliothèque Marguerite Durand, the Bibliothèque nationale de France, the Centre du documentation of the Mouvement français pour le planning familial, Editions Grasset, and the Institut National d'Audiovisuel. Particular thanks go to the Institut Mémoires de l'édition contemporaine and José Ruiz-Funes. This project would not have taken shape and been completed without support from the following: the Fulbright Foundation, the U.S. Department of Education, and the Woodrow Wilson Foundation; at Berkeley, The Doreen B. Townsend Center for the Humanities, the History Department, and the Institute for International Studies; the Mellon Foundation, which supported both an initial travel grant and a Postdoctoral Fellowship in Interdisciplinary Studies at Washington University in St Louis; and Bucknell University, which provided late and invaluable sponsorship. Thanks to Berghahn Books for permission to republish a version of chapter 18 that appeared in Axel Schildt and Detlef Siegfried, eds., *Between Marx and Coca-Cola: Youth Cultures in Changing European Societies, 1960–1980* (New York: Berghahn Books, 2006). Abby Miller, Deirdre Moran, and especially Sam Brawand helped inestimably with the bibliography. Jane McWhinney, a superb reader, worked wonders with the final text.

I cannot express to the following what I hope they already know. On that side of the pond, Jean-Yves Blum Le Coat, Julie Chansel, Fabienne Couvert, Paul Crouzet, Maxime Dahan, Andrea Dillon, Rosalie Foucard, Miguel Gomez, Julien Goodman, Jean-Pierre Haget, Michelle Hoffman, Charlotte de l'Escale, Rachel Levieux, Jessica Lundgren, Arnaud Lebassard, Stéphanie Lebassard, Karine Martin-Haget, and Martine Zejgman. On this side, Charlotte Avant, Alisa Berger, Gentle Blythe, Beth Bromley, Josh Burke, Judy Daniels, Michael D'Andrea, J.P. Daughton, Shea Dean, Henry Elsesser, Kath Elsesser, Amy Garland, Dan Geary, Sarah Houle, Nate Johnson, Sara Moyn, Danielle Merida, Karen Panitch, Dave

Radke, Amy Reticker, Roberta Ricci, Richard Roston, Mack Starks, Erich Strom, Jennie Sutton, and Amy Symons. Elizabeth Durden took certain chapters by the horns. I have learned many things from Sam Moyn. Véronique André gave more than she should have for this project; je serai toujours reconnaissant.

This book is dedicated to those who come next. Among others, Sarah Riley, Evan Riley, and Will Riley, as well as Finley Symons Burke, Margaux Dahan, Mahealani D'Andrea Daniels, Emma Gianni Ricci De Lucca, Ellie Elsesser, Hank Jr Elsesser, Wilbur Elsesser, Félix Legrand, Benjamin Martin, Juliette Martin, Lily Moyn, Madeleine Moyn, Nathaniel Panitch-Daughton, Henry Panitch-Daughton, Dylan Reticker Radke, Carmen Rafanell, and Rose Roston.

On days when theory grows grey, you keep green life's golden tree.

Abbreviations

APL	Agence de presse libération
CAP	Comité d'action des prisonniers
CERFI	Centre d'étude, de recherche et de formation institutionnelle
CRS	Compagnies républicaines de sécurité
FGERI	Fédération des groupes d'études et de recherches institutionnelles
FHAR	Front homosexuel d'action révolutionnaire
FLN	Front de libération nationale
GIP	Groupe d'information sur les prisons
GIS	Groupe d'information de santé
GITS	Groupe d'information des travailleurs sociaux
GP	Gauche prolétarienne
GTPSI	Groupe de travail sur la psychothérapie et sociothérapie institutionnelle
IP	Institutional Psychotherapy
MLF	Mouvement de libération des femmes
OAS	Organisation armée secrète
OPP	Organisation des prisonniers politiques
PCF	Parti communiste français
PS	Parti socialiste
SPI	Société de psychothérapie institutionnelle
SR	Secours rouge
UJC(ml)	Union des jeunesses communistes marxistes-léninistes
VLR	Vive la révolution!

Preface to the Second Edition: 1968 at Fifty

Fifty years is a long time. Those who can remember their own experiences at twenty are seventy now. Others who were "born late" grew up shadow-boxing with the legacies of the Sixties, the era symbolized by 1968. For those who have come of age more recently, all that seems as far away as the Second World War or the invention of the railroad. It was another century. Today some still wish the Sixties had never happened and that we could go back to the days before the terrible Fall; others claim that, finally out from under the shadow of '68, new social and political movements might thrive. Many people unknowingly act out dynamics and tensions of the Sixties without understanding why. For all the diverging views according to generation and perspective, much of what matters today still relates to forces unleashed in the 1960s and 1970s, from human rights to terrorism to religious politics to economic disorder to the infinite variations on life and life-style around the world. Even many contemporary political and cultural blockages stem from positions seemingly frozen in place for some fifty years. In another way, where distance has intervened and memories have faded, forgetting becomes the occasion to discover. Comparisons at the time to the revolutions of 1848, "failed" events that still help us understand the nineteenth century, make more sense than ever. On 26 June 1968, Hannah Arendt wrote to her old friend Karl Jaspers: "It seems to me that the children of the next century will once learn about 1968 the way we learned about 1848." We continue to learn. Perhaps 1968 – "the beginning of a long struggle," "the year the dream died" – is far enough away that we can see it ever more clearly. How did we get here? What are paths forward? On its fiftieth anniversary the signature year of the Sixties appears both far away and close at hand, remote and fresh.[1]

Every ten years, 1968 is commemorated. Such honouring is typically reserved for wars, marriages, disasters, or … revolutions. In this case what we often celebrate is a fundamental sense of possibility. Whether or not 1968 merits such anniversary observances is a separate issue. Every decade personal memoirs are trotted out, even as memory stretches further toward history. National histories (such as this one) continue to form a common ground of understanding. In the 1990s, 1968 could be folded into the history of the Cold War, just ended, and local and regional portraits began to emerge. The year 2008 brought new appreciation for the global, transnational Sixties and non-iconic localities and connections. The golden anniversary is a big one. Dangers of overestimating the prerogative of the present notwithstanding, we do seem further away from the events of 1968 than we did ten years ago, not only in an obvious literal sense but more importantly as a question of collective imagination. The timescale clearly looks different as I write in 2017 from how it did in 2007 when this book was published.

The crash of 2008 and then Brexit and Donald Trump in 2016 may have helped instigate a rupture that both distances us from the Sixties and may enable us to see that time anew. Economic crisis, inviting comparisons with the Great Depression, and the elections of 2016, undermining the European project and conjuring the ghosts of interwar fascism, have altered our horizons of historical thinking. Faced with deeper historical memories of capitalism in crisis and angry populism that recall the 1930s, postwar and even post–Cold War timelines no longer seem as adequate as before in appraising the Sixties. On this level, we are less and less obliged to refer to 1968. Think back to the presidential elections of 2007–08 in France and the United States: Nicolas Sarkozy calling for the "liquidation" of the legacy of 1968 and Barack Obama fending off criticism that he was friends with the Sixties radical Bill Ayers. Such melodrama seems minor compared to the subsequent economic collapse and the new populism. We should be careful, of course. Overestimating the present can obscure how the past escapes all attempts to exhaust it and remains an endless reservoir of possibilities on which to draw. Events continue to irrupt and surprise.

In other ways the circumstances of 2008 and 2016 – together with a third kind of shock event in the new century, terrorism since September 11, 2001 – bear direct connections to the Sixties. Terrorism involves a kind of violence that "we" in the West supposedly got over in the 1970s when far-left radicalism dissolved. Since then, exceptions like Utøya, Norway, aside, right-wing outsider violence in North Atlantic societies has never been taken as seriously; white people tend not to be labelled terrorists. The economic collapse of 2008, both unforeseen and inevitable, marked the apparent crisis of a cycle that also began in the 1970s: neoliberal economics rising to predominance out of that decade's stagflation crisis with which the postwar boom ended. For observers on both the left and right, the counterculture of the Sixties had abetted the rise of post-industrial capitalism. That no fundamental reforms to the casino of global finance have been made since 2008 does not alter the fact that neoliberalism may now face challenges it did not during the decades of its ascendency. So too does the phenomenon of contemporary populism relate to the Sixties in multiple ways. Anti-elitism, identity politics, and emotive attempts to represent the true "people" could already be found on the radical left during the Sixties, when the term *populism* often referred to now-distant communist peasant insurgencies. The social movements of Occupy Wall Street (U.S.), Insoumise (France), Syriza (Greece), and Podemos (Spain) are successors of this Sixties left, and the sensibilities of a Bernie Sanders or a Jeremy Corbyn come directly from that time. It is important, though, not to draw false equivalences: contemporary right-wing populism channels anti-pluralist anti-elitism into its own distinctive forms of moralizing identity politics, combining ressentiment over neoliberal globalization with fears about terrorism and rage against immigrants.[2] It repudiates decades-long trends: Brexit and far-right parties from the Netherlands to Italy to Hungary undermine post-national European cosmopolitanism; Trump's openly racist supporters reject seeming progress in race relations signalled by the Obama presidency. This is how things look in the summer of 2017.

Should all this really be laid at the feet of the Sixties? One should not exaggerate, but there seems little doubt that we are still fighting over 1968. Pieces of the puzzle of the present such as populism, neoliberalism, and the politics of terrorism were cut in the Sixties, even if they subsequently combined in unforeseen ways. In many countries, division reflects different political and cultural paths that emerged in that era. Post-1960s cultural and political conflict continually takes on new forms while remaining stubbornly locked in place. Like neighbours in an old feud, we may not remember when or how or even why we started fighting. Many urban and urbane, educated, and secular elites do show contempt for people who are not like them. Right-wing populism is not merely toxic to democracy (as if that were not enough); it also cannot deliver on its promises. And as the history of the twentieth century reminds us, nothing good comes from vitriolic nationalism. We have ended up on a road that, if it did not begin in the Sixties, at least branched there. Fifty years is nothing at all.

From Revolution to Ethics recalls other pathways that came out of the Sixties. It is a story of inspiring social action and emancipatory striving and thus a cautionary tale for those inclined to read our times only darkly. The principal themes of the book, it seems to me, continue to resonate: many people today pursue "values" that can trace their genealogy in part to 1968, principles such as openness, freedom, equality, solidarity, and dialogue – what I refer to as the ethics of liberation (7, this volume). These are powerful, not empty words, and while open to interpretation, they also inspire and guide meaningful activity all around the world. Countless persons experience the capacity, responsibility, and burden of determining how to live their lives, how to be a self among others, to relate to institutions and states, and to imagine humanity as a whole. Not everyone, to be sure, shares this fate; constraint in the form of repressive regimes, restrictive conventions, violence, poverty, and so forth is real; the refugee is a principal figure of our time. And loud voices today fantasize about returning to allegedly monolithic pasts. Yet plural striving also describes our real global historical condition as much as terrorism, neoliberalism, and populism. The fact that there is no single answer to questions posed at varied levels of experience – from the self's relationship to itself to humanity and nature as a whole – does not mean that there are not answers, efforts, and projects that share a basic sensibility: *another world is possible*. Many people realize this promise in their immediate lives and strive to establish it for others now and in the future.

This history of the present shows how French activists, writers, and thinkers in the 1970s were already grappling with how to live and thrive amid contemporary multiplicity and complexity. Why France? Because the student and worker strikes in that country during May–June 1968 were among the most potent and prominent events of the era. They opened a period of heightened social action and were linked to globally influential styles of French thought. On the level of both myth and reality, May '68 was one of the most significant happenings of the twentieth century. And French history still matters more generally. In 2017 the worldwide populist trend was repudiated with the defeat of Marie Le Pen and the Front National. For decades French people across the political spectrum have resisted neoliberal economics and its social and cultural consequences. The country has had considerable experience with terrorism, especially since the 1980s, even as it faces distinctive challenges with respect to Islamist violence (large Muslim population, militantly secular Republicanism). A populace that did not fall for the populist temptation, sustained criticisms of neoliberal capitalism, and the rejection of political violence – such characteristics, too, bear direct historical relationships to May '68 and the Sixties. Also not to be underestimated is a key fact of late-twentieth-century global cultural history: the worldwide exportation of French thinkers such as Michel Foucault, Jacques Derrida, Jean-François Lyotard, Gilles Deleuze, and others. Clustered together as "French theory" or "'68 thought" and inspiring intellectual styles such as poststructuralism and postmodernism, their ideas shaped aspects of transnational university and public life for decades. The distinctive history of France since the Sixties continues to hold lessons for those of us who are not French.

Many French activists and thinkers influenced by the events of May–June 1968 were committed to emancipatory ideas and projects. Minimally, emancipation or liberation is shorthand for the process of recognizing the fact and realizing the ideal that my freedom is tied to yours. Emancipatory politics in "the '68 years" had often been framed within a revolutionary paradigm: the quest for sudden, total historical change and a salutary new beginning. Historical dynamics unleashed by the '68 moment indeed led to a sea change; during the 1970s liberation took new forms while in many ways remaining true to the emancipatory ethos of 1968. The proof of continuity depends on how actors found alternative outlets for liberational values, desires, and goals while retaining commitments to them. The ethos of 1968 gave rise to a new paradigm: since then, ethics has been one way to describe the multitudinous ways that people strive to more fully realize principles of openness, freedom, equality, solidarity, dialogue, and so forth. Below, I will explain what I mean by ethics. For now, we can note that everywhere around the world today one finds people labouring in ways large and small to give voice to the voiceless, to reject violence, to have their and others' dignity recognized. There are many sources to these efforts; the social movements and intellectual innovations of the '68 years are among them. These then are also legacies of the Sixties: taking our own desires seriously, including the desires for recognition and fulfillment, while understanding ourselves to be part of larger wholes with others who have their own desires; attending to those who are left behind, diminished, and hurt by powerful state and economic interests; building bridges between parties who are opposed; telling states and institutions to get off our backs and, alternatively, asking them for help and to care for our needs; fighting for a common humanity and care of the environment. Such legacies form a vital counter-current to other inheritances such as terrorism, neoliberalism, and populism. They are new traditions not to be underestimated.

Looking back ten years after the book was published, four themes in particular stand out. First, social action requires effort, risk, and the demanding task of building alliances. Such lessons need to be constantly relearned, and today new generations are acquainting themselves with the possibilities and challenges of activism. One inspiring example in *From Revolution to Ethics* is the Groupe d'information sur les prisons, discussed in Part I. Involving writers, teachers, social workers, doctors, family members, and prisoners themselves, the Groupe investigated and exposed the "intolerable" conditions of French prisons. In our own era of migrant camps and the prison industrial complex (over two million prisoners in the U.S.), such attempts to illuminate the hidden corners of society need to be recalled and revived. Mobilization on behalf of others takes work and sacrifice but also the wisdom to step out of the way so that people can speak for themselves.[3] Second, we still are coming to terms with the world-historical changes of the Sixties with regard to gender and sexuality, changes whose significance may someday be measured on the scale of centuries. Part III examines the 1970s gay liberation and women's movements, focusing on debates over the meaning of the liberation of desire and campaigns against sexual violence. I highlight certain dilemmas that surfaced during the years of the sexual revolution and that we continue to face: How to be true to one's desires? Where are their limits? What do non-repressive and reciprocal intimate relationships look like? What to do about rape, sexual violence, exploitation, and harassment? Third, we remain in the orbit of the human rights and humanitarian worldviews that crystallized during the 1970s. Human rights have been an ethical as opposed to a political approach to international affairs, and as a model have yielded both notable accomplishments and abysmal failures. Looking back, the fact that fin-de-siècle humanitarianism emerged during the same years as the worldwide "return of religion" is becoming clearer. The New Philosophers discussed in Part IV pioneered the kind of media-oriented, historically pessimistic, and religiously inflected humanitarian principles that have helped shape geopolitics for decades.[4] They also demonstrated that ideas matter, our actions always determined in part by notions of what is possible or dangerous. The New Philosophers' rejection of politics, though, continues to haunt us. This last thought brings me to a fourth appreciable motif of *From Revolution to Ethics*, the suggestion with which the book concludes: the fact that ethics is not enough. Before I address this point, however, I need to explain what I mean by ethics.

The term *ethics* has a number of senses throughout this book. First, ethics (in the singular) is one kind of precise, self-conscious reflection on the normative aspects of experience. Philosophers write treatises on ethics, and by the end of this story about 1970s France one finds thinkers who explicitly placed ethics at the centre of their thinking. We will call this *ethics in general*. The key point is that around 1968 ethics in this sense was not a predominant theme in French intellectual life, and by the late 1970s and early 1980s it was. Something happened. There is little doubt that the revolutionary paradigm was reconfigured in the decades after 1968. Up for interpretation is what this transformation meant.

Second, the term *ethics* describes the substantive values of 1968, those aforementioned principles such as openness, freedom, equality, solidarity, dialogue, and so forth. Ethics (in the plural) were on display in the ethos of 1968: *the ethics of liberation*. I characterize these ethics as antinomian, from *anti-nomos*, meaning against law. The book traces how the contradictory ethics of liberation were worked through over time in their relationship to the self, intersubjectivity, institutions, the state, and humanity. For instance, the ethics of liberation helped drive the dramatic evolution of social mores during the Sixties, and such processes in turn helped lead to a revival of ethics in general.

The dynamics set in motion by the ethics of liberation point to a third, speculative meaning of the term in this book: *ethics as an explanation of historical change*. I follow the tensions and conflicts between the antinomian, immanent ethos of '68 and various kinds of transcending limits it encountered. Such tensions and conflicts drove change. Like all histories this is an interpretation, a constructed narrative. But it is also true that things really happen in history and the historian tries to show how and why they did. The model of historical change pursued here is that of immanent transvaluation, to borrow a concept from Friedrich Nietzsche. Both continuities and changes were involved as the largely implicit *ethics of liberation* transformed into explicit *ethics in general*. As the antinomian ethos of 1968 engaged different limits, its means of expression altered, the star of revolution set, and that of ethical fascination rose. I rely throughout on such naturalistic metaphors: tides coming in and out, caterpillars metamorphosing into butterflies, etc. In sum, the reader should be aware at the outset of the multilayered uses of the term *ethics*, uses that complicate the simple argument of the book and push the story out into the general intellectual, cultural, social, and political history of France during the 1970s.

There remains the question, *why* ethics? The biography of the book provides a partial answer. The dissertation on which it is based was written 1998–2001, but the questions that motivated it emerged when I was an undergraduate during the late 1980s and early 1990s, closer to 1968 than we are now. In a way *From Revolution to Ethics* is already thirty years old.

Like others in my peer group, as a student I was deeply influenced by French theory.[5] Such ideas offered some of us avenues of critical thought in a moment of foreclosed political possibility. The Sixties cast a shadow over Generation X (as someone said, a cohort that used to blame things on the Baby Boomers and now blames things on Millennials). It was an oddly common experience: nostalgia for an era through which one had not lived. French theory's focus on language, textuality, power, desire, theoretical practice, and so forth provided a vocabulary with which to come to terms with the United States of the Reagan-Bush years. French thought, which seemed both exotic and familiar, energized. Yet I was also uncomfortable with unresolved questions: If everything was language or power, how were social movements possible? What of progress and emancipation? At the time, more serious minds were also wondering about the normative contradictions of poststructuralist and postmodern thought. The issue of ethics thus emerged for me as a genuine problematic. When it came time to write a dissertation, this question became linked to another: What was the story of Foucault, Derrida, et al. in the historical context in which some of their most influential ideas had germinated – namely France in the 1960s and 1970s? Historical study seemed to offer a way to approach the fact that the Anglo-American reception of French theory played fast and loose with varied thinkers. Such were the original warrants for the project. In truth, as is often the case, the dissertation and eventual book turned out very different from how they were originally conceived. Spending time in France, in archives and listening to people's memories of the Sixties, pushed the project in directions beyond a focus on ideas alone. The book expresses the historical moment in which it was conceived and written even as it reconstructs the post-1968 years.

Let me return to the fourth theme mentioned above: ethics is not enough.[6] "Ethics is a necessary and yet thoroughly insufficient condition for social and political life [that] can never take the place of genuine political analysis and mobilization," I wrote in conclusion, linking this critical point to the post-1968 revitalization of civil society, the search for healthy forms of conflict that keep the "democratic wager" alive, and the need for "citizens who are willing to take the risks of engagement and confrontation" (345–7, this volume). At the time others were amplifying the critique of contemporary ethical fascination that is now more widespread than ever. To take one example, already in 2004 Jacques Rancière had denounced the "ethical turn" for its "indistinction": "the kind of thinking in which an identity is established between an environment, a way of being, and a principle of action." Where ethics pointed toward "an unprecedented dramaturgy of infinite evil, justice, and reparation" focused on past traumas, in contrast politics could envision divisions between oppression and the oppressed, concrete injustice and justice, and thus the possibility of futures where domination would bend to emancipation. In invoking the ethical turn, Rancière had in mind human rights and humanitarianism; privileging outsiders, victims, and Others; consensus (as opposed to political "dissensus"); and even George Bush's initial name for post–September 11 action in Afghanistan, "Operation Infinite Justice."[7] One might add the return of religion in the late twentieth and early twenty-first centuries, from political Islam and religious Zionism to fundamentalist Christianity, Catholic integralism, and Hindu nationalism. Such a situation indeed seems a far cry from the emancipatory aspirations and ethos of 1968 – the era in which Rancière himself came of age.

Yet such critiques of the ethical turn, with which I tend to agree, are also incomplete. Rancière's own notion of politics itself drew on simplistic formulas of the past, and his suggestion that the divisions or "cuts" of politics are "always ambiguous, precarious, and litigious" can also be applied to the ethical turn.[8] This book might have been called *From Revolution to the Pursuit of Emancipation beyond Politics Alone*, but even that would not capture the point. In short, two things are true at once: the ethical turn bore certain continuities with the emancipatory ethos of 1968, and it is important to criticize and move beyond it. This seems a properly dialectical approach to grasping where we are historically, how we got here, and how to move forward, the unrealized possibilities of roads not taken as well as undervalued resources ready at hand. Merely denouncing the ethical turn is only a half measure. In a thoughtful and rigorous review of *From Revolution to Ethics*, Knox Peden noted of my concluding, glancing critical position that it was "curious" that I was "brokering such a distinction [between ethics and politics] so late in the game" when the book had "done so much to compromise the notions of ethics and politics as potentially exclusive historical categories." He usefully observed an "interminable ... ambivalence" that might frustrate some readers but that also remains faithful to a complex historical story.[9] Paradoxically, ethics can be interpreted both as leading to anti- or non-political stances and as a way of framing the political itself. Here we are: simplistic narratives, political or moral, cannot do justice to the complexity and plurality of our world-historical condition; we are all porcupines to some and hedgehogs to others (343, this volume). And at the same time history does have sides; domination and oppression exist.

Ethics alone, for instance, offers little response to neoliberalism; if anything, they often fit hand in glove.[10] "It is exceedingly difficult to adjudicate," writes Alberto Toscano, "the difference between the values that shore up a new spirit of capitalism and the ethical contributions to liberal democracy that revolutionaries brought about largely despite themselves."[11] Likewise, it is important to make the qualitative distinction between populism's noxious jingoisms and dangerous cults of personality, on the one hand, and democratic equality and fairness, on the other hand.

The challenge, of course, is to articulate how and why such distinctions are drawn and then to successfully mobilize social action around them. Democracy as an ideal, a way of life, and a system of governance includes both political ethics and ethical politics. There is little doubt that "genuine politics of struggle and collective enunciation" (347, this volume) remain both needed and elusive in our historical moment. By the same token, it is also true that without the lodestar of ethical orientation, struggle and collective enunciation themselves can get lost. Western militaries and jihadists also struggle; populism likewise reflects collective enunciation. Simply asserting moral norms is not enough either, for ethics speaks to practical and theoretical plurality. What "1968" promised and continues to promise is a world not compelled by market utopianism, terror/counter-terror, religious fundamentalism, and the tyranny of the crowd. *From Revolution to Ethics* presents a history that exceeds purely political categories and leaves other problems unresolved. It focuses on the political and cultural left, which one character in this story, Maurice Clavel, defined as those who prefer justice to order. Needless to say, the difficult task is to create orders that are just. One of the principal accomplishments of the Sixties was to have multiplied and expanded the sites and means of emancipation: new forms of freedom for the self, emergent possibilities for mutuality and equality in interpersonal relationships, greater lived awareness of how institutions and laws can both liberate and constrain, the pursuit of recognition and fulfillment in spaces below, including, and beyond the state. One might approach the actors, movements, and ideas in this book as imperfect and distant examples as well as inspiring and relevant models: those denouncing prison conditions and asserting prisoner dignity, liberating desire from shame and guilt, mobilizing against sexual violence, rejecting politics as usual for the sake of a critique of injustice everywhere, reflecting on human beings' "relationship" and "obligation" to one another (Jean-Paul Sartre) and on "the conscious practice of freedom" (Foucault) (5, this volume).

From Revolution to Ethics appeared shortly before the fortieth anniversary of 1968 and contributed to a largely unanticipated publication frenzy, not least on the French events of May–June 1968.[12] The book did not resonate in France where, as is well known, the notion of French theory has never made much sense; its concern for ethics intersected disjointedly with French debates on the Sixties in 2008 understandably pushing away from the Parisian student milieu toward other locales and especially toward social and labour history. So too, in part because it had been conceived in another time, the book's attention to a single country was out of step with a new focus on the global Sixties, and its consideration of intellectual life and ideas also contrasted with the emphases of many studies. Expectedly, some Anglo-American scholars remain more interested in applying and extending the theoretical insights of French theory than in the much more prosaic task of situating and explaining – historicizing – ideas. I say all this to emphasize one of the virtues of *From Revolution to Ethics*: it does not fit. Triangulating a number of different approaches to the Sixties, its unconventional, even marginal approach opens up new spaces.

A book is fulfilled by its readers, especially critical ones.[13] Many reviews phrased things more clearly than I had. James Winders compared the cumulative effect of the book to the "slow emergence of a photograph in a darkroom"; Bénédicte Delorme-Montini said that ethics were present in a "latent state" in the "unconscious of May." Some (Breckman, Delorme-Montini, Moyn, Toscano) latched onto the political issue discussed above. While noting "a dogged ambivalence on political questions," Peden was persuaded that "Maoism was a democratizing impulse in France"; the impersonal and immanent category of the "intolerable" enabled "institutional mediation." Re-reading the book now, I am struck by how much the state is everywhere in it: as a foil, target, and recourse for emancipation. Others (Horn, Leslie, Schneider) tended to bring their own assumptions about ethics to the table; yet the categories of "the individual," "rights," and the "unlimited rights to the individual," for instance, were not the culminating meaning of the historical field. Indeed, one of the main points is that a simplistic Marxism-to-liberalism tale is not accurate. If liberalism is a species, liberation is not just a genus; it is a domain. A principal complaint was that the book was too "teleological," meaning that the beginning predetermined the end (Breckman, Jackson, Moyn). I understand why readers might have this impression: naturalistic metaphors (caterpillars to butterflies), the reconstruction of the immanent logics of change-in-continuity, and the ironies and "cunning" of history were involved. It is hard to write history without a little Hegel; all books reach their conclusions. However, my intention was closer to Nietzschean immanent transvaluation than to totalizing Hegelianism. There was nothing preordained or necessary about what transpired; things might have turned out otherwise. Since the ethical turn happened, though, one is left with the challenge of showing how it did and explaining why. Some historians' appropriate disciplinary commitments to contingency and representation have made them hesitant to answer such questions (beyond the conventional go-to interpretation that dominant power always manipulates). Curiously, in contrast to worries about teleology, others found the "*petites histoires* ... more compelling than the grand narrative" (Judaken, also Peden and Reader). Moyn expressed both positions: on the one hand, he wondered if I tried to solve "empirical uncertainty" (why did one trajectory win out among others?) by suggesting that things were "fated by foreordained necessity"; on the other hand, he found "dubious [the] idea that a huge panoply of different moves harmonized at all." Coherence without fate is plausible, but as author I am responsible for any failure to convince. Ulrich Johannes Schneider, who would have preferred a more internalist history of ideas, helpfully pointed out that intellectuals in this book appear as "speakers" as well as "thinkers." Finally, a line by Esther Leslie stays with me. For her, this is a story of those "who lived and thought and fought, then lived and thought and fought some more." She meant it critically, but I take it to bind together the book's personages with its readers.

What would I do differently now? There is a list – engaging other dimensions of feminism and gay liberation in Part III; giving Emmanuel Levinas, Vladimir Jankélévitch, and Paul Ricoeur more attention (I had run out of gas); including environmentalism; etc. – but the main change I would make would be to Part II. I was somewhat unfair to Gilles Deleuze and Félix Guattari, who would not have appreciated my genealogical approach to their collaboration. Moreover, my own judgments of the anti-Oedipal project detracted from historicizing it more deeply. An interest in psychoanalysis, concern about links between vitalism and Nazism – whatever the reasons, I ended up more critical than necessary of Deleuze and Guattari's immanent vitalism. My worry about "literal" schizophrenics was itself a bit "paranoid," as the authors would have said. Moyn, for instance, was right to point out the tension between ethics as a historical actor's category and as an author's position. In this case, I tended to moralize. Alan Schrift indicated a missed opportunity: more might have been made of Deleuze's own contrast between ethics and morality. Not that the contradictions and problems I identified were not real. Rather, it would have been better to say: the anti-Oedipal philosophy of desire was a theoretical high-water mark of the antinomian ethics of liberation, and some in the historical field – psychiatrists, feminists, the New Philosophers, Foucault – criticized it themselves. I also now see more clearly than before the need to take seriously Foucault's 1977 statement that *Anti-Oedipus* was the "first book of ethics to be written in France in quite a long time" by which he meant the project of fighting the "fascism in us all, in our heads and everyday behavior": our own love of power and domination, our own desires to be subjugated by others (171–2, this volume). At stake is the possibility of non-fascistic dispositions and ways of being. Such a prospect seems more vital than ever.

What, then, to make of 1968 at fifty? Consider an analogy. The philosopher Ricoeur and historian Foucault each separately described Karl Marx, Nietzsche, and Sigmund Freud as having founded traditions of critical thought that have led in myriad unanticipated directions. With them, Foucault said, interpretation became an "infinite task."[14] For many generations now, extensions and variations on Marx's, Nietzsche's, and Freud's ideas have far surpassed what they wrote, their thought serving as wellsprings, generous sources that continue to flow. Likewise, perhaps ideas and forms of social action from the Sixties have been similarly generative, exceeding their original moment and giving rise to multitudinous projects and ways of being that ultimately cannot be stopped or held back. In lieu of what Ricoeur called the "hermeneutics of suspicion," could one refer to a critical hermeneutics of emancipation? Did an era open distinguished in part by multiplicity and open-endedness? There are many temporalities to 1968: generation, memory and forgetting, beginnings and endings, fatigue, commemoration, eventfulness, historicization, repetitions, reservoirs of possibilities, family feuds, extended timelines that reach forward to today and back into the pre-1968 past. Such temporalities give us relief. They turn our attention away from our frantic present, providing perspective (a notion no less true for being trite) and, more importantly, resources. Insofar as one reaches for its sense of possibility and embraces what is alive, fifty years later 1968 is still, as the opening epigraph by Michel de Certeau says, "*becoming* an event."

If it might be too much to observe a swing of the pendulum back from ethics to revolution, the latter term is certainly back among activists, academics, and even mainstream politics (Sanders, Corbyn, even Emmanuel Macron).[15] Powerful words like revolution can never entirely escape their prior meanings even if they are not held to them. There are more stirrings of left-wing and radical politics than a decade ago, from writing and rethinking to the reacquisition of organizational and street protest know-how. Reflecting on the Sixties may be newly worthwhile, and histories such as *From Revolution to Ethics* make a difference. The past matters, and the future is undetermined. Today, if one knows how to listen, there are intimations, murmurs of possibilities. One hears them wherever people conceive and create a world beyond terrorism and militarism, elitism and mass rage, the reduction of human beings to market relations, and environmental degradation. To learn from the past, to think, and to act in concert – these are the best means by which to increase our familiarity with that elusive pronoun: we.

July 2017

NOTES

1 On the multiple times and spaces of 1968, as well as references to the above citations, see my "Writing on the Wall: 1968 as Event and Representation," in *Scripting Revolution: A Historical Approach to the Comparative Study of Revolutions*, ed. Keith Michael Baker and Dan Edelstein (Stanford: Stanford University Press, 2015). For a snapshot of the annus mirabilis see Bourg, "1968," in *A Dictionary of Cultural and Critical Theory*, ed. Michael Payne and Jessica Rae Barbera, 2nd ed. (Malden, MA: Wiley-Blackwell, 2010), 491–6.

2 Jan-Werner Müller, *What Is Populism?* (Philadelphia: University of Pennsylvania Press, 2016), 2–3, 7, 19, 21, 101–2. John B. Judis, *The Populist Explosion: How the Great Recession Transformed American and European Politics* (New York: Columbia Global Reports, 2016).

3 Perry Zurn and Andrew Dilts, ed., *Active Intolerance: Michel Foucault, the Prisons Information Group, and the Future of Abolition* (Houndmills, UK: Palgrave, 2016). Groupe d'information sur les prisons, *Intolérable*, ed. Philippe Artières (Paris: Gallimard, 2013).

4 On Bernard-Henri Lévy's itinerary from the 1970s to the present see Bourg, "From the Left Bank to Libya: The New Philosophy and Humanitarianism," in *Human Rights and Humanitarian Intervention: Legitimizing the Use of Force since the 1970s*, ed. Norbert Frei, Daniel Stahl, and Annette Weinke (Göttingen: Wallstein Verlag, 2017).

5 The following draws on Bourg, "Response Essay," *H-France Forum* 4, no. 3 (Fall 2009): 78–89.

6 Some still look favourably on the ethical turn. Antonio Y. Vásquez-Arroyo, *Political Responsibility: Responding to Predicaments of Power* (New York: Columbia University Press, 2016), ch. 2. Dave Boothroyd, *Ethical Subjects in*

Contemporary Culture (Edinburgh: Edinburgh University Press, 2013), ch. 1.

7 Jacques Rancière, "The Ethical Turn of Aesthetics and Politics" [2004], in *Aesthetics and Its Discontents* (Cambridge: Polity, 2009), 110 and passim.

8 Ibid., 132.

9 Knox Peden, "The Maoist March through the Institutions," *Radical Philosophy* 149 (May–June 2008): 46–9, citation from 49.

10 Peter Bloom, *The Ethics of Neoliberalism: The Business of Making Capitalism Moral* (New York: Routledge, 2017).

11 Alberto Toscano, "Beginnings and Ends: For, Against, and Beyond '68," *New Formations* 65 (Autumn 2008): 94–104, citation from 102.

12 Robert Gildea, "Forty Years On: French Writing on 1968 in 2008," *French History* 23, no. 1 (2009): 108–19. Daniel A. Gordon, "History at Last? 1968–2008," *Modern & Contemporary France* 17, no. 3 (August 2009): 335–42; "Memories of 1968 in France: Reflections on the 40th Anniversary," in *Memories of 1968: International Perspectives*, ed. Ingo Cornils and Sarah Waters (Oxford: Peter Lang, 2010). Julian Jackson, "The Mystery of May 1968," *French Historical Studies* 33, no. 4 (Fall 2010): 625–53.

13 Bénédicte Delorme-Montini, "Régards extérieurs sur 1968," *Le Débat* 149 (March–April 2008): 66–82. Alan Schrift, review, *Philosophy in Review* 28, no. 2 (April 2008): 86–9. Peden, "The Maoist March through the Institutions." Moyn, review, *The Sixties: A Journal of History, Politics and Culture* 1, no. 1 (June 2008): 93–6. James A. Winders, review, *The American Historical Review* 113, no. 3 (June 2008): 928–9. Keith Reader, review, *Modern and Contemporary France* 16, no. 3 (August 2008): 351–2. Toscano, "Beginnings and Ends." Warren Breckman, review, *The Journal of Modern History* 81, no. 1 (March 2009): 207–9. Gerd-Rainer Horn, review, *Le Mouvement social* 228 (July–September 2009): 183–4. Esther Leslie, review, *Intellectual History Review* 19, no. 3 (2009): 386–7. Jonathan Judaken, review, *H-France Forum* 4, no. 3 (Fall 2009): 73–9. Ulrich Johannes Schneider, review, *French Politics, Culture & Society* 28 (2010): 135–8. Julian Jackson, "The Mystery of May 1968." I agree with Michael Scott Christofferson much more than before. Christofferson, review, *H-France Forum* 4, no. 3 (Fall 2009): 61–8. Bourg, "Response Essay."

14 Michel Foucault, "Nietzsche, Freud, Marx" [1964], in *Essential Works of Foucault 1954–1984*, vol. 2, *Aesthetics, Method, and Epistemology*, ed. James D. Faubion, tr. Robert Hurley et al. (New York: New Press, 1998), 274. Paul Ricoeur, "The Conflict of Interpretations" [1962], in *Freud and Philosophy: An Essay on Interpretation*, tr. Denis Savage (New Haven: Yale University Press, 1970).

15 Emmanuel Macron, *Révolution* (Paris: xo Éditions, 2016). In his July 2017 Versailles discourse, Macron said that "progressivism is … a shared ethics of action and responsibility." http://www.elysee.fr/declarations/article/discours-du-president-de-la-republique-devant-le-parlement-reuni-en-congres. He commented in a 2015 interview that his mentor Ricoeur represents "another path from May '68." Macron, *Macron par Macron* (La Tour d'Aigues, France: Éditions de l'Aube, 2017), 22.

Figure 1. One version of the May 1968 graffiti "It is forbidden to forbid." Here, the legal notice "Défense d'afficher" [Post No Bills] has been rewritten to prohibit prohibition. © Bruno Barbey/Magnum Photos.

Figure 2. Students throwing paving stones on 6 May 1968 at Place Maubert-Mutualité. © Jean-Pierre Tartrat/Gamma Presse.

Figure 3. Workmen repairing Boulevard St-Germain on 7 May 1968 near the café Les Deux Magots. Sand beneath the paving stones. A beach? © Agence France Presse/Getty Images.

Figure 4. The Sorbonne courtyard on 14 May 1968. Louis Pasteur holds a red flag. © Bruno Barbey/Magnum Photos.

Figure 5. The same Sorbonne courtyard (from the left) on 25 May 1968. Tracts and newspapers burn in a pile. A stoic Victor Hugo is joined by Karl Marx, Vladimir Lenin, and Mao Tse-tung. © Guy Le Querrec/Magnum Photos.

Figure 6. Groupe d'information sur les prisons demonstration walking through the Cour Vendôme en route to the Ministère de la Justice on 17 January 1972. In the background in front of the middle column is René Schérer; in front of the right-hand column is André Glucksmann. To his immediate right in the centre is Claude Mauriac. Michel Foucault, Jean-Paul Sartre, and Michelle Vian are walking together. In the foreground left to right are Alain Jaubert, Gilles Deleuze, and Daniel Defert. © Elie Kagan/BDIC.

Figure 7. Following the demonstration, Foucault and Sartre held a press conference at the Agence de presse libération. © Elie Kagan /BDIC.

Figure 8. Gilles Deleuze and Félix Guattari. © Xavier Martin.

Figure 9. René Schérer and Guy Hocquenghem. 9 June 1987. © Sophie Bassouls/CORBIS SYGMA.

Figure 10. Nadja Ringart (left) in 1970 working on the Mouvement de libération des femmes paper, *Le Torchon brûle* [*The Burning Dish Towel*]. Ringart co-authored with Françoise Picq the June 1971 article, "Your Sexual Revolution Is Not Ours," which appeared in the Maoist paper, *Tout!* © Martine Franck/Magnum Photos.

Figure 11. "Ten Hours Against Rape" meeting held by the Mouvement de libération des femmes at the Mutualité meeting hall on 26 June 1976. © Martine Franck/Magnum Photos.

Figure 12. Mouvement de libération des femmes posters from the mid-1970s anti-rape campaign. © Bibliothèque Marguerite Durand.

Figure 13. Bernard Pivot (left), host of the literary television round table, *Apostrophes*, with Maurice Clavel. This 27 May 1977 broadcast was entitled "The New Philosophers: Are They on the Left or the Right?" © Sophie Bassouls/CORBIS SYGMA.

Figure 14. The same broadcast. Seated left to right, Clavel, Bernard-Henri Lévy, and André Glucksmann. Also participating were François Aubral and Xavier Delcourt. © Sophie Bassouls/CORBIS SYGMA.

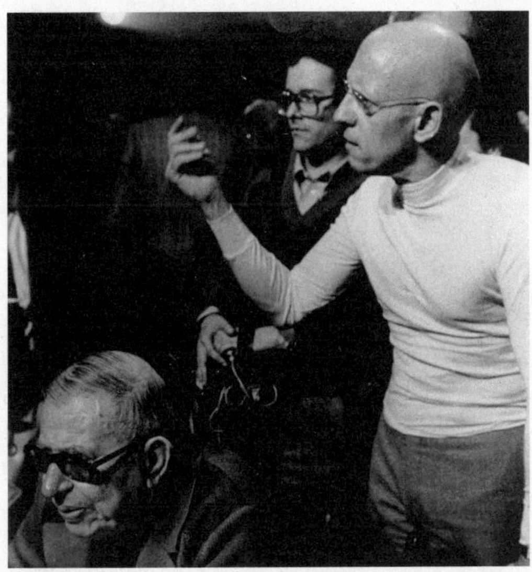

Figure 15. Jean-Paul Sartre and Michel Foucault at a reception for Soviet and Eastern European dissidents at the Théâtre Récamier on 21 June 1976. The event was designed to counter Leonid Brezhnev's concurrent state visit to France. Other participants included Roland Barthes, Simone de Beauvoir, Gilles Deleuze, André Glucksmann, Benny Lévy, and Laurent Schwartz. © Despatin-Gobeli/Fonds Michel Foucault/IMEC.

Figure 16. Vladimir Jankélévitch at a 7 December 1981 demonstration at the Soviet embassy in Paris in support of dissident Andrei Sakharov then on a hunger strike. Martial law was declared in Poland six days later. © Patrick Zachmann/Magnum Photos.

FROM REVOLUTION TO ETHICS

Perhaps May '68 is *becoming* an event in that we are required to *make* less of it ... The true literature about May 1968 is already less (and will soon cease to be) the literature that talks about it. After a first span of time, that of the chroniclers and of defensive or apologetic reactions, after a second span of time of analyses centred on the event, comes a third one of self-reflection for each human science and each institution ... A surfeit of strategies, methodologies, and epistemologies picks up where the last episodes of the "May '68" soap opera left off. They are no longer attracted to the historical object but to the instruments of thought and of action that it brought forth.

Michel de Certeau (1969)

We need to find real limits, but writing a literature that "shocks" will not get us there. This society is in the end not very "shockable." Our enemy, on the contrary, is this consumer society, this freedom that devalues everything. It is by constructing certain criteria more than by breaking taboos that we can move forward. Now, all criteria, all moral thought are devalued. As Friedrich Nietzsche said, the danger is nihilism. Nihilism advertised as something liberating.

Doesn't that connect with an essential thing [Alexandr] Solzhenitsyn has taught us, that morals and ethics, far from being something repressive, could be points of resistance, the only possible subjective position for resisting power?

Exactly. We're taking up here a very devalued term. We were so caught up with the idea of the intellectual terrorist who shattered taboos, for whom the moral was nothing other than bourgeois morality. At the same time, we kept our idea of the moral for the "other side," for socialism, communism, anarchism, for an ideal society. But in our society, we were against ethics. That's an awful thing. Because if you follow this guide wire of ethics you encounter many things, many limits. Limits are less in expression than in principles. This society is a hypocritical society; it's necessary to unmask that hypocrisy, but not under the flag of nihilism. The [Russian and Eastern European] dissidents have a very moralizing discourse. Our society has its own very amoral discourse: happiness, purchasing power, consumption. We find ourselves caught between these two terms: nihilism and consumption.

Susan Sontag, Interview with Guy Scarpetta (1978)

Introduction

On 22 May 1968, there was no weather in Paris. The weathermen were all on strike. That same day professional athletes unfurled a banner on their stadium that read, in a playful Marxist tease, "Soccer to the soccer players." The mostly female employees at the major department stores in the capital left their posts but not the premises, which they occupied. In Lyon, workers at the Berliet factory climbed out onto the marquee and rearranged the name of their company to spell *liberté*. Novelists Michel Butor and Nathalie Sarraute joined others in taking over the Société des Gens de Lettres de France, an organization dedicated since the nineteenth century to protecting authors' rights. That same day, by only eleven votes, the National Assembly defeated a measure that would have censured the government and effectively called for new elections. Later that night, the representatives passed a resolution granting amnesty to students arrested in riots that had exploded earlier in the month.

In the afternoon, President Charles de Gaulle announced a seemingly ill-conceived television address for two days later, when he would propose a yea-or-nay national referendum on his government. His plan would be briefly ridiculed as straw-grasping by an old, out-of-touch man – briefly, that is, before the prevailing winds soon shifted to his advantage. Also that afternoon, student leader Daniel Cohn-Bendit, who a day earlier had declared that the "tricolour flag must be torn up to make a red one," was refused re-entry into France after a short trip to Germany. News of his interdiction quickly spread, sparking violence in the centre of Paris that lasted until four in the morning and led to sixty-five arrests. By 22 May 1968 the popular revolt unleashed by French university students three weeks earlier had become the largest general strike in twentieth-century Europe, as six or seven million professional and blue-collar workers had stopped working. The major labour unions declared (also on 22 May) that they were ready to negotiate with the government. It was yet another day in the electric eight weeks between May 2nd and June 30th when a modern Western democratic nation seemed to court the possibility of a leftist revolution.[1]

What is remarkable about "the events" [*les événements*], as the student and worker revolts came to be called, is that many people believed at the time that a monumental social and political revolution might be underway. The feeling was shared by both friends and foes of the "French Revolution of 1968." The country was turned upside down by spontaneous and sometimes carnivalesque revolt, and many participants later recalled how liberating it had been to talk to strangers in the street, where the rules of everyday life were suspended. That spring, de Gaulle himself noted that "France never carries out reforms except in the course of a revolution." Still today, despite the brief effervescence of the actual happening, French public opinion polls continue to treat it as the most important episode in French history since the Nazi Occupation.[2]

And yet, as every historian of the events must note in his or her second breath, by the beginning of June the tide had turned. Elections at the end of the month gave de Gaulle more power than he had previously held, and by the time the warm vacation days of August arrived, order had been restored. For some, May–June 1968 (I will throughout refer to "May" as a shorthand) passed into memory, but for those who wanted to "continue the fight," it soon became a touchstone, a rallying cry, and a myth. In spite of their immediate outcome, the events opened – symbolically and in fact – an era of radical agitation and cultural and political upheaval that reached fever pitch in the early 1970s before dropping off sharply around 1974. In many ways, though, the "'68 years" – *les années soixante-huit* – continued until the May 1981 election of François Mitterrand as president, creating a period that historian Pascal Ory refers to as "between the two Mays." It was possible during those years to decide that the May revolution, judged according to what it promised and what it subsequently delivered, apparently turned out to be a failure. In 1981 the former editor of *Esprit*, Jean-Marie Domenach, could ask with genuine – if forlorn – curiosity, "Why did the terrific explosion of May '68 change society so little?"[3]

On the contrary. In the years after 1968, France did experience a revolution. In 1968 that word – *revolution* – was on everyone's lips. By the early 1980s and especially by the 1990s, everywhere one turned, there was talk of *ethics*. What had been revolutionized was the very notion of revolution itself.

This book tells the story of how ethics became increasingly fascinating to French activists, liberal professionals, and intellectuals in the years following the events of 1968. My narrative follows the arc of this turn to ethics. Like the previous decade, the 1970s was a time of significant, far-reaching change, popular social and political movements, cultural transformation, and intellectual innovation. After 1968 *ethics* gradually became a preferred term, lens, and framework for grappling with many aspects of life: from interpersonal relationships (especially matters of desire, sex, and gender) to institutions (universities, prisons, and psychiatric hospitals) to politics (violence, law, the state, and human rights). Before 1968 the tides of interest in ethics had been receding. After that year they began to come back in. By the early 1980s a paradigm shift had occurred. Even though the ethical turn had multiple sources, and even if 1968 had other consequences, one of the "gifts" – with all the ambiguity that term implies – of May 1968 has been ethical fascination.[4] There is no better sign of the indirect and complicated process underway from the late 1960s to the early 1980s than one of May 1968's celebrated graffitied slogans – *It is forbidden to forbid* – a paradoxical subtext of this book.

From Revolution to Ethics is not a history of ethics but the history of a phenomenon. My aim is twofold: to show *that* a turn to ethics occurred, and to demonstrate *how* and *why* it did. This is not to say that ethics was not a concern before 1968; in some circles, it certainly had been. Yet the preponderance of references to ethics in post-1968 France demonstrates a historic sea change and paradigm shift. In 1993 Cornelius Castoriadis wrote: "For approximately the past twenty years we have witnessed an apparent return to the offensive of a discourse that makes ethics its paramount authority."[5] Jean-Paul Sartre and Michel Foucault, for example, in their final years, assigned ethics a primacy it had not previously held in their thought. In a 1980 interview Sartre said: "Essentially, ethics is a matter of one person's relationship to another ... By 'ethics' I mean that every consciousness, no matter whose, has a dimension that I didn't study in my philosophical works and that few people have studied, for that matter: the dimension of obligation."[6] And in 1984 Foucault commented: "For what is ethics, if not the practice of freedom, the conscious practice of freedom? ... Freedom is the ontological condition of ethics. But ethics is the considered form that freedom takes when it is informed by reflection."[7] Although they each meant something different by the term, neither thinker had previously afforded ethics such pride of place. Their individual "turns" exemplified a broader development as the theme became explicitly foregrounded in qualitatively and quantitatively distinctive ways. Lending itself to a variety of instrumentalizations, ethics became a leitmotif of the late twentieth century.

Beyond demonstrating that an ethical turn occurred, I offer an interpretation and explanation of how and why it did. In examining May 1968 and the dynamics that followed in its wake, it becomes clear that the seeds of post-1968 ethical fascination were already present in 1968, and that the ethical turn reflected a transvaluation of May's contestatory energies. Through a gradual change-in-continuity, the 1970s achieved a self-consciousness about ethics and proliferating uses of that term. Insofar as the turn to ethics was a development, it marked a shift from the implicit to the explicit, from the unconscious to the self-conscious, and from the potential to the flowering. The ethical turn incorporated a number of overlapping, perhaps seemingly contradictory factors: a "turn" in the sense of a new currency given the ethical, a "return" in the sense of the revival of ethics, and a metamorphosis involving both continuity and discontinuity of 1968's implicit ethics of liberation. Overall, May 1968 set in motion dynamics that oscillated between two poles – ethos and law/limit – that led to an explicit foregrounding of the question of ethics.

Granted, the language of ethics was almost entirely absent among the actors of the May events.[8] But, as we note in chapter 1, those events had many sides. Alongside reform-minded protestors and officials responding with moderation, many protagonists still spoke the language of "revolution." Workerist rhetoric unquestionably predominated in 1968, and the marxisant tradition's longstanding suspicion toward ethics, morality, and other forms of value-talk was reinforced. If one spoke of "norms" in 1968, one did so mostly to criticize and reject them. Norms were the smoke and mirrors of bourgeois culture – consumer society, work, nationalism, family, religion, and morality – to be dispelled by the revolution. However, the worldview of a class-based revolution proved ill-equipped to capture the complexity of the era's contestatory spirit. The rhetoric of revolution often concealed non-revolutionary, democratic substance. But in 1968, electoral politics centred on the state also seemed inadequate. The ethics of liberation accordingly emerged in those social spaces where class-based revolutionary – and even reformist – politics were judged insufficient. For example, the popular statement "the personal is political" was in essence eminently ethical; 1968 itself implied an ethics, the ethics of liberation, with both critical and affirmative sides.

One of the most important aspects of May 1968 was its manifestation of an antinomian revolt against norms. The word "antinomian" can be traced back to the sense given it by sixteenth-century Protestantism; namely, that moral law is not binding on Christians who experience grace. In general the term means a rejection of laws of various kinds – *anti-nomos* – and it is important here because 1968 unleashed an antinomian *ethos* that served as an antipode to *law*.[9] While 1968 did not boil down to complete anti-authoritarian antinomianism, it was precisely that element that became important for the ethical turn. In the story of May 1968's contribution to later ethical fascination, what matters, as Michel de Certeau has said, is not "the historical object" of May 1968 but "the instruments of thought and action that it brought forth." The events were fuelled by an antinomian rejection of the juridical laws of the French Fifth Republic, the social laws of convention, and the moral laws of tradition. Eventually, such antinomianism would even target the marxisant "laws of history" that had enabled the May "revolution."

Yet antinomianism does not mean simple transgression; it also suggests the rejection of norms seen as constrictive in favour of a redemption that will come "outside the law." Looked at this way, May's ethics of liberation contained a decidedly affirmative impulse. As Jean-Marie Domenach observed in August 1968: "The key point is this: in the name of what is this critique of society carried out? We have made out the answer, and it is not a paltry one: in the name of the desire to live to express oneself, to be free."[10] The "values" of the moment included: imagination, human interest, communication, conviviality, expression, enjoyment, freedom, spontaneity, solidarity, de-alienation, speaking out, dialogue, non-utility, utopia, dreams, fantasies, community, association, antiauthoritarianism, self-management, direct democracy, equality, self-representation, fraternity, self-defence – and romance. The May events presented an *épanouissement* – an opening toward self-realization. The ethics of liberation was quintessentially modern, involving what Jürgen Habermas has called, in a phrase borrowed from Immanuel Kant, "emancipatory interest."[11] No matter how "liberated" we are – or think we are – we are not as liberated as we can and should be. In 1968 laws were broken in the name of something beyond what those laws could offer: more freedom, more communication, more expression, more equality. The activists of May were saying, freedom is not free enough, equality is not equitable enough, imagination is not imaginative enough. This was the phenomenon that Lionel Trilling in 1968 called "modernism in the streets."[12] Many people wanted to reject an "old world" in order to give birth to a "new world," no matter how inchoate and vague. Although the notion of revolution gave some an orienting compass, advance planning was not part of the script of May's spontaneous happening. As slogans of the era said, *Be realistic, demand the impossible. It is forbidden to forbid.*

The slogans encapsulated a liberational spirit that refused easy reduction, a desire to suspend the rules of everyday life and to experience extraordinary modes of social interaction. Graffiti painted on walls revealed a sense of play; perhaps "it is forbidden to forbid" was less a tricky and circular syllogism than a passing, clever, or ridiculous thought. The slogan, though, also demonstrated the great difficulty of escaping norms. The statement "there are no rules" can itself be taken as a rule; to break the law or to deny one's conscience is still a mode of relating to the law or one's conscience. Transgression, overstepping boundaries, upsetting codes – these phenomena could be considered as norms themselves. Another version of this "Liar's Paradox" is that the transgressor respects the violated law enough to make it worthwhile to break in the first place. On the surface this could look like sheer antiauthoritarian refusal. However, the beliefs behind the ethics of "forbidden to forbid," although not explicit in 1968, and often wrapped in heavy revolutionary packaging, were not hard to discern. Almost by definition there seemed a hesitancy to articulate and explicate a "new law." To do so risked "recuperation" by the status quo, reverting to the very norms one claimed to have broken – the *category* of norm, if not particular norms. The ethics of refusal was caught on a paradoxical double-edged blade when "it is forbidden to forbid" was applied to itself.

Such ambiguities became apparent during the 1970s. It took time to work out the contradictions of what might be called utopian refusal, a phrase that captures both the antinomian and the redemptive thrust of the ethics of liberation. But such contradictions were not maintained over the long term. As Robert Maggiori, the philosophy columnist for the newspaper *Libération*, says, it took time "to express this 'ethics' [*morale*] which in '68 could not be 'formulated' theoretically but was 'inherent' in all its actors."[13] This process was by no means straightforward. One essential factor in working out the contradictions of the ethics of liberation, and the ethical turn to which it led, involved the decline of revolutionary-political modes of social experience. In the decade or so after 1968, France experienced an unprecedented interruption in its nearly 200-year-old tradition of the living revolution, which saw the events of 1789 as a promissory note for future historical accomplishment.[14] Whether in the guise of Republican or even Marxist trappings, the appeal of revolution had occupied a consistent and coherent place in French political culture from the 1790s to the 1970s. After 1968 a serious reconsideration of this inheritance took place.

It is too soon to say whether this reconsideration will be permanent; however, it is certain that late in the twentieth century, at the hands of some of its most dedicated helmsmen, the ship of modern revolution ran aground in the country that had given the term so much of its colour and significance. During the 1970s, there was considerable disappointment and frustration as the anticipated "great evening" – *le grand soir* – of the revolution failed to materialize. France simply de-Marxified in new ways, the Cold War ending in Paris before the Berlin Wall fell. Remarkably, radical politics had provided some of the most important resources for overcoming radical politics: Marxism was present at its own funeral. The end of the politics of the living revolution, which was concretely embodied in French Marxism, coincided with the return of the theme of political ethics. The ethically problematic aspects of revolutionary politics led to a re-evaluation of political ethics, the political, and ethics *tout court*. One of the by-products of this transformation on the intellectual-political Left was thus a return – first implicit, then explicit – of ethical approaches to thought and action. As Dominique Lecourt reported in 1999: "The 'return to morality,' which set in in the early 1980s, unquestionably corresponds to the retreat of the political vision of the world that had crystallized around the idea of revolution."[15]

In the same years, a rapid and sweeping evolution of social mores took hold in France. Related ineluctably to a postwar economic modernization that was nothing short of miraculous given the state of France at the end of World War II, 1968 crystallized and provoked a modernization in daily life, beliefs, behaviours, and mores. The culturally conservative and still powerfully Catholic middle-class morality of Gaullist France, already challenged in many ways since the late 1950s, was shaken on multiple fronts. The 1970s saw the dramatic eruption of "new social movements" and the rapid transformation of social life from a regime of "formality" to one of generalized "informality."[16] By the 1980s irreversible changes had taken place in popular culture and in matters regarding state censorship, youth, race, and especially sexuality and gender. The 1970s marked a pivotal transition in which France liberalized and became flexible – even though contemporary France remains to this day traditionalist and culturally conservative in its own recognizable manner. To some degree, Domenach was right to have asked about the extent to which 1968 had really changed France.

At the same time, at the socio-cultural level, the disruption of traditional moral codes, from religious moralism to the dogmatic moral purism of French Communism, similarly forced a reconsideration of moral and ethical issues in the public sphere. With greater spaces of personal liberty came increased reflection on and self-reflexivity about moral and ethical questions. In post-traditional societies the burden of moral identity shifts from external authorities to individuals, and traditionalism itself becomes elective. So in late modern France, changes in social mores raised new ethical and moral questions and led to old questions being asked anew. Partially as a result, the era gave birth to widespread and sometimes innovative treatments of norms and also to ethically positioned participation in civic life.

On yet another level, during the 1970s, the ethics of liberation occasionally fizzled out in dead ends. Aspects of the 1960s never made it to the 1980s. As a result, the turn to explicit ethical fascination sometimes entailed breaking with or overcoming the limits of the ethics of liberation. In other ways, however, there was great continuity in the ethics of liberation, even if the languages in which this ethics was expressed changed dramatically. Transvaluation involves both the continuity and the change inherent in metamorphosis. From still another perspective, the turn to ethics marked a return to older intellectual traditions, which is why some commentators see it as a traditionalist, deradicalizing, even anti-political reaction. Ethical fascination moved away from the issue of liberation in such ways as to forget or conceal one of its most critical origins.

These dynamics – disappointment with revolution and a shift to post-Marxism, an evolution of social mores, occasional dead ends of the ethics of liberation, the transvaluation of the ethics of liberation into ethical fascination, and the ethical turn as cyclical return – form the heart of this book as it follows the evolution and direction of the turn to ethics.

By the 1980s the "turn" had been accomplished as ethics replaced revolution in French intellectual politics and tradition in the sociocultural sphere and as ethical fascination moved beyond the specific ethics of liberation. By then, several different, often conflicting models or schools of ethical fascination had emerged. Certain liberal professionals – doctors, lawyers, psychiatrists, teachers, journalists, writers – played a tremendous role in pushing ethics beyond earlier religious, Marxist, and sometimes even Republican-humanist configurations. In post-1968 France, intellectuals confronted the normative dimensions of violence, the law, prisons, mental illness, desire, sex, gender, and citizenship in unprecedented ways. Some of the most interesting contributions to ethical revival were made by "revolutionaries" and so-called anti-humanists. May '68 had promised a transformation of selves in relation to themselves, to others, to institutions, to the state, and to humanity in general, and such a transformation was in fact effected; often unexpectedly, sometimes with unhappy consequences, and never, of course, to the extent of fulfilling utopian aspirations.

The story of the ethical turn is to a great extent indistinguishable from the broader history of French intellectual and cultural life in the 1970s. Irrespective of the ethical question, some readers may profit from this book's treatment of that more general history. In fact, since I focus on the arc of the ethical turn, on getting to the final destination, many chapters do not explicitly discuss "ethics." *From Revolution to Ethics* contributes to two discussions: first, to the largely unwritten history of what is known outside of France as "French theory," and second, to existing English-language histories of postwar France. To begin with, there is a significant overlap, both direct and circuitous, between the ethical turn and an infamous coterie of French theorists who flourished in France during the 1960s and 1970s, including Louis Althusser, Roland Barthes, Jean Baudrillard, Guy Debord, Gilles Deleuze, Jacques Derrida, Michel Foucault, Félix Guattari, Luce Irigaray, Julia Kristeva, Jacques Lacan, and Jean-François Lyotard. From different generations, sometimes at odds with one another, usually (sometimes unfairly) stamped with the brand of postmodernism and sharing worldwide acclaim, these thinkers, upon close inspection, form a motley crew.[17] Still, some of them were associated with the ambience of poststructuralism (known in France as late structuralism), which thrived from the mid-1960s to the late 1970s. In broad brushstrokes, a number of family resemblances within this field can be identified: a concern about the opacity of language, suspicions about the unified self, doubts about historical progress, valorization of desire, and anxieties about power. The buzzwords of French theory which gathered around these topics – terms such as discourse, difference, the other, decentring, absence, and indeterminacy – were set against categories such as universalism, origins, representation, and metanarratives. French theorists were neither the first nor necessarily the most lucid critics of modern thought and experience, but they successfully helped focus attention on the problem of intellectual and practical "foundations" and added substantially to the "legitimation crisis" of the late twentieth century.[18]

It should come as no surprise that French theory raised a number of ethical quandaries, since it appeared to undermine many of the basic categories of traditional religious, philosophical, and even commonsensical thought and action. It was precisely the apparent ethical deficit, moral relativism, and nihilism of French theory that many of its critics – from the Right and the Left – decried.[19] By the 1990s much ink had been spilled in response to attacks of this nature, in attempts to think through the ethical lacunae of French theory, or otherwise in efforts to grapple with the ethical implications, applications, dilemmas, and dead-ends of postmodernist and poststructuralist thought. Furthermore, numerous attempts have been made, especially by English-speaking sympathizers, to qualify the field of French theory as decidedly, even basically ethical.[20] The belated recognition of ethics-and-French-theory in the 1990s tended to conceal the fact that the theme of ethics had already been significant in the 1970s. As a historian, it seems to me that there is a story to tell about French theory and ethics in the context in which these ideas emerged and how 1968 contributed to the emergence of both French theory and the ethical turn not as a matter of disembodied ideas but on the ground of historical events and circumstances.[21] I have elected to focus on the socio-institutional camp of French theory, figures like Foucault, Deleuze, and Guattari, though the "textualist" camp of Derrida, Barthes, Kristeva, and others also contributed to the ethical turn.[22]

The second field to which *From Revolution to Ethics* contributes is the historiography of postwar France. My admittedly revisionist account is an attempt to steer the straits between reigning neo-liberal and nostalgic historical treatments of 1968 and its aftermath, both of which rely on what Julie Stephens has helpfully called the "'death of the sixties' narrative."[23] The neo-liberal trend is represented by Tony Judt's indictment of postwar French intellectuals' "irresponsibility" in their attachment to Communism. Elsewhere dismissing May 1968 as "an angry hiccup" that has since acquired "a mystique out of proportion to its significance," Judt has nevertheless noted the ethical turn, writing that "one dominant theme in French intellectual life since the late 1970s has been the moral inadequacy of the French intellectual of the previous generation." I do not, however, agree with his assessment that "few thinkers in France have so far undertaken to construct a moral vocabulary for liberal politics, an ethics ... of democracy."[24] *From Revolution to Ethics* proposes that May 1968 and the dynamics of revolutionary politics did contribute, albeit unintentionally, to a renewal of democratic ethics that cannot be reduced to liberalism alone.

Kristin Ross's analysis of the May events, their prelude, and their inheritance shares a curious parallel with Judt's neo-liberal critique. At first glance the parallel seems surprising; if Judt is dismissive, Ross is wistful. She claims that a revolution took place in 1968 but was eventually betrayed by some of May's protagonists. She leans toward opposite conclusions to those of Judt about the future of revolutionary politics, but implicitly validates the judgment that May ended in failure. She, too, weighs the ethical turn, interpreting it as a flight from genuine politics to cultural questions and personal meaning as well as to the sanctimonious "pity" and "ambulance politics" of humanitarian organizations like Doctors Without Borders.[25] Ross sees in the 1970s' turn to ethics the defeat of revolution, whereas I maintain that this turn proved 1968's success. Ethics is much more than "pity," and the turn to ethics was far more than the "reactionary" by-product of a betrayed revolution. It is worth pointing out that Judt sees French theory as unworthy of comment, whereas Ross uses theories that originated in the era under examination. *From Revolution to Ethics* attempts to explain changes and continuities during the pivotal years after May 1968, an event that was more than a dismissible anachronism but less than an authentic, defeated revolution.[26]

The ethical turn, it seems, has largely been misconstrued. Setting aside the important evaluative question as to whether the contemporary revival of ethics has itself been a positive or negative development, it seems a tall enough order to try to identify how it has taken place. It is not often reported that one version of the famous graffiti slogan, written at the Sorbonne, proclaimed: "Interdit d'interdire. La liberté commence par une interdiction: celle de nuire à la liberté d'autrui": "It is forbidden to forbid. Freedom begins with a prohibition against impairing the freedom of another."[27] This slogan was more than a truism of the Anglo-American liberal tradition, though it would be dishonest not to recognize its compatibility with a certain liberal sensibility. This is a crucial point: the liberational *épanouissement* of 1968 was not incompatible with liberalism, but neither could it be reduced to it. One is hard-pressed to find a '68-er who recalls that the lesson of May was to do whatever one wanted in one's own backyard, and few French Marxists woke up one day simply to embrace free-market capitalism. As we will see in chapter 1, the 1980s in particular witnessed critical assessments of the "nihilistic" and "hedonistic" consequences of 1968, but these tended to say more about the Mitterrand era than about the 1960s. I take exception to the view that post-1968 intellectual-political histories of France ought to be subtitled *How the French Stopped Worrying and Learned to Love Anglo-American Liberalism*. It is one of my aims here to fill the gap in the historical understanding of French theory and to unsettle the seemingly dried and fixed, failed-revolution-return-to-liberalism version of post-1968 French intellectual life.

Of the twenty-five chapters of *From Revolution to Ethics*, the first and last serve as bookends. The four principal case studies that form the core of the book are structured by the tension between the themes of ethos and law.[28] I use the term "ethos" to refer to the character or spirit of 1968 and the manifold liberational aspirations it unleashed, whereas by "law" I refer to limits of various kinds – of history, of the state, even of experience. The story of the post-1968 period is the story of May's immanent antinomian ethos encountering transcending or transcendental laws.[29] I follow those forces and dynamics from revolutionary contestation against the state and its institutions (Part I) to the vicissitudes of the liberation of desire as it pertains to institutions, intersubjectivity, and legality (Parts II and III) and then to the translation of postures of rebellion and dissidence into supra-statist humanitarianism (Part IV). Only then, in the final chapters, will we see the ethical turn completed.

Chapter 1 gives a brief account of the events of May and June 1968 and examines some later French interpretations of them. The dynamics of cultural memory have been such as to harden a number of negative views of what "1968 did" to France.[30] Unfortunately, important "positive" aspects of 1968's legacy, including the ethical turn, have been neglected. Although the normative contradictions of May's antinomian ethos seemed to lead to a tension between liberational intentions and political-liberal consequences, our understanding of May's inheritance will be enriched by exploring how those real contradictions also led to a more extensive phenomenon. In the era of ethics, politics itself is, for better or worse, covered under that umbrella term. My presentation of the May events and later interpretations sets the stage for the subsequent detailed account of the turn to ethics from the late 1960s to the early 1980s.

The chapters in Part I examine one of the most influential of post-1968 French leftist groups, the Maoist Gauche prolétarienne. This faction promoted two Maoist principles in particular: the need to investigate what the people wanted, and the belief that revolution was necessarily violent. Largely symbolic Maoist violent agitation, however, encountered the inconvenient fact of the French Fifth Republic, its police, and its criminal justice system. Many activists found themselves in jail, especially when the Minister of the Interior, Raymond Marcellin, rolled back basic civil liberties. The presence of detained militants in French prisons brought to the surface the Maoist strategy of investigating what was happening behind prison walls. As prisons became increasingly politicized in 1970–71, public attention and calls for investigations into the "carceral universe" brought lawyers, journalists, and other liberal professionals to the defence of inmates. In February 1971, integrating aspects of French Maoism with the Dreyfusard and Social Catholic traditions, the Groupe d'information sur les prisons was founded under the inspiration of Michel Foucault. Seeing its role as publicizing the prisoners' complaints, the Groupe circulated information about the "intolerable" conditions inside French penal institutions. In contrast to the quasi-violent Maoist practice of "popular justice," the Groupe d'information sur les prisons contributed to a deradicalization of the

French far left, which found itself caught between the languages of rights and revolution. It was difficult to hold to antinomian revolt when the laws of the state put one behind bars. The Groupe's contribution to the ethical turn was to have delegitimized revolutionary violence and to have implicity asserted the principles of participatory self-representation.

Part II turns to the signature text of early-1970s French antinomian liberationism: Gilles Deleuze and Félix Guattari's *Anti-Oedipus*, published in March 1972. Criticizing psychoanalysis and what it called "familialism" in favour of a "schizoanalytic" unleashing of desire, *Anti-Oedipus* was immediately associated with the popular French reception of anti-psychiatry, which criticized psychiatric institutions much as the Groupe d'information sur les prisons had criticized prisons. In 1977 Foucault called *Anti-Oedipus* "a book of ethics, the first book of ethics to be written in France in quite a long time." To understand how this admittedly perplexing book could be considered a work of ethics, my analysis turns to the origins of the anti-Oedipal project: first, to Guattari's formative experience with a movement in French psychiatry called Institutional Psychotherapy, and then to Deleuze's prior interest in Benedict de Spinoza's ethical philosophy. Before they met, each had individually formulated a coherent ethical standpoint: institutional and philosophical ethics respectively. Yet their collective philosophy of schizoanalysis, in taking madness as a normative model, risked raising as many ethical problems as it solved. Although Foucault praised *Anti-Oedipus* for offering an "antifascist" ethics, I argue that Deleuze and Guattari's embrace of madness as a model for social critique presented an ethical hurdle for 1968-era liberationism. In Part II, therefore, we see the high-water mark of May's antinomian ethos set against the "laws" of psychoanalysis, the family, the state, and even economics. Here, the contribution to the ethical turn was largely indirect, pushing antiauthoritarianism to an extreme that, even if some saw an ethics at work, proved to be a barrier for other, notably feminist, liberational aspirations.

The philosophy of desire was found in the streets as much as in books. Part III explores conflicts between two groups of militants associated with the sexual revolution, groups that broke down largely along lines of gender. The most celebrated gay activist of the era, Guy Hocquenghem, advocated a "dark homosexuality" that took on stridently masculinist tones. Tensions arose between Hocquenghem and other male activists, and feminists, who seriously doubted that women were served by the crass liberation of sexual desire. These tensions came to a boiling point in mid-1970s debates over sexual violence and the law. Between the passage of a law guaranteeing reproductive freedom (1974) and the advocacy of new laws punishing perpetrators of sexual violence (1976–78), French feminism changed its emphasis, moving from a radical position "outside the law" (*hors la loi*) to a reluctant embrace of Republican law as a vehicle for women's liberation. In the mid-to-late 1970s the philosophy of desire entrenched itself in advocacy of intergenerational sexual relations, notably between men and boys. At this moment many male activists accused feminists of "moralizing" in their efforts to draw limits on desire and sexuality around the issues of violence and children. Numerous feminists maintained that, where the pleasure principle met the reality principle, the ethics of desire required limits – and sometimes the law. The conflict between ethos and law became explicit at this juncture; though the competing ethics of desire and of reliance on the legal system were unresolved, the terms of the debate were no longer primarily those of revolution.

In the mid-to-late 1970s talk of ethics shifted from being an implied topic in public discourse to an explosively explicit one. Part IV considers a loosely affiliated group of thinkers, the New Philosophers, people like Bernard-Henri Lévy and André Glucksmann, who burst onto television screens and into the popular press in 1976–77. They were young and charismatic, and almost all of them had participated as radicals in the events of 1968. The New Philosophers were decried by politicians, academics, and journalists for allegedly equating Marxism with the Soviet Gulag. Though they have since become a symbol for sloppy, sound-bite thinking, their true cultural significance related to the legislative elections of 1978 – to speak against Marx at that moment was to threaten the Left's electoral prospects. More deeply, however, the New Philosophers represented a return to a classic figure in French culture: the moralist. Their moralism bore an uncanny resemblance to the seventeenth-century French religious-cultural tradition of Jansenism, which, in drawing a strict line between the immanent, messy world and a transcendent God, cultivated the tragic attitude of being "in the world but not of it." Under the inspiration of their "uncle," the eccentric Maurice Clavel, the New Philosophers lay claim to morality and religion against revolution. Building on a wave of interest in Eastern European and Russian dissidence (on the rise since the 1974 publication of Alexandr Solzhenitsyn's *The Gulag Archipelago*), the New Philosophers were seen to embody the wholesale return of an ethical critique of politics and the birth of late-twentieth-century humanitarianism. The ethical turn was thus in full swing by the time the 1970s ended.

Complementing the first chapter, the last before the Conclusion serves as a second bookend. It surveys the multiple ways that, by the early 1980s and the opening of the Mitterrand era, the ethical turn was accomplished. This was the moment, for instance, of postmodernism, the Solidarity movement in Poland, AIDS, Holocaust denial, and biotechnological advances – all of which placed ethics on the public agenda in France and elsewhere. Thinkers who had long championed ethics – Paul Ricoeur, Vladimir Jankélévitch, and Emmanuel Levinas – were given unprecedented attention. Both Jean-Paul Sartre and Foucault made ethics a theme of explicit concern, and we will examine their individual ethical turns in detail. For the remainder of the twentieth century, in distinctively French ways, sometimes building on the ethos of 1968, sometimes rejecting it, sometimes applauding ethics, sometimes decrying it, a variety of thinkers grappled with the ethical dimensions of contemporary experience.

In the conclusion, I note the ultimate destination of the turn to ethics that began in the post-1968 years: its contribution to the truly popular explosion of ethical fascination throughout the West during the 1990s.[31] Further, understanding the ethical turn will allow us to re-evaluate the legacy of the Sixties so as to show the poverty of both "Right" and "Left" interpretations of that era. A repercussion of the tension between *ethos* and *law*, the turn to ethics fits between these poles in a number of ways. But there was also a distinctively French cast to these dynamics. The turn to ethics demonstrated how 1968 contributed to a renewal of civil society and to the peculiarly Gallic understanding of how *associations* and *institutions* occupy the social space between atomized individuals, and the state and its laws. Finally, I conclude on the critical point – the reader should be aware at the outset – that ethics is a necessary yet insufficient condition for social and political life.

From Revolution to Ethics follows a number of themes with regard to the ethical: the self, others, institutions, the state, and "humanity." The four principal case studies indicate the flows, cross-currents, overlaps, and cumulative effects of these themes. The narrative as a whole moves from one scene to the next like a slide show or a collection of short stories. From revolt against the state (Maoism), the nascent ethical sensibility shifted from institutions (prisons and asylums) to the individual (the philosophy of desire, sexual liberation), and back to the state (embodied by law). The New Philosophers projected aspirations for liberation beyond revolutionary and reformist politics in the name of metaphysical resistance and human rights. One can sense the vibrations of May's antiauthoritarian antinomianism as they moved forward into the ethics of violence, the "intolerable," madness, desire, limit thinking, law, antipolitical denunciation, and humanitarianism.

The turn to ethics was not straightforward. It took time. Now and then it involved dead ends. It was, however, an unmistakable legacy of the dialectics sparked by *les événements* of May 1968.[32]

I

Cobblestone Beaches: Normative Contradictions of the May Revolt

We live today under an entirely new régime ...
What men of other times sometimes sensed in their music,
We realize each day in practical reality.
What was for them in the domain of the inaccessible and absolute,
We consider as something simple and well-known.
Nevertheless, we don't scorn those men;
We know what we owe their dreams ....
Today,
For the first time,
We can retrace the end of the old regime.

Michel Houellebecq (1998)

What happened in May 1968? One of the most popular versions of how "the events" transpired, a story whose ink had dried before the last barricade had been taken down, recounts how student unrest at the University of Paris campus at Nanterre in the spring of 1968 moved to the Sorbonne in early May. Built in 1964 in the suburbs of Paris to alleviate overcrowding at the Sorbonne, Nanterre had become the symbol of all that was wrong with the French educational system. The campus was a series of ultramodern glass and concrete superstructures rising out of surrounding slums. With few non-institutional public or social spaces, classes were soon overcrowded there as well. Political meetings were forbidden; one could not move furniture or cook in dorm rooms. An initial focus for student dissatisfaction was the fact that men and women, assigned to live in separate buildings, were not allowed to visit one another. In April 1967 male students camped in the entrance to the women's dormitory.[1] The issue was temporarily quieted by the decision later in the year to allow male students over twenty-one to have female visitors. Men under twenty-one could have female visitors if they had written permission from their parents. Illustrating the absurdity of the rule, nearly 90 percent of males secured this signature. Women still could not receive male visitors.

In November 1967 students briefly went on strike against the general working conditions at Nanterre. Photographs of the many plainclothes policemen appearing on campus were taken, enlarged, and tacked to bulletin boards. On 8 January 1968 the Minister of Sports, François Missoffe, came to dedicate a massive new swimming pool and was accosted by a young sociology student named Daniel Cohn-Bendit, who asked him why so much attention was given to the swimming facility when issues more pressing to the students – like sexual freedom – were not being addressed. The government official told Cohn-Bendit that if he had a sexual problem then he should jump in the pool and take a swim. "Danny the Red" replied: "Yes, that's what they used to say to the Hitler Youth."

After further protests against the presence of plainclothes policemen, Nanterre sociology students went on strike again in mid-March 1968, demanding basic changes in the operation of the university, such as the removal of outdated curricula and greater freedom of association. They also threatened to boycott their exams. These preliminary tensions reached a boiling point on March 22nd when, following the arrest of students for participation in a protest against the Vietnam War, others took over the administration building, writing on the walls: "Professors you are past and so is your culture!" and, in reference to signs posted in public toilets: "Please leave the Communist Party as clean on departing as you would like to find it on entering!" The activists christened themselves the March 22nd Movement. On 28 March the dean closed Nanterre for four days, which resulted in surging attendance at the series of mass meetings that followed. On 22 April a collectively written manifesto called for the rejection of the capitalist-technocratic university and for solidarity with the working class. In response to growing student involvement, a clear escalation of rhetoric, and outright clashes between leftist and right-wing students, the university was closed indefinitely on Thursday, 2 May. The next day Cohn-Bendit and several other leaders were summoned to appear before the university disciplinary committee at the Sorbonne the following Monday. It was to be a long weekend.

In the wake of the events at Nanterre, students in the Latin Quarter staged a small but vocal demonstration in the courtyard of the Sorbonne on Friday, 3 May in support of their fellow students. The rector of the University of Paris, fearing more provocation, jumped the gun and called his ministerial superiors. The Sorbonne was to be closed for only the second time in its 700-year history (the other time had been in 1940). By five o'clock the police had arrived and, instead of simply dispersing the crowd, filled their vans with demonstrators. As the first of these vans pulled away, the growing crowd of students and onlookers at the Place de la Sorbonne suddenly intervened. Spontaneous and unorganized, the chant went up: "Free our comrades." A police vehicle was blocked, its windows smashed, and the first of the three-pound paving stones – *pavés* – thrown. Sporadic fighting spread through the Latin Quarter, and 600 students were arrested. That night the largest national student union and the junior faculty union voted to go out on strike. On Sunday, 5 May, four of the arrested demonstrators were sentenced to prison. The ad hoc coalition of students and young teachers responded with three demands: reopen the Sorbonne, withdraw the police from the Latin Quarter, and release those arrested.

On Monday, 6 May, Cohn-Bendit and seven others walked into the Sorbonne singing the *Internationale* as a mass march wound its way through Paris en route to the Latin Quarter. In preparation for the expected confrontations with the police, some demonstrators donned hard hats and motorcycle helmets, placed wet cloths over their mouths to protect them from tear gas, and carried iron bars and table legs. The chant "CRS-SS" began to be heard, provocatively conflating the French police with the Nazis. Between Monday and Friday, 10 May, however, demonstrations were generally peaceful, as student leaders and the university negotiated. An agreement to reopen the Sorbonne fell through, since the university had no power to release the arrested students. That week high-school students in Paris and university students in other cities joined the strike. President Charles de Gaulle was noticeably quiet, except for a useless "We cannot tolerate violence in the streets." Shocked by the initial severe intervention of the police, segments of the general population of Paris seemed sympathetic to the students. Numerous action committees began to form with no clear structure or agenda, and the leaders of the movement described themselves simply as spokesmen who were part of the crowd. Failed negotiations and mounting tensions came to a head on the night of 10–11 May, the Night of the Barricades. When the government again refused to free the imprisoned students, a crowd of 15,000 turned the narrow streets of the Latin Quarter into a fortified maze with barricades fashioned from cars, street signs, stones, and mattresses. The police moved in. Feeding the drama, the events were carried live on the radio. The serious fighting started at 2:00 a.m. and ended at dawn: 367 wounded; 460 arrested; 188 cars overturned or burned.

On Saturday, 11 May, as people inspected the charred and uprooted aftermath, Prime Minister Georges Pompidou returned to Paris from an official visit to Afghanistan. His deputies had been running the show. Back at the helm, he suddenly reversed the government policy of clearing the Latin Quarter, freed the jailed students, and gestured toward conciliation. Not only was the move too late; it also whetted the appetites of the demonstrators. The students, together with the trade unions with whom they had already begun negotiations, called for a one-day general strike, and on May 13, a march of eight hundred thousand, led by the students, with national political leaders of the Left buried in the crowd, crossed Paris. That night, the students took possession of the Sorbonne, initiating one of the twentieth century's most joyously chaotic experiments in spontaneous collectivism – part carnival, part twenty-four-hour-a-day revolutionary plenary session. The student soviet lasted in one form or another until 16 June, when the police cleared the Sorbonne.

Beyond the political agitation that began to touch national parties and leaders, and alongside the revolutionary rhetoric and its economic-class vocabulary, it was the libertarian spirit of the Sorbonne and then at the nearby Théâtre de l'Odéon that did the most to create the mythos of May 1968. Some participants revelled in the suspension of the ordinary rules of everyday life. Of the many slogans of *la jolie mai* – the lovely days of May – one above all served as an exemplary expressive and organizing principle: *prendre la parole* [speak out].[2] People found themselves talking openly with others, addressing groups, debating, and speaking up as they had never done before. The spontaneity, ease, and openness were formative for thousands and would be recalled for a long time. A few realized that talking about revolution was itself their so-called revolution, but the defining characteristic of the moment was a gushing forth of hopes, anticipations, imaginings, fantasies, and illusions. This exuberance left its mark in the graffiti on walls and facades all over Paris: "Speak to your neighbours" ... "I hate writing on walls" ... "Don't take the elevator, take power" ... "We are all German Jews" ... "Labour unions are whorehouses" ... "Embrace your lover without putting down your gun" ... "Imagination is taking power" ... "I am coming all over the paving stones" ... "Art is dead, liberate daily life" ... "Shame is counter-revolutionary" ... "I dream of being a happy idiot" ... "I love you! Oh, say it with paving stones!" ... "International solidarity with the African-American people." And the most well-known: "It is forbidden to forbid" and "Underneath the *pavés*, the beach!" At the Ecole nationale des Beaux-Arts, from mid-May until the school was cleared by the police on 27 June, the Atelier Populaire created the most famous poster art of the movement. About a thousand artists in teams of 200 worked day and night to produce about a hundred thousand posters from 350 designs.

After the one-day general strike of 13 May, the workers threw their in lot with the students. The initial trickle (on 14 May, about 200 workers were on strike) reached a head on 15 May when workers from Renault, one of the largest state-owned industries, downed tools. By 19 May approximately two million workers in all professions were on strike. With occasional exceptions, the workers and students did not come together. Yet, it was the involvement of the workers that escalated the revolt into a genuine national crisis. By 22 May there were roughly six or seven million strikers.[3] Many of them, directly inspired by the students and motivated by less abstract aspirations than "speaking out," took disparate action. The national labour unions, and with them the Communist and Socialist parties, were initially skeptical about the student revolt. Only when rank-and-file workers took control of factories one at a time, with little national coordination, frequently locking themselves inside their work premises, did union leaders begin to see that they perhaps had a role to play. The lumbering and staggered response to the events on the part of the national labour and political Left was matched only by the equally maladroit steps of the de Gaulle government.

Between 15 May and 29 May the crisis reached its climax with five main elements involved: students, the government, unions, political parties of the Left, and the silent majority of French citizens. The radical factions among the students won the debate on the tactical question of revolution versus reform, but they were unable to relate their multifaceted cultural program, which tended toward the anarchic rather than the organized, to a more widely appealing political one. Saturday, 25 May saw the most violent street fighting of the month. The student quarter overflowed, and several fires were set at the Stock Exchange. Reacting with a degree of impulsiveness that the students might have admired, the government waffled between wanting to broker peace with them and relying on the police to regain order. Such inconsistency succeeded in alienating both the students and the police. De Gaulle cut short a planned visit to Romania to make the curious remark: "Reform yes, bedwetting no" [*chienlit non*], which, though not without a certain reassuring appeal to many French adults, was hardly proactive. The major unions were divided on whether to pursue moderate objectives (wage increases and job security) or to push for a new government – or more radically still, to seek worker control of workplaces. Over the weekend of 25–26 May, the government and the labour unions negotiated, but when labour leaders submitted the "Grenelle accords" (with numerous concessions to the government) to the workers on Monday, 27 May, many workers rejected the proposals, thus upping the ante. The opposition parties of the Left – the Communists and Socialists (by no means happy partners) – could also not agree on a course of action, locked as they were in the strategy of biding their time until the still-distant 1971 elections. The Parti communiste français (PCF) had been particularly dismissive of the student uprising for its anarchic "misjudgment" of the needs of the working class. Unprepared psychologically or programmatically for the sudden wave of social unrest, the PCF and Parti socialiste unifié were caught between wanting to ride that wave toward more seats in the National Assembly and advocating new elections – or, more dramatically, seeking a new constitution. Only on 23 May did the Communists agree to ally themselves with other Left parties but, as evidenced by a mass meeting on Monday, 27 May, the aspiration of aligning students, workers, socialists, communists, and more marginal radicals behind the Left's candidate, the tragic Pierre Mendès-France, former Minister and advocate of decolonization, proved too great an undertaking. As for the silent majority of the French citizenry, their tolerance – or even tacit support – for the events receded, one might say, in direct proportion to the length of the lines at the empty gas stations.

May 29th was the decisive day when history did not turn. That morning, de Gaulle abruptly cancelled his normal Wednesday, 10 a.m. cabinet meeting. By that afternoon, the radio was reporting, "We have lost General de Gaulle." He had disappeared. Without even informing Prime Minister Pompidou, de Gaulle had been driven to a helicopter pad, flown to an airfield, and taken to the French military base at Baden-Baden, Germany. Rumours spread that he and his wife had large suitcases with them. That afternoon, half a million people demonstrated on the streets of Paris. Overnight, it seemed almost certain that de Gaulle was withdrawing from power. But there was an ominous silence from the government. The night passed in a power vacuum. The next morning, just as mysteriously, de Gaulle returned to Paris and at 4:31 p.m. addressed the nation. There would be no backing down, he said, appealing to what the Left would call the "party of fear." France was threatened with subversion, he continued, and the entire situation was a Communist plot. The National Assembly would be dissolved and new elections held. He mentioned neither the students nor the deal negotiated with the unions. In a political culture with a long tradition of the cult of personality, de Gaulle's eleventh-hour show of confidence reassured a startled and increasingly uneasy public. By that afternoon, with a spontaneity that rivalled that of the left-wing demonstrations, an immense crowd of citizens rallying to the president's message massed in the heart of Paris and marched from the Place de la Concorde to the Arc de Triomphe. They shouted slogans like "Communism will not succeed!" and nastier taunts like "France for the French!" and "Cohn-Bendit to Dachau!" Tricolour flags took the place of the red and black ones that had previously filled the streets.

The speech and demonstration of 30 May signalled a shift in momentum away from the workers and students, who themselves were surprised by the tremendous anti-climax. Within a few days, the strikes began to break and the government reclaimed strategic positions like post offices. On 23 and 30 June national elections gave more power to the Right than it had held before the May events. And a new chapter in French history had unmistakably opened.

The question "Why May?" is inseparable from the voluminous commentary that followed on its heels. Many explanations focused on the student milieu, emphasizing, for instance, the postwar demographic boom that had increased the population of French university students (from 150,000 to 600,000 between 1955 and 1968). Schools themselves were known to be organized according to the injurious principles of "centralization," "authoritarianism," and "elimination" (rigid classicism, exams reinforcing social hierarchies, and impersonal formality between students and teachers). Many French youth were dissatisfied with the perceived technocratic function of education. In their view, students were only being trained as expert managers and administrators of a postwar society undergoing the rapid modernization and unprecedented economic growth of the period known as the *trente glorieuses*, or "thirty glorious years."[4] Paradoxically, attacks on "consumer society" were voiced among students from precisely this advancing middle class; in a culture of plenty, their expectations of life, society, and history were heightened.[5] Student radicalism, leaning on recycled "revolutionary" thought and action, had intensified in 1965–67. The Communist student union especially experienced conflicts and schisms, and spawned a number of far-left *groupuscules* (small groups). Building on earlier agitation against the Algerian War, which had concluded in 1962, mobilization against the Vietnam War intensified in step with American intervention. French student *tiers-mondisme* ("Third World-ism") flourished from the early 1960s until the mid-1970s. Despite rapid turnover in membership, various student groups and unions provided a high coefficient of continuity in political mobilizations. International student unrest, with the exception of events in Germany and the looming Vietnam situation, seems to have had little direct impact on French students.

Stronger influences were found in the more general historical situation of France during the 1960s: its Cold War position, half-imagined, half-real, as situated between East and West; the repressed and not-yet-worked-through experience of the Vichy years; the conflation of the Liberation, Republican values, and revolution in the political imagination; and older legacies of state centralism, charismatic politics, un-time-tested constitutions, the political importance of intellectuals, and French exceptionalism. There is also the not-to-be-exaggerated fact that, as Paul Berman and H. Stuart Hughes have suggested, the postwar European generation found itself not fighting a war and yet confronted with the moral examples – the courage, ambiguity, and unpardonable collaboration – of their parents; the generation of 1968, as it were, in search of an event.[6]

Explanations of the May events also address the fact that, in the face of a slight economic downturn, there had been a number of wildcat worker strikes in recent years and notably in the spring of 1968. However, the momentum for May '68 undeniably came from the student milieu, with its complex, sometimes conflicted mixtures of revolution and revolt. Trotskyists, Maoists, Castroists, and others who saw themselves in the line of Marxism-Leninism blurred with those with more anarchistic or generally antiauthoritarian tendencies, such as the Situationists (who had led a sizeable student strike in Strasbourg in 1966) and the March 22nd Movement from Nanterre, as well as with those who were religiously affiliated or claimed no party whatsoever.[7] The Trotskyists and the March 22nd Movement saw their memberships swell in May and June, ahead of all others. There was general hostility toward the Parti communiste français, which, in part through its student union, had already been discredited, and whose Stalinism and negotiations with the government further damaged its credibility.

The technocratic mission of the university fuelled criticisms of bureaucracy in parties, structures, and institutions. Students looked to earlier critiques of the capitalist social order for inspiration. Henri Lefebvre's attentions to everyday life or the writings of former members of the Socialisme ou Barbarie group – Edgar Morin, Claude Lefort, and Cornelius Castoriadis – seemed suddenly prescient and newly relevant. Herbert Marcuse's popular influence emerged in and through the events themselves.[8] The only author most members of the Nanterre movement had read was Jean-Paul Sartre.[9] Everywhere in 1968 one saw signs of protest against the prevailing economic, social, and political systems, claims for liberation against alienated life, and spontaneous expressions of conviviality.[10] With the exception of the more or less ritualistic street violence between the plastic-suited police "Martians" and the helmeted, rock-throwing students, challenges to the dominant order took the form of romantic communitarianism, a generalized antiauthoritarianism, and utopian experiments in direct democracy.

And yet contestation, liberationism, spontaneity, and other expressions of May's ethos were almost always garbed in "workerist" rhetoric. Class conflict was the lingua franca for articulating a host of aspirations and efforts that in essence were not actually reducible to class struggle. Many protagonists believed they were indeed launching a marxisant revolution, with students in the vanguard role of providing an initial impetus and the working classes being expected to take up the baton and, befitting the paradigm, validate the authenticity of a genuine revolution. Even some critics of the would-be revolutionaries – including de Gaulle, who, as we saw, linked revolution and reform – tended to see radicals' projects within the same moral universe as the French Republic itself, which also traced its origins to insurrection and radical change. The sweeping and indelible events of May 1968 – from the President of the Republic's mysterious crisis of confidence, to the non-stop "General Assemblies" at the Sorbonne and the Théâtre de l'Odéon, to the café patron, short of change, told by a waiter to take her coffee for free since there was a "revolution" underway – strike the contemporary observer (at least this one) as at once remarkable and strange.

Still, these brief accounts of what happened in May 1968, and why, omit a great deal. The events were experienced differently in various parts of Paris, in other cities, or in the countryside. It made a difference if one listened to the radio or was directly involved. For many of the foreign nationals in Paris that month, some of whom were there for peace talks between the United States and Vietnam, the events were a mere backdrop or at most an inconvenience. Some remember 1968 as a formative, halcyon happening; others saw it as a reckless party for *les enfants gâtés*, spoiled children. Now as then, May can amount to a historical Rorschach test, upon which one projects a range of perspectives, emotions, and judgments. In the early 2000s, for instance, I learned something essential about May 1968 in the Vosges mountains of eastern France, the region where Joan of Arc was born. When I asked villagers young and old what 1968 had meant to them and how it had changed their lives, they answered, "Nothing" and "Very little," respectively. But the fact that not every person in France was directly affected does not at all diminish the events' historical significance. As we shall see below, in subsequent decades attitudes toward the events came to serve as a barometer of changing cultural moods and political persuasions.

Obviously, the prologue at Nanterre described above begs the question of the deeper sources, accumulating forces, and contributing factors that combined over years to produce the events. Perhaps most significantly, May 1968 transpired in the context of the global ferment of "the Sixties," outside of which it is incomprehensible.[11] But our story is limited to France. This will help draw the boundaries of inquiry and avoid the relative pitfalls of international histories. In addition, some revisionist historical scholarship has begun to relativize the events of that year in light of the "long 1960s," which stretched from the late 1950s to the mid-1970s. This reappraisal has contributed greatly to measured and nonpartisan assessments of the era. I intend this book also to be revisionist in its way. Yet there is no escaping the fact that the events of 1968 were a watershed; they were understood at the time and since to have been unexpected and spectacular. In France, May 1968 was singular, emblematic, and prototypical all at once, opening a period of magnified political activism that dwarfed pre-1968 stirrings. Revisionism cannot change the fact that the events amounted to the largest general strike in twentieth-century Europe and opened a historical period. A pivotal moment in an invariably more complicated history, May 1968 is our point of departure for an adventure of ideas, intellectuals, culture, politics, and public life in France from the late 1960s to the early 1980s.

May 1968 was lived as a mass of discrete, interrelated experiences suggested by that term: event.[12] Events mark history and divide it into chapters. Like the Kennedy assassination or September 11, 2001, for Americans, one is led to ask the question: *Do you remember where you were when ...?* Something along the lines of a shock to French society transpired, a shock that would be mulled over, celebrated, disavowed, and denounced for decades. For as much as some experienced *les événements* as a chaotic suspension of everyday rules, a surge of utopian and revolutionary anticipations, and a "taking up of speech," one clear observation is that they marked the age of proliferating commentary.[13]

As early as May 1969 Michel de Certeau wrote a helpful bibliographical article emphasizing the themes of "authority crisis," the relative proportions of repetition and originality in the events, and the interpretive crisis that had emerged as existing conceptual tools proved insufficient to the task of explanation. That crisis, however, promised further movement toward "interdisciplinarity" and new roles for intellectuals in society, he added.[14] Little more than a year after De Certeau's assessment, Philippe Bénéton and Jean Touchard published a review essay that oriented understanding of the May events for the next thirty-odd years.[15] They proposed eight different interpretive categories that had appeared in the avalanche of commentaries over the preceding two years:

1 The conspiracy of an inflammatory minority (de Gaulle, Pompidou, Raymond Marcellin, François Duprat);
2 a university crisis (Raymond Boudon, Pierre Bourdieu and Jean-Claude Passeron, Edgar Faure);
3 a youth rebellion (Raymond Aron, Edgar Morin, André Stéphane);
4 a metaphysical revolt or a crisis of civilization (Maurice Clavel, Jean-Marie Domenach, Jacques Maritain, Edgar Faure, André Malraux);
5 a new kind of class conflict giving birth to new social movements (Alain Touraine);
6 a traditional type of social conflict related to economic contraction and anarchistic trouble-making (the PCF);
7 a political crisis for the Fifth Republic (Raymond Aron, Pierre Avril);
8 a convergence of chance circumstances.

It is worth pausing on the two most celebrated of these commentaries, largely written as the events were unfolding: *La Brèche* by Claude Lefort, Edgar Morin, and Cornelius Castoriadis (former members of Socialisme ou Barbarie), and *La Révolution introuvable* by Raymond Aron.[16] The essays in *La Brèche* stressed the originality of the revolts, the role of young people in rejecting technocratic and bureaucratic society, and the opening of a "breach" that might (it seemed at the time) lead toward groundbreaking social and political transformation. Whatever their predictive errors and exaggerations, due perhaps to the heat of the moment and to sympathies with the students, the analyses of *La Brèche* have a certain freshness in their depiction of the urgency, openness, and imagined possibilities of the moment. Aron's more circumspect evaluation, perhaps because it was more fault-finding, has stood the test of time in a different way. Presenting himself as a new Alexis de Tocqueville, the voice of moderation and reform, Aron encapsulated in a single word – "psychodrama" – his judgment that the students were acting out childish antiauthoritarianism with no clear aim. That catchword, though, covers up Aron's own ambivalences and worries about May.

Admitting that he mostly had in mind only the university crisis, perhaps because he had been absent in California from 15–23 May at the crucial moment when the student revolt passed to more general unrest, he acknowledged that the French university system needed real reform, that there was a general "moral crisis" in the West, and that Morin and Lefort were right to suggest that May '68 demonstrated "the fragility of the modern order." That fragility, he said, derived from the nature of modern society itself, which required self-discipline and complex forms of cooperation in order to function, and which was thereby susceptible to "minorities" performing "paralysing actions" (a judgment remarkably similar to diagnoses of twenty-first-century terrorism). To Aron's mind, France had at that moment "gone further than any other country in the discovery of her own vulnerability." Convinced of the need for "intermediary bodies" (such as labour unions) between the state and the French people, and insisting that the university was the "best guarantor" of freedoms in the Republic, Aron pleaded to give the "constitution a chance to last for a time." To his mind, behind chaos lay violence, and there is no mistaking the kind of violence he meant when he expressed concern for the fragility of the Republic and intermediary institutions; namely, the memory of fascism. On two different occasions he linked his diagnosis of the stability of the Republic to the fact that he was a "Frenchman of Jewish origins." (We will see below in Parts I and II how the label of fascism was marshalled in post-1968 France by different actors for varied purposes.) For Aron – caught between the "revolutionary propensities of the French people," which he condemned, and the "emotional and moral revolt" against alienated society, "which cannot be translated into a political program" – the core of the matter was that criticism without a positive alternative vision ended in "nihilism."[17]

The merit of *La Brèche* and *La Révolution introuvable* was that, whether approving or denunciatory, they captured the fact that 1968 represented something unanticipated, unsettling, and uncertain. Subsequent French interpretations have generally gathered around those positive or negative poles, viewing May 1968 either as the sign of a marvellous new beginning or, with increasing frequency after the mid-1970s, as the sign of nihilistic, individualistic, and anti-political tendencies. Obviously, French accounts have been unable to treat the events apart from subsequent developments, and May has continued to play its role as an intellectual, cultural, and political Rorschach test. With punctual regularity, the anniversary years of 1978, 1988, and 1998 witnessed an upsurge in interpretive accounts. It has thus seemed difficult to talk about 1968 without crediting that year as the origin of real social, cultural, and political transformation. Again, in recent decades, judgments have slipped into the orbit of polemic and negation, and even nostalgic accounts can be refreshing when they restrict themselves to the events and concern themselves less with consequences. Glowing testimonies, though, have become rare.[18]

On the twentieth anniversary of the May events, *La Brèche* was republished with additional essays by Lefort, Morin, and Castoriadis written between 1978 and 1988. Their originally positive assessment was now qualified by terms like "ambivalence," "contradiction," and "complexity," the post-1968 period having left unrealized May's "other possibilities."[19] Also in 1988, Laurent Joffrin, similarly stressing the mixed legacy of '68, reduced Bénéton and Touchard's eight categories of interpretation to five: May had been a conspiracy, an antiauthoritarian tantrum, a failed proletarian revolution, an original event worthy of sociological and philosophical reflection, or (as he himself saw it) a democratic revolt.

> In spite of its fascinating flight toward the wholly unimagined [*impensé*], the revolt moved forward in step with a democratization of society that had been underway for over two centuries. The events of 1968 did not herald the socialist revolution; they prolonged the French Revolution ... [They were] not a failed revolution but a great reformist revolt, a democratic insurrection ... Behind the messianism of revolutionaries, one indeed oscillated between an individualism that collapsed onto itself and an individualism of civic participation ... [If] the real reason for all that was a raw but salutary leap toward more democracy, the fight was worth being fought.[20]

Joffrin could derive an overall positive tally from the calculation of May's ambiguities, but his division of its inheritance into democratic participation and individualism pointed to a predominant interpretive tendency between 1978 and 1988 that, spotlighting non-participatory and self-interested individualism, was less sympathetic.

One of the harshest critiques of May, which linked the events to modernization and a newly emergent individualism, came from the Left in 1978. In his *Modest Contribution to the Discourses and Official Ceremonies of the Tenth Anniversary*, Régis Debray, the former student of Louis Althusser and close associate of Ernesto Che Guevara, blasted May 1968 for having performed a vital function in the development of late modern capitalism.[21] The events, he said, had served mainly to clear away the antiquated values of an older France that had been holding back the expansion of market forces in the country. The "revolutionaries" had wanted to destroy capitalism, but they had served as unwitting accomplices to its growing domination. Debray's attack needs to be understood in the specific context of the breakdown in 1977 of the Union of the Left, the Communist and Socialist parties' partnership, a breakdown that sealed the Left's electoral defeat in legislative elections the following year (an episode examined below in Part IV).

The suspicion that 1968 had bolstered rather than undermined capitalist culture was taken to another level by Gilles Lipovetsky in a series of articles written from 1979–82 and republished in 1983 as *L'Ere du vide: essais sur l'individualisme contemporain*. Following up on Aron's concerns about narcissism, he concluded that 1968 had instigated a "second individualist revolution" of "personalization."[22] The events had inadvertently magnified cultural hedonism, leading many people to retreat into the isolated, private spheres of individual fulfillment. As a result, social and political life had been fractured and undermined. Lipovetsky shared Debray's belief that the actors of May 1968 had in fact helped consolidate the social order they believed their collectivism would overturn. This perspective has implications for the ethical turn, which in some quarters did indeed involve a retreat from politics and a privatization of the normative dimensions of experience.

In its occasional stress on and valorization of the individual, the ethical turn was sometimes compatible with liberalism, a concept typically concerned with individual rights guaranteed by laws of nature or of the state. Aron, for example, had emphasized individual freedom but in the context of worries about social stability being guaranteed via intermediary bodies. From their admittedly different political perspectives, Debray and Lipovetsky were surveying a society whose growing rigidity made issues of stability seem beside the point, given that atomistic individualism was impairing the very mediatory institutions and associations that Aron had defended. Their writings, of course, in many ways said more about the years 1976–83 than about 1968; in other words, they described exactly the moment when the ethical turn was being accomplished. (We shall return to the question of the nature of the relation among ethics, liberalism, and democracy. As I have already suggested, the turn to ethics, while compatible with liberalism, cannot be reduced to it.)

Luc Ferry and Alain Renault followed in the same vein. Their *La Pensée 68: essai sur l'anti-humanisme contemporaine* (1985) proposed a tidy schema of four different kinds of interpretation of 1968: uncritical and sympathetic expositions (Sartre, Morin, and Castoriadis); the view that "history" was working at cross-purposes and "behind the backs" of the 68-ers (Debray and Lipovetsky); a "phenomenological" claim that 1968 was a new beginning and a radical caesura (Lefort); and their own position of "interpretive pluralism," which was indebted explicitly to Aron's "sociological" method.[23] Ferry and Renault's proposal to "integrate understanding and explanation" seemed attractive enough. Oddly, however, the interpretive pluralism they put forward turned out to be somewhat flawed in conception and execution. The authors wrote more of an erratic polemic than a sociological account. The essence of 1968 as a whole, they implied, overlapped with the "anti-humanist" thought of Michel Foucault, Jacques Derrida, Pierre Bourdieu, and Jacques Lacan; in other words, with French theory. The way in which Ferry and Renault blamed these thinkers for what was wrong in post-1968 French politics and culture bears on my interest in the normative contradictions of 1968, the slogan "Forbidden to forbid," and the ethical turn. Foucault and company were accused of having shared an epistemological project of abolishing facts and questioning the "constraints" of knowledge.[24] Once constraints in the field of knowledge were undermined, epistemological relativism reared its head. *Consequently*, Ferry and Renault deduced, a relativization of facts culminated in a relativization of values: "The idea that everything could be represented as valid, and that no norms need be imposed institutionally on the play of desire, for example, was gradually developing. From the disintegration of norms to the rise of neonihilism was but a single step, which, when taken, rather easily undermined the fragile order of existing society." Again, as it had been in Aron's case, the admission of French society's fragility and the risk of nihilism was quite remarkable.

> The relationship between the 1968 crisis as a critique of norms ("It is forbidden to forbid") and the critical work on normativity itself by French philosophers of the sixties should not necessarily be regarded in a simplistic and caricatural way as the establishment of a cause/effect relationship: Neither cause nor effect, '68 philosophy is part of a meaningful whole whose importance it illuminates while being illuminated by it. With this in mind, the observations outlined in *The Elusive Revolution* are all the more interesting when Aron (anticipating Debray's and Lipovetsky's analyses) adds this description of the future "'68 generation": The lucky ones, Aron concluded, will escape from this situation where the cultural norms (norms defining a collective ideal) are crumbling, not by joining an "order that might replace it" (through political action) but "by withdrawal and apathy, by retiring to their country cottages."[25]

As a result, said Ferry and Renault, the spirit of '68, the spirit of nihilism and relativism, needed to be exorcised by calling upon the enchanting powers of the responsible citizen-individual of the liberal tradition. They invoked ethics, specifically a Kantian ethics of individual responsibility, as a solution to problems introduced by May 1968. And yet, in another sense, Ferry and Renault were themselves symptomatic of French intellectual culture after the ethical turn. Again, foregrounding the figure of the individual said a lot about French political culture under Mitterrand during the 1980s.

Prioritizing the individual, however, minimized other aspects of the inheritance of May 1968's "ethics of liberation" and what Joffrin called the "democratic insurrection," such as dialogue, equality of condition, intersubjective association, shared horizons, participation, and protest, which could not be simply reduced to a liberalism centred on the individual. It is precisely this interpretation of May 1968 as nihilistic and individualistic that is in question; the turn to ethics, which did eventually *also* include the kind of post-political move about which Lipovetsky, for instance, was concerned, did not amount merely to the formulation of individualized solutions to problems introduced by the events. For this reason, the positive role played by the energies of 1968 in the ethical turn has remained unacknowledged.

Even three decades later, as the predictable slew of commemorative works appeared, interpretive divisions still appeared between those favourably disposed (most often veteran *soixante-huitards* reciting strained caveats and frank ambivalences), and those so critical as to dismiss or to call to a close the period inaugurated by 1968. The former-Trotskyist-turned-Socialist-politician Henri Weber described the multiple, at times inconsistent "ambitions" of 1968 as having been "democratic and liberational [*libertaire*]," "hedonistic and communitarian," and "romantic and messianic." Echoing Joffrin, he concluded: "What remains of May '68 is the ferocious and visceral attachment to individual liberty and equality of rights and opportunities, in a word, democracy."[26] In one of the most thorough studies of post-1968 French radicalism, Jean-Pierre Le Goff also spoke of "democratic passion," borrowing the term from Olivier Mongin but insisting that the reinvigoration of contemporary political life required nothing less than abandoning May's "impossible inheritance." To Le Goff, the legacy of 1968 represented an "impasse." Far-left movements of that era had appealed to the traditions of the French Revolution and earlier workers' movements, but their emphasis on "desire" and immediacy had sabotaged the "sacrifice" and discipline necessary for "collective action." In other words, said Le Goff, caught between "neo-Leninism" and "*les désirants*" (the party of desire we will see in Parts II and III below), and enchanted by the idea of a "blank slate," cultural leftism unintentionally destroyed both the "myth of revolution" and the "rational and ethical foundations of politics." In addition to confirming Lipovetsky's view that the era had intensified hedonistic individualism, Le Goff cited other symptoms of post-1968 anti-democratic malaise: 1980s "consensus" politics characterized by emphasis on human rights, tolerance, and the "right to difference"; postmodernism's "new sophists," who embraced the nihilistic "desert" of post-political life; the disorientation of the Left under Mitterrand; media spectacle; and outright reaction. To some extent, Le Goff's judgment built on his earlier studies of contemporary management practices, in which transparency, participation, and individual initiative had become principal, if insidiously constraining norms. He emphasized on this occasion that neo-liberal market culture reflected the "recomposition" of some aspirations found in 1968. The radicalism of that era had been enthralled with the notion of a "blank slate," a view that had tragically been fortified by 1980s and 1990s neo-liberalism. Reinvigorating structurally modest democratic politics, Le Goff concluded, therefore meant abandoning the illusion of total and immediate life transformation. All-or-nothing thinking and the fantasy of an absolute beginning were stumbling blocks en route to mundane yet relevant political citizenship.[27] While Le Goff's treatment had the merit of entering into the cultural and intellectual history of *les années '68* in some detail, politically, his argument extended the Lipovetsky, Ferry, and Renault line: May 1968 had indeed become in French cultural memory not a defeated revolution but the origin of a decline. As Aron had worried, France had become a nation of country cottages and their disengaged, atomistic, and consuming inhabitants.

We have seen how descriptions of what transpired in May 1968 were intimately bound to explanations of why the events erupted, and that those explanations tended over time toward re-evaluations of 1968's significance. The intervening decades have witnessed a transition from description to explanation to meaning. There had been immediate, colourful sketches of students in a time of abundance, who conjured revolution while fomenting revolt. Others had speculated about the eventfulness of events. Then came the plethora of explanations: crises of authority and interpretation (de Certeau); conspiracy, university eruption, youth rebellion, a metaphysical revolt, a crisis of civilization, new social movements, traditional social conflicts, political strife, and chance (Bénéton and Touchard); and subsequent reduction (Joffrin's five explanations, Ferry and Renault's four).

I have drawn the most simplistic division possible among interpretations of 1968, along both positive and negative axes. Obviously, both aspects were present. From the brief survey above, so-called negative interpretations have predominated. If Lefort, Morin, and Castoriadis saw May as opening a revolutionary "breach" in history, they subsequently conceded that any rupture had closed and that 1968 ambiguously gestured toward other, unrealized possibilities for social and political life. Joffrin and Weber also noted May's inconsistent ambitions while maintaining – lest one forget – that the movements associated with it had been democratic at heart. Pushing the balance into the deficit column more explicitly, a range of analyses have insisted that the partisans of May 1968 ironically achieved the opposite of what they had wanted, their collectivist aspirations having reinforced liberal capitalist individualism. Each in his own way – Debray, Lipovetsky, Ferry and Renault, and Le Goff – criticized 1968 for its deleterious consequences, including the advancement of market capitalism, widespread depoliticization, the rise of hedonistic individualism, and the nihilistic undermining of humanistic culture.

It is remarkable how these accounts have worked fields first tilled by Raymond Aron. For he, too, had concerns about the destructive effects of individuals who had no clearly articulated political program and no apparent regard for the mediatory institutions of civil society. To be sure, the issue of the Fifth Republic's stability was not as pertinent in the 1980s and 1990s as it seemingly was in 1968, when the constitution was ten years old; and predominant anxieties had shifted from threatened individual freedom to the threat that individual freedom was the be all and end all of social and political life. Nevertheless, the judgment that May 1968's "revolutionary" excesses were harmful and that its "positive" self-understanding was essentially "negative" has risen to prominence in France.

As we have seen, the slogan "It is forbidden to forbid" illustrated the great difficulty of escaping reference to norms. Antiauthoritarian antinomianism in itself seems to valorize the intentional transgression of laws and limits. In fact, such action can be interpreted as relying on unstated and implicit normative visions: the desire to break with norms can itself be considered normative. Wrapped in dense "revolutionary" and political fabric, 1968's virtually unmentioned "ethics of liberation" was at once critical, affirmative, implicit, and ambiguous. Critique is usually carried out in the name of something. The May revolt's affirmative ethics was largely hidden behind critique, since categories like values, norms, and ethics were themselves considered suspect. The situation was bound to lead to confusion, in the same way, for instance, that a critique of freedom might be misinterpreted as merely a rejection of freedom instead of an effort to push freedom, as it were, out of freedom's way. So, while the merit of Aron, Lipovetsky, Ferry and Renault, and Le Goff's analyses was to have identified May 1968's attack on a variety of social, political, cultural, and intellectual norms, they were mistaken to conclude that such critiques ultimately had "nihilistic" intentions and ramifications. Though it would have been appropriate to use the word *nihilistic* to describe negation as an end in itself, the evidence suggests that this stance was not the prevalent message and self-understanding of May's protagonists.

Were there unanticipated consequences in the aftermath of 1968? Of course there were; the turn to ethics was one such consequence. Can the events of May 1968 themselves, as well as the substantive changes that transpired in French social, political, cultural, and intellectual life, be reduced to the de-politicized individualism of the nihilistic marketplace? Of course not. Aron himself had called the May events a "moral revolt." What makes post-1968 France and the forms of thought it brought forth so exciting is that efforts to articulate ethics often took surprising forms that were unrecognizable to some people's minds and to some ethical traditions.

Part of the misrecognition of the ethical turn as one legacy of May 1968 is the tendency to view the post-1968 period through the lens of political history, especially as a shift from revolutionary politics to liberal politics. In truth, the relationship of the ethical turn to politics is thorny. A number of overlapping elements tensely coexisted within the same historical field. One might consider Aron's liberal view that 1968 was anti-political since it menaced the institutional stability of the Republic, that orderly prerequisite to any healthy political life. Later critics like Le Goff also underscored 1968's anti-political consequences, not because liberal politics were threatened but because they had become "Americanized" – depoliticization being one of the unfortunate fruits of May's hedonistic and nihilistic individualism. Still, one might observe how radicals of the era, including the counterculture and new social movements, attempted to politicize many aspects of everyday life beyond commonly recognized "official politics" of elections, parties, reform, and state power. We will be concerned with this phenomenon in Parts I and II below. In Part III, the tensions between the opponents and defenders of lawful politics reach a breaking point. Yet, as we will see in Part IV, electoral politics continued their staid grind in the 1970s, even if enlivened by theories of "self-management" [*autogestion*] and by the contributions of the new social movements, both of which were commandeered at a certain point by the Socialist and Communist parties' Union of the Left (1972–77). Furthermore, drawing on the energies of 1968 – at the edges of electoral politics and in the context of mid-1970s debates on totalitarianism – thinkers like Claude Lefort, Marcel Gauchet, and Pierre Rosanvallon revived political philosophy. They posed basic political questions anew at the very moment when the revolutionary paradigm was coming undone; that is, between May's "failure" and the Socialist Party's electoral success at the polls in 1981. Lipovetsky, Ferry, and Renault's attacks were published in what became known as the liberal and Tocquevillean moment, and related in turn to the late-twentieth-century renaissance of French Republicanism. Thus, one needs to be clear that any decline of the revolutionary paradigm and ascendancy of liberalism were part and parcel of a more general problematization of the political during the 1970s, which involved the rejection of revolution, depoliticization, attempts to politicize everyday life, the continuing saga of electoral politics, and the revival of political thinking.

The turn to ethics was partly related to this problematization of the political. As I shall later demonstrate, 1968's revolutionary politics themselves contained the seeds of the turn that ultimately substituted ethics for revolution. In this process, the attempt to politicize everyday life, de-politicization, and the turn to ethics formed a pertinent cluster of circumstances. A strong case can be made that the revival of political philosophy, de Tocqueville, liberalism, and so forth, by the late 1970s and early 1980s was itself one of the positive consequences of 1968's legacy, as social action and protest not only helped undermine the revolutionary paradigm but also contributed to the need to rethink French political culture. It is worth observing that the post-1968 problematization of the political brought forward the requirement that politics proceed under the star of ethical concern. Some political matters in the late twentieth century could be seen as subordinate to ethical prerogatives. Not that politics ever lives up to ethical limitations, but in the era of ethics one finds phenomena that bespeak a supercession of politics by ethics. Indeed, the presence of ethics has become an interpretive grid for judging pure political reasoning, for example, in cases of humanitarianism and human rights or in instances when French traditions of political violence have been sidelined (the strikes of 1995 and riots of 2005 and 2006, though serious, did not de-stabilize the Republic as the events of 1934 and 1958 did). Politics since the 1960s has shown itself susceptible to a variety of ethical concerns, obsessions, and limits, and it was harder in the late twentieth century to take seriously older forms of political reasoning according to which all sorts of means were justified in the name of desired ends. The twentieth century began with Vladimir Lenin's observation that making an omelet meant breaking eggs; it ended with the assertion of the rights of chickens.

May's "liberal" critics – Debray, Lipovetsky, and Le Goff – had criticized 1968 for the atomization to which it led in spite of its solidaristic intentions. Ferry and Renault, like Aron, criticized the era for not being liberal enough, that is, for not clearly formulating and founding a politics of rights and limits. Again, the fundamental critique was that 1968 had enhanced market capitalism, depoliticization, hedonistic individualism, and nihilism. In this light the story of revolution-to-liberalism has a downward trajectory. But the same developments can also be viewed differently. Within this amplified capitalist framework, official politics ceased to be the primary forum for individuals to work out their relationships to themselves, one another, institutions, and humanity in general. By the late twentieth century, ethics seemed a framework more appropriate to the tasks of living than politics. Certainly, the ethical turn was at points compatible with the economic and political liberalism that came to predominate in the 1980s and 1990s, but it also included elements at odds with the liberal imaginary. To grasp this we need to draw a contrast – suggestive and not strict – between the liberal and the democratic sides of liberal-democracy. In gross terms, liberalism sees the individual and rights at the heart of political life, and democracy focuses on legal and social equality. The ethos of 1968 was thus one place where the heart of democracy and democratization could be felt beating.

Considering the affirmative sides of 1968 means taking seriously its democratic impulses. With Joffrin and Weber, and in a different way with Lefort, Morin, and Castoriadis, one can note that the spirit of '68 and of "the after-'68 period" [*l'après-68*] was in part a democratic spirit. I do not mean democracy only in the sense of a citizen's relationship to the state, electoral processes, and rights guaranteed by law – those liberal hallmarks; although some so-called revolutionary rhetoric and acts had liberal-democratic ramifications that actually protected civil liberties in the early 1970s (Part I), and contributed to legal reforms in the mid-1970s and early 1980s (Part III). Beyond the liberal-legal framework, the democratic spirit of '68 also penetrated daily life, interpersonal relationships, and mores. It led to a revitalization of civil society, new forms of associational life, and critical institutional engagements. It brought about reassessments of what it meant to be a citizen in late modern society and catalysed remarkably influential and creative intellectual work in a variety of fields. It eventually reached out beyond the structures of the state to visualize new forms of universalism. The implication of this interpretation is that there is a link between the democratic impulses of 1968 and the ethical turn. We are confronted with the fact that May's "revolutionary" rhetoric contributed to a reinvigoration of democracy, notwithstanding some of the deleterious developments discussed above. Ultimately, democracies do maintain the liberal virtues of individual freedom and law, and there is no doubt that some sides of 1968-era radicalism were illiberal. In fact, in Part III below we will see that some feminists chose law over anti-legal radicalism. Yet liberalism does not exhaust democracy, especially democracy's concern for equality and sociability. Democratic society in its fullest and most realized sense is neither entirely liberal nor illiberal.

In 1980 Lefort made this penetrating observation, worth quoting at length, about France "since 1968":

> The inability to conceive of [human rights] politically ... has had strange consequences: whether they concern the family, women, children, or sexuality, whether they concern justice, the function of the magistrates, or the condition of prisoners ... we have seen either changes in legislation or the rise of new demands that ... testify to new collective needs ... If we wish to conceive of a new relationship to the political, we should begin by recognizing that it is beginning to take shape before our eyes. So our first task is not to invent; it is to interpret, to raise to the level of reflection a practice which is not silent, of course, but which, being necessarily diffuse, is unaware of its significance in society at large ... Faced with the demand for or defense of a right, [a movement] has to respond according to its principles, according to the criteria of the just and the unjust and not only of the permitted and the forbidden.[28]

The citation is replete. To begin with, the contrast between the criteria of the just/unjust and the criteria of the permitted/forbidden reaches the essence of the "forbidden to forbid" mantra and its paradoxical, contradictory, and implicit normativity. In what follows we will indeed encounter "new demands," "collective needs," and "changes in legislation" related to women, children, and sexuality; prisoners; and the mentally ill. Above all, though, our pursuit of the ethical turn of the 1970s is an effort "to raise to the level of reflection" a practice that remains otherwise scattered and dispersed. In this specific context, Lefort was musing on the difficulties of articulating human rights from a political point of view and contending with the fact that a "new relationship to the political" was emerging. That new relationship involved new reworkings of and reflections upon political ethics, politics, and ethics *tout court*.

Neither a nihilistic and relativistic sign of Western civilization's decline nor an authentic but failed nineteenth-century revolution, May 1968 was an ambiguous event that opened a period of significant transformation in French politics, society, culture, and intellectual life. Attempts to blame the 1980s and 1990s on the 1960s are largely just that – attempts to blame. Later developments, while obviously not unrelated to *les années soixante-huit*, have dynamics and a momentum of their own. This story of the post-1968 ethical turn is thus a partial corrective to interpretations of 1968 that have predominated in France.

May 1968 was neither the best nor the worst of times. The total revolution its partisans believed they were executing did not arrive, but neither did the events of that spring amount simply to an infantile tantrum, worthy of their critics scorn. There was genuine social unrest that began in a minority student milieu and eventually affected the highest levels of government and large swatches of the French population. No one can deny the unforeseen shock of the events. Though dramatically suggestive in retrospect, Pierre Viansson-Ponté's famous *Le Monde* article of 15 March 1968, claiming that "France was bored," cannot be granted any predictive credit.[29] There had been preliminaries, and the totality of contributing factors – demographic, economic, political, social, cultural, and intellectual – has been the subject of ceaseless comment and analysis at the time and since. In the context of international student uprisings, circumstances in France reached levels of intensity and national crisis witnessed nowhere else. Even voices of caution like Raymond Aron's fretted over the "fragility" of French institutions and the state. To speculate on whether the Fifth Republic might have collapsed if circumstances had evolved differently might be an amusing counter-factual exercise, but in point of fact it did not. France did not experience a "revolution" in the familiar sense of the word. The institutions of the Fifth Republic held, and more than one observer noted that the weaker ones of the Fourth Republic likely would not have. Behind the chants in the streets, addressed to de Gaulle, that "ten years was enough" lay the fact that the previous Republic had lasted only twelve years (October 1946–September 1958). The government *was* a target. Yet 1968 marks the beginning of the Fifth Republic's transition to its post-Gaullist era, during which it achieved a stability guaranteed by more than the force of the General's personality. Jean Ferinot certainly exaggerated when he wrote: "One can say, correctly I believe, that General de Gaulle died not in November 1970, but two years earlier, in the spring of 1968."[30] Nevertheless, the writing was on the wall.

The events of 1968 opened a period. Surprising and unprecedented though it was, May '68 was not a lightning flash that vanished as suddenly as it appeared. In the decade that followed, the nature of the Fifth Republic and the role of the state in national life would be challenged through a continuing intensification of citizen demands upon the government and its institutions. Those demands materialized in the field of civil society, that very intermediate public space about which Aron, for instance, had expressed concern. The languages and symbolic practices of "revolution" contributed to an enlivening of civil society, to a liberalization of "private" mores, and to reforms by the French state. Cultural contestation was occasionally the growing point of civil society. There was sometimes a slip between what social actors thought they were doing and what (within the limits of interpretation alone) was *really* going on "behind their backs." To be sure, there was no shortage of illusion, hyperbole, and theatre in May; and thus also no lack of disillusionment and deflated dreams in the years that followed (the least explored topic of 1968 is the number of suicides related to its "failure"). The mélange of revolutionary intentions and democratic consequences, and the gradual shedding of the former in order to reveal the latter, would be one of the most important legacies of 1968. The ethical turn wove both continuity and originality in complex layers and patterns, and the story is not one of simple tragic decline or of comic resolution. As for the events themselves, the inheritance of May 1968 is ambiguous and contradictory. But contradiction – the realm of refusal, incoherence, impasse, and paradox – also generates dialectical and dialogical movement.

Even if many of the cobblestones in the Latin Quarter are today paved with asphalt, it is true, as anyone who has watched workers repairing the streets can attest, there *is* sand beneath the streets of Paris. A beach? ... well ... .

PART ONE

The Sabre and the Keyhole: French Maoism, Violence, and Prisoner Dignity

Even though the economic and political motives for the explosions of popular violence are obvious, the explosions can only be explained by the fact that these motives were *morally* appreciated by the masses ... Theirs is an attempt to put together a *moral* society ... a society in which man, no longer alienated, will be able to find himself in his real relationship with the group. Violence, spontaneity, morality: for the Maoists these are the three immediate characteristics of revolutionary action.

Jean-Paul Sartre (1972)

La Santé [Prison], 24 January 1971
My dear [Daniel] Guérin,

Thank you for your solidarity. It is as precious for my comrades as it is for me. The support on the exterior of the prison is decisive. It is not a question of a handful of prisoners and the apparatus of the state, but a combat between freedom and oppression.

Fraternally,
Alain Geismar

The prisoners occupy the prisons like the workers occupy the factories. The prisoners now want to – they must, they can – explain themselves directly to the population on questions that ought to trouble society as a whole: Why are we in prison? Who goes to prison? Why the prison? For whom? Against whom?

Groupe d'information sur les prisons (1972)

2

A Press Conference

On 5 January 1972 a press conference was held to discuss a revolt that had erupted the previous month at the prison in Toul, France, several hours by train east of Paris.[1] The revolt had begun as a peaceful work strike, and through the mediation of the prison chaplain, the administration had promised the prisoners that some of their demands would be met. When that promise was broken several days later, the prisoners occupied and destroyed part of the prison. Riot police had to be called in to quell the rebellion. Not all the facts of the situation had made it into the mainstream newspapers, and Toul was hardly mentioned on state-run French television. The press conference had thus been called by the Agence de presse libération (APL) to share the prisoners' version of how the events had escalated and to comment on the "hell-like" living conditions behind the walls. This was not the first such press conference. The APL, formed the previous June under the aegis of the Maoist group, the Gauche prolétarienne (GP), was designed to publicize the diverse activities of the far-left movements, which had proliferated after the events of May 1968.[2] The Maoists believed the mainstream press was in cahoots with the state, the unions, the bourgeoisie – in short, those reactionary forces that opposed the revolutionary forces of workers and their allies. Since 1968, there had been no shortage of situations about which to pursue a self-proclaimed, retributive "propaganda" campaign. In the years known in France as the "far-left period" [*les années extrême-gauche*], workers, college and high-school students, women, gays, immigrants, and other social groups promoted the French version of the New Left. Violent clashes between the French government and its foes had intensified dramatically since 1968. In this context, Toul was no anomaly.

At the 5 January 1972 press conference, Michel Foucault spoke in person and a message from Jean-Paul Sartre was read. Sartre represented the point of view of the Comité de vérité de Toul, a group loosely affiliated with the GP, set up on 14 December 1971. Sartre had been associated with the Gauche prolétarienne since the spring of 1970, when the group had come under heavy attack by the government for its radical activities. Sixty-eight years old and going blind, the elder statesman of French letters found renewed energy by rising to the defence of his Maoist friends. "What is a prisoner?" Sartre wrote: "He is a man detained against his will. Why is he detained? Because he dared to revolt individually against our sinister society." Giving the specific example of juvenile auto theft, Sartre generalized crime to stand for political conflict between the state and the citizenry as well as for class conflict between those with means and those without. People steal, he said, because of their lot in life; crime itself is political, since it is a response to an economically and politically unjust society. The plight of prisoners bore a synecdochic relation – an example of a larger case that is also a metaphor for that case – to the situation of all people disenfranchised by the state and bourgeois society. Behind prison walls, the warden is "king ... he interprets the law as he wants"; "suspicion" and "denunciations" characterize an environment where "life is unbearable." Prisons are a focal point of a system in which it is "impossible to live and most of the time to die": "No matter what one thinks of a car theft, is it warranted to turn the thief into an animal, into an other-than-man? In fact, the prison administration does not punish them in our name: society represses us as it does them." Since life outside the walls can be presumed to parallel life within them, by the same logic, the prison revolt at Toul was exemplary, a "model" of the struggle "for justice, for dialogue." Sartre concluded by asking if the events at Toul might not be viewed as the "beginning of our struggle against the repressive regime that holds all of us – even those who do not enter prison – in a concentration camp universe." The comparison of French society, exemplified by the prison, to the Nazi concentration camps was fraught, dense, and extreme; labels of "fascist" and "resistance" still had significant currency in 1970s France. The old existentialist exhumed his notion of "choice" between clean and dirty hands – between quietistic non-intervention and political engagement – but the question, too, was loaded. "Don't forget," he added dramatically, "that man himself, his freedom, and his meaning depend on it."

Foucault, for his part, spoke on behalf of the Groupe d'information sur les prisons (GIP).[3] Formed eleven months earlier in February 1971, the GIP had concentrated its activist efforts solely on prisons, places that had recently attracted much attention in the wake of the arrest and incarceration of numerous leftists. Foucault was the driving, if self-effacing, force behind the GIP. While fresh as a lecturer at the Collège de France, he was also living the life of a political activist for really the first time. In his remarks at the 5 January press conference, Foucault stressed the institutional regime of the prison system: "Toul is not a monstrosity in the penal system. It is the penal system itself." Justice in France, he said, works in the following way: a person violates a law and is put in prison "in the name of the law." Once the prisoner enters the prison, the penal system refuses him or her recourse to the law: "Law and right stop there where the prison begins. Justice puts the prisoner outside the law [*hors la loi*]." The prisoner then "belongs" to the rule of "the arbitrary, violence, uncontrolled repression, and the secret." The revolt at Toul was remarkable because it was a movement of the prisoners themselves "against the powers that be in order to assert and command respect for their rights." It was an action that dared to say that the emperor had no clothes, thus exposing the naked force of the penitentiary system. It was a "political movement" whose reverberation would be felt in other prisons as well as the public at large. Spreading word of what was happening in the prison was essential, since speaking out might prevent repression and "silence." Still, Foucault suggested, it was important to see the difference between "support" outside the walls and the fact that prisoners themselves had to say "what must be."

Most of Foucault's remarks were devoted to the principle that those outside support those inside. He read a list of six proposals for change that had been collected through an "investigation," a survey having been passed around prisons and among former prisoners. The prisoners wanted: an end to censorship; an equalization of working conditions in prison with those outside; the establishment of juridical mechanisms to prevent guard abuse and allow prisoners to defend themselves against accusations made against them; the standardization of an otherwise arbitrary parole process by making legal counsel consistently available; the revocation of the *casier judiciaire*, a permanent prison record that caused great difficulty for post-prison employment; and finally, in order to counter the bias and corruption of prison administrators, independent commissions composed of outside persons (former prisoners and families of prisoners) who would be allowed to enter prisons to check on the conditions of inmates, interview them without guards present, and develop an "informed opinion."

While leaving to prisoners themselves the task of articulating the content of the changes they wanted, Foucault did mention the "campaign" of support on the outside: "This campaign is the responsibility of all: former prisoners, families of prisoners, lawyers, doctors, psychiatrists, chaplains, and all who are concerned with prisons." Whereas for Sartre engagement was a response to collective oppression mirrored on each side of the prison wall, for Foucault, it was a series of strategic alliances among those affected by and concerned about imprisonment. "It is necessary," he concluded, "that around each prison a group of investigation or struggle be formed, ready to support the fight of these men who, on the other side of the walls, struggle against justice, for their rights." The phrase "investigation or struggle" was significant, since the GIP was doing much to advocate "investigation" itself as a form of "struggle." In the spirit of participation and direct democracy that characterized Foucault's remarks, someone then read aloud an anonymous "testimony" of a prisoner who had participated in the revolt.

The 5 January 1972 APL press conference is notable if only for the status of the intellectual figures who came to the defence of the Toul prisoners. Alongside Sartre's text and Foucault's intervention, the philosopher Gilles Deleuze spoke, as did the prison psychiatrist, Edith Rose.[4] Rose's remarks on 5 January, with other comments made at another press conference held on 16 December 1971, cast her in the role of a whistle-blower.[5] Her revelations on psychiatric mistreatment and the correlations between criminalization and pathologization within the justice system served as a model for Foucault and Deleuze's later conversation (4 March 1972) on what they called the "specific intellectual," by which they meant liberal professionals, intellectuals, and informed people engaging critically on the basis of their own expertise rather than in the name of generalized criteria such as "revolution" or "justice."[6] David Macey notes that the 5 January press conference was reported in *Le Monde* only two days later. Sartre's comment was quoted at length; Foucault's was not even mentioned. Not only was Sartre ... well ... Sartre, but his association of Toul with the Nazi concentration camps surely made better copy than Foucault's attempt at passing on the complaints of those behind the walls. "Foucault's one comment at the time," writes Macey, "was that it was so sad to see *Le Monde* devoting so much time to Sartre and failing to mention the prisoners' demands."[7]

The APL conference is also interesting for its direct contrast between two former intellectual adversaries who had only recently met. (They had engaged in a brief polemic in 1966 on the question of humanism and antihumanism – Sartre calling the author of *The Order of Things* (1966) "a positivist in despair," Foucault replying in kind that the *Critique of Dialectical Reason* (1960) was "a nineteenth-century man's magnificent and pathetic attempt to think the twentieth century."[8]) Although they had shared the platform at a rally held at the Mutualité meeting hall on 10 February 1969 over the police evacuation of the University of Vincennes, hotbed of radicalism, they did not actually meet until 27 November 1971.[9] Foucault and Sartre would be seen together at numerous protests and demonstrations throughout 1972 and for the rest of the decade. Lastly, the press conference is interesting for the way in which the two philosophers' respective arguments diverge – Sartre remaining invested in a quasi-revolutionary belief in broad revolt against alienated society, Foucault trying to articulate a delicate balance between the spirit of direct democracy (very much of the moment) and a role for concerned allies. While both were clearly attempting to connect the events at Toul to a context beyond the prison, their visions of the nature and means of this connection could not have been further apart: for Sartre the lives of *prisoners* were unbearable; whereas for Foucault it was *prison conditions* that were "intolerable." Sartre was arguing *for* revolutionary justice on behalf of an oppressed class of people; Foucault, criticizing the penal institution, was arguing *against* the judicial system and ultimately against the category of justice itself.

Perhaps more significant than the meanings immediately generated by this particular situation is the way the press conference represented a convergence of forces and discourses that went beyond the particular occasion of Toul, the APL, the Comité de vérité de Toul, the GIP, or even Sartre's and Foucault's comments. The press conference, like Sartre's prisons, bore a synecdochic relation to broader cultural and political meanings about revolution, violence, law, justice, and intellectuals in France, meanings that were coming more clearly into focus in the years after the May events. The conference was not necessarily exemplary, since it was but one scene in a larger narrative. Nor was it a pivotal moment, in the sense that it culminated past trends. Still, one can see the convergence of forces and discourses that had accumulated, some since 1968, some for much longer. More specifically, it was a moment in which currents and countercurrents in the particular field of post-1968 French Maoism came together. Prisons had come to the fore due to the dialectics of far-left activism and state repression. Leftists, by no means all of them Maoists, had upped the ante after 1968, engaging in dramatic forms of violent or pseudo-violent protest, and the French government had taken a hard line in return. Demonization had been mutual. The policy of zero tolerance by the government landed more than a few radicals in jail, and their presence in French prisons led directly, as we will see below, to a politicization of prisons themselves. Out of this politicization and the subsequent mobilization on behalf of prisoners, notably through the efforts of the GIP, came a re-evaluation of revolutionary violence and the difficult genesis of another *ethos*. Prisons were one site where the meaning of contestation quickened and evolved in 1970s France.

Sartre represented the figure of revolutionary justice longing to stand, sabre in hand, above the King's head placed on a chopping block. Foucault was like a member of the crowd, twisting his neck to get a better view of what was going on inside the prison, peering through a keyhole in a barred and locked door. Therein lay the difference between two approaches to revolution, violence, law, justice, prisoner dignity, and ethics.

3

Violence and the Gauche prolétarienne

"Of all the Maoist organizations after May 1968," Christophe Bourseiller writes, "the most important numerically as well as in cultural influence was without question the Gauche prolétarienne."[1] During the six years of its existence from 1968–74, the group was so omnipresent that, as another observer put it, "when in France one said, *les Maoïstes*, it was usually assumed one was referring to the Gauche prolétarienne."[2] Most of the young leaders of the GP, and a good number of its members and sympathizers, came from the youthful cultural elite of France, as witnessed by the trajectories of many former GP-ists in the 1970s and 1980s. Names that might be familiar would include Alain Finkielkraut, André Glucksmann, Serge July, and the late Benny Lévy. At the time, they were able, quite remarkably, to pull some of the most prominent French intellectuals into their sphere of influence: Jean-Paul Sartre, Michel Foucault, Gilles Deleuze, Maurice Clavel, Simone de Beauvoir, and Jean-Luc Godard. *Les Maos* were briefly at the centre of a romantic-revolutionary maelstrom which, when it was over, had contributed in no small way to major changes in French political culture. Paul Berman's enticing description captures the GP sensibility: "They had a swaggering air, half-brilliant and half-crazy, full of dash and combativeness, a style of leather jackets and alarming slogans, which is to say, they were rebellious, thuggish, hostile, alluring. A familiar enough style in twentieth-century Europe: a posture of extremism and violence, slightly dandified."[3]

The GP officially formed in October 1968 from elements of the recently collapsed Union des jeunesses communistes marxistes-léninistes (UJC(ml)), which had been founded in December 1966 by students at the Ecole normale supérieure on the rue d'Ulm in Paris. The principal animators had been greatly influenced by the theoretical Marxism of their teacher Louis

Althusser and had embraced Maoism in an effort to cultivate radicalism out from under the sway of the Parti communiste français (PCF). Between 1966 and 1968, the members of the UJC(ml) had engaged in two specific political programs: they had gone to farms and factories to undertake "investigations" [*enquêtes*] of real live farmers and workers in order to supplement and ground their highly abstract Marxism; and they had been active in the popular Left opposition to the Vietnam War. Since the Maoist method of "investigation" became essential for the GIP, it is worth saying a brief word about it.

Mao Tse-tung had discussed the program of "investigation" in detail for the first time in the midst of a civil war against bourgeois nationalists and defenders of the feudal order. The title of the first section of his May 1930 essay "Oppose Book Worship" declared bluntly: "No Investigation, No Right to Speak."

> Unless you have investigated a problem, you will be deprived of the right to speak on it ... You can't solve a problem? Well, get down and investigate the present facts and its past history! When you have investigated the problem thoroughly, you will know how to solve it ... Investigation may be likened to the long months of pregnancy, and solving a problem to the day of birth. To investigate a problem is, indeed, to solve it.[4]

Investigations yielded knowledge to be used in struggle. When the Red Army arrived in a locale, "it would first [make] itself familiar with the class situation of the locality and then [formulate] slogans suited to the needs of the masses." The investigation was designed "to dissect the different social classes" in order to "understand" them and thereby elaborate the "correct tactics" for the struggle. In the process the Party would learn who its friends and enemies were. The 1930 essay concluded with a seven-point plan on the "technique" of investigation, instructing investigators to: hold "fact-finding meetings and undertake investigations through discussion"; include relevant people; prepare a questionnaire; participate directly in the investigation and make one's own notes; and "probe deeply" into "a particular place or problem" in order to glean lessons for the future. Those lessons required an attitude of "humility" on the part of the investigator/activist. In 1941 Mao drove home the point, counselling the investigator: "First direct your eyes downward, do not hold your head high and gaze at the sky. Unless a person is interested in turning his eyes downward and is determined to do so, he will never in his whole life really understand things in China."[5] Indeed, for French student Maoists, the experience of leaving the crème de la crème shelter of the Ecole on the rue d'Ulm to face farmers and workers was likely a humbling one.

By 1967 the tactic of investigation had created tensions in the UJC(ml) between those committed to Althusser-inspired theoretical practice and those who took the empirico-practical lessons of hands-on experience to heart. Preoccupied with its own internal organizational conflicts and suspicious of the anarchistic spirit of Nanterre, the group largely underestimated the events of May 1968. That fall, the UJC(ml) split up and some of its members – Olivier Rolin, Jean-Pierre Le Dantec, Jean-Claude Vernier, Tony Lévy (Benny's brother), Jean Schiavo, Maurice Brover, and Jean-Claude Zancarini (a.k.a. "Tarzan"), among others – formed the Gauche prolétarienne.[6] Benny Lévy, the undisputed leader of the GP, later recalled:

> In Paris a group of not more than forty, fundamentally united by the struggle against liquidationist positions ... decided to put out [the newspaper] *La Cause du peuple* with the theme: "What's new is the practice of maximum proletarization" and apply the thesis "power is at the end of a gun" to the concrete conditions in France. That was basically our program. There were not many other ideas; it was a direction. We would engage ourselves and then we would see.[7]

The GP first undertook a relentless, often perverse self-criticism [*auto-critique*] over why the UJC(ml) had misread the May events. Mao's texts were instrumental in this process; as a GP document asserted unambiguously in October 1968: "All error goes back to an incorrect interpretation of Mao."[8] May's defeat was explained by pulling out a favourite trump card in the Marxist deck; departures from the correct theoretical and practical line – revisionism – had clouded the situation. Caught in too rigid a formula of workerist revolution, the UJC(ml) had ignored Mao's correct view that class struggle needed to adapt to local political and cultural situations. They had thus misjudged the antiauthoritarian ethos of the May events. In October 1968, it seemed that "in the last analysis" the situation involved "a struggle between those who still want to make a revolution and those who do not." The students in May could be applauded (after the fact) for their "audacity and organization." So too, the "liberal professions" – doctors and lawyers were specifically named – had "under the effects of the May tempest" proved to be "extremely progressive."[9]

The notion of linking Maoism with May's ethos was put into practice during the winter and spring of 1969 as the GP welcomed members of the March 22nd Movement and former student union leaders, like Alain Geismar and Serge July, into its ranks. The group read with interest

Geismar and July's analysis of the situation in France, *Vers la guerre civile*, written between May 1968 and March 1969. It did not take long for the GP-ists to become known as "Mao-spontex," or Maoist-spontaneists. The name was originally an insult – *Spontex* was the brand name of a cleaning sponge – intended to belittle the group's embrace of antiauthoritarianism as an element of revolutionary contestation. The marxisant tradition had long criticized spontaneism as an anarchistic error. The first issue of the *Cahiers de la Gauche prolétarienne*, published in April 1969 under the title "From the Anti-Authoritarian Revolt to the Proletarian Revolution," illustrated the GP's diverging vision.[10] The publication claimed that the GP would draw on the best of the May student movement, fuse it with Maoist practice, and end up with a genuine proletarian movement. Acknowledging students and liberal professionals as allies in a "revolutionary" struggle did not fit certain revolutionary blueprints, but on this occasion May's ethos proved stronger than the law of revolutionary orthodoxy.

From the fall of 1968 to the spring of 1970 the GP gained its reputation for brash adventurism. Of the many forms of action it pursued – among high-school and university students, soldiers, factory workers, immigrants, doctors, members of the women's movement, and others – one in particular bears closer examination, since its dynamics will lead us to the issue behind prisons; namely, violence. In October 1968 the GP's "most burning questions" concerned "ideological struggle, the fight against the legal establishment, mass political organization, forms of propaganda and agitation, [and] mass struggle against repression through violence."[11] It did not take long for "violence" to become, to borrow a Freudian term updated by Althusser, an overdetermined category meant to carry the political and ideological weight of inculcation, confrontation with the legal establishment, propaganda, and direct struggle against repression. This promotion of violence arose in part from a narrow and ultimately foolish judgment of the situation in France, of which this December 1968 text was representative:

> 1. We are actually in a *period of intense class struggle*, a period when the bourgeoisie fights to save its skin. 2. The means of economic, political, and ideological action of the bourgeois dictatorship are considerably weak, and oblige it to *have recourse as soon as possible to brutal repression*, in an effort to erase what it cannot fight by other means ... One should see that this situation is totally *new*.
>
> Above all, we must not neglect *the constructive role of violent struggle against repression*: if its principal aspect is to *protect* the masses and the communists who work among them ... its secondary aspect is to *accelerate* political work.[12]

Through its soul-searching self-criticism in the autumn of 1968, the group arrived at the judgment that in May the UJC(ml) had placed too much emphasis on the "self-defence" of workers in factories and had thus trivialized student-led street violence as "petit-bourgeois." Violence could be a "launching pad," however, and should be regarded as an offensive tool as well as a defensive one. Ultimately, the GP would refer to violence as "defensive" or "offensive" according to the ideological needs of the situation. For instance, early on it called for the formation of "a strong and courageous revolutionary organization" whose task would be "to mobilize the greatest number of people" in order to repel attacks by the police, right-wing provocateurs, and even rival communist and leftist factions. This action was allegedly defensive, a response to the fact that "the powers that be search for confrontation in the street."[13] The Minister of the Interior, as we shall see in the next chapter, gave a different version of the situation.

It was in any case determined that hesitancy to use violence had contributed to the defeat of the May movement. Consequently, in the post-May era, violence needed to be a primary means of resuscitating revolutionary politics. If in the mind of the public the GP was inextricably linked to Mao's 1938 slogan that "power was at the end of the gun," it is worth noting, however, that (as we will see shortly) the group's violence was often symbolic, intended to have a catalysing or exemplary function. Still, its embrace of violent action set it apart from other radical groups. Clashes with the police, with other student groups, and with the PCF and the Confédération générale du travail (the largest Communist labour union) were key aspects of the spontaneist-Maoist experiment, experiences providing the raw materials for new directions. The judgment that such visions reflected a whimsical romanticism (since France was *not* going to have a proletarian revolution) needs to be balanced with the observation that they were efforts to grapple with and explain social conflict. There *was* in fact intense confrontation between the French government and the far-left student groups. Whether or not Marxist explanations of class struggle made sense, the serious, consistent, and mutually inflammatory violence between the French state and leftist activists was real. The French government felt threatened by the student groups and stepped up repressive measures to silence dissent. Although the GP subsumed this fact under a predetermined explanatory formula – revolution – it was nevertheless a response to something that was actually going on. With no precise starting point, revolutionary violence and police violence fed on one another and had consequences.

The idea that the "development of violent resistance to the police [was] one of the most important factors of the revolutionarization of the masses" was put into practice in the spring of 1969 in the wake of violent clashes between police and high-school students. A first premeditated and organized confrontation between the GP and the *forces d'ordre* occurred on 15 June 1969 at the Montrouge market outside Paris.[14] Two days later the GP returned to the factory at Flins, site of intense fights a year earlier between the police and workers (with a few students) that had led to a young worker, Gilles Tautin, drowning.[15] Olivier Rolin, leading the 1969 action, spoke of avenging Tautin's death. The day's conflict was bloody – the GP fighting PCF security teams [*service d'ordre*] and the police at the same time. Numerous GP members were arrested. Also in June 1969 a group attacked the Flins factory office off the Champs Elysées with rocks and metal bolts, fleeing before the police arrived. The GP began to make its presence felt in factories throughout France; they organized small business owners and farmers; and they made headway in mobilizing immigrant workers through championing the Palestinian cause. Shopkeepers and small business owners, or *petits commerçants*, were once the home crowd of Poujadisme, a populist right-wing movement in the 1950s, and it was unusual for leftists to consider organizing them. The GP's efforts at doing so bothered Sartre in particular. The GP also set up shop at the experimental University of Vincennes, where academics caught in the wake of May 1968, such as Hélène Cixous, Deleuze, Foucault, Jean-François Lyotard, and Michel Serres, began teaching when the campus opened in early 1969.

As the summer of 1969 ended, Benny Lévy pushed for a new political line. According to Bourseiller, he felt that "the situation in France in 1969 was comparable to the Nazi Occupation. Faced with 'the bosses' armed gangs,' police repression, and PCF 'collaborators,' a 'New Resistance' had to be launched." The second edition of the *Cahiers de la Gauche prolétarienne*, subtitled "Pour la résistance" (May 1970), contained an article, "Construire le Parti communiste révolutionnaire prolétarien," written the previous October. Lévy later cited this text as marking the moment when the call went out for "non-armed but violent partisan struggles of a symbolic character." After September 1969, "dozens and dozens" of violent actions were claimed by the Nouvelle résistance populaire (NRP). Olivier Rolin was the leader of this loosely organized and highly clandestine guerrilla wing of the GP.[16]

Two well-publicized conflicts took place in the fall of 1969. The first occurred on 14 September 1969 at the Arguenteuil immigrant shanty towns, which had been slotted for demolition by the local government, which happened to be Communist-controlled. The GP defended the immigrant community bodily against the PCF *service d'ordre*. More spectacular was an action on 19 November 1969. About fifty GP-ists, "armed with Molotov cocktails and iron bars" attacked the police station on the rue Halle-Puget in Marseille. On the way to the attack, they handed out a tract that read, "We are going to attack the neighbourhood police station. Why? Because the cops are the guard dogs of the bosses, and they make us live in their shit ... The people can no longer tolerate that these dogs try to bite us. For one eye, we'll take two, for one tooth, the whole mouth." Windows were broken and a truck burned. By the winter of 1969–70, about 500 people were actively associating themselves with the GP, and a group of disciplined, covert operatives had emerged. Commitment to the GP was total, "twenty-four hours a day, in the service of the most unfairly treated and of the revolution"; life for its members was "austere, without downtime, without distractions, everything turned towards militant goals." Alongside violent provocations like Arguenteuil and Marseille, in early 1970 came another genre of action that was quintessential GP: public, dramatic, and Robin Hood-esque. GP activists stole several thousand Métro tickets in Paris in the middle of the night of 23–24 February 1970 and then distributed them gratis to delighted commuters the following morning. On 8 May they robbed the Parisian specialty food store Fauchon in broad daylight, and delivered the looted delicacies to nearby poor suburbs.[17]

But the acts of the GP never escalated to the point of outright terrorism. This remains somewhat of a historical quandary, given the clear development of violent terrorism in 1970s Germany and Italy. (We will along the way offer a partial explanation.) The absence of a major leftist terrorist movement during these years in France would be significant for mid-to-late-1970s debates on the French state and Republican law. With these facts in mind, a global, structural account of GP violence needs to be considered in order to isolate the two elements – state repression and the search for alternative sites of struggle – to be considered below.

As Isabelle Sommier shows in her valuable study of political violence, its decline, and the "mourning" it inspired in post-1968 France and Italy, the GP was obviously not alone on the far left in its embrace of violence as a legitimate method.[18] Her contrast of French Maoists and Trotskyists with Italian far-left groups hinges on the important fact that the new figure of the terrorist emerged in 1970s Italy while most French '68-ers strongly disavowed political violence after 1974. Although her study tends to lack a sense of historical development, as she treats the period from 1968 to 1973 as a consistent and synchronic whole, her work helps to explain GP violence. According to Sommier, "the encounter of demonstrators with repressive structures" was the most important factor in the passage from talk of revolutionary violence to the act. Contemporary interpreters like André Glucksmann spoke of the "revolutionary use of repression." Direct provocation of the state would reveal the force and violence, ordinarily concealed behind a pacific front, upon which the state was in fact ultimately based. Furthermore, defensive violence could be a form of dialogue with "the people," a means of educating and mobilizing them. Violence, Sommier says, thus had a "cathartic function." In terms Sartre expressed rather unambiguously, there was the "bad" violence of the state and the "good" violence of the revolutionaries.[19] Violence was "necessary" and "inevitable": since the state was violent by definition, revolutionaries had to use violence not only to defend the people but also to provoke the state into showing its true colours. The GP spoke in terms of the "fascization" of the French state and of being the genuine inheritors of the French Resistance. This identity was evidenced by the name Nouvelle résistance populaire. Simone de Beauvoir summarized their sensibility, which she said Sartre actually found "unsound" and "clumsy," in this way: "The GP likened its activities to those of the Resistance and the Communist Party's to those of the collaborators ... it spoke of the 'occupation' of France by the bourgeoisie and of the 'liberation of the country.'" Symbolically, the reclamation of the French Resistance reached a high point on 18 June 1971 when leaders of the GP joined former members of the French Resistance, including Maurice Clavel, Vladimir Jankélévitch, and Jean Cassou, in placing a bouquet at Mont Valérin, the Resistance shrine. Co-opting the Resistance as a way to legitimize violence was a rhetorical tactic in a strategy of "prolonged struggle" [*lutte prolongée*] that would have neither easy nor immediate successes. Violence, for the most part intended to be more defensive than offensive, became organized and mobilized.[20]

Sommier goes on to underscore the "unreal and surreal representations" of the working class by the GP. Cut off from actual workers for a variety of reasons – mostly by ignoring the fact that the majority of workers wanted nothing to do with revolution – the "masses" became an *imago*. Repeatedly confronted with this reality – which Sommier compares to the "deep bitterness" one feels over a "lover's deception" – the GP experienced a "cognitive dissonance" that fed upon itself. Her explanation of this dissonance is suggestive: the GP Maoists were a prestigious elite who experienced an "inverted reflex-effect"; by swinging from pure theoretical practice (the Althusserianism of the UJC(ml)) to pure un-thinking practice (the workers were *the* historical agent), they ended up idealizing the workers in unique ways compared to other French or Italian groups. Committed to an organizational structure of a minority who *knew better*, they unconsciously "invested" the workers with "mythic representations." The moral of the story is that GP violence was entirely "symbolic" and "theatrical." The stage was in fact a stage, and it was located in the "distance that separated [the GP's] objective restraint from its very war-like subjective sense" of itself. Its revolutionary theatre revolved around the attempt to "seduce" the masses through acts of "social banditry," to denounce every sign of government, business, and union calls for order, and to revenge particular incidents through reprisals.[21]

Two aspects of Sommier's compelling analysis are unsatisfying. She explains that Italy experienced terrorism in the 1970s and France did not because the Italian state was more fragile and more repressive; whereas in contrast French state repression from 1968 to 1974 was "temperate" or "restrained." She points to the "brief prison sentences" assigned French radicals, adding that the "question of legitimacy was hardly asked" in France where "state construction" was "old and achieved."[22] Perhaps when compared to the Italian case these points have some validity. Yet even if she seems right about GP cognitive dissonance and its violence being largely symbolic, Sommier overlooks the role of real repression in France in the 1968–74 period, repression in which protection from arbitrary search and seizure as well as freedom of the press, speech, organization, and assembly were denied to those judged as threats by the French state. Police presence was "ubiquitous" on the streets of Paris for several years after May 1968.[23] In brief, if French Maoists were out of touch with the "masses" they desired to inspire, if they idealized violence and practised it on a symbolic stage, at the same time, talk about "fascism" and "resistance" and calls for defensive resistance – though certainly exaggerated and often hysterical – were not merely plaintive cries. From the perspective of civil liberties and some of the basic principles of democratic practice, at least, there *was* real repression. I shall return to this point below.

The second aspect of Sommier's analysis that begs a supplement is her discussion of the attempted "substitution" of immigrants and prisoners for the working class as revolutionary agents, once the working class was found wanting. In her view, these new sites and figures of struggle failed to transubstantiate the project of class revolution; that is, to change its substance while maintaining its form. Immigrants and prisoners were purportedly not interested in revolution, and they were disorganized and perhaps unorganizable in ways the working class presumably was not. Attempted substitution was thus ersatz. Sommier does admit that "attention paid to the marginal [i.e., immigrants and prisoners] could be an appropriate return to the groups' roots: ethical indignation, antiauthoritarianism, the breath of liberationism, etc."[24] However, she underestimates the extent to which the return to those roots could play a constructive role in at least two ways. First, once resistance to repression, say, in the prisons was seen as an end in itself and not as a means toward a further, phantasmic goal of destabilizing the dominant political and economic order, the will to violence diminished. Second, with the decline of violence as a realistic strategy and the cultivation of political intervention based in part on "ethical indignation," resistance to "oppression" would occur at particular times and in particular places that could not be assimilated to a general philosophy of history along the lines of revolutionary Marxism. What seemed ersatz for class revolution was actually the introduction of social action models with great historical, theoretical, and ethical possibility.

The strategies of French state repression from 1969 to 1972 landed a number of revolutionaries in jail. Their presence in prisons provoked a reconsideration of the strategy of non-participation with French legal structures and of the commitment to violent revolution. What could be accomplished through violence against the state by those *within prison*? The prison situation also served as the "handmaiden" – as Marx had said violence was for revolution – to the birth of organizations that played key roles in the transition from revolutionary political violence to a non-violent ethos grappling with what a "people's democracy" might mean within the limits of the Fifth Republic's judicial institutions.

4

The President's Man and the State's Thumb

Raymond Marcellin was named Minister of the Interior on 31 May 1968, in the midst of the May crisis. Until his replacement by Jacques Chirac in February 1974, he commanded the government response to political unrest during the post-1968 period. His approach was summarized in his account of the events of May 1968, *Public Order and the Revolutionary Groups* (1969), in which he spelled out his understanding of the dynamics of the movement's ethos and the government's response. He wrote his account, he explained, because "we could once again be confronted with events of the same genre."[1] The goals of revolutionaries like the Maoists, Castroists, Trotskyists, and March 22nd Movement, who were active prior to 1968 and thus played a capital role in the May events, were none other, he said, than the "overthrow of the government by force and the destruction of Republican and democratic institutions." Talk of university reform, the Vietnam War, and worker demands were mere "pretexts" for this subversive project. To Marcellin's mind, all such revolutionary groups followed a predictable script: they called for demonstrations over any topic at all, demanded that the police evacuate the scene, and when they did not, sent in "shock groups" to provoke police response. These incitements to violence would then be followed by a campaign of "psychological war" whereby the revolutionaries would publicize "the lie" of police provocation and exaggerate police brutality, the use of tear gas, "disappearances," and expulsions. Marcellin was obsessed with the idea that these groups were directed and financed by "foreign" influences, their leaders having "official or secret contacts with foreign states."[2] Such paranoia was worthy of a Joseph McCarthy. The claim, true or not, was instrumental; the threat of a conspiratorial subversion of the French state served as a fundamental rationale for measures taken against the students. The students, Marcellin suggested, were not interested in the university, Vietnam, or the workers, but were agents of foreign powers trying to overthrow the state. This argument was bound to resonate with one particular circumstance: The Fifth Republic was ten years old, and the Fourth had only lasted slightly longer before collapsing.

On 12 June 1968 Marcellin banned eleven leftist groups under the *Law of 10 January 1936*. The law had been passed to protect the Popular Front from right-wing fascist violence and was based on the French legal principle, in effect since the *Law on Associations of 1901*, that political and social groups had to be registered with the state. Such a principle, he wrote, justified the proscription of groups who "tried to undermine the Republican form of government or whose activity attempted to subvert the re-establishment of Republican legality."[3] Nevertheless, the groups Marcellin banned continued to function; they were "followed very closely" and files were opened on them by the Court of State Security (Cour de Sûreté de l'Etat). This court merits some explanation, since it introduces an entire category of postwar French legal approaches to violent rebellion.

The Court of State Security was an extraordinary court that had been established by the National Assembly on 15 January 1963. Henry J. Abraham describes its creation as a "direct result of terrorist activity by both civil and military elements in the government's attempts to settle the difficult problem of Algeria."[4] The Court, intended to replace the Military Court of Justice, was composed of civilian and military judges; there was no jury.[5] Only the French version of the Supreme Court of Appeals – the Cour de Cassation – could reverse its judgments. The law establishing the State Security Court had specified seventeen categories of charges according to which persons could be accused of violating state security, from armed rebellion to "provocation of or participation in" a riot, traffic disruptions, "confinement" [*sequestration*], and theft.[6] The particular targets of this law had been the right-wing terrorists of the Organisation armée secrète (OAS), who launched a bloody campaign to keep Algeria part of France. Yet in 1968 other measures from the era of the Algerian War were on the books which could be applied across the political spectrum. The "assignment to residence" law had been promulgated in 1955; it said that police in Algeria could relocate a person suspected of aiding the Algerian insurgents – the Front de libération nationale (FLN) – to "a place remote from his normal place of residence or to an internment camp."[7] In 1958 that measure was extended to apply to those who aided the FLN in metropolitan France itself, and on 2 February 1961 another law was passed to cover all persons accused of attacking the security of the French state.

Between 1958 and 1961 a series of criminal law procedures were declared, without legislative consent, when de Gaulle's government twice assumed its "special powers" granted the president by the constitution of the newly established Fifth Republic. Military tribunals could try persons suspected of aiding the FLN; the police could detain persons without charges for longer periods of time; and provisions were made for depriving an accused of his or her citizenship if the charges related to state security. The ordinance of 4 June 1960 abolished the distinction between external and internal threats to state security, but held on to the category of the "political regime," that is, special benefits for prisoners convicted of crimes whose motives were political.[8] After all, a war against terrorism was underway.

Against this backdrop, Marcellin's strategy in 1968 and subsequent years appears in a certain light. Besides the active collection of information to be used in the Court of State Security, other post-1968 measures that built on those of the era of the Algerian War included: "the expulsion of all foreigners who do not observe political neutrality" (Daniel Cohn-Bendit had been denied re-entry to France for this reason); the banning of all public demonstrations sponsored by revolutionary groups; the application of criminal law against "instigators of disorder"; Article 30 of the *Code Pénal* allowing "in emergency cases, the police commissioners to personally do all that is necessary" to prevent crimes against "state security," including the use of "preventive surveillance"; and finally, the coordination of all the police forces in France under the Ministry of the Interior. Those forces, Marcellin wrote, ought to be "more numerous, more mobile, and better equipped." In May and June 1968 these legal-juridical measures were put into practice. When the police evacuated the public buildings occupied by the students – the Sorbonne was cleared on June 16th – Marcellin justified the action in the following communiqué: "The State indeed has the primary obligation to assure public order, the function of public services, and the general application of laws. In exceptional circumstances, it has to make good on this essential obligation through the abusive use [*l'usage abusif*] of a particular juridical rule."[9] Here one found an extraordinary instance of the top policeman in France advocating a policy of breaking the law to save it. And the rhetoric and policies of law and order would only intensify throughout the 1970s. It was President Georges Pompidou himself who made the following Rousseauean claim at a press conference on 24 June 1971: "Order, as you have said, is respect for the law. The law is the expression of the general will. By consequence, what has to happen? Well, when someone breaks the law the police are there to seize him, and *la justice* can condemn him ... There are individuals and groups who refuse not only the law but also the expression of the law, who refuse the means by which the general will translates itself: elections."[10]

In his account of May 1968, after itemizing the methods he used as Minister of the Interior to contend with the uprising, methods that would be built on after that year, Marcellin concluded with a surprising "political" rebuttal. Revolutionary groups, he claimed, were out of touch with France; they proposed not less bureaucracy but more; they wanted a society of "underconsumption" to replace the society of consumption; their denunciation of imperialism said nothing that de Gaulle himself had not already said; their anti-capitalism – the call for "the suppression of economic freedoms" – could only be followed by the suppression of "private and public freedoms." The government did not "repress" a particular "ideology" or set of "political opinions" but violence and violations of the law. When Marcellin added, "there is no civilization without freedom," he courted performative contradiction, since it fell to him to decide both who the enemies of civilization were and how liberties might be curtailed. Marcellin's remarkable concern that the "establishment of collectivism, statism, totalitarianism[, and] dictatorial tyranny" was a real possibility in France shows how seriously he took the actions and rhetoric of the revolutionary groups. On another level, ironically, it shows how much the French judicial system itself was still subject to fears of revolution. Ten years after 1968, Marcellin wrote, referring to the general who repressed the workers' rebellion of 1848: "I hope I will never find myself called back one day to play Cavaignac."[11] He meant, called back to restore order *again*.

It was strange that Marcellin took groups like the Gauche prolétarienne as seriously as they took themselves. Everyone was fighting the repressed ghost of "fascism."[12] Far-left militants accused the Fifth Republic and its police of fascistic repression, comparing themselves to "partisans" of the French Resistance, as we saw with the NRP in the previous chapter. As we will see in Part III, some leftists were happy to associate *criminality* with *revolution*. Marcellin and the presidents under whom he served – de Gaulle and Pompidou – saw in 1968 and subsequent agitation an anti-Republican, anti-legal recourse to force that evoked images of the Occupation or the chaos of the Algerian years. Believing that the Republic had inherited the mantle of the Resistance, Marcellin in turn called far-leftists fascistic. Not that the perspective of law and order should in any way be surprising; as Max Weber said, modern states legitimize violence through monopolizing it. The Minister of Interior's effort at maintaining social order, however, generally tilted toward the extremes of its own mission. He was a scrupulous employee. As Maurice Rajsfus has shown in his tirelessly detailed book on police repression and violence between May 1968 and March 1974, the campaign to re-establish order in France during the period of the "*extrême-gauche*" involved a series of group dissolutions, censorships, arrests, preventive detentions, harsh sentencing (*pace* Sommier), and new laws that expanded the powers of the state and diminished the rights of individuals to organize into groups and to engage in even non-violent political activity.[13] It was as if the chaos and instability of the Algerian years needed to be paid for by the students of 1968. To be sure, the government had tolerated some radical mischief – recall Pompidou's indulgent waffling mentioned in chapter 1 – and the spirit of reform could at times be felt trying to endure between the dynamics of revolutionarism and repression; but the overall tone and timbre of the moment was captured by the fact that between 1 June 1968 and 20 March 1972, 1,035 individuals were sentenced to French prisons for crimes related to political action.[14] In the summer of 1968 the Ministry of the Interior controlled 83,000 police directly, 13,500 of whom were riot police, the Compagnies républicaines de sécurité (CRS). The Ministry of the Armed Forces had 61,000 *gendarmes* at its disposal for domestic service.[15] The 1969 national budget asked for more.

Of all the ways the state responded to 1968-era radicalism, none was more infamous than the "*Anti-Casseurs*" [anti-person-who-breaks-things] law passed on 30 April 1970.[16] With the ministerial banishment of revolutionary groups having proved ineffective, the new law held that anyone who could be linked – even tangentially – to a demonstration or act where harm to persons or damage to property was done could be charged with responsibility for that destruction. Guilt could readily be established by association. Barton Ingraham summarizes the measure in the following way: "Also punishable by this law were (1) deliberate refusal to move from places where a demonstration was taking place after an official order to disperse had been given, (2) illegal occupation of private and public buildings, (3) violence committed against public officials, and (4) false imprisonment [*sequestration*]."[17] The act caught the GP, which by then had become one of the most visible and prominent far-left groups, in its net. The group's paper, *La Cause du peuple*, had been seized in March and April, and the organization itself would be outlawed on 27 May, less than a month after the *Anti-Casseurs* law was passed.

In March 1970 the editor of *La Cause du peuple*, Jean-Pierre Le Dantec, was arrested and charged with attacking state security. It was the first time since 1881 (except under the Occupation) that an editor had been arrested in France. In light of this development, someone suggested that Jean-Paul

Sartre be enlisted to help protect the GP and its paper.[18] The move seemed a logical next step in the GP's program of building alliances between intellectuals and workers. Sartre agreed on 27 April to become the director of *La Cause du peuple.*[19] This is not to say that there were not serious differences between Sartre and the Maoists (over Palestine and Israel, over the role, mentioned in the previous chapter, of shopkeepers and small business owners [*petits commerçants*] in the revolution), but relationships began, notably the mutually influential one between Sartre and Benny Lévy that lasted until the former's death in 1980.[20] During the early 1970s Sartre identified himself as a godfatherly fellow traveller of the Maoists, writing in their defence, participating in demonstrations, sneaking into factories, testifying in trials, and overseeing publications. The first issue of *La Cause du peuple* under Sartre's symbolic direction appeared on 1 May, the day after the paper's interim editor, Michel Le Bris, was arrested and the *Anti-Casseurs* law was passed. In the beginning of May, the GP focused its energies on saving its paper from seizure and censorship and on the defence of their two arrested leaders, Le Dantec and Le Bris. But on the day their trials were scheduled, 27 May, the government banned the GP and arrested around 500 people in Paris.

Sartre stepped up to his new role as the public defender of the now-outlawed Maoists. On 4 June 1970 he, along with Simone de Beauvoir and Michel Leiris, helped found "The Friends of *La Cause du peuple*," a group of intellectuals, at least sympathetic to the Maoists' politics, mobilized around the issues of free speech and freedom of the press. Later in the month (20 and 26 June), Sartre, de Beauvoir, François Truffaut, Louis Malle, Claude Lanzmann, Robert Gallimard, and others distributed the paper on the streets of Paris, in open defiance of the government ban and with the media in tow. The authorities would not touch the renowned Sartre – de Gaulle had famously said in 1960 after Sartre visited Algeria, "You don't arrest Voltaire!" – and instead went after the real GP leadership. Alain Geismar, the official spokesperson for the group, was arrested on 25 June. Held in detention until his 20–22 October trial before the criminal court and his 24 November trial before the Court of State Security, he would be sentenced to eighteen months in prison and released early on 24 December 1971.[21] At a 25 May 1970 meeting at the Mutualité held in support of Le Dantec and Le Bris, an undercover policeman had recorded Geismar's speech, which was alleged to be seditious and in violation of the *Anti-Casseurs* law. The banning of groups, the censorship of publications, the arrest of militant leaders, the *Anti-Casseurs* law – all of these elements added up to two realities: 1970 was not the greatest moment for civil liberties in France, and those defending democratic principles and freedoms happened to be speaking the language of revolution. What activists intended to achieve is in some sense beside the point, because one of the historically significant outcomes and consequences of radical rhetoric and practices was an enlivening of debate in the public sphere about civil liberties and, as we will see below, about conditions in French prisons. If reference to "fascism" was often hysterical, on both sides, police and juridical repression was nevertheless very real. In June 1970, two groups – the Secours rouge and the Organisation des prisonniers politiques – were formed to deal with the fact that the government had cracked down and that large numbers of leftists, among them the Maoist leaders, were in jail.

5

Popular Justice and Incarcerated Leftists

Confrontational dynamics between the French state and far-left activists meant that hundreds of militants were being incarcerated. In 1970 activists focused on French prisons as sites of contestation in new ways. For example, the trial of four soldiers accused of distributing leftist tracts and the trial of the Maoist Roland Castro, both in February 1970, elicited much public notice. Jean-Paul Sartre spoke at Castro's trial on 23 February, and that night Maoists stole the Métro tickets in the incident recounted above. One of the consequences of this kind of publicity was a transformation in the strategies and sensibilities of leftist politics, notably around the themes of violence and justice. While prisons were obviously not the only focus of the early-1970s French far left – mobilizations of farmers, workers, soldiers, women, high school students, and so forth continued – prisons were a quickening point where radical politics encountered a number of limits. The French situation also needs to be understood in a wider context; namely, the contemporaneous politicization of imprisonment throughout Europe and North America.[1] In the United States, Angela Davis was arrested in October 1970, and George Jackson achieved notoriety between the January 1970 Soledad incident, when three black prisoners were shot to death by a guard, and his August 1971 murder. Attica exploded the following month.[2] The American and French radical movements were in dialogue – note, for instance, Jean Genet's links to the Black Panthers and Régis Debray's impact on Bay Area radicalism; and Jackson and Attica were widely discussed in France.[3] Furthermore, spurred on by the events of Prague in 1968, the French non-Communist Left critique of the Soviet Union and Eastern Bloc was moving into high gear over prisons, violated civil liberties, repressive "revolutionary justice," and dissidence. In short, "radicals" in jail were not a local phenomenon in the early 1970s.

In France, as elsewhere, encounters with the legal system called for new strategies, or as a prominent slogan in the late 1960s and early 1970s put it, for "expanding the resistance." A lawyers' union – the Syndicat de la magistrature – had formed in June 1968, coinciding with but not necessarily prompted by the heat of the May events. Eventually a more radical association – the Mouvement d'action judiciaire – was created in the early 1970s; the first issue of its review, *Actes*, appeared in January 1974. Lawyers like Robert Badinter (the future Minister of Justice, 1981–86), Georges Kiejman (future Minister *délégué* under Mitterrand), Tiennot Grumbach (Pierre Mendes-France's nephew), and Denis Langlois were enlisted in the defence of arrested militants. Langlois wrote a practical handbook on the labyrinth of the French judicial system.[4] In a context of inflamed confrontation and exaggerated rhetoric, with actions of the French state being compared to "fascism" and those of leftists being punished as "seditious" by the courts – a new emphasis on law and rights emerged in leftist discourse and practice. As one internal Maoist document put it in the fall of 1970: "The role of lawyers is very important in an era witnessing the rise of a new fascism where the judicial system is charged with applying profligate laws (notably the *Anti-Casseurs* law)."[5] Like teachers and journalists, lawyers were liberal professionals whose activities helped fulfill one sought-after goal of the post-1968 far left: the unity of intellectuals and workers. In the case of the legal defence of jailed militants, such unity took the precise form of liberal professionals working with "revolutionary" activists, many of whom had by no means sprung fully formed from the factory floor.

Between lawyers serving "the movement" and necessary engagement with the police, judicial, and penal institutions of the Republic, a certain revolutionary discourse came to the fore: "class justice" or "popular justice" or "savage justice" was contrasted to corrupt and ostensibly fascistic "bourgeois justice." Through the destruction of a false democracy, it was maintained, a "new" democracy, the "people's" democracy, would be constructed. In the black and white moral universe of the far left, especially among the Maoists, where the repressive state was bad and the "people" were good, "justice" emerged as a common denominator, a fulcrum, and a point of contrast. What the state called justice was in fact injustice; consequently, the "people" had to assert their own justice. One association created in the fall of 1969, Défense Active, described its mission as developing "active defence against the repression of political actions by class justice" and "active defence against repression in daily life."[6] The tasks were equivalent.

Those in the early 1970s who mobilized within or on the frontiers of a discourse of popular justice placed themselves within a French tradition with a long history. The notion of popular justice, of course, pointed back to the French Revolution, vendettas of the populist crowd, emergency powers of the state, Revolutionary Tribunals, the September Massacres, the Committee for Public Safety, and other "extraordinary" institutions of the Terror. Popular justice during the French Revolution was best summed up by Danton's phrase: "Let us be terrible in order to dispense the people from being so."[7] The supposed or real differences between crowd violence and institutional violence would continue to be debated during *les années '68*. In the late nineteenth century, one form of 1790s popular justice had been revived under very different circumstances. During the Dreyfus Affair, Truth and Justice Commissions played a role in the formation of extra-statist associations like the Ligue des droits de l'homme et du citoyen, whose mission was less the execution of popular justice than making the Third Republic's juridical institutions live up to themselves.[8] In the early 1970s, the Ligue came out against leftist recourse to popular justice.[9] The very different types of acts following the Liberation in 1944 – for instance, shaving the heads of women who had collaborated – also evoked the rhetoric and practice of popular justice. So too, in the years before and after World War II, the French debated – denounced or rationalized – the historical significance of Soviet "revolutionary" justice.[10]

These precedents notwithstanding, it was more recent mobilizations during the French-Algerian and American-Vietnam wars that provided the real impetus for the serious emergence of "popular justice" talk and tactics in post-1968 France. For example, in June 1957 the torture and murder of Maurice Audin, mathematics student and Communist, was covered up, leading to the formation of the Audin Committee, which investigated and publicized the French army's more general use of torture in the 1950s and early 1960s. The committee's bulletin was called *Truth-Justice*.[11] In 1966, following the assassination by French government operatives of the Moroccan nationalist Mehdi Ben Barka, the Comité pour la vérité sur l'affaire Ben Barka was formed. It continued to publish its findings into the 1970s.[12] In 1966–67, the Russell International War Crimes Tribunal, under the leadership of the aging but active Bertrand Russell, with the French participation of Sartre, Simone de Beauvoir, Laurent Schwartz, and Gisèle Halimi, more explicitly combined the form of the investigative commission with that of the court. As Russell stated in his opening speech on 13 November 1966:

> We do not represent any state power ... We lack *force majeure*. The procedures of a trial are impossible to implement. I believe that these apparent limitations are, in fact, virtues. We are free to conduct a solemn and historic investigation,

uncompelled by reasons of state ... We must record the truth in Vietnam. We must pass judgment on what we find to be the truth. We must warn of the consequences of this truth ... I have lived through the Dreyfus Case and been party to the investigation of crimes committed by King Leopold in the Congo ... May this Tribunal prevent the crime of silence.[13]

As we shall see in short order, Sartre, with the Maoists, played a significant role in promoting a rhetoric of popular justice. In the longer term, the formulation of an extra- or non-statist view of justice – demanding that state juridical institutions answer to a "higher law" – would be one factor contributing to the emergence, by the late 1970s, of extra-statist human rights discourse.

The Secours rouge international had been an interwar Communist organization supported by the Soviet Union but with independent national committees. Formed in 1924, it was dedicated to providing "material, moral, political, and juridical aid" to victims of oppression, particularly those who had gotten into trouble with "bourgeois justice."[14] In France the organization was meant to function alongside the Communist Party, but rather than mobilize the masses politically or get them to join the Party, it offered them direct, immediate aid. Prisoners and their families were among those it assisted. It looked after "particular causes that mobilized people often on ethical, political, juridical bases," and its effects were at times "ambiguous."[15] The PCF's humanitarian organization, Secours populaire, had been founded in 1945 out of the ashes of the interwar Secours rouge international.

In 1970, in response to the immediate repression of far-left groups (but also as a slap in the face to the PCF), a new Secours rouge (SR) was founded. Weeks after the GP was banned and the "The Friends of *La Cause du peuple*" had formed, on 11 June, eighteen former French Resisters and FLN activists, Christian radicals, lawyers, academics, and the *sui generis* Sartre signed the founding SR manifesto. A Secours rouge was declared again necessary, given an obviously intensifying "systematic repression" of the French people by "the powers that be," a situation in which "the principles of rights and jurisprudence" were threatened.[16] The manifesto went on to itemize the ways in which this repression had manifested itself: police in the factories, expulsions and arrests of immigrants, mass firings, black lists of militants, dissolution of revolutionary groups, political repression in the army, seizure of newspapers, and so forth. In responding to this crisis of law and justice in France, the SR proposed: "to be a legally declared democratic association, independent of all organizations and open to everyone.

Its essential objective will be to assure the political and juridical defence of victims of repression and to give them and their families material and moral support with no exceptions." In the beginning, the SR "supported all movements on the far left and was not linked to one particular organization."[17] Though many jailed activists in the summer of 1970 were Maoists, there were also Trotskyists, anarchists, and non-aligned radicals. Still, the Maoists were generally in the front seat of SR actions. De Beauvoir recalled:

> The organization included the main leftist groups, *Témoignage chrétien*, and a number of well-known people. Its chief purpose was to resist the wave of arrests initiated by Marcellin after the dissolution of the GP. A great many militants were in prison. What had to be done was to collect information on their cases and decide what action to take. Several thousand people belonged to Secours rouge, and primary committees were set up in various districts of Paris and in the provinces ... Although generally speaking the committees were politically eclectic, it was the Maoists who were the most active and who more or less took them over.[18]

The SR divided its energies between legal matters (preparing the defence of arrested militants) and public demonstrations meant to dramatize specific cases, say, of police brutality. Rhetorically at least, the group maintained that the general situation of police repression was opportune since it gave the far left something to rally around and against which to define itself. Even while holding on to revolutionary language and class as criteria of social analysis, SR circles throughout 1970 and 1971 spoke of general democratic struggles against injustice, and for liberties.

> Against division, injustice, an arbitrary order propagated by the powers that be, we must defend unity, justice, and liberties ... All our practice shows that at all moments and in no matter what campaign, "fighting for liberties" is always necessary. We must therefore defend fundamental liberties: freedom of expression, of association, of public meetings, of demonstrations, all the rights of citizens. These liberties are necessary in order to conquer new freedoms in business and in society: for example, the freedom to contest injustice.[19]

Thus a new leftist emphasis on rights was born within the framework of revolutionary militancy.

Nowhere was the SR's blurring of class and "liberty" politics more apparent than in the theory of "popular justice" and the practice of the Popular Tribunal. On 4 February 1970 sixteen miners had been killed by an explosion at Fouquières-les-Lens. On 17 February the NRP burned the offices of the state company in charge of the mine where the explosion had occurred (the theft and distribution of Métro tickets took place that same month). Four Maoists and two others without apparent political affiliation were charged with the crime, and their trials was set for 14 December at the Court of State Security. Under the leadership of Serge July, the SR and the GP organized a Popular Tribunal to be held at Lens to coincide with the state trial. In a tract, Sartre wrote: "The facts are clear: sixteen men were killed. Since it was 'bad luck,' bourgeois justice does not intervene; it only shows up to pronounce a sentence against those who wanted to avenge the dead." At Lens, Sartre played the role of the prosecutor – an extension of his role as executive president with the Russell Commission – weaving together the testimonies of miners and their families on the malfeasance of the mining company and the inaction of the police. General work conditions were put on trial along the lines of a criminal law proceeding. The mining "accident" was examined: the explosion had taken place, it was suggested, because the mining company had placed profit over safety. Doctors testified on the condition of "black lung." Indictments were handed down. To the criticism that such a tribunal was pure theatre, de Beauvoir replied that "a condemnation of this kind has its effect: it is an urgent warning to employers and it is a way of arousing public opinion." As a later account described it, at Lens "the idea of a tribunal for judging the true criminals, the true wrong-doers, the true wreckers [*casseurs*] was born."[20]

The January 1971 issue of the GP's *Cahiers prolétariens* discussed the Lens tribunal in detail. Intended neither as a media event nor as only a mockery of judicial process, the Popular Tribunal – "an ideal-type example" of SR action – was meant to "deliberately violate bourgeois law since it tried to install another, and make the State Security Court appear as a parody of the Popular Tribunal."

> The Popular Tribunal showed to the vast majority of the miners, in a scientific and irrefutable manner, that silicosis and "accidents" were murders and not just bad luck. The unity of miners, doctors, engineers, painters, intellectuals, under the direction of the miners and led by their accusations, permitted this mass demonstration to operate ... Faced with a "justice" based on lies, crimes, or hypocrisy, faced with a "justice" that condemns the worker and lets the guilty boss go free, our people are thirsty for another justice, for a justice in which the people can express themselves, make charges, and impose its law.

The Secours rouge was committed to class war; it was not a "pacific organization." It had its "own weapons, which, like all arms at the stage of ideological revolution, combine an illegal character and a symbolic character."[21] Lens was thus a theatre of justice, but one in which the divide between the performers and audience was intended to be bridged in a populist fusion; the people's law was higher and more authentic than the distorted judicial institutions of the Republic, which showed themselves to be alienated from the ultimate source of their authority: the people.

What made this action a success in the eyes of some SR members was that it put the idea of "popular sovereignty" into practice. The specific issue was class injustice: miners had been killed by the willful negligence of the mine owners; the bourgeois legal system seemed only to want to punish those who had taken justice into their own hands by setting fire to the mine offices. The true victims – the miners – were seemingly abandoned by state justice. Ironically, though, the Popular Tribunal took on the form of demands for justice before the law, punishment for wrongdoing, and the preservation of rights. Of course, the Lens proceedings set themselves up outside the state apparatus, as an alternative to and judge of it. They expressed to some degree an anti-representative and illiberal desire to take matters into one's own hands. Certain contradictions lay down this road, and we will see in the next chapter how Michel Foucault, Sartre, and the Maoists took different positions on popular justice.

Another Popular Tribunal was planned for 27 June 1971 at the Cité Universitaire in Paris. A petition signed by 230 intellectuals was circulated, calling for a "popular trial of the police organized by SR." Sartre wrote in another tract: "A popular tribunal is an excellent means of sharing information among the masses, before whom a complete dossier can be opened on political circumstances that official justice has kept totally or partially secret; and it is also an excellent occasion for them to not passively accept the decisions of class justice but instead exercise their judgment of a concrete case about which we will give them all the facts."[22] Though the government had forbidden the 27 June meeting the day before it was to take place, numbers of people turned out, and thirty were arrested. On Tuesday, 30 June, a press conference was held by the SR to denounce the threat to "freedom of expression" in France. At this moment, certain ambivalences about the Popular Tribunal became apparent. An SR meeting held 10–11 July 1971 revealed divergent opinions about its goals and value. Conflating the languages of class and justice seemed to bring inherent tensions between "revolution" and "bourgeois society" to the surface. While there was general consensus about contrasting "popular" and "bourgeois," there was disagreement over what forms this contrast should take: "popular tribunals, popular trials, or simply investigative commissions?"[23] Would these measures be open or clandestine?

Would they privilege celebrated cases or focus on less-well-known experiences of injustice? Would sentences be given? Who would carry them out? How far should it go? To accuse the French judicial system of being unjust and illegitimate was one thing, but the attempt to set up parallel judicial practices ran into numerous difficulties.

Not surprisingly, the inability to resolve questions about the ultimate ends of popular justice was, in the spirit of self-criticism, blamed on an amalgam of organizational rigidity and chaos. The July 1971 SR meeting in Paris in fact ignored the December 1970 Lens tribunal, maintaining that the idea of the Popular Tribunal had emerged only after a 9 February demonstration in which a young militant, Richard Deshayes, had been gravely wounded by a tear gas canister fired at his face.[24] Popular Tribunals had failed to take hold in any massive way, and efforts at judging police acts descended into "popular celebrations," or, in the case of the "Commissions for the Investigation of Police Brutality," the refusal "to substitute themselves for official justice." In detailing how "the political conditions" that would have made the June 1971 Popular Tribunal a success "had not been fulfilled," the SR representatives present at the July meeting suggested that the group had failed to apply one basic lesson: "It is *all* progressive political forces that can act, *each in its own manner.*" This lesson had been learned during prisoner hunger strikes in September 1970 and January 1971, to which we now turn. Like lawyers, those who worked in prisons and prisoners' families brought motives and sensibilities that differed in many ways from those of young radicals.

Let us first backtrack a little. The previous June, the same month in 1970 the SR was founded, the National Committee of the GP created a new section within its ranks, the Organisation des prisonniers politiques (OPP) and put it in charge of the advocacy and defence of arrested militants.[25] Benny Lévy asked Nicole Linhart, the wife of the rue d'Ulm Maoist, Robert Linhart, to be in charge. The OPP was given three tasks and ideological lines to pursue. First, it would centralize and coordinate all links between militants in prison and those outside. Second, it would promote the policy that a militant in prison was still "active" and not "dead." This translated into a campaign to have the "political" status of militant prisoners recognized: "The campaign for obtaining the "political regime" aims to force the enemy to recognize us as a political force and not as a band of criminals – as communists and not as thieves. The people mobilize behind communists, not behind thieves. ... The car thief, the common law criminal, reflects society; the communist transforms it."

Some French Resisters during World War II and members of the Front de libération nationale and the Organisation armée secrète during the Algerian War had been granted the status of the "political regime." That status allowed them to maintain a sense of political identity and activity while incarcerated. As summed up by René Pleven, the Minister of Justice (also known as the Garde des Sceaux – literally, Keeper of the King's Seals), the political regime gave prisoners the right to: "separation from other categories of prisoners, placement in an individual cell or room, the possibility of ordering books and daily newspapers from outside the prison, to write and to receive visitors every day [and to be] relieved of all work duties."[26] Marcellin and Pleven had refused to grant the "political regime" to 1968-era *énragés* [angry young people], even if some jailed militants claimed the status, as did, for example, eight activists from Bordeaux given two- to four-year sentences for having thrown Molotov cocktails in May 1968.[27]

Beyond coordination of activities and pursuit of the political regime, the OPP was lastly entrusted with making the prisons a "new front of struggle against despotism." The sorts of revolutionary campaigns underway in factories needed to be transplanted to the prisons, since these "modern Bastilles" were focal points for the struggle against oppressive bourgeois society. As we saw Sartre claim in chapter 2, prisons served as a metaphor and stand-in for French society as a whole.

On 1 September 1970 incarcerated leftist militants declared a hunger strike. That same month the Maoists arrested for having distributed their paper, *La Cause du people*, went on trial. The hunger strikers' goal was to achieve recognition of the political status for prisoners whose crimes had political "motives."[28] The manifesto of the strike was careful to say that achieving political status was one step in "denouncing the present scandalous conditions" experienced by all prisoners. Some of the hunger strikers' demands – for instance, an increase in the number of authorized visits and an amelioration of prison conditions in general – could just as easily have been made by non-militant "common law" prisoners. But the clear aim of the hunger strike was to publicize the fact that jailed militants were, in spite of their motivations and beliefs, considered common criminals: isolated, divided, and forbidden to meet together. Echoing the sensibility expressed in the SR, families of the striking prisoners became involved, petitioning Pleven to grant the "special regime."[29] On 22 September, all hunger strikers held in preventive detention, save one, were sent to the hospital. Alain Geismar, incarcerated since 20 June, followed the next day. The circumstances gained public attention. At a 24 September Rolling Stones concert in Paris, a Maoist militant had been invited to speak on the strike in front of the crowd of 10,000, and the Stones followed him by breaking into their song "Street Fighting Man." The Supreme Court of Appeals then recognized the political nature of the crimes of one individual, Michel Julien, who had been convicted for writing a slogan on a wall while he was already in prison.[30] When the Supreme Court of Appeals granted him "political regime" status on 28 September, the hunger strike ended. In their final tract, participating militants hastily declared victory. Having "thus opened the way for new struggles inside the prison," they were prepared to undertake another hunger strike if the "political regime" was not applied universally and completely.[31] Threatening another hunger strike was a prescient move on their part, despite the fact that over the course of the month around twenty imprisoned militants were quietly released on "provisional liberty" and the "political regime" was applied in particular prisons like Rennes and Saint-Nazaire.

The promised application of the "political regime" for incarcerated leftists remaining inadequately fulfilled, a second hunger strike was planned for December 1970 but postponed until January 1971.[32] Inflaming the rhetoric, the OPP claimed that even fascist regimes like those in Spain and Greece permitted certain rights to prisoners that were refused in France. Those rights were not specified, but, the group said, "when the Minister of 'Justice' refuses to let a political prisoner see his newborn child at least once, he has nothing to envy in the jails of Brezhnev, Husak, or Franco."[33] "The scandalous conditions made for us," the statement announcing the new hunger strikes concluded, "result ... from a deliberate system of persecution. We want this to end and we will pursue the hunger strike until our dignity is recognized." Passing reference was made to the idea of connecting the situation of "political" and common law prisoners – militants and car thieves, as it were. However, the difference between militancy and crime, traceable to Marx's distinction between the proletariat and lumpenproletariat, remained important to many activists. Even if most prisoners could be seen as "rebels" [*révoltés*], a qualitative gap lay between "revolt that leads to the theft of mopeds and revolt that leads to the practice of resistance ... we are Maos, [not] 'thugs' [or] 'common law criminals.'"[34] In other words, since their crimes lacked a properly political explanation and self-understanding, common law prisoners still needed the inspirational and exemplary direction of sacrificial Maoist militants.

In contrast, the rhetoric around the hunger strike was less sparing in its call for militants outside the prison walls to support militants inside. Such support played an essential role in keeping people in different prisons, or even within the same prison, informed. The judgment was made in January 1971 that during the September hunger strike outside assistance had been "extremely insufficient," an "ideologically negative" trend that had not abated: "The comrades in prison receive relatively few letters; their families and lawyers are taken lightly. Some sort of an absence of solicitude is visible in our ranks ... an absence of generosity in our relations with them." Mobilization outside the prison was therefore crucial for the hunger strike's success. In January 1971, doctors joined family members in supporting the prisoners, and the Philosophy Department at the University of Vincennes sent a letter to prisoners encouraging them to enroll in correspondence courses, which would allow professors to visit them and pass messages.[35]

From the fall of 1969 to the spring of 1970, clandestine Maoist violence had increased. In the late spring and early summer of 1970, French authorities intensified their efforts at breaking the small but visible movements of the far left. Responding to this situation, in June 1970, groups like "The Friends of *La Cause du peuple*," Secours rouge, and the Organisation des prisonniers politiques were formed to focus activist energies on the protection of civil liberties and the legal defence of incarcerated militants. In September "political prisoners" went on a hunger strike; in December the Popular Tribunal of Lens was held, dramatizing the rhetoric of "popular justice"; and in January 1971 another hunger strike took place. Some members of the far left had their sights set on *la justice* – the judicial system (police, courts, and prisons) as well as popular justice, people's tribunals, and acts of class vengeance.

6

The Groupe d'information sur les prisons

Michel Foucault was the driving force behind the Groupe d'information sur les prisons.[1] Although the topic of prisons resonated with his earlier scholarly work on madness and confinement, his involvement as a prison activist in the 1970s owes much to his long-term companion, Daniel Defert.[2] Joining the GP after it was banned by the government in May 1970, Defert was asked by Benny Lévy to work with Secours rouge, but he had deferred and the job was given to Gilbert Castro. With Jacques Rancière, Defert turned his efforts to the OPP and the strategy of politicizing the common law offenses of which militants were accused.[3] The Maoist strategy of the "investigation" (introduced in chapter 3) found new prominence at this time. It was to be crucial in the mobilizations around the prisons and, unintentionally, in the surpassing of French Marxism-Leninism. In 1970 the best way to aid political prisoners was, Defert determined, to follow the model of "going to the factories, going to see the farmers, and mobilizing people around trials." This investigative militancy led Defert, against the grain of the OPP, to advocate the inclusion of common law prisoners in the GP's contestation. We have just seen that even into January 1971 efforts were made to distinguish militant from "common" criminals. Inspired in part by the role of intellectuals in "The Friends of *La Cause du peuple*," Defert felt that fellow-travelling intellectuals had a two-fold task: "to mobilize people and to create insecurity in the prisons."

Defert went to the GP leadership and suggested that Foucault be invited to participate in the prison campaign. Though the leaders were "enthusiastic" about the idea, Defert did not want to ask Foucault himself, aware that his partner was already over-committed, having begun his prestigious new position at the Collège de France in December 1970. "Seeing that an answer was not forthcoming, the GP came as a delegation to ask him,"

Defert recalls: "He was very happy. So the GIP was born not exactly by the direction of the GP, nor really from Foucault, but between the two [*dans l'entre-deux*]." Foucault's presence, though, marked an immediate departure from the Gauche prolétarienne ambience. He was not willing to play a shepherding role akin to Sartre's: "Foucault absolutely did not want to let himself be guided by the GP. He did not at all share their modes of work and ideology." (The divergences of Foucault and the Maoists and of Foucault and Sartre will be discussed below.)

Foucault's first move was to ask a judge, Serge Fuster, known publicly by the pseudonym Casamayor, to participate in the new prison effort. Casamayor had been active in the denunciations of French torture during the Algerian War and in the Ben Barka Affair.[4] A Catholic, he was "one of the more important moral personalities in France" at the time.[5] As a sitting judge, however, he could not openly participate in a movement meant to bring critical attention to the criminal justice system. Casamayor suggested that Foucault go to see Jean-Marie Domenach, the editor of the review *Esprit*. Domenach represented the tradition of left-wing Social Catholicism that pointed back to the Resistance, Emmanuel Mounier's school of personalism, and the worker-priest movements of the 1950s. In agreeing to sign the inaugural GIP manifesto, Domenach became an important strategic ally on many fronts, one of which was especially significant: "In the prisons, there was the tradition of religion, notably, chaplains and social workers. In Domenach, we immediately had the support of an important part of the prison personnel." Foucault and Defert also went to see Pierre Vidal-Naquet. A historian of ancient Greece, Vidal-Naquet, like Casamayor, had been very active in the critique of the French Army's use of torture during the Algerian War and had written the definitive account of the aforementioned Audin Affair. Vidal-Naquet was a distant relative of the Dreyfus family and identified himself within the Dreyfusard tradition of secularized French Jews who defended the Republic in the name of universal values of justice. Though not a great presence in the day-to-day function of the GIP, Vidal-Naquet also signed the group's manifesto.[6] It was an important symbolic convergence of the Social Catholic and Dreyfusard Republican traditions, and of those two traditions with Foucault's more-difficult-to-pin-down orientation. As Defert comments: "We immediately left the GP to form alliances with people and social movements linked to moral and religious values, but essentially to the value of justice." Danielle Rancière, involved in the GIP from the beginning, referred to Domenach and Vidal-Naquet as "democratic personalities."[7] David Macey comments: "The experience of Vichy and then Algeria had bred in both men a deep distrust of – and even contempt for – a legal system which had compromised itself both during the Occupation, when magistrates and judges condoned the deportation of Jews, and during the Algerian war, characterized as it was by flagrant breaches of both human rights and French law."[8]

Foucault's name appeared alongside those of Domenach and Vidal-Naquet on the GIP manifesto read by Foucault at a press conference on 9 February 1971 at the Chapelle St Bernard, a low-ceilinged room resembling an American high-school cafeteria located beneath the Montparnasse train station. In January eleven militants had begun a hunger strike at the Chapelle (as had others at the Sorbonne and the Halle-aux-Vins) in solidarity with the hunger strikes then taking place inside the prisons. There had been some press coverage, as well-known figures such as Yves Montand, Simone Signoret, Vladimir Jankélévitch, and Maurice Clavel had stopped by to express their support.[9] Furthermore, on 27 January Maoist activists had thrown Molotov cocktails at the Petit Rocquette prison in Paris; late in the night on 29 January, the NRP shot fireworks over the La Santé walls and promised the prisoners over a loudspeaker that they would soon be liberated; and on 3 February, two police cars on the rue de la Santé had been burned.[10] On 8 February, the Minister of Justice, René Pleven, agreed to call a commission – composed of a high-level bureaucrat, a judge, two lawyers, a law professor, the chief chaplain for the prisons, and René Cassin, Nobel Peace prize winner and partial author of the United Nations Declaration on Human Rights – to evaluate the "political regime" statute.[11] This was seen as a partial victory, and the hunger strike was called off. At the press conference called to announce the end of the hunger strike, Pierre Halbwachs, spokesperson for SR and son of the sociologist Maurice Halbwachs who had died in Buchenwald in 1945, called Foucault to the microphone. Foucault read the announcement for the creation of the GIP:

> There is no one among us who is certain of escaping prison. Today more than ever. Police control is tightening on our everyday life, in city streets, and on the roads; expressing an opinion is once again an offense for foreigners and young people, and anti-drug measures are increasingly arbitrary. We live in a state of "custody" ... They tell us that the prisons are overcrowded. But what if the population is over-imprisoned? There is little information published about prisoners; it is one of the hidden regions of our social system, one of the dark compartments of our existence. It is our right to know. We want to know. That is why, with magistrates, lawyers, journalists, doctors, and psychologists, we have created the Groupe d'information sur les prisons.
>
> We propose to let people know what prisons are: who goes there, and how and

why they go; what happens there; what the existence of prisoners is like ... This information is not going to be found in the official reports. We will ask those who, for one reason or another, have some experience with prison or a connection with it. We ask them to contact us and tell us what they know. We have composed a questionnaire they can request. As soon as we have a sufficient number of results, we will publish them.[12]

Copies of the questionnaire were then distributed to those present. While the status of the political prisoners would remain a concern for the GIP, from its inception, the group placed its emphasis on the common law prisoners.[13] This emphasis was not wholly original, but it was now foregrounded in ways it had not been by SR and the OPP. The organizing method of the GIP – the investigation – showed how the group began in a Maoist milieu, was at first close to the GP, SR, and the OPP, and then moved in new directions. Foucault was remembered as repeating the refrain: "This is the GIP, not Secours rouge, and not the Gauche prolétarienne."[14] Still, the GP and the GIP worked together in early 1971 on a report that discussed how general conditions inside the prisons – hygiene, food, walks and exercise, solitary confinement, the confiscation of personal belongings, the *mitard* (a lightless, heatless solitary cell), and work – "totally break the individual physically and morally."[15]

Originally there was a plan to hold a trial on the model of the Popular Tribunal. In their 1976 essay on the history of the GIP, Defert and Jacques Donzelot described the sense that "something new took form at the Popular Tribunal at Lens" when doctors had testified on the medical conditions of miners, speaking from a position of "social practices" and not "prestige."[16] Following this "impetus," the GIP sought to use intellectuals and perform investigations similarly. No doubt through Foucault's doing, the idea of having a trial was, according to Danielle Rancière, "let go very quickly."[17] Interest settled on the method of investigation. "We were somewhat within the spirit of the investigative work we did in the GP with workers," Rancière recalls. Like the GP *enquête*, the GIP questionnaire circulated in the spring of 1971 built on "preliminary knowledge" obtained by militants who had been jailed with the common law prisoners.[18] The questionnaire was a written version of what had been an oral, Maoist-*spontex* technique.

The model of militant work for the GP or the Maoists in the factories was important. Essentially, we waited outside the factory doors and distributed tracts that, because we had information from militants inside [*les établis*] or from other contacts, discussed what was happening inside the factories. In this way we tried to give the workers a certain consciousness of their own situation and sometimes mobilize and get them to join the GP. It was a model we wanted to use for the prisons. But it was more complicated.[19]

It was complicated mainly because no prisoners came out the front door at the five o'clock whistle.

Gathering information from prisoners necessarily entailed the mediation of the prisoners' families and those who worked inside prisons. With greater force than either the SR or the OPP, from the beginning, the GIP actively solicited the support of prisoners' families. An initial "Letter to the Families of Common Law Prisoners" asked family members to mail "detailed descriptions of detention with places, dates, and names of prisons" to Foucault's home address, the GIP headquarters.[20] But the real momentum was created by going to the prison walls themselves. Danielle Rancière canvassed at La Santé prison.

We organized as we had at the GP with one intervention group for each prison, just as there had been one intervention group for each factory ... We noticed very quickly that people waited in front of the prison for visiting hours at one o'clock in the afternoon or something. The families arrived much earlier as to not to lose time, whereas the lawyers entered the prison directly ... We distributed our tracts to these groups of people in front of the prison and also in the nearby cafés ... We had to put them at ease and then ask them to help us gather information ... They were a little nervous but they took our tracts and read them. They spoke freely and tried to obtain information and give it to us.[21]

The recruitment of families as equal and even privileged allies in the prison struggle meant a break with one strain of revolutionary belief: the conviction that the family was a bourgeois construct, as far from a revolutionary agent as one could get. Yet, given their unique access to the prisoners, involving them reflected a simple acceptance of the reality of the situation, a victory of pragmatism over ideology. In May 1971, an "Association of Families of Prisoners" was announced.[22] This was an autonomous initiative of the families, advertised by the GIP. It was a first sign of the consequences of the GIP's enormous emphasis on self-representation.

The other group mediating between the GIP and the prisoners was made up of professionals who worked inside the prison: educators, psychiatrists, social workers, doctors, and nurses. Many of the prison service personnel had Catholic affiliations. In any effort to further its distribution, the GIP questionnaire was printed in *Esprit*, one of the few journals authorized in prison. Defert comments: "The prisoners did not read [*Esprit*], but the social workers did."[23] The service personnel also played an important role in contacting the families. Many of these nurses, social workers, and psychiatrists had worked in prisons for many years and had been "waiting for this movement for a long time ... Fundamentally, they were disgusted, but they were isolated and could do nothing."[24] Their participation was significant, and not only because less than a year later, following the revelations of Edith Rose, the Toul prison psychiatrist, Foucault and Gilles Deleuze would speak of "specific intellectuals." The SR and OPP had already faced the inevitable need of mobilizing lawyers on behalf of detained radicals. While this mobilization made sense in light of post-1968 attempts to unite intellectuals and workers, it had nevertheless introduced an ambivalence into the Marxist-Leninist cohort: bourgeois elements were being enlisted for the revolutionary struggle. The GIP went one step further. Like families, members of the service professions had unparalleled access to the prisoners. That was the reality. All those who wanted to bring information from behind the walls into the public sphere were welcome. The implication was that the issue of prisons had priority over class identity. To be sure, some of the core members of the GIP, notably Foucault, did not share the motives of the Social Catholics any more than those of the Maoists. "[The Catholics] wanted reforms in prison because they love the prison," recalls Daniel Defert: "They love punishment, redemption ... a spiritual project. Foucault showed well [in *Discipline and Punish* (1975)] that the prison acts on the soul. It models the soul, produces the soul. Believers like to talk about the soul. We were not on the side of the soul. There are people who don't understand that."[25] Foucault rejected the heroization of prisoners that was often implied in Social Catholic rhetoric, where prison occasioned conversion and redemption.[26] However, ideological commitments were considered of secondary importance and subordinate to the project of disseminating information about life behind the walls.

In the spring of 1971, besides enlisting the support of prisoner families and prison service workers, the GIP also attracted important intellectuals to the prison information campaign. Deleuze, the Rancières, Jean-Claude Passeron, Robert Castel, Hélène Cixous, Jacques Donzelot, Jean Genet, and, later, Claude Mauriac all participated. In its practice, the GIP embodied the idea of "interclass solidarity."[27] Its primary directive – gathering information on prisons with the goal of disseminating it – occasioned the coming together of "intellectual" information gatherers and "non-intellectual" information providers. "To inform is to struggle," one GIP document said.[28] At the same time, GIP intellectuals were deliberate about their desire that the true "investigators" would be the "investigated." It was radical participant observation: the prisoners knew better than anyone what was happening in the prisons. The GIP intellectuals saw their role as presenting prisoner information with as little re-presentation as possible. They thus tried to walk a delicate balance between, on one hand, using their prestige and social positions to bring attention to the situation in the prisons, and on the other, cultivating a self-effacing role whereby they merely passed on information they received. As its manifesto clearly stated, the GIP was not intended as a prison reform movement: "It is not for us to suggest a reform. We only want to make the reality known."[29] The first published *enquête* put the view starkly – "We are not dreaming of an ideal prison" – and Defert continues to maintain that the GIP "did not propose reforms. The prisoners proposed them ... If the prisoners had demands we could make them known because our goal was to give them their own voice. Demands came out of the prison ... They were not the demands of the GIP."[30]

The call for self-representation was very much of the moment. The years 1970–72 saw broad calls for "direct democracy" in France, particularly in factories and workplaces, where it was known as *autogestion*. Notwithstanding the fact that such approaches could seem naïve and unreflective, a new appreciation for autonomy and participation, which was to have lasting effects, made itself felt. Again, surprisingly, this democraticizing sensibility emerged within circles for whom revolution was a fundamental project. Danielle Rancière, for instance, saw the spirit of direct democracy partially "inherited from the Maoists" whose *spontex* practice held that "in order for things to change, it was necessary that people revolt and take charge of making their own demands."[31] For Defert, the "base" of activism was giving expression to those who had no expression: "The GP supported those people who were revolting who had no representation in traditional worker organizations. We did the same thing: we supported the prisoners who had no means of expression."[32] In spite of proximity and influence, the GIP moved away from one key GP line: whereas the latter maintained that self-expression and self-representation were means toward revolutionary ends, for the GIP, self-expression and self-representation were ends in themselves. If there was a background framework it was the unspoken conviction that information itself could be critical and that bringing concealed secrets into the light of public discourse was a way to denounce them.

The first fruits of the investigation were borne in late May 1971.[33] The forty-seven-page *Intolerable Prisons: The GIP Investigates in Twenty Prisons* was published on 28 May by the radical publishing house, Champ

Libre. The questionnaire was reproduced together with compiled responses on a range of topics, from visiting rights and mail censorship to suicides and strikes. Foucault wrote the introduction. Among other institutions, such as psychiatric hospitals, courts, universities, the military, and the media, prisons were "masks" of "political oppression." Noting that the "exploited class" had been aware of this fact for a long while, Foucault observed that something new was happening. In a phrase that evoked Alain Touraine's discussion of "new social movements," Foucault said that "new social groups" – intellectuals, technicians, lawyers, doctors, journalists – now found the connection between institutions and dominant political power "intolerable" in the way that the "exploited class" long had. Both Touraine and Foucault were right that liberal professionals were in unprecedented numbers bringing the spirit of radicalism into their own specific fields and métiers. In his introduction to *Intolerable Prisons*, Foucault went on to detail four criteria of the "*investigation-intolérance*," clarifying its goals and limits.[34] First, GIP investigations were intended to indirectly attack "oppressive power" by challenging its exercise under particular umbrellas ("justice, technique, knowledge, objectivity"). Each investigation was thus a "political act." Second, each investigation was meant to be a "first episode in a struggle." It was therefore important that the investigations focus on specific sites, since it was only at prison X or prison Y that a revolt might occur. Third, investigators represented a united "attack front," joining groups like prisoners, lawyers, and prison service personnel that were sometimes separated by (illusory) conflicting interests. Finally, the investigations reflected the principle of self-representation. The "investigators here are those being investigated themselves"; it was for them "to find their voice" [*prendre la parole*]. The GIP would publish three more investigations: on the "assassination" of George Jackson, the "model prison" of Fleury-Mérogis, and prison suicides.[35]

As Foucault's introduction to the first investigation demonstrates, the notion that the GIP was *only* passing on factual information was a little disingenuous; the evaluative moment in the investigative process was concealed by a rhetoric of quasi-objectivity (*We're just passing along the facts*). In truth, collection, selection, and dissemination of information were interested; that is, they were activities performed with an *interest*, in *the name of* something. Or so Foucault's introduction suggested. But what was this interest? In the name of *what* was the prison investigation conducted? What were the ethics of this procedure? I shall return to these questions below.

Three incidents between the late spring and early fall 1971 helped push the GIP beyond its initial formation. On 1 May, Foucault, Domenach, Danielle Rancière, and others were arrested while protesting the *casier judiciaire*, the permanent criminal record that often blocked former inmates' chances for employment. They were charged with distributing tracts that did not list the printer's name and address. The detainees were verbally assaulted at the police station. Foucault filed suit, but nothing came of it.[36] Then, when the journalist Alain Jaubert was severely beaten by police on 29 May after attempting to come to the aid of a wounded demonstrator, Foucault and others from the GIP participated in a counter-investigation, the so-called Jaubert Commission. Jaubert, it was alleged, had been targeted for carrying out his journalistic duties. The commission's report, released on 21 June, included contributions from a diverse range of intellectuals, including Deleuze and Denis Langlois.[37] The last set of incidents involved continuing violence in prisons: on 27 July a prison guard at Lyon, Albert Collomb, had been killed with a weapon smuggled into the prison in a care package, and on 22 September a nurse and guard in the Clairvaux prison were murdered after having been held hostage by two inmates.[38] The Attica prison riots had taken place from 10–14 September, and the GIP organized a mass meeting at the Mutualité on 11 November to demonstrate its solidarity and discuss the situation in France – a film on American prisons was screened and French ex-prisoners told their stories.[39] The next day, Minister of Justice Pleven took away the right of all prisoners in France to receive Christmas packages, a right dating to 1958. This provocative gesture lit the fuse on an already tense situation. A new wave of hunger strikes and, now, riots broke out in prisons throughout France.[40]

This was the moment of the prison revolt at Toul described in chapter 2. A brief rebellion occurred on 5 December when prisoners presented a list of demands to the administration. More violent revolts on 9 and 13 December were put down by riot police. Elements of the GP, SR, and the GIP converged on the scene to support the prisoners and publicize their demands. Robert Linhart arrived with other Maoists to try to find out what was happening and to organize a protest. The GP had a fierce internal debate on whether to publish a special issue of *La Cause du peuple*. Linhart, André Glucksmann, and Foucault argued that it was important to do so; Benny Lévy, Jean-Pierre Le Dantec, and Christian Jambet took the losing side in arguing that not all revolts were of equal importance with regard to class struggle.[41] On 9 December, the GIP proposed for the first of several times that independent investigative commissions be allowed inside the prison. The SR-connected

Comité de vérité de Toul was formed on 14 December. More than once, its meetings descended into chaos as prison guards arrived to have their say and were confronted by former prisoners. The psychiatrist, Edith Rose, held her press conference on 15 December, and Pleven responded by forming another commission, headed by Robert Schmelck, to study her allegations. On New Year's Eve, GIP and GP militants launched fireworks over the walls of several prisons.

"Toul is not an exception," a GIP tract said in January 1972.[42] This was true. There were over thirty revolts and hunger strikes in December 1971 and January 1972 at prisons such as Nîmes, Amiens, Rouen, Melun, Limoges, and Fleury-Mérogis. The APL press conference, with Foucault's participation and a message from Sartre, took place on 2 January. The Schmelck report, published on 8 January, concluded that although discipline in the prison had been unnecessarily harsh prior to the December riots, gangs might have been responsible for the troubles. Furthermore, Edith Rose's allegations could be neither proved nor disproved.[43] The next day, Pleven spoke at a press conference after meeting with Prime Minister Jacques Chaban-Delmas and Minister of the Interior Raymond Marcellin:

> I can only reaffirm what I said to you when, at the end of last month, I proposed a set of measures that must be studied with care because this administration will not make generalizations or extrapolate. You know that there are about seventy establishments under the penal administration. What exists at Toul does not necessarily exist elsewhere ... I affirm my confidence in the personnel of the penal administration and in the directors of the correctional facilities ... I have decided that before the end of the month I will propose to the government an ensemble of measures. We are under pressure but we are serious. And we must study things with care, which is what I have done with my colleagues.[44]

The rhetorical contrast – if Toul was not exception for the GIP, it *was* for Pleven – could not have been greater.

Later in the month, after a revolt at the Nancy prison on 15 January 1972, the demand for an independent investigation was repeated in a petition signed by Sartre, Foucault, Maurice Clavel, Claude Mauriac, Halbwachs, Deleuze, Georges Kiejman, Michèle Manceaux, Alain Jaubert, Marianne Merleau-Ponty, Hélène Cixous, and others.[45] "The Schmelck Commission revealed nothing that was not already known," the petition read, "promised only what was indispensable to it. The prisoners understood this right away ... Like the prisoners we are asking that a GIP commission be authorized to: 1) enter the Nancy prison; 2) assess the condition of the injured and the treatment they have received; 3) inform ourselves on the state of transferred prisoners; and 4) see that the demands of the prisoners are examined seriously." Pleven publicly denounced the outside agitators for provoking unrest within the prisons. But the coalition of prominent intellectuals and professionals strategically assembled to support the prisoners was strongest at this time. Though their motives for supporting the prisoners diverged, many nevertheless shared the sense that the situation was *intolérable*. On 17 January, the day before Pleven announced some rather modest reforms for prisoners with light sentences, Foucault wanted to publicize a document he had received from the Melun prison. Most of the above signatories converged on the Ministry of Justice.[46] A tense confrontation ensued between the demonstrators and the CRS. Foucault had his foot struck with a gun butt. Alain Jaubert and Marianne Merleau-Ponty were placed in a police van. A chant went up – "We must not lose Marianne" – referring both to Merleau-Ponty and to the female symbol of the Republic since the French Revolution. Jaubert and Merleau-Ponty were almost immediately let out of the police van through the quick negotiations of Claude Mauriac. The Republic would not be put behind bars. After the rally, Foucault and Sartre held a joint press conference to explain what had happened and read statements passed along by several prisoners.

When one looks closely at GIP documents and Foucault's interviews and published writings from 1971, the denial that the GIP was advocating prison reforms seems equivocal. To be sure, from the GIP manifesto forward, the group's rhetoric tilted toward emphasizing its disinterest in promoting reforms not proposed by prisoners themselves. But on a few occasions Foucault stepped in the opposite direction. In an interview published in August 1971 but probably given in May, he said, "I believe that now a reform of the entire penal code is necessary, a reform that goes to the root of things [*une réforme en profondeur*]. We need a new Beccaria, a new Bertin. I do not have any pretension of being a new Beccaria or Bertin, because it is not for a theoretician to reform states."[47] With greater subtlety, Foucault in July 1971 said: "It is not a question of proposing an ideal prison. I believe that by definition the prison is an instrument of repression." The first phrase denied utopian solutions; the second implied at least a denunciation of the way things were. Together they added up to a demand that something be done without specifying exactly what.[48] *That* reforms were necessary was implicit in the GIP's very existence; *what form* those reforms took depended on the prisoners. If the prisoners wanted to revolt and not ask for reforms, the GIP would convey that information, too.

Thus the GIP's own approach to reform was more implicit than explicit, and concerned institutions more than persons. This annoyed some Catholic participants in particular, who were generally less ambivalent about prison reform. One might recall Defert's distinction of Foucault's view of the prison from a prototypical Catholic one. There were ultimately conflicts between the GIP and *Esprit* on this question.

If in the end Foucault and the GIP parted company from the orientation of Social Catholics (with whom they nevertheless had important alliances), they also distanced themselves from the Maoists. In March 1971 Foucault deliberately contrasted the GIP's version of the "investigation" with that of the Maoists. In an article published in the Maoist paper, *J'Accuse*, on 15 March, he wrote, "This is not a sociological investigation. It is a question of giving voice to those who have an experience in prison. Not that they have the need to 'gain consciousness': consciousness of oppression is there, perfectly clear."[49] Foucault here articulated his view that information about prisons and prisoners' experiences did not need to be explained or narrated. Assimilating such information into a conceptual framework would have turned the *enquête* into a sociological project; fitting it into a political narrative would have reduced it to an episode, say, in historical revolution.[50] In an interview published on 18 March, three days after the *J'Accuse* piece, Foucault elaborated further: "We are not playing the role of an investigative commission. We want to be an information group that searches, provokes, distributes information, and locates targets of possible action."[51] Of course, Foucault continued to use the term "investigation" throughout the duration of the GIP's existence, and he eagerly participated in the "counter-investigation" over the Jaubert Affair in June 1971, even if that forum departed from the GIP's *modus operandi*. Overall, though, Foucault distinguished the GIP's use of the investigative method from that of the Maoists.

We saw above Foucault's hesitation to identify the GIP's activities too closely with the Maoists, as well as Danielle Rancière's admission that the idea of the group holding a Popular Tribunal was "let go very quickly." Foucault's and the GIP's distance from the GP was put in even starker relief in a February 1972 interview with Foucault conducted by Benny Lévy and André Glucksmann on the theme of "popular justice."[52] Ironically, in this discussion Foucault went some distance onto the Maoists' terrain by admitting that class conflict between the bourgeoisie and the "popular classes," the latter under the leadership of the proletariat, was real. His concern with Maoist popular justice and tribunals was that they mimicked the juridical forms of the bourgeoisie, in other words, laws and courts. When claimants presented themselves before a judge or a tribunal, conflict was "suspended" by a mediating third. His critique of these forms of justice sounded very similar to classic Marxist attacks on the systematic distortions of the bourgeois legal state. There was indeed such a thing as popular justice, Foucault maintained, but the effort to institutionalize it was flawed. Popular justice was "anti-juridical" in spirit, even if it sought to punish class enemies or educate the masses.[53] The implication was that popular justice should express the popular will with minimal institutional formalization and mediation.[54]

For his part, Lévy argued for a "dialectical" view of the Popular Tribunals.[55] Dangers of aping bourgeois forms notwithstanding, authentic popular justice could make productive use of the form of the court, as had been done at the Lens tribunal, he said. The people required forms, like the Chinese Red Army or a state apparatus, to shape their "revolt" into "revolution." Lévy and Glucksmann's interview with Foucault ended somewhat in a dialogue of the deaf, with Lévy dreaming of a "fusion" of the masses, to be accomplished via the mediation of revolutionary institutions, and Foucault cautioning that the form of the law had created "dangerous" classes (which Marxists rewrote as the lumpenproletariat) and that the form of the court reinforced the division of labour.[56] "The revolution can only take place," Foucault remarked dramatically, "via the radical elimination of the judicial apparatus."[57] Such a statement reflected less Foucault's commitment to revolution than his characteristic adaptation to the rhetoric of his interlocutors and his suspicion, concretized in the GIP, that judicial forms – the law, court, and prisons – created as many problems as they solved.

Foucault's real break with the Maoists came from his refusal to employ the category of popular justice as a conceptual counter-balance to bourgeois justice. Deleuze later suggested that Foucault found in the difference between the "theoretical or juridical status of the prison" and its "practice ... a whole system of humiliation, a system that breaks people and that is not part of the system of deprivation of freedom ... uncontrolled justice inside the prisons."[58] From this point of view, Popular Tribunals merely re-enacted what was wrong with French justice; violence inside the prisons was both meaningless and suicidal; and the GP's acceptance of the French juridical distinctions between "political" and "common law" prisoners, though perhaps not without strategic value, rewrote the distinction between revolutionary and lumpen elements. "I think one of the accomplishments of the GIP," says Defert, "was to erase that notion of lumpenproletariat from political vocabulary."[59]

Rather than trying to substitute one genre of justice for another, the normative criteria of the GIP were expressed in the group's practice, which was radically democratic and negative, asserting, however indirectly, the dignity of prisoners. In March 1971, Foucault said that the prisoner experiences the "absence of all real rights ... he is totally disarmed" by justice.[60] From one point of view, at the heart of the GIP's project was an old political question: Does a citizen who has violated the social contract (thus ending up in prison) still deserve the rights and dignities that accompany citizenship? As Deleuze's comment cited above suggests, the GIP was interested in the dangers of over-imprisonment, of an environment that did more than simply deprive a prisoner of his freedom, that acted on a prisoner not only *negatively* (taking away his or her freedom), but *positively* (reducing his or her dignity) as well. A GIP petition described this situation well,

> Political power manages the daily life of prisoners in a quasi-feudal manner to the point of considering them as beings stripped of all their rights of personhood and citizenship. The prisoner is put in prison in the name of the law, but once he enters the police station or the prison he is no longer under the law, but subject to the arbitrary, violence, uncontrolled repression, and the secret. Law and right stop there where the prison begins. As Michel Foucault says: "Justice puts the prisoner outside the law."[61]

If the French Republic stood for the rule of law and justice, and law was seen as the instantiation of democracy, another set of principles was needed to cover that field and those persons placed outside the law in a non-democratic space. Perhaps dignity could be seen as a juridical category; I would argue that it is an ethical category. In any case, it served a functional role for the GIP that "popular justice" did for SR and the GP.

The GIP's and others' *right to know* and the prisoners' *right to dignity* reflected each other. In May 1971 Foucault asked: "By what right are we held back from knowing what really goes on in there? ... By what right do the powers that be keep [what goes on inside prisons] secret?"[62] The state justified its closed-door policy on prisons as appropriate and juridically legitimate. The GIP's challenges to the control of information and its assertion of the right to know pointed directly to civil society and the general public. The right to know was a social right in a democracy, a right that in turn referred back to the issue of political and juridical rights. To ask about what was "going on in there" was tantamount to asking what rights prisoners had. Defert and Donzelot commented in 1976: "Our essential question [to the prisoners] was: Do you have the right to ...?"[63] Again, this was an ambivalent position. Speaking not of Foucault, but more generally of the GIP milieu, Danielle Rancière notes:

> At the time we were very critical of the language of the rights of man. We were very much subsumed in Marxist criticism, the critique of Marx himself. No one wanted or dared to invoke the rights of man. But at the same time, the problem was striving for the rights of which prisoners could not be deprived. The privation of liberty was a punishment, but this privation could not lead to the suppression of all rights, whether it was the right to information, the right to health, or the right to dignity, moral dignity. That was what seemed revolting to us and against which we tried to struggle ... We did not speak like that, but that is what was at stake.[64]

Hindsight clarifies what was cloudy at the time, but this statement captures exactly the tensions and ambiguities of the GIP's proximity to and distanciation from Marxist-Leninist theory and practice. Though hostile both to the languages of rights and revolution, Foucault and the GIP nevertheless drew on both discourses. The birth of rights talk within the immanent field of marxisant theory and practice – the ethos of 1968 – would be one of the most significant developments of 1970s French culture.

The languages of rights and revolution were combined in subtle ways in the notion of the "intolerable." As a flyer from the spring of 1971 had put it: "The situation in prisons is intolerable. Prisoners are made to live a life without the dignity of a human being. Their rights are not respected. We want to bring this scandal into the light of day. [They] are placed in a situation where their dignity finds itself ridiculed in all possible ways." During the Jaubert Affair, Foucault had even referred to "our *constitutional* rights"; namely, the provision in the Declaration of the Rights of Man and Citizen that "society had the right to demand every public officer to account for his administration." The GIP manifesto referred to making "reality known." This reality included not only prison conditions but also the "factual discontentment" of many French people "a propos of the prison [and] the judicial system." Between the prisons and the public, speaking as an individual, Foucault summed up his position in this way: "Simply, I perceive the intolerable."[65] The intolerable was a way of saying, "No." There was no need to elucidate the values and criteria upon which something was judged intolerable; the intolerable simply *was*.

The normative form of the GIP, largely a result of Foucault's influence, was *negative* and *radically democratic*. It was negative first of all because the GIP, by its very presence, was saying "No" to the intolerable. Moreover, its effectiveness came from defining itself negatively, saying what it was not: on the face of it, the group was not proposing reforms, speaking for the prisoners, advocating revolt, or for that matter, necessarily advocating anything at all. The tactics of the GIP thus bear some formal similarities to the slippery negative logic of Socrates when he claimed that he knew only that he did not know. Drawing up a program would have defined and locked down the GIP, limited it, made it a target. But the negative moment did not mean that one ought to say nothing. On the contrary, the call went out for people to employ whatever skills they had at their disposal. For his part, as an intellectual-citizen, Foucault declared: "I am simply trying to see, to make appear, and to transform into a discourse readable by all, that which is insupportable for the most unprivileged classes in the present justice system."[66] This came close to the position of the "specific intellectual" embodied by Edith Rose (and the example, evoked later, of Robert Oppenheimer who spoke against nuclear weapons as a nuclear physicist). But in his own terms, Foucault was not a specific intellectual in what he did with the GIP. Nor was he a revolutionary intellectual or fellow traveller à la Sartre. Intellectual "analysis" was needed. Foucault said: "We need analyses in order to be able to give meaning to this political struggle that is beginning ... The problem is not a model prison or the abolition of prisons ... The problem is the following: to offer a critique of the system that explains the process by which contemporary society pushes to the margins part of the population. There you have it."[67]

What Foucault called analysis, Deleuze in a later interview called thinking:

> Michel [Foucault] called the GIP an information group, but "information" is not quite the right word: the GIP was a kind of experiment in thinking ... He saw things, and like all people who know how to see, who see something and see it deeply, he found what he saw to be intolerable. For him, to think meant to react to the intolerable, to something intolerable he had seen ... Thinking was an experiment, but it was also a vision, a grasping of something intolerable ... I believe for him it functioned as ethics. But the intolerable was not a matter of ethics. That is, his ethics were to apprehend or to see something as intolerable, but it was not in the name of morals that something was intolerable. This was his way of philosophizing, his way of thinking. In other words, if thinking did not reach the intolerable, it was not worthwhile to think.[68]

Deleuze's mention of ethics, in fact prompted by Paul Rabinow and Keith Gandal in their interview with him, brings us finally to a consideration of the power of the *negative* and of *implicit denunciation* in the articulation of a *radically democratic ethics*. The fact that the phrase "Information is a prerequisite for democracy" drones on and on in the internet era makes it no less true. What made the GIP's democratic practice radical was not the information conveyed, but the effort, in Deleuze's words, "to create a place where people would be forced to listen to" the prisoners.[69] Ultimately the GIP's radical democracy was negative, in the specific sense of criticizing existing social institutions without proposing to replace or reform them. The group's efforts, however, seem a far cry from the label of "nihilism" that we saw attached to the ethos of 1968 in chapter 1. The GIP's radical democracy was further evidenced by its rapid decline after 1972 (many far-left groups disappeared about the same time) and by the emergence of a new group, the Comité d'action des prisonniers (CAP) in December 1972.[70] The CAP was an organization created for prisoners by prisoners and in which intellectuals had no role analogous to the one they had played in the GIP. It marked a culmination of the principle of *prendre la parole*. Once a social group gains autonomy it no longer needs people to speak on its behalf. Defert's somewhat sharp dismissal of the CAP as a group that did not have much impact needs to be seen at least partially in this light, since one of the casualties of 1970s France was going to be the French intellectual as master and spokesperson.[71]

7

These Modern Bastilles

Since the taking of the Bastille by the revolutionaries of 1789, prisons have occupied a privileged place in modern France's relationship to democratic rights and revolutionary aspirations. From Honoré Mirabeau's reflections on his imprisonment on the eve of the Revolution and Alexis de Tocqueville's nineteenth-century ethnography of American prisons to literary expressions like *The Count of Monte Cristo* (1845) and *Papillon* (1969), French prisons have been an imaginative barometer of the qualities and quantities of Republican freedoms, rights, and justice.[1] Furthermore, in modern France prisons have also served as a symbolic testing ground for the inheritance of the French Revolution and for social violence – from jailed revolutionaries in 1848 and 1871 to the detention of both Algerian and right-wing militants during the Algerian War. The entanglement of *soixante-huitards* with the French judicial establishment and the emergence in the early 1970s of associations mobilized around the prisons, most notably the Groupe d'information sur les prisons (GIP) – these developments are chapters in a much longer story. The most important late-twentieth-century book on early modern French prisons, Foucault's *Discipline and Punish* (1975), was itself symptomatic of the historical moment in which it was written. Rather than take a closer look at that book, tempting though it is, I would like to delve a little more deeply into its context.

World War II had set in motion dynamics in the French penal system that 1968-era radicals would encounter. When the Fourth Republic proclaimed that the mission of prisons was the "amendment and social reclassification of the convict," some could hear the reforming voices of individuals who had themselves a few years before been prisoners in labour camps, prisoner of war camps, and concentration camps. In the late 1940s and 1950s educators were introduced into prisons, a measure that sometimes led to conflicts with prison guards. This reformist theme, emphasizing rehabilitation over repression, altered slightly when the Fifth Republic was founded in 1958. New attention was paid to "security" concerns: in 1955 and 1957 prison guards at La Santé prison had gone on strike; in 1957 prisoners there had revolted. Most significantly, however, France was at war in Algeria. Though the notion of the "special regime" had emerged as early as 1832, strikes by some of the 6,400 jailed Algerian insurgents and sympathizers in early 1959 led to the recognition of politically motivated prisoners as "Category A" prisoners, with the special rights discussed above. In the early 1960s, some of the 1,700 jailed partisans of the right-wing Organisation armée secrète (OAS) also received the "special regime" status.[2] When two OAS prisoners escaped from La Santé with help from a prison guard on 4 September 1963, de Gaulle was incensed. Obsession with security and prevention of such escapes would occupy much French penal policy until the mid–1970s. Fanning the flames of far-left agitation, de Gaulle granted amnesty to most of the remaining OAS prisoners in June and July 1968.

As we have seen, between 1968 and 1972, the prevailing winds of the French judicial and penal systems blew decidedly in the direction of increasing repression. There were exceptions. At the trial of Le Dantec and Le Bris, the judge refused the government's request to permanently ban *La Cause du peuple*. On 17 July 1970 the category of "preventive detention" was replaced by "provisional detention." Minister of Justice Pleven was obliged to begrudgingly grant "special regime" status to incarcerated militants, and the commissions he authorized (the Parodi Commission on the "special regime" in early 1971 and the Schmelck Commission on the Toul revolts later that year) facilitated modest reforms. For instance, in December 1973 a greater variety of publications were allowed into prisons. But strife in the prisons continued. The point of emphasizing conflict over peaceable reform here is that it was primarily discord that led to the transformations whose significance in fact surpassed the specific questions of prisons and even violence.

In May 1973, prisoners in Lyon revolted, and the next month, the head doctor of the French penal system was assassinated. On 22 February 1974, Patrick Mirval, a repeat offender jailed for having stolen fifty-seven francs from an automated teller machine, died under suspicious circumstances at the Fleury-Mérogis prison while being transported under guard. His death sparked great controversy. The most significant and destructive prison revolts of the 1970s occurred later in 1974. In late July and early August nearly one-third of French prisons were consumed by riots. Six prisoners were killed, and eleven prisons partially or totally destroyed. The summer 1974 revolts were significant because in the midst of them, prison guards went on strike. The French penal system was in open crisis. President Valéry Giscard d'Estaing, shaking prisoners' hands on an August 1974 visit to the Lyon prison after the revolts had subsided, said: "A prison sentence is detention and nothing more than detention." His liberalizing, reformist agenda included mass amnesties for convicts with short sentences and granting some prisoners visits outside the prison for up to five days. For the remaining years of the decade, though, and into François Mitterrand's tenure, French penal policy was in some ways characterized by indecision and hesitation between policies of "security" and "humanization" – as has been the case since medieval times.[3] Though Mitterrand's election was followed by a number of progressive measures (abolition of the death penalty and the Court of State Security, installation of visiting rooms without glass or metal barriers between prisoners and their visitors, access to television and print media), the 2 February 1981 law passed under the sponsorship of Alain Peyrefitte entitled "Security and Liberty" captured the tensions of the era with an almost Orwellian flair.

The activities of the GIP bring to mind George Bernard Shaw's comment in 1924 that "imprisonment cannot be fully understood by those who do not understand freedom. But it can be understood quite well enough to have it made a much less horrible, wicked, and wasteful thing than it is at present."[4] The GIP did not claim to understand either freedom or imprisonment, but however indirectly, it targeted horror, wickedness, and waste. Between the January 1972 demonstrations at the Ministry of Justice and the December 1972 formation of the CAP, Foucault and company kept up their agitation as revolts and hunger strikes continued throughout the country. But the GIP occupied a small corner of far-left militancy, for which 1972 proved to be the beginning of the end. The February 25th murder of the activist Pierre Overney by a factory guard was the Kent State of the French far left: its most dramatic and publicized event, but also the signal of decline. The entire independent Left attended Overney's March 4th funeral, but as Louis Althusser recalled saying to himself that day, "It isn't Overney they are burying today but the politics of leftism."[5] To some extent, the collapse of the GIP at the end of the year reflected the fortunes of the broader far-left milieu as much as it did its own self-cancelling rhetoric.

"Popular justice," too, received its greatest public exposure in the spring and summer of 1972, an exposure that also marked its decline. Four days after Overney's funeral, on 8 March, the NRP kidnapped Robert Nogrette, a member of the management at Renault, where Overney had been shot. He was held for three days and then released. The public outcry was directly proportional to the NRP's wild estimation that revolutionary violence was passing from the symbolic to the pragmatic stage.[6] The practice of popular justice was more openly contested within the Maoist camp several months later, in May, when the daughter of a miner in Bruay-en-Artois was murdered and a local notable suspected of perpetrating the crime. Far-left activists descended on Bruay and made a lot of noise about duplicitous official justice, but the assumption that "the proletariat" had been raped by the "bourgeoisie" drove a wedge in the GP itself.[7] (We will see in Part IV how the issue of rape – and not just as a metaphor – would again divide the far left.)

That Chinese Maoism proved to be a democratizing influence and impulse in France may come as a surprise. In the early 1970s some of the most adamant defenders of such standard democratic themes as freedoms of the press and of assembly, human rights, and popular political participation were actors who spoke in terms of revolution and class warfare. Almost in spite of themselves, some Maoist revolutionary activists brought democratic questions into public discourse. For a quality of Chinese Maoism like the "investigation" to move onto centre stage and shed its class-based meanings, other aspects of Maoism – such as the primacy of revolutionary violence – had to retreat. The decline of the French Maoist impulse for violence was related to a variety of factors: the presence of older intellectuals and liberal professionals who cautioned against the terrorist route; tensions internal to Maoist ideology, in which vanguardist and populist impulses collided, causing symbolic violence to decline once popular support diminished; and, most important, it seems, the dynamics of a contest between marginal revolutionaries and a modern state, the outcome of which was largely structurally guaranteed. As Isabelle Sommier has shown, French Maoist violence was largely symbolic. State power was decisive for shifting the terrain of contestation from the factory to the judicial system. The courts and jails were places where the revolutionary pleasure principle and its fantasies – revolutionary violence was largely a phantasm under the Fifth Republic – met the unavoidable reality principle of state power. The results should not have been a surprise. As suggested by the consolidation of left-wing support for those who were arrested and imprisoned, the strategy of non-participation with the "bourgeois" political institutions of the Fifth Republic – which continued, for example, in the boycott of elections – became discredited and fell apart. Sartre's prolonged talk of revolutionary violence in his meetings with the Baader-Meinhof terrorist group in 1974, for instance, made him seem lonely, fragile, and out of touch.

More promising were the multiple information groups that were born and thrived in the wake of the GIP's experience. Such groups formed around specific professional identities or social issues: the Groupe d'information de santé (GIS) for health, the Groupe d'information sur les asiles for mental illness, the Groupe d'information des travailleurs sociaux (GITS) for social workers, and the Groupe d'information sur la répression for workplace safety.[8] The GIS was created after the December 1970 Lens trials, at which doctors had testified on silicosis and other illnesses affecting miners.[9] The organization became involved in a variety of public health issues, notably the struggle for reproductive rights. Its 1973 pamphlet, *Oui nous avortons!*, for example, led to its being indicted for endangering public morals because it detailed the so-called Karmen method of abortion.[10] Since Foucault was among those registered as responsible for the publication, he was also brought up on charges. Another publication from the following year declared the aims of the association:

> The GIS taken upon itself the tasks of developing an intolerance for the health system in France, both freeing up and correcting information on health problems, and struggling against false propaganda that confuses an increase in the use of medicines with an improvement in the conditions of health. For the GIS, improving the conditions of health means improving the conditions of life in all its aspects – at work, on public transport, in leisure time, and in private – a life often without liberty, initiative, and joy [*épanouissement*]; a life that is truncated and fragmented. What we call the struggle for "improving the conditions of life" is in fact a struggle for life. It is also a struggle for health.[11]

In chapter 12 we will see Deleuze give a sophisticated philosophical rendition of this manner of endorsing the forces of life. As the GIS saw it, knowledge about health had become the exclusive domain of specialists, and consequently, a democratization of information and knowledge was needed. Referring to the larger project of "unblocking" information in a variety of social contexts, the GIS pamphlet concluded:

> Whether it is a question of asylums, prisons, social work, or the way that the sick are cared for ... information is truncated, unilateral, sometimes even dishonest, provided sometimes by unscrupulous journalists looking for scandal, sometimes by *specialists* who deign to give up a little bit of their knowledge to "mass education." To inform is already subversive in itself ... Information is indeed never neutral; the

person who informs [*l'informateur*], doctor or not, always has another goal besides the apparent one. He can want to bring his listener to reflect, to go deeper, to understand, then to participate and stand up for himself, or ... he can comfort the listener with received ideas and put him to sleep.[12]

In another example of the rise of the model of the information group, the GITS, the social workers' information group, echoed the notion of information as revelatory, declaring its intention "to denounce all attacks that public and private authorities make on the social worker when he takes seriously the defence of persons society has entrusted to him."[13] The GITS had been formed in late 1971 when two teachers were sent to prison for refusing to give a judge the name of a student who had injured another. The group included teachers, social assistants, psychologists, and psychiatrists who worked with "marginal" populations – juvenile delinquents, the homeless, and so forth. Such marginal populations, they said, were "secreted" by modern society in the same way that the nineteenth century had produced the proletariat. To function, contemporary "repression" required more "agents" and a greater variety of them. Certain liberal professionals thus found themselves caught in an "ambiguous" situation: Was their role "assistance or repression? The defence of the social order or the defence of the victims of this social order?" Building on this acknowledged socio-professional ambiguity, the GITS said that its purpose was not necessarily to defend social workers. On the contrary, social workers themselves sometimes needed to be criticized and ambivalences brought to the surface. The defence of *les marginaux* required that difficult questions be asked and that information circulate. Like the GIP, the GITS retained a certain proximity to revolutionary talk, not only in its comparison of marginal populations and the proletariat, but also in an appeal to Lenin's thought, with which one pamphlet at least concluded: "When the bottom can't take any more and the top can't take any more, then the situation ripens."

In some respects, prisons are the lowest common denominator of the state's relationship to its citizenry. And behind the activities of the Secours rouge, the OPP, and the GIP, that relationship was very much the question of the hour. Pompidou's France, although by no means as brutal as leftist hysterical rhetoric claimed it to be, was nevertheless not a model for civil liberties in the Fifth Republic – even if things had come some way since the era of the Algerian War. Harsh judicial and police activity manifested imagined and often paranoid worries among advocates of law and order concerned about the stability of the Fifth Republic. One crucial question of the moment was: Could the Fifth Republic survive the era in which it was shepherded by de Gaulle's forceful personality? If so, what would it look like?

The contributions of the GIP, in spite of its self-effacing structure and perhaps even because of that self-effacement, played a crucial role in overcoming the excesses of the far-left period – excesses perpetrated by leftists and the Ministry of Justice alike. The desire for prisoners to be counted as citizens was a desire to refashion the Fifth Republic at the moment of its post-Gaullist transition. The state remained the object of liberational expectations – the Garde des Sceaux was accountable to the prisoners – but those expectations evolved from wanting a radical substitute for the rules of the "bourgeois" game to grudgingly accepting those rules. One could not opt for non-participation in prisons in the same way one could with respect to elections.

Handmaidens to self-represented reforms – this was a reality-based direction for liberational energies to flow. Prisons were "factories" where the raw materials of hope for total social transformation and dreams of starting history fresh went in; and self-representation, the "specific intellectual," and a vaguely understood ethical criterion of reference – the intolerable – came out. The rhetorical force of the "intolerable" came from its vagueness and the way it functioned as a moral fulcrum; its meaning was both obvious and not obvious. It represented a kind of limit-thinking that had little to do with the more ethically ambiguous "transgression" and valorization of criminality that (as we shall see) some were celebrating with regard to prisons in the 1970s. And yet, the intolerable was not unrelated to other early-1970s activism and reflection on institutions, individuals, and the contradictions of constraint – namely, anti-psychiatry and the philosophy of desire. Because in France the relations among the state, institutions like the prison and the psychiatric hospital, and individuals were so highly conductive, the new ethics being worked out would affect everyday relationships bounded by borders more porous than the walls at La Santé or Toul.

PART TWO

Spinoza on Prozac: From Institutional Psychotherapy to the Philosophy of Desire

By *virtue* (*virtus*) and *power* I mean the same thing; that is, virtue, in so far as it is referred to man, is a man's nature or essence, in so far as it has the power of affecting what can only be understood by the laws of nature.

Desire is the actual essence of man ... By the term desire, then, I mean all man's endeavours, impulses, appetites, and volitions, which vary according to each man's disposition, and are, therefore, not seldom opposed one to another, as a man is drawn in different directions, and knows not where to turn.

Benedict de Spinoza (1661–75)

There are too many laws, too few civil institutions ... I believe that the more institutions there are, the more people are free ... It is necessary that our institutions be numerous and composed of few persons. We must diminish the number of constituted authorities.

Saint-Just (1793–94)

To speak of Institutional Psychotherapy can only be an ethical discourse. The permanent risk of pathetic and polemic variations.

Jean Oury (1973)

8

Anti-Psychiatry and the Philosophy of Desire

In the years following the events of May 1968, militants of the far left directed their efforts against the French state and its institutions. Certainly, they protested against the conditions of the French educational system, both in universities and high schools, and, through encounters with police and judicial institutions, brought unprecedented attention to the "Bastilles" of the twentieth century – the prisons of the Fifth Republic. Those dynamics yielded innovative coalitions such as the Groupe d'information sur les prisons (GIP), and other groups mobilized around immigrants, health, and psychiatry. Among institutions targeted by information groups, two in particular overlapped: prisons and psychiatric hospitals. We have previously seen how the GIP had mobilized in support of Edith Rose, the psychiatrist at the Toul prison who denounced conditions there. As Michel Foucault in particular made clear throughout the 1970s, linking his earlier and recent research, prisons and psychiatric hospitals shared a basic paradoxical function: to confine and to reform.

In France, all prisons and most psychiatric hospitals were state institutions, and in them state power dealt with minority, marginal, and (to use Foucault's term) "dangerous" populations. Of course, the revolutionary ethos of the immediate post-1968 period rejected both straitjackets and palliatives. Thus, alongside prison revolts and heated public debate on the "carceral universe," in the late 1960s and early 1970s psychiatry and its institutions found themselves confronted with analogous agitation. It was not accidental that jails and asylums appeared together as "hot" sites. Institutional relationships themselves, even apart from their ties to the state, were subject to new forms of criticism and activism. In Part I we saw the dynamics of violence and protest lead to a shift of radical attention from the state to the institution of the prison; here in Part II we will observe the contributions of anti-psychiatry and the philosophy of desire to a shift in attention away from institutionally mediated relationships to the social field of intersubjectivity. Furthermore, in both Parts I and II ethics remains largely *implicit* – the ethical turn is underway but still concealed. Whereas the direct democratic category of the "intolerable" examined above was generally "positive," in the sense of having a discernible ethical anchor point, here we shall view the implicit quality of the turn more negatively, in the sense of there being an absence, lack, or breakdown of an ethical point of reference.

Anti-psychiatry was an international radical tendency generally inclined toward viewing madness as socially constructed. It brought the spirit of antiauthoritarian revolt to the mentally ill and their caregivers.[1] The somewhat looser category "philosophy of desire" included anti-psychiatry in its scope but implied a more general valorization of the unconscious, volitional, and passional aspects of thought and experience.[2] The importance of anti-psychiatry and the philosophy of desire for the larger arc of the 1970s ethical turn is, though no less crucial, indirect. They represented the culmination and high water mark of the antinomian spirit of 1968, the rejection of laws and norms in the name of a liberational ethos. As the critical spirit of the times tuned to the categories of mental health, questions that had been popularly asked earlier in other – notably British – anti-psychiatric milieux were now posed in France with newfound intensity: Was normalcy tantamount to normalization? Was psychiatry merely the furthest reach of an array of social and political institutions whose intention, or at least effective function, was to quiet all kinds of rebellion? Was it not society itself that was mad? Anti-psychiatry counselled unleashing madness's creative and contestatory energies. The old notion of madmen as seers was exhumed, and schizophrenic fragmentation and fantasy became models for revolution. The notable signature text of the philosophy that championed desire as a weapon against rationalization and repression, Gilles Deleuze and Félix Guattari's *Capitalism and Schizophrenia: Volume 1: Anti-Oedipus*, published in March 1972, criticized psychoanalysis and its "familialism" in favour of a "schizo-analytic" unchaining of "desiring machines" whose only *raison d'être* was to desire.[3] By exploring its genesis and, as Deleuze and Guattari would have put it, its "lines of flight," we will find that as far as the ethical turn was concerned the anti-Oedipal philosophy of desire largely involved a detour. *Anti-Oedipus* brought to the fore the ethical stickiness of the antinomian spirit of 1968; and an examination of its origins will help us better to understand that work and the debates around it. We shall consider the book and its reception in the next chapter.

Insofar as *Anti-Oedipus* concretized a broader cultural ambience of post-1968 antinomianism, it represented a kind of roadblock – a barrier to be overcome and a problem to be solved. The philosophy of desire and its anti-psychiatric and anti-Oedipal wings raised several practical and theoretical ethical quandaries. Was madness really a worthwhile criterion of social analysis? Was the liberation of desire always good? Were all limits to be overcome? If so, in the name of what? In crystallizing, expressing, and exemplifying certain aspects of the 1968-era ethos, the philosophy of desire indirectly provided the rationale for some to abandon *les années soixante-huit*. As we shall see in Parts III and IV, feminists and the New Philosophers rooted their ethical assertion of limits in a direct rebuttal to and departure from the *désirants* – the party of desire. On the other hand, we will have to grapple with Foucault's surprising 1977 claim that *Anti-Oedipus* was a "work of ethics." (We will consider this claim in chapter 9 and then again in greater detail in chapter 13.) It remains an open question the extent to which a coherent ethics could be derived from the philosophy of desire, in Deleuze and Guattari's hands an anti-Oedipal theory grounded in schizophrenic incoherence. What was ethically problematic – in the sense of thorny and questionable – can thus be considered as a factor contributing to the explicit emergence of the ethical *problématique* – in the sense of theme or subject matter.

As will become clear below, my approach to this question will also be indirect, turning from the book and its reception back in time to Guattari's and Deleuze's individual paths during the 1950s and 1960s. Much of this section is thus devoted to establishing how their distinctive trajectories – Guattari's experiences with the postwar French movement of Institutional Psychotherapy and Deleuze's unique brand of theory, drawing in the late 1960s on the history of philosophy and especially Benedict de Spinoza – furnished the raw materials for their collective work. Though each of their paths had encountered the ethical thematic prior to 1968, the *Anti-Oedipal* project, in posing a number of ethical dilemmas, broke the assumed mathematical rule that the sum of one ethical stance and another ethical stance equals two ethical stances. What might seem at first glance a circuitous route in the story of the ethical turn is in fact a necessary approach. Although we will turn back to years prior to 1968, we are indeed on our way forward. Some aspects of radicalism proved to be resources for the ethical turn while others did not, and we might consider here the extent to which the "barricades of May" served in part as obstacles en route to ethical fascination. At the intersection of institutions, psychiatry, madness, desire, and revolt the ethical turn continued to be made, even though this detour in some ways became a dead end.

The explosion of interest in anti-psychiatry after May 1968 thus further illustrates how a reappraisal of revolutionary strategies on the far left coincided with a reassessment of the role of institutions in French national life.[4] Before 1968, psychiatry was not separated from neurology in medical schools and was dominated by physicians with no separate training in psychopathology. To be sure, calls for splitting psychiatric studies off from the medical faculty had emerged prior to 1968 and increased in the months before the May revolts. That measure, however, was only adopted in December 1968 and January 1969.[5] To some extent, the formation of a separate discipline of psychiatry also represented a change in attitude toward the non-biological aspects of mental disorder and thus also toward methods like psychoanalysis, until then marginalized by the medical establishment.

A second major reform in the practice of French psychiatry was the belated application in 1971 of an organizational method first proposed immediately after World War II: *sectorisation*. This meant the creation of mental health centres according to demographic zones (the proportion of one facility for every 70,000 French citizens was proposed) and could be compared most closely to the Anglo-American model of community mental health centres.[6] Although sectorization had been seriously considered in the early 1960s, when the Ministry of Health had circulated some memos on the idea, the 1968-era reforms marked the first significant restructuring of psychiatry in France since the immediate postwar period.

Many saw the French anti-psychiatry movement of the early 1970s as following the path laid by the English spokespersons of anti-psychiatry, R.D. Laing and David Cooper, the Italians Franco Basaglia and Giovanni Jervis, and American fellow traveller, Thomas Szasz. The French sensibility certainly was related to the timing of the French translation of Laing and Cooper in particular.[7] The French anti-psychiatric milieu included various groups: practising analysts and psychiatrists committed to "humanizing" mental health practices, non-pragmatic and abstract followers of the psychoanalytic theorist Jacques Lacan, and left-wing activists bringing the gospel of antiauthoritarian revolt to the mentally ill. For example, the sixth issue of the leftist newspaper *Marge* (April–May 1975) called rather unrealistically for "the destruction of psychiatry, the liberation of all the 'mentally ill,' the suppression of all asylums."[8]

As Sherry Turkle has suggested, French anti-psychiatry had as much to do with shifting positions among French psychoanalysts and psychiatrists as it did with any common theoretical front. The marginality of French psychoanalysis gave it cause with the anti-psychiatric movement, whereas in the Anglo-American context, "anti-psychiatric stances [had] tended to imply anti-psychoanalytic ones."[9] The Lacanian cast of some French anti-psychiatry created a situation in which highly abstract psychoanalytic theory sometimes butted heads with the pragmatic orientations of practising analysts and psychiatrists.[10] At the same time, practising Lacanians, such as the children's psychoanalyst Maud Mannoni, whose *La Psychiatrie, son "fou" et la psychanalyse* (1970) was a runaway success, found themselves allied with psychiatrists who cheered many of the "humanizing" aspects of the general anti-psychiatric program.[11] Other psychoanalysts smiled smugly as familiar truths about the underlying madness of reason dawned upon others, while many psychiatrists not surprisingly resisted all criticism. Crying pox on both the psychiatric and psychoanalytic houses, sociologist Robert Castel diagnosed as "*psychanalysme*" a Lacanian anti-psychiatry unable to criticize itself.[12] Elsewhere, many left-wing activists saw the mentally ill as another population ripe for revolt, and a few philosophers became identified with the storm.[13] The last case will be important to us here.

French anti-psychiatry was one piece of a larger cultural mosaic that in the 1970s became known as the philosophy of desire. That sensibility reached deeper into the past, drawing on older cultural constellations such as surrealism, libertinage, and a natively French, crypto-Catholic eroticism. During the May events, the libertarian disposition of groups like the Situationist International and the March 22nd Movement did much to encourage people to, as the wall graffiti said, "Take one's desires for reality." After 1968 there was an unprecedented popular interest in the thought of Herbert Marcuse and Wilhelm Reich, both of whom gave eros and desire a privileged position in their thinking.[14] Above all, the philosophy of desire related to the sexual revolution of the 1960s and 1970s, and, as we will soon see, the nascent women's and gay liberation movements, which appeared in their popular forms in France only after 1968. In the early 1970s, a pervasive cultural sensibility held that *desire* – amorphous, polysemic, irreducible desire – lay at the heart of any relevant social and political thinking. It was both the problem to consider and the solution to which to turn. In the wake of failure on the May barricades, and as leftist *groupuscules* were digging in for a period of heightened agitation, *les désirants* were among the many who were shifting politics from the arena of state power to that of everyday life, from adjudication among political subjects to the constitution of subjectivity. Between the state and its citizens, however, were institutions such as prisons, psychiatric hospitals, schools, and families, which, like the streets where protests transpired, were sites disturbed by the revolutionaries of desire. The philosophy of desire thus amounted to an ambience and set of challenges.

Actual philosophers of desire shared rough, sometimes feuding family resemblances. Notable texts in the philosophy of desire were Guy Hocquenghem's *Homosexual Desire* (1972), Jean-Paul Dollé, *Le Désir de la révolution* (1972), and Jean-François Lyotard's *Libidinal Economy* (1974). The theme of desire was more generally in the air, even for those like René Girard and Jean Lacroix who were less inclined to assess its revolutionary potential.[15] Above all others, though, Deleuze and Guattari's *Anti-Oedipus* epitomized this cultural current, and in it anti-psychiatry, the philosophy of desire, and revolutionary politics intersected.

The authors' collaboration had begun on 5 April 1969 when the psychoanalyst and activist Guattari wrote the philosopher Deleuze a letter saying how much he valued Deleuze's recent publications. Deleuze responded in a May 13th letter in which he said that he, too, had admired Guattari's work from afar and had for some time sensed the parallels in their itineraries.[16] Over the next two and a half years, they moved slowly forward on the *Anti-Oedipus* project. As Deleuze recalled:

> Félix and I decided to work together. It started off with letters. And then we began to meet from time to time to listen to what the other had to say. It was great fun. But it could be really tedious, too. One of us always talked too much. Often one of us would put forward some notion, and the other just didn't see it, wouldn't be able to make anything of it until months later, in a different context. And then we read a lot, not whole books, but bits and pieces ... And then we wrote a lot.[17]

Write a lot they did. Their first joint publication, "La Synthèse disjonctive," a forecast of an important theme in *Anti-Oedipus*, appeared in 1970.[18] Although Deleuze apparently destroyed many of his papers before his 1995 suicide, hundreds of pages of notes exist in the Félix Guattari Archives in Caen. Most of the book seems to have been worked out between August 1969 and August 1971. On 26 April 1971 Guattari wrote to Deleuze: "This time I wanted to make an outline, but I sense that we still have to dig around for it."[19] From November 1971 through the March 1972 publication, Deleuze lectured on *Anti-Oedipus*'s themes at the experimental University of Paris at Vincennes, and reported that especially after the book began to sell well, all sorts of crazy people had been showing up at his classes. A mutual friend, Arlette Donati, later recalled Deleuze having said that Guattari was the "diamond" and that he was the "gem cutter."[20]

Anti-Oedipus was immediately and, for some, indelibly associated with anti-psychiatry in France. Sherry Turkle claims that it was "something of an antipsychiatric *cause célèbre* in Paris 1972–73."[21] In truth, Deleuze and Guattari directed almost all their energy against psychoanalysis, not psychiatry, putting themselves at odds with some Lacanian quarters of the anti-psychiatry sensibility. Overall, *Anti-Oedipus* exemplified the philosophy of desire in the way its "schizo-analysis" targeted the socio-political canalization of desire. Its overall view of madness and schizophrenia as revolutionary modes of being struck a chord with their general milieu, appealing to many on the far left who, though perhaps not centrally concerned with madness and psychiatry, were on the lookout for alternative languages to work through the post-1968 experience. Even if many readers did not always understand its dense and (as we will see in the next chapter) "nonsensical" character, they identified with its revolt against norms. With *Anti-Oedipus*, the *soixante-huitard* antinomian revolt – the redemptive desire to throw off all recourse to law – reached its most technically elaborate and fully philosophical expression. Its uses of the category of *desire* made the book refract the cultural moment in which it appeared.

This second Part will take the following route: I will first present some of the core arguments of *Anti-Oedipus*, especially its valorization of desire, and survey its immediate reception. This résumé will lead to a set of problems related to the anti-Oedipal framework, notably Foucault's claim that *Anti-Oedipus* was a "work of ethics." Rather than discussing these problems directly, I first historicize them by tracing the genesis of the anti-Oedipal project in Guattari's and Deleuze's respective itineraries before that project was born. The majority of this section (chapters 10–12) will thus consider Guattari's experiences with Institutional Psychotherapy and Deleuze's late 1960s philosophical writings, which became the tributaries for *Anti-Oedipus*. The encounter of Deleuze and Guattari gave rise to an original worldview that was more than the sum of its parts. In chapters 13–14, we shall return to the claim that *Anti-Oedipus* was a work of ethics and suggest how the philosophy of desire's embrace of the schizophrenic sublime led it to positions others would then criticize as blind. The 1970s ethical turn was not a straight line. In order to trace its path and follow its trajectory beyond *les années soixante-huit*, we have to take a switchback itinerary.

9

Anti-Oedipus: Redux and Reception, Ethics and Origins

Anti-Oedipus was the opening chapter in a collaboration between Deleuze and Guattari that lasted until the latter's death in 1992.[1] This bizarre, hermetic book offers among the best performative rebuttals to Ludwig Wittgenstein's claim that there is no such thing as a private language. It is at points so obscure and opaque that one often wonders what the authors were trying to say. A number of volumes have been published whose specific aim is to walk readers through the anti-Oedipal wilderness.[2] The book does not explicitly address the question of ethics. Rather, in step with much contemporaneous French theory, it examines ontological, epistemological, and political issues in an original idiom. Its objective was to challenge the construct of the Oedipus complex, both in the social form of the nuclear family and in Sigmund Freud's psychoanalytic diagnosis of it. *Anti-Oedipus* makes at least three basic arguments: (1) desire is productive, (2) Freud made a mistake by trapping desire in the family, and consequently, (3) psychoanalysis should be replaced by "schizo-analysis" in order to truly grasp the function of what the authors called "desiring machines." The overall purpose was to update the contrast between capitalism and revolution by charting the relationships among desiring machines, "familialism," and schizophrenia. This argument culminates in the contrast between paranoid "molar" formations like the family, which regulate desire, and schizophrenic "molecular" formations of "nomadic" parts, which express desire's inherent machinations.

A distinctive understanding of desire lay at the heart of this system. Rejecting a traditional Western view of desire as lack or privation – found from Plato and Augustine to Jacques Lacan – Deleuze and Guattari maintained that desire is a productive force. In other words, desire is not empty; it is not conditioned by absence and want. Rather, it is full, lawless, purely immanent, and essentially unconditioned by objects and transcendence. To imagine desire as the hunger or search for an object is to have misapprehended a secondary situation that develops through the trapping or channelling of desire by "law" into a regulated and controlled economy.

One can immediately see the anti-psychoanalytic implications of this view. Generally speaking, according to the classic Freudian perspective, desire develops its dynamism in the tension between, on one hand, the subject's wishes and organic drives, and on the other, the objective socio-historical conditioning of the superego and the reality principle. Even in the archetypical Lacanian depiction, the inaccessible Real, which is the absent Other not a concrete object, always defies both Imaginary fantasies and Symbolic representations. In ways analogous to the functioning of the Freudian superego and reality principle, the Lacanian Symbolic is also that externally imposed limit on our constitutively divided subjectivity – "le 'nom' du père," as Lacan famously put it, playing on the French homonym, means "the 'name' of the father" and suggests "the 'no' of the father." In short, according to the psychoanalytic paradigm, desire is always desire for something; that is, yearning for some "thing": for Freud, an object we can have within limits; for Lacan, an Other we can never have. Desire is thus bound to what is lacking, and is therefore to some extent constituted by that otherness which it cannot possess. As we will see, if psychoanalysis ascribes a basic transcendental structure to desire, whereby the desiring subject is cut off from the "object" or law that arouses desire, in contrast Deleuze and Guattari's anti-Oedipal view is centred on the basic immanence of desire's senseless (*non-sens* means without meaning or direction) workings. The authors designated their understanding of full, productive desire by their well-known and difficult category of the "desiring machine."

Part of the difficulty of Deleuze and Guattari's view of desire is that their text approaches it in different ways and describes it variously. Desiring machines, like other machines, produce. That is what they do – it is their essence and their history. Anterior to individuation (and certainly to the experience of individuals) desire runs in a continuous and nonpersonal "flow" or "*hylé*" (primary matter prior to its formation into things). Deleuze and Guattari's use of *hylé* brings to mind the pre-Socratic notion of *hylezoism*, or the belief that matter itself is alive. Into the flow of desire come "machines," which interrupt the *hylé* and condition it. The "interruptions" or "cuts" brought about by the machines are in fact part of the flow itself. When a machine interrupts the flow of desire, "schizzes" – "building blocks" or "partial objects" (the latter term was Melanie Klein's)

– break off. One might think of schizzes as the drops of water that splash off a hand when it is passed under a running faucet. Through their interruptions, breaking-offs, and reconnections, desiring machines produce, distribute, circulate, and consume. The flow and the machines operate together and thus in some sense merge. At one point, desiring machines evoke the image of a primal body that eats, copulates, and defecates in a pure continuum. In fact, that continuum, it turns out, is nothing more than various machines hooked up to one another in endless chains. At this level, machines operate according to a leg-bone's-connected-to-the-knee-bone kind of reasoning. The *hylé*, machinic interruptions, and chains of machines – these are all equivalent.[3]

The figure of the desiring machine was intended to bypass the traditional split between organicism and mechanism. By way of imagistic examples, one could consider the factory scene in Lars Von Trier's film *Dancer in the Dark* (2000), where Björk sings a musical number to the syncopated rhythms of grinding and pounding industrial machinery. Or, more abstractly, Marcel Duchamp's attempt in his *Bride Stripped Bare by Her Bachelors* (1915–23) to blur the mechanic and organic by indirectly representing sexual consummation as a network of gears, pumps, and conduits. Nevertheless, in my view, their insistence that desire was not anchored in a vitalistic nature, as it had been for Freud, was unconvincing: a covert naturalism was the first principle of their philosophy of desire. (We see the importance of this link with Henri Bergson in our discussion of Deleuze's Spinozism in chapter 12.)

Anti-Oedipus, the authors declared, was a work of "materialist psychiatry" that examined the function of "desire in machines" and the role of "production in desire"; that is, the relationship between "social production" and "desiring production." The difficulty was to discuss the "process of production" as process and not reduce it to something else. Freudian psychoanalysis was precisely this kind of reduction. Desiring machines were betrayed by psychoanalysis and the bourgeois family, which were two sides of the same coin in the sense that Freud's diagnostic model mirrored and reinforced a socio-historical institution. Deleuze and Guattari called this complex "familialism," by which they meant that the family was the primary arena where desire was captured and socialized and that psychoanalysis effectively abetted and reinforced this capture. Freud constantly returned desire to the Oedipal family drama where it was effectively contained. To be sure, Deleuze and Guattari were ambivalent about Freud and even more so about Lacan. Since desiring machines passed through the various stages in the formation and imprinting of the social unconscious,

Freud had been right to emphasize the unconscious, but in the authors' view, the good Viennese bourgeois doctor had got it wrong. The unconscious, according to Deleuze and Guattari, was itself social. Rather than being an organic naturalism à la Freud or a linguistic operation à la Lacan, the anti-Oedipal unconscious was the product of relations of production, distribution, circulation, and consumption. So, in some sense the Oedipal cycle did in fact describe the experience of modern family life, but only because familialism symptomatized capitalism, the predominant social order. The family was, after all, a bourgeois institution. For this reason, Oedipal "truth" deserved all the more to be subverted. Freud needed to be melted down in a marxisant cauldron.[4]

If familialism was a constellation inherent in capitalist civilization, capitalism involved a particular way of organizing and managing desiring machines. If the "nature" (a word antithetical to the authors' self-understanding) of desiring machines was to produce, distribute, and so forth, then capitalism reflected a specific kind of structuring and commanding "culture." In other words, desiring machines were a kind of primordial content and capitalism a kind of overlaid form. In *Anti-Oedipus* capitalism was described as a historical form characterized by disaggregation and reorganization. Under its reign, desiring machines were "de-territorialized" (they flowed in the market) and paradoxically "re-territorialized" (they were canalized and locked down in institutions like the family). Two tendencies could thus be found in capitalist societies – de-territorializing "schizophrenia" and re-territorializing "paranoia." Deleuze and Guattari went on to draw a contrast between "schizzes," on one hand, and "codes," on the other. Familialism demonstrated what happened when schizzes were channelled into a code, frozen in place, and robbed of their productivity. The Oedipal represented a "displaced or internalized limit [to capitalism] where desire lets itself be caught." Caught within the family, desire could not flow toward the "exterior limit" of capitalism and the "absolute limit" of all societies, which Deleuze and Guattari called schizophrenia.[5]

Apart from its figurative uses, in English, schizophrenia most frequently refers to "a mental disorder occurring in various forms, all characterized by a breakdown in the relation between thoughts, feelings, and actions, usually with a withdrawal from social activity and the occurrence of delusions and hallucinations." Clearly, the authors wanted to rescue some sense of the original Greek root, meaning "to split," as in "schism." Although their use also approached the term "schizophreniform" (resembling schizophrenia), it also seemed close to "schizoid" (resembling schizophrenia, but with milder or less developed symptoms) if not "schizophrenogenic" (tending to give rise to schizophrenia).[6] Deleuze and Guattari said in passing that they were not interested in the "clinical entity" of schizophrenia but in "schizophrenization as a process." A number of interpreters were troubled by this sleight of hand, and in chapter 13 we take a closer look at their efforts to separate the "entity" from the "process." In any case, etymologies and ambiguities notwithstanding, in *Anti-Oedipus* schizophrenia was understood as a model that "sets in motion decoded and deterritorialized flows that are restored to desiring production." In other words, schizophrenia itself was a capitalist form, but in the way that, as Marx had said, capitalism itself was revolutionary. Capitalism showed schizophrenic tendencies whose amplification might explode its other, "paranoid" tendencies, which tried to prevent productive desire from getting out of hand (or, so to speak, out of family). In *Anti-Oedipus* capitalism, schizophrenia, and revolution were all related in an immanent field.

Particular lessons could be drawn from having divided the capitalist world into two tendencies: the paranoid and the schizophrenic. The re-territorializing paranoid tended toward "molar" structures (the family, the fascist state) and the de-territorializing schizophrenic toward "molecular" formations of "nomadic" parts (May 1968, the women's and gay liberation movements).[7] If psychoanalysis counselled the family, "schizoanalysis," teased out "beneath the familial reduction the nature of the social investments of the unconscious [and] beneath the individual fantasy the nature of group fantasies." In this way, the nomadic would be unleashed. A "nomadic" subjectivity would mean letting schizzes – those "partial objects" and "building blocks" of desire – be themselves without reduction. For example, a sexual organ would not be considered a symbol signifying a transaction between a parent and a child, but a machine wanting to "hook up" with another machine. Flowing desire itself is presumed to be "revolutionary" when it confronts the molar formations of capitalism, when schizzes overflow the entropic reductions of desire to Oedipus and familialism. Both historical and natural, desire is productive and – here was the great normative implication of the book – ought to be left alone to realize itself. One should allow desiring flows to flow. The authors concluded:

> The task of schizoanalysis is ultimately that of discovering for every case the nature of the libidinal investments in the social field, their possible internal conflicts, their relationships with the preconscious investments of the same field, their possible conflicts with these – in short, the entire interplay of the desiring-machines and the repression of desire. Completing the process and not arresting it, not making it turn about in the void, not assigning it a goal.[8]

Anti-Oedipus was a popular book that elicited a range of contemporary responses. Weighing some of them serves to illustrate not only the high stakes of the debate around anti-Oedipalism and the philosophy of desire, but also the way that readers read selectively, singling out certain themes. Comments by the authors themselves also did much to push the reception of their work in particular directions. While the French cannot be accused of being poorer readers than anyone else, the so-called intellectual "affairs" that regularly punctuate contemporary French cultural life often revolve around highly redacted and partial reformulations of complex issues and themes. The tyranny of the sound bite has a long history (in France, 1950s existentialism was a crucial turning point) and the sound-bite dynamics at play over *Anti-Oedipus* in 1972 were intensified several years later in the New Philosophy controversy we study in Part IV. Deleuze and Guattari's book resonated with, reflected, and served as a lightning rod for its cultural moment. In the early 1970s the energies of 1968 were somewhat diffused but still potent; the search was on to redefine revolutionary fervour and locate alternative languages and sites for its expression.

In a two-page spread dedicated to the book in *Le Monde* (28 April 1972), Roland Jaccard anticipated the split in interpretations that would take place in the ensuing months.[9] The "theoretical, therapeutic, and social practices" of psychoanalysts and psychiatrists would prevent them from appreciating the book, while those who saw it as a "mild leftist delirium" and believed that "signs of madness" intimated social change (perhaps only the mad could disrupt the quiet insanity of normalcy and normalization) would appreciate it. Jaccard's prediction was fulfilled immediately on the facing page. The psychoanalyst André Green chastised Deleuze and Guattari for their "psychoanalytic anarchism" on the "left flank of Lacan." Their thought, he wrote, bore resemblances to that of the young Freud – "Anti-Oedipus is ante-Oedipus" – and he took Deleuze and Guattari to task: Their "analytic paranoia is consistent with a moral rigorism that assaults the neurotic-psychoanalyst twosome. But what contempt for the suffering of the neurotic! It's not for nothing that the book that speaks of psychosis, perversion, and neurosis completely leaves out depression."[10]

Psychiatrist Cyrille Koupernik complained: "Even if familial or social factors help precipitate the shipwreck that madness is, I don't think that they are determinant, nor above all sufficient. It is even possible that they are not even necessary."[11] Practising psychiatrists dealt with the ambiguities of schizophrenic symptoms being mixed with others. The appeal to a "biological, inhuman, ahuman, protopersonal desire" was "stunning," but the problems attendant upon a philosopher borrowing an uncertain category – schizophrenia – from a practical medical science were legion. Koupernik gave the example of having watched an Algerian boy on television whose mother had just been killed. The boy stared stony-eyed at the camera. Satirizing the anti-Oedipal attack on the nuclear family, Koupernik commented acerbically that the boy "didn't know his happiness."

The two philosophers featured in the *Le Monde* dossier – François Châtelet and Kostas Axelos – were more generous. Châtelet, Deleuze's colleague at the University of Vincennes Philosophy Department, having already organized a discussion of the book with Deleuze and Guattari, said simply that *Anti-Oedipus* was sure to provoke, since "the materialist combat in its work obeys absolutely no logic."[12] The book had made an "opening" [*percée*] and, like the work of the Roman philosopher Lucretius, it could not be expected to "obey the religious and scientific pieties of its time." *Anti-Oedipus* asked the right question: "Why do men fight for their servitude as if it were their salvation?" In the context of 1970s French intellectual-cultural politics, this was among the most important questions raised in the book. As we see in passing much later in chapter 25, Etienne de La Boétie's book *On Voluntary Servitude* (1552) experienced newfound attention during this decade.

Axelos, for his part, in another commentary posed a series of speculative and open-ended questions, addressing Deleuze as *tu*.[13] In one of his more pointed challenges, he asked ironically: "Honourable French professor, good husband, excellent father of two charming children, loyal friend, progressive who demands deep reforms in all domains where exploitation and oppression are inflicted and who demands actions that are immediately effective – would you want your students and children to follow in their "effective life" the path of your life or, for example, that of [Antonin] Artaud?" Artaud (1896–1948), of course, was one of the twentieth century's archetypical "mad" artists, whose "Theatre of Cruelty" was intended to transgress and transcend ordinary experience. Though they did in fact claim Artaud as a forerunner of their "materialist psychiatry," Deleuze and Guattari would respond to queries such as Axelos's by saying that pragmatics of this kind, and for that matter the worries of psychoanalysts and psychiatrists, hit too low and outside to strike the target they were aiming for. But the question, as Axelos put it otherwise, of whether *Anti-Oedipus* was "a slogan or a concept" would continually haunt discussions of the book.

In response to these and other criticisms, Deleuze and Guattari, in approximately seven different interviews and published clarifications of

Anti-Oedipus in 1972 and 1973, defended themselves in a number of ways. Their immediate post-publication comments highlighted certain elements of their argument. What the book actually said did not always accord with what they and others said about it, with the result that its consequences were sometimes more important than its content. One could mention, for example, the noticeable absence of any serious discussion about the three kinds of syntheses – connective, disjunctive, or conjunctive – that served as the work's organizational skeleton. (My own discussion has successfully excluded them as well.) Such precisions often seemed beyond interest, perhaps because readers (including this one) had to work so hard to identify patterns and arguments. For Deleuze in particular, this misrecognition and lack of precision was celebrated as part of *Anti-Oedipus*'s larger point. In March–April 1972 and again in April 1973, he suggested that the book as a whole should be viewed through the lens of its arguments: one ought to look for how it functioned as a kind of desiring-machine itself, since it seemed to respond to the desires of people who were fed up with the psychoanalytical model.[14] Deleuze only regretted that he and Guattari had not gotten further away from a certain "academic" language, and Guattari agreed that their tone had been too "serious." Waving off the criticisms of psychoanalysts and practically minded readers as self-interested, Deleuze cared little for the controversy or for the vicissitudes of interpretation, claiming that they had already moved on to other projects that were "less public and more fun."[15] (He may have had in mind their immediate collaboration on Franz Kafka (who had already appeared in *Anti-Oedipus*) and the second volume of *Capitalism and Schizophrenia*, entitled *A Thousand Plateaus*, not published until 1980.[16]) Guattari, however, had a slightly different reaction, commenting in a 17 January 1973 interview: "It is even surprising that the book elicited ... so many responses. We didn't anticipate any."[17]

Psychiatrists and psychoanalysts seemed to have the greatest investment in challenging the principal claims of *Anti-Oedipus*.[18] At stake were theories about the experience of *desire* and practices of managing, negotiating, and treating human desires. André Green, for instance, worried about Deleuze and Guattari's "contempt" for the psychiatric patient. In a slightly different way, others like René Girard and Jean-Marie Domenach, whose concerns were more religio-philosophical than psycho-professional, resorted to the righteous language of "suffering" in order to question the authors' lack of attention to the pragmatic implications of their lofty and difficult thought. Thinkers such as François Châtelet and Jean-François Lyotard were more receptive to *Anti-Oedipus*'s creative and imaginative "machinations." Roger Dadoun had cheered upon hearing the "life song" of desiring machines as composed by Deleuze and Guattari. But the further one went on the political Left, the more resistance one encountered, as Michel Clouscard showed in his indictment of Deleuze and Guattari's abandonment of recognizable political militancy. The reason for this criticism seemed to be that the construction of a new idiom, however critical, that dispensed with recognizable terms and forms of political action – agency, subjectivity, class, and so forth – was tantamount to leftist self-flagellation and paralysis.

More sympathetic but with thoughtful reserve, Jacques Donzelot qualified his positive appraisal by his perceptive observation on *Anti-Oedipus*'s sources: the book had blended elements of Nietzschean thought (via Deleuze) and the movement in French psychiatry known as Institutional Psychotherapy (via Guattari). Along with Jean Furtos and René Roussillon's intelligent comment that Guattari should not be forgotten as a partner in the anti-Oedipal enterprise, Donzelot's historical suggestion invites further exploration, since the schizophrenic whole of *Anti-Oedipus* was unequal to the sum of its parts.[19]

In revisiting the arguments and reception of *Anti-Oedipus*, one sees how the book resonated – or "machinated" – with its moment. But in making desire the problem and solution worth thinking about for cultural politics, the philosophers of desire raised further problems for which they did not always have the answers. The phrase *desire without limits*, a stereotypical fantasy of antiauthoritarian revolt (at least in the eyes of some its more conservative critics), was in fact an ethical minefield. Even if *Anti-Oedipus* did not make the claim for limitless liberated desire, it did not make a clear case against it. To appreciate the historicity of this dense, inventive book and how it bore a metonymic relation to its cultural moment, it is worth broaching the ethical consequences of *Anti-Oedipus* before tracing its origins.

Anti-Oedipus's attack on psychoanalysis was classically antinomian. Its attack on the bourgeois family and its psychoanalytic props amounted to an assault on normative criteria in general and on the notion of *law* in particular. The notion of law was unambiguously dispensed with, up to the point that even transgression was seen as merely the flip side of a juridical game in which all potential moves were played out ahead of time. Transgression was a dead end because the "nomadic" subject would not even recognize enough law to feel perverse pleasure in breaking it. While Deleuze and Guattari's description of the constitutive function of law was reminiscent of Lacan's, their wholesale rejection of law for the purely immanent machinations of desire was not something Lacan would have countenanced. The nature of law, they said, is to formulate a "fictitious" displacement of desiring machines; law invents prohibitions and directs desire to want what those prohibitions forbid. Displacement is a form of repression "meant to trap desire." They praised Kafka for having shown that law imposed an "eminent formal unity, and *reigned accordingly over pieces and fragments*." An empty formality governs partial objects, and in that emptiness, the law has no real object – "the verdict having no existence prior to the penalty, and the statement of the law having no existence prior to the verdict." There is no room for the happy contractualist vision of legality: "The law is the invention of the despot ... *it is the juridical form of the infinite debt*."[20] One's desires are channelled into an endlessly deferred and interest-accruing bond; that is, into bondage. Schizoanalysis will free desire from this constitutively guilty nexus.

The practical and strategic dimensions of *Anti-Oedipus* were wrapped up in the somewhat vague theory of schizoanalysis, and Deleuze and Guattari ended with a promissory note for later clarification on how "the various tasks of schizoanalysis proceed."[21] The prescriptive or normative in an explicitly positive register – that is, the criteria *in the name of which* the anti-Oedipal critique operated – was generally elided in the book. To be sure, appeals were made to "revolution," which for some readers in early-1970s France needed no explanation. But little justificatory reflection was brought to bear on those assumptions. In the end, it seemed difficult for Deleuze and Guattari to defend themselves against the charge that they weren't doing much more than valorizing desire's rebellion against normative constraints in general. Despite their continual efforts during the 1970s to explain that they were *not* merely advocating a free-for-all celebration of unfettered desire, it was not merely by chance that their work was judged in that light. Desire, as they presented it, was full and productive, unlike Lacanian desire, which was empty and lacking. It was lawless – essentially immanent and only incidentally or temporarily framed by transcendence. At the same time, some readers of *Anti-Oedipus* actually saw a kind of moralism in the book, echoing Vincent Descombes's later perceptive judgment that "Deleuze finds himself measuring *that which is* according to the standard of *that which is not*, but *which should be*."[22]

Remarkably, in the 1977 preface to the English translation of *Anti-Oedipus*, Michel Foucault made the following claim: "I would say that *Anti-Oedipus* (may its authors forgive me) is a book of ethics, the first book of ethics to be written in France in quite a long time (perhaps that explains why its success was not limited to a particular "readership": being anti-Oedipal has become a life style, a way of thinking and living)."[23] Foucault was referring precisely to the way *Anti-Oedipus* targeted the "fascism in us all, in our heads and everyday behavior, the fascism that causes us to love power, to desire the very thing that dominates and exploits us." Now, Foucault's comments perhaps said less about the climate in 1972 than about that of 1977, when the New Philosophers (see Part IV) and others were championing "dissidence" and rebellion against all sorts of totalizing logics. The idea of "voluntary servitude," already mentioned, was then being more widely discussed. And Foucault's remarks are complicated by the fact that after the mid-1970s he was growing more distant from Deleuze, to whom he had been quite close during the moment of the Groupe d'information sur les prisons and at the University of Vincennes, where they both taught. He had also become increasingly suspicious that "desire" was a useful category of either analysis or emancipation. Still, Foucault's comment is striking, both for its description (*Anti-Oedipus* was a work of ethics) and for its claim of novelty ("the first book of ethics to be written in France in quite a long time").

Foucault's evocation of "anti-fascism" clearly foregrounded the authors' debt to Wilhelm Reich, who decades before had analysed the relationship of desire to fascism and the ways in which Hitlerism had successfully appealed to and fulfilled the desires of its adherents.[24] Deleuze and Guattari had explicitly cited Reich in presenting their "materialist psychiatry." Nonetheless, it seems worthwhile to ask: in what sense could the anti-Oedipal be construed as an ethical philosophy of anti-fascism? What was the relationship between fascism and schizophrenia? What was the state of law and status of limits? Was the de-territorialization of desire itself, against all tendencies toward re-territorialization, an ethical pressure point? Fairly or not, some of *Anti-Oedipus*'s critics had worried about an aestheticized schizophrenization that ignored the bodies of clinically diagnosed schizophrenics and about an "anything goes" liberation of desire. We will thus have to square Foucault's far-from-self-evident claim that *Anti-Oedipus* was a work of ethics with the apparent ethical dilemmas posed by madness and desire. To accomplish this task, we now turn to the historical and intellectual sources of Deleuze and Guattari's project. The route is indirect, like *Anti-Oedipus*'s contribution to the ethical turn.

It is already well known that the sources of the book rest in the itineraries of its two authors since the 1950s: Guattari's experiences at the La Borde psychiatric clinic and Deleuze's as the author of idiosyncratic studies in the history of philosophy and literature and, by the late 1960s, difficult works of original theory. But we still need to establish what exactly each of these authors brought to *Anti-Oedipus*. This question is not new. Early critics of *Anti-Oedipus* in the early 1970s sometimes tried to reduce the whole of the work to its authorial parts – an exercise Deleuze and Guattari found repugnant. Nor did they warm to the idea that their work reflected a synthesis of two independent branches.[25] With my own apologies to the authors, I would like to make the following argument: Guattari had been formatively exposed to a specific, ethically coherent thought and practice in the La Bordean network – Institutional Psychotherapy (IP). That movement was a sustained experiment in institutional ethics, and Guattari's contribution to it stemmed largely from his interest in Lacanian psychoanalysis and the cross-currents of his political, intellectual, and practical experiences. Although his commitment to IP was already waning by the mid-1960s, Guattari's meeting with Deleuze marked a definitive rupture from it. That contact pushed into the background ethical aspects of his thought that had emerged in the laboratory of clinical experience. Though Guattari never ceased advocating radical praxis and was a tireless activist, the intellectual model advanced in *Anti-Oedipus* – the "schizoanalyst" – was not likely, quips Gary Genosko, to "open a technical consultancy in pragmatics."[26] But the Guattarian strain was not the only project to be altered in the encounter.

Deleuze, for his part, had by the late 1960s forged his own coherent philosophical ethics, indebted largely to Nietzschean, Spinozist, and Stoic thought. Though by no means an ethical philosopher, he nevertheless articulated positions – notably a vitalistic affirmation of life and a joyful embrace of one's own destiny – that could generally be described as ethical or more exactly as "ethological." At the same time, his idiosyncratically creative readings of canonical thinkers and works led in the mid-to-late 1960s to startling departures into literature and the elaboration of highly original, dense meditations on the themes of meaning, madness, difference, and repetition. Though desire and schizophrenia were not new themes for Deleuze, after his encounter with Guattari they came to occupy a greater role in his thinking. The anti-Oedipal schema marked a splintering and breakdown – a schizophrenization – of the Nietzschean, Spinozist, and Stoic ethics he had been assembling in the 1960s. The merging and mutual collapse of two ethically coherent stances generated a remarkable and highly original line of thinking, whose ethical implications were not entirely clear in 1972, when *Anti-Oedipus* was by no stretch of the imagination seen as a work of ethics. The philosophy of desire was moulded by Deleuze and Guattari in the contexts of antiauthoritarian revolt and anti-psychiatric agitation, contexts to which they were indebted and of which they ultimately became unwitting caricatures. No amount of psychotropic medication could have restored Spinoza to his very non-schizophrenic lucidity once Deleuze and Guattari were through with him. *Anti-Oedipus* had an ethics ... and it did not. Let us now sort out how this was the case by looking at how the book came to be written.

10

Institutional Psychotherapy and the La Borde Psychiatric Clinic

Félix Guattari's contribution to *Anti-Oedipus* was the culmination of his gradual departure from an ambience he had been part of for the previous two decades. In this chapter and the next I examine that setting and his divestment from it, a disinvestment underway even before his opportune meeting with Deleuze. The term "disinvestment" seems appropriate because we are concerned here with Guattari's gradual rejection of his standing investments in the field of psychiatric practice known as Institutional Psychotherapy and in Lacanian psychoanalysis. It is by no means an exaggeration to say that Guattari contributed prodigiously, if not singularly, to that convergence, and while it would be silly to try to divide out who brought exactly what to the table, his influence needs to be emphasized, since their joint work is often unfairly credited to his more famous collaborator. Guattari, five years Deleuze's junior, had already come to a number of methods and insights that would play a predominant role in *Anti-Oedipus* and future works. His practical experiences of living and working in the La Borde psychiatric clinic, and its experimental implementation of procedures and concepts such as the "grid," "local law," and the "vacuole," paid later dividends. It is from the framework of one of the most important and imaginative movements in modern psychiatry – Institutional Psychotherapy (IP) – that some of anti-Oedipalism's component elements and energies were drawn. *Anti-Oedipus*, however, left IP's ethical charge and limits behind.

The term Institutional Psychotherapy was first used in print in 1952 by the French psychiatrists Georges Daumézon and Philippe Koechlin.[1] Born of the experience of French psychiatry under the Occupation, IP was a postwar leftist movement in French psychiatry. It emphasized the role of the social-unconscious, and applied diagnostic and curative methods originally intended for patients to other relationships within the psychiatric institution. What psychoanalysis did on the scale of the therapist and patient, IP tried to accomplish at the level of the institution. Treating the institution as a whole meant analysing interactions among caregivers and care-receivers as well as situating the institution as part of a larger social field. More than a rallying cry for physicians to heal themselves, IP has been a pragmatic, non-utopian program of Freudian-Marxist institutional experimentation. A by no means frivolous illustration of how one might grasp IP is to consider how the contemporary academic department functions: it involves institutional and personal relationships – affections, rivalries, laughter, memories, and resentments; it must balance egos and operate within limits; it pursues sometimes divided, sometimes shared tasks, and relates to broader social and political realms. Such institutions could sometimes stand a little therapy.

Whatever IP's liberational and restorative potential, however, the circumstances of its birth were unhappy. During World War II, an estimated 40,000 mental patients had died in France, and psychiatrists and nurses had been well situated to witness the tragic uses to which institutions and categories of mental health had been put under Vichy and the Nazis.[2] The experience of concentration camps, writes Liane Mozère, brought about an "entirely ethical obligation" to respond to mental illness in new ways.[3] From its origins, IP sought to end the "segregation" of mental patients at several levels. The Saint-Alban clinic, located in Lozère in the South of France, was the most important incubator for Institutional Psychotherapy; in 1998 the newspaper *Libération* called it the "Mecca of Institutional Psychotherapy."[4] The distinctiveness of the clinic had begun to take shape shortly before the war in the era of the Popular Front when reforms such as changing the name "asylum" to "psychiatric centre" were being introduced. Saint-Alban's wartime director, Paul Balvet, had taken charge in 1936, and during the war, an extraordinary array of people, ideas, structural constraints, and psychiatric tasks converged there. Mozère comments:

> The historical "fortune" was that Tristan Tzara, Paul Eluard, the surrealists, communists, Christians, members of the French Resistance, the sick, doctors that needed to be hidden – all took refuge at Saint-Alban. The "fortune" was that a singular constellation formed there, associating Resisters, surrealists, the mad, peasants; therapeutic activities, acts of Resistance, underground publishing, networks.[5]

Jean-Claude Polack and Danielle Sabourin's certainly bloated description of the clinic at the time sets the scene:

> The hospital welcomed deserters and Resisters. The patients went into the countryside to help the peasants look for food [amid wartime shortages]. The asylum structure became permeable, fluid, a place of passage or of meeting, incandescence, and agitation. The originary situation, the primitive scene of institutional therapy; somewhere, in a brutal countryside, politics slept with madness.[6]

Among the influential actors at the clinic was the refugee Spanish psychiatrist François Tosquelles, who found his way there in 1941, fleeing Franco. Under Tosquelles's significant influence, the outer walls of the clinic were taken down, the front doors opened, and prison-like bars removed.[7] The philosopher of science and French Resister Georges Canguilhem, whose "Essai sur quelques problèmes concernant le normal et le pathologique" was first published in 1943, also sought refuge at Saint-Alban.[8] After the war, among the first interns there were the future godfather of postcolonial studies, Frantz Fanon, and, arriving in September 1947, Jean Oury, a young psychiatrist in training who went on to found the influential La Borde psychiatric clinic in 1953 and mentor Guattari.[9] Much postwar French intellectual interest in madness, normality, and pathology had its roots in the Saint-Alban "ambience," to borrow an IP term.

During the late 1940s and early 1950s, IP was a diversely formulated and diffusely situated phenomenon woven into mainstream French psychiatry; Daumézon, for example, was named secretary general of the Union of Psychiatric Doctors (Syndicat des médecins des hôpitaux psychiatriques) in 1945; and another early pioneer of the movement, Lucien Bonnafé, was given the post of technical advisor to the Ministry of Health during the early Fourth Republic. Those associated with the IP movement at the moment of its greatest legitimacy would become some of the major forces in French psychiatry into the 1980s: Jean Ayme, Bonnafé, Hélène Chaigneau, Daumézon, Pierre Fouquet, Roger Gentis, Koechlin, Germaine Le Guillant, Oury, and Tosquelles, among others. IP drew on and fed into the major intellectual and cultural currents of the twentieth century, including surrealism, phenomenology, existentialism, linguistics, structuralism, American and English group and experimental therapy, and Gestalt. It also engaged with a cast of characters as varied as Henri Ey, Jacques Lacan, Melanie Klein, Maxwell Jones, Kurt Lewin, and J.L. Moreno.

By the late 1950s, however, the movement had become more marginalized, as psychotropic drugs first became widely available and biological approaches to mental illness were renewed. Although IP seemed never to have openly challenged the neurological dimensions of mental illness (the back pages of the journal *Psychothérapie institutionnelle* (1965–68) were filled with advertisements by pharmaceutical companies), that was not where its emphasis lay. IP provided a forceful balance to the somatic model, and its small but influential circle of advocates continued their agitation into the 1960s. Changes of the 1968 era in the structural organization of French psychiatry (such as sectorization, for example), can been seen in part as the fruits of their labour. Still, 1968 and the popular French reception of Anglo-American and Italian anti-psychiatry took much of the wind out of IP's sails. Some of its advocates were resentful of a younger generation they saw as stumbling across established insights as if they were newly discovered. In the early 1980s, a period of renewed interest in IP opened among European and South American psychiatrists. That period continues today.[10]

One of the many architects of IP during the 1950s, Jean Oury, and the house that he built, merits closer attention. Pierre Chanoit is right in saying that "the place of Jean Oury in the history of Institutional Psychotherapy is singular," particularly if one bears in mind that *singulier* can also mean odd or eccentric.[11] In 1947, upon completing his psychiatric studies in Paris and looking for a first internship, Oury heard by chance that Tosquelles needed help.[12] It was a fruitful encounter. Oury commented in 1997: "From 1947 until his death [in 1994], I stayed in constant touch with Tosquelles. Neither disciple or student: a deep and militant friendship."[13] Oury spent two formative years at Saint-Alban before agreeing in September 1949 to take a temporary assignment ("for a month") at the Château de Saumery near the Loire River because that clinic was short-staffed; he ended up staying four years. The Saumery clinic provided a sharp contrast to the cutting-edge atmosphere at Saint-Alban. Faced with lingering material lack, absence of local medical coordination, and memories of patients having been deported to concentration camps, Saumery became the initial laboratory for Oury's improvisation of new approaches to psychiatric care. To cite Mozère again:

> The small size of the establishment, which in 1949 had only thirty patients, constrained the team to a polyvalence of tasks assumed by each, consequently bringing about a questioning of the tasks and status [of those who worked there] ... Foundational, this reshuffling was accompanied by an opening of the clinic to networks, or bands, outside the psychiatric world: friends of this or that person, students, militants – all who came to participate in the activities of the clinic, but also to lead theoretical discussions, games, and philosophical, political, or aesthetic debates.[14]

The structural constraints of the institution facilitated experimental methods, and Oury's version of IP would continue to reflect this mixture. Soon, however, those constraints proved too great, and in March 1953 Oury left Saumery to form another clinic, taking some of the staff and a few of the patients with him. Securing modest funding, he was able to purchase the nearby La Borde Château, a building that had seen better days, in the Département de Loir-et-Cher. Unlike Saumery, La Borde was private, with greater independence and flexibility for innovation than a state hospital, but it was also plagued by financial uncertainties and material lack. Once again, the very limitations of the situation helped bring about innovations in practice.

Though Oury was the original and principal long-term animator of La Borde, he and Guattari would be remembered as the Romulus and Remus of the clinic. When Guattari died from a heart attack in 1992, Oury wrote movingly of their forty-year-long "dialectical friendship," saying that "he was exactly the same at sixty as at fifteen."[15] They had known each other since the immediate postwar years when they had both been involved in the "youth hostel" [Auberges de jeunesse] movement, begun under the Popular Front as a means to encourage young people to travel by providing inexpensive lodging.[16] Guattari had been a student of Oury's older brother, Fernand, a high-school teacher who later played an important role in transferring the method of IP to education and pedagogy.[17] Several years later, in the winter of 1951–52, when Guattari was becoming increasingly disillusioned with his studies in pharmacy school, Fernand suggested that he go see Jean Oury at Saumery under the pretext of life and career counselling. A number of changes quickly took shape in Guattari's life. He left pharmacy school and began studies in philosophy. He broke with the Trotskyists, with whom he had been a key actor (in 1947 he had gone to Yugoslavia to pour the concrete foundations for the new University of Zagreb). He developed a great admiration for Sartre, and in 1953 first attended Lacan's famous seminars on psychoanalysis – that year on Goethe and poetry. Guattari would say that he was the first non-medical student to attend Lacan's lectures in the early 1950s and that he and Didier Anzieu were the first Lacanians at the Sorbonne. Although he also studied under Maurice Merleau-Ponty and Gaston Bachelard, the fact that some of his classmates nicknamed him "Lacan" showed where his interests were headed. Perhaps most significant of all the changes in Guattari's life were his regular late-night visits to Jean Oury and their conversations on philosophy, art, politics, and psychoanalysis. Oury, too, was influenced by Lacan, whose work he continued to engage from his first encounter in 1947 through the 1970s, at which point he tired of the way Lacan cut theory off from any dialectical exchange with clinical practice.[18] The ways that Oury and Guattari employed Lacanian theories and tactics at La Borde set them apart from other IP currents that were more suspicious of Lacan's opaque elaborations. Guattari's later rejection of psychoanalysis needs to be set against this backdrop.

Guattari was officially hired at La Borde to organize events for the patients, and was placed in charge of the Comité Intra-hospitalier de la Clinique and the Club des pensionnaires. He moved into the clinic to live full time in 1955. In his own words, he was very "interventionist," pushing the patients to participate in group events and challenging the nursing staff. He admitted that he was more of a "communist militant" of a Trotskyist persuasion than a medical or psychological professional, recalling of his early time at La Borde: "In several months, I contributed to putting into place multiple collective authorities [*instances*]: general assemblies, a secretariat, patient-staff parity commissions, sub-commissions for daily activities, an office for the coordination of individual initiative, and 'workshops' of all sorts: a newspaper, drawing, sewing, the chicken coop, garden, etc." Immediately taken up with questions of work relations and functional tasks, Guattari distinguished himself from Oury and Tosquelles who, he later said, felt that the institutional structure should be subordinated to the needs of psychiatric care.[19] In contrast, Guattari believed that "institutional functions" had a certain "autonomy." One of those functions was to prepare insulin for the patients every morning. Given his background in pharmacology, in addition to keeping the books, this was Guattari's other job.

From 1953 until the early 1970s, a variety of Institutional Psychotherapeutic techniques were developed at La Borde, as the clinic passed through several phases. A 1974 study of the clinic by the Centre d'étude, de recherche et de formation institutionnelle (CERFI), an interdisciplinary research group founded by Guattari in 1967, described four periods in the institutional life of the clinic from 1953 to the early 1970s.[20] A first period (1953–59) saw the emergence of a work structure known as the *grille*, or grid, based on a rotation of tasks and a blurring of work identities. In a second period (1959–64), new problems generated by the *grille* structure were confronted. Dealing with these difficulties led to the development of new strategies, such as an analytic procedure, referred to by the Lacanian notion of "empty speech" [*la parole vide*], which was an attempt to take into account the desires of specific individuals as well as the global needs of the institutional collectivity. Between 1965 and 1969 a third phase reflected a pattern of oscillation between too much central structure and too little. The attempt to establish an equilibrium between functional and analytical tasks led to the development of mixed patient-counsellor groups and to groups that were primarily either functional or analytic. From 1969 to 1972 (the time when the CERFI study began), an *esprit autogestionnaire*, or spirit of self-management, emerged, intensifying earlier attempts at exchanging roles but going further in the levelling of tasks. This last period, amid post-1968 fervour and attractions to anti-psychiatry, saw a temporary decline of interest in IP, after which it was reinvigorated in the 1980s. A closer look at the first two of these periods helps illustrate the kind of conceptual/practical institutional ethics that were in play during the "golden era" of La Borde. The specific procedures and techniques of Institutional Psychotherapy aimed to bring what Freud had described as the psychoanalyst's "evenly hovering attention" toward his or her patient to institutional relationships and their exponentially magnified complexities.

Between 1953 and 1959 the major preoccupation of the La Bordean milieu was *la grille*, or grid, a chart that emerged as a solution to the problem of organizing the occupational "ambience" with the goal of "group reshuffling." Oury had decided in 1953 when the clinic opened that a "management group" could make work assignments. In fact, the doctors were effectively in charge of the personnel. Beginning in 1955, as the number of infra-institutional groups increased and the financial state of La Borde became dire, new approaches to work distribution were instituted.[21] Over the next two years, building on earlier attempts to reassess the doctor-nurse work relationship, efforts focused on reassessing the division of labour between the caregivers and the service personnel. In the summer of 1957, the salaries of those two groups were equalized, and a system of rotation was set up so that those who did the cleaning, for instance, would participate in group meetings, and interns, nurses, and doctors would take their turn with the broom. "Here the maids take care of patients," someone said at the time. Inevitably, resistance to these measures arose: not only did those with status-laden work balk at performing tasks beneath them, but also, service personnel became reluctant to act as caregivers. Guattari later recalled:

> A kind of resistance developed. For example, "I was hired to be a nurse and not to do the laundry!" But that was easy to get around, once people were able to see that there was a "therapeutic coefficient" in doing the laundry as well. Oury used the term "linguistic," and Claude Poncin referred to "*situèmes*." (The laundry room being such a "linguistic locale.") We said: "You're not doing laundry, you're doing linguistics!" That worked pretty well.

After affecting the doctor-nurse relation and the care-taker/service worker relation, "group reshuffling" seeped into staff-patient relationships. In this context, "things, problems, and information began to circulate very quickly," and the term "polyvalence" was used both to describe this quality of exchange and to serve as an organizing principle: such flexibility could be mobilized against the tendency of relations within an institution to "segregate." Beyond purely functional aspects of making the clinic run – Félix cleans the kitchen on Monday, Jean-François gives the electro-shocks on Wednesday, Liane organizes the art group on Friday – all sorts of other factors had to be considered: "the affection of someone for his or her task"; the shifting popularity of some tasks over others "with no one knowing really why"; a consideration of the "psychopathology of everyday life" (gender, age, experience; "more or less paranoid accusations"); and the "circulation ... of fantasies and transferences." The *grille* was a structural attempt to marshal and direct this heightened circulation toward effects that were at the same time therapeutic and liberational.

By the late 1950s, however, problems generated by the *grille* became apparent, directly in its formal operations and indirectly in what it overlooked. As the CERFI study concluded of this period: "Since we marshalled available energies for solving such and such a problem, we had to take them from another sector."[22] The effort to shake up roles and tasks in the name of a process of "disalienation" brought about other forms of alienation. The frequently invoked term "disalienation" combined the suggestion of a vaguely Marxist project of liberation with a play on a French term for someone who is mentally ill: *un aliéné*.[23] Yet even a structure as fluid and shifting as the *grille* could not help neglecting the desires and wants of specific individuals; someone or a group of people had to organize the *grille*, someone's interests were always left out. A severing of affect and tasks (nurses liked to be nurses) led to a decline in a "certain dimension of sympathy, of 'contact' with the ambience." Given the self-reflexive nature of La Bordean praxis, this development was more or less foreseen, in the sense that Institutional Psychotherapy, like psychoanalysis more generally, involved dynamic engagements whose outcomes could not be known ahead of time. A second period of La Bordean history (1959–64) opened when strategies were elaborated to address resistances and alienations whose sources were understood to be more deeply libidinal than ego-attachments to task and status.

The *grille* had enabled desire to circulate more freely within the institutional setting, and linguistics and Lacanian thought were brought into play to deal with this polyvalent situation. Institutional structures, like linguistic structures, reflected levels and relationships of signification, and the analysis of those relationships led to new practical interventions. The early 1960s saw the emergence of a widespread interest in one-on-one psychoanalysis among staff members, and the development of information meetings and "inter-service" encounters intended to put various "sectors" into dialogue. The interaction of various sectors, say, the kitchen, medical clinic, and patients' club, brought out the "intersubjective weave" of the institution. The challenge of dealing with circulating libidinal elements that originated on the level of individual fantasies and interactions led to the consideration of the concept of "local law," or that which is "impossible to entirely recognize but which has in view ... the impossible symbolization of the ensemble of circuits in place in an institution."[24] In other words, local law covered the "non-totalized totality" of the institutional field. In order to grasp its place in the institution, while taking into account the force of individual erotic elements, the Lacanian concept of "empty speech" [*la parole vide*] was employed.

Lacan uses the notion of "empty speech" to explain the discourse of the analysand (the patient) in the therapeutic setting; one can talk and talk and not say very much. The analyst confronts the "imaginary" ego and fantasies of the analysand, who is constitutively "frustrated": he or she can never live up to his or her own self-identifications (hence his or her frustration, aggressivity, regression, and resistance, etc.). But it is out of such "empty" talk that the analyst and analysand can move toward "full speech," or discourse that acknowledges the "real" impossibility of desire's fulfillment. Lacan writes:

> Speech, even when almost completely worn out, retains its values as a *tessera* [which Alan Sheridan describes as a token of recognition, password, symbol, or link]. Even if it communicates nothing, the discourse represents the existence of communication; even if it denies the evidence, it affirms that speech constitutes truth; even if it is intended to deceive, the discourse speculates on faith in testimony ... "empty" speech, where the subject seems to be talking in vain about someone who, even if he were his splitting image, can never become one with the assumption of his desire.[25]

One of the ways Lacan believed the passage from the "obsessional intrasubjectivity" of empty speech to the "hysterical intersubjectivity" of full speech could be accomplished was in the "beneficent punctuation" achieved by bringing a psychoanalytic session abruptly to a close, thereby shocking the empty speech of the analysand. This served as one of the justifications for his notoriously "short" psychoanalytic sessions. The approach at La Borde was to take the dyadic model of empty speech and apply it to groups and institutions. Of course, institutional constraints thwarted any attempt to apply Lacan's short session technique, since one could not very well order patients to leave the hospital.

As it was exercised in the constellation known as the "training group" (otherwise described as the "vacuum cleaner of the flux of speech"), empty speech meant "the necessity of 'speaking,' independently of all *immediate* efficacy, independently of all *direct* organizational ambition." Staff and patients would speak about all sorts of psychological, social, and structural problems at La Borde without seeking to resolve specific questions directly. A space was made for speech to proliferate, and things were "worked out" indirectly and by-the-by rather than as a matter of mandate or compromise and consensus. From the notion of empty speech came the model of the *vacuolic* group. In science, a vacuole is "a small cavity or space in the tissues of an organism containing air or fluid," a meaning played with at La Borde.[26] The vacuole described for the group what transference, countertransference, and dyadic exchange did for the therapist-patient relationship. It was a recipe for complexity. As the CERFI study put it:

> The idea of the vacuole is that there is between people a zone of opacity that one must respect; it is the idea that the detour is the shortest route to settle such or such a question, such or such a difficulty. The vacuolic group rejects in its preoccupations all utilitarian references, all immediate efficiency. That is not its object. The object of the vacuolic group is the object in its psychoanalytic meaning: it disrobes without end; one can only sketch its silhouette and contours. The vacuolic group handles a white space, a *no man's land* [English in the original]. The vacuole presents itself as a pond: to advance one must go around the banks. The banks roam: one can at least guess the place and the expanse and indicate the place of the object ... There is no question of facing real difficulties without mediation; one must more so go around them, "talk about" them, independent of all worries about efficacy, of all obsession with interpretation.[27]

The strategies of empty speech and the *grille* were examples of the sub-institutions that were encouraged to proliferate at La Borde. Such practices were intended to "mediate" the primary relationship for which the clinic existed – the staff-patient, or caregiver/care-receiver [*soignant-soigné*] relationship. Such secondary mediations reflected a "fundamental detour" in the treatment of the sick, but also, as such, an effort to affect the "ambience" of La Borde.[28] Other forms of mediation would emerge later, such as mixed groups of patients and staff and, after 1968, more radical experiments at *autogestion*, or self-management.

From 1953 through the 1960s, staff at La Borde tried to combine and overlap the diagnostic tools of Lacanian psychoanalysis, ethnographic and linguistic structuralism, and existential Marxism. Of particular interest is that one found there the compatibility of two intellectual fields of the era – structuralism and existentialism – otherwise frequently opposed. As we have just seen, psychoanalytic procedures usually imagined for the one-on-one patient-therapist relationship were applied to complex work and affective relations within the institution as a whole. The institution itself had an unconscious that could be grasped – this was the Lacanian insight – structurally. At La Borde the appeal of psychoanalytic structuralism overlapped with an interest in the structuralist anthropology of Claude Levi-Strauss. The clinic was frequently described in terms of the rites, economies, and status rivalries of a primitive society. As Polack and Sabourin, for example, commented: "Neither chance not the frequent visits by structuralist ethnologues (Lucien Sebag, Michel Cartry, Pierre Clastres, Alfred Adler) explained the vogue of Levi-Straussian anthropology in the discourse of the promoters of the institution."[29]

Structural analysis helped to designate possibilities for action within the totality of the institution. But what kind of action and for what? The application of the psychoanalytic model to the collectivity and the analysis of institutional structures both pointed toward the liberational aim of "disalienation." It was in the region of work relations within the institutional body that the symptoms of "institutional illness" were localized. IP's critical assessment of labour and production was patently Marxist in inspiration:

> The politics of work were divided immediately around three fundamental, voluntarist axes: *democratic centralism, the precariousness of statuses and functions, the communitarian organization of tasks.* These elements essentially broke with the hospital tradition by importing into the psychiatric institution ethico-practical exigencies coming out of deep currents of revolutionary ideology: communist, oppositional Trotskyist, anarcho-*libertaire*.[30]

The critique of hierarchy and fixed roles implicit in strategies such as *la grille* coincided with a critique of the tendency for institutions to build up bureaucracies, a process that led to the freezing up of the institution's "historically detectable desiring fields."[31] This attack on bureaucratic closedness – indebted to Sartre's concepts of "seriality," the "practico-inert," and "non-totalized totality" in *Critique of Dialectical Reason* (1960) – was undertaken at La Borde in ways befitting a psychiatric institution.[32] By considering the specific desires of each person, that analysis attempted to keep an existential dimension from being effaced by anonymous institutional structures.[33] To a great extent, Institutional Psychotherapy emerged at the intellectual crossroads of 1950s existentialism and structuralism as well as those of Freudianism and Marxism. It was an ambitious balance that was impossible to maintain for long; thus the need for continual elaboration and adaptation.

Notwithstanding its sometimes vague self-understanding and the short-lived existence of many of its organizational elaborations, La Bordean IP was an extended project in institutional ethics. In a 1978 interview, looking back on La Borde in the 1950s and early 1960s, Oury commented: "I would say that all we were doing was an ethics."[34] At the heart of this ethics lay an acceptance of the reality of mental illness (as opposed to the assertion of its social construction or "aesthetic" appeal), the distinction between *soignants* and *soignés*, and the limits of the institution, represented by "local law." The psychiatric institution was there for a reason; it was not a hippie commune. As some brief and dismissive discussions of La Borde like to point out, electro-shock therapy continued to be practised there for many years. It thus differred from some English anti-psychiatric experiments in its non-utopian outlook. But in its tasks and day-to-day operations, efforts were made to be self-consciously critical about the circulation of libidinal investments and unconscious drives in all relationships at La Borde. Rating the success and failure of this endeavour is perhaps less interesting than noting the techniques, such as the *grille* and the *vacuolic* group, whose *raison d'être* was to answer the question: Within the limits of a psychiatric institution, what ways of living and working will bring the greatest liberation to staff and patients? Though the precise terms of that liberation could be vague – most talk of liberation usually is – attempts were made at La Borde to articulate and apply a non-functionalist pragmatics: to care for the mentally ill while self-reflexively critiquing rationalization and bureaucratization, and analysing the impossible-to-totalize totality of the institutional "ambience." These procedures rested on an ethical understanding of primary and protean desire as well as its limits within an institutional setting.

La Bordean Institutional Psychotherapy foregrounded a dynamic that, although ultimately of psychoanalytic provenance and centred on a concrete institution, offers more lessons for the later story of the post-1968 ethical turn. That dynamic can be described as the contrast between *ethos* and the *law*. La Borde certainly was an ambience, a setting, even a stage. Its characteristic spirit recognized that desire flowed within this institutional situation and that a complex web of unconscious forces permeated the atmosphere. The *grille* was even employed to cultivate this ethos, and the notion of the *vacuole* took into consideration the fact that the machinations of desire could not be handled straightforwardly. One had to arrive indirectly by strolling around the banks of the pond. And yet, the psychiatric institution existed to treat mental illness. "Local law" took account of this constitutive limitation. Intentions at La Borde were not so much curative in a strictly medical sense as emancipatory and restorative. But unlike anti-psychiatry and the philosophy of desire, La Bordean IP did not generally view mental illness itself as essentially liberatory or socially constructed. The facticity of schizophrenia, paranoia, depression, and so forth was a given, even though those phenomena had political, social, and intersubjective dimensions. One might say that the "reality principle" was at play here, with the qualification that the circulation of desire was cultivated in the name, not of normalization, but of liberation. The ethos of La Bordean IP was, one might say, checked by the twofold limit of clinical mental illness and the project of emancipation.

The reason why this *ethos/law* distinction is important is that the ethos of 1968, too, as it continued to reverberate into the 1970s, similarly encountered various kinds of laws and limits during the subsequent decade: the laws of the state enforced by the police we saw in Part I; the explicit limits on the liberation of desire we will see in Part III, limits that for some ended up having recourse to Fifth Republic legality; and the equally explicit limits of rebellion, dissidence, and ethics that we observe in Part IV. We can therefore ask if the turn to ethics was not related to the manner in which the ethos of 1968 ran up against different laws and limits. Here in Part II, if the overall turn to ethics can be seen as a parabola, *Anti-Oedipus*'s renunciation of ethically coherent limits seemingly marks the furthest points on that curve, until, *paradoxically*, we revisit Foucault's claims that the book was "the first book of ethics to be written in France in quite a long time." For the moment, whereas the contribution of the anti-Oedipal to the ethical turn was largely indirect, the contribution of La Bordean IP to *Anti-Oedipus* can be directly emplotted as a story of breakdown: from an ethically coherent institutional ethics to an apparently ethically incoherent schizophrenization.

11

Félix Guattari's Devolution

If the La Borde clinic was in part Guattari's formative school and Institutional Psychotherapy his course of study, then one might say that by the mid-to-late 1960s he was ready to graduate. In the years around 1968 he came into his own and began to hit his mature productive stride. For the rest of his life, his thinking evolved in tandem with Deleuze's and also grew in original directions (collaborations with the Italian Antonio Negri; reflections on the ecological and what he called an "ethico-aesthetic paradigm").[1] His development during the 1970s and 1980s was continuous. At the same time, there is another story of continuity to be told: from his La Bordean years to *Anti-Oedipus* and beyond. One sees this first in the eventual expression in Deleuzo-Guattarian language of themes and terms broached earlier by each of them, but notably, it seems, by Guattari. So too, he did not simply abandon psychiatric issues in the 1970s. For instance, with Robert Castel, Mony Elkaïm, and the Italian Giovanni Jervis he helped form the Réseau alternative à la psychiatrie in 1975; and he never severed his connections with La Borde even though he moved away and gradually visited less.[2]

Nevertheless, in spite of obvious continuities and links, the important chapter in Guattari's itinerary to emphasize on this occasion is an interruptive and disjunctive one. A discontinuity exists between the ethically coherent institutional practices of La Bordean IP and the confused ethical status of the anti-Oedipal. In the overall track of the ethical turn, we again touch, however paradoxically, the notion that the way forward involves a step back. In the previous chapter we backtracked chronologically to years before 1968. In this short chapter, we are again concerned with the prelude to 1968 and *Anti-Oedipus*, but we also now include a thematic devolution – a decline and deterioration but also a transfer and delegation. Insofar as

Anti-Oedipus in part reflected the influence of IP, its antinomian revolt against the institutionalization of desire dispensed with the circumscription of an ethos by institutional limits. Guattari himself had turned.

In the early 1960s Guattari continued to be oriented intellectually by the thinking of Jacques Lacan and wider IP circles. In late 1961 he completed an extended commentary on Lacan's 1955 seminar on Edgar Allan Poe's "The Purloined Letter." The commentary was written in the form of a letter to Lacan (8 December 1961) and marked a new stage in Guattari's own thought, bending Lacan's theory of "enunciation" [*l'énoncé*] to his own uses in considering "collective enunciation" and "institutional objects."[3] Perhaps significantly, just as he was starting to develop his own public voice on psychoanalysis and institutions, he began analysis with Lacan (apparently around 1962). Also during the early to mid-1960s, Guattari was involved, as a somewhat junior member, in the Groupe de travail sur la psychothérapie et sociothérapie institutionnelle (GTPSI) formed in May 1960 by some of the original instigators of French IP.[4] The group met twelve times over the next five years, ultimately dissolving to form the Société de psychothérapie institutionnelle (SPI) in 1965, which in turn published six issues of the review *Psychothérapie institutionnelle* until 1968 when it, too, folded. The organization was small, hovering at around fifteen to twenty participants, but its theoretical output – based on the various clinical experiences of 1950s IP, of which La Borde was only one example – was considerable. Oury and Guattari were more favourable to Lacan than others in the GTPSI, and Guattari more open to the influx of non-psychiatrists and non-psychoanalysts who were drawn toward the group as its reputation grew.

Guattari often worked out his own ideas in the context of the GTPSI. For example, the important distinction he drew between "subjugated groups" [*les groups assujettis*] and "subject groups" [*les groupes sujets*], a distinction clearly indebted to Jean-Paul Sartre's contrast of "serial groups" and "groups-in-fusion," appeared in talks he gave to the group in 1962–64.[5] As we have already seen in passing in the previous chapter, his engagement with Sartre and Lacan, and thus the related interchange between existentialism and structuralism, exemplified the broader sensibilities of La Bordean IP. Guattari's most important essay of the 1960s, "Transversality," was originally a presentation to the First International Congress on Group Therapy in September 1964 as part of a GTSPI round table on transference and countertransference. It was then published in the first issue of *Psychothérapie institutionnelle* (1965).[6] This was the urtext of *Anti-Oedipus*, and in it

Guattari was already making use, for example, of the *grille* (see chapter 10) in relation to schizophrenia and the political content of the unconscious, using the terms "machine," "schizzes," and "territorialization."[7] (We will return to the concept of transversality momentarily.) In 1966 he published another comment in *Psychothérapie institutionnelle*, in which he mentioned the role of "political economy" in "the production of the institution," the irrelevance of the father figure in the contemporary division of labour, the "corporeal schema of the institution," and the problem of group desire coming to supplant an individual's desire.[8] In short, the GTPSI and the SPI formed Guattari's core ambience for much of the 1960s.

But Guattari was also involved in other conversations. In the periodization of his own life, the Algerian War was a more significant turning point than the events of May 1968.[9] He had never ceased his far-left activism in the years after he had broken with the Trotskyists in the early 1950s, but he had redirected his energy into La Borde. During the Algerian War, however, Guattari attached himself to the Voie communiste, an independent Left group with Trotskyist tendencies mobilized in support of the Algerian insurgency, the Front de libération nationale. He left that group in 1964 but reconnected with similar circles when the Voie communiste collapsed and in its wake the Opposition gauche was formed in the fall of 1965 following the Eighth Congress of the PCF-backed Communist student union, the Union des étudiants communistes.[10] Guattari's activism put him in frequent touch with left-wing students. He was asked by the Mutuelle nationale des étudiants de France to serve as a technical consultant on psychological problems among students. In that capacity, he contributed an essay on "institutional therapy and the problem of mental health in the student milieu" to the Mutuelle's organ, *Recherches universitaires*, in 1964. Philosophy students at the Sorbonne also asked him to explain IP to them in 1966. The following year he ended his association with the Opposition gauche.[11]

Guattari's reactivation as a political militant thus brought him into wide-ranging contact with people from various intellectual and political networks, and the cumulative effect of these interactions facilitated a shift that would lead him away from aspects of IP (though not from La Borde) and to some extent prepare him for his meeting with Deleuze. In Oury's mind, Guattari was also largely responsible – and this was not a positive development – for the fact that growing numbers of Parisian intellectuals were descending on La Borde for weekend visits. By the mid-1960s, the clinic had acquired a reputation as a hotbed of non-Communist Left thinking about madness and social change.[12] La Borde, Lacan, the GTSPI, the

Algerian War, dissident Trotskyism, the student milieu – these wide-ranging zones of engagement, along with Guattari's love of music (he had played piano as a boy), formed the experiences out of which his theory of transversality emerged. Although one should hesitate before ascribing a thinker's theory to his or her biographical experience, in Guattari's case, such a link seems apt. Guattari himself made the suggestion. It was his own crossing back-and-forth among different intellectual and practical sites that led him to thematize the experience of "transversal" relations. His article on transversality addressed the fact that psychiatrists showed "a systematic failure to understand what is going on outside hospital walls"; in other words, the social, institutional, and political contexts in which psychiatric practices were embedded.[13]

As described in the 1965 article, "Transversality," the transversal referred to a method that considered the "effect of the social signifier on the individual," or, put differently, "a reshuffling of the givens of the Super-ego's 'welcome.'" Building on the psychoanalytic notion of transference and especially on the mathematical notion of the *transversal* as a line that intersects systems of other lines, Guattari intended his concept to address the overlapping and interwoven relations that connected the individual to various contexts.[14] The most interesting of these relations, of course, were unconscious ones. All groups – for instance, an institution, sub-institutions within it, or supra-institutional groups that existed beyond "hospital walls" – were traversed by unconscious forces. Like individuals, groups presented their own structures of manifest and latent content. A group's latent content, its "desire," was approached from the point of view of a "ground clearing" [*déblaiement*] and the "preservation of a vacuole" (see chapter 10).

The task of transversal analysis was "to modify different unconscious coefficients of transversality at the different levels of an institution," a process "sometimes leading to immense detours that can make us ask questions about the crucial problems of our era." This procedure would make it "possible for an individual to be part of a group as someone being-heard and who hears and furthermore to have access to a beyond-the-group which he or she interprets, more than simply manifests." The method of transversality would "found a new group law," one that formed a group-subject aware of its limits – its "non-sense, death, alterity" – as well as of its overlapping and interacting desires.[15] In short, transversal analysis would transform "subjugated groups" into "subject groups." The difference between subjugated and subject groups was furthermore described as the shift between two fields: "that of an alienated subjectivity that has lost sight of social alterity" and "that of a subjectivity whose vocation is to take up speech [*prendre la parole*]." This difference was one of the origins of *Anti-Oedipus*'s antithesis between paranoid molar formations and revolutionary-schizophrenic molecular ones. There is thus a clear line of descent from Sartre's "serial groups" and "groups in fusion" to Guattari's "subjugated groups" and "subject groups"... to *Anti-Oedipus*.

One significant outlet and experiment for the notion of transversality was the formation, under Guattari's inspiration, of the Fédération des groupes d'études et de recherches institutionnelles (FGERI) in 1964. The FGERI represented a collective of research groups in various disciplines (such as architecture, urban planning, film, and psychiatry) who wanted to reflect on their own practices in an interdisciplinary context. The Fédération also served as an outlet for the various professionals, writers, and scholars who had descended on La Borde. It applied methods of transversal analysis developed in a clinical setting to more strictly intellectual tasks. Here perhaps, the clinical body of the schizophrenic began to be replaced by an interdisciplinary intellectual discourse, a process that was to be exemplified by *Anti-Oedipus*. The FGERI was also a testing ground for Guattari's overflowing interests, and when the Fédération required greater stability and structure, Guattari signed on as the head of its replacement, the above-mentioned Centre d'étude, de recherche et de formation institutionnelle (CERFI).[16] Officially formed in March 1967 as an association under the *Law on Associations of 1901*, CERFI declared its principal objectives to be the following:

- to carry out studies relative to the management, conditions, and social and economic development of local collectivities, organizations of cultural activity, businesses and social institutions, etc.;
- to promote statistical research as well as economic, sociological, psychosociological, and urbanist investigations concerning urban and regional planning;
- to develop research and studies at all phases of investigation with the participation of those who will use such knowledge;
- and to organize the training of educators, teachers, cultural facilitators, nurses, administrative executives, architects, economists, etc., in the spirit of the researches themselves.[17]

In the era of Gaullist technocracy, CERFI sought to combine democratic intentions and expert knowledge in the analysis of a range of overlapping social fields. Its original members included doctors, psychiatrists, architects, psychologists, philosophers, engineers, urbanists, a television journalist, and a mathematician. Its main accomplishment was the journal *Recherches*, which began publication in January 1966. The journal claimed to be "an instrument of elaboration, a site for the *interpellation* of different scientific practices, an occasion to unveil multiple approaches that question the subject, institutions, and science."[18] Until the collective's dissolution in the early 1980s, the review published studies on architecture, childhood, pedagogy, homosexuality, capitalism, Ferdinand de Saussure, "sector" psychiatry, day-care centres, Eastern European dissidence, and Institutional Psychotherapy. CERFI also oversaw the 1967–68 publication of the last two issues of the GTPSI's *Psychothérapie institutionnelle* (nos. 5 and 6), and from 1967 until at least 1977, the group also had contracts with La Borde for CERFI members to perform certain tasks at the clinic. For example, a 1970 agreement specifying CERFI's "mission" at La Borde said that CERFI would "take charge of all the problems of the arrangement [*aménagement*] of spaces in the clinic" and that it would furthermore bring "technical competencies or experiences which the clinic's personal [did] not have," along the lines of theatre, cinema, group therapy, and collective outings.[19] Some of the contracts were signed by Oury and Guattari, the former representing La Borde, the latter representing CERFI. For friends such as these, the bureaucratic record must have been amusing."[20]

Integral connections between La Borde and CERFI notwithstanding, the research collective had interests far beyond the management and day-to-day operations of a clinic and thus also beyond the practical limitations of clinical expertise. CERFI members would at one point be referred to as the "anarchists of research."[21] The kind of interdisciplinary border-crossing instituted by CERFI would appear in *Anti-Oedipus* in the authors' diverse, wide-ranging, and sometimes superficial reliance on works from the fields of psychology, anthropology, linguistics, mathematics, and history, among other disciplines. Guattari's devolution from IP, then, occurred precisely at the "transversal" interstices of his own life experiences and of the institutions, political groups, research collectives, and identities among which he moved. What began in attempts to reorder work relations among psychiatric caregivers by taking into account the circulation of desires within an institutional setting, through splintering and dispersion became the seeds of the anti-Oedipal project – an enterprise, to be sure, that was collaborative. We now turn from the psychiatric and psychoanalytic "couch," so to speak, to the philosopher's den.

12

Gilles Deleuze's Spinozist Ethics

Until 1968, when he published his two doctoral dissertations, *Difference and Repetition* and *Expressionism in Philosophy: Spinoza*, Gilles Deleuze was known as the author of solid if idiosyncratic works in the history of philosophy and of equally distinctive forays into literary criticism.[1] The methodological pattern that emerged in the historical works had been to take a particular philosopher (David Hume, Immanuel Kant, Friedrich Nietzsche, Henri Bergson) and, by carefully explicating basic elements of his thought, to direct that thinker toward an original, though not implausible point of tension. It was a way of writing the history of philosophy and of individual thinkers from the inside out.[2] Deleuze also subjected Marcel Proust and Leopold von Sacher-Masoch to similar origamic unfoldings. These books were as much or more about their author than about their subjects. In the 1960s such creative readings earned Deleuze an iconic reputation but not a university position in Paris. The publication of the books on difference/repetition and Spinoza, along with *The Logic of Sense* (1969), marked the transition from this earlier period to the second half of his career.[3]

From 1968 until his 1995 suicide, Deleuze was renowned outside of France as a star poststructuralist and inside France as a philosopher and political activist. This biographical and intellectual transition was due to a confluence of factors: the slow-going professionalizing track of the French academy, the events of May 1968, and his not-to-be-underestimated meeting with Guattari, among others. The overall picture of Deleuze's early work and his highly original mature work – all of it difficult – cannot concern us here, but it seems worthwhile to look a little more closely at what and how Deleuze was thinking around the time he met Guattari. Not coincidentally, the Spinoza dissertation, together with an introduction to a collection of Spinoza's texts (1970) and *The Logic of Sense*, featured the concept of the ethical.[4] An examination of Deleuze's treatment of ethics between 1968 and 1970 might help shed some light on the vexed ethicality of *Anti-Oedipus*. Parts of ethical Spinozism made it into the polemic against Oedipus; parts of it did not.

In his *Nietzsche and Philosophy* (1962) Deleuze had already anticipated several of the themes explored in greater depth in his works on Spinoza.[5] He presented Nietzsche as the anti-Hegel and also as a radicalizer of Kant. Against Hegelian dialectical thought, Nietzsche had postulated a universe of active and reactive forces that arranged themselves in hierarchies. Force was affirmative by definition, as intimated by the joyous figure of Dionysus. Dialectical thought, which turned on the "labour of the negative," was actually a reactive philosophy of *ressentiment*. Kant had seemingly come closer to an affirmative philosophy, but his law-abiding moral philosophy faltered before the consequences of full autonomy: the free spirit would create his or her own values. As we see below, Deleuze's Spinozism was rooted in distinctions between active and reactive, affirmation and negation, joy and sadness. In his book on Nietzsche, he explicitly evoked Spinoza on a number of occasions, pairing Nietzsche's "will to power" with Spinoza's "capacity" and introducing the Spinoza quotation he would often repeat for the next thirty years: we do not even know what a body – an assemblage of forces – can do.[6]

An interesting interpretive question arises. Are we to consider Deleuze's later engagement with Spinoza an extension of a prior, more basic, and consistently held Nietzscheanism? Or, did it represent a departure or a development? There is compelling evidence for the latter alternative. Deleuze spent much more time in the 1970s and 1980s writing and lecturing on Spinoza than on Nietzsche. Although he continued to explore Nietzschean themes, the structural frameworks of *Anti-Oedipus* and later works were more explicitly Spinozist insofar as they described an immanent field of modalities operating in a totality. Nietzsche himself said of Spinoza: "I am utterly amazed, utterly enchanted! I have a *precursor*, and what a precursor! ... in five main points of his doctrine I recognize myself ... he denies the freedom of the will, teleology, the moral world-order, the unegotistic, and evil ... my lonesomeness ... is now at least a twosomeness."[7] The historical picture of Deleuze's Spinozism has another level of consequences: the unfortunate associational chain – Nietzsche-Heidegger-Nazi. French debates in the 1980s over Heidegger and Nazism were indeed an important sign of French intellectual culture after the ethical turn.[8] Yet there is hardly any evidence that Deleuze was influenced by Heidegger.

Despite parallels in their respective treatments of *ethos*, Deleuze's use of Nietzsche led back to Spinoza rather than forward to Heidegger.

Spinoza has proved influential for contemporary continental philosophy more generally. Lauding a collection of European essays on Spinoza written since the 1960s, Judith Butler has acknowledged "the centrality of Spinoza's influence on contemporary critical theory. [These essays show that] we have ... been speaking about him all along."[9] Alan D. Schrift has highlighted the sustained French interest in a Spinozist Marxism, and Christopher Norris has pointed out the parallels between Spinoza and critical theory.[10] For some, the seventeenth-century Dutch-Jewish thinker provided an antidote and alternative to Hegelianism. Deleuze's books on Spinoza were joined in the years around 1968 by numerous studies about and re-editions of the Spinozist corpus. For instance, Louis Althusser helped found a "Spinoza Circle" in the late 1960s. Martial Gueroult published almost 600 pages of commentary on the first section of the *Ethics* in 1968. Alexandre Matheron wrote on Spinoza's vision of individual and community the following year. Commentators later taken with Spinoza would include Alain Badiou, Etienne Balibar, Luce Irigaray, Pierre Macherey, the Italian Antonio Negri, and Jacques Rancière.[11]

To this list we might add Robert Misrahi, who had helped edit Spinoza's complete works in 1954 and the year before the May events was teaching a course at the Sorbonne on the Spinozist theme of "happiness."[12] His 1972 treatment of desire in Spinoza deserves recognition for refracting the prevailing cultural mood as much as Deleuze's *Expressionism in Philosophy: Spinoza* and *Anti-Oedipus*.[13] Here, we see a certain symmetrical coincidence between Spinoza's thought and the cultural and political climate of *les années soixante-huit*. "The numerous publications dedicated to Spinoza in recent years," Misrahi began, "only confirm in our eyes the modernity of this philosopher." His own book had emerged through conversations with "friends" who met every Saturday night to discuss Spinoza, and students who, through Spinoza, "glimpsed the promise of that transmutation of life and society which they look for so ardently in the French university." Calling Spinoza a direct source for both psychoanalysis and Marxism, Misrahi suggested: "[The] basic intention of Spinozism ... is to make man attain the fullness of his being, the complete *jouisssance* of his freedom as reflexively transmuted Desire." That reflexive transmutation of desire, which governs the evolution from "servitude to joy [and from] internal scission to the adequation of oneself to oneself and of oneself to an Other [*autrui*] is an ethical enterprise so important and exclusive, an interior path so perplexing and so revolutionary ... that one must strive for it as a whole in order to express its solar purity and diamond-sharp rigour."[14]

Misrahi tried to show how, in a supposed system of total necessity, an ethics is possible. He drew a triple parallel among: 1) Spinoza's theory of infinite substance and the finite "modes" (parts) that participate in it; 2) the system as a totality and the "wisdom" of the system; and 3) Spinoza's philosophy and Spinoza the thinker. Desire is the "privileged instrument" by which to explore these tiered relations.[15] In other words, the *Ethics* expresses and performs a triple cascade of theory-work-thinker; Spinoza the thinker mirrored the "wisdom" of the system described in his book, which in turn mirrored the theory of finite modes itself. Misrahi pointed out that Spinoza discusses desire in the third of the *Ethics*' five parts. Desire was thus the "pivot" of the work. In the nearly 400 pages that followed, Misrahi analysed the false goods and "imaginary" possibilities of existence generated by desire when it was understood as "passion," how the moral problematic hinged on the nature of reflection, and why Spinoza considered freedom as a form of reflexive desire.

In the Spinozist system, Nature exceeds the power of each individual part of it. Each individual part, or mode, exists in causal relation with other parts in the whole, and nature is the totality of forces and effects; that is, the way those parts interact in cause-and-effect relationships. Each part is a node of power that is not equal to the whole. Nevertheless, the *telos* at the heart of Spinozist metaphysics leads from the part to the whole, from the freedom of each part wrongly understood as isolated to freedom rightly understood in its connection to the necessary totality, which is God. Paradoxically, if humans overestimate their place in the world, their desires are bound to be frustrated. Misrahi pointed to an opposition between an "alienated life," characterized by an "imaginary form of desire" (precisely this over-estimation), and a "free life," characterized by a "reflexive form" of desire.[16] There is thus a difference between inadequate "passion," on one hand, and adequate desire-and-reason, on the other. Correctly understood, desire is the vehicle for moving from servitude to joy and also for seeking rational Wisdom. The Wisdom of the Spinozist totality is the reflexive knowledge that our desire fits into a system of necessity – desire and Nature coinciding in a theodicy-like coherence: "*The Spinozist philosophy of freedom is ultimately a philosophy of Desire that is at the same time a philosophy of reflection.*"[17] In Misrahi's view, this "philosophy of man saved by himself in himself without any recourse to some transcendences" showed how Spinoza was too shrewd, too wise, not to have made a place for his own freedom in the God/Nature system he described.[18] The term "pantheism," often ascribed to Spinoza by his critics, is somewhat of a misnomer: God and Nature do coincide, and from the theist point of view, this does not bode well for God. But from another point of view, the convergence works out well for nature, which becomes enlivened and self-organizing. Spinoza's is a philosophy of immanence without transcendence.

Deleuze later considered his discussion of how finite modes participate in the Spinozist totality – the way humans express God/Nature – "one of the most original aspects" of *Expressionism in Philosophy: Spinoza.*[19] Finite modes are *affective*: they express a capacity to be affected and to affect, to be acted upon and to act. In other words, they are capable of both passivity and activity. For Deleuze, Spinozist ethics revolves around this qualitative distinction, which itself is anchored in the quantitative difference between less and more. Passive and active affects exist in a relation of inverse proportions – the more of one, the less of the other. Passivity is the absence or privation of – but also the potential for – activity. Furthermore, according to Deleuze, Spinoza postulates a continuum between the extremes of passivity and activity. As far as the mode of nature called a human being is concerned, that continuum runs from passive feelings and inadequate ideas (passions) to active feelings and adequate ideas (actions).[20] We might note that Deleuze had already suggested this kind of passive/active distinction in *Nietzsche and Philosophy.* Yet there is a difference. The term *adequate* has a technical meaning for Spinoza; it means being equal to (*adaequatus*) God/Nature in the sense that humans recognize that they are free parts of a determined whole. In partial contrast to Nietzsche, then, Spinoza is presented here as advocating a developmental climb from passivity to activity, from passions to actions.

Even passivity, though, can be seen to be a kind of activity, however diminished. Nothing is completely still in Spinoza's universe of movement and interaction. So the developmental climb can perhaps more accurately be described as a step from essentially lesser powers of acting to greater powers of acting. This expansion of power will be intellectual as well as practical (for Spinoza mind and body are not different genres), and it will always involve counteractions and reactions. At the risk of anachronism, one might observe that there is nevertheless something at work here reminiscent of Hegel's master-slave dynamic in the sense that one mode's expansion (or as we will see below, "joy") may involve another mode's diminishment ("sadness"). Yet the model is not consciousness, as it had been for Hegel, but corporeality. The body becomes a model and privileged vehicle for

Deleuze's Spinoza, upsetting the traditional philosophical priority of consciousness to corporeality and introducing the force of unconscious thought.[21]

As mentioned, Deleuze was fond of quoting one particular line of Spinoza's: "We do not even know what a body is capable of."[22] This admission was a first step on the road to an ethics of joyful activity – an ethics at first glance Nietzschean but more profoundly Spinozist. The "ethical" question, says Deleuze, is: How can finite modes move from passions to actions, from being affected to affecting? In other words: "How can we come to experience a maximum of joyful passions?"[23] The phrasing is significant because it subtly introduces Deleuze's distinctive spin on Spinoza, who, through selection, interpretation, and emphasis, is pushed away from a more prosaic rendering. Certainly, Spinoza advocated joyful passions over sad passions, but he did so in the context of a climb from passion to reason and intellect, a climb culminating in the coincidence or adequation of the human and divine/natural and of freedom and necessity – a state he calls "beatitude." Deleuze will advocate no such culminating totalization, just touching ever so lightly on the theme of beatitude at the end of *Expressionism in Philosophy: Spinoza*. His creative appropriation stems from his emphasis on embodiedness at the partial expense of intellection, even if Spinozism is indeed a materialism and if from another angle we can understand Deleuze's philosophical vocation, including *Anti-Oedipus* and later works, as forms of ideational practice. In any case, his version of Spinoza's ethical question – How can we experience a maximum of joyful passions? – follows a clear demarcation between "sadness" and "joy." On one hand, passivity, privation, limitation, suffering, ill-health, and sadness – these are all ethically "bad." On the other hand, activity, plenitude, health, and joy – these are all ethically "good." As we see below, the assertion that active "joy" is better than passive "sadness" relies on a quasi-naturalism and a functionalism that have as their ultimate criterion the *ethos* of life itself.

To grasp the ethics of joyful passions invites a detour into the naturalism of Spinoza. Against Descartes and with Leibniz, Spinoza postulated an enlivened nature, says Deleuze, with a dynamic "capacity to be affected." All parts, modes, and bodies – the terms are at some point equivalent – possess this capacity, otherwise known as a body's "essence," "power of action," or "degree of power." We will use the word "capacity" to stand in for its virtual synonyms. A body's capacity to be affected is constant; even if sometimes frustrated and curtailed and other times more fully realized, a body always has some capacity to act. Thus from the "physical" point of view, bodies are always already perfect: each body in nature is essentially "active." However, from the "ethical" perspective, capacity is not always realized. A body's capacity unfortunately experiences limits, and it is from this understanding of limitation and *potentia* that one arrives at the determination that activity is ethically preferable to passivity. Again, this qualitative distinction – better/worse – is rooted in a quantitative distinction of less/more. Spinoza uses the term *conatus* to describe how every part of nature seeks to preserve itself, endure, and augment its capacity. *Conatus* more generally means an endeavour or striving as well as an impulse or force stimulating human effort – the "affirmation" of our capacity. According to Deleuze, *conatus* represents "the effort to maintain the body's ability to be affected in a great number of ways." The fewer the ways, the more capacity is limited; the greater the ways, the more capacity actualizes itself. Now, when *conatus* is "determined by an affection or feeling," even passively (suffering, imagining), it is called "desire." In other words, *conatus* is the constantly idling tendency to exist and expand; desire is the name given to *conatus* when it engages or is engaged by something. Often our desires remain on the level of (passively experienced) passions, which is why they tend to cause us so much distress. The ethical question is: How can our capacity, essence, power of acting be augmented and amplified; how can we cease to be affected by external causes that make us suffer; how can our desires express us; and how can we express the maximum of joyful desire?[24]

Spinoza's nature is a nature of "absolutely immanent pure causality" where everything is "natural" and tends toward expression or "explication." Here, Deleuze emphasizes the Spinozist view that God/Nature "emanates" or unfolds in the various modes that comprise and express it. From the aforementioned "physical" point of view of the whole, inasmuch as any one body expresses capacity, it is like all other bodies. On the level of totality, bodies are related in an economic, balanced "conformity" and equilibrium.[25] Now, from the outside, this totality may seem orderly and synthetic. Unfortunately, unlike Hegel, Spinoza provided no "owl of Minerva," or outside vantage point from which one could view parts in their synthetic unity. This is why there is no such thing as "morality" for Spinoza, only "ethics." We ourselves are fully within immanent nature where all sorts of infinitely variable and impermanent relations are established among parts. Deleuze calls these impermanent relations "encounters." Encounters modify our capacity, either increasing or decreasing it. Ethically speaking, there are "good" (better) and "bad" (worse) encounters. Those that "agree" with my body and lead it to experience "a kind of joy that increases my power of acting" are good. Other encounters that "disagree" with or can "destroy" my body are bad. A relation that is harmful to my body brings about "sadness" and a resulting diminishment of my capacity. Spinoza himself uses the example of "poison" to demonstrate this point. Poison invites sadness because it destroys positive relations in the body. Eating poison brings no joy.[26] This amoralistic stance, in which distinctions of good and bad turn on particular relations and encounters, and in which qualitative distinctions turn on quantitative ones, amounts, says Deleuze, to "an ethical vision of the world." Eliminating a totalized morality means shifting normative assessment to the level of encounters and upsetting moral traditions that rely on vertical hierarchies. The question "What can a body do?" turns out to be a "war cry" against transcendent or transcendental morality.[27]

There is a clearly articulated politics in this "embodied" kineticism that Deleuze compares to Thomas Hobbes's "natural right," and that expresses the notion that "*a body goes as far as it can, in passion as in action.*" Against the tradition of natural law, Hobbes and Spinoza agree on emphasizing "initial desire" over "final perfection," the non-self-evidentiary quality of reason (it emerges instead over time), the primacy of power and right over duty, and the priority of each individual to judge "what is necessary for his or her preservation." The Hobbesian contract emerges neither from compulsion nor from abstract rational choice, but rather from "fear of greater evil or hope for a greater good." Because humans seeks what is useful, what will bring joy and augment their power of acting, they join in association with others. Returning to Spinoza, Deleuze notes that ethical difference "does not relate to *conatus*" – to the natural inclination to endure and survive – since all persons attempt to preserve themselves. Rather, it "*relates to the kind of affections that determine our conatus*," that is, our desire. To be "free, strong, and reasonable" brings greater power of acting than being a "slave and weak man." Those who are strong and free have "joyful passions"; those who are slaves and weak have "sad passions." The slave is more cut off from his or her power of acting than is the free person. Slaves ought to be free, in other words, so that they can experience the joy of a realized and increased capacity, essence, or power.[28]

It is important to emphasize the fact that the difference between the free person and the slave is ultimately a difference of degree, not of kind. A healthy body differs in degree, not in kind from a sick one. There is a sequence and development that leads from passively received "chance encounters" that come to us from the outside to "good encounters" that we actively engage, moving us from the "inadequate" to the "adequate." As we get further away from "chance encounters" and seek out "good encounters," we experience greater joy and thus actualize our potential for active feelings and adequate ideas. From a position of childlike passivity, a condition characterized by suffering imposed by outside forces, we develop an increasing power of action by cultivating *that which brings joy.* Follow your bliss, in so many words. Deleuze seems faithful to Spinoza when he writes: "Joys that are active are born of reason." Yet the invocation of reason – reflection that leads to "adequation," when finite modes recognize and affirm themselves as part of God/Nature – leads to the recognition that something is missing here. Spinoza's account culminates in a religious experience of "beatitude" and in the political project of founding a regime that will facilitate the cultivation of "good" encounters. In *Expressionism in Philosophy: Spinoza* and later works, however, Deleuze spent little time considering either beatitude or political Spinozism.[29]

To sum up: joy is good because it is active; sadness is bad because it reflects (and adds to) the limitation of our power of acting. The active is good – and this is the essential point – because it expresses nature; it is the *nature* of nature. Joy is to the practical sphere "what affirmation is to the speculative." Spinoza's ethics, says Deleuze, amounts to a "war cry" against all that stands in the way of increasing our power of acting. We must move from states of passive and passion-filled suffering to active and rational joy.[30] The cultivation of joyful passions leads to greater power of acting, and with each expansion of our expressive capacity, we move toward a greater perception of and participation in that universality of which we are a part.

Deleuze's book on Spinoza was a crucial but by no means exclusive part of his developing thought around 1968. In some respects, it marked his last major work in a series within the genre of the history of philosophy (until a 1988 work on Leibniz), appearing almost side by side with his first two major ventures of original theory: *Difference and Repetition* and *The Logic of Sense.* We cannot pause here to read those works as closely as we have examined part of *Expressionism in Philosophy: Spinoza*, although doing so would add other elements to the picture. *The Logic of Sense* in particular reveals themes that would appear in *Anti-Oedipus*; for instance, "surface," the distinction among connective, conjunctive, and disjunctive syntheses, and the figure of the machine.[31] The only part of that book published earlier, which is some measure of an author's priorities, was a discussion on schizophrenia, Lewis Carroll, and Antonin Artaud that appeared in the August–September 1968 edition of *Critique.*[32] Furthermore, Deleuze's treatment in *The Logic of Sense* of an "ethics of Effects" and of the "event" indebted to the Stoic directive "to affirm destiny and deny necessity," also bears on my observation that he had articulated theoretically coherent ethical positions prior to *Anti-Oedipus*.[33]

Rather than pursue these promising suggestions, we now take a more critical look at the Spinozism described above. My pupose is not to propose a corrective or alternative position. Nevertheless, from the point of view of the historical field, and particularly as it concerns the story of the ethical turn, Deleuze's Spinozist ethics itself was not unambiguous or untroubled. Ethically coherent, yes; without problems, no. In fact, there are already several problems here that would be exacerbated in *Anti-Oedipus*. While, like Guattari, Deleuze also changed emphasis between the late 1960s and early 1970s, and while we can consider a parallel devolution from Spinoza to the anti-Oedipal, at the same time, his Spinozism already contained elements that would add to the vexed ethicality of *Anti-Oedipus*. In other words, Deleuze's Spinozist ethics was a tributary source for that book and already expressed the complex elements – problematic or innovative, according to one's point of view – that would contribute both indirectly and directly to the ethical turn. The potentially problematic elements at hand could be described in two overlapping ways: immanent vitalism and ethology.

To begin with, immanent criteria seem to end up referring only to themselves. Deleuze's Spinoza risks being tautological: movement is good *because* movement is good. Daniel Smith has argued that Deleuze's Spinozist ethics substitutes a "system of affects" relying on purely immanent criteria for a "system of judgment" that must appeal to transcendent or transcendental criteria.[34] It is curious, though, that Smith thinks Deleuze believed himself to have fulfilled rather than rejected Kantian ethics. The latter, one might recall, revolves around the categorical imperative, which links freedom to a law-like duty to treat other people as ends in themselves. While there is certainly a vague parallel between the concordance of freedom and necessity in both the Spinozist and Kantian systems, Spinoza's thought itself seems less to provide an amplified version of Kant than to offer the ammunition for a very powerful critique of an ethics of duty and law. We are indeed far from the Kantian model here; there was never much joyful passion in Kant's Mudville.

A short step from this problem of immanent self-referentiality is a second set of difficulties. Within this immanent system of affects, one might ask, is all action good simply because it is action? Is life good simply because it is alive? Does the distinction between active joy and passive suffering become one of more and less, *strength* and *weakness*? Perhaps between those "beasts of prey" and "little lambs" that Nietzsche famously presented in the *Genealogy of Morals*? This was not Spinoza's position at all. Although he himself said that every action involves a reaction, and while one might take this to mean that every joy results in a commensurate sadness, he also believed that interactions added up to an orderly totality, every interaction contributing to equilibrium. Yet after Nietzsche, it is more difficult to maintain Spinoza's theodicy in which, as with Hegel, the tragedy of the part is justified by the comedy of the whole. Like Nietzsche, Deleuze reached in another direction than a balanced and integrated whole to describe the *raison d'être* and ground for corporeal interaction. This other direction was vitalism.

As Deleuze said in a 1988 interview: "Everything I've written is vitalistic, at least I hope it is."[35] Vitalism is the doctrine that life is driven by a vital principle or force that is not explainable by scientific analysis alone. Nietzsche's doctrine of the will to power and Bergson's *élan vital* are both examples of vitalist formulations. Not surprisingly perhaps, vitalism in Deleuze's hands lends itself to no such tidy definition. In 1990 he wrote: "What is essential for me [is] this 'vitalism' or a conception of life as a *non-organic power.*"[36] But what is non-organic life? It is true that in some sense vitalism has typically dispensed with an organicism to the extent that life cannot be summed up by the biological, chemical, and physical. The crux of the matter, though, concerns the extent to which Deleuze's vitalism can be seen to be organic, non-organic, or somewhere in-between. Certainly the evocation of "machines" in *Anti-Oedipus* suggests a non-organic description of life, and Deleuze and Guattari spent considerable time after their book was published claiming, for instance, that "the desiring machine is a non-organic system of the body."[37] Clearly "desiring machines" are intended to be something besides a mere organic-mechanistic hybrid. Taking them seriously on this point would lead us to a discussion of cybernetics and cyborgs, which I will not presently entertain. Generally speaking, however, it does not seem that Deleuze completely extricates himself from the traditionally organicist dimensions of vitalism: singular things that are alive, want to survive, and extend their force. The reason for this conclusion is that, for Deleuze, *life* and not the *good life* is the evaluative criterion of reference.

Now it is true that Spinoza is also a vitalist – God/Nature is expressed through the embodied modes it emanates; ethics concerns the joyful augmentation of capacity, essence, and power. Still, Deleuze reads him through a Nietzschean and Bergsonian prism.[38] As already suggested, Spinoza had sought the convergence of desire and reflection in "understanding" or "beatitude." Misrahi, for example, in stressing the recognition of the part's place in the whole, paid greater attention to the *telos* at work in Spinozist metaphysics than had Deleuze. In contrast, Deleuze had underscored the *route* disassociated from ends, and seems to have creatively misread

Spinoza on this point. The problem of immanent vitalism is that one simply knocks to another level the evaluative criteria by which discriminations are made. Changing the *name* of evaluative criteria does not necessarily change the *constitutive and formal fact* that evaluation is taking place. In this case the evaluative criterion becomes, rather than law, duty, or other recognizable standards, life in search of its extension. In *Anti-Oedipus*, immanent and transcendental criteria were worked out in slightly different ways, but one can sense the Deleuzian vitalist contribution to that project. The "logic of expression," says Pierre Macherey, is "not simply a way of analyzing or thinking about life, but as 'expressing' the logic of life itself produces an ethics, in the strict sense of a way of living, a true *ethos*."[39]

This term leads us to another engaging interpretive branch that has implications for our larger explanation of the ethical turn. In 1978 Deleuze explained "ethology" as the attempt to:

> define bodies, animals, or humans by the affects they are capable of ... The approach is no less valid for us, for human beings, than for animals, because no one knows ahead of time the affects one is capable of; it is a long affair of experimentation, requiring a lasting prudence, a Spinozist wisdom that implies the construction of a plane of immanence or consistency ... Ethology is first of all the study of the relations of speed and slowness, of the capacities for affecting and being affected that characterize each thing.[40]

Deleuze was writing in the midst of an international revival of the nineteenth-century pseudo-science of ethology. Recall that John Stuart Mill had discussed "ethology" as a science of "character" in his massive *System of Logic* (1843). In the 1970s, when joined with ecological concerns and when avoiding sociobiological consequences, ethology seems to have been one of the sources for the emergence of bio-ethics in the 1980s. But one should also bear in mind that Konrad Lorenz, for example, chiefly remembered for his examination of animals' inevitable aggression, also appealed to ethology.[41]

For Deleuze, the ethological seems to refer to the ethos of interactive corporeality, the zone of physical encounters among bodies, and what he elsewhere calls the "event." Commenting on this life-ethos, François Zourabichvili writes:

> Deleuzian ethics may be summed up by the following formula: be like everyone else, on condition of being able to *take one's strolls*; or, following Kafka's expression, of "having nothing to do but take one's walks" ... The forces of the *encounter*, as

Deleuze likes to say, come unexpectedly upon us: no-one is ready for an encounter, which necessarily contains its share of violence ("too much for me") as a concomitant of the relation of forces. To take a stroll is to "extend one singularity right into the neighborhood of another," to extend every percept into another percept, following inevitably hazardous external connections or relations, and in this way, to compose the richest possible artistic disjunctive synthesis. Or grasp the *event* in things and in what happens.[42]

Paul Patton comments in a similar vein that Deleuze's "ethics of the event" concerns "our stance towards the events which befall us."[43] On the one hand, events and encounters happen to us, come to us from the outside. On the other hand, one can maintain a certain attitude or bearing in relation to them. To *take one's strolls* means to engage with events and encounters (the outcomes of which can never be known ahead of time) in a manner that is active and makes them one's own. The question is: Shall I affirm this event or encounter and make it my own? To put it in a Nietzschean tone, which is undoubtedly present in this line of thinking, shall I say Yes? Shall I love my fate (*amor fati*)? Shall I pursue joyful encounters that augment my capacity, essence, or power? "The sage waits for the event," Deleuze writes in *The Logic of Sense*, "but, at the same time, the sage also *wills the embodiment* and the actualization of the sure incorporeal event in a state of affairs and in his or her own body and flesh."[44] Some commentators like Constantin Boundas have cautioned against taking too seriously the "quietisic overtones" of the ethics of the encounter and event. In other words, the implication is that one simply affirms whatever happens, a form of fatalism – perhaps the flipside of the love of fate – that potentially raises as many problems as it claims to solve, since such activity is from one point of view quite passive. For Boundas, though, the ethics of the event is not "an ethics of the accident" – that is, of the circumstantial, arbitrary, and capricious – but rather the search for the "eternal truth of events."[45] Deleuze, after all, was a philosopher.

It is likely cultivation and engagement through the affirmation of encounters and events that Zourabichvili, for example, has in mind when he describes Deleuzean ethics in the context of a life-ethos as "the exploration of ways of living, or even of the *Character*." And yet in the same discussion he characterizes that ethics as a matter of "health."[46] We now come to a genuinely problematic aspect in an ethics that depends on vitalism and ethology. The idea of an ethics of "health" does not exactly have a trouble-free history. Beyond the social norms that qualify and frame any understanding of health, one might more specifically consider Lorenz's aforementioned ethology in which aggression invariably figured; or more dramatically, the way vitalism intersected with fascism's celebration of virile, active bodies and denigration of their opposites.[47] We touch here a debate whose scope and stakes far exceed the limited case of Deleuze's Spinoza, a debate epitomized by the dramatic if ultimately vulgar question: What is the nature of the relation between Nietzscheanism and Nazism? The immediate reply to this suggestion is obviously that fascism was in fact a machinery of death that defined, subjugated, and obliterated life.

This indeed was one of *Anti-Oedipus*'s arguments: that fascism amounted to a molar channelling, reduction, and damming up of desiring machines. Paradoxically, the authors also intimated that fascism also stemmed from the sudden on-rush and venting of hemmed-in, canalized desire. In the next chapter I assess the relationship of fascism to schizophrenia as well as Foucault's suggestion that the anti-Oedipal embodied an ethical stance. What becomes immediately clear is that one of *Anti-Oedipus*'s ambiguities, already present in Deleuze's earlier thought, relates to the uses made of a certain vitalism and ethology to garnish leftist arguments against "fascism" without squarely confronting fascism's own vitalistic currents. Why are strength, virility, and even domination not the result and excrescence of life's extension of its own capacities, essence, and power? There is also joyful expression in sadism. And yet, at the same time, is not the problem with slavery the fact that the slave experiences the sad passions of diminished joyful capacity, essence, and power?

Many of Deleuze's later interpreters and defenders have tried to explain that the kind of criticisms I have just advanced misconstrue his larger oeuvre and aims. Such problematizations are generally perceived, if not as spurious, then as misrecognizing the overall design of his fecund thought. Some readers have found ethics "ready to wear" in Deleuze. Philip Goodchild, for example, examines his admittedly under-reported ethics as a matter of "the unconscious determinants of thought and action" prevailing in an immanent ethos shared by subjects who in turn affect it. He finds in Deleuzean ethics the agreeable elements of "generosity," "faith," and "courtesy." Paul Patton sees in the overall Deleuzo-Guattarian project a fulfillment of the Spinozist ethical program of conceptualizing "an ontology which is at the same time an evaluative typology of modes of existence."[48] Of course, Deleuze's thought continued to develop beyond the limited phase (circa 1968–73) under discussion here. Later writings, alone and with Guattari, clarified some questions, deepened some analyses, and moved on to other topics and away from some of *Anti-Oedipus*'s rhetoric, caught as that book was in its expression of post-1968 radicalism. The point here, in contrast to the many systematic accounts of his thought, is to see Deleuze in a specific moment, between *Expressionism in Philosophy: Spinoza* and *Anti-Oedipus*. There may or may not be structural ambiguities to Deleuze's thought overall, but it does seem that in the years around 1968 one could identify a number of uncertainties in the effort, to put it succinctly, to derive an ethics from an ethos. Those difficulties bore a relation to difficulties endemic to the historical terrain. They interest us here insofar as they, too, contributed to the ethical turn (of which, we might observe, later readings like Goodchild's and Patton's are themselves obliquely symptomatic).

At no point during these years did the theme of ethics predominate in Deleuze's work, although prior to the publication of *Anti-Oedipus* his thought did show some degree of ethical elaboration. In his 1968 book on Spinoza, Deleuze had worked through the different modalities of the logic of expression, especially as it pertained to the desiring parts of Nature/God. We find there the model of a finite body, unable to know or grasp the totality of which it is part, affirming encounters and willing events as they come to pass. Affirmation is joyful because it is active, and it is active because it expresses nature. And, as said above, the cultivation of joyful passions leads to greater power of acting. Deleuze's Spinozist ethics turns on this constellation of nature, action, affirmation, joy, capacity, essence, and power.

We have also seen how a number of complications arise from this immanentist vitalism and ethology, complications that are of more than theoretical interest. They are of historical value and can be set into relief if, in conclusion, we return to Misrahi's intimation that Spinoza's thought resonated with the post-1968 student milieu. In many ways, Spinozism fits with the May 1968 *event*: its activism, circulation of desires, expressiveness, and joyful encounters. Bearing in mind the dangers of reductionism, Spinoza does seem to be an emblematic and representative thinker. The spirit of 1968, continuing to reverberate during the early 1970s, indeed embodied an antinomian ethos that was hostile to laws and limits. Deleuze's exemplary thought can be understood as a symptom of and also a contribution to that cultural mood. Spinoza and *Anti-Oedipus* constitute the high-water mark of the principle that it is forbidden to forbid and of an ethos that was wary of limits of any kind. To be sure, from 1972 forward, Deleuze took Spinozist encounters in surprising directions; *Anti-Oedipus* undoubtedly made many integral components of the Spinozist system unrecognizable. For Deleuze's thinking after 1968 also involved the pursuit of other themes – such as schizophrenia and madness – in which he had displayed an interest preceding his rendezvous with Guattari.

13

Schizophrenia and Fascism

We saw at the beginning of this section that Deleuze and Guattari had their first joyful "encounter" in 1969. Both had been surprised and delighted by the events of May 1968. Deleuze, like Foucault, seems to have been jolted out of a rather bookish existence and drawn, if tentatively, toward the pragmatics of militancy. For his part, Guattari, having broken with the Opposition gauche in 1967 (and the Société de psychothérapie institutionnelle having folded in 1968), was likely looking for a change. The meeting with Deleuze fit a "transversal" pattern of ruptures with existing "ambiences" and engagements with new ones. Curiously, Guattari embarked on this great anti-psychoanalytic adventure at the same moment – 1969 – that he joined the Ecole freudienne de Paris, becoming, after seven years of analysis with Lacan, a practising analyst.[1] Perhaps due to a combination of age, prior experience, and disposition, both found that they shared suspicions about the form that post-1968 militancy seemed to be taking. Behind *Anti-Oedipus*'s critique of psychoanalysis, increasingly popular for some leftist activists, were two larger and related phenomena: the mirroring by far-left organizations of the very hierarchies, discriminations, and repressions they challenged; and the mainstreaming of revolutionary passions by "recuperation" and reformism. Deleuze and Guattari wrote as a direct response to this situation.[2]

According to Arlette Donati – who, as I noted above, recalled Deleuze having said that Guattari was the "diamond" and that he was the "gem cutter" – Guattari had first envisioned signing Deleuze onto a CERFI project.[3] Deleuze, however, would have nothing of it and asked Donati to intervene with Guattari, encourage him to engage in a two-person project, and leave CERFI out of it. Guattari perhaps did not know at first what Deleuze wanted, but he was apparently slightly intimidated by the philosopher's intellect and reputation, even though, as Deleuze later noted, at that time Guattari had gone further than he in considering the unconscious as a machine.[4] The artist Gérard Fromanger, with whom Deleuze published a collaborative book, characterized conversations with him as "sessions" [*séances*] that went on for hours, process-oriented exchanges best described as an "opening."[5] He compared the experience to receiving the surprise gift of "a fruit basket or box of chocolates." Their sessions would often begin with Deleuze asking a simple question like "Why did you paint red over there?" and then one of them would talk extempore at length. Deleuze would take notes. Fromanger, incidentally, described these open-ended sessions as "an ethics of life in general." One can surmise that Deleuze and Guattari employed a similar method.

There were family resemblances between Deleuze and Guattari's earlier trajectories as well as important differences. The pair were like a rock and a flint creating sparks. The *transversal* and the *ethological*, to use their respective terminologies, interpenetrated and merged into the eccentric language of *Anti-Oedipus*. Theirs was a theory of immanent intensities seeking to break out of and break down rigid limitations, allowing desiring machines to machinate. The events of 1968 had generally amplified popular and theoretical appeals to the so-called philosophy of desire, but its component elements had preceded and anticipated the events themselves. The role of desire as a common denominator in Deleuze and Guattari's individual "lines of flight" (originally the latter's phrase) prior to their own Spinozist encounter was one example of a more extensive sensibility. Guattari's understanding of desire had developed in the context of institutional pragmatics, structures, and limits; notwithstanding his devolution, already underway by the late 1960s, it bore traces of his prior psychoanalytic and tactile experience. Deleuze, for his part, had most recently grappled with desire as one corner of an intricate philosophical tapestry, triangulating the vitalism of Spinoza, Bergson, and Nietzsche and venturing into literary-aesthetic expressions of schizophrenia.

Each brought key differences to the dialogue, differences that were borrowed and traded, and that were grounded in their earlier distinctive experiences. Deleuze superimposed Guattari's "machine" figure over his own affirmative vitalism; Guattari linked Deleuze's "encounter" and "event" with his own La Bordean/militant "collective enunciation of the masses" and "transversality." Again, however, the point is not to identify and track down what each brought to their non-synthetic mixture. "Synthesis is a big word!" Guattari commented in early 1973, abjuring the verdict that *Anti-Oedipus* was an additive sum of two parts.[6] And Deleuze later explained that the evident "hostility toward the book" was possibly due to the fact that it was co-authored; readers "try to disentangle inseparable elements and identify who did what. But since each of us, like everyone, is already various people, it gets rather crowded."[7]

In such post-publication comments, one could nevertheless sense persistent differences. Deleuze tended toward the theoretical, while Guattari more often pursued the concretely social (schools, factories, and neighbourhoods) and stressed the political and militant consequences of their theory. Deleuze seemed more interested in distinguishing their project from the work of psychoanalysis – Guattari once remarked that Deleuze "was wary of Lacan as if he were a plague" – while Guattari was willing for a time to use psychoanalytic language if only to disagree with his interlocutors over its meaning.[8] This dissimilarity was evident, again, in their descriptions of desire. In 1972–73, they often attempted to clarify and defend what they had meant or not meant by the term. Deleuze consistently maintained that desire had to be distinguished from "interest" or Freudian cathexis since it did not "depend on a lack" or "refer to any law." Guattari was at first less inclined to define their understanding of desire in opposition to psychoanalysis, cautioning in April 1972, for instance, that he and Deleuze were "certainly not going to recommend that desire be taken seriously. It is rather urgent to undermine the spirit of seriousness." Only in May 1973 did he for the first time make the strong and revisionist claim that his notion of desire was neither "borrowed from orthodox psychoanalysis or Lacanian theory" nor "intrinsically linked to individuation of the libido."[9] It was thus in clarifying what they had meant, since many people seemed unsure, that Deleuze and Guattari ended up solidifying, if not hardening, a number of points. Nowhere was this more true than in their post-publication comments on schizophrenia and fascism, comments that will return us – at last – to Foucault's claim of *Anti-Oedipus* as a work of ethics.

Deleuze and Guattari insisted that schizophrenia was not just a word. They were wise to do so. For if the term was merely a figure of speech, a metaphor, or an incantation, then *Anti-Oedipus*'s "materialist psychiatry" could, reasonably it seems, be criticized as idealist or imaginary. However, at the same time, confusion about the book grew as the pair tirelessly insisted in 1972–73 that they were not talking about hospitalized schizophrenics either. They were not, that is, except on the occasions when "real" schizophrenics were evoked as exemplars of revolutionary schizoanalysis. In other words, though they tried whenever they could to separate "schizophrenization as a process" from the "clinical entity" of schizophrenia, the latter seemed to keep sneaking back in.[10] A tension between word and object, between the linguistic and tactile was palpable. The questions thus arose: What did Deleuze and Guattari mean by schizophrenia? If schizophrenia was *not* a metaphor, what of the bodies of hospitalized schizophrenics? This was the inferred anti-psychiatric implication of their liberation of desire that troubled practising psychiatrists, psychoanalysts, and others. The authors may not have meant to hand the keys of the asylum over to its residents, but such a gesture was not incompatible with their positions in the early 1970s. Their ambiguity on this point therefore accounted for some of *Anti-Oedipus*'s abstruseness, its assimilation to the anti-psychiatry movement, and also for its troubled or vexed ethicality. While it is immediately important not to fetishize the "clinical body" of medicalized schizophrenics as some sort of stopgap or substratum pre-emptively derailing the anti-Oedipal project, on this issue the book and the authors' post-publication comments were – appropriately? – confused, fragmented, and somewhat incoherent. Was their confusion and fragmentation a clever performance of schizoanalytic flight? How far and how seriously ought one to take incoherence, especially as a ground for critical thought? Where was ethics?

For the sake of clarity, we might once more cast a glance back on earlier years. Deleuze's approach to schizophrenia and madness during the 1960s was based significantly in literature. In other words, his interest in schizophrenia as a mode of being and expression was intimately bound to language and aesthetic gesture. Now, literature obviously bears a special relationship to subjectivity and experience, and literary representations of mental anguish certainly have a long and notable history. Furthermore and specifically, modernist writing's non-conventional linguistic experimentalism throughout the twentieth century was part of more widespread interest in the "language problem." The well-known "linguistic turn" of the last century, of which French theory was a notable and infamous chapter, focused on the non-communicative opacity of language. Rather than being seen simply as a transparent medium or tool enabling human interaction, language in many corners has been recognized as a complication and a stumbling block. Not surprisingly, madness, and schizophrenia in particular, frequently emerged as paradigmatic cases of linguistic breakdown and fragmentation. For his part, Deleuze turned to figures like Antonin Artaud, Lewis Carroll, D.H. Lawrence, Marcel Proust, Leopold von Sacher-Masoch, Michel Tournier, and Louis Wolfson to facilitate his philosophical explorations of meaning, non-sense, expression, and eventfulness, explorations of a piece with his immanentist vitalism and ethology. As mentioned in the previous chapter, for example, Deleuze's extended discussion of schizophrenia in *The Logic of Sense* was centred around Artaud, Carroll, and Wolfson, and, excluding the appendices, was the only part of the book to have earlier appeared as a separate essay. In his comparison of Carroll's "surface" and Artaud's "depth," he suggested that "nothing is more fragile than a surface" and that for the schizophrenic "*there is not, there is no longer, any surface.*"[11]

The comment raises some interesting issues for the "folds" (to use a later Deleuzean term) of Deleuze and Guattari's joint thinking, since from *Anti-Oedipus* to *A Thousand Plateaus* (1980) to their last collaboration, *What Is Philosophy?* (1991), the field of immanence they championed was often presented as a surface crisscrossed by transversal movements of desiring-machines and what they later called "assemblages."[12] On some occasions they seemed to suggest that a surface was the ultimate ground for molar and molecular operations. Thus, they never allowed much room in their thinking for the "depths" of despair or other subjective experiences of mental anguish whose representation required the "spaces" of explanation, interpretation, unveiling, and disclosure. The literary-aesthetic appeal of schizophrenia, though, was that it expressed dismemberment and disassociation – core elements in theoretical antinomianism. Specifically, in his contributions to *Anti-Oedipus* and in post-publication emphases, Deleuze's philosophical reflections on vital expressionism and on the joy of affirmative desire converged with the figure of the "mad" artist. Schizophrenics were law breakers who defied reality, who engaged with the world on their terms rather than adapting to external limitation, and who were model revolutionaries – in other words, schizotypes.

When Deleuze commented after the book's publication that his favourite line in *Anti-Oedipus* had been, "No, we've never seen a schizophrenic," he could not have been speaking for Guattari.[13] It is true that in 1966 Guattari had expressed his admiration for the work of "Alfred Jarry, Franz Kafka, James Joyce, Samuel Beckett, Maurice Blanchot, and Antonin Artaud," but for him the literary coexisted with a prior and parallel accumulation of tactile experience.[14] Still, unlike Deleuze, he could say, "I'd always liked schizophrenics, been drawn to them. You have to live with them to understand this. Schizophrenics do at least, unlike neurotics, have real problems ... My first work as a psychotherapist was with a schizophrenic, using a tape recorder."[15] In the 1980s he recalled: "Before meeting Jean Oury, I believed that madness formed a map to the other side of the world: strange, unsettling, and fascinating. In the style of communitarian life that was found at La Borde during those years [the mid-1950s], I saw the patients in an entirely different light: familiar, friendly, human, ready to participate in the collective life on all possible occasions."[16] Only a befuddled literary scholar could confuse the difference between reading Artaud and having a cup of coffee with him.

It was Guattari's prior non-literary experience with "real live" schizophrenics, not to mention his training as an analyst, that made his contributions to anti-Oedipal schizo-analysis so visceral charged – and potentially problematic. Likewise, his earlier political activism provided an orientation that persisted for the rest of his life. Whereas he never abandoned political activism, he did reject the Lacanian paradigm and distance himself from institutional pragmatics. Guattari's theoretical writings during the 1970s thus conveyed a vigorous, embodied tone that complemented Deleuze's perhaps more rigorous but also more abstract thinking on corporeality. Guattari's notion of the transversal built on his own clinical, political, and biographical experiences, which found their way into *Anti-Oedipus*'s machinic operations. Was the movement from practice to theory intended to complete a circuit back into practice? There was understandable confusion on the part of some readers as to how the anti-Oedipal was supposed to be taken: as an analytics, an optics, a strategy, a tactic, or even, as Foucault would later opine, a way of life? Arno Münster, for instance, wondered if the authors were not calling "for an identification of the analyst, the patient, and the militant." Guattari's response, in which he tried to spell out the distinction between "process" and "clinical case," demonstrated the ambiguities of the enterprise:

> We don't say that revolutionaries ought to identify with free-wheeling madmen, but that they should model their action on the "schizo-process." The schizophrenic is a person who, for whatever reason, has been touched off by a desiring flow which threatens the social order. There's an immediate intervention to ward off such a menace ... The work of the analyst, the revolutionary, and the artist meet to the extent that they must constantly tear down the systems which reify desire, which submit the subject to the familial and social hierarchy.[17]

The schizophrenic him or herself was a threat to the social order, as evidenced by the pathologization and medicalization to which the patient was subjected. Furthermore, the schizophrenic exemplified the schizo-process. Anti-familialism and anti-psychiatry intersected antinomian revolution in the ambition for us to schizophrenize ourselves, without, however, going insane.

The distinction between a schizo-process and a "locked-up schizophrenic" might have been passable were it not for the fact that schizophrenics were regarded as model cases of desire's connections and disjunctions, flows and cuts. In one interview Guattari commented: "We chose as our reference a state of desire at its most critical and acute: the desire of the schizophrenic. And the schizophrenic who is able to produce something, beyond or beneath the schizophrenic who has been locked up, beaten down with drugs and social repression. In our opinion, some schizophrenics directly express a free deciphering of desire." Deleuze foregrounded the Spinozist dimensions of the valorized schizophrenic sublime. From the molecular perspective, he said, desiring machines were a "general and productive schizophrenia, finally become happy. For, one must say of the desiring machine what [Jean] Tanguely says, '*a truly joyous machine, by joyous I mean free.*'" Unhappy schizophrenia, so to speak, was blamed on the reification of desire. Putting schizophrenics in psychiatric institutions made them the opposite of joyous and free. As Guattari put it, "repressive systems of hospitalization" shut schizophrenics down, forcing them to disconnect from the "essence of their madness." "Battered down," repressed, and hospitalized schizophrenics infrequently achieved the "de-territorialization" proper to "schizzes," to put it in the idiom of *Anti-Oedipus*. In other words, schizophrenics were not permitted to be schizophrenic enough. By extension, we normalized, or Oedipalized, subjects in society at large, whose desires are also institutionalized in various ways, are similarly battered down.[18]

To be sure, the authors were cognizant of the fact that not all "real" schizophrenics were happy and joyous. They made allowances for the phenomenon of "autistic" schizophrenia. In the interview in which they did the most to explain what they thought schizophrenia to be, published in the fall 1972 issue of the Italian review *Tempi moderni*, Deleuze admitted the ambiguities and limits of the schizophrenic model: schizophrenia let loose intensities not without certain risks. Schizophrenia was "an involuntary and stupefying experience, something very, very acute ... with high levels of intensity."[19] The experience of intensity and the intensification of experience led to the "crossing [of] what biologists call a gradient, a threshold." The vitalist resonances of this view should be clear. Deleuze went on to raise the possibility that "experimental pharmaceutical treatments relating to schizophrenia – treatments that are so badly applied today – could be very productive" since they "put the problem in terms of a variation in the metabolism of intensity." Pill-popping may have seemed to hold more revolutionary potential in the 1970s than it does in retrospect, but the appeal to intensity led directly to one of Deleuze's clearest statements about aesthetic schizophrenia, in which he turned to R.D. Laing and especially to Karl Jaspers' 1922 study of schizophrenia and art.[20] Jaspers had defined the two core elements in madness as "breaking through" and "collapse." Deleuze lauded the former while granting that one could not entirely escape the "danger" and "risk" of the latter. The smashing of a "wall" and the opening of the doors of perception, to use Aldous Huxley's memorable phrase, led to an aestheticization of experience. Artaud was the heroic example of "the voice of the future," a point echoed by Guattari who called him "a 'seer' – let's use quotation marks." Yet breakthrough courted the possibility of a breakdown into the position of the "autistic schizophrenic," shut in, unable to communicate, given to fantasy, and immobilized. It thus seemed that schizoanalysis attempted to walk a line between confining institutionalization and paralytic phantasm, meanwhile availing itself of the schizophrenic body as an operational template.

Matters were complicated still further by the fact that schizophrenia was declared to express and symptomatize society and politics. In a qualification of his statement that his favourite line in *Anti-Oedipus* was "No, we've never seen a schizophrenic," Deleuze wrote: "We have never seen a schizophrenic delirium that is not first about race, racism, politics, that does not begin in all directions from history, that does not involve culture, that does not speak of continents, kingdoms, and so forth." That political register served as the Ariadne's thread by which the more general phenomenon of schizzes could be traced. As Institutional Psychotherapy had maintained earlier, psychiatry and psychoanalysis generally failed to appreciate the sociopolitical aspects of madness in general and schizophrenia in particular. Those aspects involved both experiential content ("continents, kingdoms, and so forth") and form – how the script of madness itself corresponded to social and political structures, which in the case of schizophrenia meant for Deleuze and Guattari the dispersions and flows of capitalism. They were concerned with what Fredric Jameson, indebted in part to our authors, later called the "political unconscious."

Anti-Oedipus's subtitle, *Capitalism and Schizophrenia,* suggested how schizophrenia was, in Guattari's words, "indissociable from the capitalist system" itself. They were "two poles" that shared the "common feature of non-sense"; they had both a "contingent relationship" ("modern society induces madness in human beings") and a stronger, analytic onc (capitalism could be diagnosed by "[bringing] into play the same concepts that one relies upon to interpret schizophrenia"). Furthermore, such a diagnosis meant that schizophrenia was related to revolution. If schizophrenia symptomatized capitalism, it was also, to paraphrase Nietzsche, a disease like pregnancy is a disease: schizophrenic desire could give birth to revolutionary desiring machines. The revolution would be desiring or it would not be. According to Guattari: "The capitalist economy functions through decoding and de-territorialization: it has its extreme illnesses, that is, its schizophrenics who come uncoded and become de-territorialized to the extreme, but also it has its extreme consequences, its revolutionaries."[21] In maintaining the link between capitalism and revolution, Deleuze and Guattari remained rather loyal to Marx, who had held the similar position that capitalism was the precondition for surpassing capitalism. *Anti-Oedipus* added the revolutionary potential of both desire and schizophrenia. The world was not merely deluded but mad, and not merely mad but in need of becoming madder still.

Ultimately, Deleuze and Guattari's view of schizophrenia was ambivalent, caught between the literary-aesthetic appeal of "schizzes" and the bodies of flesh-and-blood schizophrenics, between the denotational and the tactile, the model and the case. We will conclude our discussion of this ambiguity with two examples. In the *Tempi moderni* interview, Guattari said that schizophrenics had the ability to slip in and out of different "registers." While the case of the "autistic" schizophrenic shut in on him- or herself to some extent betrayed the template, that case was an "illusory image." Schizophrenics more generally displayed a fundamental disconnect and shifting among different "levels" of reality, and Guattari went on to conclude that "people who are operating on the level of social sciences or on the level of politics ought to 'make themselves schizophrenic,'" that is, break down boundaries among disciplines and cultivate the "schizophrenic's capacity to range across fields." It is fairly clear that Guattari had the interdisciplinary studies of CERFI in mind while on this occasion dismissing mental breakdown as fanciful.

The other example is the contrast of two statements by Deleuze, in which one sees the literary-aesthetic, mental illness, and the sociopolitical combined. "It would be irresponsible," he said in the interview just cited, "to ignore the danger of collapse in these processes. Even if the risk is perhaps worthwhile." Elsewhere, he declared: "As for being responsible or irresponsible, we don't recognize those notions, they're for policemen and courtroom psychiatrists."[22] Even in the homely normative language of responsibility, one ought to see here the problems in making schizophrenia an archetype of analysis and social praxis. If even psychiatrists and psychoanalysts considered that term and phenomenon ambiguous, making it into a standard for post-1968 revolutionary politics would almost necessarily lead to misunderstandings, uncertainties, and difficulties.

Anti-Oedipal schizophrenic-revolutionary "machines" targeted the sociopolitical forces that reified desire, including the "paranoid" formations of psychoanalysis, the family, and fascism. The assimilation of those three terms is obviously not above criticism, but the underlying connotation was a link between the collaborationist Vichy slogan of "Work, Family, and Fatherland" and the perceived and actually growing prevalence of psychoanalysis in post-1968 French intellectual circles. We saw in passing above in chapter 1 and Part I that the label "fascism" was bandied about during May 1968 and afterward both by advocates of revolt and by defenders of the status quo. The term lay close to the surface of French cultural memory a mere quarter of a century or so after the end of World War II and was used, for example, to describe both lawlessness and heavy-handed state action. Deleuze and Guattari's political pretensions came to the fore in their own contribution to this rhetorical inflation.

In truth, fascism had been a minor character in *Anti-Oedipus* – a consequence more than an object of analysis.[23] However, in post-publication comments the authors emphasized the split between "fascist paranoid" and "schizo-revolutionary" machines. Guattari as political militant was inclined to exaggerate: he and Deleuze were signalling the rise of what that called a "comprehensive fascism": "Like many others, we were worried about the future being readied for us, one that could make you miss the fascism of yore ... [Short of a revolution,] we can see nothing, no reason, to stop it spreading"; "a fascism that will make Hitler and Mussolini look like a joke." Such comments reveal a great deal about the heat of the moment and should not be dismissed either by critics who might only see in them proof of French theory's irrationalism and bombast or by defenders of Deleuze and Guattari who would rightly be embarrassed especially by the last line. The analysis of fascism as a sociopolitical type and form native to the modern world permitted its extension to times and places other than its Italian, German, and Spanish sites of origin. In other words, fascism was an interpretive grid borrowed from history in the same way that schizophrenia was an interpretive grid borrowed from psychiatry. The politics of *Anti-Oedipus* were plain: the book itself was a machine let loose to perform its revolutionary function in disrupting, uncoupling, and discharging molecular desire against the molar structures – the family, psychoanalysis, and above all fascism – that channelled and penned it in. In 1972–73, in this milieu, the antinomian ethos of 1968 continued to be framed by a revolution/reaction dynamic for which fascism was the code word.[24]

That Deleuze and Guattari emphasized the theme of fascism, especially after *Anti-Oedipus* was published, reveals not only the relevance of World

War II's persistent echoes but also the authors' perspective as members of a postwar cohort that had come of age before 1968. "We are part of a generation," said Guattari, "whose political consciousness was born in the enthusiasm and naïveté of the Liberation, with its conspiratorial mythology of fascism. And the questions left hanging by the other failed revolution that was May '68." They were struggling with two "large historical machinations": fascism and May 1968. Such a comparison might have seemed apt in the early 1970s, again, more or less in the heat of the moment, although in retrospect placing those historical events on a par with one another seems like an exaggeration. Yet, the authors were reflecting on types, forms, dynamics, and principles with consequences that were at once historical and contemporaneous. They saw their anti-Oedipal project as taking Wilhelm Reich's questions about the relationship between fascism and mass desire, shearing them of their Freudian-psychoanalytic limitations, translating them into new idioms, and applying them to the problem of relationships among desire, society, and history.

Recall that while on the whole criticizing him, Deleuze and Guattari had referred to Reich, as "the true founder of a materialist psychiatry." They were less generous about Herbert Marcuse. Characteristically, Deleuze noted that the psychoanalytic explanation of fascism was "ridiculous." Building on the suggestion that desires and interests were not synonymous, Guattari commented:

> Desire never stops shaping history, even in its worst periods. The German masses had come to desire Nazism. After Wilhelm Reich, one cannot avoid facing that truth. Under certain conditions, the desire of the masses can turn against their own interests. What are those conditions? That's the whole question ... If it is true that the social revolution is inseparable from a revolution of desire, then the question shifts: under what conditions will the revolutionary avant-garde be able to free itself from its unconscious complicity with repressive structures and elude power's manipulation of the masses' desire that makes them "fight for their servitude as though it were their salvation"?

We have already mentioned in chapter 9 how François Châtelet had in his *Le Monde* review of *Anti-Oedipus* highlighted the question of "voluntary servitude," originally posed forcefully by the sixteenth-century thinker Etienne de La Boétie. In some senses Reich had reformulated the question by updating it for a post-Freudian world. The critique of historical fascism also played a role in Deleuze and Guattari's attention to Kafka, who had analysed "the decaying bureaucracy of Austria-Hungary and the cultural turmoil out of which Nazi Eros [would] rise."[25]

But the ghosts of mid–twentieth-century European fascism were the object of anti-Oedipal critique insofar as they yielded lessons about ongoing and contemporaneous reifications of desire. Following the language of voluntary servitude, Deleuze noted in April 1973 that France was "rapidly approaching an era of half-voluntary and half-enforced secrecy." As we have already seen in his hyperbolic comment above, for Guattari fascism was a continuing lure and danger. In a May 1973 talk at the Milan meeting on "Psychoanalysis and Politics," entitled "Everybody Wants to be a Fascist," he discussed "the *genealogy* and the *permanence* of certain fascist machineries," concluding with the supposition that some form of "totalitarian machine" existed consistently across time, though it manifested or organized itself variously according to historical context. Fascism, like schizophrenia in a different way, was intended to be exemplary, especially in the way it demonstrated how some people desired "repression and death." The antinomian spirit of 1968 certainly defined itself as an anti-totalitarianism, either against Stalinist Communism, in the case of the Maoists and later the New Philosophers, or here with antifascism.

Claiming that "true history is the history of desire," Deleuze combined the themes of voluntary servitude and the role of desire in submission with the historical experience of fascism in ways that seemed, without mentioning Spinoza, to fit comfortably with his earlier diagnosis of "sad passions" in which desire "acts" to limit capacity rather than expand it.

> When people in a society desire repression, both for others *and for themselves*; when there are people who like to harass others, and who have the opportunity to do so, the "right" to do so, this exhibits the problem of a deep link between libidinal desire and the social field ... And don't forget fascism. It too "subsumes social desires," including the desires of repression and death. Hitler and the fascist machine gave people hard-ons.[26]

In the early 1970s, building on the possibilities of 1968, "molecular revolutions" were underway against the Oedipal, the familial, the psychoanalytic, and the fascist. As we see in the next section, these desiring revolutions explicitly included the women's and gay liberation movements.

We seem to have drifted from the theme of the ethical turn. Having briefly examined *Anti-Oedipus*'s arguments and taken a first glance at its reception, we then took a large detour by digging into its conceptual roots. We found that prior to their meeting both Guattari and Deleuze had formulated stances that were not ethically incoherent; the former in his experiences with the ethical pragmatics of Institutional Psychotherapy, and the latter in his Spinozist philosophical vitalism. In this chapter we have seen how, after the book's publication, the authors stressed the themes of schizophrenia and fascism as means of providing a "revolutionary" strategy for approaching the repressive social forms they had diagnosed. The hyperbole in some of this rhetoric is plain and might be excused for having reflected the heat of the far-left moment. Deleuze and Guattari were caught up in a climate in which inflated references to fascism were common and in which madness was one of many social forms undergoing intensive and unprecedented politicization. Though we have approached it from the angle of tributaries and sources, in *Anti-Oedipus* the antinomian ethos of 1968 reached a certain peak. The desire to throw off all law – whether that of familialism, psychoanalysis, the state, or even a revolutionary philosophy of history – in the name of liberational and antiauthoritarian mobilization found impressively sophisticated theoretical expression in Deleuze and Guattari's best-selling admonition to let desiring machines desire.

This story, which might conclude in the description of a *politics* of desire, leads us instead back to Michel Foucault's claim that *Anti-Oedipus* was a work of ethics. In his 1977 preface to the English translation of that book, Foucault insisted that it should not be considered as "*the* new theoretical reference" or as "a flashy Hegel" that provided clear conceptual answers to the problems of the day. Rather, it should be read as a book of "art," in the sense of "*ars erotica*, *ars theoretica*, *ars politica*" – a work that addressed the question, *How?* more than the question, *Why?* It was a how-to manual. Therein, in his view, lay its ethical significance. *Anti-Oedipus* had three "adversaries": purely political thinking, psychoanalytic "technicians" who reduced desire to "structure and lack," and finally, fascism.

The fascism in us all, in our heads and everyday behavior, the fascism that causes us to love power, to desire the very thing that dominates and exploits us. I would say that *Anti-Oedipus* (may its authors forgive me) is a book of ethics, the first book of ethics to be written in France in quite a long time (perhaps that explains why its success was not limited to a particular "readership": being anti-Oedipal has become a life style, a way of thinking and living). How does one keep from being fascist, even (especially) when one believes oneself to be a revolutionary militant? How do we rid our speech and our acts, our hearts and our pleasures, of fascism? How do we ferret out the fascism that is ingrained in our behavior? The Christian moralists sought out the traces of the flesh lodged deep within the soul. Deleuze and Guattari, for their part, pursue the slightest traces of fascism in the body. Paying a modest tribute to Saint Francis de Sales [author of *Introduction to the Devout Life*], one might say that *Anti-Oedipus* is an *Introduction to the Non-Fascist Life.*[27]

Foucault's gloss focused on the theme of fascism in a way that suggested both Reich's diagnosis of the masses' desire for fascism and La Boétie's much earlier assessment of the will toward servitude. The suggestion that ethics pertains to a way of living evoked both Guattari's earlier tactile experiences of pursuing emancipation within the limits of an institutional setting and Deleuze's affirmative vitalism. One hears echoes, of course, of Foucault's own mid-1970s interests in formative practices of the self and sexuality. The fact that he made his comments in 1977 and not five years earlier when the book was published is itself significant. By then many energies previously engaged in activist enterprises were being reinvested in reflections along the ethical lines Foucault identified: How do language, practices, feeling, pleasures, and thought themselves conceal the will to dominate and be dominated?

In spite of its impervious density and hermetic idiosyncrasies, *Anti-Oedipus* did offer insights into how desire formed the "parts" of familial, political, and social "wholes." To take the authors at their word, the book was a machine whose gears produced and unsettled some accepted, even very commonsensical ways of talking about desire and social production. Inasmuch as the anti-Oedipal was concerned with questions about desire's functions and operations, its "ethics" addressed the question, *How?* Its answers to that question suggested a "life style." If the anti-Oedipal was not an idealism, it had pragmatic implications. On the continuum between ethos and the law, *Anti-Oedipus* clearly leaned toward *ethos*, or in Deleuze's sense, the "ethological." But by foregrounding the descriptive, functional element and leaving their own normative criteria largely implicit, the authors seemed to invite two related but distinctive kinds of criticism: "moralizing" in the sense that descriptions of how things *are* imply affirmations of how things *should be*; and an antinomian dismantling of normativity, the consequences of which were far from self-evidently positive. We saw Vincent Descombes make the first objection in chapter 9, and René Girard had recognized both these aspects at once.[28] In a declared effort to erase "fascism" on certain levels, barring some concept of limit to the machinations of desire, there seemed to be little to prevent fascism from sneaking back in on other levels, since the basis for distinguishing "molar" and "molecular," paranoid and schizophrenic, was unclear.

From one point of view, this groundlessness fit well with the antinomian ethos of anti-Oedipalism. The question remained, however, whether schizophrenia was the only or the best response to the fascism "in our heads." If some, like Fredric Jameson, have seen the schizoid as characteristic of our historical condition, it seems just as likely that the model of the schizophrenic sublime was itself a normative claim.[29]

14

Craziness Is a Dead End

The exaltation of schizophrenia raised, I think, legitimate questions about anti-Oedipal pragmatics and their resonances with contemporary anti-psychiatry. Jean Oury, although one might, in Foucault's terminology, characterize him as a "technician" of the unconscious, represents well the limitations of using schizophrenia as a model for cultural and political analysis. In a 1984 interview, Oury recounted how once, before 1968, while he was on a ten-day vacation away from La Borde, Guattari had invited David Cooper to come and give a talk at the clinic.[1] The gist of the talk was that the patients should stop taking their medication and have sex instead. The clinic went into turmoil, and the next day one of the patients died. Oury also described the post-1968 "slippage" that occurred in the context, as he dismissively put it, of "Deleuze and all that." The philosophy of desire embodied by *Anti-Oedipus* was a "massive ideology" that "made life idiotic," and appeals to "erotic power" themselves ran to the "limit of fascism." He gave another example of an exchange he had with a co-worker at La Borde. He said hello to the person and asked him what had happened that day. The person responded, "Nothing. Nothing happened at all." Then, after a short pause, he continued, "Oh yes. My father died today." Oury commented that it was an awful time when to "shed a tear" made one seem the "accomplice of capitalism."

While he may not have been receptive to some of the positive developments related to 1968, Oury's judgment of the immediate post-1968 period was telling. As he said in 1997, the era marked "a regression, a kind of destruction of all that was being concretely constructed. So-called new ideas had in fact already been long surpassed in our group and our organizations: the critique of hierarchy, segregation, [and so forth]."[2] The practical tasks of a psychiatric institution placed real limits on the expressions, modulations, and "machinations" of desire. As it had been for Institutional Psychotherapy more generally, pragmatic institutional limitations contributed to the articulation of an ethics. In 1977 Oury commented:

> There is always ethics. It is true. Why did I always have this passion for the careful handling of space? That is ethics. It is not some nervous tic that has no context. One sees very well what ethics has to do with desire. One cannot speak of ethics without speaking of desire ... It is clear how ethics grapples with something along the lines of a kind of passage, given the articulation of all that takes place in the analytical field every day. One must intervene ... An ethical position is necessary in order to support the confrontation of the political and of collective power.[3]

If Jacques Donzelot could have precipitously seen *Anti-Oedipus* as a "theoretical extension" of Institutional Psychotherapy, perhaps it would be more accurate to say that – in its expansion of the schizophrenic beyond its clinical setting, and thus in its negation of the specificity of mental illness – rather than an extension, the anti-Oedipal implied a devolution of IP.[4] Guattari had begun moving away from IP before 1968, but through the May events and his encounter with Deleuze, that devolution was accelerated. One of its consequences was a turn away from the limitations found in a clinical setting and a move out into the expanses of literary and theoretical space. But there were more practical implications as well, if one considers the early-1970s popularity of what Sherry Turkle has called "grass roots anti-psychiatry." Recall the spring 1975 appeal in *Marge* for the "destruction of psychiatry" and the "liberation" of mental patients. The judgment that *Anti-Oedipus* contributed substantially to this sensibility would be a fair one, and Deleuze and Guattari could not at a certain point disclaim the output of their machine-book.

After 1973, and at least for the next decade, both Deleuze and Guattari went to great lengths to clarify that desire was *not* a pulsion or a vitalistic principle that simply needed to be unchained.[5] Again, it is far from clear that their disclaimers effectively exempted them from such criticisms. A vitalistic ethics of desire and life in search of extension and amplification, of "intensities" and performative mechanics, and even of self-reflective "anti-fascism" – all this was not without a certain appeal. At the same time, one can in a limited sense agree with Richard Wolin that some strains of "Nietzschean" French thought, in this case, a schizophrenic Spinozist Nietzscheanism, posed some ethical problems.[6] For his part, Deleuze himself embraced an immanentist logic that could not make qualitative differentiations, except in terms of force, magnitude, power, relation, and operation. Those terms were the normative criteria. To the questions, Why *life* and not the *good life*? Where were limits? Whence obligation? Deleuze had less to say. At the same time, a Spinozist ethical philosophy might not be expected to answer questions that Socrates or Kant, for example, might have asked. In this instance, one seems left with a choice of whether or not to accept the immanent machinations of desire as the court of final appeal, to use a metaphor Deleuze and Guattari would surely not have liked. For partisans of the philosophy of desire, the choice was clear.

PART THREE

"Your Sexual Revolution Is Not Ours": French Feminist "Moralism" and the Limits of Desire

The strength of a nation is the decency and restraint of its women.

Ernest Renan (1888)

What therefore is precisely the subject of this discourse? It is to point out, in the progress of things, that moment, when, right taking place of violence, nature became subject to law; to unfold that chain of amazing events, in consequence of which the strong submitted to serve the weak, and the people to purchase imaginary ease, at the expense of real happiness.

We must in the first place allow that the more violent the passions, the more laws are necessary to restrain them. But, setting aside the inadequacy of laws to effect this purpose, which is evident from the crimes and disorders to which these passions daily give rise among us, we should do well to look back a little further and inquire if these evils did not spring up with the laws themselves; for in this case, even if the laws were capable of repressing such evils, it is the least that could be expected from them, that they should check a mischief which would not have arisen without them. Let us begin by distinguishing between what is moral and what is physical in the passion called love.

Jean-Jacques Rousseau (1755)

15

Gender and '68: Tensions from the Start

The philosophy of desire expressed a particular far-left sensibility. But its dense theoretical formulations were themselves part of a more extensive social and political terrain. The widespread foregrounding of basic questions about desire touched the most essential intuitions and structures of selfhood, interpersonal relationships, work, play, and citizenship. The very fact that *desire* was subjected to serious self-reflection symptomized the radical nature of the criticism and contestation spurred on by May 1968. Deleuze and Guattari epitomized a highly intellectualized version of the approach to desire as the fundamental building block of social and political life. Another crucial domain where, as it were, desire's depths were plumbed, was the sexual revolution and the social movements of gender contestation associated with it – feminism and gay liberation. There were links between the philosophy of desire and the women's and gay liberation movements, but the dynamics of social activism differed from those of theoretical activism.

Feminism and gay liberation were never unified phenomena. Although feminists and some male activists often found common cause with one another in attacking the sexual and gender "old order," such solidarity did not always materialize. Advocates of sexual and gender liberation certainly came up against external limits (religious, middle-class, and/or patriarchal) to their projects. They also encountered limits within generally consonant but sometimes conflicting sexual and gender liberation movements, as various parties struggled among themselves to define what the sexual revolution promised and what it could deliver. Ironically, sexual politics sometimes fought other sexual politics all in the name of liberation.

In Part III, I discuss conflicts in France *between* certain feminists and certain male leftists over what the liberation of desire was supposed to mean.

Although the story of feminist/male leftist conflict should not for a moment be taken to exemplify or sum up relationships that were otherwise conciliatory and strategically linked, such antagonisms could be felt even as the French women's and gay liberation movements were founded in 1970–71. After simmering for several years, those tensions came out into the open, especially between 1976 and 1978, around specific questions of sexual violence and the law. Disagreements on these questions often broke down along lines of sex difference. Some men on the French far left – associated with gay liberation and the "revolutionary" appeal of criminality – were incapable of appreciating the limits of liberation and desire. A few of these men, showing the extremes to which the sexual revolution might lead, developed an eccentric discourse on intergenerational sexual relations that sometimes countenanced pedophilia. Feminists were not slow to criticize the intolerable defence of sexual violence and sex with children. Debate ultimately turned on the promises and risks of participation/collusion with French law, courts, and prisons. As in the earlier history of French feminism, 1970s sexual politics also had "only paradoxes to offer" not simply between difference and universality but also between "revolution" and "reform."[1] Such paradoxes emerged when good questions were raised about the limits of legal limits (incarceration as an end) and also when feminists who said that the sexual revolution had limits (violence against women and pedophilia) were accused of "moralism."

To "moralize" was to betray the revolutionary or progressive agenda of the Left – a betrayal of "the cause" by a supposed ally. Those who stereotypically moralized were priests and right-wing defenders of the social order. "Feminist moralism" thus meant that women were, as was said, "making the bed of" or were in bed with the political Right. The effort to draw limits within a progressive political agenda was often perceived as treachery. In pursuing limits – that not everything was permitted in the permissive society – feminists were accused of tacit support of conservative agendas, just as American feminists were accused of coziness with the "moral majority" in their anti-pornography campaigns of the 1980s. Some French feminists in turn accused leftists of a machismo indistinguishable from the same "phallocratic" bourgeois society that leftists claimed they, too, wanted to overturn.

Mid-to-late-1970s French debates on sexual violence reflected the delayed unfolding of some of the contradictions of May 1968. Conflicts between men and women on the Left over sexual and gender liberation became apparent shortly after the May events. The liberational promises of a phrase like "It is forbidden to forbid" had themselves been contradictory.

There were competing, sometimes irreconcilable answers to questions such as: Were all desires or all acts related to sexuality to be liberated? Was *everything* permitted? Was the liberation promised by 1968 a break with certain sexual norms or a utopian aspiration to break with normativity in general? If there were limits to desire, what were they based on? What happened to "revolution" and "recuperation" in the articulation of new norms and values? It took several years for some of the liberational contradictions of May 1968 to work themselves out. Gender, sex difference, and sexuality were some of the terms involved in this sorting. I do not mean to suggest that phenomena of the *sexual revolution* and *gender* are one and the same. Rather, since in 1970s France they combined in fascinating and sometimes conflicting ways, it is of interest to examine their relationship in greater detail.

Gender concerns were not highlighted during the events of May 1968 in France. Although revisionist historians will no doubt continue to find evidence to the contrary,[2] accounts of the French women's and gay liberation social movements generally contend that widespread leftist mobilization around and contestation of gender matters developed only later, around 1970.[3] Granted, the group Féminin, masculin, avenir had formed in 1967, and inasmuch as gender was linked to questions of sexuality and desire, signs of this kind of cultural ferment abounded in the student milieu. As recounted in chapter 1, the May movement could be traced to agitation at Nanterre where male students had demanded the right to visit the dorms of female students, and the Minister of Sports, François Missoffe, had told Daniel Cohn-Bendit to jump in the newly completed university swimming pool if he was sexually frustrated.

Some celebrated graffiti of the May days captured the liberational/ libertine ethos of the moment – *Take one's desires for reality*; *The more I make love, the more I make revolution* – but aphoristic expressions did little to systematize or strategize a "desiring revolution," even if such slogans helped seal the reputation of May '68 as a festival where the rules of everyday life had been suspended and speech had been taken up and proliferated [*prendre la parole*]. The Mouvement jeune révolutionnaire admitted its isolation when it claimed in one of its tracts that it "alone approache[d] the problem of women frankly."[4] While the Freudo-Marxist works of Herbert Marcuse and Wilhelm Reich would be devoured in the early 1970s, few participants of May 1968 had read them, including the "leaders" of the movement.[5] The Mouvement démocratique féminin circulated a tract addressed to "women students," which declared: "The society to be built must be the work of women as well as of men; it must give all women equal opportunity with men."[6] In the occupied Sorbonne, the two-person Comité d'action pédérastique révolutionnaire put up flyers that were immediately ripped down, and a day-care centre was organized for women trying to find a balance between the demands of motherhood and those of radical agitation.[7]

Groups and efforts such as these were hardly coordinated, and further evidence for gender and sexuality being taken up in the maelstrom of the May revolts is similarly anecdotal. It was true that sex was viewed as some kind of challenge to repressive bourgeois society, but critical energies were directed toward work and speech and generally not focused on gender and sexuality.[8] If for at least a generation afterward the French terms *jouissance* (pleasure, enjoyment, orgasm) and *épanouissement* (flowering, opening out onto) would be associated with May 1968, it was not because sexuality had immediately become political, but because politics had suddenly seemed sexy. The problematization of sexuality – and with it as a historical companion piece, the problematization of gender – did not take place until the French far left stopped expressing itself, as it still had in 1968, in the monolanguage of class.

During the extended period of radical agitation in the early 1970s the French far left began to face the challenge of diversifying the sites and terms of its liberational projects. Among radical groups open to the sexual revolution and to shifting the focus from class war to the transformation of daily life, the most important was the Maoist group Vive la révolution! (VLR), formed in the fall of 1969 under the leadership of Roland Castro and Tiennot Grumbach.[9] Castro tried to welcome groups representing specific identities – women, gays, immigrants, and youth movements – into the organization. These groups, which Alain Touraine popularized as the New Social Movements, were still framed for VLR within a Marxist-Leninist structure.[10] In a 1970 text whose title borrowed a line from the poet Arthur Rimbaud, "change life," Castro wrote: "The people oppose on all fronts of social life tit-for-tat responses against oppression, exploitation, anarchy, boredom, and capitalist manipulation. To begin to oppose on every front, everywhere, popular legality against bourgeois legality: this is the guiding principle for *changing life*."[11] As we saw previously, suspicion of "bourgeois legality," whose corollary was found in talk of "prolonged armed struggle," haunted the far left for some time. Castro's strategy was to organize autonomous groups in the form of a union that was directed by a Leninist organization but preserved the autonomy of specific parties. "It didn't work like that," he admits.[12] The contradictions of Marxism-Leninism and the New Social Movements came to a head with the publication of the infamous issue Number 12 of the VLR newspaper, *Ce que nous voulons: Tout!*, published on 23 April 1971. In the wake of increasing dissension following that issue, Castro abruptly dissolved the group a few months later.

The editors of the paper had given responsibility for the contents of the twelfth issue to a group of male homosexual and feminist activists. Many of the articles were signed by members of the Front homosexuel d'action révolutionnaire (FHAR), which had begun meeting the previous month.[13] The front page of the newspaper captured aspects of the agenda, as well as some of the dilemmas, of gay and feminist activists working together:

> Yes, our bodies belong to us.
> - free abortion and contraception
> - right to homosexuality and all sexualities
> - right of minors to the freedom of desire and to its accomplishment
>
> These exigencies raise questions about the limit points of life: about incest, rape, euthanasia, and suicide ... They have their extensions: refusal to submit one's body to the census, to pollution, to daily rhythms, to work accidents ... They exceed themselves: the free disposition of my body cannot exercise itself against those of others. This freedom only really exists in the blossoming [*l'épanouissement*] of all. They designate the ends of the revolution: the perfection of happiness.[14]

The side-by-side appearance of reproductive rights, "all sexualities," and the sexuality of minors was significant. Such terms would not again be so easily invoked together. Similarly, the question of limits, the extension of sexual matters into knowledge-power regimes (for example, the census), and the conjunction of a happy liberal vision of self-delimiting freedoms with the utopian forecast of revolutionary beatitude – these very different ramifications of "our bodies belong to us" were also to be worked over in coming years. The remainder of the articles in issue Number 12 demonstrated how collaborative strategizing between feminists and homosexuals was already leading to a number of divergent emphases.

Differences emerged in the respective agendas and perceptions of feminists and gay men. For women, the reclamation of reproductive rights and the question of the women's movement becoming *non-mixte*, or separatist, figured prominently. For men, the sexuality of minors seemed important: first of all, minors had a right to express their sexuality; second, amorous relations between adults and minors ought to be permitted. Programmatic contrasts spilled over into attitudes. Whereas one male FHAR member wrote of the "disruption of all mores, without restriction," a woman from the group spoke of how "our homosexual [male] friends are raised like others in the overestimation of pseudo-virile values," but noted optimistically: "They succeed in throwing [those values] off to the extent that they know better than anyone else the repressive significance of the hetero-cop morality [*la morale hétéro-flic*]." On the other hand, another man from FHAR decried the "legend" of gay male misogyny. Women, he said, had "opened the way," and gay men found themselves in the position of "desiring men" and "despising virility": "We claim our 'femininity,' that which women reject, at the same time as we declare that these roles have no meaning." On the question of strategic allegiances between women and gay men, a certain "Sylvie" wrote that "their struggles seem incompatible." Gay men took themselves as the "elite of the male sex [*le race mâle*]" and lived in a "world of misogynist selection ... the very opposite of the liberation of women." Mentioning a position that would be popularized during debates on pornography in 1974–75, Sylvie noted that lesbianism formed a key part of the "erotic commerce" of straight society, though she went on to say that even if lesbianism could bring a "disalienation" in consciousness, consciousness alone did little to change the "political and social situation of women."[15]

The twelfth issue of *Tout!* was, as the next number reported, a "paving stone [thrown] in the leftist pond."[16] The issue certainly made waves. Using a frostier metaphor, the editors wrote that an "avalanche of letters," laudatory and critical, had been received. The far-left press expressed dismay, especially over a printed statement by Jean Genet, who said in effect that if he had not slept with Algerian boys, then he might not have supported the Algerian insurgency during the 1956–62 war.[17] The *Tout!* staff also felt obliged to answer objections that issue Number 12 had been "anti-worker."[18] The real storm came, however, when, after complaints by a member of the National Assembly, Michel Caldaguès, and the mayor of Tours, Jean Royer, Number 12 was confiscated by the police. Its nominal director of publication, Jean-Paul Sartre, was charged with *outrage aux bonnes moeurs*, or outrage against public morals. This led Sartre to comment that "a new bourgeois offensive for moral order" had begun in which "market pornography is favoured, but those who want to conquer freedom against sexual oppression are prosecuted."[19] Bad publicity on the far left and from the government had the not surprising effect of boosting sales. Attendees at the FHAR's weekly meetings jumped from forty to around 400 within the month.[20]

The predominance of male homosexuality in the twelfth issue of *Tout!* had been fairly evident even to those involved. The position of women in

VLR was less obvious in April 1971. Matters were somewhat cleared up, if scandalously so, with the publication of issue Number 14 on June 7th, which featured the inflammatory "Letter from Mohamed."[21] As the introductory editorial note that accompanied the letter explained: "This text is serious and even provocative ... For many of us, it is difficult to swallow."[22] The "Letter" accused French female radicals of an awful racism. The proof of this racism, Mohamed said, was that French girls refused to go to bed with him. Behind the pathetic argument was a larger, more serious point about race on the far left and in the politics of everyday life: "You say that you aren't racist, that there are simply cultural and educational differences ... To make love you don't need a diploma in philosophy or science." But Mohamed added insult to injury by targeting what he called "leftist fascism": "French girls are rotten with racism; they have it in their blood like an almost incurable virus ... [They] incarnate all the evil of Europe, the bestiality of the filthy white." The editors of *Tout!*, admitting that "this text expresse[d] a male racism at the same time as denouncing a racism of colour," decided to publish it anyway since "today, Arab comrades speak of their life also ... We don't care if we're full of contradictions. We assume them." Understandably, part of the reason why women would leave both far-left organizations and the newly born gay one was that the culture of masculinity – straight and gay – played itself on very broad bandwidths.

Needless to say, the text and *Tout!*'s decision to publish it provoked the ire of some VLR feminists. The following issue of *Tout!* (30 June 1971) included both a "Response to the Letter from Mohamed," whose author said she had slept with several Arabs without any significant problems, and, more significantly, a scathing criticism of VLR-*Tout!*'s tacit support for the more questionable aspects of Mohamed's polemic.[23] This latter piece, "Your Sexual Revolution Is Not Ours," was authored by two "militants from the Mouvement de libération des femmes (MLF)," Françoise Picq and Nadja Ringart. "The numbers twelve and following of *Tout!* give a certain image of the 'sexual revolution,'" the essay said, "by taking pleasure/enjoyment [*jouissance*] and the right to enjoy oneself/come more [*plus jouir*] for basic criteria ... Since men and women are alienated, there is at present only an alienated conception of pleasure/enjoyment. New forms of pleasure/enjoyment need to be found." Even the "new image" of the liberated woman corresponded to this relational structure, since women in VLR were "fixed in this [so-called liberated] role and made to feel guilty when they no longer corresponded to it." That was to say, promiscuity was a putatively revolutionary act. Picq and Ringart called for a prolonged "deconstruction" of power on many levels in order to "at last discover our totality of being human." The question of "love" could not be posed until women were indeed "liberated." Picq and Ringart's text accompanied a mock study of the mores of the *Tout!* staff, in faux anthropological speak, entitled "Life and Mores of the 'Tuot' Tribe, or May Your Bones Rot in the Moonlight."[24]

The controversy continued in the next issue of *Tout!*, which was the newspaper's last. Although a "group of girls" struck back at Mohamed's "aberrant generalization" and "infantile logic," the final word seems to have gone to several male FHAR members. One *Tout!* editor, responding to "Your Sexual Revolution Is Not Ours," admitted that some "comrades" had tried to form "veritable harems" by telling women that any jealousy on their part was residual "bourgeois" sentiment. But, he went on to say, the phrase "enjoy oneself/come more" [*plus jouir*] could not be applied equally to straight and gay men. It was "women's fault" if they did not challenge "more subtle oppression ... at the moment when this ideology was constituted." Even if women and gay men seemed to be "natural allies," the program of the FHAR was "rather different" than that of the MLF: "Sexuality occupies the principal place in the revolt of [male] homosexuals." Echoing this sentiment, several FHAR activists, drawing up the "balance sheet" of the group's first few months, concluded that the "sensibilities" of lesbians and gay men were "frankly different and [that they had] a bit too quickly called for 'unity.'" After the summer holiday, when the group met again in September, it was likely that "two distinct movements" would be formed.[25]

16

Guy Hocquenghem's Dark Encounter with Feminism

Alliances between lesbians and gay men in the Front homosexuel d'action révolutionnaire (FHAR) were indeed short-lived in 1971. The group's weekly Thursday night meetings at the Ecole des Beaux-Arts in Paris were often contentious, and before long turned into forums for sexual cruising as much as for political discussion. The infamous "sixth floor" was reputed for its shadowy encounters. Though the FHAR was officially disbanded in February 1974, when police cleared out the building at the request of the Beaux-Arts administration, for all practical purposes, the organization flourished from March 1971 through early 1973. It did not take long for the FHAR to collapse into a kind of gay male party and for women – lesbians in FHAR as well as other feminists – to bemoan how the group fostered the "machoism" of "sex without love." In a representative example, Cathy Bernheim recounts how one weekend retreat in the country for lesbians and gay men from FHAR concluded with the men going into the local town to try to pick up boys, and the women staying at the group's lodging to discuss whether sexual liberation meant more than the right to have multiple partners.[1]

The person who did the most to represent and publicly express the male sensibility of the FHAR was Guy Hocquenghem. His writings on gay liberation give a glimpse of two important nodes in the FHAR/MLF constellation – "dark homosexuality" and its relation to feminism.[2] Hocquenghem, a recent graduate of the Ecole normale supérieure, had joined VLR in September 1970 and began attending FHAR meetings in April 1971. He had successfully lobbied for the inclusion in the first issue of *Tout!* of a text by Huey Newton on the participation of gays in revolutionary struggle, and had collaborated on the famous issue Number 12. Hocquenghem's political activism, linked with Trotskyism and experiments in communal living, had emerged after 1968 and led to his identification as a gay activist. In 1972 he was appointed as a lecturer in philosophy at the newly formed University of Vincennes, where he worked alongside Gilles Deleuze. Hocquenghem's first major publication, *Homosexual Desire* (1972), was indebted to Deleuze and Félix Guattari's *Anti-Oedipus*, published a few months earlier.[3] As we saw in Part II, *Anti-Oedipus* had attacked psychoanalysis and the bourgeois family as two heads of the same repressive dragon, promoting in their place the notion of "desiring machines" as the basic elements in a "schizoanalytic" alternative. Hocquenghem's "homosexual desire" built directly on this model.

The Oedipus complex represented a "double bind" for homosexuals: to be "normal" they had to give up their desire; to keep their desire, they had to accept identification as "perverse."[4] In a way that recalls Herbert Marcuse's notion of "repressive desublimation," the double bind also described the fact that although contemporary societies showed great tolerance in sexual matters, they were simultaneously, increasingly repressive in other ways.[5] The no-win situation of the double bind was insidious. As Hocquenghem wrote in November 1972, in a kind of elegy on the FHAR's decline, attempts to mobilize around gay "pride" had merely played to the other half of Oedipalized homosexual "shame." Such pride did not escape the double-bind game and had ended up with "gilded bars" on the social cages of homosexuals.[6] Attempts to escape the normative register had backfired.

More than the particular forms of patriarchy, capitalism, or the "sad" phallic politics of the public sphere, Hocquenghem's real enemies were normativity and normalcy, toward which he was congenitally allergic. Such strictures, he thought, could just as easily constrain leftist, revolutionary circles ("new norms") as bourgeois-Oedipal ones. It is for this reason that Hocquenghem rejected the "self-affirmation" of homosexuals associated with gay "pride." Identity, "humanism," "integration," and even political "engagement" based on hope for tolerance and the repeal of repressive legislation, were dead-end, double-bind games. Homosexuality was simply the inverse of a normative heterosexuality, and collective mobilization around identity generated new forms of normalcy and normativity. Slotting the word "sexual" in front of "revolution" guaranteed nothing, and "refusal" alone was inadequate. The sexual revolution had not yet been revolutionary enough, and to go the next step, gays needed to escape the trap of hoping for reform and integration.

One can thus understand Hocquenghem's anti-Oedipal hostility to the category of law. Since the Law of the Father, to use the Lacanian term for the "symbolic" regime of Freud's superego, signified the social, familial, and psychoanalytic forces that gave homosexuals the choice between "perversity" and "normalcy," the law in a more mundane, French Republican sense could only exclude and normalize. Hocquenghem saw proof of this conclusion in the increasing legal repression of homosexuals since World War II and in the development of new notions of criminality that relied on a connection of penalization and psychiatry (guilt was a juridical and a psychological complex; gay identity was born of a "bad conscience" [*mauvaise conscience*]). Furthermore, the justice system had its own libidinal interests. Again, Hocquenghem held out little hope for either legal and judicial reform or social integration.[7]

So what, then, did he want? Hocquenghem's view of homosexuality clung to marginality and renounced the tradition of the "discreet" homosexual who sought legitimation in assimilation. What he called "dark homosexuality" followed the literary tradition laid down by Jean Genet: a gayness whose milieu was one of thieves, prostitutes, and public sex. Homosexuality was thus the "unclassifiable inquisitor of heterosexuality" engaged in a "permanent questioning of norms." Against identity, normalization, and the double bind in their many forms, Hocquenghem asserted a "primary homosexuality that reveals the lack of differentiation of desire." Like Deleuze and Guattari's desiring machines, Hocquenghem's homosexual desire was productive, machinic, nomadic, flux-like, polyvocal, and rule-defying. Desire was present in all institutions and could be configured in "group" situations, a concept borrowed from Guattari's notion of fluid and dynamic "subject groups," which differed from "social" ones. Though they risked enacting a mere "refusal" or "reversal," the various "autonomous movements" that, according to Hocquenghem, had emerged after 1968 (women, homosexuals, and young people) rejected politics as usual or politics *tout court* in their emphasis on the everyday and the problematization of typically "private" experience. Homosexual desire exemplified the form of "producing without reproducing"; that is, expression without the Oedipal and generational services of reproductive sexuality. Following the suggestions of his former teacher René Schérer (whom I will discuss below), Hocquenghem argued that such desire might escape social-Oedipal mediation by cultivating a spontaneous and explosive "immediacy." Unsublimated desire was the "best weapon" against normalcy and normativity; homosexuals were "orgasm machines."[8]

The praxis of homosexual desire, then, resided in embracing the marginal and deviant culture of homosexuality, as constructed by the Oedipal-normative world – the culture of Genet, of prostitutes, criminality, cruising, public sex, and so forth. In contrast to the "lighted agora of sexual identity" – political recognition, legal tolerance, and social integration – Hocquenghem embraced the "dark" pole to which he had been assigned. In *Homosexual Desire*, the most extended theoretical discussion of dark homosexuality, Hocquenghem contrasts the phallic politics of Oedipus with "anal" sexuality – the realm of the private, the scatological, the transgressive, and the not-yet-sublimated. Homosexuality ultimately revolved around the group function of apolitical anal eroticism. Though in passing he also mentioned encounters between adults and children and between Frenchmen and Arabs, that group function found its full pragmatic expression in the anonymous homosexual encounter, or "pick-up machine," which exemplified a non-Oedipal sexuality free of the guilt/law complex.

> In truth, the pick-up machine is not concerned with names or sexes. The drift where all encounters become possible is the moment in which desire produces and feels no guilt ... "scattering" – the fact that homosexuals have a multitude of love affairs, each of which may last only a moment ... a system in action, the system in which polyvocal desire is plugged in on a non-exclusive basis ... Homosexual love is immensely superior, precisely because everything is possible at any moment: organs look for each other and plug in, unaware of the law of exclusive disjunction. Homosexual encounters do not take place in the seclusion of a domestic setting but outside, in the open air, in forests and on beaches. The cruising homosexual, on the lookout for anything that might come and plug in to his own desire, is reminiscent of the "voyaging schizophrenic" described in *Anti-Oedipus*. If the homo pick-up machine, which is infinitely more direct and less guilt-induced than the complex system of "civilized love" (to use Charles Fourier's phrase), were to take off the Oedipal cloak of morality under which it is forced to hide, we would see that its mechanical scattering corresponds to the mode of existence of desire itself.[9]

Hocquenghem's deep aversion to anything resembling normalizing recuperation (identity, toleration, reformism, even rebellion) provides a window on his attitude toward feminism. To be sure, Hocquenghem was the first to acknowledge gay men's debt to feminists and admit that the FHAR had come into being on a "political terrain already cleared by the MLF." The FHAR had proceeded through an "imitation" of the MLF's tactics and objectives. Their original solidarity had been based on "friendly complicity" in the rejection of patriarchal, "phallocractic" society and the bourgeois family, and sometimes by a shared desire to take "vengeance on other men." Both movements had attempted to address the "private" in new ways, had discovered that they could "ignore" castration and the Oedipal law, and had found a form of "egalitarian" or "Platonic" love between men and women. Hocquenghem even joked that since everyone had an anus, "seen from behind we are all women; the anus does not practice sexual discrimination" (in the way the phallus marks sexual identity).[10]

Beyond that, Hocquenghem had little to say about or to women. Homosexuality was implicitly masculine. There was no discussion of lesbianism in *Homosexual Desire*, and women's sexuality had only been mentioned to demonstrate the tyranny of the phallocratic Oedipus. From the summer of 1972 forward, Hocquenghem dissected the corpse of any gay male-feminist alliance. The gay movement had needed "independence" from the MLF. The two movements had "totally different ideological bases," since the MLF "apparently need[ed] to put itself in a position of relative strength with respect to male society." In another version of the claim published in *Tout!* that gays were "asking to be treated like women just when women are fed up with that," he gave the facetious example: "The girls said that they were fed up with being whistled at by guys in the street. To which the fags responded that they were asking for just that: to be whistled at, for someone to put his hand on their asses." His repetition of another comment evoked during the *Tout!* debates – that the FHAR was about sex, and feminists were stuck on love – reduced to a facile stereotype feminist insistence that the sexual revolution and women's liberation was about more than just more sex. Inasmuch as Hocquenghem's "orgasm machines" were meant to make gay liberation an "anti-humanist" movement, he saw any concern for the contextual "psychology of relationships" as retrograde. In his judgment, feminism was a humanism, and only a step away from the normalizing traps of identity, reform, and integration.[11]

He displayed this attitude in the summer of 1973 in his response to feminist criticisms of a special issue of the journal *Recherches*. That issue, entitled *Three Billion Perverts: Great Encyclopedia of Homosexualities* (March 1973), had published a variety of articles on Arab gay sex, masturbation, pick-ups, pedophilia, sado-masochism, and institutions.[12] Collaborators included Cathy Bernheim, Gilles and Fanny Deleuze, Guattari, Michel Foucault, Genet, Daniel Guérin, Hocquenghem, Georges Lapassade, and Jean-Paul Sartre. The issue was immediately seized by the police, and Guattari, the journal's director of publication, was charged with outrage against public morals (as Sartre had been for *Tout!*).[13] What had bothered some feminists was that the prominent display of male bodies and erect penises espoused a "phallocratism," perhaps of non-traditional shades, but masculinist nonetheless. In July Hocquenghem responded somewhat bitterly to what he saw as the "moral rearmament" of "Mao-feminism": "The movement is pulled between two extremes, a body with multiple organs (sado-masochist, crossing-dressing, etc.) and a new morality that aims to exclude diversity and the polymorphism of the new perverts in the name of a one and only law that distinguishes the friends and enemies of the People – excuse me – women."[14]

Hocquenghem could only see in feminist criticisms a "new law," a "new phallus," and a new norm. That a voice came from the Left was no guarantee that it was not normalizing. The crux of the matter was that feminist criticism and state censorship happened to coincide, and Hocquenghem conflated them. In his view, neo-normalizations had to be met with the same ruthless critique that was directed against the traditional Oedipal system. As he had written in *Homosexual Desire*:

> There can be no symmetry between what the gay movement advocates on the one hand and the dominant form of sexuality on the other ... Why set a limit? – if there is to be an end to the sexual norm, this must come through the concrete disintegrative process that the gay movement has begun ... We shall therefore not accuse the gay movement of failing to relate to women, lest we reintroduce thereby the very guilt we have worked to dissolve ... The danger for homosexuality, the trap of desire, lies elsewhere, in what we call its guilt-induced perversion.[15]

Hocquenghem could admit that gay male "misogyny" existed, but he had little to say about it.[16]

17

Feminism, Law, Rape, and Leftist Male Reaction

The Mouvement de libération des femmes (MLF) and 1970s French feminism embraced diverse tendencies. In regard to the specific question of conflict between female and male activists and the emergence of the charge of feminist "moralism," one development merits close examination: the changing status of law among certain feminists during the 1970s, particularly the shift from the struggle for reproductive rights (1972–74) to the struggle to have rape taken more seriously by the judicial system (1976–78).[1] These years witnessed the development from a feminist position *outside* the law (abortion was illegal) to a feminist position operating *within* the law (rape should be criminalized and punished). From defiance of a proscriptive law that forbade, many feminists moved toward a more positive evaluation of French Republican legality; it could be a site where feminists agitated for rights and justice for women, by using the judicial scene, in the words of Françoise Picq, "to drive rape out from clandestiny and insignificance" into the open.[2] There were, in fact, serious disagreements among feminists over the uses to which French justice should be put – the limits, so to speak, of legal limits.

The focus on the positive relation to law advocated by some feminists was meant to draw a contrast with a particularly vicious, if generally short-lived strain of leftist anti-feminism. During those years, the MLF had to confront a distinctly far-left hostility to "bourgeois" legality, a hostility already expressed by Hocquenghem, but which ran much deeper. The often hysterical and sometimes pathetic entrenchment in a "revolutionary" view of French law by some male leftists, who decried feminist calls for penalizing rape, did much to mobilize feminists in a positive embrace of progressive legislation. To be sure, some men and women raised serious questions about the limits of legal recourse, especially penalization. But the shift from "revolution" to "reform," seen as "recuperation" among leftists, marked not only the end of one post-1968 ambience but also a wider implementation of a certain spirit of '68 with regard to gender and sexuality. The spirit of reform had also been present in May, but now we see a deradicalizing shift among some of the very elements that in the far-left years (circa 1968–74) had sworn off any form of compromise.

The charge on the far left that feminists were instigating new forms of moralism coalesced around the issue of rape. The rape debate began in the winter of 1975–76 and concluded in the famous Aix-en-Provence trial of May 1978 and the subsequent introduction of new legislation that June. It emerged in several distinct phases and was punctuated by a discrete series of controversies, most notably in the newspaper *Libération* in March and April 1977. From an initial and incremental mobilization throughout 1976, the "*Libé*" acrimony – limited to the far left but during which some men made some outrageous statements – was followed in September and October 1977 by a full mass-media mobilization on the issue. By early 1978 some feminists were expressing doubts that the French judicial system, despite taking rape more seriously, could serve women's interests alongside its own. But such hesitations could not reverse the overall transformation, which culminated symbolically in late spring and early summer 1978 in the Aix trial and the proposed new legislation (not passed, however, until 1980).

In February 1976 lawyers representing two Belgian tourists who had been raped in August 1974 succeeded in having the case transferred from the Tribunal correctionel to the Cour d'Assises – the equivalent in the United States to bumping the charge up from misdemeanour assault to felony rape.[3] Although the trial by jury in Aix-en-Provence would not take place until fifteen months later (May 1978), the comment was made later in 1976 that "the campaign against rape truly began" with that appellate decision.[4] Meanwhile, throughout 1976, the issue of rape achieved a higher profile within the feminist movement and in public discourse. An International Tribunal of Crimes against Women was held in Brussels (4–8 March 1976), at which the lack of juridical consequences for violence against women figured significantly; the issue of female circumcision/genital mutilation began to be taken seriously in France; and Susan Brownmiller's *Against Our Will* (1975) arrived in bookstores on 23 November 1976 (translated as *Le Viol*, the same title as a book by Marie-Odile Fargier also published in 1976). Most significant, however, was the "Ten Hours Against Rape" held at the Mutualité meeting hall in Paris on 26 June and attended by close to 5,000 women. The meeting was closed to men, a group of whom stood on the sidewalk asking women what was happening inside as they came out of the Mutualité. Taking the form of a general speak-out, the discussion ran from calls for collective self-defence and vigilante justice to the recounting of tragic and painful personal experiences. The fact that the Mutualité meeting concerned rape (apparently more than the fact that it was a closed-door event) seemed to provoke resentful reactions from some male leftists. The newspaper *Libération* on several occasions published letters from men who spoke of their incredulity toward the growing mobilization around sexual violence.[5] Male leftist reaction soon reached hysterical proportions, and it is difficult in retrospect to treat it with sympathy.

Throughout 1976 and early 1977, the rape debate continued to mount in intensity, particularly as several court cases received heightened publicity. However, the real moment of conflict between feminists and male leftists (as well as among some feminists) came in March and April 1977 when the newspaper *Libération* hosted a contentious debate. The controversy would lead several women to ask: "At *Libération*, which sexual liberation are you for? Those of rapists? Is the war of the sexes the only solution you leave us with?"[6] The controversy began with a trial. Brigitte Ribaillier, twenty-six years old, had been raped in April 1976, and her aggressor had been brought before the Tribunal correctionel on assault charges. As in the case of the two Belgian tourists, Brigitte's lawyers had asked that the court declare itself incompetent and send the dossier to the Cour d'Assises. The court reached that decision on 21 March 1977. That same day, *Libération* published an interview with defence lawyer Roger Koskas, a member of the Mouvement d'action judiciaire.[7] The thrust of his remarks addressed the fact that the accused, Youri Eshak, was a twenty-seven-year-old Egyptian student at the University of Vincennes. Koskas did not hesitate to play the terms of race, sexual violence, and "bourgeois" Republican justice off one another. Marie-Odile Fargier was not exaggerating when she wrote that this "trial [would] remain one of the hardest moments of a debate opened inside the Left, and above all on the far left, on the approach to take with rapists."[8]

In his interview, Koskas distinguished between the desire to "repress" and punish the perpetrator of a crime, and his own "political reaction," which leaned toward contextualizing and explaining the crime. Ultimately, Eshak's social condition, in the form of male "sexual misery," was to blame. The argument of "sexual misery" as a consequence of sexual repression was popularized by widespread attention to the theories of Wilhelm Reich, who wrote: "The sexual misery of the patriarchal-authoritarian society is the consequence of the negation and the sexual representation which characterize it, and which provoke neurosis, perversion, and sexual crimes among all those it enslaves." One feminist responded to Koskas's cheap use of this concept by remarking: "[Women] are perfectly capable of analysing and understanding sexual misery. We have been made to feel guilty by it for far too long."[9] Koskas went on to say that feminists were only hurting themselves by appealing to a repressive juridical system whose structures and interests were fundamentally at odds with any collective campaign for changing "the ensemble of social relations."

> I say thus that their action is wrong, reactionary, and that paradoxically, they discredit the fight they want to lead. Repressing this guy will not help the relations between men and women ... They don't see that men and women are in the same shit. To appeal to repression is to situate oneself in a traditional way of seeing things: that of the weak woman who seeks protection from the code of men. What will they gain? Years in prison and exile. Nothing else.

Koskas thus used one politicized version of the trial, foregrounding race and class (the accused was an Egyptian immigrant persecuted by white bourgeois justice) to counter the feminist version of the political trial of rape. In the face-off between rape politics and race politics, the Left stared itself down.

As if Koskas's statements in *Libération* were not inflammatory enough, the following day, newspapers published accounts of what he had said in the courtroom.[10] He had denounced certain "cultured women ready to sacrifice a poor guy for a debate of ideas ... For the sake of the life, equality, and oppression of women, we pass lightly over the other victims of society ... Your struggle is abstract, as full of hate as that of the classic reactionaries. It's together that men and women will change society." The accused had been "begging for love, he committed a crime of love ... If she had consented, none of us would be here." Koskas's comments provoked such an uproar among those observing the trial that the judge cleared the courtroom. Fargier wrote of the experience of "feeling so much hostility in this voice that wanted to denounce hate." The lawyers for the plaintiff – Josyane Moutet, Colette Auger, and Monique Antoine – were completely taken aback by the venomous tirade. Moutet responded: "The most oppressed and crushed man can still turn his aggressivity against women, the designated victims." The rape of Brigitte and the charge of assault against Eshak were symptomatic of the violence women faced every day and of the ineptness of the judicial system in defending women. "The judicial system is a means used in all times, even by revolutionaries," Moutet said: "The legal procedure is the only means at our disposal at the present moment. It only represents a step, a moment in our struggle. We use it with neither joy nor satisfaction and will only abandon it when we have other means."[11]

What those other means might be was not exactly clear in 1977 and 1978. There were, of course, serious divisions among feminists with respect to the question of rape and the French legal system, especially around prison sentences. Writing of the lack of "unanimity" among feminists on the question, Michèle Solat commented in October 1977:

> We have trouble admitting that the women's movement, coming out of the oppositional Left which has denounced "bourgeois justice" since 1968, could use the current reigning institutions. Some go as far as saying that in dragging rapists in front of the Assises court, or even simply filing complaints, rape victims participate in "repression." It remains to be seen whether feminists have any other choice.[12]

Solat drew the parallel between the use of courts to dramatize the injustice of the law against abortion and to promote the campaign against rape ("to sensitize public opinion and, through the occasion of a trial, to call into question a law and its application"). But she also noted that a shift had occurred: women were no longer defendants but civil parties who "accuse." Though the "general tendency" had been to seek incarceration for rape perpetrators, there had yet to be consensus on that goal. Certain organizations that mobilized around the legal representation of rape victims – Choisir, SOS Femmes, and La Ligue des droits des femmes – had fewer qualms about penalization, perhaps because they were also seeking reforms in rape law and trial practices. Moutet and her colleagues, Auger and Antoine, belonged to the Collectif juridique de défense des femmes, a group that was wary about the effectiveness and political wisdom of seeking harsh prison sentences. They were not alone. In the midst of the Eshak affair, on 23 March 1977, *Libération* published a letter from a group calling themselves the "Cassandras," who affirmed: "The prison, system of repression that reinforces the violence of men among themselves, is not the best solution for us."[13] On 29 March the "'Rape' Commission of the 18th Arrondissement" proposed simply posting the photo and name of the rapist in the neighbourhood where he lived.[14] On 30 April Hélène Lanive wrote: "We must refuse to let ourselves fall into the circle where we have been put"; and further: "To refuse *also* prison for rapists is elementary."[15] As we will see below, the contradictions of being *for* trials and *against* punishment came to a head, especially for Moutet and others, in early 1978.[16]

Despite the diversity of feminist attitudes, their ranks closed when three inflammatory articles, written, as it were, in the spirit of Koskas, appeared in *Libération* in late March and early April 1977. The articles reflected a far-left discourse of political criminality – valorizations of criminality, politicizations of violence – that had been associated with the far left since the nineteenth century and had resurfaced in the post-1968 era of radical agitation.[17] If bourgeois justice was rotten, then there could be no compromises with it. After the Eshak trial, certain male leftists went as far as to accuse feminists of anti-revolutionary complicity with legal institutions in their prosecution of sexual violence. The articles speak for themselves. The first, by Pierre Goldman, appeared on 23 March 1977, the same day as the "Cassandras'" unavailing statement mentioned above and also the day that Jean-Antoine Tramoni, who had famously murdered the militant Pierre Overney in 1972, was himself assassinated by leftists in an act of vigilante justice shortly after being released from a two-year prison sentence. A quixotic figure of the far left, Goldman had made a reputation for himself as half-gangster, half-urban guerrilla by blending politics and crime.[18] His *Libération* article was entitled "On Rape, the Correct Application of the Law, and Despair."[19] Though he carefully recounted the logic of leftist uses of the legal system, and even more carefully the rationale behind feminists' turn toward penal law, he went on to address the "tragic ... contradictions" of this development. Though no society would likely do without law (it prevented "the savage reign of the law of the strongest, of lynching, of the vendetta" – that is, feminist vigilante justice), there remained individuals such as himself who regarded "all legal justice, all legal judgment, all legal repression as an infamy." Goldman spoke for those few who saw themselves as "determined to remain, morally and not in the sense of the penal code, definitively and absolutely *outside the law* [*des 'hors-la-loi' définitifs et absolus*]." It was a position of "marginality" and "despair" he was happy to claim.

The second article was written by Hocquenghem and published on 29 March, coincidentally four days after Jacques Chirac had been elected mayor of Paris, signalling an advance of the political Right. Implying that he needed to spell things out, the piece was called, simply, "R-A-P-E."[20] Attacking the idea that criminal penalization could serve as a deterrent, he said that the feminist pursuit of exemplary punishment was motivated by "vengeance" and that feminists were "ruthless" and had "become Amazons." In a crude and somewhat malicious contrast of feminist and gay male politics, he claimed that gay men did not ask the law to punish those who assaulted them. Gay men knew out of "good sense" that filing charges accomplished nothing; it could not undo a crime that had taken place – "justice does not help them at all": "Because who in the end has ever seen a fag complain about being *raped*? To have been beaten up, yes. But raped ... It definitely seems that the anus of the gay man is not endowed with the same transcendental qualities as the vagina. And the curious thing is, it is rape alone that makes calling on justice indispensable." The "indispensability," in Hocquenghem's mind, was proven by the fact that only in the case of rape, not the case in theft and physical assault, was some sort of post-facto realignment sought. Through judicial redress, vengeance would be assuaged and "a certain virginity, that of dignity" restored.

The third intervention was the transcript of a "dialogue of the deaf" between "Mohamed" and "Françoise," published on 5 April.[21] This was the same Mohamed who had written the inflammatory letter in 1971 to *Tout!*, in which he had suggested that French woman revealed their racism by refusing to sleep with him. He had contacted *Libération* in 1977 to comment on the absence of race from the rape debate. "My problem is not," he began, "to approve or disapprove that one sends a guy to the Cour d'Assises. My problem is to say that every immigrant, the day he arrives in France, is already in the hands of French injustice; he is already in a prison, in a vast prison." The immigrant faced repression if he decided to rebel in any way: by striking, demonstrating, or – preposterously – "taking what he is refused, which could be a woman." Though in a fleeting moment he acknowledged that women were also victims in French society, he gave race priority over gender ("Who raped whom first? It is easy to forget that and to give oneself a good conscience"), and stressed the incommensurability of the positions of male immigrants and women ("Listen. We don't have the same problems. Our political, economic, and cultural interests don't converge"). He concluded his increasingly heated exchange with his interlocutor, Françoise, with the bitter statement: "I am not waiting for anything from the West. I have no solution. I don't care. I say: You only speak of the rapist, never of the situation that surrounds him. I say: Don't claim innocence [*Ne vous déculpabilisez pas*]. Assume your responsibilities. French imperialism did not fall out of the sky ... I want you to know who we are and who you are, that's all."

These three overlapping attacks showed the fragmentation of the post-1968 far left around revolutionary criminality and the identity politics of homosexuality and race – all of which were mobilized to beat down feminist mobilization on rape. Though *Libération* was not alone on the Left in giving prominence to such anti-feminist views, the newspaper's editorial choices did not improve its image among some feminists, even though it did make some room for debate. Responses to these attacks were understandably incensed. On 28 March Josyane Moutet posed a battery of "questions to Pierre Goldman."[22] To his embrace of despairing marginality, she replied that feminists were despairing of leftists who were unable to come to terms with sexual violence. The erroneous notion that feminists were engaged in anti-liberational recuperation completely underestimated how their turn to law was strategic and situational. Moutet specified that she and Brigitte's other lawyers had not asked for a particular penalty, had not opposed that Eshak be let out on bail (which the judge had in any case denied), and had refused to make use of police testimonies. Claiming that the "dialectic of relations of force applied also to the women's struggle," Moutet emphasized the coherence of a strategy that sent "men back to their own organized violence" and ensured that "the law did not dupe" women. As for the suggestion that feminists were playing into the hands of the powers-that-be, she asked mockingly: "Are you afraid we are so stupid as to not also denounce this [judicial] machine?" – a machine structurally skewed, she acknowledged, along class lines. There was a qualitative difference between theft or attacks on institutions and sexual violence against women, crimes that point "in the most archaic direction of the patriarchal system."

The real high-point of the *Libération* acrimony followed Mohamed's intervention. On the next two days, 6–7 April, the newspaper published a dossier entitled "Rape or Violence?" in which Elisabeth Salvaresi wrote that women avoided playing the role of "rapists of the rapists" by allowing two masculine regimes – sexual violence and criminal justice – to confront one another "until they notice our absence from their game." The "violence" of the debate between feminists and "certain so-called leftist men" showed the "half-peace" that reigned between the sexes. "There is between them and us," Salvaresi concluded regretfully, "a gap of desire and of reality greater than at other times." Paul Roussopoulos wrote that the "editors of *Libération*" made a huge "error" in believing that the French justice system was a monolithic block to be denounced out of hand. Pierre Goldman's pardon for a murder conviction demonstrated the self-corrective capacity of legal systems, and Goldman himself was caught between the *hors-la-loi* status he claimed for himself and the fact that he had participated in the system in order to seek his release (having appealed his case, relied on lawyers, and accused the police themselves of having acted *hors la loi*). Goldman's "despair" was thus "theoretical," said Roussopoulos, and in performative contradiction with his actions. The *Libération* controversy, the Left's "crisis of conscience," was in the end a "museum debate" over the dusty and dried idea that French justice needed to be attacked in its totality. Men on the Left needed to face up to the poverty of their own philosophy. Roussopoulos cautioned: "*Libération* [should] not respond to me by saying that it is feminist because it sometimes grants a page to the problems of women. And the men's page? Don't look for it. It's the rest of the newspaper."[23]

On 7 April Odile Dhavernas, a lawyer with the same leftist legal defence fund as Koskas, the Mouvement d'action judiciaire, attacked her colleague's "odious act" during the March 21st trial. To Koskas's question published in *Libération* as to why women claimed the "privilege of indignation," Dhavernas shot back that she wondered why women were granted the "privilege of rape." Rape was not an "expedient means" of sexual satisfaction, it was an affirmation of "power over another," a "revenge" that had nothing to do either with desire or with enjoyment/pleasure [*jouissance*]. Koskas's suggestion that rape derived from the "irrepressible impulses of men" was abhorrent. Dhavernas said that women wanted "to have the support of [their] male comrades" in the women's movement, but if, like Koskas, men acted like "enemies," feminists would appropriately defend themselves.[24]

Thierry Lévy entered the argument by writing that feminists "disqualified themselves as lawyers and militants" when they made a criminal defendant, already in a position of weakness with respect to the law, into the "physical target of a criminal politics of elimination." They had the "gall" to try to enforce a "repressive" law and then to say that they were not opposed to letting the accused out on bail. Worse still, the "stain" of rape on the victim "was nothing when compared to that which judicial debates inflict." The rape victim, already having suffered physical and emotional trauma, would be submitted to a "thorough examination" in the courtroom that would border on "dry pornography" and would call into question whether or not "her body, her pleasure, her secrets belong to her."[25] Finally, Hélène, a judge "in training," said that she herself was outside the law, a feminist working within legal institutions in despair at the prospect of "one day [applying] this 'phallic law.'" At the base of this contradiction and despair was "a hole that emits only an infinite silence." Although other interventions followed throughout the rest of April and into the following months, one of the last comments on the Eshak trial was made in late May by Brigitte herself in an open letter addressed to Koskas. After picking apart some of his more outrageous statements, she concluded that "if repression won't improve relations between men and women, the actual state of affairs will certainly not do the job!"[26]

The *Libération* debate had the effect of placing the issue of rape more openly on the map of public discourse, and in the fall of 1977 the discussion reached a certain critical mass. High-publicity trials continued; mainstream newspapers like *Le Matin* and *Le Monde* published multipart series on the issues of sexual violence; television documentaries and roundtables appeared.[27] Broader debate on rape forced to the surface many cultural "a priori," or predispositions, which form even today part of the social imaginary: the presumed connection between rape and a permissive society (rape is more prevalent or more visible); rape as an "inevitable" consequence of irrepressible male instincts or as a socially determined phenomenon; rape as one end of a continuum of daily sexual aggression and harassment; and rape as an age-old problem receiving long-overdue and, at the very minimum, appropriate attention.[28]

Such mainstream debates set the scene for the Aix trial in May 1978 and the introduction of new legislation in June. Significantly, also in early 1978, some feminists previously committed to bringing rape cases to trial were having second thoughts. The strategy of trying rape cases before the Cour d'Assises as a means of getting the crime taken more seriously seemed to be getting out of hand. As the numbers of trials and the severity of sentences both increased, the justice system showed that it had a logic of its own that operated independently of feminist involvement. Feminists were upset that their discourse had been usurped by the judicial establishment. A state prosecutor, for instance, had said at one trial: "Think of your wives, your daughters." As one woman noted, he had spoken "in the name of women and their dignity, in order to hold on to the most reactionary and repressive discourses." As Picq notes: "The judicial machine was launched. It could not be stopped. Women wanted to use justice, and it used them. The campaign against rape would be the alibi for repression, fuelling the discourse of security."[29] *Libération* commented at the time: "No matter what the intentions or jurisdictions, the judicial machine never puts rape on trial. Only the rapist."[30] Martine Storti summed up her ambivalence upon the sentencing of an Algerian immigrant, Lakdhadar Setti, to twenty years in prison for rape, a judgment that feminists and their supporters had protested was too severe.

> I had neither the desire to renounce my and other women's struggle, nor the desire to continue in the same way, faced with this double wall of repression and the reinforcing of institutions. [At Setti's sentencing] this was the wall I hit, and I no longer know today how to move on ... We are also fighting against incarceration. And nevertheless, would I have resented it on Wednesday if Setti had been freed? There's no lack of contradictions. In my mind. In reality. In the movement feminists have embarked upon for their liberation. A struggle lived, precisely, as the most contradictory. But we have chosen to never leave ourselves shut up in a unilateral political line or discourse. Today, our struggle against rape, directed with seriousness and emotion, is at an impasse.[31]

Paradoxically, the moment of impasse from one point of view was also the moment at which rape was taken most seriously by mainstream society, a fact reflected in the Aix trial and in the new legislation.[32] If 1978 revealed fissures among feminists, it also marked the moment at which a certain campaign against rape achieved its fought-for and sought-after legitimacy.

18

Boy Trouble: French Pedophiliac Discourse of the 1970s

A final ingredient in the French sexual-political mix that brought accusations of French feminist moralism involved sexual relationships between adults and minors. The theme of "intergenerational" sex has been such a recurrent fixture of recent European and North American public culture as to have become a genuinely historic phenomenon. This has particularly been the case in light of the Marc Dutroux scandal in Belgium in 1996, accusations of pedophilia made against Daniel Cohn-Bendit in early 2001, and the priest-child sex crisis in the American Catholic Church in 2002. Acrimony on this theme, ranging from understandable outrage to hysterical and paranoid polemic, can be historicized in a broader context. Setting aside the obvious points that adult-minor sexual relations have found various forms of legitimacy since the Greeks and that societies continually wrestle with the sexuality of children, open debate on pedophilia has been widespread since the 1970s, especially in gay male circles.[1] Advocates of intergenerational sexual relations have often focused their attentions on how law governs the spaces where children, adult society, and sexuality intersect. Calls for reform of the legal regimes covering adult-minor relationships have frequently been argued on the basis of their "pedagogical" value, a rhetoric that clearly references the model of "Greek love."[2] The issue of consent finds itself sandwiched between a liberational notion that claims the denial of childhood sexuality to be repressive, and a pedagogical notion that finds adult-minor relations to be educative. The theme of "power" often seems elided, a point that feminists have championed for some time.[3] Gender differences have played out decisively in the articulation of positions toward pedophilia.

During the 1970s, calls for legitimizing intergenerational relations were taken seriously by eminent figures on the French intellectual-political Left.

An eccentric masculinist rhetoric of intergenerational relations, native to the sexual liberation movements of the 1970s, held that the sexuality of children and, among some, sex with children were frontiers of social liberation. Its popularity and occasional sophistication perhaps surprising to the outside observer, pedophiliac discourse focused on sexual liberation, pedagogy, and homosexuality (the long-standing French term for homosexual, *pédéraste*, has strong intergenerational overtones). Its advocates forcefully criticized the limits of legal limits – that liberational/juridical "impasse" mentioned above by Storti. Debate turned to the dilemma of consent and the reform of laws barring sex between adults and minors.

Two widely noted petitions published in the first half of 1977 exemplified the rhetorical power of arguments for the decriminalization of pedophilia. In January, *Libération* and *Le Monde* published "For Another Legislation on the Sexuality of Minors," written in support of three men who, after being held in preventive detention in French jails since 1973, were at last coming to trial for "indecent assault without violence on minors" [*attentat à la pudeur sans violence sur les mineurs*].[4] All three were accused of having had relations, played sexual games with, and taken pornographic photographs of a number of boys and girls under the age of fifteen. Declaring that "three years in prison is enough for caresses and kisses," the petition attacked the "disproportion" between the accused's pretrial punishment and the offenses with which they were charged. The petition furthermore highlighted a presumed disconnect between the law and the "daily reality" of French society. Although the document may well have reflected the ease with which those on the independent French Left at the time signed petitions on the fly, the names of the signatories spoke volumes: Louis Aragon, Roland Barthes, Simone de Beauvoir, Jean-Louis Bory, François Châtelet, Copi, Michel Cressole, Gilles and Fanny Deleuze, Jean-Pierrre Faye, Philippe Gavi, André Glucksmann, Félix Guattari, Daniel Guérin, Jean-Luc Hennig, Guy Hocquenghem, Bernard Kouchner, Jack Lang, Georges Lapassade, Michel Leiris, Jean-François Lyotard, Gabriel Matzneff, Bernard Muldworf, Anne Querrien, Christiane Rochefort, Jean-Paul Sartre, René Schérer, Philippe Sollers, and Jean-Marie Vincent, among others. By the end of the month, the three men in the so-called Dejager Affair had been sentenced to five years in prison. A journalist for the Trotskyist *Rouge* noted that, ironically, a rapid judgment had been reached only after the leftist press had taken up the cause of the accused and suggested that the minors had consented to the games and photographs.[5]

The second petition, an "Open Letter for the Revision of the Penal Code," was printed in *Le Monde* on 22 May 1977.[6] The previous month, as we saw in the preceding chapter, *Libération* had hosted intense and often outrageous debates on sexual violence against women and the pitfalls of "bourgeois justice." Pedophiliac discourse on "consent" coincided temporally and thematically with French feminist mobilization against rape. Also in April 1977, the Parti communiste français had finally come out in favour of decriminalizing homosexuality.[7] It was a dynamic convergence. The "Open Letter" that appeared in *Le Monde* called for a revision of the portions of the penal code that dealt with intergenerational relations. The three specific provisions in question were: the criminal charge of corruption of minors [*incitation de mineur à la débauche*], the minimum heterosexual age of consent of fifteen years, and the minimum homosexual age of consent of eighteen years. Again, the lag between laws on the books and the evolution of social mores served as the rationale for a change in legislation. In addition to many of the names mentioned above, there were new additions: Louis Althusser, Jean-Paul Aron, Jacques Derrida, Françoise Dolto, Michel Foucault, and Alain Robbe-Grillet. The petition was not mere fancy, since a state blue-ribbon panel, the Commission de révision du Code pénal, had been formed to oversee an updating of the entire penal code.[8] Foucault, in fact, had been invited to serve as a consultant to the Commission.

Though these notables of the French intellectual-political Left signed their support for the "Dejager Three" and for a reform of the penal code, a much smaller number of individuals made rethinking and decriminalizing intergenerational relations their *idée fixe*, their obsession. The most significant observation to make about this discursive constellation is the simplest: those doing the talking were exclusively men. They included Jean Danet, Tony Duvert, Michel Foucault, Daniel Guérin, Guy Hocquenghem, Georges Lapassade, Gabriel Matzneff, and René Schérer.[9] Granted, the theme of adult-minor relations had been present at the birth of the French women's and gay liberation movements. The famous twelfth issue of the Maoist publication *Tout!* (April 1971), which symbolically marked the emergence of the Mouvement de libération des femmes and the Front homosexuel d'action révolutionnaire, had made adult-minor relations contiguous with the general sexual liberation of young people. Of course, all articles on that topic had been written by men. "Marginal" or alternative sexualities were widely legitimated in the far-left press in the decade after 1968. Guérin and Schérer were both members of the editorial collective of the mid-1970s cultural revolution rag *Marge*, where they published on man-boy relations between 1974 and 1976.[10] In October 1976, the magazine *Sexpol* printed a special issue on *Childhoods*. It treated prepubescent sensuality, the dilemma of parents having sex in the presence of their children, and how post-1968 sexual education was introducing new forms of repression. Sex with children was also the topic of a letter from a self-identified pedophile.[11] Child sexuality and sex with children appeared as sub-themes within more global counter-cultural and sexual-political mobilizations.

The status of the *desires* of children and youth lay at the heart of pedophiliac discourse, itself another facet of the philosophy of desire. Talk of children's desires thus subtended more generalized agitation around the liberation of desire. When Hocquenghem defended children's own "desire to be seduced," he touched upon a fantasy that would be remarkably popular in the mid-to-late 1970s. In 1974 Tony Duvert argued for the decriminalization of child love on the basis of a straightforward application of sexual liberation to an overlooked social class. Gabriel Matzneff called children willful "igniters" [*allumeurs*] since they liked "to please," and suggested that young people make passionate, ardent lovers since they had yet to succumb to the cynicism and detachment that can characterize adult relations. The handsome and smarmy Matzneff saw his own desires for children as a reversion to the polymorphism of his own childhood desires: "I was never so tormented by the thirst for caresses and kisses as when I was twelve or thirteen years old." This reversion represented a willful refusal to join the world of adults. Even those who were skeptical about a simple freeing of young desires, like Hocquenghem, Foucault, and Schérer, nevertheless placed children's desires at the centre of their analyses. Hocquenghem's suggestion, noted above, that children desire seduction needs to be set against his criticism of Duvert for making "the liberty of the child" into the "sufficient reason for sexual liberation." As we will see, Foucault, otherwise suspicious of talk of desire, raised the issue of a child's role in seduction, linking it to the important issue of consent, and Schérer's theory of the "puerile erotic" also smuggled children's desire back into the very "system of childhood" he criticized.[12]

Whatever the various commitments to a positive view of the desires of children, there was a more general consensus about the regimes of social relations aligned against them. Hocquenghem had mentioned adult-minor sex as one possible means of disrupting the Oedipal order of reproductive sexuality because it "inspired a particular degree of civilized concern." The notion that desire could subvert repressive civilization was related not only to *Anti-Oedipus* but also to Schérer, who turned to Charles Fourier as a resource in thinking about an "immediate" quasi-anarchistic contestation of "civilization." Civilization included everything that involved the order of normalization and normality: the family, politics, the state, the police, and institutions like schools. More provocatively, Matzneff viewed "adult society" as an order that held a claim of "exclusive use" with regard to children. Parents, teachers, police, judges, and so forth made children "untouchable" in a kind of age-segregated "caste" system: old with old, young with young. Such segregation – a buzzword in French pedophiliac discourse – had as its "cornerstone" the notion that the sexual expression of young people was "harmful and disastrous" to their development. Matzneff went to the extreme of saying that adults who were authorized to deal with children perpetrated a kind of violence that approached that of "sadists" and "ogres" who "rape and kill" and which was in the end "worse" than the "soft violence" of a "bill note that is slipped into a blue jean pocket or a panty." He reserved his harshest words, however, for mothers whose animosity to child-lovers such as himself he explained as the jealousy that older women felt when men found their daughters more attractive than themselves. The lesson to be learned was that the chances of seducing a child in a broken home were better than in a tightly knit one. Matzneff's troubling rhetoric and sensibility disturb the attempt to associate him with Hocquenghem and Schérer's more sophisticated theorizing, even if such linkages are historically sound.[13]

Among the many facets of "civilization" to be undercut by intergenerational sex, education and pedagogy were singled out for attack. They seemed the strongest points of convergence for linking male homosexuality, children, and social institutions in 1970s France. The eighth issue of *Tout!* (February 1971) had published an article by a substitute teacher who had been fired when he decided to "let the children do whatever they wanted," allowing their sexuality to "express itself, even physically" as part of an "experiment in non-pedagogy."[14] The March 1973 special issue of *Recherches*, the journal directed by Guattari, entitled "Three Billion Perverts," addressed homosexuality and pedagogy in four different ways: the relationship of homosexuality to institutions; an analysis of a homoerotic Boy Scout cartoon; a petition, signed by activists at the experimental University of Vincennes, in support of a high-school teacher who had been fired for being gay; and a discussion of the tension between pederasty and pedagogy and of the "very dangerous" notion of liberating child-child and youth-youth sexual relations that alone would rewrite adult-child segregation in a new way (i.e., Matzneff's "caste").[15]

The most thorough analysis of the pedophiliac/pedagogical complex was made by Schérer, or rather, at his intersection with Hocquenghem. Schérer had been the younger man's high-school philosophy teacher and first amorous relationship. He had joined Hocquenghem at the Front homosexuel d'action révolutionnaire, and they had both taught at the University of Vincennes during the early and mid–1970s. In 1976 they co-authored a controversial issue of *Recherches* entitled *Co-ire: album systématique de l'enfance*, based in part on Schérer's Vincennes seminars on childhood.[16] When Hocquenghem's last book was published posthumously in 1994, Schérer wrote an affectionate postface invoking their relationship, and he continues today to discuss his own positions in relation to Hocquenghem's.[17] Thus it was with some measure of personal- erotic familiarity that they wrote on pedagogy and intergenerational relationships.

In a review of Schérer's *Emile perverti* (1974) and Duvert's *Le Bon sexe illustré* (1974), Hocquenghem argued that "since Rousseau" pedagogues have been "obsessed" with eradicating the pervasive sexuality of the school environment.[18] A mutually segregating – for adults and children – "system of childhood" has developed. Although "pedagogy and pederasty grow from the same tree," the two branches have offered different possibilities. Pedagogy, instituted by Socrates and exemplified by Rousseau, subjected the child to a disembodied "surveillance-viewing" [*surveillance-vue*] by the "weak and warped body" of the teacher.[19] The bodies of the student and teacher were separated and segregated, a "renouncing master" facing an "ideal child." Pedagogy consisted in the transfer of a "disincarnated" *logos* between them. Knowledge was thus a "deflection" of the pederastic aspect of the pedagogical relation. Haunted by sex on all sides, that de-sexed relation has become *the* template for other non-familial relations between adults and children.

Hocquenghem concluded his review by foregrounding the Deleuzo-Guattarian aspects of Schérer's project of dismantling the system of childhood. In order to find "a 'pederasty' finally cleared of the pedagogical perversion" and "to weave a multitude of transversal, non-pedagogical relations on cleared grounds and bodies," the "cut" of child and adult had to be mended. This reparation had nothing to do either with one's so-called inner child or with a recovery of lost innocence. On the contrary, one must, "re-establish the continuity of what was cut, reopen the floodgates of these intensive and *intuitive* fluxes that have bifurcated in compensation for the belief that the child and the adult were separated ... To circulate [*faire passer*] intensities and not ideas is the beginning of the struggle against pedagogy [of] the intuitive, non-segregating drift ... the vast tide of a re-found unity." To reduce this position, in Freudian language, to a reversion to infantile, polymorphous perversity – or in Lacanian language, to an imaginary search for an elusive Real – would betray Hocquenghem's Deleuzo-

Guattarian meaning. It seems, however, a reasonable judgment. Despite important qualifications, Hocquenghem and Schérer came close to Duvert and Matzneff's affirmation of child desires when it came to the subversion of normalizing pedagogy.

Schérer followed *Emile perverti* and *Co-ire* with ruminations in the same vein: *Le Corps interdit* (an essay collection co-authored with Georges Lapassade) (1976), *Une Erotique puérile* (1978), and *L'Emprise des enfants entre nous* (1979).[20] The latter two works completed his portrait of the social status of childhood and the logic of adult-child relations. Aiming straight for the heart of pedagogical thinking, Schérer contended not only that children were treated as potentialities, persons in formation, but also that as little-big-people, children and childhood played a functional role in the maintenance of social order. The child had a specific social function as a "pivot" and "social organizer" in the ordering of those *intensities* and *intuitive fluxes* mentioned by Hocquenghem. In the same way that psychoanalytic "familialism" had channelled and ordered Deleuze and Guattari's "desiring machines," the child had a familial and pedagogical function for the maintenance of social order. This functionality had become apparent in contemporary discourse about children's rights, especially in the debate on whether a child could consent to an amorous relationship.

There was thus a curious coincidence between the educational/pedagogical regime of *Bildung* and a juridical regime that spoke of the "rights of children" in terms of consensual contract. To Schérer's mind, the paradox was that, on one hand, children were considered "legal subjects" [*sujet du droit*] inasmuch as they were protected by law as non-consenting agents, but on the other hand, they were defined as "incapable" of being full juridical subjects because of their status as social works-in-progress. We will see with Foucault how objections to the language of rights and consent served as the *terminus ad quem* for arguments by some advocates of adult-minor relationships. Schérer was bothered by two different kinds of talk about children: first, the rhetoric that children needed "rights" as if they were "in a universal state of servitude"; and second, by an optimistic appraisal of "sexual liberation." The latter, *pace* Duvert and Matzneff, failed to account for the possibility that liberalizing social norms might involve rewriting norms at other levels. In other words, widespread acceptance of childhood sexuality was a prelude to its re-canalization – the more one talked about sex, the less one said.[21] In Schérer's half-Fourierist/half-Deleuzo-Guattarian view, the normalizing connection between juridical and pedagogical registers hinged on the fact that the social order was the order of discourse and representation.

Very much in step with the predilections of 1970s French theory, Schérer contrasted this social order with a "puerile erotic" and a "passional universe" that were "outside" or "indifferent to" discourse. The prediscursivity of children's experience, that is, its not-fully-formed nature prior to entry into the adult social and political world, held liberational potential. As Fourier had maintained, childhood was a time of *gourmandise*, a period of "transition" that did not completely obey the "civilized" order. Though he was careful to point out that he was not advocating a view of the child as an "essential being," Schérer did not completely escape the ironically Rousseauan position that set a pre-social "good" child up against the corruptions of the "bad" social order. In fact, Schérer's thorough attempt to extricate himself from the Rousseauan-pedagogical position in *Emile perverti* could be seen as a troubled dialogue – troubled for the very proximity of his position to a "naturalism" against which he was arguing. In any case, Schérer had to admit that the passion of the child could be evoked by terms such as "essential being" or the German, *Grund*, or ground. A child's passion showed an "inconsistency" and "versatility" that revealed an "incommensurable liberty" – "disordering ... subversive ... erotic ... [and] irreducible to all discourse." Lest this seem like a happily romantic, utopian outlook, Schérer gingerly phrased the child's "puerility" as the "affirmation of simulacra" – signs without reference, meaning without *logos* – and as a "reversal of Platonism."[22]

Notwithstanding this flourish, the endpoint of his analysis was to rework a role for the "pederast," or in Fourier's language, the "ambiguous ones" [*des ambiguës*]. Pederasts were ambiguous because they played the role of "pivots" between the child and adult worlds, since they too (like children) broke down fixed relations and predetermined roles: such "characters ... constantly established the transitions and accords between otherwise divergent classes according to age or disposition in the social order." The virtue of pederasty, concluded Schérer, was the fact that it will never be a generalized social fact or role. Its very lack of generalizability showed how it opened up a way of speaking about the sexuality of children that had nothing to do with the language of "rights" and "consent." Borrowing Jean-François Lyotard's notion of a "politics of incommensurables," Schérer contrasted "a non-Euclidean political space" to politics with more ordinary geometric proportions. A "topological justice" might satisfy a kind of freedom based on "attraction" in ways that rights talk never could. As he had concluded a discussion of Fourier some years earlier: "The revolution can *also* be attractive. In fact, in order *to be*, it must be attractive."[23]

Joining the attack on pedagogized child sexuality, in his own oily way, Matzneff targeted what he called "*philopédie*." "I am horrified by pederasty with pedagogical pretensions," he wrote: "One can caress a young boy without believing oneself obliged to give him a math or history lesson in the half hour that follows." But his personal and practical accounts of his own experiences – vainglorious writings that suffered from the stylistic excesses of someone who takes himself too seriously – tended toward the self-contradictory. He could slip from a discussion of his "Don Juan-esque nature" to the claim that "love is at the antipodes of the vampire egoism of Don Juan-ism." So instead of an anti-pedagogical version of pederasty, Matzneff displayed a contradictory non-pedagogical pedagogy, which nevertheless had certain lessons in mind. He was the author of what might be called "pedophilia rightly understood." And what needed to be understood in his view was that pederasty was about love not violence. Constitutionally incapable of seeing himself as doing any wrong, he was utterly convinced of the transparency between his motives and acts ("I have never wrested the least kiss, the least caress, by either ruse or force"). In a kind of odd Christian metaphysics of incarnated "flesh" and corporeal love, he distanced himself from "ogres" who abuse children by saying that he was "one who wakes people up" [*éveilleur*]. Waking up young people meant introducing them not only to sexual pleasure but also to sexual love. Matzneff's vision of love bizarrely combined traditional elements like fidelity and "the leap" with the hard-knock lessons of "love 'em and leave 'em." The great tutorial his young lovers received dealt with autonomy – by leaving them or encouraging them to leave him, he rationalized that he gave them the gift of themselves. Young people who had the great fortune of having been with him left "happier, freer, more *realized*." He called this kind of relationship a "special paternity" and offered it as a clear alternative to the familialism he detested.[24]

In part because he wanted to distinguish himself from pedophilia *incorrectly* understood, Matzneff favoured a reform of criminal law that dealt with sexual matters. So-called "ogres" should be punished because they gave well-intentioned pedophiles like himself a bad name. He had to admit that among the many pedophiles he had met, few were "Socrates."

> Too many pedophiles are tricksters; they lie to kids, they present themselves as they are not, they use pick-up methods that are extremely dishonest and cynical, justifying the kind of complaints made by feminists who identify pederastic seduction with rape. Pederasts certainly have nothing in common with sexual sadists, but they frequently behave like abusers, and to abuse means not only to deceive and to fool;

to abuse equally means to rape. As much as pedophiles mystify children, they incur similar reproaches and don't have the right to be indignant about it.

Legal reform was needed, Matzneff claimed, because repressive laws were partially responsible for reprehensible behaviour: "The day we are free to love those who we love, we will love them better." Although at one point Matzneff referred to a "we" (himself, Schérer, Hocquenghem, and Foucault) engaged in a "fight" for the amendment of articles 330, 331, and 356 of the penal code; he did not want to go too far in the revision of criminal law. Legalizing intergenerational relations would first of all not address the important pseudo-religious fact that love was a "perilous adventure" and a "leap into the unknown." Furthermore, as Matzneff admitted, he felt in "transgression like a fish in water." He preferred the impasse of being outside the law to legal legitimation. More toleration and liberalization, yes, but not so much as to spoil his savoury transgressions: "The day we see, in magazines, in the cinema, in the street, everywhere, men or women kissing twelve-year-old kids on the mouth, it will doubtless amuse me much less to pick up *les minettes et les minons*." Though Matzneff could eke out a critical insight into the regime of Republican law – "the love of the less-than-sixteen-year-old reigned until the French Revolution" and so-called progress had been a downhill slide ever since – Michel Foucault brought a slightly more nuanced reflection to bear on the juridical impasses of adult-minor sex.[25]

It would be a considerable understatement to say that Foucault's mid-1970s-to-early-1980s history of sexuality project reflected his contemporary ambience as much as it made historical claims about earlier periods. Foucault obviously expressed and added significantly to the sexual politics of that decade. It is by no means an exaggeration to claim that child sexuality lay at the very origins of his history of sexuality project. In his 1974–75 Collège de France lectures on "The Abnormals," he first discussed sexuality as a separate issue, focusing on the late-eighteenth-century emergence of the medico-disciplinary figure of the "onanist." New concerns about masturbation emerged at the same time as the "appearance of the sexual body of the child."[26] Children and sex were thus an integral part of Foucault's projected six-volume enterprise, of which only three volumes were published. In the first volume, *La Volonté de savoir* (1976), he claimed that the "pedagogization" of children's sexuality exemplified the proliferation of talk about children and sex since the eighteenth century, a proliferation accompanied by the simultaneous repression of sexuality.[27] This claim, however, can be read contextually and symptomatically; it said as much about the 1970s as it did about the eighteenth century. The same holds for the second volume of the *History of Sexuality*, in which Foucault differentiated the cases of sexual girls and boys; and also in the third volume's final section on "boys," where he described how the normative heterosexual reproductive couple borrowed from and supplanted the male pederastic relation, establishing an "order of things which is still ours today."[28] In addition to the light it sheds on earlier historical periods, the sexuality project says a great deal about 1970s France with an almost journalistic immediacy (wrapped, of course, in Foucault's smoggy rhetoric). Foucault himself often referred to his work as a "history of the present." In the context of one of his ambiences – and Foucault was a man of many ambiences – one can perhaps see why he took some of the positions – and made some of the omissions – that he did.

Some of Foucault's few direct comments on the pedophiliac discourse occurred in the spring of 1977 and the spring of 1978, in the context of the possible reform of the penal code with respect to sex and children. Two roundtable discussions – one with David Cooper, Jean-Pierre Faye, Marie-Odile Faye, and Marine Zecca; the other with Hocquenghem and Jean Danet – were significant for their direct handling of the question of sexuality and the law. They are even more important for the ways they join children's sexuality to the question of rape, and thus to a partial feminist perspective. The first discussion took place on 12 May 1977 and was published that October; it was framed as a debate on psychiatry and penalization. Foucault himself raised the problem of sex and legality, explaining that he had just received a number of written questions from the Commission de révision du Code pénal. Dismissing censorship as a non-problem (presumably for the reason, stated later in the dialogue when discussing the social "reformers" of the eighteenth century, that "private life" has "nothing to do with legislation"), Foucault declared: "There are two areas that for me present a problem. One is rape and the other is children." Clearly intending to provoke the two women discussants – Zecca and Faye – he suggested that rape might very well be punished as violence removed from any consideration of sexuality, as if there were "no difference, in principle, between sticking one's fist in someone's face and one's penis into their vagina." Zecca's objection to this prodding led him to conclude that sexuality had a "preponderant place" on the body; it was set apart and given particular legislative protection.[29]

Against this speculation, Zecca and Faye raised forceful objections about sexual violence against children – particularly against "little girls," says

Faye – claiming that such acts mixed sex and violence in ways that could not be cleanly separated. At this point Foucault shifted gears, admitting that rape could be "defined fairly easily" as "non-consent" and "physical refusal of access" – although the vague *refus physique d'accès* implied that a simple "No" was insufficient. He then launched into his "second question": children. The primary issue for Foucault (and he presented it more as a question than as an entrenched position) was the difficulty of distinguishing between rape and seduction. That a child could be an active agent in the situation of seduction – a situation presumed to be a two-way street – raised the dilemma of consent. Although perhaps intending only to provoke, his reasoning on this point was abysmal. In response to Faye's repeated assertion that between adults and children there was a structural "inequality that is difficult to define," Foucault responded: "I'm tempted to say: from the moment that the child doesn't refuse, there is no reason to punish any act." Digging himself in deeper, he further claimed that even persons in positions of "authority" could not make a child "do what he or she doesn't really want to." In a quintessential expression of exhausted anti-familialism, perhaps indebted to *Anti-Oedipus*, he claimed that one exception was the domineering authority of parents, especially wicked "stepfathers." It troubled him that "the legislation concerning the rape of a child" gave authority to the parents, who "usually" turned that power and used their children against other adults. Foucault completely passed over the potential for risks and distortions outside the family, and so too, outside law. Oddly, at this moment Foucault was relatively open to the prospects of reform and saw himself as asking the tough questions. "People may ask why I've allowed myself to get involved in this – why I've agreed to ask these questions ... But in the end, I've become rather irritated by an attitude, which for a long time was mine, too, and which I no longer subscribe to, which consists in saying: our problem is to denounce and to criticize; let them get on with their legislation and their reforms. That doesn't seem to me the right attitude."[30]

It was thus in a very different spirit that Foucault, almost a year later, on 4 April 1978, joined Hocquenghem and Danet on a radio roundtable broadcast on France-Culture: "The Law of Sexual Decency" [*La Loi de la pudeur*].[31] Not only did this moment precede the highly publicized rape trial in Aix-en-Provence but it also coincided with a press campaign on child prostitution.[32] The density of contemporaneous convergences helps situate the discourse around children, sexuality, and the law. For Foucault and his interlocutors, it was a moment of dashed hopes. What had looked like a period of reform and increased legal toleration for homosexuals, and perhaps for the specific question of intergenerational relations, had undergone an abrupt shift, said Foucault, "in the opposite direction": the "over-all movement tending toward liberalism" had been "followed by a phenomenon of reaction, of slowing down, perhaps even the beginning of a reverse process." As Hocquenghem put it, the "liberal illusion" of reformed legislation had led to the emergence of "new arguments" about the categorical separation of adults and children. Those arguments allowed a new category of social behaviour to emerge (and with it a new class of criminal perpetrators, or "perverts"): sex with children was bad, but it was "worse when children were consenting." Danet made the same point, emphasizing the way in which emergent "subtle forms of sexual supervision" could coexist with old repressive legislation.[33]

Discussing the history of that legal regime and new forms of containment, Foucault suggested that the shift underway was from an earlier phase of sexual legislation operating according to vague laws on "decency" [*pudeur*] to the present definition and protection of certain "vulnerable populations." In other times, "acts" had been punished; now "individuals" were caught up in a juridical/medical regime in which psychiatrists and psychologists played key roles. Since the old "repressive hypothesis" was no longer convincing and the sexuality of children had to be admitted, childhood sexuality was made generically distinct from adult or fully developed sexuality. As distinct, it was off limits. If adults were sexual with children, they could be accused of imposing "their" adult sexuality. For their part, children needed to be "protected from [their] own desires," since they, too, might cross the border. To some extent, this diagnosis was premonitory, since 1980s and 1990s discussions of "child abuse" were to recycle sharp distinctions between *predators* and *innocents*. In an impressive rhetoric torrent, Foucault concluded that more or less everything had become "dangerous." Children were vulnerable and in danger, and they needed to be protected from dangerous adults who threatened them. Sexuality itself became a "roaming danger ... a threat in all social relations." And finally, these developments Foucault saw – from his critical, if still vaguely ethical position – as dangerous themselves: "I would say that the danger lay there."[34]

Following this presentation, the panel was asked a number of tough questions. The first cut right to the crux of the debate in 1977 and 1978. Given that feminists were focusing on rape and asking for penalization of that crime, how did Foucault, Hocquenghem, and Danet propose to build "strategic alliances" with them? Hocquenghem referred back to the May 1977 petition, "Open Letter for the Revision of the Penal Code," in which, he said, they had been "extremely careful" not to confuse "indecent assault without violence" [*attentat à la pudeur sans violence*] and "corruption of minors" [*incitation de mineur à la débauche*] with "indecent assault with violence" [*attentat à la pudeur avec violence*]. But such a distinction was clouded over when he next tried to separate the question of "rape in the strict sense," on which feminists were right to take a stand, and "reactions at the level of public opinion ... man-hunting, lynching, or moral mobilization."

Perhaps Hocquenghem had the campaign against child pornography, with its homophobic overtones, in the front of his mind. Be that as it may, in effect, he dismissed feminist recourse to publicized rape trials by foregrounding other social anxieties, completely missing the fact that, unless feminists appealed to public opinion, there could be no change in public policy and attitudes. Hocquenghem's comment was consistent with his long-standing irritation with the anti-male echoes of some feminist discourse. The limits of his capacity to form strategic alliances in the fight against "phallocentrism" emerged at the moment when he was unable to examine the macho dimensions of his own positions. With greater subtly, Danet sought to divide the questions of rape and pedophilia on the issue of consent. Consent was a courtroom discourse, but the courts applied the criterion of consent differently in rape and pedophilia cases. Warning that he did not mean to say that "consent is always there" for children, he stressed that: "with regard to rape, judges consider that there is a presumption of consent on the part of the women and that the opposite has to be demonstrated. Whereas where pedophilia is concerned, it's the opposite. It's considered that there is a presumption of non-consent, a presumption of violence." The "system of proof" operated under different assumptions in each case.[35]

This argumentative manoeuvre, however, could not handle the next direct question, which asked point-blank what age for consent should be allowed. Foucault skirted the question, admitting that it was in fact "difficult to lay down barriers." He commented instead on two underlying issues, the presumed impossibility of childhood sexuality being directed toward adults and the belief that a child was "incapable of explaining what happened and incapable of giving his consent." Against the latter prejudice, he declared: "A child may be trusted to say whether or not he was subjected to violence." Hocquenghem used somewhat stronger language, saying that consent was a "trap" and that "no one signs a contract before making love." The linkage of consent with contract (a point echoed by Foucault) was meant to short-circuit any project of a reform of the penal code. That the parties involved here had reservations about appeals to consent, contract, and law should be clear. Their own talk of consent, concluded Hocquenghem, was meant as a kind of short-hand to say that "there was no violence, or organized manipulation in order to gain affective or erotic relations."[36] But barring an appeal to a category of limit such as law, it is difficult to see how a lack of violence or manipulation could be assessed. Such was the confidence in the transparency of motives among certain French advocates of intergenerational relations, acknowledged "dangers" notwithstanding.

19

Desire Has Its Limits

The 1970s French discourse on pedophilia continued to move forward after the 1979 formation of the Groupe de recherche pour une enfance différente but hit a major setback in the Coral Affair of 1982–84.[1] Personalities such as Foucault, Guattari, and Jack Lang were accused of having sex with boys at a group home, Le Coral, outside Montpellier. Fake photographs and documents were circulated as alleged proof. Schérer, who called the controversy "an important moment in the modern legal system's general mobilization against pedophilia," was himself charged for "corrupting youth," but the charges were dropped. The early 1980s saw a marked decline in the public legitimacy of arguments for intergenerational relations. Newspapers on the Left, such as *Libération*, which had legitimated eccentric sexual debates in the 1970s, became less willing to do so. In the gay male community, the arrival of AIDS forced a reconsideration of sexual ethics. More broadly, a new rhetoric of "abuse" emerged in Europe and North America, abetted in part by the reassertion of cultural conservatism associated with Ronald Reagan, Margaret Thatcher, and, in a slightly different way, François Mitterrand.

The last point should be softened in light of specific circumstances: the years on either side of Mitterrand's 1981 election saw the passage of a series of progressive laws that took a liberalizing and equalizing stance toward sexuality.[2] The right to choose was reaffirmed in 1979, making a probationary five-year law permanent. In December 1980 the penal code's statutes on rape were updated for the first time since 1810. In August 1982 homosexuality was decriminalized and the minimum age of consent for all orientations lowered to fifteen. Legal liberalization with an eye toward equalization represented the institutionalizing of sexual mores that had evolved since 1968. Feminists and gay activists had played inestimable roles in changing the cultural and legal status of abortion, rape, and homosexuality in France.

French pedophiliac discourse in the 1970s was thoroughly masculine. That discourse fit into a more extensive pattern on the French intellectual-political Left. With a few exceptions, in that decade masculine power and masculinity were seldom the objects of self-critical analysis by French men, a fact that explains in part the delayed emergence of critical masculinity in France.[3] At the time, one more frequently saw hysterical and paranoid reactions to feminist criticisms of male power, violence, and desire. On another hand, limits to the liberation of child desires were to some extent drawn by feminists in terms of power and violence. The utter absence of these themes in 1970s French pedophiliac discourse speaks volumes. The writings of Schérer, Matzneff, and company appeared at the same time and within the same political field as feminist mobilizations around sexual violence. In fact, the overlapping of intergenerational discourse with sexual violence discourse was only one case of a series of conflicts between men and women on the French Left between 1968 and the early 1980s. Many male French leftists in the 1970s were slow to become self-critical about violence in general, often for "revolutionary" reasons. So too, older links between radicalism and criminality returned. To be sure, the inability of male leftists to consider the masculinist features of their own positions is neither new nor specific to France.[4] There are many examples of how men and women on the post-1968 French Left have responded to criticisms of masculinity, it seems to me, with "bad faith."[5] One might recall that until recently France had a law specifying castration as a capital crime.[6]

The full charge of feminist moralism came in December 1978 in the midst of the so-called *Détective* Affair.[7] In late November the government had decided to ban the sale to minors of the marginal "true crimes" magazine *Détective*, which, in an effort to attract a broader readership, had since the early 1970s featured accounts of sex crimes. Several members of the National Assembly had sought to ban the publication on the grounds that it degraded women. They appealed for censorship by the baroque "Commission Charged with the Surveillance and Control of Publications Destined to Children and Adolescents." In the almost predictable fallout in *Libération* and *Le Monde*, feminism in general was blamed (feminists had torn down *Détective* posters the previous month). The fact that some feminists availed themselves of the French judicial system on matters of sexual violence was conflated by some with the censorship measures, which in any case many feminists did not support. Some men interpreted both situations as signs of the "recuperative" defeat of radicalism. As Liliane Kandel commented soon thereafter: "The autumn of 1978 and the *Détective* Affair could well mark, after years of fascinated terror (or prudent muteness) another moment: the tentative resumption of the right of speech and judgment by men (of the "Left," indeed "feminists") on the women's movements. Sometimes at any price: there are old accounts to settle."[8] Serge July wrote an editorial in *Libération* entitled "It Is Forbidden to Forbid, Even for Women," in which he asked rhetorically: "Are certain feminists on the way to constituting the new embryos of new moral leagues under cover of the denunciation of sexism? ... Could they not become the pilot fish of a moral reaction?"[9] Bruno Frappat, long-time commentator on gay issues for *Le Monde*, published on the same day a reflection on "feminism and repression."

> Is the defence of the freedom of women and their dignity passing by way of increased repression? Certain French feminists give the impression of thinking so, as two of their recent campaigns attest. For many months rape cases have been the object of a vigilante surveillance on the part of a group of women ... More recently, a very short campaign against the biweekly *Détective* ... ended by the magazine being banned ... It is a question here of a change in strategy that has weighty consequences.[10]

By "strategy" Frappat meant the shift from agitation outside the "law of men" toward the law as an "ally." "If we don't watch out," he concluded, "the third step in feminist groups' strategy runs the risk of developing proposals for abusive laws in the radical sense of restricting certain liberties." Leftist anti-feminism seemed to be the zenith of a certain post-1968 disdain for law and the state on the part of the far left.

The election of Mitterrand a year and a half later, in May 1981, would force a new reckoning of various parties of the Left with the state, a reckoning that generated fresh contradictions and confronted other limits. The above-mentioned legislative measures, passed on the cusp of the Mitterrand era, instantiating shifts wrought by post-1968 sexual politics, reflected the "dialectic between law and social mores," which Gisèle Halimi, the feminist lawyer most often associated with the French right-to-choice and rape campaigns, says she long tried to pursue.[11] Françoise Picq has suggested that the 1970s witnessed the shift from the "pleasure principle" of May 1968 to the "reality principle" of progressive politics having to work within the limits of existing political institutions.[12] Although she cautions against taking such an analysis too far, Picq makes a relevant point.

To return to themes raised in the Introduction, we might again observe that the antinomian ethos of 1968, which involved in part the principle of utopian refusal, contained both negative-critical and positive-constructive moments: laws were broken in the name of promised liberation. In chapter 1 we saw several commentators note that 1968 had unleashed nihilistic forces. In the Mitterand years we see a transformative evolution fully at work more than a decade after the May events. For the negative-critical manner of relating to norms is not the same as the positive-constructive. *Don't tell me what to do!* is not the same quality of statement as *How shall we live?* The pursuit of "pleasures" and the confrontation of "realities" are analytically and politically distinct. Working out new sexual ethics required at a certain point engaging with conceptual and practical limits (such as the legal limits discussed in this section). The statement "It is forbidden to forbid" had indeed been a contradictory one.

On the issue of how sexual violence and intergenerational relations intersected juridico-legal frameworks, by the mid-1970s some people on the Left were willing to say that it *was* appropriate to forbid *in the name* of liberation. Negative-critical modes were thus explicitly supplemented by positive-affirmative ones. Responding to the question: Where and how were limits on liberated desire, sexual desires and also desires for liberation, to be drawn? required moving beyond some of the rigidities of far-leftism, whether appeals to limitless desire, violence, criminality, or the kind of anti-feminism represented by Serge July's own forbidding to forbid. It required, in other words, grasping an emergent consideration of ethics, ironically an unintended consequence – a "gift" – of 1968, according to which the normative was not entirely a weapon of repression. This last view, for instance, pointed toward the notion of "moral panic," which tends to equate norms with normalization and in which valorized transgressions are tragically integrated by monolithic, dominant systems (like religious or middle-class morality).[13] The encounter by 1970s radicalism with the "reality principle" meant in essence struggling with the fact that the normative may be an inescapable social and conceptual field.

One protagonist from this story, Cathy Bernheim – feminist, former member of FHAR, and friend of Hocquenghem – sees in the charges of feminist moralism during the 1970s a failure to appreciate what the sexual revolution promised women such as herself.[14] In her view, the discourse of "anti-moralism" expressed male desires for limitless desire, a refusal to admit the ethical boundaries that began where desires went too far. In the case of sexual violence and exploitation, for example, desire was inseparable from power. In general, desire had its ethical limits:

> It was always very clear to me that social actors are moral actors. If not, we find ourselves in societies in which all is permitted and all is possible. For me it was extremely clear, and I think it was clear for many among us. But then we were taken up into the rhetoric that said, "You are moralists." For me, I was also clear that I was not going to bend over backwards in order to say that I was right. No, I knew that there must be a certain ethics [*morale*] in society and that we need to have certain actions and acts that we do not accept. I also had a strong perception of the constraints that society imposed on women. For example, when one spoke of sexual misery, I always recalled that the worst sexual misery faced by human beings in our society was that of women and not men.

The tricky part, she conceded in reference to a book by Jean-Marie Domenach, was (and remains) to articulate "an ethics [*morale*] without moralism," to find a way between a general order that is imposed on others and the articulation of an ethics that "people give themselves."[15] Where such a challenge touches upon desire and power in the form of violence, as the chapters in this section have suggested, it seems that at some point ethics must involve the state and politics in a mundane sense.

This is not to say that the law offers easy answers; on the contrary, it creates further dilemmas. Here, skepticism about juridical institutions on the part of some feminists and male activists was well founded. As Michel Foucault said at the time, everything is dangerous: not only the knowledge-power regimes of law and justice but also the fantasy of a total liberation that denies the very constraints upon which the possibility for even partial liberation depends.[16] The calculus of relative dangers demands a vigilance against inflexibility and the courage to draw limits where such limits are needed. One of the overall accomplishments of the sexual politics of the 1970s was to have sought out the possibilities of desire within and against its perimeters. More specifically, the paradox of feminist "moralism" reached in two directions at once: toward the law as a limit and toward the limits of the law. Thus did the ambiguities of relying on the state as one front of liberation become clear in the campaigns against rape in 1976–78.

Significantly, it was during those same years that another conversation emerged that more directly shunned the state and party politics in favour of an explicit embrace of ethics. As a point of departure for our treatment in the next section of that pivotal ethical explicitness, we might give a last word here to a slogan that feminists wrote on banners and graffitied on walls in the mid-1970s: "Rape is an unacknowledged totalitarianism."

PART FOUR

When All Bets Are Off: Ethical Jansenism and the New Philosophers

True eloquence mocks eloquence, true ethics mocks ethics, that is to say that the ethics of judgment – which is without rules – mocks the ethics of the mind. For judgment is that which belongs to sentiment, as science belong to the mind. Finesse is part of judgment, geometry is part of mind. To mock philosophy is truly to philosophize.

Blaise Pascal (1670)

Philosophy of the casino, the "New Philosophy" evokes the roulette table, where the ball hesitates between the black and the red before being immobilized. Place your bets. The die is cast. [*Faites vos jeux. Les jeux sont faits.*] Certain "New Philosophers," like Christian Jambet, Guy Lardreau, and Michel Guérin, are more precise: "one must wager." The wager, ultimate and fundamental act of thought: old stratagem of defacement in the gaudy colour of the philosophical "new wave." Why this resurrection of wagering thought? What horse are these new gamblers of Minerva going to bet on?

François Aubral and Xavier Delcourt (1977)

And now, as for the entire socialist ideal: nothing but a clumsy misunderstanding of that Christian moral ideal.

Morality as a means of seduction. "Nature is good, for a wise and good God is its cause. Who, then, is responsible for the 'corruption of mankind'? Its tyrants and seducers, the ruling orders – they must be destroyed" – : *Rousseau*'s logic (compare *Pascal*'s logic, which lays the responsibility on original sin).

Friedrich Nietzsche (1887)

20

The Main Event

Did May 1968 fail? The very question is misleading. History is not a laboratory test, a machine, a business, an exam, or a bad student, all of which can indeed fail or be failed. History can seldom be judged with a simple thumbs up or thumbs down. Of course, it turned out that the expectations of the revolutionaries of 1968 in France as elsewhere were foiled. Many had expected a complete reorganization of the French university, the fall of the Fifth Republic, a sustained reunion between cadres and workers, and above all a proletarian revolution ... none of which came to pass. In retrospect, one can see another kind of writing on the walls than the graffiti that decorated the halls of the Sorbonne and the walls of the Latin Quarter. Within a few years the split between expectation and achievement (May had opened a portal (*la brèche*) that the far left was committed to forcing wide) mutated into judgments about success and failure or about rhetoric and reality.

Historically speaking, May's protagonists were proved "wrong" after the fact. As we saw in chapter 1, in 1968 and for several years afterward, many in France, including Raymond Aron, Charles de Gaulle, Georges Pompidou, and Raymond Marcellin, took as self-evident that the student/worker movement and then the far-left *groupuscules* posed a serious challenge to the stability of the Fifth Republic, the sanctity of property, cultural norms, and business as usual. That challenge may have been presented through chaos, violence, and disorder, but it was neither unreal nor inconsequential. It has become easy to forget how pervasive and upsetting – *bouleversants* – contestatory movements of the era in fact were. In France from 1968 to the mid-1970s protests actually increased in intensity as some activists courted violence before making terrorism the road generally not taken. Contestation also spread into unprecedented domains – as we saw, prisons in Part I, asylums or madness in Part II, and sexual politics in Part III. My contention has been that the significance of these ersatz sites of contestation, substituting institutions and interpersonal relations for labour and class as the "stuff of revolution," was not always apparent to the actors and actresses involved. Many *thought* they were sowing the seeds of another May, opening *la brèche*, or at the very least engaging in revolutionary politics. They were in fact contributing to a turn to ethics that took place through a revitalization of civil society and democratic politics. Revolutionary politics says that ethics can wait, that ethics is subordinate to the imperatives of history, struggle, and action, or that ethics consists of those very imperatives. Democratic politics says that ethics cannot wait and must be an integral part of the historical process; that declared ends can only justify means that are chosen after deliberation, reflection, and debate; and that violence is ultimately a deal breaker. The turn to ethics would in some corners eventually involve a rejection of politics altogether.

The transubstantiation of one kind of politics for another under cover of seemingly contiguous appearances was played out in many ways in different settings. One unifying paradigmatic question had to do with the meaning and direction of history. The militants of 1968 and far-left activists in groups like the Gauche prolétarienne believed that history was going somewhere and that they could influence it; the marxisant combination of historical laws (exploitation and class conflict) with voluntarist action (class consciousness and struggle) would yield results. But alongside – or better, within – this field of thought and action, guided by a coherent, not unproblematic philosophy of history, another relation to history appeared, less a fully articulated and systematic philosophy of history than an inchoate and anti-systematic anti-philosophy of history. We saw this alternative emerge in the activities of the GIP, which steadfastly refused to represent the meaning and direction of its own activities or those of prisoners. We also saw this anti-systematicity at work in Deleuze and Guattari's anti-Oedipal philosophy, which pushed the antinomian spirit of 1968 toward those directionless and elemental "desiring machines" (whose very depiction defied meaningful representation). This deliberate breakdown of a singular, unifying, totalizing, and meaningful philosophy of history was one of the great "achievements" of the post-1968 French far left. The direct democratic ethos of the age was unprecedented.

Not that this ethos was without its quandaries and problems. I have tried to raise some of them by critically portraying Deleuze and Guattari's problematic attempt to make madness into a primary lens for social analysis and political identity. Aspects of the ethos of 1968 obviously did not work out, but rather than being some sort of global failure, they may have embodied and contributed to a considerable achievement: a step down the democratic road. Is a democratic society not one in which no one point of view can represent the entire historical meaning of life in common? I do not mean to suggest that French democratic society does not rely on philosophies of history, such as Gaullism, Republicanism, and liberalism (the 1980s saw a revival of the last two). Rather, May 1968 unleashed dynamics that by the late 1970s had both disassembled a revolutionary philosophy of history from within and introduced alternatives to globalizing political philosophies of history in the form of ethically corrected politics or the complete substitution of ethics for politics. For ethics does not offer a bird's eye view; it is neither a politics nor a philosophy of history. Despite its disappointments, May 1968 turned out to be a "successful" revolution but not necessarily for the reasons one might think.

Consider the role of feminism and the acrimony over sexual violence that we saw in the previous section. Feminists had exemplified a broader development in instigating a movement away from treating the French state and its legal and juridical apparatuses as an enemy to viewing it as a potential ally. To have appealed to Republican law and the judiciary in 1968 or during the high-water mark of the far-left period (1968–74) would have been largely foreign to the "revolutionary" mindset. The Fifth Republic and the reigning social order both had to be overturned; anything less was "recuperation." But the foolhardiness of challenging the late modern state for its monopoly on political sovereignty, let alone its monopoly on legitimate violence, became clear. In a related way, the contradictions in which the libidinal Left – *les désirants* – was mired, especially in its advocacy of limitless desire and its tacit acceptance of intergenerational sex and sexual violence, were equally clear. Masculinist defence of revolutionary violence seemed archaic by the mid-1970s. Coherently, imaginatively, and given the circumstances, bravely, French feminists brought the issue of sexual violence into the public sphere and in so doing helped bring closure to the far left's questioning of the Fifth Republic's legitimacy. Their efforts played a significant role in a larger historical transformation and also acted as a metaphor for it: desire has limits, and the antinomian must face the law – in fact it is already defined in opposition, and thus in relation, to law. The acceptance of the Fifth Republic, however qualified, meant that for some '68-ers in the mid-1970s reform came to supplant revolution. Deradicalization had its benefits, and it was one wave that François Mitterrand would ride on his way to victory in 1981. Nevertheless, paradoxically, one of the costs of the mid-1970s de-radicalization of the French far left was a slowdown in social activism, a turning away from social action toward intellectual reflection, or to put it plainly, depoliticization.

One thing to be said for a coherent philosophy of history is that it can motivate. The Maoists had reasons for putting their shoes on in the morning. Even an anti-philosophy of history can motivate in this sense, insofar as a demand to act is implicit, as in the case of the GIP and to some extent with the "desiring machine" model (more problematically so in the latter). The MLF's pursuit of the emancipation of women expressed a historical vision that combined the particular and the universal in strategically potent ways. Mobilizing in "non-mixte" settings, it politicized the personal, and then sought recourse in Republican universalism when it was expedient to do so. Still, in the mid-1970s, the moment when May's "failure" became widely discussed, or alternatively, when its hidden and unintended "success" reached fruition, certain types of social action declined. *Les Années '68* drew to a close between 1973 and 1977. The last gasp of far-left activism was the strike at the Lip watch factory in the summer and fall of 1973, during which workers decisively rejected the meddling of outsider militants. After that, street theatrics and clandestine meetings became a much less significant feature of May's ethos as it extended into the next decade. To describe it more simply, mid-1970s deradicalization might be seen as a continuity of a project with a change of language (revolution to ethics) and venue (social action to reflection). Reflection only feels like a letdown to those who think they already have all the answers.

Curiously, deradicalizion also witnessed the emergence of a new contestation of the French state, its laws, and institutions. In a sense, this challenge came from "above" rather than from "below," from thinkers directing their rhetoric toward a new extra-statist humanitarianism as opposed to demonstrators confronting the police or lawyers pleading their cases. And yet this new metaphysical critique of politics can be said to have grown directly out of the populist and direct democractic movements of 1968. The New Philosophy phenomenon of 1976–77, a constellation at once intellectual, political, and *médiatique*, illustrated disappointments with 1968-era aspirations as well as the partial translation of those aspirations into other idioms. It reflected a dialectical rupture and continuity with *les années soixante-huit* and at the same time a symbolic collapse of grand philosophies of history, of which dialectical thought itself was a celebrated example. In short, in New Philosophy we see the explicit turn to ethics we have been anticipating in the course of this book. In 1976–77, that turn received its most public and controversial exposure. It was a coming out in multiple senses: the shift from an implicit fascination with ethics to an explicit obsession, the ceremonial entry of ethics into public debate, and the accusation that the New Philosophers were debutants of the worst sort. When they burst onto French newspaper pages and television screens in 1976 and 1977, these young, mostly good-looking former *soixante-huitards* were variously denounced as a superficial media phenomenon, a publishing *coup*, or a right-wing conspiracy. Their thinking was judged ephemeral and lacking rigour. Their anti-Marxist tones appeared facilely to equate Marxism with totalitarianism and to cast aspersions on the established Left, Communist and non-Communist alike. Nevertheless, the scale of the debate they inspired was extraordinary, and at least one commentator noted that no supposed intellectual movement had provoked such wide-ranging controversy since the existentialist fad of the late 1940s and early 1950s.[1]

The short version of the New Philosophers' rise to prominence, invented at the time and repeated since in most secondary literature, had it that Bernard-Henri Lévy, a young editor at the Editions Grasset, had published a number of works by his friends and then written an inaugural article in *Les Nouvelles littéraires* (10 June 1976), christening their collective project *la nouvelle philosophie*.[2] Lévy had attended the Ecole normale supérieure and studied under Louis Althusser. He had hovered around the rue d'Ulm Maoists and experienced the May events mostly over the radio. Finding himself again on the fringes of the Gauche prolétarienne (an author he later edited, Christian Jambet, had brought him to a Nouvelle résistance populaire meeting), he was more attracted to the *tiers-mondisme* of Régis Debray and consequently went to Bangladesh, on which he published his first book in 1973. He then found himself on the margins of the Parti socialiste after Mitterrand asked him to consult for the party on the then-trendy theme of *autogestion*. After a failed attempt to launch a journal (*L'Imprévue*) with Michel Butel in January 1975, his chief editor, Françoise Verny, invited him to edit two collections with Grasset – *Théoriciens* and *Figures* – which featured books by Jean-Marie Benoist, Jean-Paul Dollé, Michel Guérin, Christian Jambet, Guy Lardreau, Michel Le Bris, Philippe Nemo, Françoise Paul-Lévy, and Gilles Susong.[3] Dollé recalls that Lévy had approached him with an open-ended invitation:

> When he [Lévy] launched his collection, he said to me, "Do you want to put out a book?" Mine was the first book in the collection. And then he asked people close to him. It is true that at the time most people, the young philosophers, were still tied to their Althusserian moorings, Maoism, whatever. There was a kind of recruitment,

but among people who knew each other. What did they have in common? Nothing. Except that we knew each other. We liked each other. There was not a collective philosophical corpus, not even a political one.[4]

Two other co-conspirators whose works were published at Grasset, but not in Lévy's collections, figured prominently in discussions of the New Philosophy: Maurice Clavel and André Glucksmann. (The latter, former secretary of Raymond Aron, we have already met in dialogue with Michel Foucault in chapter 5). The short list of names most often cited as New Philosophers were Lévy, Clavel, Glucksmann, Jambet, and Lardreau. It is important to note that the last three had been members of the Gauche prolétarienne (Jambet and Lardreau were in charge of organizing high-school students) and that Clavel had been an older fellow traveller of the Maoists (he had co-founded the Agence de presse libération). Drawing on renewed interest in philosophy and dissidence, which was on the rise since the publication of Alexandr Solzhenitsyn's *The Gulag Archipelago* in 1974 and commentaries by Glucksmann (1975) and Claude Lefort (1976), Lévy allegedly invented the "school" of New Philosophy from whole cloth.[5] His own *Barbarism with a Human Face* and Glucksmann's *The Master Thinkers*, both published in the spring of 1977, were bestsellers.[6] (We examine these works more closely below in chapter 25.) The authors' 27 May 1977 appearance with Clavel on the literary roundtable television show *Apostrophes* seemed to confirm the suspicion that Lévy had masterminded a publicity campaign. From spring 1976 until summer 1977, the New Philosophy filled the airways and hallways of France as the purported new guard saw their books and their persons discussed at length by journalists, philosophers, media personalities, political party operatives, and even the president of the Republic. Remarkably, all was to be forgotten a short time later.

The emergence of New Philosophy as a seemingly coordinated and serendipitous publishing venture, media phenomenon, and public debate that took the pulse of a generational cohort and assessed the inheritance of May 1968 had everything to do with a convergence of interwoven circumstances. These conditions might be summarized in the following way. A number of books appeared that seemed in reviewers' eyes to share family resemblances. Momentum built via media publicity and debate in the public domain. Attacks on these books and their authors contributed greatly to the perception that there was a coherent movement called New Philosophy. In fact, the critique of New Philosophy was tantamount to creating the object it criticized – arrows finding their target after they had taken flight. Even the alleged New Philosophers attacked New Philosophy. In spite of this debate without a centre, one can indeed identify intellectual characteristics common to the milieu. A brief look at the similarities and differences between New Philosophy and French theory will help identify how the former led, via an attraction to Soviet and Eastern European dissidence, to a revival of philosophy and metaphysics as well as a turn toward ethics.[7] It is this last factor which makes the New Philosophers of lasting importance.

Most of the works considered within the New Philosophy field were published before Lévy's 1976 article in *Les Nouvelles littéraires*. Books by Jean-Marie Benoist (1970), Dollé (1972), and Lardreau (1973) had been the first signs of a reshuffling with respect to 1968-era paradigms and commitments.[8] Dollé's *Voie d'accès au plaisir: la métaphysique* (1974) was the first volume published in Lévy's *Figures* collection. Philippe Nemo's *L'Homme structural* followed in 1975, along with two works by Benoist and one each by Michel Guérin, Gilles Susong, and Clavel. Thus, when Jambet and Lardreau published their *L'Ange* and Clavel his *Dieu est Dieu, nom de Dieu* in the spring of 1976, the scene was well set for Lévy's June dossier.[9] Although one might debate the extent to which that dossier, organized more as a portrait of generational contrast than as a call to arms, was a publicity stunt, certainly the advertising-copy ring of the "New Philosophers" gave birth to the view that a coherent group had arrived with an intellectual and political agenda.

The public perception of an emerging and cohesive cadre was due to an accumulation of overlapping forces. François Hourmant has shown the mounting pressures that made the affair explode between Lévy's article and the early summer of 1977: in July 1976, Gérard Petitjean published an article on the "Nouveaux gourous" in *Le Nouvel Observateur*; Claude Mauriac wrote on the New Philosophy in *Le Figaro* in August; in the fall, articles appeared in *Le Point* on the "new oracles" and in *Le Monde* on the "new lost generation."[10] More books, by Jambet, Benoist, and Dollé, soon made their way to the stores, as did Françoise Paul-Lévy's critical work on Marx.[11] The true momentum, however, seems to have come from philosophical colloquia at the Théâtre Oblique (October), a radio series on France-Culture entitled "Philosophie aujourd'hui" (November), and another series on the "lost generation" (October and November), the last published under the same title by series host Jacques Paugam.[12] In October Grasset took out a full-page ad for Lévy's collection in *Le Magazine littéraire*.

A final important site of gestation was the Centre Beaubourg's "Philosophical Mondays" series, which ran from February 1977 to January 1978. Three different meetings were held during this time on "Representation and Power," "Desire and Law," and "The Reason of the State and the Rights of Man."[13] The very titles of these meetings speak volumes about the composition of 1970s French intellectual politics. The terms *desire* and *law* mirror exactly the debate discussed above in Parts II and III – from Deleuze and Guattari's *Anti-Oedipus* to the feminist reclamation of Republican law over sexual violence. The last Beaubourg meeting on the state and the rights of man evokes the tension we will see in this current Part between the logic of the state and the metaphysics of human rights. The New Philosophy affair was thus not only a localized event in 1976–77; it was also the high point of a drama that had been playing out since 1968. Commenting on the success of the Beaubourg meetings, Glucksmann noted: "The philosophical lectures at the Centre Beaubourg attracted more people than do political meetings – very interesting! An entire generation – that of '68 – has retained the capacity to be amazed. It has known activism; now it is reflecting."[14] Thus, when Glucksmann's *The Master Thinkers* appeared in April 1977 and Lévy's *Barbarism with a Human Face* in May – the two books at the centre of the contemporaneous media storm – an extensive debate was already underway.[15]

Though the New Philosophers' names were on everyone's lips in 1977, few had anything positive to say about them. "I think their thought is worthless," said Gilles Deleuze. Jean-François Lyotard published a mocking pamphlet, *Pagan Instructions*, on the "Clavel and Lévy affair." "Latest attraction: the *New Philosophy*," wrote Maria-Antonietta Macciocchi: "The newspapers are calling their *regression* a *renaissance*." Cornelius Castoriadis called them "diversionists," and Régis Debray wrote bitingly: "A joke cannot be refuted, except when it drags on and concerns a solemn topic. The 'new philosophy' has all the attributes needed to pass for the highlight of the season." Jacques Rancière isolated with some craftiness the "ultimate paradox" by which the New Philosophers ended up entranced by the "rhetoric" of the very Marxism they claimed to denounce. Henri Lefebvre made the remark, superb in its simplicity, that he could not tell what "concepts" the New Philosophers were proposing to use. Also hard on the New Philosophers for theoretical reasons were, among others, Catherine Clément, Nikos Poulantzas, René Schérer, Blandine Barret-Kriegel, Daniel Lindenberg, Jean-Marie Vincent, and Michel de Certeau. Many of these brief critical interventions were thoughtful, much more so than the most popularized polemic, *Contre la nouvelle philosophie* by François Aubral and Xavier Delcourt – a weave of quotations and invective that brought down the general level of debate.

In *Contre la nouvelle philosophie*, Aubral and Delcourt zeroed in on the fact that the "new gurus" were trendy, reintroduced metaphysics, juggled Christianity and leftism, and painted themselves as "inheritors" of May 1968. New Philosophy, they wrote, was organized around five "slogans": Marxism is a barbarism, everything is only discourse, one must escape the political conception of the world, socialists are imposters, and one must wager. That last term was indeed a unifying theme, as we will see in the next three chapters. The authors went on to suggest that the New Philosophers, disillusioned after 1968, had become spellbound by the question of unassailable mastery and the impossibility of rebellion. Driven to a bizarre crypto-Christian metaphysics, stealthily inflicted on the public in a media blitz, they destroyed the Left and gave birth to the New Right of the late 1970s (whose architect, Alain de Benoist, should not be confused with Jean-Marie Benoist). Aubral and Delcourt's attack was warmly received by the Parti communiste français, and the link between the New Philosophy and the political Right became *de rigueur*. In 1983, for example, Serge Quaduppani commented that the New Philosophy of 1976–77 and the New Right of 1979–80 were both media-era fashions rather than genuine intellectual movements. Though motives and tactics varied among those who decried the New Philosophy's facile substance and its annoying presence, many nevertheless shared something of Bernard Weisz's sense that all of this was a "new blah-blah-blah," a view that has since been repeated *ad nauseam* in literature on post-1968 French intellectual life.[16]

The voices of the "pub-philosophes" had even less in common than the array of thinkers aligned against them. One didn't have to say anything terribly specific about the New Philosophy to talk about it. "It is a curious custom in our Parisian province," Roger-Pol Droit wrote in *Le Monde*: "At fairly regular intervals a great confused and impassioned polemic comes to pass around a movement, a group, a current, to which one assigns a cohesion for the purposes of this ritual. ... To speak of *the* New Philosophy is to chase a phantom."[17] To be fair, not all the critical voices mentioned above reduced the parts to a questionable whole, even if the tendency to do so was in the air. The circumstance bore some parallels with the existentialist and structuralist "moments" in which generalization and criticism did much to cement bonds among disparate thinkers who otherwise argued among themselves. And yet the New Philosophers were distinctive because, appearing just as television censorship was being relaxed under Valéry Giscard d'Estaing, they participated in the first wave of a rapid shift from literary to media-based intellectual and cultural life.[18] Never before had a publishing venture and print, radio, and television media lined up so well; and the first stone thrown in a pond always seems to make the biggest splash. But the mediatization of intellectual life in mid-1970s France involved more than the sound bites of young Turks and the critiques of more thoughtful Left intellectuals. It involved the entire brouhaha – reductive, vague, polarizing, accusatory, and ubiquitous. Those who decried the phenomenon *were* the phenomenon.

Amazingly, among the most vocal castigators of New Philosophy were the alleged New Philosophers themselves, who rejected the suggestion that they had a coherent program. Dollé complained that the term was "idiotic" and that "there are no gurus," and Michel Guérin added that he was "completely estranged from this 'philosophical' affair" and that he was "clearly on the Left."[19] (We will see, below and in the next chapter, the extent of the political stakes of this debate.) Glucksmann, when asked by Bernard Pivot on the 27 May 1977 *Apostrophes* show if he considered himself a "New Philosopher," replied, "Absolutely not."[20] Lévy's regret that he had ever used the term was also evident that evening, but he made his clearest statement in the special issue of *La Nef* (early 1978) dedicated to the New Philosophy. His essay "The New Philosophy Does Not Exist" was published alongside Jambet and Lardreau's exasperated "One Last Time Against the 'New Philosophy.'" The latter wrote that the New Philosophy was a "fantasy produced by the same ones who fight it."[21] Now as then, one would be in good company in dismissing the New Philosophy phenomenon. That almost no one was happy with the New Philosophy debate at the time is underscored by later impressions of the affair. Verny, Lévy's boss at Grasset and according to Jean-Pierre Le Goff the inventor of the New Philosophy brand name, when asked in the 1990s what remained of the New Philosophy, responded dryly, "Nothing ... New Philosophy did not stand the test of time."[22] Also recently, Dollé has concluded: "Now? The New Philosophers? Nothing at all. The label has no meaning."[23] The New Philosophy controversy had no centre, and the judgment of history has been almost universally dismissive.

If fans of New Philosophy were few, and nothing remains of it, why even discuss it? There are some very good reasons. Although its real objects were usually mentioned only indirectly or tangentially, if at all, and its cultural significance was almost completely elided, it was not a debate about nothing. New Philosophy was epiphenomenal in important ways. In fact, its apparent nullity is part of what made it so historically significant. Animus usually conceals deeper meaning. Again, the content of New Philosophy, though frustrating and superficial, is of interest since it gave explicit and resounding expression to the 1970s ethical turn. That content amounted to more than the public debate around it, the momentum of the affair, and the criticisms and self-criticisms of the New Philosophers. Ethics became a resource to pursue and a problem to ponder. As we see in the next chapter, New Philosophy's contribution to the ethical turn had much to do with the immediate political climate of 1976–77 and the fortunes of an electoral coalition between the Communist and Socialist parties called the Union of the Left. The true cultural significance of New Philosophy – the depoliticizing turn to ethical dissidence against the alternative of the philosophy of desire – evoked older French intellectual traditions, in particular, Jansenism, in which the moral served as a *point d'appui*, a point of reference or support, outside the realms of history and politics. Thus, as well as exploring contextual considerations – the forces of media publicity, local political climate, and older cultural traditions – our story tracks the ways in which New Philosophy as an intellectual movement helped point the ethical turn into its home stretch. In chapters 22–24 we examine works by Maurice Clavel, Christian Jambet, Guy Lardreau, Bernard-Henri Lévy, and André Glucksmann. For the remainder of this chapter we consider New Philosophy's relationship to French theory, its return to philosophy against structuralism and the human sciences, and its embrace of the model of dissidence and rebellion over revolution. These characteristics constituted an explicit embrace of ethics.

While noting the international scale of the New Philosophy media phenomenon, Günther Schiwy in 1979 judiciously pointed out the filiation between French theory and the alleged new gurus.[24] His point is pertinent. Michel Foucault, Philippe Sollers, and Roland Barthes had written some of the few positive reviews of Glucksmann's and Lévy's writings, and Roger-Pol Droit's sensitive appraisal, published on 27 May 1977 in the midst of the hullabaloo, pointed out that Jacques Lacan was a serious reference for many suspected adherents, with the exception of Glucksmann.[25] New Philosophy seemed generally consistent with earlier structuralist emphases on the passivity of the subject in the face of constitutive linguistic, epistemological, ideological, and normative structures. Preoccupation with the themes of discourse, desire, power, and the unconscious similarly brought attention to the New Philosophers' debt to strains of French theory, as did their distrust of emancipatory politics and Marxism. Some of the New Philosophers had been students of Louis Althusser, and the shift from theoretical Marxism to abstract anti-Marxism was not much of a stretch. In fact, of the five characteristics of French theory discussed in the Introduction:

emphasis on language, suspicions about the unified self, doubts about historical progress, valorization of desire, and anxieties about power – only the second did not seem germane to New Philosophy since the self as ethical agent, resister, and dissident was to reappear in what Alain Touraine later called the "return of the actor."[26]

It is worth pausing on this filiation between New Philosophy and French theory, and on the way the theme of ethics was related to both.[27] Upon closer examination, New Philosophy helps us grasp similarities, divergences, and variations among strains of French theory. One sees a clear split between the *désirant* camp we saw in Parts II and III and the New Philosophers, many of whom, having been influenced by Louis Althusser, ended up closer to Lacan or Foucault than to Guattari, Deleuze, or Lyotard (the latter two expressed their ire in their critical reviews of New Philosophy). Significantly, the New Philosophers, like the philosophers of desire, focused on marginal and particularized resistance to macro-structures and totalizing systems. As we saw in Part II, in an extension and prolongation of the antinomian spirit of 1968, the philosophy of desire represented a rebellion against norms and limits of all kinds, a celebration of immanent machinations within the threshold of lived experience, the ethics of ethos, so to speak. The contradictions of this "anti-Oedipal" posture emerged in many places, notably the sexual politics we examined in Part III, where laws and limits were reasserted by feminists as checks on the manœuvrings of desire that offered no coherent response to the question of violence. The philosophy of desire had only stumbling answers to the ways power and barbarism could be combined, from sexual violence to the Soviet Gulag. Feminists had turned to the law and the state to provide a check and limit on the machinations of interpersonal desire; similarly the New Philosophers cultivated positions of a transcendent or transcendental limit on immanent desire. Both the feminist sexual politics we saw in Part III and the New Philosophers used universal categories in ways that the philosophers of desire found unpalatable. But whereas the feminist universalism I have chosen to emphasize pointed toward a universalism embodied in law and the Republican state, the New Philosophers articulated a supra-statist vision of limit and law; that is, human rights, humanism, morality – or ethics. Their animosity toward official, party, and state-centred politics was unambiguous: looking to the state – whether French Republican or Soviet Socialist – for salvation ran the risk of tyranny and totalitarian ruin. They thus represented another step in the historical dynamics of the era.

And yet, the New Philosophers maintained a relationship to the philosophy of desire, and thus a continuation of the spirit of '68 in their championing of marginal and particularized resistance, notably, dissidence (which we will discuss shortly). The attitude of the dissident reflected a continuation of the antinomianism of 1968: the rebel, the outsider, the critic, the *refusé* who said "No" to the reigning social, cultural, and political order. As Roger-Pol Droit put it, recalling the dispositions of the New Philosophers and many people in the mid-to-late 1970s: "We might not all agree on a positive, collective historical project, but we might agree on those things to which we are opposed."[28] The conflict between the New Philosophers and the *désirant* sensibility can in part be understood as a struggle over the meaning and significance of May's antinomian inheritance, a struggle between those who rejected appeals to transcendence or the transcendental and those who embraced those categories. One might understand in this light the New Philosophers' (with the exception of Glucksmann) general embrace of psychoanalysis, for which the notion of limit, even in the Lacanian version of "the Other," presented a marked contrast to the anti-psychoanalytic tirades of the philosophers of desire.

Foucault's median position between the extremes represented by the philosophy of desire and the New Philosophers was also striking. We have already mentioned his appreciation of Glucksmann's writings. Lévy published a lengthy interview with Foucault in *Le Nouvel Observateur* on 12 March 1977.[29] In September 1977 Jérôme Bindé made a compelling suggestion: "Foucault is symptomatic of a strange zone of frankness, a margin of wandering between the leftist *désirants* and the new conceptual pessimism that dominates the media and the entire world these days."[30] And Jean-Jacques Brochier commented, in reference to the New Philosophers: "The only serious objection indeed against the discourse of power (inseparable from the power of discourse) is the underlying, confused, murmuring, quasi-inaudible *parole* of the dominated, of marginality, of the world of exclusion, confinement, and shutting in ... That is the coincidence of the true discovery of the Gulag ... and of the publication of [Foucault's] *Madness and Civilization* and *Discipline and Punish*."[31] The celebrated archeologist of marginal populations and diagnostician of knowledge/power complexes now appeared as the precursor to a cohort that was turning away from politics of any kind. We have in fact already witnessed a number of Foucaults in this book: the Foucault of the Groupe d'information sur les prisons and the Foucault of polemics against feminist rape politics. In chapter 23 we observe Maurice Clavel's embrace of Foucault's thought and how Foucault literally sat at the same table with Clavel, Jambet, Lardreau, and Glucksmann. And in chapter 25 we examine Foucault's late ethical writings. One might speculate that what made Foucault disposed toward some of the New Philosophers was his openness and search for unexpected languages and routes of thought. He also rejected lingering talk of liberation, and on that point in 1976–77 he was distancing himself from the principal heirs to 1968-era liberationism; namely, the party of desire. His move away from Deleuze was personal, and they found themselves on opposite sides of the New Philosophy debate.

After the publication of *Discipline and Punish* (1975) Foucault rapidly embraced – and then discarded – a variety of potentially fruitful avenues of thought. New Philosophy was one such passing engagement in a largely unsystematic flurry of activity. And the New Philosophers were also indebted to him, even if they clearly took unrigorous liberties with his thought. Foucault's thorny understanding of power as a social relationship – not unrelated to Deleuze's Spinoza – was taken up by the New Philosophers and metastasized into the metaphysical assumption that all societies are infused by an original and eternal evil called power. If there was an essential point of divergence between the New Philosophers and Foucault, or French theory in general, it was precisely the philosophers' embrace of the metaphysical.[32] While Deleuze, Lyotard, Foucault, and others were busy turning philosophy into theory, the New Philosophers explicitly returned to philosophy in a traditional sense. This revival of philosophy, and with it, metaphysics, religion, and ethics, was enabled by the experience of historical pessimism and the discovery of the phenomenon of dissidence.

The return to philosophy expressed a generation's historical experience, concluded Schiwy, in linking French theory and New Philospohy:

> In contrast to the militants of 1968, the "New Philosophers" no longer situated themselves with respect to the cultural revolution via the direct practice of political action, but rather deliberately within the field of philosophical reflection and the activities of men of letters. But they differed from the structuralists, for whom the revolutionary cultural function resided in the formation of new epistemological knowledges or new methodological approaches. The "New Philosophers" took the cultural revolution itself as the object of their reflection and – disappointed by the evolution of things since 1968 while at the same time being marked by structuralist thought on humans, society, and the state – they forced themselves to draw the conclusions of their own experience.[33]

The return to philosophy was a return to basic questions. "After 1968," Jean-Marie Domenach commented, "it was said that philosophers had left France. Only the initiated knew the names Jankélévitch, Levinas, or

Ricoeur. Philosophy was camouflaged in the human sciences."[34] As we see in chapter 25, the names of Vladimir Jankélévitch, Emmanuel Levinas, and Paul Ricoeur were not mentioned arbitrarily, since they were the major ethical thinkers in late-twentieth-century French philosophy. But in the era of structuralism and the human sciences, classical philosophical questions such as ethics had been overlooked. Structuralism had confidently targeted the interstices of knowledge and politics, and in post-1968 France, Marxism and Freudo-Marxism had provided stable philosophies of history from which to advocate and activate social change. But as political revolutionary hopes were unrealized – particularly in the circles of the cultural elite from which the New Philosophers came – prior, more basic questions resurfaced. As Domenach continued: "What is the goal of this life, the reason for so many efforts? What are progress, politics, and science for? These are the questions that made the New Philosophers explode onto the scene ... Political failure was transformed into metaphysical failure." In truth, these were questions that had been implicitly asked in 1968; now, however, they were more widely and directly posed, having been freed from the limits of earlier paradigms and rhetorics. Many found both structuralist politics of epistemology and post-1968 revolutionary politics lacking in 1976–77. Questions of ontology and possibility were to take precedence, and in the mood of disappointment that did in fact reign, answer to those questions were frequently dark and pessimistic. In 1977, in a twist on Immanuel Kant's question, *What can man hope for?* Foucault remarked that his generation – the generation of 1956 – had rebelled against what it had been "obliged" to hope for. In the same conversation in which Foucault made this remark, André Glucksmann said that the question of the hour was: *What is man permitted to despair?*[35]

Thus, if a single global theme can be said to have unified the otherwise disparate phenomenon of New Philosophy, it was historical pessimism. The term is apt, even if ultimately unsatisfying, since talk of pessimism and optimism depends in turn on the ends pursued. The overall gloom of the New Philosophers derived from a disillusionment with the idea that human liberation could be fulfilled in history. Many in 1968 had believed that history was an arena of human action and a meaningful process through which the potential for emancipation could be actualized. As noted above, one thing to be said for a coherent philosophy of history is that it can motivate people to act. And yet by the mid-to-late 1970s, many former '68-ers had concluded from their own experience that history amounted to the story of the defeat of rebellion and opposition at the hands of the powers that be. History in the above senses was breaking down. Some who had seen it as a sure bet changed their minds as they came to view it as a gamble whose results could not be known in advance. For a specific, well-educated cadre in the context of Gallic intellectualism and French publishing culture, concrete experiences were filtered through heady interpretation and catapulted into stratospheres of abstraction. They seemed to be saying that it was not only a cohort in a single country that experienced disappointment and pessimism, but rather humanity at all times and in all places. History became a metaphysical problem that hinged on the oddly popular assumption that *mastery* was the foundation and result, the Alpha and the Omega, of power, discourse, knowledge, desire, and politics – the very component elements of historical experience. Even "liberation," while seeming to promise a rupture with or counter-balance to domination, was not immune to the tricks and tropes of mastery since rebellious outsiders eventually became consummate insiders through cooption or "recuperation." Further, if thought itself was infused with tendencies toward domination, then politics and history as practice would have to wait. One could not simply act; one had to clean one's conceptual house. In other words, one had to philosophize, and the branch of the philosophical imagination to be pursued was ethics. The New Philosophers' return to ethics therefore emerged at the intersection of their pessimistic experience of history and their philosophical rejection of it as a field of confident action.

Yet behind this major shift from historical action to circumspect reflection on history's problematic nature lay a fundamental continuity. The events of 1968 had been formative for many of the New Philosophers, and as the aspired-to revolutionary moment of the post-1968 period receded, they retained an a priori sympathy for and attachment to belief in revolt. Revolution, one might say, involves systematic transformation and strategies that require the kind of coherent philosophy of history just mentioned. Revolt, on the other hand, can be oppositional, local, and tactical. Revolution involves many, while revolt needs a critical mass of one. To be sure, the contestatory movements of the 1960s combined the rhetoric and practices of revolution and revolt in complex ways; from Mario Savio standing on a police car at the University of California at Berkeley in 1964 inveighing against the "machinery" of American society to Mao Tse-tung's maxim, frequently quoted in the West, that "one is right to revolt." Of course, the total, systematic transformation of Western societies did not come to pass, and some greeted this dawning reality by clinging to and updating the languages of rebellion and revolt. Bernard-Henri Lévy, for instance, was not shy in his retrieval of Albert Camus and his figure of the rebel.[36] More generally, the New Philosophers rode the coattails of popular interest in Soviet and Eastern European dissidents, who in the mid-1970s were becoming the new symbols of rebellion at the heart of societies that refused to be fundamentally transformed.

Dissidence had always existed in the Soviet and Eastern European Communist regimes.[37] Of course, dissent from prevailing orthodoxies in rigid, hierarchical, anti-liberal societies comes at a high price. During the Stalinist era, the plight of dissenters was symbolized by the infamous "show trials" at which those accused by Communist "justice" sealed their death sentences or imprisonment in labour camps by publicly confessing their "crimes." After Joseph Stalin died in 1953, dissenters more often faced prison, house arrest, and psychiatric hospitalization. Some were religiously motivated; many were intellectuals. In the years preceding 1968, benefiting in part from a thaw in Cold War tensions, many dissidents sought reform by drawing attention, often by risky actions with high costs, to the contradictions between Communist ideals and reality. After 1968, as a result of events in Poland and Czechoslovakia, dissidents generally gave up hope that Communism could be reformed. But during the 1970s dissidence became a general buzzword in the West. Solzhenitsyn was granted the Nobel Prize in Literature in 1970 and Andrei Sakharov the Nobel Peace Prize in 1975, showcasing international support for Soviet nonconformist, public intellectuals. Also in 1975 the Helsinki Accords were signed, forcing the hand of Soviet authorities by getting them to agree to basic human rights protocols in exchange for improved international relations.

The theme of dissidence emerged in French public discourse at this time. One signature moment was the debates that took place in 1974–75 over the publication of Solzhenitsyn's *The Gulag Archipelago*. However, the essential factor in propelling dissidence into the limelight was the emigration of high-profile exiles to the West, including Solzhenitsyn, many of whom first stopped in Paris. French intellectuals rolled out the carpet in the ways they knew best: signing petitions, holding press conferences, writing articles, and debating the significance of dissidents *for France*. Jean Chiama and Jean-François Soulet noted in their exhaustive *Histoire de la dissidence* (1982) that despite three waves of publicity in France about dissidence – 1953–56, 1967–70, 1976–81 – the French remained largely "underinformed" about dissent behind the Iron Curtain.[38] Michael Scott Christofferson, however, has explained that French intellectuals began mobilizing on behalf of dissidents after 1956 and that associations like the Comité du 5 janvier pour une Tchécoslovaquie libre et socialiste and the Comité internationale des mathématiciens sowed the seeds of popular awareness.[39] Still, the 1970s were a turning point, since French intellectuals took over the model of dissidence for themselves.[40] Notwithstanding the poverty of the implied comparison between the Fifth Republic and the Communist bloc, the model fit the need to maintain a position of critique within a society that seemed increasingly impervious to fundamental transformation.

It was a short step from rebellion and dissidence to ethics. Here, we should understand ethics as a particular form of thought as well as the content of that form. In other words, the New Philosophers foregrounded ethics as a primary alternative to other forms of thought, such as politics, aesthetics, epistemology, and so forth; and they also cultivated a specific kind of ethics rooted in the figures of the rebel and the dissident. The latter personified the struggle of the singular against systematic, intractable powers. Ethical or moral stances replaced revolution and collective efforts at political transformation. Given the assessment that the spoils of history went to the victors, the quandary was to identify criteria according to which barbarism could be criticized and the intolerable confronted. Through their pessimism about far-reaching emancipation, their stubborn attachment to rebellion, and their admiration for Eastern dissidents, the New Philosophers and others were searching for foundations and first principles on which to construct a modest and defensive ethics of refusal and ethics *as* refusal. Needless to say, the turn to ethics was taken by some on the Left as either a reactionary move or a quasi-anarchistic stance based on the individual. Dominique Grisoni observed that, against some tenets of French theory, the human subject returned as ordinary, provisional, and resistant.[41] The focus on the individual was a pillar in the revival of human rights, a revival that was to maintain a sustained hum for the rest of the century. On human rights, too, the New Philosophers were in step with the dissenters from the East. Alhough their role should in no way be overestimated, they symbolized and popularized a broad shift in the West from radicalism to the ethical correction of politics, even if behind this shift lay important continuities.

The centrality of ethical and moral concerns to the New Philosophers was noted at the time and has since been widely accepted. "The 'New Philosophers' have effectively contributed to the rehabilitation of a moral or ethical approach to politics," wrote Sylvie Bouscasse and Denis Bourgeois in their 1978 edited dossier on the New Philosophy debates.[42] More recently, Jean-Pierre Le Goff has commented: "The New Philosophers inaugurated a social and political usage of ethics that would have numerous adaptations."[43] In the most thorough treatment of ethics and the New Philosophers, written in 1979, Patrick Pharo isolated the dynamics by which the leftism of the early 1970s gave rise, via a refusal of remaining political options, to an attachment to ethics in the mid-to-late 1970s.[44] As we have seen, New Philosophy was an unreliable umbrella term that grouped otherwise distinct thinkers together. Nevertheless, Pharo isolated the most-often cited themes in the explicit turn to ethics represented by this sensibility: "Defence of the rights of man, critique of the political and of its statist realization, rehabilitation of the individual and the intellectual, [and] affirmation of the moral as a foundation for historical action." In stressing these themes, the New Philosophy was a "space of crystallization" for more extensive changes in intellectual politics.

Leftist "sapience," Pharo said, had been characterized both by the diagnosis of a radically corrupt society that possessed its own mechanism of self-overcoming – revolution – and by an ethic of *dépassement*, or the invention of a new humanity. This "leftist myth" had showed itself to be "incompatible" with the "historical conjuncture" of 1970s France. A depression had set in. The New Philosophers' fascination with ethics and morals reflected the re-emergence of already existing elements in a Left confronted by the objective frustration of its hopes: "This political retreat is only intelligible by reference to the moral and philosophical hyperbole of leftist messianism which furnished its symbolic conditions of possibility." Detailing the shape of New Philosophy ethics, Pharo suggested that Glucksmann had kept ethics a hidden thematic; that Clavel had made explicit references to ethics; and that for Jambet, Lardreau, Lévy, and Nemo, ethics was primary. Altogether, the ethics of the New Philosophy was characterized by four theses: evil is originary; there is no sovereign good; ethical action is rooted in culture; and ethical action is the affair of the individual. Ethics and politics were sundered.[45]

Pharo was correct to identify the parallels between post-1968 leftism and the New Philosophers, parallels that marked a development rather than a rupture. His analysis of the content of New Philosophy ethics also remains useful, even if it underestimated the magnitude of the New Philosophy debate and thus missed the relevance of the immediate political climate in which it had erupted. In short, even if we accept the general outline of Pharo's argument, there seems to be much room for elaboration. Why evil? Revolt how? Why ethics? To address these questions we turn to two intersecting historical contexts: first, 1970s French politics, and second, the French tradition of Jansenism. We then take a look at the life and thought of a major animator of New Philosophy – Maurice Clavel – whose intellectual biography places the beginnings of the phenomenon well before 1968. Finally, we look more closely at texts by Jambet, Lardreau, Glucksmann, and Lévy. Jambet and Lardreau's "angelism," which had Clavel's odd religious thought as its antecedent, as well as Lévy's "atheistic spiritualism" and Glucksmann's "pleb" reflected the longing for the purity of a dream world and a rejection of the "messy" real world. Whatever their failings, and there were many, the New Philosophers' ethical turn coincided with the struggle to think through the passage from revolution to the rights of man. In 1968 many people had rejected the state in the name of revolution. Ten years later some of those same people turned away from the state in the name of human rights.

21

Between the Union of the Left and Jansenism

The ethos of the New Philosophy can perhaps be captured in a single overarching statement: disappointed hopes were displaced into metaphysical dream-states as a way of avoiding the reality of mundane political practice, which could never fulfill the fantasies of total liberation that had taken shape in May 1968. Such "mundane political practice" could be radical and revolutionary or, as we see below, reformist and state-oriented. But New Philosophers rejected both kinds of politics in favour of vague, otherworldly affirmations and first principles of a moral or ethical nature (which nevertheless bore significant resemblances to the liberational aspirations of 1968). For some, the sense of possibility associated with the May events persisted a decade later in an awkward proximity with an admission that history was not a realm where political visions and ambitions could be realized. As Jean-Denis Bredin put it, the New Philosophers' "limitation and effectiveness" derived from how "they dream[t] a society without dreaming of building it."[1] Others have referred to how they echoed Antonio Gramsci's slogan about "pessimism of the intellect and optimism of the will," even if their efforts paradoxically showed them to be overly optimistic about their own intellectual powers and overly pessimistic about the potential of resolute social and political action.

Having sampled the New Philosophy affair and its overall arguments, we now ask why it erupted when it did. Historical context – both local and on a wider scale – provides the key. New Philosophy's rejection of politics, meant a rejection of politics in general and Marxism in particular. Infamously, the anti-Marxism of the New Philosophers was epitomized by their reputed linkage of Marxism with Soviet totalitarianism – a reputation due as much to their critics' summary judgments as to their own occasionally flip stances. The New Philosophers' association with this equivalence, which further undermined both a by-then already largely discredited radical street politics and left-wing electoral politics, was an essential part of the far-reaching transformations in 1970s France. For it was in that decade that the centuries-old French tradition of the living revolution, including the twentieth-century graft of Marxism onto it, underwent an unprecedented and rapid decline. The victory of the Parti socialiste (PS) in François Mitterrand's 1981 presidential bid would immediately and paradoxically be taken as the sign of a resounding defeat of revolutionary aspirations in France, and the bicentennial celebrations of the French Revolution in 1989 were attended by all sorts of post-revolutionary expirations. So it was that the decade following one of the *grandes dates* in the history of revolution in France ironically achieved a significant undoing of the languages and practices of revolution. Ethics never was fundamental to certain Marxist traditions, and the emergence of ethics in the late twentieth century is co-extensive with the decline of those traditions. It was French electoral politics, though, that served as the accelerant for the conflagration of the New Philosophy affair. In particular, the New Philosophers became caught up in (and fed) political debates between the Parti socialiste and the Parti communiste français (PCF), linked since 1972 in a strategic coalition called the Union of the Left. Leaving revolution behind meant weighing the alternative of reform and electoral politics, which the New Philosophers also found wanting, as they cultivated instead their anti-political ethics.

Second, and more briefly, we also take history in another sense, turning to the deeper and perduring realm of French culture over an extended period of time. Indirectly and obliquely, the New Philosophers evoked coherent intellectual positions further back in French history; namely, the seventeenth-century religious and cultural movement of Jansenism. This historical dimension provides, modestly and at a distance, a comparative counterpoint. For alongside the specificity of the New Philosophers' rejection of politics in the mid-1970s, we find echoes of a more general suspicion of political agency and the kind of this-worldly can-do-it interventionism typical of modern politics, radical and reformist alike. The New Philosophers were not the first, of course, to cultivate a *contemptus mundi* view of human agency and possibility, and late modern societies can be seen to embody and express tensions that are uncannily reminiscent of early modern dilemmas. Still, the New Philosophers' disposition to be "in the world but not of it" echoed the Jansenists, who had cultivated that perspective many centuries before. Jansenism is thus an evocative reference that helps clarify the disparate media phenomenon known as New Philosophy.

Famously, France was slow to break free from its attachment to Marxism. The larger questions of this enchantment and of the fundamental French refusal to confront the terror of Communist regimes are beyond our present interest. Nevertheless, it is important to acknowledge a baseline attachment to Marxism in postwar French intellectual and cultural politics, for the undoing of that attachment and the resulting turn to ethics are of precise interest here. In postwar France, Marx was a legitimate *référence*, a looming figure on the cultural landscape. The Resistance of World War II had legitimized French Communism in particular. Between 1945 and the mid-1970s, factors postponing French critiques of Marxism or regimes built in its name included, beyond a generalized Gallic insularity, the desire to find a "third way" during the Cold War; efforts on the independent Left to temper criticisms of Communism lest they be taken as endorsements of Atlanticism; the power of the PCF, aligned with the Soviet Union, impeding independent marxisant movements; the fantastical connection between 1789 and 1917; the recent memory of the more forceful association of rightist politics with fascism; and the new life given to radicalism in 1968. In any event, the scale, noise, and consequences of searching deliberations on Marxism and Soviet totalitarianism during the 1970s were unprecedented. Why did those debates erupt when they did, and how were the New Philosophers involved in them?

Michael Scott Christofferson has offered a compelling examination of the New Philosophers as the pinnacle of 1970s French discourse on "anti-totalitarianism."[2] That discourse linked Marxian politics and Soviet totalitarianism, establishing a guilt by association that became a rhetorical *cul de sac* for the Left in general by tainting emancipatory politics with the horrors of the Gulag. Christofferson argues specifically that anti-totalitarianism was an instrumental and symptomatic discourse marshalled to indirectly grapple with the local circumstances of French domestic politics and especially the electoral fortunes of the Left. Drawing on independent Left critiques of Communism since the 1950s, and especially on post-1968 "direct democratic" movements, anti-totalitarianism gathered in polemics between the PCF and non-Communist intellectuals over the meaning, for instance, of Alexandr Solzhenitsyn's *The Gulag Archipelago* (published in French in 1974), the 1975 Portuguese revolution, and dissidence overall. Solzhenitsyn's book especially has long been understood as a symbolic and paradigmatic watershed in France's belated coming to grips with the facts of Soviet totalitiarianism. Behind these polemics, independent Left intellectuals used talk of totalitarianism to circuitously express their worries about the PCF and its electoral coalition with the PS known as the Union of the Left (1972–77). (The Union – treated in greater detail below – amounted to shared electoral platforms and the strategy of each party supporting the other's candidates if its own fared poorly.) At stake in debates about totalitarianism, Christofferson suggests, was the alleged fear of what would happen in France if the Communists came to power via its partnership with the PS, a fear, in other words, that France would have to face its own homegrown totalitarianism.

Setting aside possible doubts about the actual force of this fear factor, there is much to merit this account.[3] Christofferson argues convincingly, for instance, that anti-totalitarian discourse was an instrument; that direct democratic practices and rhetoric contributed greatly to the delegitimation of electoral politics; that the debate on Solzhenitsyn was really a debate about the PCF's attack on him; and that French supporters of Soviet and Eastern European dissidents followed the latter in moving away from advocating socialism *and* liberty, as they had previously, toward championing liberty *as human rights*. In this context, New Philosophy was a keystone event. Posturing as dissidents, accused of being media charlatans, hostile to radical and electoral politics, the New Philosophers dramatized important and timely questions about the political consequences of the Left's achieving power.

It was in this context of debates about totalitarianism that the New Philosophers were charged by their critics, not always unfairly, of having resorted to the simplistic recipe: Marx equals Stalin equals the Gulag. Such a recipe was read as an indirect attack on the Union of the Left, increasingly fragile by 1976. What mattered, as Pierre Viansson-Ponté observed, was not that revelations about the Gulag were new, but that people like André Glucksmann and Bernard-Henri Lévy "were making them here and now." The New Philosophers were accused of "making the bed of the Right at a decisive moment in the history of the Left," since "introducing the demons of the spirit of examination at this hour seemed like a sacrilege." Claude Mauriac agreed, and, while declaring his sympathy for his ex-Maoist "friends," he questioned their "use" of old news about the Gulag: their criterion of "perfection" could only harm the Left. In November 1977 David Rousset, whose name was synonymous with bringing the news of the Nazi concentration camps to France in the 1940s, said that the New Philosophers' conclusions were too hasty: "What I reproach them for is to have not pushed their examination very far and to have not founded it on very solid bases. It is nevertheless necessary to try to establish the historical filiation between Marx and the Gulag." To the question of what was original in the alleged connection between Marxism and totalitarianism, Diane

Ribardière answered: "The way it is dressed up." And René Pascal, referring to the failure of previous revelations to have any effect, remarked on the general anti-totalitarian climate: "Why then did Solzhenitsyn succeed in shaking convictions that neither Victor Serge, nor Arthur Koestler, nor Victor Kravchenko, etc. succeeded in undermining? The effectiveness of genius? Mystery of credibility? Grace of the moment? It does not matter. Things are what they are."[4] For all their shortcomings, the New Philosophers had hit a nerve.

Why? The most significant factors in responding to this question were generational and political. Perhaps like sex, Marxism can never fully be explained by parents to their children, every generation needing to figure out for itself what is already basic knowledge. It seems clear, though, that the belatedness of the reckoning with Stalinism seemed less the fault of the '68 generation than of earlier ones. From the 1940s to the 1960s, no critical debate on Marxism had been sustained or strong enough to alter that ideology's central role in French culture and politics. Yet the generation of '68 had already done the groundwork for this fight, Maoists and Trotskyists criticizing the Soviet Union and the PCF in the same breath. The Marxist tradition ironically provided the resources for overcoming Marxism.[5] Disenchantment with their own activism could only amplify this pre-existing critique: the passage from anti-Stalinism to anti-Marxism completed a logic. In terms of politics, one might first consider the international scene. French anti-totalitarianism appeared in relative conjunction with the world economic downturn after 1973, crises in China between the deaths of Lin Piao (1971) and Mao (1976), controversy over the Portuguese revolution (1975), terrorism in Germany and Italy, the end of the Vietnam War, and the reign of the Khmer Rouge in Cambodia (1975–79). As Christian Jambet and Guy Lardreau said, Solzhenitsyn's book alone could not have fired the Gulag debate in France; but together with events in China and Cambodia in particular, "*It was too much*."[6]

More important than international politics, however, was the domestic political situation in France. Christofferson is largely right here, if for slightly different reasons than he maintains. The question – What can one really hope from the Left coming to power? – in fact revealed a more fundamental one: What should the role of the post-Gaullist state be? Consider, for instance, the fact that the French translation of *The Gulag Archipelago* (June 1974) came out just a month after Valéry Giscard d'Estaing became president (19 May), Georges Pompidou having passed away on April the second. The coincidence, hardly noted at the time, was crucial, even if, as Christofferson amply demonstrates, much of the acrimony over

Solzhenitsyn's book occurred before its translation into French! The Gulag affair nevertheless came at a critical juncture in the history of the Fifth Republic. The controversy's central and unacknowledged questions were the following: What would the Fifth Republic be after de Gaulle (and after Pompidou's brief interregnum)? What kind of state should France have? What should the role of the state be? The relation of the citizen to the state? Citizens who had been activated and formed by 1968 often had different answers to these questions than professional party operatives and those who looked to the state as a legitimate arena of action.

So indeed, France's general political conjuncture was reflected in talk of Gulags and dissidence. To take one example, Glucksmann wrote in his *La Cuisinière ou le mangeur d'hommes* (1975): "The Russian dissidents [*contestataires*] can here help us to better understand ourselves ... Keeping in view our own experience, we are free to meditate on the universal treasure of resistance to *state violence*."[7] Anti-totalitarianism was therefore more than simply a debate about the specific political conjuncture of the Union of the Left; it was also a debate about the broader puzzle of whether politics *in general* could ever fulfill its charge as the art of the possible and satisfy the liberational aspirations of *les années soixante-huit*. If not, surrogates would be needed. So, while it is true that the New Philosophers emerged at the same time that the Union of the Left was collapsing, on the eve of the much-anticipated legislative elections of 1978, their target was loftier and more immodest. On the whole, they equated power and politics with barbarism. To be sure, the New Philosophers were fundamentally critical of Marxism, but they were so in a particular way. The critique of power per se preceded the application of that critique to Marxism. To interpret anti-Marxism as the driving force rather than the particular target of their attacks is thus to confuse motives and expressions.

Alain Peyrefitte, Minister of Justice, correctly identified the dual motives of the New Philosophers when he said that they claimed that "one must defy power, which is by nature bad" and also that "the worst of powers is that which weighs on minds before weighing on bodies – today a role played by Marxism."[8] The New Philosophers' flight into philosophical abstractions and the dream-state of metaphysics, culminating in their valorization of rebellion, dissidence, and ethics, was seen not incorrectly as a rejection of the electoral politics of the Left. But it was more. New Philosophy rejected politics as such.

Let us now backtrack for a moment and examine the fate of the Union of the Left in order to grasp more exactly how the New Philosophers were associated with its collapse. In June 1972 the PCF under Georges Marchais, and the PS under François Mitterrand had, together with the small centre-left Mouvement des radicaux de gauche, signed an accord for a Common Program, creating the Union of the Left.[9] The agreement consisted of both a legislative agenda and an electoral promise. "This program is a program of action," said the Preamble: "It constitutes an engagement of two parties, with respect to each other and to the country; it creates a new situation that permits the installation of a true political and economic democracy. The PCF and PS naturally conserve their personalities. They each hold on to the principles that establish their separate existences. Some of their political appreciations differ, but this does not put in question their will and capacity to govern together."[10] Differences would win out within a few years, but, for the time being, there was talk of a renewal of the Popular Front sensibility of the late 1930s. The statement of goals included provisions on employment, health care, urbanism, housing, transportation, education, scientific research, sports, cultural life, women, youth, the police, the judicial system, national political institutions, radio and television, and international affairs, among other themes. More than a political platform, it was an agenda for a complete reorganization of French society based mainly around economic democratization. Of more immediate concrete utility, both parties agreed to support on second ballots in presidential and legislative elections whichever PCF or PS candidates had won on the first round. This provision had immediate returns in the March 1973 legislative elections, with both the PCF and PS gaining seats. When the agreement was signed it seemed like a good bargain for the PCF, since it was stronger than the PS. In fact, it turned out to be a pact with the devil for the former, since it would end up losing out in the long term. (The subsequent reversal of fortunes could not have been known in advance.)

At the same time, on the Right, Pompidou's death in April 1974 was followed by the spilling over of tensions within the Gaullist Union des démocrates pour la République. Dissatisfied with the two contenders for the Gaullist legacy – Jacques Chaban-Delmas and Jean Royer – a group of UDR leaders, including Minister of the Interior Jacques Chirac, threw their support behind Valéry Giscard d'Estaing, head of the Républicains indépendants and most recently Finance Minister under Pompidou. In the closest presidential election of the Fifth Republic, on 18 May 1974 Giscard d'Estaing narrowly defeated Mitterrand, the Common Program candidate, with a vote of 50.8% to 49.2%. Giscard d'Estaing's liberalizing social measures took some of the wind out of the sails of the Union of the Left; his 1976 book, *Towards a New Democracy*, described his attempt at a compromise between liberalism and communism.[11] Still, his presidency suffered from his own troubled partnerships, with Jacques Chirac resigning as prime minister in August 1976. The president was forced to take a rightist turn to recoup his losses, as Chirac formed his own power bloc. Still, the divorce between Chirac's Rassemblement du peuple pour la République and the Républicains indépendants seemed to bode well for the Left in the approaching 1978 legislative elections, and, recognizing the danger, both parties of the Right began negotiations in 1977 to try to work out a common program of their own. Giscard lost support in his own party to the Union of the Left as he tried to keep up with Chirac, and the worsening post-1973 economic situation in France also buttressed the position of the Left.

In fact, the actual situation of the Union of the Left itself was not strong. When the trend of PS gains in the 1973 and 1974 elections continued in the March 1977 municipal ballot, the PCF began more openly to express worries that the Union might not be advantageous after all. That May, and as Lévy's and Glucksmann's books were beginning to be reviewed and shortly before the authors appeared on the television show *Apostrophes*, the PCF, the PS, and the Mouvement des radicaux de gauche met to work out the differences threatening to wreck the Union of the Left. In a ploy that was pathetically self-destructive, the PCF, having less weight to throw around than ever, tried to force changes in the Common Program by directing it toward its own policy agenda, particularly the nationalization of companies if majority control of the National Assembly was achieved. Conflicts and bickering within the coalition intensified over the summer, and the Union of the Left disbanded in September 1977.[12]

The New Philosophy debate erupted in its full splendour in May 1977, exactly as the Union of the Left was coming apart. Again, as we have seen in previous chapters, events of historical significance transpire when otherwise minor incidents converge opportunely. To express doubts about the Union in the spring and summer of 1977 was tantamount to criticizing it, and criticisms were seen as reactionary betrayal. Denis Roche began his 10 June *Libération* article on Lévy and Glucksmann this way: "The fundamental debate: What is on the political horizon in 1978 (the legislative elections and how intellectuals will 'place' themselves)?"[13] It is true that some of the New Philosophers had themselves introduced the question of the Socialists' and Communists' electoral fortunes. Lévy, an advisor to Mitterrand and the only former supporter of the Union, was on record as saying that master for master, he guessed he would take Mitterrand. Jambet and Lardreau came out strongly against the Common Program. Glucksmann pretentiously complained: "The Common Program will transform 'everything,' that is to say, Being as such ... It is dependent on the university unions to make its truth exist, the Christians to show its goodness, and the artists to glorify its beauty."[14] But again, the Union was not the principal preoccupation of the New Philosophers. It was a particular case handled in pursuit of their larger objectives.

In June and July 1977, Socialists and Communists tried to dispel the phantom of the New Philosophy with a simplistic if-you're-not-with-us-you're-against-us reasoning. *Le Matin*, close to the PS, and *L'Humanité*, organ of the PCF, were particularly feisty as conflicts within the Union and (likely) the desperate desire to hold things together were displaced onto paranoid fears of conspiratorial subterfuge. But the New Philosophers represented not so much the threat of an internal betrayal as untimely and unwanted criticism by a Left intelligentsia who, although not necessarily identified with any party, were politically influential because of their visibility and cultural cachet. Bernard Pingaud, member of the PS, decried the "temptation to irresponsibility" that the New Philosophers encouraged through their "rather banal form of dandyism." Catherine Kintzler, also a member of the PS but writing in *L'Humanité*, took Glucksmann to task after his 27 May appearance on *Apostrophes* for implying that the Gulag and the Common Program were of the same cloth (Glucksmann did in fact say, "The tribunes of the Common Program are empty"). Speaking for the PCF, J.-M. Geng, evoking Paul Nizan, called them the "new guard dogs," as politically useless as their "predecessors," Baudrillard, Guattari, and Lyotard! If the Right won the elections in 1978, he said, the "future would belong to them." *L'Humanité* also applauded Aubral and Delcourt's "empirical investigation" (see chapter 20). Pierre Juquin, member of the Central Committee of the PCF, said that the New Philosophers seemed a little "old-fashioned" and that with them "class struggle had disappeared into the heaven of ideas." The third partner in the Common Program, the Mouvement des radicaux de gauche, in a notice on Lévy's *Barbarism with a Human Face*, said somewhat more gently that the New Philosophers were "fairly representative of the French public, who, although attracted to the Left in the hopes of a better society, feared the slippages that could threaten democracy. [*Barbarism with a Human Face*] must be understood as a caution, in particular for the Radicaux de Gauche who must make sure that the Common Program is not a damper."[15]

Those who criticized the New Philosophers as saboteurs of the Union gave Lévy and company too much credit. The Union was collapsing for its own reasons, and it was easier for Socialists and Communists to find common cause in attacking would-be troublemakers than to face the meltdown of their own alliance. On the other hand, the New Philosophers' pessimistic equation of power, mastery, and politics, though couched as philosophical high-mindedness, targeted the Union of the Left only in a roundabout way, a few direct comments notwithstanding. Yet it is unmistakable that in ideological politics ideas matter. The New Philosophers' books were often addressed to the Left. One implication of their general critique of politics, as Philippe Buchon noted, was to "predict catastrophe if the Left comes to lead the state" – a wild exaggeration, if not an absurdity.[16] The real object of the New Philosophers' criticism was politics and the state as such. *No* political enterprise could accomplish the dream-like purity of dissidence and rebellion. Through a return to basic questions about what was possible and what could be hoped for in the political realm, the New Philosophers were following through on the logic of an earlier far-leftism and, for some, of Maoism. Between 1968 and 1972 they had rejected electoral politics in the name of an authentic revolution. As the potential of the supposed revolutionary moment faded, the contrast became one between still-shunned electoral politics and pure dissidence or rebellion divorced from practical action and empirical reality. Revolution against capitalist domination shifted into rebellion against any kind of domination. Circumstanially, but with far-reaching implications, the discourse of mastery most ready at hand was, of course, Marxism. Maurice Duverger, writing in *Le Monde*, suggested: "This about-face would only interest small Parisian circles if it did not correspond to a much larger movement ... The tide that carries them is deeper. It concerns the role of Marxist ideology in the West, and the use of such schemas in the analyses of contemporary societies ... Vive the New Philosophy, despite its pyrotechnics, if it helps liberate us from the new scholasticism."[17] The West was experiencing a general depoliticization during the 1970s. Marxism was one of its casualities, and a turn to an antipolitical ethics was one of its consequences. Even if Jean Creiser's prediction in the fall of 1977 that "the New Philosophy has become a political phenomenon that can only amplify itself after the failure of the Union of the Left" was mistaken, one can understand why it was made at the time.[18]

Having delved into the immediate and local historical context to help frame and explain the New Philosophy phenomenon, we now need to take historical contextualization in a more theoretical direction and, however briefly, backtrack even further in order to raise the question of ulterior sources and origins. We have already mentioned how New Philosophy and French theory appeared, according to Günther Schiwy and others, to hold parallels. Other readers drew attention to the New Philosophers' eclecticism, to their mixing of figures and themes in ways worthy of the great nineteenth-century philosophical blender, Victor Cousin. Some saw specific traces of thinkers such as Albert Camus, Immanuel Kant, Maurice Merleau-Ponty, Plato, Solzhenitsyn, and Benedict de Spinoza. Dismissive comparisons were made to Gérard de Nerval, Georges Bernanos, and Maurice Barrès, and Georges Politzer's critique of Henri Bergson was exhumed to make a parallel case. Olivier Cohen placed the genesis of New Philosophy in the defeat of Maoism and the shameless pilfering and exploitation of the ideas of Socialisme ou Barbarie, which had pioneered independent Left criticisms of Stalinism from the 1940s to the 1960s.[19] My interest here is somewhat different, for the dynamics of the New Philosophers' anti-state and anti-political ethics declared in the name of an other-worldliness bring to mind a much older French intellectual tradition: Jansenism. Despite the evident dangers of cross-historical comparisons of such magnitude – between the mid-seventeenth and the late twentieth centuries – nevertheless, bringing together Jansenism and the New Philosophers, as represented by the figures of Blaise Pascal and Maurice Clavel, seems fruitful. Several aspects of comparison present themselves: first thematic affinity (for example, the critique of worldly reason and the return to metaphysical questions); second, different but related worldviews (the crisis of modernity and Marxism, which inspired a return to early modern dilemmas and non-modern solutions); and finally, on the level of historical tradition, facets of contemporary French culture, such as statism and the belief in French exceptionalism, have lineages that go back centuries.[20]

Jansenism was a seventeenth-century theological movement within the French Catholic Church.[21] Basing its teaching on principles attributed to the theologian Cornelius Jansen, who was condemned by the Church in 1653, the movement set itself up against the dominant theology of the Catholic Reformation. The common denominator among its diverse adherents, among whom Pascal was the most well known, was their opposition to the Catholic view (associated with the Jesuits) of the role of human will in the process of salvation. Jansenists minimized the part that humans could play, stressing the inscrutability of an absolute divine will that dispensed grace for its own reasons – grace without which salvation was not possible. In short, if in the conventional Catholic view humans had some role in their own salvation, for the Jansenists nothing done in this world could influence divine will. Mankind and the world were clearly of secondary importance, and the result was a stark pessimism about the human condition. This accent on divine grace over human will in the theological hierarchy involved a return to the tradition of Augustinian spirituality, particularly its sharp division between matters human and matters divine. In Lucien Goldmann's description, Jansenism had a "tragic" outlook: God was "hidden"; history did not provide an autonomous testing ground for divine judgment; and except for those "extreme" Jansenists who retreated entirely from worldly affairs altogether, the Jansenist mentality – when pushed to its logical conclusions by someone like Pascal – led to the cultivation of the ambiguous identity of being "in the world but not of it."[22] On its surface, writes Dale K. Van Kley, Jansenism "bore an uncanny resemblance" to Calvinism, but was less activist with regard to worldly affairs.[23] God's will was so "hidden" that neither earthly rewards, nor monastic or mystical retreat from the world were trustworthy. One had to act "as if" one's actions were performed with the light of grace. This is one of the origins of Pascal's famous "wager" – it is better to believe in God even if He does not exist than to not believe in Him if He does ... to act as if God exists, though one can never be sure. (We shall see the theme of the wager take on particular importance with Clavel, Jambet, and Lardreau.)

From one point of view, the devaluing of worldly activity was "conservative," but the same position could alternatively be described as one of "passive resistance" (Alexander Sedgwick) or "explicit obedience and implicit subversion" (Van Kley).[24] The conservative aspect was to diminish human agency and possibility; the resistant or subversive side was to delegitimize ruling worldly powers. In its sharp, Manichean divisions between God and world/man, between grace and nature, and, for Pascal, between the heart and the mind, Jansenism did in fact play an important cultural and political role in delegitimizing monarchical power and cultivating counter-powers in non-official spheres. In its tragic pessimism, it held that the Church was wrong for saying that the will was good, and the Calvinists were wrong in implying that the world was good. Earthly power was earthly power, and as such inherently wicked. Indirectly and in complicated ways, as Van Kley has suggested, this cultural attitude contributed to the French Revolution by desacralizing and thus undermining the sovereignty of the king. Ironically, the tempered revival of this view by the New Philosophers came at the end of a prolonged period of the French tradition of the living revolution; namely, the Marxian graft of 1917 onto the inheritance of the French Revolution. Pessimism about the world helped lay the groundwork for the French Revolution, a rejection of this world contributing to the desire to fashion a new one; and, 200 years later, the revolutionary tradition that was born in 1789 helped revive another form of pessimism.

A number of parallels appear between the sensibilities of the Jansenists and those of the New Philosophers:

- Pessimism with regard to worldly activity, which did not pass into nihilism because hopes were placed in a realm outside human power and history;
- Persecution as a test;
- A rejection of historical action;
- The persistent demand for absolute values, but with an emphasis on the *conscience* rather than preconceived formulas and explanations;
- The rejection of dialectical thought for paradoxical tragedy;
- The metaphor of the wager;
- The transfer of focus from active resistance to passive and from the life of the body to the life of the mind;
- Politics as a (necessary) evil that would not make heaven on earth.

Alone, neither pessimism nor spiritualism nor resistance leads to a Jansenist viewpoint. It is the accumulative weight of these attitudes that suggests a Jansenist *ethics of resistance to worldly power.* This resistance is pessimistic: it will never overcome the alienated nature of the world. It is the standpoint of a permanent rebellion by a minority who lives "in the world but not of it." The Jansensists were the dissidents of their day; the New Philosophers championed that position in their own.

The local political context of 1970s France, as well as history on a larger scale, helps us grasp better what the New Philosophers were up to, why they created such a commotion, or at least how their overall position resonated with deeper sensibilities in French culture. Yet we have not yet penetrated very deeply into what they actually said. Bearing in mind New Philosophy's thematic affinities with Jansenism, we now turn to look more closely at the works of the five principal agents who, willingly or not, were associated with the media affair: Clavel, Jambet, Lardreau, Glucksmann, and Lévy. We start by introducing Clavel as the New Philosopher's "uncle" in the context of his own biographical and intellectual itinerary. He had seen the May events and the far-left period as a confirmation of a perspective he had developed earlier through his conversion to Catholicism in the early 1960s. Despite his own caveats, Clavel was the foremost exponent of a Pascalian type of religiousness in the New Philosophy milieu. In the subsequent chapter we will move more explicitly into the realm of ideas. Former Maoists Jambet and Lardreau published in 1976 and 1978 two philosophical volumes on the status and stakes of the cultural revolution after the decisive end of the far-left period. In their own turn toward a religious language of "angelism," which they nevertheless claimed was atheistic, and in their highly abstract and somewhat convoluted attempt to develop a theory of rebellion, they exemplified New Philosophy's revival of metaphysics and philosophy. In the last chapter in this section, we will look briefly at the two signature texts of the New Philosophy – Glucksmann's *The Master Thinkers* and Lévy's *Barbarism with a Human Face* – and draw general conclusions about the shift from historical action to philosophical reflection. The time for throwing stones or demonstrating in the streets had passed, but, for some, the search to continue by other means, to translate and update, and to re-found the spirit of '68 on a new basis persisted. Looking closely at some of the bestsellers of the New Philosophers, the reader may suddenly develop a sympathy for the impatience of many of their critics. We are faced with the historical significance of tedious books.

22

Maurice Clavel

When several reviewers of Maurice Clavel's 1975 intellectual and personal testament, *Ce que je crois*, claimed he was a "little crazy," they meant it as an affectionate chiding.[1] "Every group of friends needs to have someone like Maurice Clavel," wrote Mikro: "A big warm guy, hot-headed, near-sighted, and a little crazy ... You must bring this devil Clavel with you to the beach this summer." Michel Le Bris commented: "A crazy man for sure! Superb, but crazy! ... His madness ought to excuse him." And Robert Kanters added: "One says sometimes that with all his generosity M. Maurice Clavel is a little crazy ... Taking him as a whole, one sees well that it is not him that is crazy, it is our world." Even de Gaulle found Clavel peculiar. André Malraux said to Claude Mauriac: "De Gaulle does not take Clavel altogether seriously. He considers him a little crazy, but he loves him. Clavel really amuses him."[2] The description of Clavel as *un peu fou* had something to do with the fact that, as we will see, his thought seemed to meander all over the place just as he had done in his own life experiences. Born in 1920, graduate of the Ecole normale supérieure, de Gaulle's Resistance point man in the liberation of Chartres in 1944, playwright, "leftist Gaullist," a particularly unquiet Christian convert, television critic for *Le Nouvel Observateur*, supporter and friend to many post-1968 Maoists, co-founder of the Agence de presse libération, and soon to be recognized as the "godfather" or "uncle" of the New Philosophers, Clavel had traversed broad swatches of the political and cultural landscape of postwar France. If something seemed "a little crazy" about Clavel in 1975, it was that he was a highly visible presence on the post-1968 Left while at the same time extolling the notion that 1968 represented the "convulsive" return of a "repressed God" and the annunciation of a cultural revolution of unprecedented magnitude. This cultural revolution was to be post-humanist and spiritual, rejecting many core elements of modern thought, secular and religious alike. The younger *soixante-huitards* who cautiously embraced aspects of Clavel's analyses of circumstances in France usually disavowed his unambiguously Christian conclusions, ultimately leaving this "fou de Dieu" alone with his idiosyncratic philosophical and religious commitments.[3] But his perceptive, timely, and provocative assessments of post-1968 France endeared him – or made him a target – to some on the intellectual-political Left.

Clavel provoked a range of responses. At the height of the New Philosophy controversy in 1977, for example, André Glucksmann said: "[Clavel] does not operate as one is supposed to ... He says the things he feels and that he feels them; he does not speak in the name of a theory or a party or an organization ... Clavel is one of the few to say, 'I am horrified.'" Philippe Sollers called him "a fundamentally free spirit" in the book of stormy interviews he and Clavel published jointly in 1977. In an obsequious and surely exaggerated letter to Clavel, after the latter had defended *The Order of Things* (1967) in *Le Nouvel Observateur* in 1968, Michel Foucault commented: "If someone was to ask me now, as one often says today 'from where do you speak?' I would say that I spoke from that point where I am now silent, where Clavel spoke for me in passing one day on his way to say much more important things." When Clavel died, Foucault published a eulogy in *Le Nouvel Observateur* in which he compared Clavel to Maurice Blanchot (no small compliment) and wrote: "[He] was at the heart of what was undoubtedly most important in our era. By this I mean a vast and very profound change in the consciousness of history and of time as it has gradually been formed by the West." On the other hand, Gilles Deleuze accused him of being the "Doctor Mobius of philosophy," to which Clavel retorted in good humour: "I accept that last name Möbius if I might be permitted to place in front of it that charming Swedish first name, Sven." Maria-Antonietta Macciocchi decried his "retro-spiritualism," and Jean-Marie Domenach echoed her sentiment from a different basis, writing in *Esprit*: "I perceive in this Clavelian reaction the inevitable pendulum swing of fashionable anti-humanism ... But it sends us back fifty years." All in all, Clavel was a difficult-to-pin-down presence whose oddly formulated spiritual revolutionarism might have seemed ill-suited for and marginal to the heady debates on Marxism and totalitarianism that were the rage in France in the mid-1970s. And yet, throughout that decade, Clavel kept showing up at the centre of the action. Jean Daniel remarked at Clavel's funeral in 1979: "We have lost the last of the great Judeo-Christian troublemakers."[4]

With the important proviso that no one actually adhered to Clavel's exact line of thinking, and that even those who felt close to him did not hesitate to take their distance, it would be difficult to disagree with Domenach's later assessment that, as far as the New Philosophers went, Clavel was "at the head of those insurgents, sounding the charge and orchestrating the spectacle."[5] As an elder fellow traveller, says François Hourmant, "Clavel played a decisive role as animator, promoter, and cement for the New Philosophers" as they began to translate post-1968 disappointments into post-revolutionary visions of liberational thought and action.[6] As an observer/*provacateur* on the cultural scene whose commitment to the "transcendent" provided a "critical" vantage point on the intellectual politics of 1970s France, Clavel was uniquely situated to interpret the significance of cultural fields such as anti-humanism, the decline of Marxism, and the search for new foundations. Not only did he best represent the "Jansenist" sensibility of the New Philosophers (discussed in the previous chapter) but his thought was also foundational for their making post-1968 ethics explicit. He was influential in part because his message and the unrepentant exuberance with which he expressed it were at least a little "touched." Some sympathetic retrieval is in order, since many of his ideas make easy targets. No strong critique I could make would add much to criticisms made of Clavel during his lifetime.[7]

Clavel coined the term "transcendental journalist" for himself, to describe the task of drawing transcendent or theological lessons from mundane cultural and political events. Such writing was the work, he said, of "someone who sees the moment and discovers or believes to discover behind it something more fundamental and original."[8] Foucault is reported to have said, generously, that Clavel's phrase *journalisme transcendental* was the only appropriate way to describe the work of the contemporary philosopher. To some extent, philosophy had been Clavel's first and lifelong love, despite the fact that the last ten years of his life were dedicated to calling attention to the dead ends of Western secular thought. He had a particular passion for Kant, on whom he first considered writing a work as early as 1942 and on whom he ultimately did write a 650-page treatise, published posthumously as *Critique de Kant* (1980).[9] Clavel's philosophical interests had waned in the 1950s as he devoted himself to writing for the theatre, and when he experienced a five-year bout of depression and illness that culminated in his conversion experience in May 1965. Around the same time, he was enlisted by Jean Daniel to write the television column for *Le Nouvel*

Observateur. His return to philosophy in the 1960s and 1970s needs to be viewed through the changes in his personal and political identities that came with these experiences.

Clavel believed he had had a mystical experience that he later described in terms similar to other conversion narratives. "Broken," driven to the point of suicide, on a psychiatrist's couch, he had mumbled the words "Take me," ending a dark period of his life that he later interpreted as a willful resistance to divine grace. The notion of grace was central to Clavel's self-understanding. Conversion had happened to him, come to him from the outside, in spite of his resistance to it. In the French tradition of twentieth-century intellectual converts (such as Paul Claudel, Georges Bernanos, and Simone Weil) Clavel underscored the insufficiency of humans left to their own devices and, to an extreme, the passivity of conversion. "I was scoured like a kitchen sink," he was fond of saying. There was something of Friedrich Schleiermacher's "utter dependence" here, but Clavel would have refused such simple terms. As he said to Philippe Sollers: "I would add, because one often takes this passivity for being a slave: I was liberated from my little individuality and recreated as a subject." Far from being an anti-worldly or compliant contemplative, in fact, Clavel threw himself into public action. This was a convert to Catholicism who named his dog Birth Control Pill [*Pilule*].[10]

About the same time as his conversion, he underwent a transformation in his political outlook that would soon lead him from left-Gaullism to the radical Left. The first of a series of important disillusionments with de Gaulle, whom he had otherwise loyally supported since World War II, occurred with the Ben Barka Affair in the winter of 1965–66. Government operatives had kidnapped in broad daylight a leader of the Moroccan opposition, Mehdi Ben Barka, tortured him, and then brought him to Morocco, where he was killed. The resulting scandal led to clay-faced denials by government leaders, including de Gaulle, and the eventual trial of the agent-kidnappers. The president's failure to act led Clavel to accuse him of "theocentrism" and pushed Clavel further to the Left. Jean Daniel took Clavel up on his open-letter offer to cover the Ben Barka kidnapping trial for *Le Nouvel Observateur*, writing: "Maurice Clavel is not one of 'ours,' as one says; he is 'unconditionally a Gaullist at heart.' But he is honest, even in his passions."[11] Clavel thus began to garner a reputation as an independent and critical thinker unbeholden to prescribed political postures. When the trial was over, in November 1966 Daniel offered Clavel a position as television critic for *Le Nouvel Observateur*, a position he would fill for the remaining thirteen years of his life.

Sending his pre-conversion personal and political identities through the wash, so to speak, led Clavel to observe and comment on French politics and culture through new lenses. The columns of *Le Nouvel Observateur* provided one vantage point and forum, and his job as a philosophy teacher at the Lycée Buffon in Paris another. Paying special attention to Blaise Pascal and Søren Kierkegaard in his courses, he became fixated on a particular dynamic: the passage from human efforts that end in nihilism to "something else." Clavel could be vague about what this something else was going to be, but was becoming increasingly convinced that, as indicated by the emptiness of emerging media culture and the malaise among the young, France was cornered in dead ends that only a transcendence could overcome. One does not have to look very far for the psychological motives for this view: Clavel projected onto French society his personal experiences of a "lightning bolt" and "irruptive" transcendence that had helped him overcome his own depression and despair. Collective nihilism would require an analogous, total overhaul. The result was that before May 1968, in his own terms, Clavel was anticipating and cultivating the arrival of this something else. Nihilism needed to be overcome, but nihilism was also the symptom of a cultural struggle with the transcendent and thus a sign of the latter's re-emergence. God was not dead, merely repressed, and His return would be – as it had been in Clavel's own life – "convulsive" and "neurotic." Taking the imagined position of the transcendent allowed Clavel to engage in a critique of everything: Marxism, Gaullism, bourgeois materialism, humanism, the Catholic Church (as party to *aggiornamento*), and, in addition to the kitchen sink, the notion of critique itself. This last point was paramount, and Clavel developed it after returning to Kant in 1967 through reading Foucault's *The Order of Things*. More than dusting off an early love, Clavel believed he had found in that book "the *Critique of Pure Reason* of our time" and in Foucault the "new Kant."

Foucault argued in *The Order of Things* that knowledge emerges in a particular era according to a basic paradigm he called an *episteme*. The era of humanism and the human sciences was based on a different *episteme* than that of the "classical" era of the late Renaissance and early modernity. Famously, Foucault ended his book with the provocative claims that "man" was therefore an invention of recent date and that, given the historical nature of shifting *epistemes*, he might someday disappear like a line in the sand washed away by waves. Of course, this is one of the sources for Foucault's often being identified within the matrix of "anti-humanist" French theory. For his part, Clavel read this famous "end of man" as the "end of man without God."[12] He believed he had already personally experienced an effacement of himself as a self-sufficient knowing and rational being; his identity as an autarchic individual had given way to the identity of a subject dependent on the transcendent.[13]

Despite Foucault's friendliness to and occasional public support of Clavel, the latter's spiritualist interpretation of anti-humanism contradicted the spirit of Foucauldian research. Foucault had not criticized modern humanism as a prelude to religious revival, even if Clavel did cleverly pursue a counter-modern route that Foucault's work had inadvertently opened up. Reading him allowed Clavel to return to one of Kant's most famous phrases: that he had "limited reason to make room for faith." Clavel took the solitary from Köningsberg seriously on this point, but in doing so ran up against a central commonplace of contemporary Kantian scholarship – that Kant had actually given reason the run of the philosophical house and squeezed faith into an attic crawl space. What struck Clavel was the sharp divide between the realm of reason and the realm of faith, between the finite and the infinite. In short, with help from Kierkegaard and Pascal, the experience of the limits of reason actually opened the door for faith. What lay beyond the rational subject's capacity to master and know (the Kantian noumenal) provided a datum of experience that was nevertheless intelligible. *Connaissance*, or understanding, differed from *savoir*, or knowledge. As we will see, in a twist, distinguishing metaphysics from faith, Clavel also eventually distanced himself from Kierkegaard and Pascal whom he accused of being metaphysical thinkers. Though its full elaboration took several more years, the essentials of his perspective were already in place before 1968.

Kant and Foucault had both shown the limits of reason. Kant had exposed as "dogmatism" the presumptuous efforts by previous thinkers to out-think reason's limits. Foucault, as noted, had implicitly undermined the anthropocentric *episteme*, centred on human reason and knowledge, in which Kant operated. Clavel took two lessons from these converging critiques: first, reason, caught in its own impasses, opened the way for an "absurd" faith, absurd because it could entertain no dialogue with reason. The position was essentially fideistic: one had the simple option to believe or not, that is, to take Kierkegaard's "qualitative leap" from one order to the other. Second, modern philosophy since Kant had tended to ignore Kantian critical limits and – a hefty generalization to be sure – had attempted to refound the noumenal in the world and to reinstate metaphysics as Spirit, history, will to power, etc. Modern philosophy had thus fostered the kind of dogmatisms Kant had sought to outlaw. "Killing" God had meant divinizing humans. In Clavel's view, Foucault's work had exposed precisely the "dogmatic" condition of the modern subject by showing the impasse at which a human being is both "the transcendental subject and empirical object of his own activity." This modern condition was the dogmatic slumber – to evoke Kant's phrase describing his own thought before he had read David Hume – from which Clavel wanted others to awaken.

Another way that Clavel approached Foucault, though on this occasion at a great remove from Kant and unintentionlly approaching the philosophers of desire we met in Part II, was in his analogy between faith and madness. In his *Ce que je crois* (1975), he referred explicitly to two thoughts he had borrowed from Foucault, whose interest in madness had also predated 1968: "This madness that made the reason that denies madness. Reason left to itself is mad." One way to describe the limits of modern reason, therefore, was precisely to refer to the pre-rational structures that subtended rationality. Furthermore, this undermining of the myth of modern rationality's self-sufficiency recast the alleged autonomy of reason as itself irrational. Of course, Clavel would overlay his own religious significations on this critique of modern rationality, but the parallels of this view with the late-1960s and early-1970s valorization of schizophrenia by the anti-pyschiatry movement and the libidinal Left are worth noting. For the philosophers of desire had, too, maintained that madness broke open the closed circuits of modernity, reason, and centred subjectivity. Yet against the disordering and de-territorializing flows of Deleuze and Guattari's schizzes, Clavel postulated a decidedly more orderly, metaphysical version of madness, arranged under the labels *faith*, *revelation*, and *transcendence*. Clavel's attack on the philosophers of desire, whom he viewed as nihilists, emerged in his 1977 exchange with Sollers, in which he severely criticized calls for a "liberation of the body":

> You [Sollers] seem to be a supporter [of this view], along with several other inheritors of May like Deleuze and Lyotard, who push the events in the direction of an absolute liberation of desire, in the direction of that sexual revolution which you yourself actually do not seem entirely to want, since yesterday you nodded in agreement when I cited [Jacques] Lacan's view of the sexual revolution as a trap for fools [*piège à cons*] ... [You seem to be] on the side of letting things go and giving in to an absolute abandon to nothingness, that is, to the funfair of sex and other stupid things *that soon and unrelentingly lead to all other dominations of this world*, as either their goal or consequence.

One can see what would have bothered Deleuze and Guattari as well. Willfully embracing an anti- or postmodern religiousness, Clavel was unattached to a particular vocabulary: God, the "great Other Thing," "divine transcendence or human self-transcendence, it does not matter." His point was that transcendence, like madness, was "beyond" or "other than" reason. The "Promethean ... self-creation" of modern humanism had emerged through the denial of a transcendent element present at its birth. The death of "man without God" made necessary the irruption and return of the "repressed God" (a term he took from Kierkegaard). Such an event would certainly be "convulsive," and humans could not effect this return by themselves: "No one searches for God; God searches for us." Clavel claimed that his "thesis" was "simple, radical, Copernican." It certainly was simple. As Jacqueline Piatier summed it up succinctly: "death of God, death of man, long live God."[14]

"There. That's it. We have arrived," Clavel later recalled saying the morning of 3 May 1968. "Where?" his wife asked. "In the middle of Foucault," he replied. May was the kind of transcendental irruption he had been waiting for, and Clavel savoured the events as an observer who wanted to "listen." He resigned his teaching position after the Night of the Barricades (10–11 May) and wrote occasional pieces for *Combat*, the vestiges of his lingering Gaullism suffering a final blow. Firm in his "spiritual" interpretation of the events – May was the "Pentecost of the Invisible Church" – Clavel saw two tasks for himself: make sure that the rift opened by the May events did not close and make clear to all his position on Marxism. If 1968 was indeed an irruptive, transcendental event, the way forward required expanding and exploiting that opening. In contrast to many of May's actors, however, Clavel felt that secular revolutionary discourses and practices were inadequate for the task – they emerged from the very world that was potentially being blown over. Even before 1968 he had rejected the choice between Marxism and capitalism, since both were symptomatic of the Promethean dogmatism he wanted to overturn. To Clavel, when students embraced Marx or Freud, they were acting, says Günter Schiwy, on a "misunderstanding": what was really transpiring, he said, was that they were unknowingly welcoming the transcendent. "1968," he said to Sollers in 1977, "produced a tear, a fracture, not of a formula or a political regime, but of a civilization, a fundamental ground ... For me, May '68 reversed the philosophy of the past two centuries. My position is much more radical [than yours, Sollers]. May '68 was a rupture, the breaking of all old modes of understanding. ... I believe, Sollers, that we are in an emptiness much bigger and in a nothingness much more radical than you maintain." As he asserted in his *Qui est aliéné?*, written in the summer of 1969, the Marxist diagnosis of alienation could not grasp a more basic schism between humans *with* God and humans *without* God, a cultural form of alienation traceable to the story of the Fall. "Alienation is from a transcendence, or it is not," he would say in 1975.[15]

That Clavel was alone in his interpretation of May did not prevent him from throwing himself into the role of fellow traveller to the *gauchistes*. During the Ben Barka Affair, he had declared: "I must be on the Left, since I prefer, it seems to me, justice to order." In the far-left period (1968–74), Clavel was an active presence in what he described as a "strange fraternity that links me to the leftists, from whom I am separated by age, life, genre, belief, etc. ... They and I are in this world like fish out of water." He was particularly instrumental in organizing the leftist press. As of December 1969, he directed the publication *Défense Active*, a precursor of *Secours rouge* (see Part I). As a result of the Jaubert Affair in the summer of 1971, Clavel helped found the aforementioned Agence de presse libération, agreeing to serve as director. Though his participation was short-lived, he also helped launch *Libération* in January 1973. Clavel thus frequented the Gauche prolétarienne milieu as other elder fellow-travelling intellectuals had. Like Mauriac, Foucault, and Sartre, his presence helped dissuade younger radicals from the path of violence and terrorism: since the cultural revolution was metaphysical, violence could do nothing to make it happen. Richard Deshayes, shot by the police on 9 February 1971, was a former student of his, and when Christian Riss was shot on 23 July 1971, Clavel dramatically announced: "The Republic is in danger."[16] Clavel furthermore played a key role in linking the language and images of the French Resistance to the Maoist campaign. With Jean-Pierre Le Dantec he organized the 18 June 1971 visit by Maoists and veterans of the war to the Resistance shrine at Mont Valérin.[17]

The most famous anecdote about Clavel concerns his 13 December 1971 appearance on French television. Invited to debate with Jean Royer, the conservative mayor from Tours and future presidential candidate, on the question, *Mores: Is Society Guilty?*, Clavel had prepared a short film. The producers of the television show, finding it too critical of President Pompidou, cut out the offending phrases. Clavel shocked the live audience by appearing briefly in front of the cameras, announcing that he would not participate in the broadcast, gathering his papers, and departing with the words, "Messieurs les censeurs, bonsoir!" The incident was seen retrospectively as the prelude to the liberalization of television under Valéry Giscard d'Estaing. In short, Clavel was present as a man of the Left.

Clavel moved among circles that otherwise had little in common. Even someone on the Royalist Right like Monseigneur le Comte de Paris referred to Clavel when he died as "without doubt, with Bernanos, the clearest spirit I have met ... I loved and admired his clear thought, his focused and pure life, and the courageous fights he made for his faith, for his ideas, for his friends, with that leftist sensibility that I love. [!]"[18] Clavel's flexibility derived in part from the fact that he thought just about everyone was wrong and therefore did in fact have a great deal in common. When Clavel crossed a sensibility he detested, he did not mince words. This was the case with the philosophy of desire, as we have seen in his dialogue with Sollers, and also with Christian-Marxist dialogues, popular during the 1960s and 1970s (related in France to Roger Garaudy and later to Solzhenitsyn). His animus toward Marxism was magnified when he saw a renunciation of transcendence in Christians' attraction to greater worldliness. "These famous 'Christian-Marxist' colloquiums that I hate!" he wrote.[19] On the 3 October 1975 episode of *Apostrophes* entitled "Is God a Marxist?" Clavel soundly trounced the advocates of rapprochement, Jacques Guichard and Michel Clévenot. His most celebrated phrase on the Christian-Marxist phenomenon was that its adherents, "afraid of being the last Christians ... will end up being the last Marxists." Transcendental journalist, reader of Kant and Foucault, odd Catholic mentor to the far left, Clavel was uniquely positioned to assist in the deradicalization of certain *soixante-huitards*.

One strain of the Clavelian project deserves closer examination, since it bore decisively on the New Philosophers and on the articulation of an ethical turn; namely, the Pascalian dimension. It is here that Clavel most clearly evoked the Jansenist sentiment. Pascal, the seventeenth-century natural philosopher, mathematician, and religious thinker, best remembered for his *Lettres Provinciales* and *Pensées*, cultivated the division between limited human rationality and faith in a transcendent God, between the mind and the heart. Pascal viewed belief as absurd, difficult, and what we would call neurotic. The human being, he said, is a simple "reed" lost in an infinite universe and needing God. Now, although Clavel was ultimately to disavow his proximity to Pascal, the affinities between the two thinkers were noted, for instance, by reviewers of *Ce que je crois* (1975).

> His book is in its own way an "anti-philosophical" book. It is written in the tradition of Pascal. (*Panorama d'Aujourd'hui*)

> There is a lot of Pascal in Clavel, the Pascal of the *Apology* but even more of the Pascal of the *Provinciales*, making fun of the good fathers who are always rushing to keep up with the tastes of the day. (*Le Figaro*)

Three hundred years later to find a new Pascal denuding and bringing to light *the misery of humans without God*, the misery of humans with God being lightly passed over in silence? Or the vision of a new world that, by affirming the spiritual, restoring the Absolute individual and by this fact giving rights to the excluded and the marginal? One wants to say: too beautiful to be true, like a novel. In many ways, *Ce que je crois* is indeed the best novel that Clavel has given us. (*Le Monde*)[20]

What was it about Clavel that reminded some readers of his precursor? Both thinkers philosophized the inadequacy of philosophy and grappled with the themes of tragedy, infinity, fideism, and a qualified pessimism.

For both Clavel and Pascal, the human drama was tragic. The Biblical Fall had established an unbridgeable gap, an alienation, between the divine and the human. Leaving Eden, humankind had entered a world without God. According to Clavel, however, this tragedy had magnified in the modern era. Modernity was an "original sin raised to the second power" that embodied the "conflictual and tragic return of an Origin," that is, the Fall. Modern human self-assertion exacerbated a basic, post-lapserian human condition. We late moderns found ourselves further down a road already identified by Pascal. "What is new since Pascal?" Clavel wrote:

Today does not our global society, our culture in its indistinct density of this thing called Man, in brief our "human world" – in the sense of modern philosophy – seem to assume, symbolize, incarnate, concretize, or if you prefer, reproduce ... all the traits that Pascal attributed to the unhappiness of our sinful condition? ... Does not our entire culture rejoin and re-choose original sin in raising it to the second power by proposing communal liberation to itself? In fact is not original sin a decisive human liberation – to be oneself, to make oneself the centre of oneself – and by the same token, a fundamental alienation? ... If the revolution at the end of the eighteenth and the nineteenth centuries was fundamentally neither economic nor political but cultural, if it was *the cultural revolution of the death of God in men*, what was for Pascal, psychologist of the solitary individual, the misery of individual man without God would have worked its way into the communal structures and today at last into communal feeling.

There were also curious if indirect parallels here to Foucault's (among others') view that modern history was not simply a story of progress and emancipation with a happy ending. Clavel, too, foregrounded the tragic aspects of human self-assertion, downplaying individual agency and collective historical action in the *saeculum*. Yet unlike Foucault and other critical thinkers, and like other Christian thinkers, Clavel made modernity a chapter in soteriological history. For him, there existed a way out of our postlapserian tragedy, a way out suggested by the Pascalian question: "Why does man, a finite being who is reduced to nature, have an infinite *amour-propre*?" In short, Clavel's argument was: humans are finite; God is infinite; humanity's infinite self-love gestures toward the transcendence of human finitude; thus the infinite from which humans are alienated persists as a repressed trace, and humans are the vehicles by which the infinite might re-enter, or better irrupt, within the world.

Between human tragedy and redemptive infinitude, Clavel admitted that faith was absurd and more specifically that Christianity was "indefensible." Fideism, the reliance on faith indifferent to ratiocination, was a "*necessary moment and necessarily the first.* One must pass via that first moment. Abraham believed it." Faith was a matter of the "heart" and not the "head." It was at this point that Clavel's religiousness courted, as we have seen above, the non-rational discourse of madness. The return of the repressed God would in his eyes be "neurotic." Clavel seemed comfortable resting with this indefensible "first moment" of fideism, since it allowed him to criticize others – the philosophy of desire, Christian-Marxist dialogues – without having to elaborate or defend a systematic vision. This lack of systematicity highlighted one frustrating aspect of his rhetoric: his dogged insistence that he knew only what he did not "know" in any philosophically coherent way. (Thus, the importance to him of Socrates that we will see momentarily.) The reasons of his "heart" were inscrutable. Yet, although one might have assumed that his thinking had quietistic implications, Clavel was actually closer to what Lucien Goldmann called "moderate Jansenism." Rather than throw one's hands up and passively wait for the Second Coming, one must work within the world, one's work illuminated by faith. In his own way, Clavel performed this Pascalian move, not only by studying quietly at his desk, as Pascal had done, but also by actively cultivating the cultural revolution that would accompany the return of the transcendent, whose exact form remained mysteriously imprecise. Thus Clavel's pessimism about human action was qualified, as he made clear in his exchange with Sollers, when he spoke of Lacan's "lucidly and profoundly pessimistic philosophy" being a philosophy "almost Pascalian in hollowness," in which desire and power conspire indefinitely:

> But what is that except the naked and blind acceptance of a truly despairing politics? [It is] a despair that nothing in the world can ease (though I would say it *must* be eased) ... a despair that can be broken, broken and not resolved, only by an absolute revolt at the source of which certain of us – I include myself but I am also

thinking of [Christian] Jambet and [Guy] Lardreau in *L'Ange* – have searched for in transcendence.

The transcendent is completely other than the human. God is infinite. Humans are finite. Humans are the portal for the irruption of the divinely transcendent within the immanent world. These familiar theological themes were taken up by Clavel with the curious addition, prophetic in tone, that such an irruption was then underway. May 1968 had been a sign and further signs abounded that the God repressed by modernity and since the Fall was stirring.[21]

Ultimately, unlike Pascal, Clavel was not shy about taking on an audacious prophetic tone, which led some like Luce Giard to complain: "I do not like the familiarity with which Clavel authorizes himself to speak for God." Giard's comment might have been addressed to Clavel's avowal that: "In truth I do not speak of God, I speak around him, I clear the ground, I encircle little by little His mystery and I preserve it."[22] Such confidence departed from Pascal's more searching, tentative, and existentially apprehensive approach. Certain that the immanent return of the transcendent was underway, Clavel had no need for the famous Pascalian wager. Yet in another way, a cultural revolution of the transcendent was a gamble *un peu fou*. For his ethics of grace and absurd faith, his pessimistic anthropology and messianic expectations, Clavel deserves credit for having written himself into the diffused cultural traditions of Jansenism.

The same month that Bernard-Henri Lévy's New Philosophy piece appeared in *Les Nouvelles littéraires* (July 1976) and just after *Dieu est Dieu, nom de Dieu* had been published, Clavel invited a dozen of his "friends" to his house outside Vézelay.[23] It was a Who's Who of the former Gauche prolétarienne circle: the radical priest Robert Davezies, François Ewald, Alain Geismar, André Glucksmann, Christian Jambet, Guy Lardreau, Michel Le Bris, Jean-Pierre Le Dantec, Benny Lévy (a.k.a. Pierre Victor), Jean-Claude Meunier, and Jean Raguenes. The purpose of the meeting was to draw up a balance sheet of the disappointed militant hopes of the post-1968 period. Those present had shared May 1968, Maoism, defeat, and retreat. "We were mistaken," Clavel wrote, "But in what? Where? ... For certain among us the retreat became implicitly spiritual." The gathering at Vézelay thus called them out of their various new commitments (Le Dantec was involved in the Brittany separatist movement; Benny Lévy was Sartre's secretary; Ewald, formerly of the Comité de vérité et justice from Bruay-en-Artois, had become Foucault's secretary at the Collège de France;

Jambet and Lardreau were teaching philosophy in Auxerre) to assess their collective experience. To be sure, Clavel's published account made it seem that there was more of a *Zeitgeist* than there actually was within the disparate group. The "chemical precipitation" that marked the meeting at Vézelay was nonetheless significant.[24] The following year Glucksmann, Jambet, and Lardreau returned to Clavel's house, bringing Foucault and Sollers with them. Their conversation was filmed for the television show *La Part de la vérité* and aired on 4 July 1977.

The first meeting was also an important symbolic moment in the mid-1970s revival of philosophy, especially of the figure of Socrates. We have already mentioned this revival above in chapter 20, involving a return to metaphysics, religion, ethics, and fundamental questions, and a move beyond the methods and foci of the human sciences and structuralism predominant in the latter 1960s and early 1970s. This revival of philosophy was paradoxical, embodying a philosophical critique of philosophy. It combined a return to classic texts and debates, and a continuation of French theory's anti-totalizing mission, with a fight against rival positions within the French theory matrix, especially against the philosophy of desire. The appeal to Socrates, the anti-philosophical philosopher par excellence, was a deliberate stand against the Dionysian *désirant* current. Clavel would have us believe that the Socrates arrival came by way of his own suggestion.[25] His own *Nous l'avons tous tué ou "Ce juif de Socrate!..."* was a meditation on Plato's betrayal of Socrates. Michel Guérin had already written on Socrates in 1975, and Jambet was about to publish *Apologie de Platon: essais de métaphysique* (1976).[26] As we see in chapter 24, Socrates would also be important for Glucksmann in *Les Maîtres penseurs* (1977).

Socrates resonated for some in 1970s France: the corrupter of youth, the dialectical thinker averse to totality, the author of *inscientia* – the wisdom born of admitting that one does not know the truth. The importance of Socrates, and philosophy more generally, for working through post-1968 disappointments and the "anti-totalitarian moment" is further evidenced by a group, established in late 1974 by former members of the Gauche prolétarienne, called the Cercle socratique. The undated founding text of the Cercle stated: "We propose a meeting on Friday, Saturday, and Sunday of All Saint's Day. We intend to examine the following theme: Where are we in the definition of a theory of revolution and subversive practice in France? This meeting will lead to absolutely no organizational reconstitution [of the GP] but an exchange in a place of free reflection." Attached were a list of participants for a meeting in Lyon, including Benny Lévy, Jean

Schiavo, J.-B. Grasset, Olivier Rolin, Christian Riss, and André Glucksmann (though Glucksmann's name was crossed out) as well as notes for a presentation by Michel Grandjean under the title "Emmanuel Levinas: Alterité, Exil et Parole."[27] As we will see in chapter 25, Levinas was the most important figure associated with the ethical revival. This is the earliest textual link I have found between the Maoists and the ethical discourse that would later predominate. The return to philosophy, from Socrates to Levinas, was a significant symbol of the more general transition underway in the 1970s.

Lastly, the July 1976 meeting at Vézelay was important because it brought Clavel into renewed contact with Jambet and Lardreau, the two thinkers who, with Michel Le Bris and Glucksmann, shared most closely the sensibility of the New Philosophers' "uncle."[28] In March 1976, when Bernard-Henri Lévy gave Clavel a copy of Jambet and Lardreau's *L'Ange*, Clavel immediately devoured it on a train. It was the sought-after proof of the breakthrough he had been trumpeting: "It is as if I had already read it," he wrote, "so much had I been waiting for it."[29] He had just enough time to squeeze a footnote into the corrected proofs of *Dieu est Dieu* to say that their work had not been available to him in time for him to itemize all the similarities between his book and *L'Ange*.[30] To be sure, Clavel later gauged his divergence from Jambet and Lardreau in the following way: "What opposes me to the authors of *L'Ange* [is that] in my conception of Being, of the present and imminent future, I have no need of their fabulous wager-challenge [*pari-défi*] on and toward the 'outside-the-world.' When this 'outside-the-world' returns, it will return to break and re-penetrate this world. The elsewhere is there. The impossible becomes possible and has no more need of us than God of man."[31] Clavel distanced himself from the notion of the wager, because where others felt the need to bet, he was certain of an outcome as only a believer could be. Yet, as Jean-Jacques Brochier would note: "One sees what in *L'Ange*, despite all qualifications, would please Maurice Clavel so much."[32]

23

The Angel in the World

Christian Jambet and Guy Lardreau's *L'Ange*, published in March 1976, was originally intended to be the first of three volumes in a work entitled *Ontology of the Revolution*, with volumes 2 and 3 to discuss the *Soul* and the *World* respectively.[1] In fact, only the *World*, subtitled *An Answer to the Question: What Are the Rights of Man?*, would appear two years later in late 1978 with the series title conspicuously absent.[2] The shift between these two publications shows dramatically, at a level of great and stubborn abstraction, the political-cultural shift from revolution to ethics, from residual Maoism to the rights of man. Jambet and Lardreau's embrace of metaphysics was an effort to think their way out of post-1968 disappointments, an effort significant for its exemplifying tendencies within the New Philosophy matrix as well as its response to other alternative intellectual-cultural positions, notably the philosophy of desire and Lacanianism. Three months before Bernard-Henri Lévy's June 1976 *Les Nouvelles littéraires* article, which allegedly christened the New Philosophy phenomenon, *Le Nouvel Observateur* had called *L'Ange* the "manifesto of the 'new' philosophy." Roger-Pol Droit lauded it as an "astonishing book ... the coming of a new, coherent, autonomous thought," and Marcel Neusch called it "the only philosophical reflection on the 'cultural revolution.'"

This assessment was quickly contested. Bertrand Poirot-Delpech wrote: "[Jambet and Lardreau] push the spirit of outrageous rebellion to the point of risking paternalistic recuperation by the haziest and most intolerant of Christians"; and Michel Field sniped: "The first reflex after the first twenty pages of reading is to shut the book back up, furious. The 'form' is indeed unsupportable ... [This book] joins the most formidable anti-Marxist offensive we have known in France without a doubt since fashionable existentialism." It would be hard to sidestep the fact that Jambet and

Lardreau's invocation of the figure of the "Angel" as heir to the notion of cultural revolution was brazen and idiosyncratic. Although they were quick to avow their atheism, their curious dialogue with Christianity – as Gilles Hertzog said, "between Mao and Jesus" – brought them, perhaps unintentionally, into Maurice Clavel's camp; the meaning of 1968 in general and the Maoist adventure more specifically had been metaphysical. Claude Mauriac echoed Clavel's interpretation in a review of *L'Ange*, in which he wrote: "I know that their [the Maoists'] combat was that of the absolute."[3] Lardreau and Jambet's willingness to entertain Christian metaphors also meant that they came closer than other New Philosophers to the logic of an ethical Jansenism, a logic that in turn led them to the rights of man.

Whether *L'Ange* represented the blooming of May's metaphysical seedlings or not, Lardreau and Jambet placed post-1968 disappointments at the origin of their reflections. Their activist efforts with the Gauche prolétarienne frustrated, they "retired to the desert" and posed the basic question: Is revolution even possible? Though the desert image was only a metaphor, Lardreau in particular found in the early Christian ascetics a parallel experience of supposed cultural revolutionaries who felt obliged to flee from worldly engagement. It was in the "a-theistic" uses of Christian "angel" talk, based in turn on a "dialogue" with Jacques Lacan and Immanuel Kant, that the authors felt they had a found an idiom in which to express their "revolutionary" aspirations and disappointments. As Lardeau described it, their ambition was "against all powers and domination, to maintain the hope that despite everything another world is possible. To designate this possibility, no other image presented itself to us than that of the Angel."[4] Jambet and Lardreau might well have stopped there, with the assertion of an unsubmergible hope. But in an excruciatingly long-winded and vague series of arguments, the authors attempted to found and justify their aspirations. The high-minded argument of *L'Ange* was slippery in the sense of sliding from one gross philosophical point to the next.

History, they said, was divided into the "struggle" between "oppressor and oppressed," or the "two worlds" of the Rebel and the Master. These worlds were not defined, but rather described rebellion/resistance or mastery/domination in general. The Rebel and the Master, as well as their different discourses, were separated by "the wager, the choice." Albert Camus had said nothing different. Yet Lardreau and Jambet further complicated the Rebel/Master relation by adding a psychoanalytic gloss indebted especially to Lacan. Lardreau drew an analogy: the Rebel bore the same relation to the Master as "desire" bore to the "law." For Lacan, desire was empty and impossible to fulfill, the always opaque Other divided from the Imaginary, the fantasy of its fulfillment, and the Symbolic, the realm of language and representation. Desire differed from sexual relations as well, since the latter involved the structurally frustrated attempt to consummate – to bring together and bridge – what was constitutively alienated. With this Lacanian etiology of desire as a starting point, Lardreau and Jambet suggested that rebellion, like desire, was checked by the Master's law, and that if one might "completely separate sex from rebellion," that is, give up on the (Imaginary) fantasy of consummating rebellion in (Symbolic) "reality," then one might be able to conceive rebellion in a new mode. The point was to break out of the fixed and constitutively alienated cycle of desire/law and Rebel/Master, in which desire and rebellion were constantly reduced and contained. The notion that desire and rebellion always ended up being reduced and contained fit well with the disappointment of many *soixante-huitards* that their radical efforts had ended up solidly "recuperated" by the powers that be. Consider also, for example, the way the feminist critique of the liberation of desire struggled with the machismo of men's liberated desires and furthermore wrestled with qualms about appealing to the judicial system over sexual violence (Part III). By the mid-1970s the image of rebels eventually becoming masters themselves struck a chord; by the Mitterrand era it would be a truism.

To maintain the possibility of a rebellion neither contained by the Master nor transformed into mastery, Lardreau submitted the image of the Angel as a sexless body. The figure was a deliberate riposte to the philosophy of desire. Where Gilles Deleuze and Félix Guattari, for instance, had insisted on corporealization, Jambet and Lardreau spiritualized the metaphor of the body. Echoing Foucault's contemporaneous investigations into the history of sexuality, Lardreau followed the old Christian distinction between flesh and body in order to suggest that, even if the Master controlled all discourse related to flesh and sexuality, there remained the possibility of discourses and practices of the body that escaped the Master's clutches. The idea of the Angel's sexless body thus broke open the circular, reductive economy of rebellion/mastery and desire/law; it intervened as a kind of non-dialectical third term between Rebel and Master, and angelism represented the possibility of an "autonomous" discourse of the Rebel. Now, these fanciful assertions by Lardreau were made in the tone of a general exhortation, supported by scant argument and justified only by a kind of axiomatic wagering. In other words, Lardreau was betting on the fact that hope and the Rebel – themselves wagers on another level – were still possible.[5]

In *L'Ange*'s most thorough engagement with the Pascalian theme of the wager, Jambet focused on one basic contradiction of the Rebel/Master structure: "There can be no end to the conflict of the two histories," since an end to conflict would mean the "triumph of the Master"; while at the same time, "an end is needed, a victory; otherwise the Master is eternal." Damned if you do, damned if you don't. The Angel represented the metaphysical vantage point from which this contradiction could be gauged: the possibility that the Master was not all there was, the possibility of a sexless body, discourse, and practice that eluded the Master. As a point of indecision, the Angel also represented a wager, betting on the possibility of the Master not always winning. It seemed, said Jambet, that the Master and Rebel also wagered – the former betting that there was nothing to oppose him, the latter gambling that there might be something else besides submission to the Master. "To wager," he wrote, "is nothing more than to link oneself up to one history – against the other, says the Rebel; against nothing, says the Master. Therefore you must wager." Jambet distinguished his notion of the wager from Pascal's by suggesting that neither the "fear of death" nor the "will to live" were at play. Recall again that Pascal had said it is better to bet that God exists even if He does not, because the benefits outweigh the costs if He does exist and you do not believe in Him. In contrast, Jambet remarked amusingly, his wager was meant to "hesitate between God and Lacan!" – one could not really revolt, but neither could one not *not* revolt. This gamble at an impasse led Jambet to conclude that he would "constantly return toward ethics." The wager that the Master was not all there was and that one might choose between the Master and the Rebel – this was an entirely formal and conditional approach to the possibility of ethics.[6]

Several readers noted that *L'Ange*'s significance was precisely a turn toward the moral or ethical, a turn linked to the Pascalian element of the wager. Philippe Nemo, in a generous review of his "friends'" book, although criticizing them for not seeing that the modular Angel is Satan and that rebels must have masters in order to play their role successfully, remarked: "When the Good, the Rebel, is impossible, one can only wager on it as a 'necessary illusion' … Here the authors meet Pascal in an admirable 'meditation on the Wager' that I have not yet read closely enough to determine if it is an attempt to announce a metaphysics, an ontology (as they say), or a religion." Marcel Neusch observed that Jambet and Lardreau's cultural revolution was characterized by "conversion and ethical change." François Ewald saw the return of a Sartrean revolutionary morality of good intentions "thirty years behind":

> The philosophy of the revolution thus becomes an *ethics*, a morality of absolute purity in all points comparable to Kant's. The solution to the problem of political power, always impure, becomes a moral solution, a call to austere revolutionary will, to a "you must therefore you can." The revolution will be moral or it will not be. And this morality has its categorical imperative: *you will not work and you will not enjoy yourself*, work and *jouissance* being the two arms of mastery. One must thus denounce, on one hand, Marx, *Capital*, and "proletarian droning" [*rabachis prolétarian*], and on the other, Deleuze and *Anti-Oedipus*, as two counter-revolutionary impostures.

Here we see New Philosophy's rejection of both Marxism and the philosophy of desire, its lingering (and fading) attachment to talk of revolution, and its explicit turn to the ethical. Jambet and Lardreau furthermore confirmed the suspicion of some that their ethical wagering bespoke a rightward political turn. In an interview with Gilles Hertzog, the authors answered his question, "What is the good question for you? Today and provisionally?" in this way:

> It is that of knowing to choose, very prosaically, the best master among masters. To know how to choose that master according to an ethics, a morality, a sense of good and bad. And after all it is the position of a man like Raymond Aron who says that the best master is the one who tortures the least. Aron has the dignity to judge the master according to the least oppression he brings us. Yes, this type of a position has a certain dignity, because it is a point of view that keeps to the moral.

Certainly, ethics was not the central preoccupation of *L'Ange*. However, it was precisely that element that was foregrounded in the work that followed two years later, *Le Monde*. Although the authors cautioned against reading the "lyrical ease of an itinerary" from one book to the next, and despite the fact that the latter work criticized the "will to purity" of angelism, the trajectory from Maoist revolution to the ethics of rebellion and then to the rights of man continued.[7]

With the exception perhaps of Lévy's somewhat lighter *The Testament of God* (1979), no other work of New Philosophy treated political ethics as explicitly as Jambet and Lardreau's *Le Monde*.[8] Its reflections on autonomy and universality intersected a number of converging, sometimes conflicting figures and themes: Kant, Freud, Jean-Jacques Rousseau, the status of "revolution," the philosophy of desire, feminism, and the rights of man. Emphasizing that there is "no question more pertinent today than *What are the rights of man?*" Lardreau made explicit a number of previously dispersed cultural elements when he added: "If man has disappeared from the horizon of our thought, how can we think the rights of man?" This single, pregnant question identified the great transformation underway from 1960s structuralism and 1970s French theory to the revival of liberalism in the 1980s. That question turned on a more basic one, also posed by Lardreau: "Under what conditions is an ethics possible?" *Le Monde* was to serve as a propaedeutic that considered formal and foundational questions: what it meant to have a "moral attitude," rather than articulating a systematic ethics. The principal stumbling block in approaching this question was the "Idea" of revolution, an idea, as Lardreau and Jambet admitted, they had happily reclaimed in *L'Ange*. If the first book had been about Rebels and Angels standing up to Masters, the second was about the moral attitude, autonomy, universality, and how Freud could be used to supplement Kant.[9]

In typically quixotic fashion, Lardreau linked revolution to politics in general. Politics was the "historically optimistic" project to do away with human "evil." The "only fundamental question" behind the political imagination, therefore, was "What is evil?" The answer was simple and dark: this world was a place of "suffering, unhappiness, inequality, injustice ... and death." In a parallel with the GIP-era too fitting to go unmentioned, Lardreau called this life-is-suffering facticity of experience the "intolerable." Revolution, or politics more generally, had tried to do away with evil in the world by trying to *master* evil, making the intolerable tolerable, under the assumption that "it was possible to finish with *this* world." Once the notion of revolution collapsed, and with it pure political thinking, Lardreau suggested, one was left with the desire to oppose or refuse evil in the world. In other words, revolution and politics had within them an ethical imperative that persisted even if the outer shell of the political imaginary was removed. Thus, the impulse to do away with evil continued even if the historical realization of that impulse seemed unlikely or impossible; even without the dream of revolution, the intolerable remained intolerable. Remaindered opposition to the world's evil was the source of Lardreau and Jambet's "moral attitude," or the search for that which "makes the least barbarism possible, that there be between men *a little gentleness* ... that the truth of their separation does not throw men against each other in the pursuit of the pure singularity of their desire [which is barbarism]." *Le Monde* would try to steer the straits between barbarism and mastery and make the moral attitude into a principle of resistance to both.[10]

Lardreau turned first to Kant to think through this problem. To his mind, a "rupture, an abyss" lay between the Kantian noumenal world of intelligibility and the phenomenal world of sensibility: between the moral ideal of autonomy and universality, on one hand, and its actualization in the world, on the other. The actualization of the moral idea in the world, the harmonization of morality and nature, would mark the utopian "Heavenly City" about which Kant had been more optimistic than Lardreau the late-twentieth-century ex-revolutionary. Although Kant might have really thought this harmonization possible, Lardreau maintained that the Heavenly City was an impossibility *ipso facto*. The Sovereign Good was structurally unrealizable, and there was thus a "deep-seated pessimism in Kantian thought," even if Kant did not realize it. Although Lardreau did not comment at length, it was not lost on him that the notion of non-sensible intelligibility evoked the figure of the Angel – angels having been viewed by scholastic philosophy as non-sensible intellect. Like the Angel, Kant's possible-impossible moral intelligibility was heuristically useful, a way of seeing things, a regulative ideal that allowed one to have a moral attitude, as he said, "*under the idea of liberty*" and "*under the idea of the universal.*" These were ideas that could motivate. The moral attitude was intelligible, because possible, even if it was not actualizable, because impossible: "The Kantian formulation is not: [act] that your maxim *can* become; but: that you can *want* it." In sum, Lardreau claimed that the possibility of a moral attitude depended on the intelligibility of autonomy and universalizability, not their realization – a point of view that could be "glimpsed" at the limit of the possible and the impossible.[11]

Lardreau next qualified this discussion by introducing the Freudian insight that desire complicated the intelligible ideals of autonomy and universality. The notion of autonomy was called into question because, given the unconscious, the self could never be fully present to itself. Desire was "the real by which the illusion of universalism [came] to smash itself to pieces." Desire suggested difference: differences within a person but also people's different desires. The psychoanalytic conflict between desire and the "universal" – the superego for Freud or the Symbolic for Lacan – meant that the moral attitude would be found "in the back and forth, if one could put it thus, between Kantian solutions and Freudian exigencies." Lardreau then suggested that if Freud complicated Kant – the self is more incongruous than the Enlightenment maintained – Kant could be solicited in turn to supplement Freud. At play was a conflict between the universal and desire that amounted to a tension between "two great aspirations": the recognition of the universal rights of man (Kant) and the acceptance of the right to difference (Freud).

The latter was a demand Lardreau tied specifically to the women's and gay liberation movements, which made themselves known as the "demands of the singular and particular against the despotic universal." These movements of desire were opposed to mastery; their aim was to shatter despotic universality. Paradoxically, they also raised the need for a non-despotic universalism in the following way: if one really liberated desire's "irreducible singularity" and "pure difference," then the death drive would be liberated as well. In other words, desire without the kind of constraint suggested by an appeal to the universal could only result in the collision of different singularities; such a collision would be violent and culminate in barbarism. If one recalls the overlap between Spinoza and Hobbes mentioned in chapter 12, it seems that Lardreau was in essence suggesting that the philosophy of desire à la Deleuze, Guattari, and Guy Hocquenghem must end in a war of all against all.[12] The moral attitude was thus a response to barbarism threatening on two fronts: the tyranny of the universal as a totalizing mastery, and the chaos of clashing, irreducible libidinal differences.[13] In brief, Freud and Kant could be used to supplement one another ... difference checking universality and universality checking difference.

Following up on these reflections, Lardreau next asserted that human non-relation lay at the heart of the problem of the moral attitude.[14] What did non-relation mean? First, it meant that the self was in a state of non-relation with itself – the self was divided, absence preceding and precluding full identity and autonomy. Non-relation also meant that different selves did not get along; desires clashed. As Lardreau had said at the outset, the world was the stage of "suffering, unhappiness, inequality, injustice ... and death." The distinction between human relation and non-relation was the hinge on which the difference between politics and the moral attitude turned. Politics, for Lardreau, took human relation as its basic problematic: How does a human community negotiate and handle its divergent interests and passions? From negotiations among free individuals to the harmonization of collective ends, politics is a project that tends toward the horizon of the universal. In short, politics concerns my relation with myself and the relation between myself and all other members of the human community. In contrast, the moral attitude assumes human non-relation as its starting point and dilemma: I am not immediately autonomous because my self is divided, and my interests and passions inevitably collide with those of others. I am incomplete, and we can't all get along. The universal vocation of politics remains elusive if not impossible, and so the moral attitude comes forward as a conditional response to the unresolvable dividedness of individual and collective human experience. Politics fails to rid the world of evil, and the moral attitude is a necessary, though inadequate stopgap measure. This crux – between human relation and non-relation, between the political and the moral – next led Lardreau to treat Rousseau's account of the difference between political and moral autonomy.

In the *Social Contract* (1762), Rousseau had distinguished, on one hand, the individual as a desiring subject whose self-interest preceded and threatened the universalism for the social bond, and on the other, the post-natural individual as a contractual party capable of harmonious concordance: the difference between the Will of All and the General Will. For Lardreau, the Will of All (as well as its difference from the General Will) confirmed his view of the individual's "non-conjunction" with itself and with others, and hence the warrant for the moral attitude. Within the field of the social contract, composed of "interchangeable" political subjects, there persisted a "remainder" of desire's basic a-sociability. Championing the General Will over the less estimable Will of All, Rousseau had "dreamed of reducing and abolishing" particular and differential desires, and thus approached the structural dividedness of the subject negatively, as an injunction *not* to disrupt the harmonization of egos promised by the General Will. Human non-relation, however, underpinned the autonomy and universality of the social contract. Consequently, for Lardreau, the political project of the social contract could never resolve individual and collective human conflict. A "moral attitude," charged with the quasi-psychoanalytic task of ensuring that the subject was not deceived about its own fundamental dividedness, was needed. There were two principal forms of deception: first, allowing oneself to be pummelled into submission by the Master, and second, inflicting one's desire on others – becoming a Master. In order to articulate the moral attitude and avoid deception, the category of the individual had to be preserved, but a happy contractualist vision of individuals willing harmonization would not suffice.[15]

Lardreau next distinguished two levels upon which the individual operated: the relation of subject to Master, and the relation of subject to another subject. His analysis dealt primarily with the first case. In general, though, the theory came down to this distinction: on one hand, facing a political order that threatened to master particular desires, the individual could be considered a moral category; on the other hand, between two subjects the individual had to be subsumed under the principle of universality lest conflicting desires descend into barbarity. Universality and autonomy were not the problem; what counted was where and how they were employed. Autonomy was a limit on the Master; universality was a limit on autonomy.

Barbarism was the overall threat. In the political realm, the barbaric threat (for which "the state" was a shorthand) involved the negation of the subject's desire; in the interpersonal realm, that threat was the subject itself, and how its desire negated other subjects and their desires.

As a response, the "moral attitude" could be described as a series of checks that had three levels, or moments. First, the individual provided a check on political mastery – the Rebel held a moral posture vis-à-vis the Master; Camus had been right. Second, in the interpersonal realm, the individual had to be checked by an appeal to the universal, since individual desires clashed; Kant had been right. Finally, and completing the circle as a reprised but slightly different version of the Camusean point, one had to watch out for the universal that checked interpersonal barbarism, because the universal was itself the home court of mastery. For example, the modern state could adjudicate conflicts among citizens under the sign of its universality, but it could also totalize and oppress; thus dissidents, '68-ers, and advocates of "difference" were right to rebel. Overall, though (and with apologies to Saul Alinsky), rules without rebels and rebels without rules were equally problematic. Autonomy and universality were thus flexible tools that, depending on their arenas, conditioned the moral. The formality of this description makes the reader hungry for some specific content – What universality? – but unfortunately a clear response was not forthcoming.

Jambet and Lardreau's ethics seemed to come down to this axiom: Resist the Master up to the point where you start to become the Master, then stop there. Even the assertion of autonomy against mastery risked making the self into a master: "Old ruse of all ethics ... being 'the master of oneself,' that is to say, a voluntary slave ... What deceives in autonomy is not that which recognizes itself as a limit, but that which, reaching its limit, affirms itself as absolute." But the authors went on to make clear that the grounds for the moral attitude were ultimately groundless, requiring a post-rationalist Pascalian leap. That leap began with Lacan's suggestion that it was impossible both to fulfill desire and to renounce it completely, and that its true horizon was the world of suffering:

It is true that the [Lacanian] maxim, *do not give ground on or to one's desire* [*ne pas céder sur son désir*], necessarily finds its limit in an "as long as it does not desire barbarism." *Necessarily* as long as one has made the choice of "civilization" and life – I would willingly say of *kindness*. An absolutely contingent and gratuitous choice ... a choice that, furthermore, is decided in the "heart" ... facing the horror of suffering, tortured bodies and humiliated souls, the putrid smells that come to us from open graves and camps. No one is taken "reasonably" there, but for us, we make this choice, gratuitous and without value – without value, since all value would already be given to us there.

Nothing lay behind the choices between the Master and the Rebel, politics and the moral attitude, barbarity and civilization. One wagered. Yet once the choice was made, Jambet and Lardreau insisted, a systematic logic of autonomy and universality, rights and duties held. Against the Master one asserted one's autonomy and right as a limit; in interpersonal relationships one found one's autonomy limited by universal duty. Rousseauean and psychoanalytic qualifications notwithstanding, this was pure Kant. "The universal," the authors surmised, "is the pivot where duties and rights are articulated. Where the rights of each subject are recognized, there is the duty to recognize them for others as 'rights of man.' The universal is that which authorizes me to posit *at once*, in the same gesture, *autonomy and its limit*."[16] Marx and Mao had been replaced by Kant and Pascal. Revolution had given way to human rights.

In conclusion, Lardreau anticipated an objection to his retrieval of universal moral philosophy: that the "right of difference" took precedence over duty-limited right. The right to difference had been broached as part of the third moment or level mentioned above. Although universalism promised to mitigate the clash of desires (Kant over Hobbes), it also risked reification as a new form of mastery; therefore difference (rebels, dissidents, '68-ers, and so forth) ought to have the last say. Now, the reclamation of the right to difference was obviously a hallmark of French theory and a leitmotif of post-1968 social activism. We have, for instance, seen the logic of differentialism at work in the philosophy of desire, in Deleuze and Guattari's embrace of schizophrenic margins, and in Hocquenghem's dark homosexuality. The "right to difference" was an organizing principle of the post-1968 far left, insofar as the mobilization of youth, students, women, gays, prisoners, mental patients, and so forth represented the breakdown of a single, unitary philosophy of history and the multiplication of the forms and agents of social action. In short, the claim to the right to difference, to the circulation of irreducible and divergent singularities, prolonged the antinomian ethos of 1968 and its claims against limits and laws. From Lardreau and Jambet's post-Maoist Lacanian perspective, however, the notion of a right to difference was incoherent. Difference, or as they put it, human non-relation, wrecked the universal and culminated in barbarity. If one spoke of a *right* to difference one had already committed to universalization, since rights-talk itself was a universalizing discourse. Thus, according to Lardreau, the call for the right to difference, for non-barbaric difference, was a happily universalist (and utterly prosaic) one: "tolerance" and "soft autonomy."[17] The mention of tolerance reintroduced the question, without answering it, with which *Le Monde* had begun: Can the intolerable ever be tolerated?

To illustrate their mediate position between right and difference in which the moral attitude culminated, the authors invoked the women's and gay liberation movements. The terms were exactly those we had seen at play in Part III in the disputes between, on one hand, feminists pursuing limits on sexual desire and consequences for sexual violence, and on the other, advocates of the philosophy of desire and intergenerational sexual relations who valorized differences. And yet, in spite of his call for a renewal of universalistic tolerance, Lardreau had some harsh words for the women's movement in particular as an example of the contemporaneous "right to difference" sensibility. He wrote, evoking the then-current debates over sexual violence:

> It is not without significance that the liberational desire of women conceals sometimes a troubling echo of savagery ... We have worked too hard to break with the "proletariat" for us to accept "woman," and just as we do not want to choose between Hitler and Stalin, we do not want to choose between rape and castration. It is true, in fact, that women do not castrate anyone, even when they are raped every day – but it is also true that one hears sometimes in their voice the muffled echo of the desire to subjugate, just as one had heard in proletarian discourse. Because the abjection of male violence reigns at this moment, women are at the forward posts of resistance to barbarism – none are more convinced of this fact than us. But in order for their revolt not to carry behind it the remnants [*lambeaux*] of the same terror they fight, they must recognize that the target of their revolt, by way of male domination, is sexual difference as such.[18]

One can read here clear echoes of the anti-feminism we saw earlier. Peter Starr's criticism that the authors' "angelism" acted out a form of castration anxiety is perhaps justified.[19] One might read in those lines an inability to appreciate difference as such – the very risk inherent in the preference for universalism against which Jambet and Lardreau had warned.

Obscure, slightly pretentious, and in the end somewhat banal, the analyses of Lardreau and Jambet in *L'Ange* and *Le Monde* were nevertheless significant for the cultural sensibility they represented. Especially in their rejection of the "philosophy of desire" current in favour of an impossible out-of-this-world ethics, the authors came close to Clavel and especially to a certain Jansenist *esprit*: pessimism that fell short of nihilism, anti-political moralism, hopes displaced outside the realm of history (in favour of grandiose, ahistorical metaphysical claims), the hunger for absolute values, conscience, and the wager. Jean-Marie Benoist gave the best description of this sensibility, including himself in the diagnosis:

> That which a certain Left does not support, beyond the anti-Marxism avowed by the New Philosophers, is the sign – beyond scientism – of a spiritualism of a Pascalian type: the hidden God, a God who speaks by figures in my case, an illuminatory fideist God for Clavel; reading the Fathers of the Church for Jambet and Lardreau. An entire repressed makes its return, and all the followers of little Father [Emile] Combes, the de-Christianizers mobilize against this danger: flat rationalists from the Enlightenment, obstinately relentless with their "*écraser l'infâme*," they barely stomach that one speaks anew of God. They would like to guard the empty shell of the progressive enunciation without realizing that their *Aufklärung* is nothing but a field of ruins where chemical death hovers.[20]

Certainly in Clavel's case, such "spiritualism" was one consequence of anti-humanist criticisms of the Enlightenment. One might also consider how the old Jansenist belief that persecution was a kind of spiritual test might have resonated with some of the New Philosophers who were criticized from all corners. Just as significant was their paradoxical and tragic outlook, which represented the breakdown of the historical dialectics to which some of them had earlier been committed.

24

The Dialectic by the Side of the Road

André Glucksmann's *The Master Thinkers* was considered among the more serious of the books associated with New Philosophy. Not that it was any freer from the rhetorical excesses of its peers, nor that it escaped an almost journalistic lightness in its discussion of that headiest of historical fields – nineteenth-century German philosophy. But there was a line of reasoning in Glucksmann's book that steered clear of Christian Jambet and Guy Lardreau's heavy foundation laying and, in relative terms, avoided Bernard-Henri Lévy's pomposity. *The Master Thinkers* offered a philosophical history of modern domination and resistance. Its main thesis was that the grandiose conceptualism of nineteenth-century German thinkers was a precondition for the twentieth century's disastrous political violence. The writings of Johann Gottlieb Fichte, G.W.F. Hegel, Karl Marx, and Friedrich Nietzsche can't be said to have *caused* the Holocaust, the Gulag, the Chinese Cultural Revolution, and the Vietnam War, but these phenomena were inconceivable without pre-existing forms of thought. "German idealism," Glucksmann wrote, "set forth a program, and our very materialistic century is putting this program into practice." Many of Glucksmann's readers inaccurately ascribed to him the view that Marx drew the Gulag's blueprints and Stalin merely implemented them.[1] A great irony of the moment was that the New Philosophers were accused of being superficial and lightweight by people who had clearly never read their books attentively. Again, the brouhaha was the event itself. Glucksmann's book, however, invites our attention here because it, too, reinforced the ambient primacy of ethics to politics. *The Master Thinkers'* treatment of "Germany" led to the rebellious counter-principle of "the *pleb*," which, although a minor character in the book, turned out to be, in addition to the stuff of cover blurbs and pigeonholes, the basis for a metaphysical ethics.

The Master Thinkers began with an elliptical meditation on François Rabelais's characters Gargantua and Panurge, in *Gargantua and Pantagruel* (1532). Toward the end of the first book of that work the giant Gargantua founds the Abbé de Thélème, which comically and satirically inverts the dreary rule of medieval monasticism by constituting a joyful utopia of sensuality and luxury. Gargantua lays down a "law" for the Thélèmites, the famous "Do What Thou Wilt." Within the walls of the abbey each person may pursue what he or she wants. Glucksmann focused on the fact that this voluntarist free-for-all emerges as a command; the Thélèmites are exhorted to obey only themselves. Now, it is worth noting (as Glucksmann did not) the parallels between Gargantua's command and the graffiti of May 1968, "It is forbidden to forbid." Both capture the paradox of command and license, of ethos and the law, that has occupied us throughout this book. Here, Glucksmann pointed out that after having established the law that everyone should do what he or she wants, Gargantua leaves Thélème behind. The law cannot be challenged and in some respects slips invisibly into the background. Glucksmann views this anecdote as modelling later relations between leaders and followers, all the way to Mao's "You are right to revolt." The law is that there is no law. In contrast, as we will see below, Panurge in his wandering "outside the walls" of Thélème represents a form of resistance inassimilable to the logic of leaders and followers, even of those beholden to the rhetorical lure of liberation.[2]

Glucksmann's "Germany" referred both to the country and, metaphorically, to modernity as a whole. Following a well-trod path, he argued that modern German history was primarily the tale of attempts to achieve a nation-state. The fact that this history eventually included Hitlerism, however, occasioned a more general indictment of a modernity born on the magic date of 1789. The French Revolution and Napoleon, in their pretense of combining revolution, science, and the state, lay at the origin of "Germany"'s troubles. The events of 1789 and Napoleon's view that "nothing must resist the construction of the state" provided a historical challenge. If the late-blooming Germany was to have its own revolution, it needed ideas and plans. If it was to be a nation, it needed a state. The construction of a post-revolutionary nation-state was thus the central intellectual project of major nineteenth-century German thinkers (the argument was compelling when considering Fichte and Hegel; much less so with regard to Marx and Nietzsche). Marxism played a special role in consolidating and instrumentalizing the program of the master thinkers, since Marx was the "most operational" of the group, even if he had remained stuck on the issue of the state. Comparing the exploitative relationship between the property owner and the worker to that of a rapist to a rape victim (we saw in Part III the rhetorical weight of such an image in 1977 France), Glucksmann charged Marx with ultimately telling the story of "capitalist rape" from the point of view of the perpetrator. Nietzsche, a figure who otherwise would seem to fit poorly alongside Fichte, Hegel, and Marx, saw domination everywhere, moving from Marx's preoccupation with "things" to the power relation between "wills," and articulated a pared-down, essential version of the master thinkers' program. Altogether, the way forward in the nineteenth century involved bringing a new spirit of "seriousness" to thought that sought to link texts to territory, class, or power. Glucksmann thus revived the older idea that Germany had experienced the French Revolution on the philosophical plane. Fichte, Hegel, Marx, and Nietzsche overvalued the power of their ideas. The attempt to refashion the world according to ideas, of course, had consequences, and not only the obvious example of Hitler. "This 'Germany,'" Glucksmann wrote, "is perfectly contemporary, having its seat in the modern heads of the modern world, in the Pentagon in Washington just as in any concentration camp deep in the Cambodian countryside."[3]

We should pause on one theme – law – which fuelled Glucksmann's account from Thélème to the present day.[4] The relationship between "guns and pens" turned on law. Thélème had been subject to a law; by obeying it, one became free. Law was a "text" that organized human experience, and it served as a criterion of knowledge that transformed politics into a science. This view held for Hegel's *Reichstaat* as much as for Marx's economic laws. Even Nietzsche said that the "greatest ambition [of] style" is "to make itself law."[5] Law embodied power – the capacity to act and achieve effects. Recall that for Deleuze and Guattari, law represented a limit to the power of desire. However, Glucksmann's distinctive construal of transcendence and immanence added to the shifting understanding of law and ethos. Here, he explicitly appealed to Foucault's arguments in *Discipline and Punish* (1975) that law is part of an immanent field of powers rather than merely transcendent to it, and that power operates via language and knowledge as well as through institutions.[6]

Glucksmann distinguished between the "externality" of law (Gargantua imposed his law on Thélème from the outside) and the immanent function of law (Gargantua departed and the Thélèmites lived according to a law without beginning or justification). Externality preceded internality. Law was imposed from the outside on the subjects who obeyed it, and the law's subjects were formed and fulfilled by the law they obeyed.[7] Glucksmann emphasized that setting up a law required *theoria* – a way of seeing, a perspective, expressed in words and usually written down. "Texts enslave," he said plainly. Hitler and Stalin, too, had been "holding texts," and their regimes had been fundamentally reliant on law (just not liberal-democratic law). "Rule *over* is first a rule *of* … law," and the "mythology of law" ultimately declared: "I can because I know, I am power because I am knowledge." The tragic horrors of the twentieth century related to the merging of law, text, and knowledge: bureaucrats applying rules and calculating their effects, the exclusion or destruction of those who did not fit the rules of the social game, and theories of history setting themselves up as "*the* science of decision."[8] But Glucksmann was clear that he was directing his critique at reigning powers as such, the West as much as earlier fascist regimes and persistent Communist ones. According to the law of Thélème, the most effective regime of obedience and submission was one in which one felt free – experiencing what Etienne de La Boétie had called "voluntary servitude."

Into this totalizing picture of law, text, and knowledge, Glucksmann inserted a mild and highly qualified appeal to resistance. He celebrated the wandering Panurge, the *inscientia* of Socrates, the indomitable "Jewish" spirit, and the populist "pleb." Panurge is a character in *Gargantua* who, as his name suggests, is a libertine free spirit. In contrast to Thélème's ordered and walled freedom, Panurge represents the open road. Pantagruel comes across him and is delighted by his witty and carefree approach to life. Panurge obeys no laws and is a crafty troublemaker, seducing and manipulating his way along, until it becomes apparent that he lacks the courage that comes with committing to a particular person or situation. For Glucksmann, Panurge captures a certain antinomian slyness unbound by the laws of the city, even laws that command one to do whatever one wants. So, too, Socrates bucked the laws of his city and never set down any law himself. He knew only that he did not know (*inscientia*). It is difficult to derive a totalizing or totalitarian logic from such positions.

Glucksmann, in step with Maurice Clavel, Michel Guérin, Christian Jambet, and others who embraced Socrates, celebrated the principle of "interruption" represented by the corrupter of Greek youth. Such a principle, he said, was at play in May 1968, in the mobilization within the United States against the Vietnam War, and in Soviet dissidence. Interruption and contestation were "history's secret, the mainspring of civilization, the locomotive of expansion!" Anticipating the dialectician's objection that such interruptions unknowingly serve the "ruse of history" by which oppositions reinforce the existing order, Glucksmann contended that the figure of Socrates was deeply troubling to a thinker like Hegel, who considered

Socratic skepticism and irony as merely underdeveloped forms of a science that reached maturity in Plato. Socrates broke the law of the city, whereas Plato, forerunner of later seriousness, wrote the law of the city. Calling attention to the relevance of *inscientia* to the twentieth century, Glucksmann went on to ponder the bloody and ultimately senseless battle of Verdun during World War I: "What sense is there there? What positive knowledge? Aren't we led instead to say that we *don't* understand or know? Ought we to begin to admit that we don't understand, to be astonished?" The disasters of the twentieth century had showed that the dreams of total knowledge and social organization embodied in the natural-cum-political laws of the Enlightenment tradition were false or, worse, nightmarish. Nevertheless, continued Glucksmann, we can still respond to "the practical truth of calamities" according to a principle no more sophisticated than the fact that "blood speaks for itself." Even if we no longer have confidence in the "ideal truths of theoretical paradises," one still has one's "conscience."[9] That one does not have all the answers may turn out to be a good thing.

As had Clavel's contemporaneous *Nous l'avons tous tué ou "Ce juif de Socrate!..."* (1977), Glucksmann linked Socrates and his positions of *inscientia* and conscience with Judaism. In the end anti-Semitism was the only value the German master thinkers – Fichte, Hegel, Marx, and Nietzsche – truly shared with their twentieth-century inheritors. Jews were given a special role in the metaphysical project of nationalism. Fichte called Judaism a state within a (German) state, while Hegel labelled Jews "anti-state." "In order to establish a modern law and state," Glucksmann commented, "the German has to kill the Jew within himself. Hegel does not rule out the possibility that the Jew too can become modern, that is, can kill the Jew within *himself*." Furthermore, Jews became a symbol for all who allegedly stood in the way of "the law"'s inexorable triumph. The animus directed against Judaism thus had become the template for attacking all who wander:

> Under the name of "Jew," condemnation is cast upon an entire little world that is liable to escape from the state by crossing its frontiers and, by violating these, to upset the disciplinary society. The Europe of states strives to shut out the "fringe people" ... Though the state's "Jew" is not necessarily Jewish, the young states nevertheless did show a marked tendency to try out on the Jews all the treatments destined for every disturbing element ... The epithet "Jewish" was to be applied to every form of community outside the state, every form of collective life outside oversight by the central administration, every subversive possibility whereby the individual escaped from the alternative between private life and public service.[10]

This line of argument, too, was Foucauldian. The nineteenth century had seen the rise and concretization of modern social homogeneity. Populations who did not assimilate were marked for attack. From Panurge to Socrates to Jews, Glucksmann moved next to his final concept of the *pleb*, which captured his own anti–master-thinker metaphysics of popular revolt.

The *pleb* was the people, spontaneous and uncontrolled. For thinkers like Fichte and Hegel, the *pleb*, once shaped into a citizenry and obedient to a state, became a people as a whole. They were raw material to be given form by modernity and rationality, the blank slate on which the new "law" was to be written. Fichte, Hegel, and Marx dismissed the *pleb* as "riff-raff," an "unassimilated residue upon which all the winds of revolt are likely to blow. If this *residue* is kept in minority status, it is a problem for the police: if it attains majority status, numerically or ideologically, then the result is revolution." The master thinkers wanted to save the *pleb* from itself and educate and shape it through the very force of their ideas. The interpretive line here was remarkably similar to the line Glucksmann had pursued in his 1972 *Les Temps modernes* conversation with Foucault and Benny Lévy (above, chapter 5), where he had joined the GIP-era chorus in defending what Marxists called the "lumpenproletariat" against the monochromatic model of an ordered, homogeneous, and disciplined working class. The kernel of Glucksmann's Maoist radicalism, which he had renounced by the publication of *La Cuisinière et le mangeur d'hommes* (1975), had grown in unanticipated directions. In *The Master Thinkers* he described how the Chinese Cultural Revolution had destroyed not only persisting hierarchies but also older forms of popular revolt. It was those forms of popular revolt, decontextualized and made into a metaphysical principle, that needed to be revived, cultivated, and continued. For the May 1968 slogan, *the beginning of a prolonged struggle*, he might have substituted *the continuation of a struggle already underway for a very long time*. That struggle, more Sisyphean than revolutionary, was unlikely to culminate in any widespread reversal of fortunes. Still, as Clavel, Jambet, and Lardreau had done, Glucksmann gratuitously asserted his own hypothetical first principle: that the master "can be resisted and thereby held back and reduced." It was an old story and the same old story: those inside Thélème's walls against those outside. The unmediated populism and direct democracy of 1968 was related both to contemporaneous figures like Vietnam War protestors and Eastern European and Soviet dissidents and, more deeply, to Panurge, Socrates, and Judaism. We thus should admire those who resist and esteem the "fraternalization of ignorance," which is democracy.[11]

The master thinkers were German-speaking alchemists of nineteenth-century modernity. Oriented toward the future and criticizing other master thinkers who had preceded them, Fichte, Hegel, Marx, and Nietzsche each thought what he said was original and unprecedented. Prototypically, they came to see themselves as replacing God by resolving the contradictions of a battlefield world. Hegel's impression of Napoleon as the world-spirit on horseback might well have served as an epigraph for *The Master Thinkers*, and Nietzsche's vision of the Eternal Return captured the cyclical pattern of thinkers who, one after another, made "laws" out of their texts as they thought their way across the vast expanses opened up by the French Revolution. Knowledge, text, power, certainty, the state, law – these were their marching orders in their pursuit of "one indivisible point ... [for] truth and morality."[12] These last words had been Pascal's. Ironically, in contrast to others in his cohort, Glucksmann said that he preferred René Descartes's "provisional morality" and its tentative make-do-ness to Pascal's absolutism. The impulse to find an Archimedean point, to make the "outside" a new "inside," was the problem. Now as in centuries past, resistance and wandering were phenomena found outside the gates.

In chapter 21 we saw Bernard-Henri Lévy's role as orchestrator, editor, and promoter of New Philosophy. Certainly his name more than all others is tied to the phenomenon, and his *Barbarism with a Human Face* can be considered the *nec plus ultra* of the affair. It is an exasperating read. The gross generalization, fanciful abstraction, contradictory sleights of logic, and obscure formulations characteristic of the works of the New Philosophers appeared in his case in a stunningly pretentious tone. "I am the bastard child of an unholy union between fascism and Stalinism," the book began. Still, *Barbarism with a Human Face* was superlative in its synthesis of circulating themes, in its unintentionally symptomatic representation of the cultural and political climate of France in 1977, and in its explicit formulation of the ethical turn. Lévy, as editor and Left-Bank *flâneur*, almost in spite of himself excelled at capturing aspects of the historical mood. He pushed buttons because he was onto something. Of particular note is that he conveyed, in the form of a critique of May 1968, almost all the elements I have found of interest in following the turn to ethics. He renewed the language of the "intolerable" first introduced by the GIP, and he criticized GP-era popular justice; he treated Deleuze and Guattari as the emblematic figures of the philosophy of desire and acknowledged that school of thought as the most significant current to emerge from 1968, before criticizing *les désirants* as being beholden to a naturalism they claimed to have left behind; he rejected the path of reformism or engagement with the Fifth Republic and furthermore spurned the PS and the Union of the Left, which he believed, too, were encumbered by outdated worldviews; and finally he said all this with exemplary New Philosopher bombast and abstraction. He concluded, in addition, by naming one hidden mainspring of the cultural and political history of 1970s France: ethics.

To be fair, even if one has to get to it by whacking away at the rhetorical underbrush, *Barbarism with a Human Face* had an argument. Lévy essentially offered a pseudo-Lacanian psychoanalytic and ethical critique of "Old Left" Marxism and "New Left" philosophy of desire. He proposed a groundless wager of voluntarist rebellion against the historical materialism of revolution in either its workerist or *désirant* guises. The problem, though, is the density of that rhetorical underbrush. The argument was deduced from grandiose and casually asserted metaphysical claims peppered with odd, stilted paradoxes (power is nothing *and* everything; progress *is* catastrophe). It was Lévy's contention that both the Old and New Lefts operated on the basic Enlightenment principle that people are dominated by lies foisted upon them, lies that can be exposed by an elite who point out this truth. Knowledge can dissolve power once the proletariat gains consciousness of its own true interest or once desire is freed from its repressive shackles. To attack this "political optimism" and substitute his own appeal to "pessimism," Lévy turned explicitly to Jambet and Lardreau's *L'Ange*.[13]

As we saw above, Lévy asserted that "mastery is the law of this world," and that power is not a *thing* but rather an effect whose cause, like the unconscious, is unknown. Parting company with the "Deleuzeans" for whom power was also an effect, "emanation," or "hemorrhage," Lévy substituted a straightforwardly psychoanalytic model of "the Prince" (equivalent to mastery and power) as an *imago* or a fantasy. The critique of the philosophy of desire, though facile, was historically significant and reflected the assertion of a psychoanalytic schema of which limitation and law were constitutive elements. Of course, the "Deleuzean" antinomian alternative continued, then as now, to resonate with some people. Yet the anti-psychoanalytic appeal of the immanent machinations of desire sounded very different in 1977 than it had in 1972. In France, five years is enough for a generation or a regime change. Lévy's Lacanian tilt, explicitly indebted to the neglected Pierre Legendre, led him to the claim that fantasies, at first not real, can become so. To this "imaginary" world of power and mastery there was no natural alternative to be recuperated. As Rousseau had said, the social contract could not be undone. To live in society, history, and "reality" as well as to have identity and desire, was to inhabit the Prince's "theatre" and experience the effective eternality of power.[14] Power had no outside to which one might appeal.

If Lévy had stayed with this point, oversimplified as it was, his book would not have been so outrageous. Its truly maddening quality, however, stemmed from the facility with which he jumped from theme to theme and, like a magician drawing scarves from a hat, tied together a jumble of diverse material. The sheer length of his list of equivalences was preposterous. Not only did reality = the world = the Prince = mastery = power = desire = identity = society = history, but furthermore, all these = the state = the individual = knowledge = language = capitalism = technology = socialism = progress = barbarism = totalitarianism. In short, all reality/existence was a game rigged in advance, one amorphous and totalized setup for inescapable domination.[15] His conclusion was a willfully embraced "pessimism" – and indeed, by the last page, one does find oneself in a dark mood, if for reasons slightly different than those Lévy had intended.

Like Glucksmann, Lévy followed his totalizing diagnosis with a far-fetched prognosis. Having once believed in liberation, in the transformational possibilities of progressive politics, we are told, Lévy now faced the fact that the twentieth century was a barbaric era. Like Clavel, Jambet, and Lardreau, Lévy cast the immediate historical situation as a deeper and more long-lasting metaphysical predicament (in comparison, Glucksmann's foray into the nineteenth century seems modest). By the same token, responses to local historical situations had to be similarly metaphysical. Against the nightmare of the Prince, Lévy counterposed the "dream" of the rebel. The "intolerable also exists, and ... we must resist it with every breath." As it had been for the GIP, the intolerable simply is; it requires no definition or theoretical elaboration. Lévy's response to the darkly portrayed world was to cultivate the role of the rebel as "*moraliste*" and to foster an anti-political ethics. Rebels are "deserters" who reject society, "eternal prisoners" who cannot alter the fundamental rules of the world's game. Their posture is thus deliberately "anti-progressive." Rebellion is a "negation" and a "wager," signalling the emergence of "dualism" and fissures within the monochromatic totality of the world.[16] Despair and paralysis are reasonable temptations in a world without redemption, but they, too, are germane to the order of the "Master." Rejecting those temptations becomes the new Archimedean point for rebellion as ethics and the ethics of rebellion:

> And then? Precisely then, we have to know how to say no. *No* to the temptation of warm surrender. No to abandonment and to the intoxication of saying "What's the good of it?" ... This project makes sense only if it is governed by an ethics which can be flatly called an ethics of *lucidity* and *truth*. Pessimism is of no value unless it brings forth at the end a slender but solid ground of *certainty* and *refusal* ... No matter where it may come from, resist the barbarian threat.[17]

How? First of all, *intellectuals* should forgo the historically established role of "counsellors to Princes" (no doubt Lévy had in mind his own proximity to Mitterrand but he ignored his own advice when with Clavel and others he accepted Valéry Giscard d'Estaing's invitation to lunch at the Elysée on 7 September 1978). Furthermore, in a deliberate subterfuge of an earlier Maoism, Lévy beseeched intellectuals to "give up 'serving the people.'" The point was not to "remake" or change the world, but to bear witness, see, and speak. The "antibarbarian intellectual" was thus to have three identities: that of the "metaphysician" ("in an angelic sense") who would "*think, without believing it*, the impossible thought of a world freed from lordship"; that of the "artist" who would represent the horror and tragedy of the world with "no ulterior motives," creating "order" out of "disorder"; and that of the "*moraliste*" along the lines of "Kant, Camus, or Merleau-Ponty"[!] who would display "a morality of courage and duty confronting the dismal cowardice of submission to facts."[18]

Lévy's refusal of any positivity – of any assertion of what one is *for* and not only *against* – was a deliberately anti-political stance. "We are now in the disturbing position," he concluded, "of having nothing left with which to decide political questions but the most fragile and uncertain tools. It is time, perhaps, to write treatises on ethics." It is true, however, that, using the phrase "provisional politics" as well as echoing Glucksmann's evocation of Descartes's provisional morality, Lévy went so far as to say that, given alternatives like Nazism and Stalinism, French socialism in 1977 might not be so bad, a "lesser evil in a world overcome by evil." Similarly, liberalism was preferable to totalitarianism since it (as well as capitalism) made allowances for differences and rebels. Overall, his conclusion was decidedly "anti-Marxist," and he chided the PS for having drawn from May 1968 merely the lesson of keeping Marxism alive. Moreover, Lévy criticized "resistance," especially as formulated by Deleuze, Guattari, and Foucault, when it came too close to the immanence and materialism of "the world" against which he wanted to rebel. Resistance could be reactionary, as populism and *poujadisme* demonstrated. Rebellion supposedly differed, given its dreamy appeal to transcendence, as when Lévy bemoaned modern politics' attack on religion and the "limit" of a "bond and a social adhesive" that for thousands of years had restrained power from realizing itself absolutely: "The twilight of the gods, a prelude to the twilight of men."[19] Religion and morality, Lévy determined, must return. He followed through on this suggestion with his *The Testament of God* (1979). In an older "revolutionary" language, one would say that reaction had set in.

If it is true that behind Marxian claims to epistemological and political truth lay a fundamental wager about history, as Lucien Goldmann suggested, then the New Philosophers represented a breakdown of Marxist dialectics into more basic component elements. The turn away from Marx toward Kant and Pascal, for instance, seems almost a complete inversion of the development Goldmann had traced in *The Hidden God* (and his earlier book on Kant).[20] Pascal had almost come to the dialectic but had been caught in the tragic separation of "two worlds"; Kant had come a little closer, but only Hegel and Marx had been able to articulate a fully dialectical thought. The New Philosophers undertook a chiasmus, for which Kant served as the mid-point: the confident wager on the immanent dialectics of history dissolved into a more basic, uncertain wager on a transcendence that refused fully to show itself.[21] The Pascalian sense of "being in the world but not of it" was very much present in the New Philosophers' ethical rejection of politics, especially their refusal of the Common Program of the Left. Electoral politics – driven by interest, guided by compromise, and promising at best only reforms – could never have fulfilled the utopian hopes of 1968. The disappointment that emerged in the mid-1970s must be understood in relationship to the hopes that persisted. As I have suggested, utopian dreams were displaced into non-historical metaphysical reflection. It was not coincidental that – for Lévy, Jambet, and Lardreau – psychoanalysis seemed one appropriate discourse by which to measure dreams against reality. The Lacanianized Rousseau, for example, was marshalled against the Spinozism of the philosophers of desire. The New Philosophers' tragic pessimism walked the line between unwarranted optimism and unacceptable cynicism.

With apologies to Voltaire, if the New Philosophers had not existed, it would have been necessary to invent them. While they may have contributed marginally to the defeat of the Left in 1978, the real responsibility for that defeat lay not with the anti-political "moralists" but with the bickering of the Union of the Left, torn as it was by its own competing visions and the necessities of political compromise. To ask if the New Philosophers were on the Left, or to assume that they were on the Right, misses the fact that they were drawing another distinction: between statism (cultivated by both the Left and Right) and an anarchistic anti-statism. Under Giscard d'Estaing, the French state achieved a new measure of stability by moving to the centre, modernizing, and liberalizing. At the same time as robbing the Left of some of its animus, this realignment helped foreground the notion that the state could not solve all problems. The state was the problem. As Jean-Marie Domenach recalled:

> At that moment indeed there was no longer any true political debate in France. De Gaulle had disappeared, the energy crisis had started, ecological consciousness asserted itself ... "There is no history but that of the State," Jean-Paul Dollé affirmed, and Michel Le Bris announced with aplomb: "I conceived the project to write the end of politics" ... Their pastry-cutter formulas ("The State is evil." "The more State there is, the more Evil takes hold") certainly could not make political reflection advance, but they opened, or rather reopened, doors that were closed.[22]

One door reopened onto civil society. In creating a space of public debate to which the state had no welcome contribution, the gamble for an anti-political ethics helped reintroduce the theme of civil society into political and cultural life. Here, the New Philosophers confirmed and contributed to widespread developments that other thinkers in the late 1970s and early 1980s would consider more directly. New Philosophy's ethical Jansenism was neither fully political nor private; it exposed the limits as well as the virtues of anti-statism, and the election of François Mitterrand in 1981 would be the strongest challenge to that ethics. As Patrick Pharo was led to ask: "Confronted with the possibility of political participation, what will the moral attitude become?"[23]

While the New Philosophers were in the limelight, however, ethical and moral concerns predominated. That predominance and the almost universal denunciation of New Philosophy were to some extent contiguous. Success made them easy targets. The difficulty of talking about ethics without moralizing was written into the controversy. "Reference to the ethical," Jean-Pierre Le Goff has concluded with respect to the New Philosophers, "has the symbolic advantage of indignation against all massacres and miseries of the world. It allows one to situate oneself right away on the good side of the debate, giving to the interlocutor the role of the self-righteous conformist, if not the accomplice of barbarism."[24] One can understand how such self-satisfied rhetoric could seem smug and insular and thus easy to criticize. In making explicit part of an ethical discourse that had been gestating since 1968, the New Philosophers were introducing into the public domain a distinctly French concern for human rights and ethical politics that was to develop into a sustained buzz in the 1980s and 1990s. Some of the weaknesses of that rhetoric, and the limits of ethics, were already apparent among the New Philosophers. But none of that was new. In fact, the figure of the *moraliste* and the aspersions cast upon him evoked an older set of debates. As Alain Peyrefitte, Minister of Justice (and, incidentally, former Minister of Education who had resigned in May 1968), put it:

> New Philosophy only refounds an old tradition. The intellectual who refuses to be a dupe of power, the apolitical intellectual is a classic figure in our history ... Power seems only legitimate in their eyes if it *opposes* another power – considered by definition as oppressive. Starting with the idea that all power is might, one arrives at the conclusion that counter-powers alone are morally good ... It is a brilliant, deep, and seemingly new appearance of the old refusal of Antigone when faced with Creon.[25]

The New Philosophers represented the challenge of tragedy and of religious and metaphysical drama. Yet as it had been for Greece, whose breadth of reflection on ethics could not be reduced to its theatre, so too in France, other thinkers would re-centre ethical fascination in languages that were less dream-like. The turn had been made.

25

John Locke Was Not French, or The Varieties of Ethical Experience

The moral problem is not the "rights of man." It is the rights of "others."

Vladimir Jankélévitch (1979)

But ethics is also thinking that tars all thought and all politics with its own impotence.

Jacques Rancière (1995)

In the late 1970s and early 1980s a rumour swept through certain circles in France: hope had mutated into something more insidious than simple despair. The hopes of a revolutionary generation, aspirations whose echoes had been felt throughout the decade after 1968, had now faded into disillusioned disappointment. Worse still, the 1970s seemed less to have fulfilled utopian aspirations, provoked class warfare, and brought about profound social rearrangement than to have nourished exactly contrary phenomena. Rather than destroying consumer society in favour of less materialistic values, or radically reworking the hierarchies of social order by "freeing up speech" [*libérer la parole*], the '68-ers had seen that society and order recover with little difficulty, reflecting at most only mild reform. Momentary disaggregation, so the rumour went, had been followed by re-aggregation, sometimes in subtle and less easily criticizable forms. Political possibility appeared to contract, and many aspects of society were presumed to be worse off than before. A period of "historical depression" had set in.[1]

Like other rumours, this one mixed exaggerated truths and outright fibbing with a desire to cling onto something sure. We encountered it above in chapter 1, in the suggestion that 1968 had ushered in an unprecedented ascendancy of market-friendly, depoliticized, and nihilistic individualism. Nevertheless, the legacy of 1968 was more ambiguous than simply gloomy.

Alongside an emergent individualism, checks on the individual as the touchstone of political and social life had arisen. These diverse checks formed a rich relational texture and, as we note in the Conclusion, included institutions and associations. Citizenship admitted very "thick description." New legislation modernized the penal code and concretized evolving sexual and social mores. A new spirit of supra-statist and extra-territorial humanitarianism emerged – from talk of the "intolerable" conditions of French prisons to the popular reception of dissidence in the mid-1970s to the success of organizations like Doctors Without Borders, founded in 1971. A fantastical anti-psychiatry, rather than leading to a liberation of schizophrenia, had by the early 1980s led to very real reforms in psychiatric practice and a revival of the school of Institutional Psychotherapy. Above all, thinking about ethics had returned. The accelerating atomization of late modern culture did not prevent people from invoking age-old questions anew: What makes a life worth living? – and asking modern ones: How ought we live together?

Of course, new spaces of civil and private liberty had opened up in post-1968 France. Paradoxically, late modern individual experience found itself simultaneously elevated and made irrelevant. Recall that Gilles Lipovetsky had denounced "personalization" in the context of the depoliticization and de-socialization of public life. Certainly one of the unhappy sides of May's ambiguous legacy involved a breakdown of collective projects and of history as a forum for inspired participation. On this point one might interpret French theory's predilection for the model of fractured and decentred subjectivity symptomatically. On the whole, however, at the end of the 1970s and early 1980s (or even today), one would have been hard-pressed to find in France large numbers of people advocating an anti-statist, free-market liberal order composed of hungry and covetous self-starters. Alexis de Tocqueville was not a utilitarian; French Republicanism was not Anglo-American liberalism; John Locke was not French.

It is now high time to examine the achieved ethical turn and its distinctively French markings. We have traced the ethical thematic throughout this book, at first in its implicit, underground flows, and in Parts III and IV as it broke through the surface. By the late 1970s and early 1980s, ethics was bubbling up everywhere. If there was a certain logic to the foregrounding of the ethical thematic at that time, it was that it came at a moment when the threads of political, cultural, and intellectual history were becoming frayed. The intellectual history of post-1968 France that we have recounted involved a number of key individuals who at pivotal moments contributed to and epitomized notable changes. By the late 1970s, however, the path becomes twisted and intricate; in short, complicated. As the era of the "master thinkers" passed, it became more difficult to narrate straightforwardly the shape, itinerary, and destination of that route. We can now observe that the turn to ethics, with its variety of meanings, occurred at the same moment that intellectual life diversified in new ways – or better, that its diversity was newly acknowledged. Perhaps ethics is just that attempt to grapple with complexities and contingencies that cannot be reduced to simple storylines and master *bien-pensants*?

In the late 1970s and early 1980s, then, the ethical turn was accomplished. Since it manifested itself at many sites and moments, our concluding selection must perforce be deliberate. We first notice how the years just before and into the Mitterrand era, which itself began with the presidential election of 1981, were characterized by a sense of malaise for some on the Left. Disenchantment with official politics continued one strain of the post-1968 ethos, but at the same time, since the New Philosophers, ethics was gaining ground in several arenas – from the linkage of postmodernism and ethics by Jean-François Lyotard to "moral" interpretations of the Polish Solidarity movement. Early in his administration, Mitterrand established a National Ethics Committee to oversee scientific, especially biotechnological, research. The AIDS crisis brought a new consideration of sexual ethics. Looking at a number of intellectual fields and thinkers in what follows, we shall touch briefly on the reassertion of political theory and historical writing, and then on three philosophers – Paul Ricoeur, Vladimir Jankélévitch, and Emmanuel Levinas – who had long reflected on ethics and now found themselves thrust into the limelight. We shall finally delve a bit more deeply into the personal ethical turns of two major characters, Jean-Paul Sartre and Michel Foucault. In their last years, these two thinkers gave ethics a pride of place unprecedented for either of them. If in the beginning was the act, our story draws to a conclusion with the passage to reflection.

In May 1981 François Mitterrand was elected president of France. The evening the election results were announced, in Paris, especially in the neighbourhoods around the Place de la Bastille and the Place de la République, people took to the streets, singing, dancing, and celebrating until late into the night. The Left seemed almost to breathe a collective sigh of relief as elusive and longed-for electoral victory was achieved after an extended period of frustration. Mitterrand had run against Charles de Gaulle in 1965 and against Valéry Giscard d'Estaing in 1974, losing the latter contest by less than one percent of the total vote. As we saw in Part IV, the legislative elections of 1978 had also ended in disappointment for the

Left when the Union of the Left (between the Socialists and Communists) had fallen apart. The pressures on those results cannot be underestimated. Expectations had been very high that the cultural and political energies of 1968 would find belated electoral expression in 1977–78. With the Right in disarray, the major question of 1978 was: If not now, then when? After the defeat, even Mitterrand, overcome by disappointment, had considered hanging up his hat. Thus it was a great reversal of fortune when, three years later, he and his Socialist Party received a mandate by capitalizing on the desertion of the PCF by the party faithful and on conflicts on the Right between Giscard d'Estaing and Jacques Chirac. If those in the streets in early May 1981 were singing some version of "happy days are here again," the only historical precedent they could have pointed to would have been the Popular Front of the late 1930s.

As in 1968, France experienced no overnight, cataclysmic transformation when Mitterrand came into power. In the first years of his administration, there were significant reforms: on the legal front (the sexual-political legislation mentioned in Part III above as well as the abolition of the death penalty and of the Court of State Security); with regard to French cultural politics (under the direction of the Minister of Culture Jack Lang); and, more moderately, in economic terms (though widespread nationalizations did not take place, labour unions found greater receptivity at the Elysée than in previous administrations – that is, until liberalization got underway in 1983). Signs of socialist redesign were, however, limited to the first few years of the first Mitterrand administration. The international economic and political situation led Mitterrand to policies that would never have been accepted into the Socialist Party's pre-1981 platform; and in 1986, France entered the period of political compromise known as *cohabitation* (the president and prime minister representing opposite political persuasions), which lasted for the rest of the century. It also did not take very long for *les années Mitterrand* to gain a reputation as a period rife with scandal and political corruption. The turn to ethics did not mean that people acted more ethically, but that behaviour was judged by ethical yardsticks. Far from a socialist revolution, Mitterrand's chief legacy is popularly held to be the number of grandiose architectural and urban projects he had set in motion before he died.

Whatever the sensibility of the 1980s (a period that largely surpasses the terrain of this study), there is no doubt that 1981 represented the symbolic culmination of a period opened by 1968. Mitterrand's ascendancy marked the arrival in power – the *arrivisme* – of some members of the generation of 1968 known henceforth as *la gauche caviar.* Perhaps even more than in other European countries, some former French radicals found themselves at the centre of political and cultural power in the 1980s, especially within Mitterrand's government and as journalists. The contemporaneous equivalent to Roland Castro, Régis Debray, and Gisèle Halimi visiting Mitterrand's Elysée would have been the unlikely spectacle of Tom Hayden, Huey Newton, and Gloria Steinem being asked to dinner in the Reagan White House. And yet, despite the confirmation of some post-1968 trends (notably in legislation) and the legitimization of some former radicals, the Mitterrand years were ultimately a great letdown to many 1968-ers. It seemed that the Left had been so accustomed to being outside the corridors of power (what else had it known?) that the notion – let alone the experience – of being inside those twisting and sometimes poorly lit passageways startled, upset, and overwhelmed. It was not uncommon in the early to mid-1980s to hear talk on the independent French Left – that political, cultural, and intellectual field at the core of this book – of "emptiness," a "vacuum," and the "dark." Disappointment had been a temptation throughout the 1970s, as utopian hopes were frustrated and liberational energies found new forms of expression; but judgments made in the 1980s about 1968 and the 1970s probably said more about the Mitterrand years. De Gaulle, Pompidou, and Giscard d'Estaing had given the Left the moral authority of the outsider, and the reality of the Mitterrand era reinforced a sense of malaise that contrasted with the high expectations of the post-1968 years. Both May 1968 and May 1981 saw brief expressions of euphoria followed by prolonged attempts to recapture something of that suspended moment. The singing that welcomed the Left to power in May 1981, like the student commune thirteen years before, was joyous but fleeting, and became a place marker in the memories of some French men and women.

Notwithstanding their many faults, the New Philosophers had in 1976–77 foreshadowed a wider-ranging skepticism and deflation with respect to politics, first between 1978 and 1981, when one could reasonably wonder if the Left was ever going to come to power, and then after 1981, as the dispiriting realities of outsiders-turned-insiders set in. Pessimism about political reasoning and the need to appeal to extra-political moral or ethical correctives were of the hour. It seemed possible to ask questions that had been "forbidden" under the marxisant paradigm.

There is a larger story to tell about this ethical stance toward politics, which could be seen variously as anti-political, non-political, or supra-political, and whose great symbol was human rights and humanitarianism. The independent Left played a central role in placing human rights on the public agenda in the last quarter of the twentieth century. In January 1978, the Comité des intellectuels pour l'Europe des libertés was created to champion human rights against the force of states and nations. The anti-totalitarian debates that Michael Scott Christofferson related primarily to dynamics in French domestic politics focused continuing attention on Soviet and Eastern European dissidents and then shone a spotlight on the horrors of the Khmer Rouge and the calamity of the Vietnamese "boat people." The Soviet invasion of Afghanistan as well as the January 1980 arrest of Andrei Sakharov, who had won the Nobel Peace Prize in 1975, led to protests in Paris. The Polish Solidarity movement, founded in September 1980, provoked an outpouring of support, and the declaration of martial law in Poland in December 1981 led to widespread denunciation.[2] It was not simply a question of the Left's belated discovery of human rights issues; the point is that the independent, non–party-affiliated Left in particular took a leadership role in publicizing and denouncing "intolerable" conditions everywhere.

The end of the post-1968 period cannot be gauged by electoral politics alone. The crucial elements in French intellectual-political culture that had accrued over the 1970s were not reducible to party politics. Still, the political, in its fading revolutionary echoes, disappointing Mitterrandist accession, and soon-resurgent Republican guises, was an important marker of a changing climate. Mitterrand's election in 1981 came in the midst of what some described as a period of disenchantment, from the legislative elections of 1978 to the economic liberalization of 1983. Jean Baudrillard, for instance, published a scathing collection of essays on "the divine Left" between 1977 and 1984, in which he tested his theory of simulation, the collapse of a difference between reality and its representation, on a *médiatique* political elite whose "desire to do good" fell flat before an indifferent public.[3] Neither romanticized radicalism nor unglamorous reformism inspired. Stanley Hoffmann's observation in the early 1960s that France tended to waver between the "saviour" and "game" models of politics puts this evacuation of the political in the late 1970s and early 1980s into perspective.[4] The 1970s proved to be an interregnum between the eras of de Gaulle and Mitterrand, the two pharaonic rulers of postwar France. The ethos of 1968 had tended toward the gambit – from rebellion in the streets to the wagers of the New Philosophers – and even before Mitterrand was elected, a sense of "game over" was palpable. Emblematically, confident acts of political will undertaken with the backing of a secure philosophy of history had been replaced by introspective analyses of "voluntary servitude." Some '68-ers had surrendered their Little Red Books for analysts' couches; others had thrown themselves into scholarly work; still others had signed on as the first guinea pigs in the new and brightly lit laboratories of post-print media culture. There was thus a certain disarray in the late 1970s, a fragmentation of previously coherent standpoints, factions, and battle lines, and a fraying of the historical *fil conducteur*, or unifying thread. It seemed more difficult than it had been in the early to mid-1970s to identify clear tendencies and pivotal moments (May 1981 was an exception in this regard). It was in this context that ethics made its vigorous return.

In retrospect one sees that there had been scattered signals throughout the 1970s of explicit ethical concern. In 1972 Pierre Verstraeten had written on Sartre, morality, and violence; and Kostas Axelos had written on ethics in the context of his larger project on the "game" [*jeu*] of life in the age of technocracy, a game that we play and which plays us. In July 1973 two of the most significant "moral personalities" in France since the Algerian War, Pierre Vidal-Naquet and Laurent Schwartz, published the "Manifesto for Truth and Morality in Politics." Also that year Jacques Bouveresse, in lonely engagement with Anglo-American philosophy, published a discussion of the ethical dimensions of the thought of Ludwig Wittgenstein. In 1974 the Centre d'études et de recherches Marxistes dedicated its annual meeting to the theme of "morality and society." The aging scholar Etienne Souriau attempted to sketch an ethics "on a purely aesthetic basis" in 1975. The following year the Socialist Party leader, Colette Audry, could write sympathetically of "militants and their morals." In 1977 André Gorz exhumed and published his *Fondements pour une morale*, written some twenty years before. In 1978, immediately following an issue dedicated to the New Philosophers, *La Nef* published a special issue called *Une Morale pour demain?*, and in 1979 the former militant Denis Langlois isolated the moral dimensions of the personal-is-political question: "How can one change the world if one is not capable of changing oneself? ... The moral is, in fact, the only worthwhile response to a system that despises the individual and believes that everything can be bought, that everything is corrupt." There were many other dispersed and anecdotal signs throughout the 1970s of renewed interest in the language, theory, and practice of *la morale* and *l'éthique*.[5]

Ethical fascination took off at a juncture in which several forms of thought and intellectual projects returned to prominence. Just as ethics had been on the ropes in the moment of structuralist and poststructuralist theory, so too, political thinking (as opposed to the politicization of thought), historical writing, and canonical philosophy had also found themselves sidelined from the mid-1960s to the mid-1970s. With the exception of circles around Raymond Aron, French political theory was largely not a lively field. Philosophers and historians, of course, continued to ply their trades, but in terms of dynamic scholarship and perspectives, the 1960s and most of the 1970s saw the influence of thinkers who spoke of structures, language, and desire, and who criticized the humanistic classicism of the academic mainstream. Political, historical, and philosophical thinking that did not engage the era's thinkers of *référence* – Karl Marx, Sigmund Freud, and Friedrich Nietzsche – was involved in conversations other than those in which significant intellectual innovations were taking shape. Setting aside the considerable complexities that this snapshot occludes, the point to make here is that one of the most important accessories to the explicit emergence of ethics was the fact (and, as important, the pervasive *sense* of that fact) that intellectual fields marginalized by Parisian intelligentsia in-crowds – such as political theory, history, and philosophy – made a comeback in the mid-to-late 1970s.

Before we turn to the philosophers Ricoeur, Jankélévitch, Levinas, and especially Sartre alongside the philosopher-historian Foucault, a brief word on the political and historical is in order. We already mentioned in passing in chapter 1 that a general problematization of the political in the 1970s led in part to political reflection. Building on the ethos of 1968, remaining on the borders of official party politics, and participating in debates on totalitarianism, thinkers like Louis Dumont, Marcel Gauchet, Claude Lefort, Pierre Manent, and Pierre Rosanvallon revived political philosophy, often with a historical cast. Their reassessments of the meanings, histories, and possibilities of the political meshed with other corresponding developments, from the advocacy of human rights to calls for a revitalization of French Republicanism to new interest in Anglo-American thought (Bouveresse no longer so alone) to debates in reviews such as *Esprit*, *Commentaire* (founded in 1978), and *Le Débat* (founded in 1980). The "Tocquevillean moment" saw the political, and thus political ethics, brought to centre stage, just as Mitterrandism landed with a dull thud. In the years shortly before his death in 1983, Raymond Aron seemed to receive belated recognition for positions he had maintained for decades.[6]

François Furet's groundbreaking reassessment of the French Revolution bestrode the fields of revived political reflection and renascent historical writing. His declaration that "the French Revolution is over" contributed substantially to drawing a significant chapter in the French history of the living revolution to a close, leaving marxisant assessments behind, putting the issue of political representation and language on the interpretive agenda, and setting the stage for the Republican hoopla of the bicentenary celebrations of 1989. But Furet was not alone in re-energizing the discipline of history. Different generations associated with the Annales school of historiography overlapped in the 1970s. Fernand Braudel's landmark revised three-volume study of civilization and capitalism appeared in 1979, at the very moment when "New History" was picking up the reins from Braudel's generation.[7] But the pertinence of the study of history had particular, even ethical meaning in the late 1970s and early 1980s as the scandalous (and scabrous) figure of Robert Faurisson started spouting his nonsense, achieving notoriety by denying the Holocaust at the same moment that anti-Semitic violence had increased markedly (several bombings and assassinations between 1979 and 1982, including the death of Pierre Goldman mentioned in chapter 17). The French debates around Holocaust denial, or *négationnisme*, which crystallized in the late 1970s and early 1980s, brought the ethical dimensions of history and memory to the fore and also to some extent foreshadowed the Heidegger controversies of the late 1980s.[8]

If political thought and history lay at the margins of the ethical turn, philosophy largely occupied its centre. François Dosse links the return of ethics to the rediscovery and popularization in the late 1970s and early 1980s of three philosophers who, though tirelessly productive, had been largely ignored during the structuralist era: Paul Ricoeur, Vladimir Jankélévitch, and Emmanuel Levinas. Each of these thinkers had put ethics at the heart of his mature thought (although in Ricoeur's case ethics was a by-product of his interest in hermeneutics). This return to philosophy, and specifically to ethical and moral concerns, was a return to loose religious identifications and questions. Again, the New Philosophers had symbolized farther-reaching and more serious developments. As Dosse comments:

> Structuralism had been an attempt to get free of philosophy, whose proximate end was endlessly proclaimed in the name of Science and Theory. Yet, as structuralism waned, philosophy, ostensibly dethroned, regained its prior place at the center. The 1978 issue of the review *Critique*, entitled "Philosophy after All," announced, "The End of the End of Philosophy." The avoidance of a certain number of properly philosophical questions, by choosing the social sciences, had led people to think that with structuralism, questions on ethics and metaphysics were made obsolete once and for all. Yet, with the major shift underway in the mid-seventies, these were the very questions that were to dominate French intellectual life for quite some time.[9]

Dosse went on to name Ricoeur, Jankélévitch, and Levinas as the three thinkers most prominently linked to revived interest in philosophy and ethics. Olivier Mongin, in his solid analysis of the "mutations of the intellectual landscape" from the 1970s through the 1990s, claims that Levinas and Ricoeur were most prominently identified with the ethical theme in the 1980s.[10]

Ricoeur (1913–2005), a French Protestant, had long included ethics within his reflections on interpretation, the human sciences, and narrative.[11] Though only in *Oneself as Another* (1990) did his hermeneutical reflection fully engage the dialectically ethical relation between self and other, the other within the self, and the self's "solicitude" toward others, nevertheless, the theme of ethics itself had appeared as early as his *History and Truth* (1955).[12] Ricoeur's synthetic hermeneutics had over the long term made room for the ethical as one dimension of interpretive activity. Having found receptive audiences in the United States, where he began teaching in 1960, he was marginalized in France during the heyday of structuralism. His own brush with the May events had come at Nanterre where he, like Levinas, then taught. After being dean there for a time, he resigned amid continuing, disagreeable agitation. During the 1970s, when he was close to *Esprit* circles, his synthetic thought began to be more widely received, especially as the revival of philosophy cited by Dosse began to take shape. In 1975 the first of a series of collections published in his honour appeared, and more recent ones have dealt specifically with his contributions to moral philosophy.[13]

Marcel Gauchet suggests that, even more than by the hand of Ricoeur, ethical revival passed first by way of the attention paid to Jankélévitch in the late 1970s and then, in the 1980s, through an explosion of interest in the thought of Levinas.[14] Long-time professor of philosophy at the Sorbonne, Jankélévitch had written on moral philosophy since the end of World War II. A former disciple of Henri Bergson, he published his first books in 1933, one on *la mauvaise conscience* and another on F.W.J. Schelling. His voluminous writings from the 1940s through the 1970s had been appreciated by only the tightest of unfashionable academic circles. He was, however, renowned as a marvellous teacher and, especially in the years after 1968, always had numerous devoted students. Born in 1903 in France of Russian Jewish origins, Jankélévitch was always adamant that the Holocaust lay at the core of his postwar moral thinking. "Forgiveness died in the death camps," he wrote in 1971. Active in the Resistance after having lost his teaching post under Vichy, he later claimed that after 1945 he had forgotten the German language, and never visited that country again. Jankélévitch's moral philosophy, says Judith Friedlander, was squarely in the tradition of "the universalistic tradition of an ethical Judaism."[15] For him, moral problems were universal problems, and he devoted much time to considering philosophically the sense and coherence of everyday experiences such as lying, evil, virtue, austerity, boredom, death, forgiveness, love, and nostalgia. He was described as offering a "non-existentialist treatment of existence." His own idiosyncratic thinking was not easily assimilated to any school, which perhaps contributes to explaining why he remained outside the spotlight in France for so long, and maybe also why he was all but ignored in English-language studies of French philosophy until the late 1990s.[16] Alongside his moral philosophy, throughout his life Jankélévitch also wrote on music (especially Claude Debussy and Gabriel Fauré) and was an avid devotee of the piano.

Long identified with the political Left in his own "solitary" way, Jankélévitch was deeply affected by the May events, commenting in 1979: "In 1968, I truly began a new life."[17] Occasionally the target of student hostility (having been older than thirty) and invariably accused in the uproar of being a mandarin, he nevertheless saw in May a continuity with his own thought and experience: "I had colleagues who told me: 'If they win, that will be the end of moral philosophy!' I believed fervently [*dur comme fer*] that moral philosophy would continue to exist anyway. The language of the leftists was riddled with moral terms, their revolt had no sense outside an ethical one." After 1968 Jankélévitch was inundated with requests to supervise theses, "Toward 1969," he said, "I found myself with 130 or 140 theses to direct ... I would return home joyously at night with twenty more theses, as if I had been off hunting." His contributions to the generation of 1968 were repaid as some of its members acknowledged his influence on them, and especially as his fame grew in the last years of his life. As Dosse writes, somewhat hyperbolically: "His efforts were rewarded and his concerns adopted by the entire intellectual world at the very moment of his death in 1985."[18] Illustrating his belated arrival, a Festschrift was published by former students in 1978, and in 1979 an issue of the journal *L'Arc*, a good index of relevance in Parisian eyes, was dedicated to him.[19] From the late 1970s until his death, he also appeared more regularly in the daily and weekly press, especially by granting interviews – probably because at long last he was being invited.[20]

One name above all others has been linked to the late-twentieth-century revival of ethics: Levinas.[21] His international stature grew tremendously during the 1980s and 1990s as he came to be seen as a corrective to some of the more difficult implications of French theory, while at the same time having been an acknowledged influence on persons such as Jacques Derrida, Lyotard, and Luce Irigaray – a corrective, in other words, from within. Born in Lithuania in 1906 to a Jewish family and having grown up in the rich Ashkenazi context of Vilna, Levinas emigrated to France in 1923. In the 1930s he was one of the first to introduce German phenomenology to France. His mature work rested on two tomes, *Totality and Infinity* (1961) and *Otherwise than Being, or Beyond Essence* (1974). But Levinas was also known since the 1950s for his Talmudic commentaries, which he himself saw as distinct from and parallel to his more strictly philosophical work. That work revolved around the phenomenological relationship between the self and the Other [*Autrui*]. What came to be called his "ethics as first philosophy" stressed the asymmetrical priority of the Other vis-à-vis any fundamental ontology of the self. The subject became a hostage to the demands of the Other's "face," to a certain "command" from an exteriority that proscribed any unrestrained exercise of freedom. Levinas can thus be seen as having mined the phenomenological legacy of the 1920s and 1930s for resources that led to fundamentally different conclusions from Sartrean existentialism and which also resonated with certain Judaic traditions. The theme of alterity, or otherness, was inexorably bound to thinking about ethics in some circles in the 1980s and 1990s, and Levinas's contribution to reconceptualizing the philosophical relationship between the self and other cannot be understated. The particular way he took secular philosophy and Judaism seriously, each on its own terrain, made him immensely attractive to some members of the generation of 1968 who found themselves searching for ways to create a dialogue among cultural traditions, rigorous thought, and ethical relevance. Like Jankélévitch, Levinas also experienced a belated popularity, although on quite a different scale, as he came to be invoked by key figures of the 1968 generation as well as by the *vedettes* of French theory mentioned above. In 1984 *Le Monde*, hardly the pulse-taker of the avant-garde, could "justly claim that Levinas was 'à la mode.'"[22]

Though experienced and expressed quite differently, the Judaism of Jankélévitch and Levinas played a crucial role in their late-1970s and early-1980s rediscovery. It is no secret that some members of the French generation of 1968 eventually turned to religion as they deradicalized, sometimes in outright conversion and belief, sometimes by considering the religious heritage in politics, and sometimes by engaging religion as a worthy interlocutor for certain problems. We have already seen this phenomenon (in Part IV) in the context of the Clavel-Lardreau-Jambet interchange.

Bernard-Henri Lévy and André Glucksmann had in passing also evoked Judaism in their 1977 writings. Lévy's *The Testament of God* (1979) went even further, explicitly asserting the ethical traditions of "Jerusalem" as correctives to the politics of "Athens."[23] Although, like much of Lévy's work, the book was taken to task for its scholarly inaccuracies, it was culturally significant for Levinas's unquestionable presence, even in watered-down form. The reputation of "BHL" as a connoisseur of superficial generalization was fixed two years later when his *L'Idéologie française* described anti-Semitism as structurally wedded to the very idea of France.[24] That book elicited heated controversy, but it appeared at the same time as the resurgence of anti-Semitism and the assertion of Holocaust denial. In his evocation of Levinas and focus on the issue of anti-Semitism, Lévy resonated with the broader *air du temps*.

In the late 1970s and early 1980s certain prominent leaders of the May movement re-engaged with Judaism, with which they identified as secularized Jews but from which they had been cut off for a variety of reasons, ranging from familial assimilation to leftist political renunciation.[25] Alain Finkielkraut's term "imaginary Jew," although referring to himself, also described the sensibility of a generation that had grown up in the shadow of the Holocaust but that knew little about Judaism's multiple traditions, histories, and cultures.[26] Like Lévy, Finkielkraut counted himself a disciple of Levinas, as did the former leader of the Gauche prolétarienne, Benny Lévy [Pierre Victor], who had read Levinas before 1968 and returned to him in the mid-1970s in the context of a deradicalizing turn to Judaism via philosophy.[27] Benny Lévy's reconversion to Judaism involved a full embrace of religious practices and Talmudic study. As we shall now see, the privileged role of Levinas in his thinking proved to be decisive in his powerful influence on Sartre, whose secretary Lévy was until Sartre's death in 1980.

Benny Lévy's infamous reputation as the leader of the Gauche prolétarienne was surpassed only in the late 1970s when, as Sartre's secretary, he was accused by Simone de Beauvoir and others of the Sartrean "family" (and eventually even by Raymond Aron) of having exercised untoward influence on the aging philosopher.[28] Sartre had arranged for Lévy to serve as his secretary first of all because, blind and in failing health, he needed someone. The two had become acquainted during the Maoist adventure (as we saw in Part I). Sartre solved the immigrant Lévy's visa troubles by writing directly to Giscard d'Estaing and asking for special consideration (which was granted). In frequent daily contact from the mid-1970s until Sartre's death, Lévy read to Sartre, helped him with his correspondence, travelled with him, and engaged him in extended conversation. Some of

Sartre's long-term intimates complained that the younger man disrespectfully bullied Sartre, although there was much evidence that Sartre enjoyed Lévy's challenges, claiming, for instance, that the latter had a better memory of his earlier writings than he did himself and that Lévy's earnestness sometimes amused him.[29] Lévy's influence was clear in the dialogue between them published in 1980 under the title *Hope Now*. Although the "philo-Semitism" of that work should be related to Sartre's long-standing defence of Israel and the parallel influence of his adopted daughter Arlette Elkaïm-Sartre (who was returning to Judaism alongside Lévy), it is fair to conclude that Sartre's somewhat random musings on Jewish messianism, for instance, strongly reflected Lévy's presence. To his credit, Sartre's curiosity never faded as his body deteriorated, and Lévy also helped Sartre look back over his career, criticize himself, and tease out continuities. The two planned a collaborative project entitled *Power and Freedom*, of which only the published 1980 interviews (among more unpublished ones) provided a glimpse. It was Lévy's interest in Levinas and in ethics that helped return Sartre to a theme he had touched, abandoned, and circled around over the previous thirty years.

Sartre had studied ethics in his preparatory course work around 1929, and when he himself taught ethics in his brief stint as a *lycée* teacher in Le Havre during the 1930s, he relied entirely on prepared textbooks. Phenomenology had given Sartre an orientation for a humanist ethics, the signs of which were present as early as his 1936 article "The Transcendence of the Ego." In "Existentialism Is a Humanism" (1946), Sartre suggested that in making one's existential choices, one was also choosing for everyone else. This stance ambiguously evoked Kant's similar linkage of autonomy and universality. Sartre's biographer noted that his attraction to the "marginal," already present in the prewar period, eventually put him at odds with the "communist ethics of the new man." It was unquestionably World War II, however, that brought ethics to the centre of Sartre's attention. De Beauvoir, for instance, whose prewar attempts at a "pluralist morality" Sartre had disparaged while the two studied in the Jardin du Luxembourg, was "quite taken aback by the rigor of his moralism," which revolved around the theme of wartime "resistance." Although between 1945 and 1948 Sartre worked away at the ethics project announced at the end of *Being and Nothingness* (as some critics wondered how that missing link would fit in his system of self-affirming authentic freedom), he ultimately rejected the project for being too idealistic and purely philosophical, although others like de Beauvoir and Francis Jeanson took up the challenge of existentialist ethics. Sartre's compromise with himself on the question of praxis led him by the late 1940s toward a political pragmatism that was at best ambiguous and expressed in his fellow-travelling with the PCF. His rupture with Albert Camus was to some extent symptomatic of his having buried the ethics project in the face of emergent Cold War politics. Sartre himself later amiably eulogized Camus in 1960 as "the present heir of that long line of moralists whose works perhaps constitute what is most original in French letters ... [He] reaffirmed the existence of moral facts within the heart of our era and against Machiavellians, against the golden calf of realism."[30] Raymond Aron would later eulogize Sartre as a moralist as well. However, throughout the 1950s, Sartre himself largely forgot about ethics in favour of an awkward mix of voluntarist freedom and materialist revolution.

The mid-1960s brought a new development. According to Thomas Anderson, Sartre's 1964 lecture entitled "Ethics and Society," held in Rome at a conference sponsored by the Italian Communist Party, marked the emergence of a "second ethics."[31] This second ethics, characterized by the search for "integral humanity," differed from the idealistic ethics of "authenticity" of the wartime and immediate postwar years. Anderson also suggests that this second ethics built directly on Sartre's *Critique of Dialectical Reason* (1960), particularly in its emphasis on historicity, materialism, and group identity. (Sartre had touched on ethics in that work, but not given the theme any serious treatment.) The Rome lecture can be seen as the ethical contribution of this middle-Sartrean period. De Beauvoir apparently considered this talk "the culmination" of Sartrean ethics. Sartre's intention seemed to have been to correct the idealism and solipsism of the earlier, abandoned ethics project by enlivening ethics with that materialism and attention to collective historicity that had led him into the Communist temptation. By the mid-1960s, Sartre was clearly considering fellow-travelling a deviation. He began the Rome lecture with the words: "The historical moment has come for socialism to rediscover its ethical structure, or rather, to unveil it." Scientific socialism had culminated in the Stalinism that was criticized even within the Soviet Union. The problem lay in Marxism's habit of "sending ethics on vacation" – something Sartre himself had done from the concluding promissory note in *Being and Nothingness* through to the political-ontology of *Critique of Dialectical Reason*.[32] By 1964 the task in Sartre's mind was to constitute ethics historically and dialectically, avoiding the obviously unethical Communist practices so blatantly betraying the "revolution," to which he nevertheless remained committed. It is not at all clear that Sartre fulfilled his objectives.

In his Rome lecture Sartre described moral experience as being made up of two elements; as Anderson says, its "prescriptive" and its "possibility" features.[33] On one hand, there were norms, rules, codes, and so forth; and on the other hand, there was the fundamental possibility of following or not following them. Reiterating the classic existentialist position, Sartre said that an individual was free to follow or not follow a norm, and therefore free to determine his or her "pure future."[34] Sartre's Marxist leanings, however, led him to note the conditioning aspects of norms; that is, their historical and inherited character. Any notion of choice and futurity emerged within a socio-historical context. One's relationship to norms thus had two dimensions: an unconditioned freedom that preceded and was the precondition for any relationship to norms, and the historical condition of existing norms. Sartre's next move in the Rome lecture was entirely gratuitous, but not really surprising: capitalist society divided those who were open to their "pure future" from those who were locked (using a term from *Critique of Dialectical Reason*) in the "practico-inert" paralysis of existing normative structures. A fuller collective realization of "man," Sartre claimed, was the same thing as the "future" that made free choices possible. In other words, history tended toward greater "'human plentitude,' 'the fully alive human organism,' human life as the possibility 'of realizing in itself and for-and-through others integral man.'"[35]

Now, beyond a sympathetic identification with the working class (for which no argument was made), Sartre also mentioned colonialism and how the colonized could grasp a fuller experience of being human than could colonialists.[36] History had a meaning and a direction [*sens*]; its "true ethics" lay in the notion, says Anderson, that "The unconditioned possibility to become *man* is the ultimate unconditioned moral norm which guides [men and women's] praxes and through them all of history ... Insofar as the ontological structure of every moral norm embodies an unconditional obligation, it calls us to create an unconditioned future, one which transcends all systems."[37] The transcendence of systems implies destroying and overcoming the practico-inert. To act ethically is to act as if one's actions opened a future of greater possibilities for all. This formulation strongly evoked Kant.

Anderson makes the appropriately critical observation that at this point Sartre did not necessarily escape the idealism he felt had plagued his "first" ethics. To make this ethical account adequately material, Sartre based the notions of freedom, possibility, futurity, and vague human fulfillment (mixed with working-class and anti-colonialist sympathies) on the fact of human need. Need lay at the root of the human experience of overcoming the practico-inert. "It is our own needs," Anderson comments, "that cause us to experience moral norms to be obligatory or prescriptive." The fact that needs require fulfillment formed the originary template of obligation. Though Anderson does not consider this objection, Sartre seemed oddly close to Abraham Maslow's "hierarchy of needs" and hardly clarified matters by simply asserting that necessity and freedom in the end converged. Still, however unsatisfactorily to the non-Sartrean, Sartre did attempt to resolve some of his earlier "idealist" impasses by basing moral actions on the fulfillment of material needs, a fulfillment that took place over historical time and had the species as its audience and goal – my needs are human, and human needs converge. He explained the importance of enlivening structures that tended toward inertia, drawing a line between the practico-inert of capitalist reification and the dynamism of workers and anti-colonialists. Finally, he proposed to explain how imperfectly realized, sometimes deeply flawed, systemizations of ethical impulses (such as Marxism) could contain degrees of truth. After all, one major preoccupation of postwar French intellectuals had been to save Marxism from itself. The human need to become more fully human, to achieve "integral humanity," lay at the core of Sartre's "second" ethics.[38]

Sartre's Rome lecture made frequent reference to the struggles of anti-colonialism, especially to the recently concluded Algerian War. It was in this context that he had written his famous preface to Frantz Fanon's *Wretched of the Earth*, which had offered a fairly straightforward endorsement of the restorative and enlivening qualities of political violence.[39] Thus it was not surprising that the Rome lecture concluded with a number of practical suggestions for those who agreed with him that integral humanism had a class and revolutionary dimension. As in *Critique of Dialectical Reason*, violence was justified if it came from the masses, was strategically effective, and – most slippery of all – was "humanized."[40] Violence was exactly the issue on which Sartrean "morality" got hung up between the Rome lecture and his later discussions with Benny Lévy. As we saw in Part I, the post-1968 years renewed talk about – and the exercise (symbolic, at least) of – political violence in the context of what Annie Cohen-Solal calls the "ethics of revolutionary heroism."[41] As Sartre remarked in his preface to Michèle Manceaux's 1972 book on the Maoists and in his published interviews with Lévy [Pierre Victor] and Philippe Gavi, *On a raison de se révolter* (1974), his idea of morality was integrally linked to that of violence. At the same time, prior to his close relationship with Lévy, Sartre was also beginning in the early 1970s to sever morality and violence.[42] France did not know serious terrorism in the early to mid-1970s (the 1980s were a different story), and Sartre's 1974 trip with Lévy to visit the members of the Baader-Meinhof group in prison was something of a sad episode. He came closest to bridging the impasse of violence, however, in the *Hope Now* interviews with Lévy, in which Levinasian ethics was an important background force.

In those interviews, what seemed new was Sartre's use of the word "obligation." In the Introduction, I cited Sartre as saying: "By 'ethics' I mean that every consciousness, no matter whose, has a dimension that I didn't study in my philosophical works and that few people have studied, for that matter: the dimension of obligation." Late in his life Sartre reconsidered the relation between self and other at the origin of his wartime existentialism. He seemed newly concerned with the problem of how that relation was rooted in connection not opposition. In the *Hope Now* interviews, he used the term "requisition" to describe the demand or "inner constraint" placed on consciousness through its relations with others. Rather than the famous "being-in-itself" and "being-for-itself" around which *Being and Nothingness* revolved, Sartre now spoke of a kind of being-for-others that had clear Levinasian resonances:

> [In] my earliest studies, like the great majority of ethicists, I was looking for an ethics in a consciousness that had no reciprocal, no other (I prefer *other* to *reciprocal*). Today I think everything that takes place for a consciousness at any given moment is necessarily linked to, and often is even engendered by, the presence of another – or even momentarily by the absence of that other – but, in all events, by the existence of another. To put it differently, each consciousness seems simultaneously to constitute itself as a consciousness and, at the same time, as the consciousness of the other and for the other. It is this reality – the self considering itself as a self for the other, having a relationship with the other – that I call ethical conscience.

The other (Sartre did not distinguish between others as people and others as things) made demands on the self. Its "requisition" was itself a kind of structural limit on consciousness. Rephrasing part of the argument of the Rome lecture, Sartre went on to describe the mutual "dependence" of selves and others as a kind of "freedom" rooted in possibility: "It is characteristic of ethics that an action, while it seems to be subtly constrained, also presents itself as capable of not being undertaken."[43] In the relation between two selves, then, intersubjective and mutually dependent freedom found its expression. Sartre gave his on-going dialogue with Lévy as an example of how relationships could embody freedom; their dialogic collaboration had opened up new paths of thought for both of them. He also said that ethics was the intentional object of their long-term mutual project.

The focus on ethics also reintroduced the question of revolutionary violence, or what both Sartre and Lévy referred to as "fraternity-terror." Returning to his confidence and optimism about historicity and the future, Sartre revised his long-standing belief, which he now explicitly traced to the French Revolution, that violent means could accomplish the revolutionary end of "fraternity." He defined fraternity as full human connection and, implicitly evoking the Rome lecture, the satisfaction of shared needs. While violence in a limited sense (such as the anti-colonial struggle) could break up systems that held back fraternal relations, violence alone was insufficient to establish properly fraternal relations. But far from denouncing violence outright, the most one can say is that Sartre ended in a kind of ambiguity most clearly expressed in his admission: "But to tell you the truth, I still don't clearly see the real relationship between violence and fraternity." In contrast, Lévy was somewhat more lucid about the difficulty of setting violence and ethics into dialogue.

Nevertheless, the primacy of ethics for both of them came through as the interviews concluded. Responding to Lévy's prompts, Sartre spoke of the significance of Jewish messianism for him as a non-Jew. His pronouncements lacked analytic precision and for some were barely cogent. In his understanding, Judaism's version of the "end" of time was compatible with – and might be an alternative source for – the "revolutionary" futurity and hope that he desired but which needed to be unburdened of their Marxist baggage:

> [The Jewish "end" is] the beginning of the existence of men who live for each other. In other words, it's an ethical end. Or, more exactly, it is ethics. The Jew thinks that the end of the world, of this world, and the upsurge of the other will result in the appearance of the ethical existence of men who live for one another ... We non-Jews are searching for an ethics, too. The question is to find the ultimate end, the moment when ethics will be simply and truly the way in which human beings live in relation to each other. The rules-and-prescriptions aspect of ethics will probably no longer exist – as has often been said, for that matter. Ethics will have to do with the way in which men form their thoughts, their feelings ... [It is] through a kind of messianism that one can conceive of this ethics as the ultimate goal of revolution ... Jewish reality must remain in the revolution. It must contribute the power of ethics to it.[44]

It was this reasoning that led many to see Lévy's late and looming influence on Sartre. But even if Lévy's share in the collaboration did push Sartre in directions he might not have wandered into on his own (from Flaubert to messianism?), his "last words" seem largely consistent with his orientation since the Rome lecture. At the end of his life, then, Sartre returned to the ethical dimension of human experience, a familiar problem whose solution continued to elude him. Of course, some of Sartre's contradictions (unfounded attachment to "revolution," the quandary of an ethics of violence) were never ultimately resolved. Lévy's intervention and the posthumously published *Notebooks for an Ethics* (1983) did much, however, to fix in the public's mind the impression that Sartre had been a thinker concerned with ethics within that particular French tradition of the *moraliste*. When Sartre died, Aron indeed observed that his life had expressed the "drama of a moralist lost in the jungle of politics."[45] It is worth noting that Foucault, too, claimed that term, saying in 1980: "In a sense, I am a moralist, insofar as I believe that one of the meanings of human existence – the source of human freedom – is never to accept anything as definitive, untouchable, obvious, or immobile."[46]

Time will tell if it is true to say that "Foucault may well be remembered as one of the major ethical thinkers of modernity."[47] But it is certainly true that in the last years of his life, and ever since in the hands of his many commentators, the "final Foucault" became associated with the turn toward ethics.[48] Foucault's own turn might be read as an attempt to answer critics of earlier works who were worried (sometimes hysterically so) about the dark implications of his treatments of knowledge, power, and disciplinarization. He himself suggested that his late-1970s and early-1980s work on ethics marked a third period in his development, following earlier concentrations on epistemic matters and then on power complexes. He hinted at times that he had grown sensitive to criticisms that his studies counselled nihilism or despair, and one can certainly speculate about the growing importance of ethics toward the end of his own life. Just as interesting as this ethical turn is the fact that something about Foucault's works, through the first volume of the *History of Sexuality*, *La Volonté de Savoir* (1976), had invited worries about moral and political agency and, by implication, raised certain ethical questions. In earlier chapters we have seen several Foucaults: an activist mobilized around the "intolerable" conditions of prisons, a participant in debates about the sexuality of children, an influence on Maurice Clavel, and in limited senses a kindred spirit of the New Philosophers. The final Foucault is yet another figure, and though one might have imagined some continuity between an earlier moment, say, the condemnation of the "intolerable," and an explicitly articulated ethics, this does not seem to be the case. Viewed in the context of 1970s France,

Foucault seems to have been a versatile thinker who showed up at significant turning points.

Foucault had made passing references to ethics in his earlier works. Most of these references were casual and, although they sometimes indicated positive usages, they more often dismissed the normative as a "bad" thing or tried to fit ethics within the framework of aesthetics. In his 1954 introduction to the French translation of Ludwig Binswanger's *Dream and Existence*, he had mentioned in passing the "ethical content of dreams"; a 1963 discussion distinguished ethics from literary transgression; three years later he suggested that André Breton had "re-moralized" writing by "de-moralizing" it and by initiating an "ethics of writing," focused on form over content; in *The Order of Things* (1966) Foucault wrote that a "moral system," in the sense of norms based on ontological presuppositions about "man," was impossible for modernity; in 1967 and 1968 he said that politics and sexuality were more fruitful categories of analysis than *la morale*; and his famous article "What is an Author?" (1969) named "indifference" as "the most fundamental ethical principle of contemporary writing," a kind of "immanent rule" that touched on the themes of "expression" and "death." In 1970 Foucault called for a strategy by which one might "pervert" the "wicked morality of thought," and in the context of literature, he again discussed the transgression of "sexual morality." He noted in 1972 that the medical profession "guards morality," and in 1974 that the proletariat was "impregnated" by bourgeois morality to the point that the working class and labour unions secreted a kind of "moral puritanism."[49]

Around the time when *La Volonté de Savoir* appeared, Foucault began to use the terms ethics and morality in slightly different senses. In 1976, in a discussion of the body's relationship to medicine and health, he spoke of the eighteenth century's "private ethics" and the "*morale* of the body." In a convergence of his earlier references to aesthetic-literary ethics and his later interest in "truth-telling" and the "practices of the subject," Foucault in 1977 described the "immanent ethics in Western literary discourse" as having culminated in the "search" for what was "hidden," "difficult," "most forbidden," and "scandalous." Such an ethics made a "duty" out of telling one's "secrets." The observation was significant for the way he merged suspicions about the formation of the confessional subject with the kind of transgressive liberationism he had previously advocated but from which he would henceforth distance himself. Also in 1977, he referred to the "*morale* of knowledge" as presenting the "real" as "acute, sharp, angular, unacceptable. Thus irrational?" This was also the year in which Foucault (as we saw above in Part II) called Deleuze and Guattari's *Anti-Oedipus* a "work of ethics." By 1978 he had already formulated some of the concepts that would appear in the posthumously published second and third volumes of the *History of Sexuality*, such as the separation of "moral ideas and ethical taboos" [*interdits éthiques*] from "techniques" and "mechanisms of power." He gave as an example the Christian notion of "flesh" operating within the "interior of subjectivity." Only in 1979 did Foucault finally seem to claim for himself some positive use for the language of ethics and morals. In the midst of the general clamour around the Iranian revolution, in which he made some infamously controversial comments, he mentioned his own "theoretical ethics" [*ma morale théorique*], which he described as "anti-strategic." Such an ethics led one: "to be respectful of a singularity that rises up, to be intransigent when power violates the universal. A simple choice, a difficult work ... to watch out for ... that which breaks up and agitates history and guards over, from a little behind politics, that which must unconditionally limit politics."[50]

Between the spring of 1981 and his death in June 1984, Foucault moved explicitly and at times emphatically toward the ethical thematic. One can distinguish among various intonations and enunciatory contexts: ethics as a topic of historical retrieval, as a scholarly method or practice, and as a life practice, especially in Foucault's increasing willingness to speak about homosexuality as a gay man, connecting themes of his scholarly work with contemporary social movements and questions. To be sure, these various levels of analysis overlapped and interpenetrated. In rough terms the "last ethics" seems to have been divided into two periods: 1981–82 and 1983–84. A first constellation of comments appeared in interviews published in the independent gay press, special issues about contemporary homosexuality, and book reviews: *Gai pied* (April 1981), *Christopher Street* (October 1981), *Libération* (1 June 1982), *The Advocate* (June 1982), and *Salmagundi* (fall 1982). Foucault spoke, for instance, of his doubts about a simple-minded liberation of desire that focused singularly on mobilization "against oppression." Instead, the search for an elusive "pleasure" should replace talk of desire, and greater emphasis should be placed on the development of new "modes of life," "lifestyles," "existential choices," "ways of relating," "types of existence," "relational rights," the "art of life" (elsewhere, the Greek *techne tou biou*), "friendship," a "gay style," and "invention."

The articulation of criteria for living, in the specific context of homosexuality, coincided with a restructuring of the history of sexuality project's conceptual core. In 1981 and 1982 Foucault was working through analytical themes that had surfaced in his treatments of Greek and early Christian sexual ethics: *ascesis*, the "permanent hermeneutics of oneself," "technologies of the self," "techniques of self-analysis," "subjectivation," the contrast between ethics and a normative "code," "truth telling," and the "care of oneself" [*epimeleia heautou*]. Foucault insisted that he never favoured the straightforward application in the contemporary era of pre-modern Greek or Stoic ethics, despite the fact that he often seemed to esteem them. The claim, for example, that Greek sexual ethics was reserved for an elite few (likely to resonate with some intellectuals' sense of themselves) was balanced against the obvious fact that few in antiquity truly exercised freedom, due to the non-freedom of the many. Nevertheless, Foucault at times suggested that some older ethical questions, and questions about the *form* of those questions, were worth asking in contemporary settings. Behind such interrogations, however, lay an underlying skepticism about his own construction of a systematic ethics, since it was for "people ... to build their own ethics."[51]

One possible moment of transition to the second period of the late ethics occurred in remarks published on 21 January 1983 in *Libération* in the midst of a plagiarism scandal involving one of Mitterrand's personal advisors, Jacques Attali. Linking his own scholarly activity to the principle of truth telling that he had analysed as part of the shift from Stoic to early Christian ethical regimes, Foucault said that the "technical rules" of the scholar ("documentation, research, verification") themselves involved an "ethics": "between *technique* and *éthique* there are not many differences."[52] The "principle" of this ethics was "to respect technical rules and to make known which ones are used." It was an ethics "with respect to others" in the sense that one's truth-telling procedures affected and implicated one's audience. The claim resonated with Foucault's sense that the relation between "knowledge" and "care of oneself" had to be reconsidered. In the modern era, knowing oneself had taken precedence over caring for oneself, whereas for the Greeks, knowledge of oneself had been a subcategory of a general care of oneself [*epimeleia heautou*]. Following these remarks during the Attali scandal, Foucault's fullest discussion of ethics came several months later, in April 1983, in a series of interviews at Berkeley, where the theme was broached in large part through the prompting of his interlocutors.[53]

It was beginning with these interviews, and until his death, that Foucault did the most to link his scholarly research to the contemporary world. "Our problem nowadays," he said, may be similar to that of Greece insofar as Greek ethics concerned "moral conduct" more than "religious problems." Perhaps we, too, were trying to disconnect ethics from social and legal "institutional systems" and practise "an aesthetics of existence" as the Greeks had done. Once again separating desire and pleasure, he reiterated his critical point that "liberation movements" had failed to found a "new ethics." The search for such a new ethics was part and parcel of his scholarly research into the history of "problematics" and related to his conviction that everything was "dangerous." Scholarly research on past eras introduced new ways of seeing the present and acting on it: "a treasury of devices, techniques, ideas, procedures, and so on [that might constitute] a certain point of view which can be very useful as a tool for analyzing what's going on now – and to change it." The project of a "history of morals" or a "genealogy of ethics" could yield information about an "art of life" [*techne tou biou*], taking care of oneself, or the *bios* that required no "analytical or necessary link" with "social or economic or political structures." Scientific knowledge did not yield an ethics. The latter turned on a difference between a "code" and an "act." Fundamentally, ethics defined "the kind of relationship you ought to have with yourself, *rapport à soi*." This relationship Foucault divided into four components, commented upon at length by others: ethical substance, mode of subjection [*mode d'assujettisement*], ethical work, and *telos*. It is significant that he also included a question that had been largely absent from most of his mature work; namely, the dialectic between the self and the other: "What I want to ask is: Are we able to have an ethics of acts and their pleasures which would be able to take into account the pleasure of the other? Is the pleasure of the other something that can be integrated in our pleasure, without reference either to law, to marriage, to I don't know what?"[54] Like Sartre, Foucault was discovering others at a relatively late stage.

In a second published Berkeley interview, Foucault connected ethics to politics and to a philosopher's "*ethos*." Confirming the judgments of several of his interlocutors, who commented that he seemed to have been paying greater attention to ethics in recent years, Foucault remarked: "In fact what interests me is much more morals than politics, or in any case, politics as an ethics."[55] This was a far cry from his position in the late 1960s when he had said that *la morale* was not an interesting topic of study. Ethics was now a "practice" and *ethos* a "way of being." He gave the example of Poland – a theme of continual reference for Foucault especially from December 1981 forward, following the military coup that crushed the Solidarity movement – and proposed a kind of ethical positioning that would face up to the inadequacy of a simple "political" response (involving "paratroopers" and "armoured cars"). An ethical response would involve the fundamental "nonacceptance of what is happening there, and a nonacceptance of the passivity of our own governments." (It is true that one could hear in this statement echoes of the GIP's emphasis on the intolerable.) Such an "attitude" was ethical as well as political inasmuch as it exceeded a mere "protest" and worked to "oblige" governments to take account of it. In another conversation about Poland, with Edmond Maire, the General Secretary of the Confédération française démocratique du travail labour union, published in May 1983, Foucault again spoke of ethics in relation to "unionism" and the question of "personal behaviour" and an "ethics of pleasure."[56]

During the last six months of his life, Foucault continued to amplify these themes. In perhaps the most concise statement of his thinking on ethics, presented in a January 1984 interview, he teased out the notion of ethics as a "practice of freedom," again setting ethics against the idea of liberation alone. Since everything was dangerous, forms of liberation raised new problems and posed new questions. "With regard to sexuality," he wrote, "it is obvious that it is by liberating our desire that we will learn to conduct ourselves ethically in pleasure relationships with others." The practice of freedom itself was an ethical problem. Referring to volumes 2 and 3 of his sexuality project, to be published later in 1984, Foucault described ethics as "the conscious practice of freedom." Ethics was "linked to the game of truth" and related to an "*ethos*," or a "way of being and of behavior." Ethics was always already political in the sense that, as in ancient Greece, some persons were free and others were not ("a slave has no ethics"). Again, the self's relationship to the self, especially in the notion of the care of the self, and the self's relationship to others lay at the heart of any ethics. The care of the self minimally involved the "active" constitution of subjectivity through a negotiation of various practices found in a person's culture and milieu. Although "the care of the self [was] ethically prior" to the care of others, such regard almost inevitably implicated others since it was a "way of limiting and controlling power," notably "power over others." Thus, "a person who took proper care of himself would, by the same token, be able to conduct himself properly in relation to others and for others." If the ethics of the self dealt with the practice of freedom, the "*ethos* of freedom [was] also a way of caring for others," and the philosopher was a person "who cares about the care of others." In other words, although "the care of the self [was] ethical in itself," ethics was not "synonymous" with the care of the self: it admitted something more; namely, others. The "very stuff of ethics" was the "freedom of the subject and its relationship to others."[57] The notion of "governmentality," which described various levels of interaction ("freedom, the relationship of the self to the self, and the relationship to the other") was a more robust vision of freedom and relationships than a "legal concept of the subject." The latter, as with the version of a liberating, transgressive subject, Foucault eagerly jettisoned.

In April 1984 Foucault gave an interview in which he referred to "an ethics of existence" involving "freedom" and a "form of life." Connecting his scholarly work with the contemporary moment – in what is as close to a smoking gun as we have – he continued: "If I have been interested in Antiquity, it is because, for an entire series of reasons, the idea of a morality as obedience to a code of rules is now disappearing; it has already disappeared. And this absence of a morality responds and must respond to a search for an aesthetics of existence."[58] The phrase "aesthetics of existence" has often been taken to express the most radical and potentially relativizing consequences of Foucault's Nietzscheanism. In the context of his last ethics, however, Foucault's reliance on the term "aesthetics of existence" seemed to mean something more than a free-for-all invention of existential precepts out of whole cloth. Rather than the self either following prefabricated moral codes or pretending it could completely liberate itself by simple-minded transgression, autonomy meant that the self would have to decide how to be in an *ethos* that included others. The aesthetic and ethical converged to the extent that the subject acted in and for itself through the very non-solipsistic process of weaving meaning and direction [*sens*] in relation to others from the found cultural materials of, say, collapsed moral codes. The scholar had the precise task of presenting data (for Foucault the historian, such data included logics and modes of thought exhumed from the past) for others to use in the "search" for an ethics, a style, a way of being. Historical reflection provided raw materials that could be used in the elaboration of ethics.

In a May 1984 interview published in *Le Magazine littéraire*, François Ewald asked Foucault directly about the connection between his historical work and contemporary questions. Foucault replied that he was writing the "genealogy [of] a problem expressed in terms current today." He was referring to certain moral sexual codes having collapsed rather easily in recent years, a collapse that led to circumstances in which "the problem of an ethics as a form to be given to one's behavior and life [had] arisen once more. In sum, people were wrong when they believed that all morality resided in prohibition and that the lifting of these prohibitions in itself solved the question of ethics."[59] Liberation was not enough for living. Drawing in part on materials from the past, ethics would also require elaboration, invention, and construction in relation to oneself and to others. His point was that "autonomy," too, was a "dangerous" and difficult challenge.

Also in May, Foucault had his last interview with Paul Rabinow. In explaining his hesitation to engage in "polemics," Foucault admitted: "A whole morality is at stake, the morality that concerns the search for the truth and the relation to the other." He portrayed this morality as a dialogue, involving questions and answers, problems and research, in which "the rights of each person are in some sense immanent in the discussion." Such procedures could lead to the "necessarily temporary result" of collective identifications in a "we." He also repeated, in stark terms, the self-periodization of his works, a trajectory that terminated in the ethical problematic: from madness ("objectivity" and "a game of truth") to delinquency ("a politics and a government of the self" and "relations of power") to sexuality ("the elaboration of an ethics and a practice in regard to oneself" and "forms of relation to oneself and to others").[60] In the last interview of his life, on 29 May 1984, Foucault repeated this tripartite division of his own work, and concluded by reiterating the relevance for the contemporary world of pre-Christian thought about ethics:

> Beginning with Christianity we have ... an appropriation of morality by the theory of the subject. But a moral experience essentially centered on the subject no longer seems satisfactory to me today. Because of this, certain questions pose themselves to us in the same terms as they were posed in antiquity. The search for styles of existence as different from each other as possible seems to me to be one of the points on which particular groups in the past may have inaugurated searches we are engaged in today. The search for a form of morality acceptable to everybody in the sense that everyone should submit to it, strikes me as catastrophic.[61]

As the editors of *Dits et écrits* said in their introduction to the republished version of this interview, the title given in *Les Nouvelles littéraires* (28 June 1984) – "Le Retour de la morale" – was unfortunate.[62] The last Foucault did not advance a return to ways past, but rather the construction of ways of living that would build on the accomplishments of the liberation movements of the post-1968 period and surmount their contradictions.

With good reason, Sartre and Foucault are generally held to have represented two very different approaches both to intellectual questions and to the public role of the intellectual. The era of the committed intellectual, instigating social change through his or her writing and commentary, was seen to have passed even before Sartre's death, as television and radio replaced the power of print, as diffuse social change after 1968 undid social hierarchies, and as Foucault's model of the "specific" intellectual replaced that of a post-Dreyfusard "universal" one represented by the aging Sartre. At the same time that this judgment seems well founded, there is another level, that of the broader historical context, on which their paths appear convergent. Both Sartre and Foucault, shortly before their deaths, each in his own idiom, came to make ethics a central preoccupation. As we have seen, for Sartre, this represented something of a return to earlier dilemmas; he had flirted with the ethical theme, been distracted, and invested himself elsewhere since the 1940s. And yet, he returned again to the problematic, first in the mid-1960s and then after 1968.

For Sartre, the principal stumbling block in considering ethics seems to have been his treatment of violence, for which, until the very end, he always found some justification in a reasoning that subordinated means to obstinately "revolutionary" ends. His ultimately ambiguous attachment to violence put real constraints on how far he could go toward making ethics primary. There is substantial evidence that after 1968, and above all in his connections to the Maoists and especially to Benny Lévy, Sartre did want to make ethics primary. He had found in the Maoists' *ethos*, as he had written, a combination of "violence, spontaneity, and morality." In a late return to some of his earlier phenomenological researches, Levinas's alternative "ethics as first philosophy," mediated through Lévy, proved to be a resource. The extent to which Lévy unduly influenced Sartre – or to which Sartre came to recognize self-critically the lacunae in his own earlier undeveloped ethical thinking – will likely remain an open question.

Foucault for his part also came to focus on ethics in the last years of his life, similarly recasting his prior work as a series of stages that either culminated in ethical questions or belatedly foregrounded a theme that had been present all along. As in so many other cases, Foucault preferred to let his scholarly work do most of the talking for him, consistent with his insistence on being a "masked philosopher." Although speaking as a self-effacing activist in 1971–72 on the "intolerable" conditions of French prisons may have formed the first link in a conceptual chain of ethical concern, it was rather the mid-1970s turn toward the history of sexuality that brought Foucault face to face with the ethical problematic. Both the prison and sexuality studies represented a direct response to the post-1968 French climate. If *Discipline and Punish* concentrated in part on the institution as an interface between subjects and the state (alongside more general concerns about knowledge, power, and discipline), the *History of Sexuality* set its sights on the ultimately deceiving promises of personal liberation. In Part I we saw the GIP contest the state's penal institutions, and in Part III we noted Foucault's hostility toward the notion of a legal subject in debates on the sexuality of children. But what remained inadequately developed in those debates, and which he did address from the late 1970s forward, was the issue of how one's relationship to one's own desires and pleasures implicated, affected, and potentially "endangered" others. Foucault's late sensitivity to ethical complexity – the self's relationship to itself, to others, to institutions, and to the state: taken together, what he called "governmentality" – ought to free him from undeserved charges of nihilistic amorality. His expressed interest was in "relations of power," relations that assumed "at least a certain degree of freedom on both sides." As he said plainly: "The idea that power is a system of domination that controls everything and leaves no room for freedom cannot be attributed to me."[63] The scholar had a role to play in furnishing the materials for others' ethical elaborations, elaborations not without their own risks and dangers, but which nevertheless confronted the fact that autonomy is something neither found fully formed nor existing in isolation from others, relationships, institutions, the state, and history.

In 1983 and 1984, Foucault was asked how his new emphasis on freedom and on the modulations of the relational self compared with Sartre's views on the same questions. Foucault showed himself on one occasion to have a limited familiarity with Sartre's thinking, leaning on a default version of Sartrean wartime "authenticity," which he saw at work in the latter's more recent studies on Flaubert and Baudelaire.[64] He contrasted his own notion of the self as a "work of art" with Sartre's version of the same idea, claiming that the difference was in Sartre's having submitted artfulness to a criterion of authenticity/inauthenticity. Foucault said that in contrast he, like Nietzsche, emphasized the creative aspect of self-creation. Speaking somewhat in "bad faith" himself, he gave an at best abbreviated version of his own position, which as we have seen, took self-relation quite seriously. Furthermore, his position actually seemed close to Sartre's, if one recalls, for instance, the latter's 1946 comment that "The moral choice is comparable to the construction of a work of art."[65] Whatever the similarity in the proto-aesthetic qualities of their respective visions of freedom – and it is likely that the systematic differences far outweigh any resemblances – the late Sartre and Foucault most resembled one another in the fresh centrality they gave to ethical questions of *relation* and *others*. Such momentary connections were much stronger than coincidental and much weaker than causal. They both discussed ethics explicitly more or less at the same moment and exemplified a broader sensibility. The evidence of their different ethical turns points the way toward a more general promotion and reception of the theme – the opening stages, as it were, of a popular fascination with ethics that would crescendo in the 1990s.

In 1980 the Belgian Chaïm Perelman published a "historical introduction to moral philosophy." Alfred Grosser followed his 1969 reflections on the foundation of a "political morality" with a 1981 call for "moral engagement." Also that year, Jankélévitch published *Le Paradoxe de la morale*, a short meditation on being and love; and in 1982 Levinas reprinted a series of interviews with Philippe Nemo – both of these works introducing their thought to wider readerships. In 1982 Marcel Conche published his somewhat dry treatise called *Le Fondement de la morale*, which relied heavily on Montaigne; André Jacob traced the transition from "dialectics to ethics"; and Angèle Kremer-Marietti published a short introduction, *La Morale*, in the Presses universitaires de France popular collection *Qui suis-je?*, a sign that the theme was ready for general consumption. The years 1983 and 1984 saw the high-water mark of this first phase of *fin-de-siècle* ethical fascination. Sartre's *Cahiers pour une morale* (1983) were printed the same year as works on ethics and morals by Jean-Luc Nancy, Bernard-Henri Lévy, Robert Misrahi, Jean-François Lyotard, and another text by Jankélévitch. In 1984 works appeared by Luce Irigaray, André Comte-Sponville, and an essay by Edgar Morin on European antinuclear campaigns in the face of Pershing and SS-20 missiles. That same year, the association SOS Racisme was founded, leading to talk that a new "génération morale" had arrived.[66]

At the beginning of this chapter we discussed the paradoxical desertion and ascendancy of politics by the intellectual-political Left in the years between the legislative elections of 1978 and the early years of the Mitterrand administration. That is, as the last hopes that a socialist France would be much different from a non-socialist France dissipated in the face of the short-of-the-mark reality of Mitterrandism, politics ceased on a heightened scale being the be-all-and-end-all (it never had been for some and had become less so for increasing numbers since 1968). Symptomatic of this dual accomplishment of electoral politics and evacuation of the political on the Left was the return to history and, for some, to the particularity of religious-cultural identity. Again, attention to basic questions reflected and expressed a thorough reshuffling of social and political life. It seemed as if more questions and more kinds of questions were posed with fewer and fewer certain answers. Fundamental questions about the individual's relationship to him- or herself, others, institutions, the state, and humanity seemed to be raised with greater openness than had been possible during previous years, notably when intellectual frameworks such as Marxism and structuralism were predominant. Fascination with ethics was both a by-product of this reassessment and one of the forms that reassessment took. By the early 1980s ethical perspectives were being foregrounded, with greater or lesser degrees of seriousness, in a variety of fields, but notably in intellectual work on politics, history, philosophy, and religion. Two of the most noteworthy keystone intellectual debates of that decade – on Heidegger and Nazism and on the bicentenary of the French Revolution – were both highly ethically charged.

It would be a mistake, however, to assume that the alleged *pensée soixante-huit* simply dried up when Mitterrand came to power. Olivier Mongin has suggested that the Kant/Nietzsche debate formed one of the central dynamics of 1980s intellectual politics. Alongside new appreciations for the political-moral individual, the so-called differentialist side of the equation also received significant treatment. Sartre and Foucault attempted to situate the individual ethically in relations to others and in networks of practices and pre-existing contexts. The influence of figures like Ricoeur, Jankélévitch, and Levinas marked the emergence of currents of thought that were inassimilable to simple liberal individualism. Structuralism's subversion of the subject had itself been undermined, and some of the more far-fetched dreams of May '68 had faded, but it would be wrong to conclude that the gates were therefore wide open to unrepentant endorsements of a liberal economic and political order composed of unfettered individuals.

No tidy tally of the 1968 period is possible, since its legacy remains ambiguous. For instance, one of the fruits of that era – new commitments to human rights – could either be a powerful tool of human liberation or an empty rhetoric. From one point of view, dilemmas at the close of the twentieth century were little different from those in the middle of that century, when de Beauvoir had discussed the "ethics of ambiguity," by which she meant the incomplete and unrealized project of one's being-in-the-world. The individual, she wrote, "is defined only by his relationship to the world and to other individuals ... Man is free; but he finds his law in his very freedom."[67] In disparate forms of critical or relational approaches to the individual, or even in persistent engagement within the civil-social sphere, there remained something of the *spirit of May 1968* well after its predominance on the historical stage had passed. What remained was the hope that there might be more to late modern life than consumption or nihilism or brute force, and that one language that ought not be ignored, even if when taken alone it might prove to be insufficient, is the language of ethics.

Post-1968 France had experienced no shortage of reflection on, concern about, or confrontation with the ethical dimensions of human experience. If it is true to say that ethics presupposes at least some appeal to the individual or to particularity, it would be false to find in the "defeat" of May 1968 a simple resurgence of schools of thought and a reassertion of practices that could only operate in terms of individuals and "elementary particles," to evoke Michel Houellebecq. Some French men and women had grown increasingly self-reflexive about ethics by the late 1970s and early 1980s, a development remarkable for the distance that seemed to separate those years from the late 1960s and early 1970s. New languages were being transposed and older ones dusted off. Seen in this way, the post-1968 period slips into the ceaseless continuum of historical continuity.

But from another perspective, there is some specificity to questions asked in 1970s France about the individual's relationships to his or her milieu, queries that can be taken as having had an ethical cast. Transhistorical questions, perhaps, and punctual responses: What is undemocratic in a democratic society? What are the terms of social solidarity in late modern life? How did the "revolutionary" paradigm ironically make a positive contribution to civil society? Does a citizen who violates the social contract still deserve to be treated as a member of the contractual community? How can finite human beings have an infinite self-love? How can we tolerate the intolerable? Where are the limits of my desire? Why do men and women desire servitude of various kinds? It is remarkable how many such questions, and many of the debates on the intellectual-political Left in 1970s France, evoked the figure, not of Freud or Marx, nor even of de Tocqueville, but someone deeper in the French collective imagination: Jean-Jacques Rousseau. Looking back, one sees that many of those affected by May 1968 could claim a special lineage. Gilles Deleuze and Félix Guattari, for example, had noted in *Anti-Oedipus*: "The unconscious is Rousseauistic, being man-nature. And how much malice and ruse there is in Rousseau!" And Guattari wrote in his journal in August 1971: "Rousseau: the first leftist militant. With all his ambiguities and ambivalences. A prototype. Artifice as power of Nature. Entirely the opposite of a romantic or realist nature. The artificiality of desire on a stage conspiring in the form of nature." Gabriel Matzneff said that "childhood is in the image of the age, at once cruel and Rousseauistic." Bernard-Henri Lévy called Rousseau his "master." Guy Lardreau saw the constitutively divided "will of all" as the warrant for the "moral attitude." And even Georges Pompidou said that Republican law expressed the general will.[68] Great was the number of Rousseau's children.

Conclusion

We live in the age of ethics. Ethics has become, as Jean-Paul Sartre said of Marxism in the early 1960s, the "impassable philosophy of our times."[1] In the decade following the end of the Cold War, ethics appeared as a problem and a solution in novel and hard-to-miss ways. The inflation of the term has been truly impressive. Corporate malfeasance and criminality have been met with calls for self-monitoring business ethics. Medical practices and advances in science, for instance in genetics, are greeted with a chorus of ethical prognosticators. Human rights and humanitarian intervention have become the standard ethical correctives to *Realpolitik*, although the distance between rhetoric and practice remains wide. The ethics of war deals with smart bombs minimizing "collateral" damage and with serious, troubling consideration of the use of torture in the fight against terrorism. People for the ethical treatment of animals and advocates of safer sex have tried to introduce ethical perspectives into public life. The private lives of public officials have been put under ethical scrutiny by a hyperactive and prurient media. At the turn of the twenty-first century, ethics was the largest growth field in American philosophy departments. Books on ethics have proliferated, from dense theories hawked in the catalogues of academic presses to lighter fare pushed by the self-help industries. The prosaic deed of throwing away one's garbage has become an ethical act if one has the right recycling containers to set out by the curb. Obviously, ethics is always a concern, but an unprecedented fascination for ethics has made itself felt on an international scale. Such fascination has drawn on many sources and appealed to many audiences, with varying degrees of seriousness. It has lent itself to meanings that are progressive or conservative, religious or secular; for this reason, one can refer to it as a sign of the times and as a token of our historical moment.

The French case has been a particularly telling example of a larger historical phenomenon in the West. In December 2000, Sophie Dufau could write in *Libération* that the ethical "question has left the philosophers' boudoirs and invaded cafés, research centers, businesses, and bookstore shelves."[2] In May 2001 long-time observer of the French cultural scene, Roger-Pol Droit, remarked:

> Ethics has already been chic for a number of years. We are busy with it a little bit everywhere. In the medical and life science disciplines, obviously, but also in businesses, international relations, and public administration. Often without bothering to really reflect ... what matters is to want to act. To show oneself determined to return to principles, to find rules to announce, recommendations to transmit, resolutions to make. All this is henceforth right and good. It matters little if most of the time the whole is confused, the results without interest, the formulations laughable. What's important is the new label: "ethics" is a good sign. We've even seen Christian Dior put out a line of beauty products called *Ethique* (no doubt the name *cosme-éthique* was not serious enough). In short, ethics is on the way to becoming a nail polish for the conscience, for which unfortunately, there is no polish remover on the market.[3]

Droit made this stinging comment in the context of a favourable review of Monique Canto-Sperber's *L'Inquiétude morale et la vie humaine*, in which he applauded her continuing campaign for rigorous moral philosophy to be taken more seriously in France. In the philosophical domain, Canto-Sperber certainly helped lead the charge in the 1990s; Droit called her "without contest the central figure in this endeavour." She began in 1993 directing the *Philosophie morale* collection at the Presses universitaires de France. In 1996 she helped bring to light the massive *Dictionnaire d'éthique et de philosophie morale*, and two years later she edited a special issue of *Le Magazine littéraire* on "The New Morals."[4]

Popularity and saturation are conditions for a certain kind of critique. Canto-Sperber has spent as much time bemoaning the inevitable simplifications and lack of "reflection" that have accompanied a popular ethical turn as she has contributing to that shift. Thus, even the foremost spokeswoman of an ethical revival insists on the critical separation between serious and lightweight moral reflection. As remains the case in France, intellectual modulations and cultural trends often refract more general developments in French society and politics. It was in this broader context that Roger-Pol Droit expressed concern about the possibility that, despite the efforts of Canto-Sperber and others, "the recent charms of the ethical" and the "reviviscence of moral philosophy" might lead to "a more or less subtle form – crafty or masked – of a return to moralism and the normalizations that accompany it." Such worries have haunted talk of ethics for some time. As Eric Dupin has put it: "Assimilated to order and constraint, the moral does not get good press on the Left."[5] Alain Badiou, for instance, has excoriated contemporary ethics talk in France, which hovers between the two poles of Levinasian "otherness" and Kantian rights, as the out-and-out symptom of reaction against radical politics. Dominique Lecourt has blasted pop-ethical philosophers such as André Comte-Sponville ("Ethics, you will tell me, is their sole concern. But in this domain we have seen that they merely manipulate what have been the central tenets of the tradition for centuries") while holding on to the contrasting project of "an inventive ethical thinking." Others whose endorsements and criticisms of ethics talk in the 1990s seem serious enough to mention would include Jean Baudrillard, Luc Boltanski, Régis Debray, Jean-Marie Domenach, Luc Ferry, Alain Finkielkraut, Emmanuel Levinas, Gilles Lipovetsky, Jean-François Lyotard, Robert Misrahi, Paul Ricoeur, Lucien Sève, and Tzvetan Todorov.[6]

The truly popular ethical fascination of the 1990s and early 2000s, as well as critiques of it (the Latin root of fascination means spell or witchcraft) are the ultimate destinations of the ethical turn I have traced in *From Revolution to Ethics*. The historical question has been: Where did such widespread contemporary interest come from? I have proposed that a major source of this recent ethical revival was the contestatory impulses of "the Sixties," whose energy fuelled the ethical turn. This development involved both change and continuity. What changed was the fading of a revolutionary politics and its replacement by a host of ethical orientations (of which political ethics was but one facet). But this sea change also concealed great continuity: the terms, practices, and imaginative framework of "liberation" had changed but something of its essential core remained. Rather than disappointment and conversion, one might speak of transvaluation and the passage from action to reflection. The point, again, is not that no one was speaking of ethics before 1968, nor that it is impossible to find "revolutionaries" in France today. Between total change (disillusioned revolutionaries converted to ethics) and absolute continuity (there was nothing new since people have always referred to ethics), the transvaluations of revolution-to-ethics explain the era's continuity-in-change. Even if there are other stories to tell about the effects of May 1968 and even if the ethical turn had additional sources, it is indisputable that 1968 set France on a road toward ethical fascination. I have tried to respond to the question of *why* 1968 yielded the turn to ethics by showing *how* this occurred. The devil is in the details. In lieu of painting a portrait of "failed revolution," as some have done, I have laid out multiple grounds for considering 1968 to have been a "successful" revolution, bearing in mind that such a success ironically defied the categories of 1968's protagonists and critics.

To be sure, I have only recounted a few episodes from a vast and more complex history. This story of the ethical turn has examined revolutionary and far-left groups, intellectuals in the public sphere and in their theoretical writings, and debates in newspapers and on television. It has reached down to the day-to-day lives of men and women profoundly affected by the May events, up toward electoral politics and the French Fifth Republic, and further toward the universally human. The story of how the ethical turn came about has dealt with the social facts of violence and mental illness; with institutions like prisons and psychiatric asylums; with laws, civil society, and citizenship; with gender, sex, and desire; and with theoretical models of the self, association, and political action. The ethical turn can be read in a number of ways: as an ersatz liberational discourse replacing a failed revolutionary paradigm; as an attempt to grapple with evolving social mores; as straightforward reaction; and as a return to a form of thought neglected in France during the 1960s, to mention a few. No corner of the historical field is exempt from ethical implication, and I have shifted among different levels: selves, others, institutions, the state, and humanity. As a historical narrative, this book has explored implicit and explicit ethics as well as unintended consequences, meanings behind and beyond what historical actors believed they were saying and doing. I have substantiated my interpretation by marshalling evidence to show historical dynamics and engines of change. By way of conclusion, let me now offer an evaluation of the turn to ethics in contemporary France. What did it mean?

The historical significance of the ethical turn touches three themes: the legacy of "the Sixties," "perennial" questions about social and political life, and elements distinctive to France. First of all, the ethical turn allows us to re-evaluate the legacy of the Sixties in a way that shows the insufficiency of both "Right" and "Left" interpretations of that era. Varying and conflicting views of the French events of 1968 demonstrate the contested legacy of the 1960s – debates about the significance and impact of the era's political, social, and cultural movements. To take the example of the United States for a moment – and to speak generally – one might divide interpretations of the 1960s over the past thirty years roughly into two camps: Right and Left. To adherents of the ideal-typical Right position, the 1960s represented a moral breakdown, a collapse of traditional moral codes related to the nation, family, sexuality, and so forth. For normative experience, ethics, and morality, the era was negative. A politically and culturally revived evangelical Christianity, itself with roots in the Sixties, has responded to "moral relativism" since the early 1980s through the reassertion of moral absolutes and totalities, that is, with appeals to "family values" and moral rigorism. On the other hand, adherent of ideal-typical Left positions on the 1960s have been more positive. As they see it, the restrictions of moralizing authorities were broken open by cultural and political rebellion. Social movements, from feminism to environmentalism, sought to define and practise new ways of living, to imagine and inhabit new – in principle, more liberated – social spaces. What the Right would call relativistic nihilism, the Left might refer to as another major step in the move to a post-traditional society with new spaces of freedom and diversity. The Left sees the call for moral rigorism as a nostalgia for a homogeneity and simplicity inadequate to historical reality.

Just as there might always be a little truth in every joke, so too, there is truth in such absurdly general snapshots. To some degree, this Right-Left picture itself is merely the latest chapter in a much longer story of modernity, a story about progress and reaction, secularism and religion, toleration and illiberalism, and so forth. More precisely, though, the Right-Left bifurcation symptomized developments in late-twentieth-century society, from the marketing of the counter-culture to the neo-traditionalist search for fixed certainties – or perhaps just for an orientation – in an uncertain world. The "culture wars" of the 1980s and 1990s, those pitched battles between multiculturalists and defenders of the Western canon, are further evidence of this divide.

My aim in raising these Right and Left ideal-typical descriptions is mainly to criticize both of them. Against the belief that the 1960s brought a breakdown of "values," ushering in an era of hedonism and nihilism, I suggest that the "spirit of 1968" had a rich and provocative ethics with a powerful, if admittedly contradictory, legacy. That ethics was implicit from the start. The Right is wrong that the Left simply deserted ethical experience for an anything-goes relativism. For its part, the Left is wrong and fruitlessly cornered when, clinging to antiauthoritarianism, it conceives of ethical experience first and foremost as a matter of repression and external constraint. Ethics and norms are not only forms of control, and the turn to ethics was not merely reactionary. The 1960s were not an enemy of the good life or living ethically. The good life and living ethically do not require neo-traditionalist moral absolutism. Leftists who emphasize the negative side of norms ("don't tell me what to do") are lost, to quote an old Leninist line, in "infantilism." The view that ethical experience is an avoidable or peripheral dimension of social and political life is unconvincing.

Normative criteria are always present, even when they do not appear to be. We cannot escape relating to norms, even if that relation is one of rejection or critique. Moral and ethical philosophies in their many colours are only the most self-reflexive forms of the more basic sociological experience of the ethical. Uneducated people have complex ethical standpoints in their day-to-day lives, in contrast to the ways they may deal with epistemological or aesthetic matters. From this point of view no era is exempt from ethics talk; such chatter forms part of the constant murmuring backdrop of the social world. Yet the normative is not simply a monolithic, normalizing field, as literature on "moral panic," for instance, tends to assume. In addition to being the material of control or repression, normative criteria are also, more positively, cultural artifacts that minimally enable us to get by and might even open up the further possibility of a good life.

With this suggestion in mind, one can see how the movements of the 1960s succeeded, but not in the way their Left protagonists hoped or their Right antagonists feared. The 1960s helped sow the seeds of a rebirth of ethics: ethics in general and particular kinds of ethics. As a member of Generation X, I have wanted this book to contribute to a critique of the 1960s generation. Retaining what was positive of the 1960s and its legacies requires a sober assessment of its excesses and dead-ends. One generation is not obliged to fight the ghosts of another. Thus between antiauthoritarianism ("don't tell me what to do") and moral rigorism ("do this"), there remains the pertinent ethical question, *How ought we to live together?* There is a related modernist project to reinvigorate: taking seriously the question, *Is a non-repressive morality possible and what would it look like?*

My second point is that ethical questions can be seen as "perennial." The elements at play in post-1968 France can be found throughout European modernity and, from a still greater distance, throughout Western civilization. One way to systematize the historical siftings and transformations I have examined is with the admittedly abstract distinction between an immanent *ethos* and a transcendent or transcendental *law*. Ethos refers to ways of being, to the immanent field of existence, to sensibilities and mentalities as they are lived. It describes an ambience and a character, portraying how people do things. An ethos approaches the notion of culture, or what Pierre Bourdieu and others have called *habitus*. From one perspective, an ethos simply *is*. A law, on the other hand, stands outside an ethos, limiting, conditioning, and organizing it, often in a normative sense. Defining what cannot be or ought to be, a law is transcendent, or transcendental, to an immanent ethos. A law is a limit that divides and separates. It regulates and binds what an ethos distributes and circulates. Where an ethos is by definition variable, law generally marks the (even temporarily) invariable. Ethos leans toward the descriptive and law toward the prescriptive.

Ethics might be imagined as occupying a space between description and prescription, splitting the difference between a loosely normative and descriptive *ethos* (what people think and do) and a tightly normative and systematic *law*, limit, or morality (what people ought to think and do). Although containing elements of two extremes, ethics can be reduced neither to simple descriptions of what people think and do irrespective of norms, nor to the strictures of, say, legal and moral systems. To be sure, many phenomena partake of both ethos and the law. For example, the early modern populist ritual of *charivari* was an event characterized by chaotic collective fusion (the ethological), and at the same time, the ritual was performed according to a fairly consistent and predictable set of rules.

The distinction between ethos and law has formed the backbone of this book. The ethics of liberation can be approached by imagining a continuum between two poles: an immanent ethos and a transcendent or transcendental law. May 1968 was an antinomian revolt, an event characterized by an intense and visceral ethos. It was a happening that people experienced, and, as many commentaries have indicated, submitting *les événements* – the spontaneity, expression, and *parole* of May – to a single explanatory framework, or law, has proved difficult. The possibility of explanation is somewhat conditioned by the object explained. In this case there was in fact a deep rejection of law, notably the laws of convention, the laws of bourgeois, religious, and Communist morality, and the laws of the French state. May's festive revolt significantly addressed the transformation of everyday life, the here-and-now relationships of people. The antinomian, in this sense, was a claim for immanence, if one sets aside the religious origins of the term (the substitution of one kind of relation to the divine for another). There was an almost Dionysian quality to the spirit of '68. The events affected the immanent *ethos* of France: the ways people did things in relationship to themselves, others, institutions, and the state. The transformation of an implicit ethics of liberation into an explicit fascination with ethics involved reacquainting May's immanent *ethos* with the notion and experience of limits, as the legacy of 1968 was worked over, struggled with, and digested during the 1970s.

A principal exception to this wholesale rejection of law was the pervasive marxisant insistence on a certain kind of law; namely, the revolutionary laws of history (class struggle, the proletariat as historical agent, violence as the handmaiden to revolution, and so forth). Hannah Arendt identified Marxism's "law of movement" as that prerogative which gave the revolutionary certain knowledge about the meaning of history of which he or she was part.[7] In the terms used here, the revolutionary laws of history ruled ethos. In 1968 marxisant class struggle and workerist rhetoric framed the spontaneous happening of the May revolt. There was thus a tension between May's spontaneity and its Marxist-Leninist features that demanded discipline and sacrifice for long-term and historically guaranteed victory. The radicalism of the 1968 era thus sometimes found itself caught between its antiauthoritarian or antinomian ethos and a certainty about the revolutionary laws of history. As exhaustion with revolution and doubts about the laws of history set in during the 1970s, the dynamics of May's ethos and the question of its limits – that is, ethics – were foregrounded.

For some, the story of post-1968 France was the story of the persistence of May's ethos, its continuing, if fading, resonance across the 1970s. That ethos, in its antinomianism, refused and resisted containment. Perhaps inevitably, it encountered limits and laws. At various moments during the 1970s, May's ethos was conditioned and checked by the police, judicial system, prisons, psychiatric institutions, psychoanalysis, gender, childhood, the state, and the very notion of humanity. In Part I we saw militants encounter limits imposed by the legal and penal systems and then how prisoners were placed "outside the law" [*hors la loi*]. Leaving aside revolutionary rhetoric for talk of the "intolerable," the direct democratic spirit of the moment implicitly demanded that state power, too, be subject to limits. Demands for change, however, had to emerge from the prisoners' own ethos. Furthermore, at roughly the same time, in a quintessential expression of French theory, Gilles Deleuze and Félix Guattari tried in *Anti-Oedipus* to think with and remain faithful to the experience of an ethos without submitting it to the regulatory strictures of law. Their anti-psychoanalytic theory of "desiring machines" valorized the antinomian impulses of desire's flows and drifts. As Deleuze, who rigorously explored the philosophical meanings of the ethological, had said in his earlier book on Nietzsche: "The encounters of forces [are] alien to every law."[8] And yet even *Anti-Oedipus* described schizophrenia as capitalism's "exterior limit" and the Oedipal as its "displaced or internalized limit." The school of thought with which Guattari had been associated before 1968, Institutional Psychotherapy, had formulated idea-practices such as the "local law" in order to handle desire within the limitations of an institutional setting.

Another case of the tension between ethos and law can be shown in the conflicts between feminists and male leftists over the limits of desire. Was the sexual revolution about the antinomian rejection of all law? The rejection of sublimation for pleasure? How were new limits to sexual desire and pleasure to be defined? The dynamics of the women's movement led some feminists to a qualified embrace of Republican law. In contrast, one found an opposite entrenchment in positions beyond the law by advocates, usually male, of revolutionary criminality and sexual libertinism. For their part, the New Philosophers also continued the rejection of law in its statist forms, opting instead for an imaginary space of humanist universalism *above* the laws of states – in other words, for a *higher law*. On one hand, they transformed the "molecular" and marginal ethos of May, which had circulated *below* and *outside* the state, into a supra-statist order – "humanity." On the other hand, they submitted the laws of the state to a "higher law," whether that of dissidence, metaphysical limits, or the wager of human rights.

By the early 1980s, there was thus a clear divide between those who embraced the category of the *legal* and those who clung to an *ethological* perspective, between the advocates of limits and the partisans of the marginal. The crucial fact is that *both* these fields lend themselves to ethical elaboration and problematization. This assessment confirms Olivier Mongin's observation that French intellectual life in the 1980s could to some extent be understood as a debate between the supporters of Kant and those of Nietzsche. The fact that Michel Foucault, particularly in the last years of his life, proved willing to walk the line between these thinkers, weighing both ethos and law, makes his work among the most fruitful of the era.

The complex ways in which ethics is spoken of in the contemporary period are themselves symptomatic of our *ethos*. If we consider ethics not as a phenomenon but as an optic, a way of seeing, interpreting, explaining, and evaluating historical reality, we see that limits to ethos appear on a variety of levels and in a variety of arenas. The self is a limit to the chaotic and dispersive qualities of the decentred subject. Other people are limits on my own self. Institutions limit and condition selves, structuring the interpersonal domain. States continue to limit selves and institutions, and in some situations the human has come to serve as limit on the prerogatives of states. One could go further and see how the environmental model offers limits even on the ethos of the human.

In the early twenty-first century, ethical limits in one arena are not necessarily applicable to other arenas: the ethical limits of one's sexual life do not yield obvious lessons, say, for corporations or human rights groups. Mono-models, such as free-market liberalism or traditional religion, sometimes presume to provide answers to what are in fact incongruous levels of human experience. No single system can completely answer the questions of how one ought to be a self, with others, a member of institutions and civil society, a citizen of a nation-state, and a member of the human race. Ethics stresses the local and the variable, which is part of the reason why we now witness a proliferation of ethical discourses. Arthur Schopenhauer once compared modern individuals to a species of porcupines: too close for comfort, and we stick out our quills and fold in on ourselves; too isolated, and we long for the warmth of companionship, communication, and proximity. The current reign of ethics, to my mind, is symptomatic of our attempts to come to terms with a historical moment in which we are all intensely aware of prickling some people and nestling with others.

The final lesson to be gleaned from this analysis concerns elements that are particular to French history. I have traced the ethical thematic in a variety of arenas: the self, others, institutions, the state, and humanity in general. Among these five forms, one in particular merits a closer look, since it is distinctive to France and illustrates an important and useful contrast to Anglo-American culture: institutions and the related category of associations.

One spoke during the 1970s, especially in the United States and Germany, of the "long march through the institutions" as the New Left shifted gears from "outsider" street politics to "insider" participation and reform. In France the far left contributed directly to a reinvigoration of civil society through its institutional challenges and associational formations; for example, fighting censorship, setting up commissions to investigate police brutality, advocating transparency with respect to state actions, and internationalizing the fight for justice and human rights. One of the great ironies of 1970s France is that some of the principal voices in the revitalization of civil society were speaking in marxisant-revolutionary tongues. Some social actors who thought they were sowing the seeds of class revolution were actually reinvigorating social and political life. Contestation of institutions, which in France often pointed toward the state, led to a quickening of associational civil society.

The French have a slightly different sense than do North Americans of what institutions and associations are. In French, *institution* and *association* are actions before they are things. In addition to signifying, as it does in English, "a custom, system, or organization that has existed for a long time and is accepted as an important part of a particular society" (such as marriage, law, national defence, and educational or health establishments), *institution* also has connotations that are more activist and approving.

"Institutional food" tastes better in France. Institutional procedures, rules, organisms, and structures are there to serve people. If they do not do their job, they can be modified or replaced. To give one example, the psychiatrist Jean Ayme, in distinguishing the English and French senses of the term in respect to his own field, has written:

In contrast to Anglo-Saxon usage, for which the institution is the hospital, where "deinstitutionalization" results in the taking care of patients outside the hospital; in French, *institution* first of all means the action of instituting, then it means "all that is invented by men in opposition to the facts of nature" (Littré) ... The word institution does not have a pejorative connotation in our language. It has on the contrary creative, transformative, if not revolutionary implications. Saint-Just said that the more society creates institutions, the more man is free. Indeed it was the French Revolution that created *new institutions* in the face of a monarchical system that had concentrated all powers in a single man, powers that he possessed by divine right. Everyone must submit to these new institutions, created by the elected representatives of the people, but they are improvable and revisable.[9]

In short, an institution in France is never just a building, but can be an association, a corporatist group, a union, or a political party; a "site of memory" [*lieu de mémoire*], a national holiday, a museum collection, or a cultural practice. Even in the United States, baseball is an institution. Filling in the social space between a state and its citizens, institutions can constrain, repress, and make people conform, but they can also liberate and socialize. This last point had been made by Emile Durkheim at the turn of the twentieth century and then by a host of institutional critics in the postwar period, including proponents of Institutional Psychotherapy, Institutional Pedagogy, and Institutional Analysis, as well as the *sui generis* Cornelius Castoriadis, who described the self-instituting of society as a creative act.[10]

Alongside this general understanding of *institution* and critical engagements with it, one might draw attention to a particular kind of institution, *association*, which also carries distinctively French connotations. The contemporary French use of the word refers to the *Law on Associations of 1901*.[11] Article One of that law states that an association is "an agreement whereby two or more persons group together, in a permanent manner, their knowledge or activity for a purpose other than making a profit." Such associations have the legal status of moral persons and thus differ from businesses and unions. Consequently, one can draw a distinction between market civil society and non-market associative civil society. The flourishing of associative life in late twentieth-century France was truly impressive. In the 1950s around 5,000 associations were created each year; in the 1960s around 10,000; in the 1970s, 25,000; in the 1980s, 40,000; and in the 1990s, 60,000. In the early twenty-first century, about 40 percent of the French adult population belonged to at least one of the approximately 700,000 associations in the country.[12]

One key moment in this proliferation came in the early 1970s when Raymond Marcellin pre-emptively banned "The Friends of *La Cause du peuple*," the group formed by Sartre, Simone de Beauvoir, Robert Gallimard, and others to defend the Gauche prolétarienne's newspaper. On 16 July 1971, the Conseil constitutionnel ruled that Marcellin's measure was illegal (a decision reaffirmed on 16 July 1991). A series of similarly intended rulings followed, expanding the autonomy and force of democratic associational life. The *Law of 1 July 1972*, an act of hate-crime legislation, outlawed groups of collaborators or those promoting racist propaganda. On 15 December 1977 the Cour d'Assises in Paris established a legal precedent when it agreed to receive the association Choisir as a civil party in a rape case. On 9 October 1981 the right of foreigners to form associations was protected. On 25 February 1983 the Conseil national de la vie associative was founded.

In post-1968 France, associational civic life was revitalized.[13] One source for this revitalization was the energy of contestation, often revolutionary in rhetoric but democratic in substance. Contestation of the state and institutions occurs within civil society, and it is no surprise that this social space became energized. As we saw in chapter 1, in May 1968, Raymond Aron had been concerned about the weaknesses of institutional "intermediary bodies" in France. Such worries, it turns out, were unfounded. Now, there is no guarantee that institutions and associations are good medicine for the human virus, and associational civil society lends itself to a variety of instrumentalizations.[14] Still, it was post-1968 critiques of and public debates around particular institutions such as prisons, psychiatric hospitals, the family, even "canons" and language, that modelled the ethical enlivening of intermediary civil spaces. Social, cultural, and political ferment thus contributed to an operation of translation, as revolutionary idea-practices were transmuted and updated into democratic idea-practices that included the ethical turn.

This view has consequences for political culture. If in the United States institutions are believed to connect us to the past when faced with an endlessly opened future (for example, the institution of marriage must be "protected" against homosexuals), in France, in addition to this time-bound sense, institutions also have the power to free the nation from its past. One is reminded of Saint-Just's remark that "the more institutions there are, the more people are free."[15] This is not to say that institutions necessarily enliven civil society (Saint-Just's revolutionary machinery had its victims; today's prisons still exclude and repress), but rather that there is something to be gained by viewing institutions as part of civil society. There is in France a view that civil society is not "empty." It is, like the spaces of the La Borde psychiatric clinic, or Spinoza's Nature, or Deleuze and Guattari's desiring machines, full. There is a density to social space in France that offers a counter-model to the model of Anglo-American space as composed of free-market individuals. (It is not incidental, I think, that in the seventeenth century, Descartes and Spinoza came out against the vacuum, and English thinkers such as John Locke favoured it.[16]) In our moment, as atomized individuals collide in the vastness of North American space, when September 11th opened a period of renewed militarized state power, it is worth reciting that truism of French political culture, intimately bound to the themes discussed here – *L'Etat, c'est nous* – The state is us. How ought we to respond to the institutionalization of our desires?

Ethics is a necessary and yet thoroughly insufficient condition for social and political life. Critiques of the ethical turn, especially those which see in ethics an evacuation of and a pale substitute for genuine politics, are not without merit.[17] I agree wholeheartedly that ethics can never take the place of genuine political analysis and mobilization. To this extent, the legacy of late-twentieth-century ethical fascination is a tremendous stumbling block. Politics involves conflicts among competing "interests and passions." Political ethics concerns how one comports oneself – and how one ought to comport oneself – with respect to the political *agon*. For large parts of the nineteenth and most of the twentieth centuries, radical politics in particular beheld ethics with a quizzical gaze, those on the Left assigning them an ambiguous place in their projects, suspicious that speaking of ethics or norms was inherently reactionary and moralizing. It is harder to get by today without taking account of the varieties of ethical experience, and this development has by and large been a good thing. But ethics is not enough.

What remains striking about the post-1968 turn to ethics is how it was related to social activism and to conflicts in civil society, conflicts that make civil society vital and democracy real. The assertion of conflict as a general principle in society and politics need not lead to a celebration of conflict for conflict's sake: one has therapy for that. The mention of therapy is not negligible since the search for healthy forms of conflict is precisely what democratic theory and practice pursue. But the search for healthy forms of conflict proceeds on the assumption that conflict is a general good – that movement is generally better than stasis, action better than inaction, interaction better than isolation. The problem today is not that there is too much conflict in civil society, but that there is not enough of the right kind. Many of us feel ourselves to be, as de Tocqueville said, "more than kings and less than human." Democracy should be noisy. That there are no guarantees is precisely the democratic wager. Perhaps without the political dimension, without citizens who are willing to take the risks of engagement and confrontation, ethics drifts toward lonely acts and high ideals. If ethics emerged at a certain moment in recent history to correct certain rigid political forms, then perhaps politics – genuine politics of struggle and collective enunciation – can enable us to move beyond this unsurpassed horizon of our times, overcoming certain of its limitations while at the same time taking with us some of the lessons the ethical turn has wrought.

Notes

INTRODUCTION

1 Dansette, *Mai 1968*. Joffrin, *Mai 68*. Labro et al., *"This Is Only a Beginning."* Rajsfus, *Mai 68*. Seal and McConville, *Red Flag/Black Flag*. Seidman, *The Imaginary Revolution*. It is certainly true that the May events had preliminaries in France and took place in a context of global upheaval. On the former see Seidman, *The Imaginary Revolution* and Ross, *May '68 and Its Afterlives*. On the latter see, for instance, Marwick, *The Sixties*. Such preludes and broader considerations will not detain us here since they would not significantly alter my account of the ethical turn that transpired in France after 1968. In addition to having been a significant event in itself, "1968" was also a symbol for more extensive contestation during "the Sixties," which themselves included the 1970s.

2 Charles de Gaulle, cited by Aron, *The Elusive Revolution*, 18. Robert Frank, "Introduction," in Dreyfus-Armand et al., eds., *Les Années 68*, 21. However, a November 1969 poll of 200 Parisians concluded that the most "memorable events" in history were: World War I and World War II (39%), Napoleon (13%), 1789 (11%), and May 1968 (8%). Muraz, *La Parole aux Français*, 233.

3 Ory, *L'Entre-deux-mai*. Domenach, *Enquête sur les idées contemporaines*, 15.

4 On the surprise gifts of May 1968, see my "Les Contributions accidentelles du marxisme au renouveau des droits de l'homme en France dans les années 1970," *Les Libéralismes au regard de l'histoire*, Special Issue of *Actuel Marx* 32 (September 2002).

5 Castoriadis, "Le Cache-misère de l'éthique," *Lettre internationale* 37 (summer 1993); repr. in *Les Carrefours du labyrinthe*, vol. 4, *La Montée de l'insignificance*; "The Ethicists' New Clothes," in Castoriadis, *World in Fragments*, 108. Others have noted the ethical turn in passing: Arendt, *On*

Violence, 23–4; Dosse, *History of Structuralism*, 2:282–7; Hirsch, *The French New Left*, 199; Jay, *Downcast Eyes*, 543–86; Le Goff, *Mai 68*, 413, 452–6; Moyn, *Origins of the Other*, 236; Ross, *May ' and Its Afterlives*, 167–8; Schrift, *Twentieth-Century French Philosophy*, 70–4; Starr, *Logics of Failed Revolt*, 154.

6 Sartre and Lévy, *Hope Now*, 68–9.

7 Foucault, "The Ethics of the Concern for Self as a Practice of Freedom," in Foucault, *Ethics*, 284.

8 See, however, Niel, *Le Mouvement étudiant*, 78–87.

9 *Oxford English Dictionary*, 2nd ed., s.v. "antinomian." Chris Rojek usefully connects the British antinomian tradition to one critical intellectual for whom the 1960s were formative. See his "Stuart Hall and the Antinomian Tradition." For a rough application of the term to 1960s protest, written at the time, see S.N. Eisenstadt, "Generational Conflict and Intellectual Antinomianism." I do not mean antinomian in the sense of a "foundational heteronomy," which Kerstin Behnke links to Romanticism and Søren Kierkegaard but that also derives from Immanuel Kant's "antinomies." Behnke, "Fragments, Not Wholes."

10 Domenach, "L'Idéologie du mouvement," *Esprit* 8–9 (August–September 1968), cited by Philippe Bénéton and Jean Touchard, "Les Interprétations de la crise de mai–juin 1968"; "The Interpretations of the Crisis of May/June 1968," in Reader, ed., *The May 1968 Events in France*, 30.

11 Habermas, *Knowledge and Human Interests*, 197–213.

12 Lionel Trilling, cited in M. Berman, *All That Is Solid Melts into Air*, 12.

13 Robert Maggiori, personal communication, July 2001.

14 Khilnani, *Arguing Revolution*, 121ff. Kaplan, *The Decline of Radicalism and the Triumph of the Left in France*, has argued that French radicalism truly ended during the Mitterrand years (1981–95). Much debate on this issue has centred on François Furet's book, written between 1971 and 1978, *Interpreting the French Revolution*.

15 Lecourt, *The Mediocracy*, 98.

16 Touraine, *The May Movement* and Touraine, ed., *Mouvements sociaux d'aujourd'hui*. Agnès Heller, remarks made at the Sorbonne conference, *'68 dans l'histoire et dans la culture politique européenne* (February 1999).

17 Measured accounts of postmodernism locate its sources elsewhere than in French theory. Anderson, *The Origins of Postmodernity*.

18 Habermas, *Legitimation Crisis*. A few examples from the innumerable commentaries on French theory that help draw a picture are: Dosse, *History of Structuralism*, 2 vols.; Pavel, *The Feud of Language*; Jay, *Marxism and Totality*, 512–17; Frank, *What is Neostructuralism?* 14–18, 83; Sylvère Lotringer and

Sande Cohen, "Introduction: A Few Theses on French Theory in America," in Lotringer and Cohen, eds., *French Theory in America*, 1–9; A. Berman, *From the New Criticism to Deconstruction*, 172–6; Sturrock, ed., *Structuralism and Since*, 2–17; Merquior, *From Prague to Paris*, 190–9, 253–60.

19 Amid numerous examples, see on the one hand, Himmelfarb, *On Looking into the Abyss*, and on the other, Habermas, *The Philosophical Discourse of Modernity*; Dews, *Logics of Disintegration*; Sokal and Bricmont, *Fashionable Nonsense*.

20 John Rajchman, *Truth and Eros*, has related the question of ethics to Lacan's and Foucault's revival of an old philosophical sense of *eros* as a love of truth. Todd May, *The Moral Theory of Poststructuralism*, has argued for poststructuralism as a form of ethical consequentialism. Claire Colebrook, *Ethics and Representation*, has seen poststructuralist ethics as the latest chapter in the story of modern autonomy, caught since Kant in the "antinomy" between anthropologism (the view that humans are immanently self-sufficient) and anthropomorphism (the view that nature is like us). The explosion of English-language scholarship on Emmanuel Levinas has done much to bring the theme of ethics to prominence. See works by Bettina Bergo, Robert Bernasconi, Richard A. Cohen, Simon Critchley, Adriaan T. Peperzak, and Edith Wyschogrod, among others. As a more general phenomenon, postmodernism has also been (endlessly) linked to ethics. See, for example, Bauman, *Postmodern Ethics* and *Life in Fragments*; Hoffmann and Hornung, eds., *Ethics and Aesthetics*; Madison and Fairbairn, eds., *The Ethics of Postmodernity*; LaFountain, ed., *Postmodern Ethics*.

21 Some have seen the presumed failure of 1968 as the motor driving French theory. Beran, *In the Wake of Failed Revolution*, 128, 154ff. Starr, *Logics of Failed Revolt*, 2–3, 8, 10, 34.

22 Baker, *Deconstruction and the Ethical Turn*; Critchley, *Ethics, Politics, Subjectivity* and *The Ethics of Deconstruction*.

23 Stephens, *Anti-Disciplinary Protest*, 2. I discern parallels between Stephens's view and my own, but her emphasis on the counter-culture's ludic "psychedelic Bolsheviks" (Jerry Rubin) underestimates the normative aspects of aesthetic play and inventiveness.

24 Judt, *Past Imperfect*, 3–4, 11, 316, 318. Judt, "Review of Capdevielle and Mouriaux, *Mai 68*," 842–3. Judt reinforced his account in *The Burden of Responsibility*. Cf. Khilnani, *Arguing Revolution*; Lilla, *The Reckless Mind* and Lilla, ed., *New French Thought*.

25 Ross, *May '68 and Its Afterlives*, 12, 32, 57, 167, 180. See my review essay "Hello to All That: Rescuing May 1968." Feenberg and Freedman, *When Poetry Ruled the Streets*, also write in the nostalgic vein.

26 I thus share Michael Scott Christofferson's judgment that 1968's direct democratic spirit had significant consequences during the 1970s. Antitotalitarianism, on which he focuses, is an important part of the more widespread ethical turn. Christofferson, *Intellectuals Against the Left*. I am also sympathetic to Michael Seidman's dispassionate engagement with facts on the ground. However, his judgment that May was a "modest" event leading to no significant changes in later years is conjectural, since his account stops in June 1968. Seidman, *The Imaginary Revolution*.

27 Besançon, ed., "*Les Murs ont la parole*," 42. The phrasing strongly evokes article 4 of the Déclaration des droits de l'homme et du citoyen of 1789.

28 The contrast breaks somewhat with Ancient Greek treatments of *nomos* or *dikē* in relation to *physis*, and of *ethos* in relation to *pathos* and *logos*. For certain readers, the category mistake would be confusing Aristotle's *Nicomachean Ethics* with his *Rhetoric*.

29 For a psychoanalytically informed discussion of May 1968, ethos, and law, see Kristeva, *Revolt, She Said*, 21–7. Much has been written on Martin Heidegger's grappling with the ethos/ethics tension in his 1946 "Letter on 'Humanism,'" in Heidegger, *Pathmarks*, 268–76.

30 On memory and 1968 in general see Passerini, *Autobiography of a Generation*. On the dynamics of French memory see Ross, *May '68 and Its Afterlives*.

31 Garber, Hanssen, and Walkowitz, eds., *The Turn to Ethics*. Davis and Womack, eds., *Mapping the Ethical Turn*. Marchitello, ed., *What Happens to History?*

32 Of many methodological points that might be made, I will note only that I have borne in mind older models of the social history of ideas as well as disparate attempts at what might be called reconstructive philosophical history. Gay, *Weimar Culture*; Hughes, *Consciousness and Society*; Schorske, *Fin-de-siècle Vienna*; Buck-Morss, *The Dialectics of Seeing*; Goldmann, *The Hidden God*; Mannheim, "Conservative Thought"; Starobinski, *Jean-Jacques Rousseau*.

CHAPTER ONE

1 Michael Seidman has helpfully reported earlier agitation around similar issues at the university at Antony. See his *The Imaginary Revolution*, 37–43.

2 De Certeau, *La Prise de parole*; part. trans. in de Certeau, *The Capture of Speech*, esp. 1–40.

3 Prost, "Les Grèves de mai-juin 1968."

4 Pierre Vidal-Naquet, "Outline of a Revolution," in Schnapp and Vidal-Naquet, eds., *The French Student Uprising*, 12–14. Fourastié, *Les Trente glorieuses*.

5 Capdevielle and Mouriaux, *Mai 68*, 293–4. Cf. Joffrin, *Mai 68*, 317. Vidal-Naquet, "Outline of a Revolution," 44.

6 Paul Berman, "The Moral History of the Baby Boom Generation," in Berman, *A Tale of Two Utopias*. H. Stuart Hughes, "The Moral Equivalent of War," in Hughes, *Sophisticated Rebels*.

7 Bensaïd and Weber, *Mai 1968*. Gombin, *Le Projet révolutionnaire*.

8 Michel Trebitsch, "Voyages autour de la révolution: les circulations de la pensée critique de 1956 à 1968," in Dreyfus-Armand et al., eds., *Les Années 68*, 71–5.

9 Daniel Cohn-Bendit, cited in Bourges et al., *The Student Revolt*, 78.

10 Ivan Illich popularized the last term a few years later in his *Tools for Conviviality*.

11 I have these works in mind for the following discussion: Dreyfus-Armand et al., eds., *Les Années 68*; Kurlansky, *1968*; Marwick, *The Sixties*; Passerini, *Autobiography of a Generation*; Ross, *May '68 and Its Afterlives*; Seidman, *The Imaginary Revolution*; Suri, *Power and Protest*; *Thesis Eleven* 68, no. 1 (2002).

12 On events, see Roland Barthes, "L'Ecriture de l'événement," *Mai 68: la prise de la parole*, Special Issue of *Communications* (1968); "Writing the Event," in Barthes, *The Rustle of Language*; Lefebvre, *The Explosion*; De Certeau, *The Capture of Speech*; Deleuze, *The Logic of Sense*.

13 Posner, ed., *Reflections on the Revolution in France*. Reader, *The May 1968 Events in France*.

14 De Certeau, "A Literature of Disquiet: A Year Later," in de Certeau, *The Capture of Speech*, 61–76.

15 Bénéton and Touchard, "Les Interprétations de la crise de mai-juin 1968"; "The Interpretations of the Crisis of May/June 1968," in Reader, ed., *The May 1968 Events in France*.

16 Morin, Lefort, and Coudray [Cornelius Castoriadis], *Mai 1968*. The revised edition includes essays from 1978, 1986, and 1988. Aron, *The Elusive Revolution*.

17 Ibid., xiii, xviii, 5, 7, 10–11, 19, 26, 33–4, 76–7, 106–7, 114, 119–20, 125. The references to Judaism appear on ibid., xv, 14.

18 For a biting commentary at the turn of the twenty-first century that struggles with post-1968 phantoms, see Lindenberg, *Le Rappel à l'ordre*. Hervé Hamon and Patrick Rotman's engrossing reportage, *Génération*, succeeds in capturing sensibilities without trying to sum up what it all meant. See also the photo-collage by Benjamin Lambert, *Défense d'interdire*. Other works that lay the groundwork for a non-polemic historiography are: BDIC, *Mémoires de 68*; Dreyfus-Armand et al., eds., *Les Années 68*; Seidman, *The Imaginary Revolution*.

19 Edgar Morin, "Mai-sphinx" [1978], in Morin et al., *La Brèche*, 147, 152; Morin, "Mai si, Messie non" [1978], ibid., 153; Cornelius Castoriadis, "Les Mouvements des années soixante" [1986], ibid., 196–7; Claude Lefort, "Relecture" [1988], ibid., 210.

20 Joffrin, *Mai 68*, 309–10, 321, 324.

21 Debray, *Modeste contribution aux discours et cérémonies officielles du dixième anniversaire*; part. trans. "A Modest Contribution to the Rites and Ceremonies of the Tenth Anniversary." See also Weber, "Reply to Debray."

22 Lipovetsky, *L'Ere du vide*, 7–8. See also his "'Changer la vie' ou l'irruption de l'individualisme transpolitique," *Pouvoirs* 39 (1986); "May '68, or the Rise of Transpolitical Individualism," in Lilla, ed., *New French Thought*. Cf. Bell, *The Cultural Contradictions of Capitalism* and Lasch, *The Culture of Narcissism*.

23 Ferry and Renault, *French Philosophy of the Sixties*, 33, 38–60.

24 Ibid., 62–3.

25 Ibid., citing in part Aron, *The Elusive Revolution*, 126.

26 Henri Weber, "Trente ans après," in Weber, *Que reste-t-il de mai 68?* 10–11, 18.

27 Le Goff, *Mai 68*, 15–20, 457–65. Seidman compares Le Goff's distinction between "neo-Leninism" and "*les désirants*" to the contemporaneous American distinction between "rads" and "freaks." Seidman, *The Imaginary Revolution*, 7.

28 Claude Lefort, "Droits de l'homme et politique," *Libre* 7 (1980); "Politics and Human Rights," in Lefort, *The Political Forms of Modern Society*, 261–2. Cf. Marcel Gauchet, "Les Droits de l'homme n'est pas une politique," *Le Débat* 3 (July–August 1980).

29 Pierre Viansson-Ponté, "Quand la France s'ennuie," *Le Monde*, 15 March 1968.

30 Ferinot, *8 h 15*, 9.

CHAPTER TWO

1 Comité vérité Toul, *La Révolte de la Centrale Ney, – décembre* . *La Révolte de la prison de Toul: délinquance sociale et justice gauchiste*, Special Issue of *Négation* avant-premier numéro (1971). Macey, *The Lives of Michel Foucault*, 274–5. Eribon, *Michel Foucault*, 231–2. The press conference is presented in "L'Enfer de Toul: textes de la conférence de presse du Groupe d'information [sur les] prisons et du Comité pour la vérité [de Toul]. Toul 5 janvier," *APL Informations: bulletin quotidien de l'Agence de presse "Libération," Bullétin spécial* 122 bis. (6 January 1972). Archives of the Gauche prolétarienne at the Bibliothèque de documentation internationale contemporaine (BDIC), University of Paris-X, Nanterre. F Δ Rés. 576/5.5.2.

2 Founded by Maurice Clavel and Jean-Paul Sartre, the APL would help lay the foundations for the newspaper *Libération*, whose first issue appeared 18 April 1973. On Clavel, see Part IV below.

3 Artières, Quéro, and Zancarini-Fournel, eds., *Le Groupe d'information sur les prisons*. Robert, "Les Luttes autour des prisons *1971–1972*."

4 "A propos des psychiatres dans les prisons (Intervention de Gilles Deleuze à la conférence de presse du Comité de vérité de Toul, le 5 janvier 1972)," *APL Dossier* 12 (9 January 1972). "Les Psychiatres et Toul: solidarité avec le docteur Rose," *APL Dossier* 13 (10 January 1972). Michel Foucault Archives at the Institut Mémoires de l'édition contemporaine (IMEC), Paris. GIP2.Dj–04.

5 On 16 December 1971 Rose gave Foucault written authorization to make public her letter denouncing the conditions at the Toul Prison, a letter addressed to the president of the Republic, the Minister of Justice, and the president of the Conseil d'ordres des médecins. IMEC: GIP2.C01–01. Her letter appeared two days later in "Toul: la voix des insurgés se fera entendre dans toute la France," *La Cause du peuple–J'Accuse*, 18 December 1971. Cf. *Le Monde*, 26–27 December 1971, and Foucault, "Le Discours de Toul," *Le Nouvel Observateur* (27 December 1971); repr. in Foucault, *Dits et écrits*, 2:236–8. Rose wrote, "Society itself and those who lead it must be informed about the way we protect society ... I have absolutely no political leanings and no religious opinions. I am someone with good intentions [*de la bonne volonté*]."

6 Michel Foucault and Gilles Deleuze, "Les Intellectuels et le pouvoir," *Gilles Deleuze*, Special Issue of *L'Arc* 49 (1972); "Intellectuals and Power," in Foucault, *Language, Counter-Memory, Practice*.

7 Macey, *The Lives of Michel Foucault*, 278, referring to Claude Mauriac, *Le Temps immobile*, vol. 3, *Et comme l'espérance est violente*, 354.

8 Cohen-Solal, *Sartre*, 449; Macey, *The Lives of Michel Foucault*, 172.

9 Mauriac, *Et comme l'espérance est violante*, 291.

CHAPTER THREE

1 Bourseiller, *Les Maoïstes*, 105. On French Maoism, see also Kessel, *Le Mouvement "maoïste" en France*, 2 vols. Hess, *Les Maoïstes français*. Jarrel, *Eléments pour une histoire de l'ex-gauche prolétarienne*. Fields, *Trotskyism and Maoism*. Van der Poel, *Une Révolution de la pensée*. On Maoism before 1968 see my "The Red Guards of Paris: French Student Maoism of the 1960s," *History of European Ideas* 31, no. 4 (2005).

2 Fields, *Trotskyism and Maoism*, 99.

3 M. Berman, *A Tale of Two Utopias*, 267.
4 Mao Tse-tung, "Oppose Book Worship" (May 1930), in *Selected Readings from the Works of Mao Tsetung*, 40–50.
5 Mao Tse-tung, "Preface to *Rural Surveys*" (17 March 1941), in *Selected Works of Mao Tsetung*, 3:11. Cf. Ross, *May '68 and Its Afterlives*, 109–13.
6 Bourseiller, *Les Maoïstes*, 104. Hamon and Rotman, *Génération*, 2:22.
7 "Un Dirigeant politique" (Interview with Pierre Victor [Benny Lévy]), in Manceaux, *Les Maos en France*, 197–8.
8 "Projet de résolution politique" [October 1968], BDIC: F Δ Rés. 576/3.3.1. A variant draft is in Kessel, *Le Mouvement "maoïste" en France*, 2:221–34.
9 "Autocritique de la Direction" (October 1968), in Kessel, *Le Mouvement "maoïste" en France*, 2:252. "Projet de résolution politique."
10 Geismar, July, and Morane, *Vers la guerre civile*. On violence, see texts written between September 1968 and January 1969: 136–7, 140–56, 158–79, 256, 330–3, 362–4. "Un Dirigeant politique," 193. Macey, *The Lives of Michel Foucault*, 218. "De la révolte anti-authoritaire à la révolution prolétarienne," *Cahiers de la Gauche prolétarienne* 1 (April 1969).
11 "Projet de résolution sur la crise et les méthodes pour la surmonter" (17 October 1968?), BDIC: F Δ Rés. 576/3.3.1.
12 "'Texte proposé à la discussion des camarades' par les ex-GPA de Saint-Cloud, Boulogne-Point du Jour" (December 1968), in Kessel, *Le Mouvement "maoïste" en France*, 2:295–6.
13 "Pour un mouvement révolutionnaire" (September 1968?), BDIC: F Δ Rés. 576/3.3.1. "Autocritique de la Direction" (October 1968), 244–5.
14 "Information," *Supplément au Bulletin Intérieur, no. 11 de la GP* (May 1969?), ibid., 323. Bourseiller, *Les Maoïstes*, 109.
15 Ibid., 111.
16 Ibid., 114–15. "Pour la Résistance," *Cahiers de la Gauche prolétarienne* 2 (May 1970). "Un Dirigeant politique," 203. Rolin's post-facto account is published as Antoine Liniers [Olivier Rolin], "Objections contre une prise d'armes," in Furet, Liniers, and Raynaud, *Terrorisme et démocratie*.
17 Bourseiller, *Les Maoïstes*, 120, citing in part *La Cause du peuple* 14 (10 December 1969). Ibid., 117–19. Hamon and Rotman, *Génération*, 2:130, 155–6, 169–71.
18 Sommier, *La Violence politique et son deuil*.
19 Sartre's relationship to violence continues to be a sticking point decades after his death. Santoni, *Sartre on Violence*. Wormser, ed., *Jean-Paul Sartre, violence et éthique*.
20 Sommier, *La Violence politique*, 55–7, 66–9, 84. Cf. Glucksmann, *Stratégie et révolution en France 1968*. De Beauvoir, *All Said and Done*, 431–2. Sartre's

position did not prevent him from describing French prisons as part of a "concentration camp universe" or from overseeing the publication of a special issue of *Les Temps modernes* 310 bis. (1972), entitled "Nouveau fascisme, nouvelle démocratie." Le Dantec, *Les Dangers du soleil*, 220–4. Hamon and Rotman, *Génération*, 2:355–6.

21 Sommier, *La Violence politique*, 120; 130; 126; 127–8; 60, 77, 89–93, 158; 89; 93–4.

22 Ibid., 162, 150.

23 Interview with Susanna Barrows, recalling Paris during the early 1970s.

24 Sommier, *La Violence politique*, 130–1, 134.

CHAPTER FOUR

1 Marcellin, *L'Ordre public et les groupes révolutionnaires*, 11.

2 Ibid., 14, 21–2, 33–9, 51.

3 Ibid, 53–4.

4 Abraham, *The Judicial Process*, 259.

5 Ingraham, *Political Crime in Europe*, 240 n57.

6 "Atteintes à la Sûreté de l'Etat" (Law no. 63–22, 15 January 1963), in *Bulletin Législatif Dalloz*, 49.

7 Paraphrased by Ingraham, *Political Crime in Europe*, 236.

8 Ibid., 236 n35, 237 n36, 237–40.

9 Marcellin, *L'Ordre public*, 54–6, 60–4.

10 Pompidou, *Entretiens et discours*, vol. 1, *1968–1974*, 152–3.

11 Marcellin, *L'Ordre public*, 66–71, 74–5. Marcellin, *L'Importune vérité*, 41.

12 Kimbro, "*Les Lieux de Mémoire.*"

13 Rajsfus, *Mai '68*.

14 *Le Monde*, 21 March 1972, cited in Fields, *Trotskyism and Maoism*, 118.

15 *The Observer*, 2 June 1968, cited in Glucksmann, *Stratégie de la révolution*, 9.

16 Law no. 70–480 (8 June 1970), tendant à réprimer certaines formes nouvelles de délinquance, *Journal officiel de la République française: lois et décrets* 132 (8–9 June 1970), 5234. See the changes in the *Code Pénal*, esp. Art. 184, 231, 314, 341.

17 Ingraham, *Political Crime in Europe*, 243.

18 For Le Dantec's first-hand account of the Maoist circle from the rue d'Ulm through his imprisonment at La Santé, see his *Les Dangers du soleil*.

19 Le Bris, *L'Homme aux semelles de vent*.

20 Gavi, Sartre, and Victor, *On a raison de se révolter*. See also, Sartre and Lévy, *Hope Now*, discussed in chapter 25.

21 *Minutes du procès d'Alain Geismar*. A few hours after Geismar's conviction by the Court of State Security, the NRP briefly kidnapped the Gaullist deputy Michel de Grailly in the name of "popular justice."

CHAPTER FIVE

1 von Tagen Page, *Prisons, Peace, and Terrorism*.
2 Cummins, *The Rise and Fall of California's Radical Prison Movement*.
3 White, *Genet*, 521–44, 560–8. Cummins, *The Rise and Fall of California's Radical Prison Movement*, 196–8.
4 Langlois, *Guide du militant*. Cf. Langlois, *Les Dossiers noirs de la police française*.
5 "Pour une politique juste v-a-v des camarades emprisonnés" [fall 1970], BDIC: F Δ Rés. 576/5.5.1.
6 "Manifeste de la 'permanence,'" *Défense Active* 1 (December 1969), 4. Maurice Clavel was director of publication. Anne Querrien, close to Félix Guattari, was responsible for membership. The group, having changed its name to Défense Collective, was debating in November 1972 whether or not it should disband because of a "spontaneous" shift from aiding "exclusively militants" to aiding "all those who suffer repression" (immigrant workers, prisoners, women, soldiers, the homeless, young people), IMEC: GIP2.Di–01.
7 François Furet, "Terror," in Furet and Ozouf, eds., *A Critical Dictionary of the French Revolution*, 140. Danton also declared: "When the justice of the tribunals begins, the justice of the people will end." Brian Singer, "Violence in the French Revolution: Forms of Ingestion/Forms of Expulsion," in Fehér, ed., *The French Revolution and the Birth of Modernity*, 158. For wider discussions of "citizen, peer, and popular justice" from Roman Antiquity to Imperial China to the French Revolution, see Société d'histoire du droit, *Justice populaire*.
8 Zola, *Humanité-vérité-justice*. Reinach, *Vers la justice par la vérité*. On the Ligue des droits de l'homme et du citoyen from its founding until World War II, see Perry, "Remembering Dreyfus."
9 Levine, *Affaires non classées*, 347–76.
10 Gide, *Retour de l'URSS. Koestler, Le Zéro et l'infini*. Merleau-Ponty, *Humanism and Terror*. Judt, *Past Imperfect*, 101–50.
11 Schwartz, *A Mathematician Grappling with His Century*, 336–45. Vidal-Naquet, *Mémoires*, 2:60–73, *passim*. Vidal-Naquet, *L'Affaire Audin*. Schwartz, *Le Problème de la torture dans la France d'aujourd'hui*.
12 Comité pour la vérité sur l'affaire Ben Barka, *L'Affaire Ben Barka, Enseignements et lacunes du premier procès*, and *La Mort de Mehdi Ben Barka*. On Clavel and Ben Barka, see Part IV. The event has continued to elicit

attention: Guérin, *Les Assassins de Ben Barka*; Violet, *L'Affaire Ben Barka*; Boukhari, *Le Secret*.

13 Limqueco and Weiss, eds., *Prevent the Crime of Silence*, 57–9. Cf. Dedijer and Elkaïm-Sartre, eds., *Tribunal Russell*. Sartre and Elkaïm-Sartre, eds., *Tribunal Russell* II. The Tribunal continued after Russell's death in 1970, holding hearings on Central and South America (1974–75), Germany (1978), and Native Americans (1980). On Halimi, see Part III.

14 "Resolution of the First International Conference Regarding the Question of Organization" (14–16 July 1924), in Executive Committee of the IRA [International Red Aid], *Ten Years of International Red Aid in Resolutions and Documents*, 34. *Qu'est-ce que le Secours rouge international?* "Statuts de la Section Française du Secours rouge international" (1931), repr. in *Secours rouge* 1 (January 1971).

15 Interview with Daniel Defert (June 1999).

16 "Appel pour le Secours rouge" (11 June 1970), in *Secours rouge* 1 (January 1971).

17 Interview with Defert.

18 De Beauvoir, *Adieux*, 5.

19 "Projet de résolution: sur l'orientation politique du Secours rouge" [after December 1970; possibly September 1971?], BDIC: F Δ Rés. 576/5.8; IMEC: G.5.5a.

20 De Beauvoir, *All Said and Done*, 437–9. Sartre, *Sartre by Himself*, 105–6, citing the film *Les Mineurs* (1972). Secours rouge, *Tribunal populaire pour juger les crimes patronaux*, BDIC: F Δ Rés. 576/5.10. Sartre, "Un Procès populaire," *Cahiers prolétariens: élargir la résistance* 1 (January 1971), 77. "Projet de résolution: sur l'orientation politique du Secours rouge."

21 "Le Secours rouge, instrument de l'unité populaire," *Cahiers prolétariens: élargir la résistance*, 68, 75–6.

22 "Appel pour un Tribunal Populaire," Supplément to *La Cause du peuple* (June 1971), BDIC: F Δ Rés. 576/5.8.

23 "Le 10 et 11 juillet s'est tenu à Paris…" [July 1971], IMEC: G.5.5a.

24 Ibid.

25 "Pour l'union des prisons et des bases d'appui" [June 1970?], BDIC: F Δ Rés. 576/5.5.1.

26 With permission, prisoners could receive visitors in their rooms. Ministère de la Justice, *Régime pénitentiaire spécial*, 17. The "special regime" was set forth in section D490–95 of the *Code de procédure pénale*. Although the code made no explicit mention of political prisoners, the regime had been granted to left- and right-wing militants during the Algerian War. Martineau and Carasso, *Le Travail dans les prisons*, 108–9.

27 They went on a hunger strike in May 1969. Comité de soutien aux détenus (Bordeaux) and Comité pour la liberté et contre la repression (Paris), *Huit détenus politiques de Bordeaux déclarent*.

28 "Déclaration des emprisonnés politiques" (1 September 1970), in *Les Prisonniers politiques parlent*, 4–5.

29 "Petition des familles" and "Les Familles soutiennent les grévistes de la faim" [September 1970], BDIC: F Δ Rés. 576/5.5.1.

30 On the Rolling Stones concert, see *Les Prisonniers politiques parlent*, 12–13.

31 "Communiqué des détenus politiques des prisons de France" (28 September 1970), ibid., 8.

32 "Grève illimitée de la faim des prisonniers politiques" (14 January 1971) and [Letter from the Vincennes Philosophy Department], [November 1970], BDIC: F Δ Rés. 576/5.5.1.

33 "Pourquoi une nouvelle grève de la faim dans les prisons?" ibid. Gustav Husak was the Czechoslovakian Communist Party Secretary who led the repression against Alexander Dubcek's supporters after 1968.

34 "Grève illimitée de la faim des prisonniers politiques," ibid.

35 "A l'initiative du 'Secours rouge' des médecins lancent un appel en faveur des emprisonnés politiques" (January 1971), ibid. [Letter from the Vincennes Philosophy Department].

CHAPTER SIX

1 Marc Kravetz, "Qu'est-ce que le GIP?" *Le Magazine littéraire* 101 (1975), 13. "Un Philosophe militant," *Le Monde*, 21 February 1975. Philippe Artières, "L'Ombre des prisonniers sur le toit: les héritages du GIP," in Eribon, ed., *L'Infréquentable Michel Foucault*. Boullant, *Michel Foucault et les prisons*.

2 Foucault, *Madness and Civilization*, 38–64, 199–220. Cf. the foreword to the first edition of the book, in Foucault, *Dits et écrits*, 1:162. Before 1971 Foucault's explicit references to prisons could be counted on one hand. *Dits et écrits*, 1:504 [1966], 2:19 [1970]. See also the testy interview with N. Meienberg, *Tages Anzeiger Magazin* 12 (25 March 1972), likely conducted in January of that year; "Le Grand enfermement," ibid., 296–306. Foucault makes the contradictory statements: (1) "I would like it if one established absolutely no relation between my theoretical work and my work with the GIP. That means a lot to me. But there probably is a relationship"; and (2) "That annoys me if you say that there is absolutely no relation between *Histoire de la folie* and my work with the GIP." Ibid., 296, 305. Unless otherwise noted, what follows is reconstructed and quoted from an interview with Daniel Defert (June 1999).

3 Macey, *The Lives of Michel Foucault*, 261.
4 Salas and Verleyn, "Casamayor l'insoumis." Some of his significant publications into the early 1970s included: *Où sont les coupables?*; *Les Juges*; *Combats pour la justice*; *La Justice pour tous*; *La Police*.
5 Interview with Defert.
6 Interview with Pierre Vidal-Naquet (September 2000). Vidal-Naquet, *Mémoires*, 2:363. The "simplism" of French Maoism "disgusted" him. Ibid., 278.
7 Interview with Danielle Rancière (April 1999).
8 Macey, *The Lives of Michel Foucault*, 263.
9 Ibid., 260. Eribon, *Michel Foucault*, 226.
10 Vimont, *La Prison politique en France*, 469.
11 The report was made public 16 September 1971. Ministère de la Justice, *Régime pénitentiaire spécial*. Pleven called it the "special penitentiary regime," observed Daniel Defert and Jacques Donzelot, "to get around the term 'political regime.'" Defert and Donzelot, "La Charnière des prisons," *Le Magazine littéraire* 112–13 (May 1976): 33.
12 "Création d'un groupe d'information sur les prisons," *Esprit* 3 (March 1971): 531–2, cited in Eribon, *Michel Foucault*, 224–5. The text was also published in *La Cause du peuple*, 17 February 1971, and excerpted in *Le Monde*, 10 February 1971. Foucault, *Dits et écrits*, 2:174–5.
13 "Où en est la commission Pleven?" [March 1971?], IMEC: G.5.1d.
14 Danielle Rancière, cited by Macey, *The Lives of Michel Foucault*, 264.
15 "Rapport fait par les détenus politiques maoïstes à l'intérieur de la GP et du GIP" [early 1971], IMEC: G.5.4d.
16 Defert and Donzelot, "La Charnière des prisons," 33.
17 Interview with D. Rancière.
18 "Rapport fait par les détenus politiques maoïstes à l'intérieur de la GP et du GIP."
19 Interview with D. Rancière.
20 "Lettre adressée aux familles des détenus de droit commun et aux prisonniers de droit commun" [late January, early February 1971?], IMEC: G.1.6.
21 Interview with D. Rancière. See also Foucault and Vidal-Naquet's description of interactions with families at La Santé in "Enquête sur les prisons, propos receuillis par Claude Angeli," *Politique-hebdo* 24 (18 March 1971); partially repr. in *Dits et écrits*, 2:176–82.
22 "Droit à l'information sur les prisons" [after 1 May 1971], IMEC: G.1.5a.
23 Interview with Defert.
24 Interview with D. Rancière.
25 Interview with Defert.

26 For example, Lemonnier, ed., *Lumière sur l'échafaud.*
27 Interview with Defert.
28 "Discussion sur l'information," [n.d.], IMEC: G.1.6.
29 "Manifeste du GIP," *Dits et écrits*, 2:175. Cf. "Je voudrais au nom du GIP …" [January 1972?], IMEC: G.1.5b. Macey, *The Lives of Michel Foucault*, 266.
30 *Intolérable les prisons: le GIP enquête dans vingt prisons*, citation from back cover. Interview with Defert.
31 Interview with D. Rancière.
32 Interview with Defert.
33 A second questionnaire had been distributed to lawyers and people who worked in the court system but its results were not published. Macey, *The Lives of Michel Foucault*, 262.
34 Ibid., 268–9.
35 *Intolérable les prisons 2: le GIP enquête dans une prison modèle: Fleury-Mérogis. L'Assassinat de George Jackson. Intolérable 4: suicides de prison (1972).* Deleuze edited and wrote parts of the last *enquête*. See "H.M.'s Letters," in Deleuze, *Desert Islands and Other Texts.*
36 Macey, *The Lives of Michel Foucault*, 270–1. "Droit à l'information sur les prisons," IMEC: G.1.5a.
37 Foucault, "Rapports de la commission de l'information sur l'affaire Jaubert" (21 June 1971), in *Dits et écrits*, 2:199–203.
38 Favard, *Les Prisons*, 20. Macey, *The Lives of Michel Foucault*, 272–3. Pompidou refused for the first time to grant a stay of execution, and the two murderers, Claude Buffet and Roger Bontems, were executed on 28 November 1972.
39 [Call for a meeting at the Mutualité for Thursday 11 November 1971], IMEC: G.1.7. Notes written in early 1971 show that, as the GIP was getting started, Foucault had thought particularly about the status of American blacks in prison. Foucault, "Qui sont les détenus?" [late January, early February 1971?], IMEC: G.1.1a.
40 "Lettre à M. Pleven" (22 November 1971), IMEC: G.1.7. "De nouveau dans les prisons," [December 1971?]; and "Pleven supprime les colis de Noël aux détenus" [December 1971], IMEC: G.1.5a.
41 Hamon and Rotman, *Génération*, 2:379–81. Macey, *The Lives of Michel Foucault*, 264.
42 "Hier, des prisonniers de Fleury-Mergis se sont révoltés," [n.d.], IMEC: G.1.5a.
43 Macey, *The Lives of Michel Foucault*, 281.
44 [Pleven meets with Prime Minister Jacques Chaban-Delmas and Minister of the Interior Raymond Marcellin on the Schmelck report], TF1, J20H (9 January 1972), Institut National d'Audiovisuel, Paris.

45 [Untitled], [16 January 1972], IMEC: G.1.5a. "Un Groupe de personnalités réclame la constitution d'une commission du GIP sur la mutinerie de Nancy," APL *Informations* 130 (16 January 1972).

46 "L'Agitation pénitentiaire," *Le Monde*, 19 January 1972. Macey, *The Lives of Michel Foucault*, 281–2. Jaubert and Artières, *Michel Foucault*.

47 Cesar Beccaria (1738–1794) was the great Italian Enlightenment advocate of prison reform. Was Foucault referring to Louis-François Bertin (1766–1841), journalist and advocate of constitutional monarchy? Or did he misspeak and mean to say Alphonse Bertillon (1853–1914), founder of anthropometry (or *bertillonage*), used in the physical identification of criminals? "Un Problème m'intéresse depuis longtemps, c'est celui du système pénal" (Interview with Jélila Hafsia), *La Presse de Tunisie* (12 August 1971), in *Dits et écrits*, 2:206.

48 Foucault, "Je perçois l'intolérable" (Interview with G. Armleder), *Journal de Genève: samedi littéraire* 170 (24–25 July 1971), in *Dits et Ecrits*, 2:204.

49 Foucault, "Sur les prisons," *J'Accuse* 3 (15 March 1971), in *Dits et Ecrits*, 2:175.

50 For a critique of the political uses of sociologizing 1968, see Ross, *May '68 and Its Afterlives*.

51 Foucault and Vidal-Naquet, "Enquête sur les prisons: brisons les barreaux du silence," in *Dits et écrits*, 2:176. The difference between an "'investigative commission,' a judicial term" and an "information group" is repeated by Defert and Ewald in their introduction to the GIP manifesto. Ibid., 174.

52 Foucault, "Sur la justice populaire: débat avec les maos" (5 February 1972); "On Popular Justice: A Discussion with Maoists," in Foucault, *Power/Knowledge*.

53 Ibid., 6, 8, 13, 27–9.

54 For a fruitful comparison of these dynamics in the French Revolution, see Singer, "Violence in the French Revolution," 161, 164–8.

55 Foucault, "On Popular Justice," 10, 20.

56 Ibid., 2–3, 20, 24, 26, 30. Foucault might have had in mind the fact that most of the victims of the September Massacres of 1793 were common-law prisoners, *les gens sans aveu*. Singer, "Violence in the French Revolution," 154–8.

57 Foucault, "On Popular Justice," 16.

58 Deleuze, "The Intellectual and Politics: Foucault and the Prison" (Interview with Paul Rabinow and Keith Gandal), *History of the Present* 2 (spring 1986). Also trans. as "Foucault and Prison," in Deleuze, *Two Regimes of Madness*. Deleuze suggested that Foucault was able to "retain his independence vis-à-vis the GP, and at the same time deal with them" precisely because he had not been involved in 1968 and had little previous experience to prejudice him.

59 Interview with Defert.

60 Foucault, "Enquête sur les prisons: brisons les barreaux du silence," in *Dits et écrits*, 2:180.
61 [Petition signed by, among others, several sociologists from the University of Paul Sabatier], [n.d.], IMEC: G.1.6.
62 Foucault, "La Prison partout," *Combat*, 5 May 1971, in *Dits et écrits*, 2:193.
63 Defert and Donzelot, "La Charnière des prisons," 34.
64 Interview with D. Rancière.
65 Foucault, "La Situation dans les prisons est intolérable ..." [n.d.], IMEC: G.1.5a. "L'Article 15," *La Cause du peuple* (3 June 1971), in *Dits et écrits*, 2:198–9. Foucault referred to article 15 of the Declaration of the Rights of Man and Citizen. "Manifeste du GIP," in *Dits et Ecrits*, 2:175. "Un Problème m'intéresse depuis longtemps, c'est celui du système pénal," ibid., 208. "Je perçois l'intolérable," ibid., 205.
66 Foucault, "Un Problème m'intéresse depuis longtemps, c'est celui du système pénal," ibid., 208.
67 Foucault, "Le Grand enfermement," ibid., 306.
68 Deleuze, "The Intellectual and Politics: Foucault and the Prison," 1.
69 Ibid., 2.
70 Serge Livrozet, *De la prison à la révolte*. Cf. Livrozet, *Aujourd'hui la prison*, 280–92. On Livrozet and the valorization of criminality in 1970s France, see Part III below. The creation of the Comité d'action des prisonniers was preceded by the formation of two other organizations within the GIP milieu: the Groupe multi-professionel in Lyon and the Association pour la défense des droits des détenus.
71 Interview with Defert. Defert and Donzelot, "La Charnière des prisons," 35.

CHAPTER SEVEN

1 Mirabeau went from the dungeon of Louis XVI's Château de Vincennes to the presidency of the National Assembly in eleven years. Falque, *Sortie de prison*, 191. Beaumont and de Tocqueville, *Du système pénitentiaire aux Etats-Unis et de son application en France*. Dumas, *The Count of Monte Cristo*. Charrière, *Papillon*.
2 Favard, *Des prisons*, 15, 18–20. Bonnemaison, *La Modernisation du service public pénitentiaire*, 11. Fize, *Une Prison dans la ville...*, 84, *passim*. Vimont, *La Prison politique en France*, 465–6.
3 De Beauvoir, *All Said and Done*, 433. Froment, *La République des surveillants de prison*, 207, 211, 216–18. François Boullant, "1974: 'l'affaire Mirval,'" *Prison et résistances politiques: le grondement de la bataille*, Special

Issue of *Cultures et conflits* 55 (2004). Cuau, *L'Affaire Mirval*, with forewords by Foucault and Pierre Vidal-Naquet. Favard, *Des prisons*, 9–10, 22, 184. Fize, *Une Prison dans la ville...*, 79.

4 Shaw, *Imprisonment*, 85.

5 "Events were very quickly to prove me right." Althusser, *The Future Lasts Forever*, 232.

6 Hamon and Rotman, *Génération*, 2:404–19.

7 See Macey, *The Lives of Michel Foucault*, 301–5.

8 Groupe d'information sur la répression, *Lutte de classes à Dunkerque*. Another organization, the Groupe d'information et de soutien des travailleurs immigrés, formed to provide legal and social support to immigrant workers (and which continues to exist today) developed in a milieu apart from the GIP. Philippe Artières, "L'Ombre des prisonniers sur le toit: les héritages du GIP," in Eribon, ed., *L'Infréquentable Michel Foucault*, 104–5. Collectif d'alphabétisation and Groupe d'information et de soutien des travailleurs immigrés, *Le Petit livre juridique des travailleurs immigrés*.

9 Michel Foucault and the members of GIS, "Médecine et lutte de classes," *La Nef* 49 (October–December 1972). Comité d'action santé, *Médecine*.

10 GIS, *Oui nous avortons!*

11 GIS, *La Médecine désordonnnée*, 7.

12 Ibid., 95. Cf. [GIS tract] (14 May 1972), IMEC GIP2. Di–15.

13 GITS, *Le Travail social contre qui?* 164–7.

CHAPTER EIGHT

1 Cooper, *Psychiatry and Anti-Psychiatry*. Sedgwick, *Psycho Politics*.

2 Descombes, *Modern French Philosophy*, 26, 172–90. Cf. Silverman, ed., *Philosophy and Desire*. Edgar Morin, "Mai '68: complexité et ambiguïté" [1986], in Morin et al., *La Brèche*, 177–8.

3 Deleuze and Guattari, *Capitalisme et schizophrénie*, vol. 1, *L'Anti-Oedipe*; *Anti-Oedipus: Capitalism and Schizophrenia*. Deleuze had been an active member of the Groupe d'information sur les prisons. Deleuze, Michel Foucault, Denis Langlois, Claude Mauriac, and Denis Perrier-Daville, "Questions à Marcellin," *Le Nouvel Observateur* (5 July 1971). Deleuze, "Ce que les prisonniers attendent de nous...," *Le Nouvel Observateur* (31 January 1972); "'What Our Prisoners Want From Us...,'" in Deleuze, *Desert Islands and Other Texts*. Deleuze, Jean-Paul Sartre, Simone de Beauvoir, Mauriac, Jean-Marie Domenach, Hélène Cixous, Jean-Pierre Faye, Foucault, and Maurice Clavel, "On en parlera demain: les dossiers (incomplets) de l'écran," *Le Nouvel Observateur* (7 February 1972).

4 Tilkin, *Quand la folie se racontait*, 21–61. Jacques Postel and David F. Allen, "History and Anti-Psychiatry in France," in Micale and Porter, eds., *Discovering the History of Psychiatry.*

5 "Graves problèmes professionnels et sociaux," *Le Monde*, 15 February 1968. "Psychopharmacologie et psychiatrie," *Le Monde*, 14 March 1968. "Réforme de la législation des malades mentaux," *Le Monde*, 12 April 1968. "Projets disassociant la neurologie et la psychiatrie sucitent inquiétude," *Le Monde*, 12 December 1968. "Création de certificats distincts de neurologie et de psychiatrie," *Le Monde*, 8 January 1969.

6 Sectorization was fully applied only in 1985. Chanoit, *La Psychothérapie institutionnelle*, 19. Fourquet and Murard, eds., *Histoire de la psychiatrie de secteur*, Special Issue of *Recherches* 17 (1975).

7 Laing, *The Divided Self* (1959) [*Le Moi divisé* (1970)]; *The Self and Others* (1961) [*Soi et les autres* (1971)]; *The Politics of Experience* (1967) [*La Politique de l'expérience* (1969)]; and *Knots* (1970) [*Noeuds* (1971)]. Laing and Esterson, *Sanity, Madness, and the Family* (1964) [*L'Equilibre mental, la folie et la famille* (1971)]. Cooper, *Psychiatry and Antipsychiatry* (1967) [*Psychiatrie et antipsychiatrie* (1970)]; *The Death of the Family* (1970) [*Mort de la famille* (1972)]. See Pierre Fédida, "Psychose et parenté (naissance de l'antipsychiatrie)" [Review of Laing and Esterson, *L'Equilibre mental, la folie et la famille* and Cooper, *Psychiatrie et antipsychiatrie*], *Critique* 257 (October 1968). Félix Guattari, "Laing divisé" [Review of Laing, *Soi et les autres*, *Noeuds*, and Laing and Esterson, *L'Equilibre mental, la folie et la famille*], *La Quinzaine littéraire* 132 (1 January 1972); "The Divided Laing," in Genosko, ed., *The Guattari Reader*; and as "Laing Divided," in Guattari, *Chaosophy*. See also Basaglia, *L'istituzione negata* (1968) [*L'Institution en négation* (1970)], and the review by Guattari, "La Contestation psychiatrique," *La Quinzaine littéraire* 94 (1 May 1970); "Franco Basaglia: Guerilla Psychiatrist," in Genosko, ed., *The Guattari Reader*. Guattari then criticized Laing's experimental Kingsley Hall for prolonging Oedipal "familialism." Guattari, "Le 'Voyage' de Mary Barnes," *Le Nouvel Observateur* (28 May 1973); in Guattari, *La Révolution moléculaire*; "Mary Barnes, or Oedipus in Anti- Psychiatry," in Guattari, *Molecular Revolution*; also trans. "Mary Barnes' 'Trip,'" *Anti-Oedipus*, Special Issue of *Semiotext(e)* 2, no. 3 (1977); in Genosko, ed., *The Guattari Reader*; and in Guattari, *Chaosophy*.

8 *Marge* 6 (April–May 1975).

9 Sherry Turkle, "French Anti-Psychiatry," in Ingleby, ed., *Critical Psychiatry*, 150–1. Cf. Turkle, *Psychoanalytic Politics*.

10 Blond, "L'Antipsychiatrie, le réel, l'imaginaire et le symbolique."

11 Mannoni, *La Psychiatre, son "fou" et la psychanalyse*. See Paul-Claude Racamier, François Tosquelles, and Cyrille Koupernik in *L'Antipsychiatrie*, Special Issue of *La Nef* 42 (January–May 1971). Racamier et al., *Le Psychanalyste sans divan*, on the celebrated experiment of community mental health in the XIIIe arrondissement of Paris. Roger Gentis and Horrace Torrubia, "Présentation" (8 March 1972), *Folie pour folie*, Special Issue of *Partisans* 62–3 (November–December 1972). Koupernik, *L'Antipsychiatrie*.

12 Castel, *Le Psychanalysme* and *La Gestion des risques*.

13 Delacampagne, *L'Antipsychiatrie*.

14 A preliminary index of Marcuse and Reich's considerable impact during *les années soixante-huit* is found in the number of first French editions of their works appearing at that time. For Marcuse, following translations of *Soviet Marxism* and *Eros and Civilization* in 1963, nothing until 1968 (3 books), 1969 (3), and one a year from 1970 through 1973. For Reich, since translations of a collection of essays (1934) and *The Function of Orgasm* (1952), nothing until 1966 (1), 1968 (1), 1970 (1), 1971 (2), 1972 (3), and one a year from 1973 through 1975. Reich's books sometimes went through three or more editions in the 1970s.

15 Hocquenghem, *Homosexual Desire*. Lyotard, *Libidinal Economy*. Dollé, *Le Désir de la révolution*. Girard, *Violence and the Sacred*. Lacroix, *Le Désir et les désirs*. See also Cauchard, *Force et sagesse du désir*. Cariou, *Freud et le désir*. Clouscard, *Néo-fascisme et idéologie du désir*. Houziaux, *Le Désir, l'arbitraire et le consentement*.

16 Guattari, *Letter to Deleuze*, 5 April 1969. Deleuze, *Letter to Guattari*, 13 May 1969. IMEC: [non-coded].

17 Deleuze and Guattari, "Sur Capitalisme et schizophrénie" (Interview with Catherine Backès-Clément) (2 March 1972), *Deleuze*, Special Issue of *L'Arc* 49 (1972); repr. in Deleuze, *Pourparlers*; "Gilles Deleuze and Félix Guattari on *Anti-Oedipus*," in Deleuze, *Negotiations*, 14.

18 Deleuze and Guattari, "Le Synthèse disjonctive," *Klossowski*, Special Issue of *L'Arc* 43 (1970). Cf. Deleuze and Guattari, *Anti-Oedipus*, 75–84.

19 Guattari, "Cette fois je voulais faire un plan ...," Félix Guattari Archives, IMEC: N16–20c. These fifty-eight pages are a close reading of Deleuze's work on Spinoza. See Guattari, *The Anti-Oedipus Papers*.

20 [Interview with Arlette Donati], IMEC: I01–26c.

21 Turkle, "French Anti-Psychiatry," 161.

CHAPTER NINE

1 We cannot here do justice to Deleuze and Guattari's larger project and other writings, in which the authors built on some of *Anti-Oedipus*'s themes while leaving behind some of its insularity. Rather, our task is limited to examining this publication, its reception, and then its origins; in other words, a specific historical configuration. Scholarship on the pair, especially Deleuze, continues to flourish, reinforcing Foucault's oft-cited dramatic quip in 1970 that "perhaps one day, this century will be known as Deleuzean." Foucault, "Theatrum Philosophicum," in Genosko, ed., *Deleuze and Guattari*, 1:305. This three-volume collection is essential. Ronald Bogue's older *Deleuze and Guattari* is a simple introduction. See also Khalfa, ed., *An Introduction to the Philosophy of Gilles Deleuze*; May, *Gilles Deleuze*; Stivale, ed., *Gilles Deleuze* and his earlier *The Two-Fold Thought of Deleuze and Guattari*. Gary Genosko has done the most to restore Guattari to his rightful place as equal collaborator. See his *Félix Guattari*.

2 Holland, *Deleuze and Guattari's* Anti-Oedipus; Massumi, *A User's Guide to Capitalism and Schizophrenia*.

3 Deleuze and Guattari, *Anti-Oedipus*, 1–4, 22–4, 36, 46, 283–5.

4 Ibid., *Anti-Oedipus*, 3, 22–4. A more complete depiction of desiring machines' productive processes would discuss the "connective," "disjunctive," and "conjunctive" syntheses, ibid., 5–22, 36–41, 110–11; and also the near-Comtean view of "savage, barbaric, and civilized societies," ibid., 261–6.

5 The discussion would be further complicated by considering the claim that the modern capitalist machine "oscillates" between "immanent regulations" and "transcendental resurrections." Ibid., 13, 15, 23, 25, 33–5, 38–40, 44–5.

6 *Oxford English Dictionary*, 2nd ed., s.v. "schiz" ... "schizophrenogenic."

7 "The molar-molecular opposition, as an opposition, depended on the perspective in *Anti-Oedipus* between flux and code. Indeed, fluxes being the universal element, the different types of molar-molecular coding depend on a difference in coding." Guattari, "L'Opposition molaire-moléculaire" [n.d.], IMEC: ET01–62. The molar-molecular distinction would serve as a template for Deleuze and Guattari's later distinction between the "arboresque" and the "rhizome." Deleuze and Guattari, *A Thousand Plateaus*, 6–7, *passim*.

8 Deleuze and Guattari, *Anti-Oedipus*, 113, 136, 266, 271, 277–83, 382. Cf. 322, 343.

9 Dossier on *Anti-Oedipus*, *Le Monde*, 28 April 1972, 18–19. Roland Jaccard reported that *Anti-Oedipus* sold out its first edition in three days. See also Jaccard, *L'Exil intérieur*.

10 André Green, "A quoi ça sert?" in Dossier on *Anti-Oedipus*, *Le Monde*, 28 April 1972.

11 Cryrille Koupernik, "Un Délire intelligent mais gratuit," ibid.

12 François Châtelet, "Le Combat d'un nouveau Lucrèce," ibid.

13 Kostas Axelos, "Sept questions d'un philosophe," ibid. Deleuze had already dedicated a review essay to Axelos: "Faille et feux locaux: Kostas Axelos," *Critique* 275 (April 1970); "The Fissure of Anaxagoras and the Local Fires of Heraclitus," in Deleuze, *Desert Islands and Other Texts*.

14 "Deleuze and Guattari, "Sur Capitalisme et schizophrénie" (Interview with Catherine Backès-Clément) (2 March 1972), *Deleuze*, Special Issue of *L'Arc* 49 (1972); repr. in Deleuze, *Pourparlers*; "Gilles Deleuze and Félix Guattari on *Anti-Oedipus*," in Deleuze, *Negotiations*, 22–3. "Deleuze et Guattari s'expliquent" [with Maurice Nadeau, Raphaël Pividal, François Châtelet, Roger Dadoun, Serge Leclaire, Henri Torrubia, Pierre Clastres, and Pierre Rose], *La Quinzaine littéraire* 143 (16 June 1972); "Deleuze and Guattari Fight Back...," in Deleuze, *Desert Islands and Other Texts*; "In Flux," in Guattari, *Chaosophy*, 95, 98, 100–1. Deleuze, "Lettre à Michel Cressole," *La Quinzaine littéraire* 161 (1 April 1973); repr. in Cressole, *Deleuze*; repub. as "Lettre à un critique sévère," in Deleuze, *Pourparlers*; part. trans. "I Have Nothing to Admit," *Anti-Oedipus*, Special Issue of *Semiotext(e)* 2, no. 3 (1977); also trans. "Letter to a Harsh Critic," in Deleuze, *Negotiations*, 7–9.

15 "Gilles Deleuze and Félix Guattari on *Anti-Oedipus*," 24. Deleuze, "Letter to a Harsh Critic," 9–10.

16 Deleuze and Guattari, *Kafka* and *A Thousand Plateaus*.

17 Guattari, "Psycho-Analysis and Schizo-Analysis" (Interview with Arno Münster for the *Frankfurter Rundschau*) (17 January 1973), *Anti-Oedipus*, Special Issue of *Semiotext(e)* 2, no. 3 (1977); "Molecular Revolution and Class Struggle," in Guattari, *Molecular Revolution*; "The Best Capitalist Drug," in Guattari, *Chaosophy*, 213.

18 See the discussions in Chasseguet-Smirgel, ed., *Les Chemins de l'anti-Oedipe*. Jacques Hochmann and A. Andre, "La Comtesse du regard, essais de 'familialisme' appliqué," in "La Mort d'Oedipe et l'anti-psychanalyse," Special Dossier in *Esprit* 40, no. 12 (December 1972).

19 René Girard, "Système du délire," *Critique* 306 (November 1972), repr. in Girard, *Critique dans un souterrain*; "Delirium as System," in Girard, *"To Double Business Bound"*; repr. in Genosko, ed., *Deleuze and Guattari*, vol. 2. Jean-Marie Domenach, "Oedipe à l'usine," *Esprit* 40, no. 12 (December 1972); "Oedipus in the Factory," *Salmagundi* 30 (summer 1975). Jean-François Lyotard, "Capitalisme énergumène," *Critique* 306 (November 1972); repr. in Lyotard, *Des Dispositifs pulsionnels*; part. trans. "Energumen

Capitalism," *Anti-Oedipus*, Special Issue of *Semiotext(e)* 2, no. 3 (1977); repr. in Genosko, ed., *Deleuze and Guattari*, vol. 2. Roger Dadoun, "Les Machines-Désirantes," *La Quinzaine littéraire* 142 (1 June 1972). Clouscard, *Néo-fascisme et idéologie du désir*. Jacques Donzelot, "Une Anti-sociologie," *Esprit* 40, no. 12 (December 1972); "An Anti-Sociology," *Anti-Oedipus*, Special Issue of *Semiotext(e)* 2, no. 3 (1977); repr. in Genosko, ed., *Deleuze and Guattari*, vol. 2. Jean Furtos and René Roussillon, "'L'Anti-Oedipe,' essai d'explication," *Esprit* 40, no. 12 (December 1972).

20 Deleuze and Guattari, *Anti-Oedipus*, 50, 62–3, 110–11, 114–15, 198, 212–13, 268. Cf. Deleuze and Guattari, *Kafka*.

21 Deleuze and Guattari, *Anti-Oedipus*, 328.

22 Descombes, *Modern French Philosophy*, 180.

23 Foucault, "Preface," in Deleuze and Guattari, *Anti-Oedipus*, xii.

24 Reich, *The Mass Psychology of Fascism*.

25 Deleuze, "Letter to a Harsh Critic," 7. Guattari, "The Best Capitalist Drug," 220.

26 Genosko, "Introduction," *The Guattari Reader*, 17.

CHAPTER TEN

1 Georges Daumézon and Philippe Koechlin, "La Psychothérapie institutionnelle française contemporaine," *Anaïs portugéses de psichuiatria* 4, no. 4 (1952).

2 Lafont, *L'Extermination douce*.

3 Mozère, *Le Printemps des crèches*, 99.

4 Eric Favereau, "Fou de fou," *Libération*, 27 June 1998. On the history of Saint-Alban, see "Saint-Alban: Mythes et histoire: les premières rencontres de Saint-Alban (juin 1986)," Special Dossier in *Information psychiatrique* 63 (October 1987).

5 Mozère, *Le Printemps des crèches*, 97.

6 Polack and Sabourin, *La Borde ou le droit à la folie*, 29.

7 Jean Ayme, "Essai sur l'histoire de la psychothérapie institutionnelle," in Delion, ed., *Actualité de la psychothérapie institutionnelle*, 35. Chanoit, *La Psychothérapie institutionnelle*, 16.

8 Canguilhem, *The Normal and the Pathological*.

9 Macey, *Frantz Fanon*, 144–53. Centre d'étude, de recherche et de formation institutionnelle (CERFI), *L'Institutionalisation des collectifs de travail*. *Histoires de La Borde: dix ans de Psychothérapie institutionnelle à la clinique de Cour-Cheverney (1953–1963)*, Special Issue of *Recherches* 21 (March–April 1976). *Recherches* was the journal of CERFI.

10 Martin, ed., *Pratiques institutionnelles et théorie des psychoses*. Delion, ed., *Actualité de la psychothérapie institutionnelle*. Chanoit, *La Psychothérapie institutionnelle*. A rare English example of methods closer to IP than anti-psychiatry was Barton, *Institutional Neurosis*.

11 Chanoit, *La Psychothérapie institutionnelle*, 24.

12 "Traitement, formation et recherche sont inséparables" (Interview with Jean Oury), *Cinquante ans d'organisation des institutions psychiatriques*, Special Issue of *Psychiatrie française* 28, no. 1 (March 1997). See also Oury, *Il, donc*.

13 Oury, "Traitement, formation et recherche sont inséparables." Oury, Guattari, and Tosquelles, *Pratique de l'institutionnel et politique*. Guattari's contribution partially translated as "Institutional Practice and Politics," in Genosko, ed., *The Guattari Reader*; and also as "Institutional Schizo-Analysis," in Guattari, *Soft Subversions*.

14 Mozère, *Le Printemps des crèches*, 102.

15 Oury, "Une Dialectique de l'amitié," *Le Monde*, 1 September 1992. Joughin, "Translator's Notes," in Deleuze, *Negotiations*, 186 n1.

16 The following biographical information about Guattari is taken from a set of remarkably candid and unpublished autobiographical interviews that he gave in 1984 (to which I was given access but not the right to take notes). Guattari, [Autobiographical Interviews], IMEC: I01–25b (10 July), d (23 August), e (29 August), and f (1 October).

17 Oury and Vasquez, *Vers une pédagogie institutionnelle* and *De la classe coopérative à la pédagogie institutionnelle*.

18 In a letter to Lacan (11 January 1980), Oury wrote: "It has already been thirty-three years, you know, since I first met you at the rue de l'Ulm in 1947. I have always attentively followed, sometimes relentlessly, what you have said or written. For nine years, at the end of each week, for two hours, I 'improvise' in public on the theme of analytic theory; a didactic exposé in order to initiate auditors to your work, and to read you with greater profit, articulating my discourse in light of the problems that are asked in the institutional field and in psychosis. It is an ethical approach and at the same time a salvaging of a discourse that has too great a tendency to dissolve itself in verbiage." IMEC: D02–16. Six days earlier, on 5 January 1980, Lacan had dissolved the Ecole freudienne de Paris.

19 Guattari, "De Léros à La Borde," IMEC: ET05–25; part. trans. from *La Quinzaine littéraire* 250 (1977) as "La Borde: A Clinic Unlike Any Other," in Guattari, *Chaosophy*. Guattari, [Autobiographical Interviews], IMEC: I01–25e.

20 CERFI, *L'Institutionalisation des collectifs de travail*, 12–13. Cf. *Histoires de La Borde*.

21 A sample *grille* from the early to mid-1960s lists the following tasks: animation, use of time, economic responsibilities, sport, culture, and financial committee. IMEC: D03–14. See also Guattari, "La Grille" (Exposé fait au stage de formation de la clinique de La Borde) (29 January 1987), IMEC: ET04–13; CERFI, *L'Institutionalisation des collectifs de travail*, 16, 19–20; CERFI, *Histoires de La Borde*, 77–104; and Guattari, "Le S.C.A.J. Messsieurs-Dames" [1957], in Guattari, *Psychanalyse et transversalité*, 35–8. Deleuze's foreword to this book is translated as "Three Group-Related Problems," in Deleuze, *Desert Islands and Other Texts*.

22 Oury and Guattari, "Sur les rapports infirmiers-médecins" [September 1955], in Guattari, *Psychanalyse et transversalité*, 7–17. Guattari, "La Grille," 6–7, 10–11, 15, 18. CERFI, *L'Institutionalisation des collectifs de travail*, 22–5.

23 Oury, "La Désaliénation en clinique psychiatrique" [1956], in Oury, *Psychiatrie et psychothérapie institutionnelle*.

24 CERFI, *L'Institutionalisation des collectifs de travail*, 27, 29, 30.

25 Jacques Lacan, "The Function and Field of Speech and Language in Psychoanalysis" [1953], in Lacan, *Ecrits*, 40–6.

26 *Oxford English Dictionary*, 2nd ed., s.v. "vacuole."

27 CERFI, *L'Institutionalisation des collectifs de travail*, 31–2. On the vacuole, see also Guattari, "Transversality" [1964], "Integration of the Working Class and Analytical Perspective" [1966], "The Group and the Person" [1966–68], and "Machine and Structure" [1969–71], in Guattari, *Molecular Revolution*, 15–16, 203, 37, 115.

28 CERFI, *L'Institutionalisation des collectifs de travail*, 4, 8.

29 Alfred Adler (1934–), the French anthropologist whose research focused on North Africa, should not be confused with Alfred Alder (1870–1937), the Austrian psychologist. Polack and Sabourin, *La Borde*, 33.

30 Ibid., 34.

31 CERFI, *L'Institutionalisation des collectifs de travail*, 1.

32 On Guattari's use of these Sartrean terms see his "De Léros à La Borde," 4.

33 For Oury, the existentialist dimension was related to Søren Kierkegaard. Oury, "Analyse de l'entourage immédiat du malade dans le cadre de la thérapeutique institutionnelle" [1957], in Oury, *Psychiatrie et psychothérapie institutionnelle*, 35–6.

34 Oury, *Il, donc*, 51. Cf. ibid., 175–9.

CHAPTER ELEVEN

1 Guattari, *The Three Ecologies* and *Chaosmosis*.

2 Elkaïm, ed., *Réseau alternative à la psychiatrie*.

3 Lacan, "Seminar on 'The Purloined Letter'" [26 April 1955], *Yale French Studies* 48 (1974). Guattari, "Notes sur un système général de transposition des chaînes signifiantes" (8 December 1961), IMEC: ET04–20. Published as "D'un signe à l'autre," *Recherches* 2 (1966); repr. in Guattari, *Psychanalyse et transversalité.*

4 Jean Ayme, "Essai sur l'histoire de la psychothérapie institutionnelle," in Delion, ed., *Actualité de la psychothérapie institutionnelle*, 47–9.

5 Guattari, "Introduction à la psychothérapie institutionnelle (Extraits d'interventions faites au GTPSI)" [1962–3], in Guattari, *Psychanalyse et transversalité*. Guattari, "Le Transfert" [1964], in Guattari, *Psychanalyse et transversalité*; "The Transference," in Genosko, ed., *The Guattari Reader*.

6 Guattari, "Transversalité," *Psychothérapie institutionnelle* 1 (1965); repr. in Guattari, *Psychanalyse et transversalité*; "Transversality," in Guattari, *Molecular Revolution*. Oury claimed that the article was written in 1959 and had the subtitle "Données d'accueil du Surmoi." Oury, "Métapsychologie et institutionnalisation," in Delion, ed., *Actualité de la psychothérapie institutionnelle*, 302. An excerpt of the conclusion appears under the title "Rôle et place du complexe de castration dans les strutures de transversalité de la psychothérapie institutionnelle," in IMEC: ET01–36. The text is accompanied by a registration form for Guattari and Oury for the Congrès International de Psychodrame dated 1 August 1964.

7 Guattari described, for example, "a grille of correspondence between the phenomena of the slippages of meaning with psychotics, especially schizophrenics, and mechanisms of increasing discordance that install themselves at all levels of industrial society in its neo-capitalist and socialist bureaucratic phase, such that the individual tends to have to identify with an ideal of 'consuming= machines=consuming=producing=machine.'" Guattari, "Transversality," 14. On "territorialization," see ibid., 17.

8 Guattari, "Intervention," *Psychothérapie institutionnelle* 4 (1966).

9 Guattari, [Autobiographical Interviews], IMEC: I01–25a.

10 Dissent within the Union des étudiants communistes in 1965–66 led to the formation of other independent Trotskyist and Maoist groups, including the UJC(ml) discussed in chapter 3.

11 F.G. [Félix Guattari], "Lettre à l'O.G." [Bulletin of the *Opposition gauche*], 1967. Personal papers of Liane Mozère. Parts of the collectively written *Neuf thèses de l'Opposition gauche* were republished in Guattari, *Psychanalyse et transversalité.*

12 [Interview with Jean Oury], IMEC: I01–26b (29 November 1984).

13 Guattari, "Réflexions sur la thérapeutique institutionnelle et les problèmes d'hygiène mentale en milieu étudiant," *Recherches universitaires* (1964); repr.

in Guattari, *Psychanalyse et transversalité*. Guattari, "Réflexions pour des philosophes à propos de la psychothérapie institutionnelle," *Cahiers de philosophie* 1 (1966); repr. *Recherches* 1 (1966) and in *Psychanalyse et transversalité*. Guattari, [Autobiographical Interviews], IMEC: I01–25b. Guattari, "Transversality," 11.

14 *Oxford English Dictionary*, 2nd ed., s.v. "transversal."

15 Guattari, "Transversality," 11, 13, 18–20, 23. For applications see Genosko, ed., *Deleuze and Guattari*, vol. 2, part 6.

16 See Janet H. Morford's essential sketch "Histoires du CERFI."

17 "Présentation du CERFI," IMEC: D03–12.

18 "Présentation du *Recherches*" (March 1969), IMEC: D03–24.

19 [Contract between CERFI and La Borde] (28 October 1970). [Accords et correspondance et divers entre le CERFI et la clinique de La Borde], IMEC: D04–06.

20 The CERFI study of La Borde noted that "the history of CERFI and the history of La Borde are intimately overlapped." CERFI, *L'Institutionalisation des collectifs de travail*, 5.

21 Morford, "Histoires du CERFI," 209.

CHAPTER TWELVE

1 Deleuze, *Difference and Repetition* and *Expressionism in Philosophy: Spinoza* (hereafter cited as *Spinoza*). The latter was Deleuze's second book with Les Editions de Minuit, following Deleuze and Léopold Sacher-Masoch, *Masochism*, based on a 1961 essay. He had published all his earlier philosophical books with the more academic Presses universitaires de France: *Empiricism and Subjectivity*, *Nietzsche and Philosophy*, *Kant's Critical Philosophy*, and *Bergsonism*. As he would for Spinoza, Deleuze edited collections of the writings of Hume (1952), Bergson (1957), and Nietzsche (1965). Deleuze and Foucault cowrote the introduction to the first volume (1967) of Nietzsche's complete works published with Gallimard. Deleuze's earlier literary work, also with the Presses universitaires, included *Proust and Signs* (1964). The second edition (1970) added an essay on the "literary machine," and the third edition (1976) added another essay on *la folie*.

2 Deleuze, "Letter to a Harsh Critic," 5–6.

3 Deleuze, *The Logic of Sense*.

4 Deleuze, *Spinoza: textes choisis*. Three chapters were added to, and the selection of Spinoza's texts dropped from, the 1981 reprint, *Spinoza: philosophie pratique*; *Spinoza: Practical Philosophy* (hereafter cited as *Practical Philosophy*).

5 Deleuze, *Nietzsche and Philosophy.*

6 Ibid., 3–14, 39–42, 52–72, 91–3, 111–14. See 39, 62, for the references to Spinoza.

7 Nietzsche, *Letter to Overbeck* (30 July 1881), cited in Kaufmann, *Nietzsche*, 140.

8 Wood, "French Thought under Mitterrand." The controversy revolved around Farías, *Heidegger and Nazism.*

9 Judith Butler, cover text, Montag and Stolze, eds., *The New Spinoza.*

10 Alan D. Schrift, "Is There Such a Thing as French Philosophy? or Why Do We Read the French So Badly?" in Bourg, ed., *After the Deluge.* Norris, *Spinoza and the Origins of Modern Critical Theory.*

11 Althusser, *The Future Lasts Forever*, 356. Gueroult, *Spinoza*, vol. 1, *Dieu.* See Deleuze's positive review, "Spinoza et la méthode générale de M. Gueroult," *Revue de métaphysique et de morale* 74, no. 4 (October–December 1969); "Gueroult's General Method for Spinoza," in Deleuze, *Desert Islands and Other Texts.* A second volume of Gueroult's extended study, cut short by his death, appeared in 1974 as *Spinoza*, vol. 2, *L'Ame.* Matheron, *Individu et communauté chez Spinoza.* Montag, "Preface," *The New Spinoza*, xiii–xvi. Negri, *The Savage Anomaly.* Michael Hardt and Antonio Negri's *Empire* and *Multitude* are eminently Spinozist books.

12 Robert Misrahi, personal communication (2 November 2003).

13 Misrahi, *Le Désir et la réflexion dans la philosophie de Spinoza.*

14 Ibid., 7–8.

15 Ibid., 12–14.

16 Ibid., 376.

17 Ibid., 378. Cf. Spinoza, *Ethics*, IV, Appendix, §32, in *Works of Spinoza*, which Misrahi cites and says "sums up Spinozism." Misrahi, *Le Désir et la réflexion dans la philosophie de Spinoza*, 373.

18 Ibid., 379.

19 Deleuze, correspondence with Martin Joughin, "Translator's Preface," in Deleuze, *Spinoza*, 11.

20 Deleuze, *Spinoza*, 245–6. Cf. Deleuze, "On the Difference between the *Ethics* and a Morality" [1970], "Index of the Main Concepts of the *Ethics*" [1970], and "Spinoza and Us" [1978; rev. 1981], in Deleuze, *Practical Philosophy.*

21 Deleuze, "On the Difference between the *Ethics* and a Morality," 17–19, 29. Cf. Deleuze and Guattari, *Anti-Oedipus*, 276 n.

22 Deleuze, *Spinoza*, 226. Spinoza, *Ethics*, III, 2, n.

23 Deleuze, *Spinoza*, 219–21, 246.

24 Ibid., 222–31. *Oxford English Dictionary*, 2nd ed., s.v. "conatus."

25 Deleuze, *Spinoza*, 228–34, 237. Cf. Deleuze, *The Logic of Sense*, 13.

26 Deleuze, "On the Difference between the *Ethics* and a Morality," 19. Deleuze, *Spinoza*, 239–42. Cf. Deleuze's discussion of evil as "the reduction of our power of action and the decomposition of a relation." Strictly speaking, evil is nothing. Ibid., 246–54.
27 Ibid., 255–7. Deleuze, "On the Difference between the *Ethics* and a Morality," 18.
28 Deleuze, *Spinoza*, 258–62.
29 Ibid., 262–8, 274.
30 Ibid., 270–2.
31 For example, see Deleuze, *The Logic of Sense*, on surface (4–11, 103–4); connective, conjunctive, and disjunctive syntheses (42–7, 67); and the machine (71–3).
32 Deleuze, "Thirteenth Series of the Schizophrenic and the Little Girl," in *The Logic of Sense*, 82–93. Deleuze, "Le Schizophrène et le mot," *Critique* 255–6 (August–September 1968); "The Schizophrenic and Language: Surface and Depth in Lewis Carroll and Antoine Artaud," in Harari, ed., *Textual Strategies*.
33 "Stoic ethics," says Deleuze, "is concerned with the event; it consists of willing the event as such, that is, of willing that which occurs insofar as it does occur." See Deleuze, *The Logic of Sense*, 4–8, 19, 22, 50–1, 53, 62, 74–81, 143, 146–7. He relies on Goldschmidt, *Le Système stoïcien et l'idée de temps*. Cf. Deleuze, *Nietzsche and Philosophy*, 25–7, on chance, necessity, and destiny. Deleuze and Parnet, *Dialogues*, 62–6. See also the helpful comments of Constatin V. Boundas, "Editor's Introduction," in *The Deleuze Reader*, 8–9.
34 Daniel W. Smith, "The Place of Ethics in Deleuze's Philosophy: Three Questions of Immanence," in Kaufman and Heller, eds., *Deleuze and Guattari*, 252–3. Cf. Smith, "Introduction: 'A Life of Pure Immanence': Deleuze's 'Critique et Clinique' Project," in Deleuze, *Essays Critical and Clinical*, lii–liii.
35 Deleuze, "On Philosophy," in *Negotiations*, 143.
36 Smith, "Introduction," xiii–xv, citing Deleuze, "Lettre-préface," in Buydens, *Sahara*, 5.
37 Guattari et al., "In Flux," in *Chaosophy*, 99.
38 See Todd May's discussion of Deleuze's "Holy Trinity" – Spinoza, Bergson, and Nietzsche – in his *Gilles Deleuze*, ch. 2.
39 Pierre Macherey, "The Encounter with Spinoza," in Patton, ed., *Deleuze*, 147.
40 Deleuze, "Spinoza and Us," in Deleuze, *Practical Philosophy*, 125. Cf. Deleuze, "On the Difference between the *Ethics* and a Morality," in ibid., 27.
41 Mill, *A System of Logic, Ratiocinative and Inductive*; Ruwet, *Introduction to Ethology*; Chauvin, *Ethology*; Ropartz, *Qu'est-ce que l'éthologie?*; Lorenz, *The Foundations of Ethology*. For ethology in the history of ideas, see Fred

Willhoite, "Ethology and the Tradition of Political Thought," *Journal of Politics* 33 (1971).

42 François Zourabichvili, "Six Notes on the Percept," in Patton, ed., *Deleuze*, 209. Emphasis added. See note 33 above.

43 Paul Patton, "Introduction," in Patton, ed., *Deleuze*, 14.

44 Deleuze, *The Logic of Sense*, 169.

45 Boundas, "Editor's Introduction," in *The Deleuze Reader*, 9.

46 Zourabichvili, "Six Notes on the Percept," 208. Cf. Smith, "Introduction," xv.

47 See Theweleit, *Male Fantasies*, 2 vols., which draws on Deleuze and Guattari.

48 Philip Goodchild, "Deleuzean Ethics," *Theory, Culture & Society* 14, no. 2 (1997): 41, 46. Paul Patton, "Deleuze and Guattari: Ethics and Post-Modernity," *Leftwright Intervention* 20 (1986); repr. in Genosko, ed., *Deleuze and Guattari*, 3:1160. Both Goodchild and Patton set ethology against Alasdair MacIntyre's neo-Aristotelian ethics.

CHAPTER THIRTEEN

1 Guattari, "So What?" in Guattari, *Chaosophy*, 10. His first reference to Deleuze in print was in "Machine and Structure," an essay "intended" for the Ecole freudienne de Paris but published in *Change* 12 (1971). This essay, along with two other delivered to the Ecole freudienne ("Money in the Analytic Exchange" [May 1971], and "The Role of the Signifier in the Institution" [November 1973]) are translated in Guattari, *Molecular Revolution*. His 17 April 1970 intervention at the congress of the Ecole freudienne was published as "Réflexions sur l'enseignement comme envers de l'analyse," in Guattari, *Psychanalyse et transversalité*.

2 "Gilles Deleuze and Félix Guattari on *Anti-Oedipus*," in Deleuze, *Negotiations*, 15. Guattari et al., "In Flux," in Guattari, *Chaosophy*, 93–4. Deleuze and Guattari, "Entretien avec Deleuze et Guattari," in *C'est demain la veille*; "Capitalism: A Very Special Delirium," in Guattari, *Chaosophy*, 59–60; also trans. "On Capitalism and Desire," in Deleuze, *Desert Islands and Other Texts*, 265–6.

3 [Interview with Arlette Donati], IMEC: I01–26c.

4 "Gilles Deleuze and Félix Guattari on *Anti-Oedipus*," 13.

5 [Interview with Gérard Fromanger], IMEC: I01–26b. According to Fromanger, Deleuze said that he and Guattari used the polite *vous* form with one another for the reason that one could show great affection with *vous* and be dismissive with an informal *tu*. Cf. Deleuze and Fromanger, *Fromanger*. Deleuze, "Hot and Cool," in Deleuze, *Desert Islands and Other Texts*.

6 Guattari, "The Best Capitalist Drug," in Guattari, *Chaosophy*, 220.

7 Deleuze, "Lettre à Michel Cressole," *La Quinzaine littéraire* 161 (1 April 1973); repr. in Cressole, *Deleuze*; "Lettre à un critique sévère," in Deleuze, *Pourparlers*; part. trans. "I Have Nothing to Admit," *Anti-Oedipus*, Special Issue of *Semiotext(e)* 2, no. 3 (1977); also trans. "Letter to a Harsh Critic," in Deleuze, *Negotiations*, 7. The last phrase would be repeated in the opening line of Deleuze and Guattari, *A Thousand Plateaus*, 3.

8 Guattari, [Autobiographical Interviews], IMEC: I01–25g. On Deleuze's animus toward psychoanalysis see also Deleuze and Lyotard, "A propos du département de psychanalyse à Vincennes," *Les Temps modernes* 342 (January 1975); "Concerning the Vincennes Psychoanalysis Department," in Lyotard, *Political Writings*; also trans. "On the Vincennes Department of Psychoanalysis," in Deleuze, *Two Regimes of Madness*. Deleuze, "Relazione de Gilles Deleuze," in Verdiglione, ed., *Psicanalisis e Politica*; "Five Propositions on Psychoanalysis," in Deleuze, *Desert Islands and Other Texts*; and the slightly different version "Four Propositions on Psychoanalysis," in Deleuze, *Two Regimes of Madness*.

9 Guattari et al., "In Flux," 95. Guattari, "Everybody Wants to be a Fascist," *Anti-Oedipus*, Special Issue of *Semiotext(e)* 2, no. 3 (1977); repr. in Guattari, *Chaosophy*, 225–6. "Gilles Deleuze and Félix Guattari on *Anti-Oedipus*," 19. On differentiating desire from what it was not, see Guattari et al., "In Flux," 97, 105–6. Deleuze and Guattari, "On Capitalism and Desire," in Deleuze, *Desert Islands and Other Texts*, 263, 266–7; also trans. "Capitalism: A Very Special Delirium," 54, 61. Deleuze and Guattari, "Bilan-programme pour machines désirantes," *Minuit* (2 January 1973); repub. as "Appendice," *L'Anti-Oedipe*, 2nd. ed.; "Balance Sheet – Program for Desiring-Machines," *Anti-Oedipus*, Special Issue of *Semiotext(e)* 2, no. 3 (1977): 117, 131. The "Balance Sheet" is reprinted in Guattari, *Chaosophy*. Deleuze and Guattari, "Capitalismo e schizofrenia" (Interview with Vittorio Marchetti and Caroline Laure), *Tempi moderni* 12 (Autumn 1972); "Capitalism and Schizophrenia," in Deleuze, *Desert Islands and Other Texts*; also trans. in Guattari, *Chaosophy*, 76–7.

10 Deleuze and Guattari, *Anti-Oedipus*, 113. Cf. ibid., 136. "Gilles Deleuze and Félix Guattari on *Anti-Oedipus*," 23. Guattari et al., "In Flux," 97.

11 Deleuze, "Thirteenth Series of the Schizophrenic and the Little Girl," in *The Logic of Sense*, esp. 82, 86. "Le Schizophrène et le mot," *Critique* 255–6 (August–September 1968); "The Schizophrenic and Language: Surface and Depth in Lewis Carroll and Antoine Artaud," in Harari, ed., *Textual Strategies*. The discussion in Deleuze, *The Logic of Sense*, was based on Wolfson, "Le Schizo et les langues ou la phonétique chez le psychotique," *Les Temps modernes* (July 1964), and was a prelude to Deleuze, "Schizologie," foreword

to Wolfson, *Le Schizo et les langues*; repr. *Critique et clinique*; "Louis Wolfson; or, The Procedure," in *Essays Critical and Clinical*. See also the article "Schizophrénie et société," *Encyclopædie Universalis* 14 (1975); "Schizophrenia and Society," in Deleuze, *Two Regimes of Madness*. Deleuze's contribution, "Schizophrénie et positivité du désir" (733–5), appeared alongside "Schizophrénie et schizo-analyse" (735–6), written by Henry Duméry, a Catholic scholar who had published several works during the 1950s and 1960s on Maurice Blondel, phenomenology, and Christianity. The association of Deleuze and Duméry suggests the inheritance of a tradition of philosophical intuitionism, to which both Bergson and Blondel were heirs in the late nineteenth century.

12 Deleuze and Guattari, *What Is Philosophy?*

13 Deleuze, "Letter to a Harsh Critic," 12, referring to Deleuze and Guattari, *Anti-Oedipus*, 380.

14 Guattari, "The Group and the Person" [1966], in Guattari, *Molecular Revolution*, 27.

15 "Effondrement d'une vie pas encore vécue. Perte du 'Je' (Extraits du journal de R.A.)" [1955] and "Monographie sur R.A." [1956], in Guattari, *Psychanalyse et transversalité*. "Gilles Deleuze and Félix Guattari on *Anti-Oedipus*," 14–15.

16 Guattari, "De Léros à La Borde," IMEC: ET05–25; part. trans. from *La Quinzaine littéraire* 250 (1977) as "La Borde: A Clinic Unlike Any Other," in Guattari, *Chaosophy*.

17 Guattari, "The Best Capitalist Drug," 221–2.

18 Deleuze and Guattari, "On Capitalism and Desire," in Deleuze, *Desert Islands and Other Texts*, 266; also trans. "Capitalism: A Very Special Delirium," 60. Deleuze and Guattari, "Balance Sheet – Program for Desiring-Machines," 130–1. Deleuze and Guattari, "Capitalism and Schizophrenia," 78.

19 Ibid., 85–6.

20 Jaspers, *Strindberg and Van Gogh*.

21 Deleuze, "Letter to a Harsh Critic," 12. Jameson, *The Political Unconscious*. Deleuze and Guattari, "On Capitalism and Desire," in Deleuze, *Desert Islands and Other Texts*, 273; also trans. "Capitalism: A Very Special Delirium," 72–3. Deleuze and Guattari, "Capitalism and Schizophrenia," 77, 80.

22 Ibid., 82–3, 89–90, 92. "Gilles Deleuze and Félix Guattari on *Anti-Oedipus*," 24. Deleuze was evoking Foucault, *The Archaeology of Knowledge*, 17.

23 Deleuze and Guattari, *Anti-Oedipus*, 29, 102–4, 256–7, 277–8, 293, 340–9, 366, 380.

24 "Gilles Deleuze and Félix Guattari on *Anti-Oedipus*," 18, 24. Deleuze and Guattari, "Capitalism and Schizophrenia," 80–1. Deleuze and Guattari, "Balance Sheet – Program for Desiring-Machines," 135. Deleuze and Guattari,

"On Capitalism and Desire," in Deleuze, *Desert Islands and Other Texts*, 269; also trans. "Capitalism: A Very Special Delirium," 66.

25 Guattari et al., "In Flux," 93, 95–6, 114. Deleuze and Guattari, *Anti-Oedipus*, 118. Guattari, "The Best Capitalist Drug," 220–1.

26 Deleuze, "Letter to a Harsh Critic," 9. Guattari, "Everybody Wants to be a Fascist," 234–45. Deleuze and Guattari, "On Capitalism and Desire," in Deleuze, *Desert Islands and Other Texts*, 263, 267–8; also trans. "Capitalism: A Very Special Delirium," 54, 63.

27 Foucault, "Preface," in Deleuze and Guattari, *Anti-Oedipus*, xii–xiii.

28 Girard described as Nietzschean what I refer to as the antinomian. Girard, "Système du délire," *Critique* 306 (November 1972), repr. in Girard, *Critique dans un souterrain*; "Delirium as System," in Girard, *"To Double Business Bound"*; repr. in Genosko, ed., *Deleuze and Guattari*, vol. 2.

29 Jameson, *Postmodernism, or The Cultural Logic of Late Capitalism.*

CHAPTER FOURTEEN

1 [Entretien avec Jean Oury] (29 November 1984), IMEC: I01–26b.

2 "Traitement, formation et recherche sont inséparables" (Interview with Jean Oury), *Cinquante ans d'organisation des institutions psychiatriques*, Special Issue of *Psychiatrie française* 28, no. 1 (March 1997).

3 Oury, *Il, donc*, 175, 179.

4 Jacques Donzelot, "Une Anti-sociologie," *Esprit* 40, no. 12 (December 1972); "An Anti-Sociology," *Anti-Oedipus*, Special Issue of *Semiotext(e)* 2, no. 3 (1977); repr. in Genosko, ed., *Deleuze and Guattari*, vol. 2.

5 See Deleuze and Parnet, *Dialogues*, 78–9, 90–1, 95–8. Oury, Guattari, and Tosquelles, *Pratique de l'institutionnel et politique*, 62; "Institutional Practice and Politics," in Genosko, ed., *The Guattari Reader*, 128; also trans. as "Institutional Schizo-Analysis," in Guattari, *Soft Subversions*, 272–3.

6 Richard Wolin, "The Grandeur and Twilight of French Philosophical Radicalism," in Flood and Hewlett, eds., *Currents in Contemporary French Intellectual Life*.

CHAPTER FIFTEEN

1 Scott, *Only Paradoxes to Offer*.

2 Dreyfus-Armand et al., *Les Années 68*, esp. Part II. Khursheed Wadia, "Women and the Events of May 1968," in Reader, *The May 1968 Events in France*.

3 On the women's liberation movement see, among others: Picq, *Libération des femmes*; Pisan and Tristan, *Histoires du* MLF; Association la Griffonne [Martine Bosshart et al.], *Douze ans de femmes au quotidien*; Duchen, *Feminism in France*; Rémy, *De l'utopie à l'intégration*. On gay liberation see J. Girard, *Le Mouvement homosexuel en France* and especially Martel, *The Pink and the Black*.

4 Mouvement jeune révolutionnaire, "L'Ecoute des étudiants," *Bulletin JR* 2 [n.d.], Bibliothèque nationale, 4-LC2-7280.

5 Cohn-Bendit, cited in Bourges et al., *The Student Revolt*, 78.

6 Schnapp and Vidal-Naquet, *The French Student Uprising*, 435.

7 Martel, *The Pink and the Black*, 15–16. Mozère, *Le Printemps des crèches*.

8 See, however, Gagey, *La Révolution sexuelle*, printed in July 1968. Other movements that considered the issue of sexuality and gender were reformist or associational in nature. Mouvement français pour le planning familial, *D'une révolte à une lutte*. Martel, *The Pink and the Black*, ch. 3, discusses the gay organization Arcadie.

9 Hamon and Rotman, *Génération*, 2:106–7. On VLR see also Bourseiller, *Les Maoïstes* and Fields, *Trotskyism and Maoism*.

10 Touraine, *The May Movement*.

11 Vive la révolution!, *Changer la vie*, 16.

12 Interview with Roland Castro (May 1999).

13 Several of the articles were reprinted in September 1971 as Front homosexuel d'action révolutionnaire, *Rapport contre la normalité*. For the history of the FHAR see Martel, *The Pink and the Black*.

14 *Tout!* 12 (23 April 1971).

15 Christiane, "Pourquoi nous avortons"; "Des filles, et un mec"; Un Militant du FHAR, "Vie quotidienne chez les pédés"; Un Pédé mineur et devenu joyeux, "Les Mineurs ont droit au désir: 15 Berges"; Un Homosexuel, sale étranger, dangereux communiste, "Le Triangle rose: lettre ouverte aux hétérosexuels communistes"; Un du FHAR, "Non, on n'est pas des obsédés"; Une du FHAR, "Elles sont unissantes, les filles qui s'embrassent!"; Un du FHAR, "Homosexuels"; Sylvie, "Pas d'accord: une lettre." Ibid.

16 "Le Pavé de l'homosexualité dans la mare gauchiste," *Tout!* 13 (17 May 1971).

17 "Happily for Genet, he did not fall in love with ... a parachutist ... This is how petit-bourgeois individualism will win out." "Tout ou rien," *Lutte ouvrière*, 4 May 1971, cited in Front homosexuel d'action révolutionnaire, *Rapport contre la normalité*, 24–5. The Genet text had been followed by a satirical petition signed by "343 bitches," an ugly riff on a petition published in *Le Nouvel Observateur* (5 April 1971) and signed by 343 women saying that they had had abortions. The *Tout!* petition said that its signatories had been "fucked by Arabs."

18 Christian, ouvrier du Livre, "Notre dernier numéro est-il anti-ouvrier?" *Tout!* 13 (17 May 1971).
19 "A trial will only make evident what everyone senses: the decay of bourgeois mores and the new sense of a revolution that aims also to transform daily life." Jean-Paul Sartre, *Tout!* 15 (30 June 1971). On 16 July 1971, the Conseil constitutionnel said that the banning of newspapers by the government was illegal.
20 "FHAR," *Tout!* 13 (17 May 1971).
21 The controversy introduced another element into mounting tensions between male leftists and feminists: race. That theme hovers around 1970s debates on gender and sexuality on the French far left, but unfortunately, it cannot be treated thoroughly here.
22 "Lettre de Mohamed," *Tout!* 14 (7 June 1971).
23 Hélène, "Réponses à la lettre de Mohammed" [sic] and Militants du MLF, "Votre libération sexuelle n'est pas la nôtre," *Tout!* 15 (30 June 1971).
24 "Vie et moeurs de la peuplade 'Tuot' ou que vos os pourrissent sous la lune," ibid.
25 Un Groupe de filles, "Encore une fois sur Mohamed"; Un du FHAR et de Tout, "Réponse au texte des femmes"; and Quelques-uns du FHAR, "Bilan," *Tout!* 16 (29 July 1971).

CHAPTER SIXTEEN

1 Interview with Cathy Bernheim (March 2001). Guy Hocquenghem recounted this weekend meeting in "Femmes et pédés" [November 1972], *L'Après-mai des faunes*, 190. See Gilles Deleuze's foreword to this collection translated in Deleuze, *Desert Islands and Other Texts*.
2 Marshall, *Guy Hocquenghem*.
3 Hocquenghem, *Homosexual Desire*.
4 Ibid., 87. The "double bind" theory was taken from Gregory Bateson et al., "Toward a Theory of Schizophrenia," *Behavioral Science* 1, no. 4 (October 1956). See Deleuze and Guattari, *Anti-Oedipus*, 79, 110.
5 Hocquenghem, *Homosexual Desire*, 94.
6 Hocquenghem, "Towards an Irrecuperable Pederasty" [July–October 1972], in Goldberg, ed., *Reclaiming Sodom*, 241, 244–5.
7 Ibid., 233, 235, 237–9, 243–4. *Homosexual Desire*, 50, 58, 63, 73, 96, 133, 135, 140, 142, 145. "Un Transversalisme éhonté" [July 1973], in Hocquenghem, *L'Après-mai des faunes*, 196–7, 199, 203. Hocquenghem entitled an introductory section in *L'Après-mai*: "Neither Law nor Self" [*Sans loi ni moi*]. Cf. *Homosexual Desire*, 142, where he says that "autonomous"

groups "create a law for themselves." In *L'Après-mai*, he writes: "The revolutionary field plays the game of morality where Capital cheats and wins" (20).

8 Hocquenghem, "Towards an Irrecuperable Pederasty," 233, 242, 245. *Homosexual Desire*, 50, 72, 95, 107, 111–12, 142, 144. "Femmes et pédés," 138, 144, 146, 188. Hocquenghem's "groups" are elsewhere described as "positions" and "miniscule obessions," in other words, the "micro-politics" discussed by Guattari, Deleuze, and Foucault. Hocquenghem, "Un Transversalisme éhonté," 203. Hocquenghem makes the interesting suggestion that homosexuals have a different relationship to time than heterosexuals, since they are normally outside the cycle of reproductive sexuality. Homosexuals thus experience old age in "intense" ways. Hocquenghem, "Femmes et pédés," 107.

9 Hocquenghem, *La Dérive homosexuelle*, 18. *Homosexual Desire*, 97–101, 131–2. "Towards an Irrecuperable Pederasty," 237. Cf. "Un Transversalisme éhonté," 199. On the positive link between homosexuality and criminality, see *Homosexual Desire*, 67.

10 Hocquenghem, "Towards an Irrecuperable Pederasty," 235, 241–2. *Homosexual Desire*, 77, 101. "Femmes et pédés," 188–9. Cf. *Homosexual Desire*, 140.

11 Hocquenghem, "Towards an Irrecuperable Pederasty," 241–2. "Femmes et pédés," 187, 189–90.

12 *Trois milliards de pervers: grande encylopédie des homosexualités*, Special Issue of *Recherches* 12 (March 1973).

13 Guattari's contribution to the issue is translated as "In Order to End the Massacre of the Body," in Guattari, *Soft Subversions*. His response to the censorship was published as "Trois milliards de pervers à la barre," in Guattari, *La Révolution moléculaire*; "Three Billion Perverts on the Stand," in Genosko, ed., *The Guattari Reader*; "Letter to the Tribunal," in *Soft Subversions*.

14 Hocquenghem, "Un Transversalisme éhonté," 199–200.

15 Hocquenghem, *Homosexual Desire*, 139–40.

16 Bill Marshall and Frédéric Martel are too soft on Hocquenghem's writings on feminism. They are both more dismissive of the "excesses" of 1970s French feminism than they are of Hocquenghem's own distortions. In some sense, they rewrite the problematic at another level. Marshall, *Guy Hocquenghem*, 11–12, 93. Martel, *The Pink and the Black*, 98, where he calls Hocquenghem a "radical" on rape who had recovered his "verve."

CHAPTER SEVENTEEN

1 Legal-activist struggles for the right to choose lie outside our present discussion. One might mention the strategy of the "political trial" advocated by

Gisèle Halimi and the association Choisir, on one hand, and radical feminist tactics of anti-legalism and non-complicity, on the other. The passage of the Veil Law in December 1974 signified the shift from removing a repressive law to supporting new laws. Paradoxically, the turn toward law, and the form of universalism it implied, led to a break with a form of "revolutionary" universalism and a reaffirmation of the particularity of women. One feminist wrote in December 1976 that rape was "the third great battle of French feminists after those for contraception and abortion." Emmanuelle Plas, "Viol: briser le mur du silence," *L'Unité*, 3 December 1976. For a long-term view of rape in France, see Vigarello, *A History of Rape*.

2 Picq, *Libération des femmes*, 249. Cf. 235, 241–3. See also Emmanuèle Durand, "Le Viol," *Libération des femmes: année zéro*, Special Issue of *Partisans* 54–5 (July–October 1970) and Mai, "Un Viol si ordinaire, un impérialisme si quotidien," *Les Femmes s'entêtent*, Special Issue of *Les Temps modernes* 333–4 (April–May 1974).

3 Association Choisir/La Cause des femmes, *Viol*, 31. Marie Cardinal, "Le Viol est un crime," *Le Monde*, 3 February 1976.

4 Plas, "Viol: briser le mur du silence," *L'Unité*, 3 December 1976.

5 Simone de Beauvoir, "Quand toutes les femmes du monde...," *Le Nouvel Observateur* (1 March 1976). Pia Paoli, "Le Circoncision des femmes," *Le Monde*, 18–19 April 1976. Brownmiller, *Le Viol*. Fargier, *Le Viol*. Roger-Pol Droit, "La Fin du silence" [Review of Brownmiller and Fargier], *Le Monde*, 19 November 1976. Cathy Bernheim, "Le Viol est pour les femmes, ce que le lynchage est pour les noirs" [Review of Brownmiller], *La Quinzaine littéraire* 251 (1 March 1977). MLF, "Manifeste contre le viol," *Libération* (16 June 1976). Christiane Chombeau, "Un Millier de femmes ont participé aux 'dix heures contre le viol,'" *Le Monde*, 29 June 1976. The idea of separatist activism had, of course, been a question in France since the early 1970s, especially since an infamous May 1970 meeting at Vincennes where men had shouted at women gathered for a feminist meeting: "Power is at the tip of a phallus." Several feminist groups had broken with one another on that very topic (the group Femmes en lutte, for example, did not participate in the "Ten Hours Against Rape" for that reason). "Courrier: en marge de la journée sur le viol: paroles au masculin III," *Libération*, 6 June 1976.

6 "Une Commission du 'viol' dans le 18è," *Libération*, 29 March 1977.

7 "L'Avocat de son agressor: 'ce n'est pas la répression qui va améliorer les rapports entre hommes et femmes,'" *Libération*, 21 March 1977.

8 Marie-Odile Fargier, "Un Tribunal qui refuse de juger," *Le Matin*, 22 March 1977.

9 Reich, *L'Irruption de la morale sexuelle*, 33–4. Ginnie, "'Il est très difficile d'avoir une attitude tranchée...,'" *Libération*, 29 March 1977.

10 Martine Storti, "La 16ème chambre correctionnelle se déclare incompétente," *Libération*, 22 March 1977.

11 Josyane Moutet cited in Odile Dhavernas, "Pourquoi les femmes ont-elles le privilège du viol?" *Libération*, 7 April 1977. Françoise, "Réponse à Maître Koskas," *Libération*, 29 March 1977.

12 Michèle Solat, "Les Féministes et le viol: III. comment lutter?" *Le Monde*, 20 October 1977.

13 "Les Cassandres et la sexualité masculine," *Libération*, 23 March 1977.

14 "Une Commission 'viol' dans le 18è," *Libération*, 29 March 1977.

15 Hélène Lanive, "'Il faut refuser de se laisser inscrire dans ce cercle où on nous a mises,'" *Libération*, 20 May 1977.

16 To be sure, some radical feminists experimented with vigilante justice [*la justice sauvage*], punishing perpetrators of violence against women by direct, extra-legal means. Such acts were comparatively rare and, though bearing directly on the debates at hand, will not be examined here.

17 The discourse included Maoist "popular tribunals" and the Groupe d'information sur les prisons (discussed in Part I). It also touched on Hocquenghem's linkage of homosexuality and criminality, and especially Serge Livrozet's advocacy of prison revolt. Livrozet, *De la prison à la révolte* and *Aujourd'hui, la prison*. A representative statement was Guy Laumont: "Le Féminisme et le viol," *Le Comité d'action des prisonniers: journal des prisonniers* (May 1977). Laumont, serving time in the St Joseph prison in Lyon, wrote that only a "total revolution" could resolve the problem of rape and that "it is not by going to hide in the dirty robes of magistrates that the solution will be found."

18 In 1974 Goldman was convicted of the murder of two (female) pharmacists and sentenced to life in prison. At his trial, luminaries of the intellectual-political Left spoke on his behalf. Pardoned in 1976, he was murdered in September 1979. Goldman, *Dim Memories of a Polish Jew Born in France*. Hamon and Rotman, *Génération*, 2:596–603, 657.

19 Pierre Goldman, "Du viol, du bon usage de la loi et du désespoir," *Libération*, 23 March 1977.

20 Hocquenghem, "V-I-O-L," *Libération*, 29 March 1977; repr. in Hocquenghem, *La Dérive homosexuelle*.

21 "'Un Viol en cache toujours un autre': une lettre de Mohamed sur le viol et le racisme," *Libération*, 5 April 1977.

22 Josyane Moutet, "Questions à Pierre Goldman," *Libération*, 28 March 1977. See also Mariella Righini, "'Nous ne sommes pas des procureurs,'" *Le Nouvel Observateur* (28 March 1977).

23 Elisabeth Salvaresi, "Ne pas être les violeuses de nos violeurs," and Paul Roussopoulos, "Un Débat de musée," *Libération*, 6 April 1977.

24 Odile Dhavernas, "Pourquoi les femmes ont-elles le privilège du viol?" *Libération*, 7 April 1977.

25 Thierry Lévy, "La Salissure des débats judiciaires," ibid.

26 Brigitte, "Réponse à l'avocat de la défense," *Libération*, 30 May 1977. Cf. Brigitte, "La Misère sexuelle n'explique pas tout," *Libération*, 9 September 1977.

27 "La Grande peur des femmes," Dossier in *Le Matin*, 6–10 September 1977. Michèle Solat, "Les Féministes et le viol," Dossier in *Le Monde*, 18–20 October 1977. See also Claudine Hermann, "Le Viol et la violence," *Les Temps modernes* 375 (October 1977). Elisabeth Salvaresi, "Un Dialogue de sourdes aux *Dossiers de l'écran*," *Libération*, 20 October 1977.

28 Yolande A., "Rompre le mur du silence," *Le Monde*, 1 January 1978. Jacques Ellul, "Le Viol et le désir," *Le Monde*, 3 January 1978.

29 Picq, *Libération des femmes*, 242. Martel, *The Pink and the Black*, cites this passage and implies that it was the chief lesson to be drawn from the feminist rape campaign (85).

30 Béatrice Vallaeys and M.C. Husson, "Le Mans: du procès du viol au procès d'un violeur," *Libération*, 27 January 1978. Laurent Greilsamer, "'La Prison n'est pas une solution,'" *Le Monde*, 27 January 1978. Mariella Righini, "Le Prix du viol," *Le Nouvel Observateur* (25 March 1978).

31 Martine Storti, "Viol: '20 ans, c'est pas possible,'" *Libération*, 24 February 1978. See also her "Des dangers de la reconnaissance du viol sans violence," *Libération*, 22 February 1978.

32 For discussions of the Aix trial and subsequent legislative debates, see Vigarello, *A History of Rape*, 206–14, and Association Choisir/La Cause des femmes, *Viol*. See also Halimi, "Viol: le crime culturel," *Le Nouvel Observateur* (22 May 1978). Anne Tonglet and Araceli Castellano, "Insoutenable débat: le vôtre," *Libération*, 12 May 1978. Cathy Bernheim, "Je suis moins désespérée qu'il y a quelques années," *Libération*, 18 May 1978. Monique Antoine, Colette Auger, and Josyane Moutet, "Les Avocats et la répression," *Le Monde*, 4 May 1978. "Contre le viol, la prison?" *Le Nouvel Observateur* (29 May 1978).

CHAPTER EIGHTEEN

1 Lewis Gannett has called man-boy relations "the closet's final frontier." See his article by that name in *The Gay & Lesbian Review* 7, no. 1 (31 January 2000). Tsang, ed., *The Age Taboo*. Geraci, ed., *Dares to Speak*. Weeks, *Sexuality and Its Discontents*, 226–9.

2 Ibid., 226. For one feminist account of sex and pedagogy, see Gallop, *Feminist Accused of Sexual Harassment.*

3 For French feminist criticisms, see Rochefort, *Les Enfants d'abord* and Sebbar, *Le Pédophile et la maman.* Tony Duvert denounced Sebbar for her "puritanism and dishonesty." Duvert, *L'Enfant au masculin*, 45. See also Tsang, ed., *The Age Taboo.*

4 "Pour une autre législation sur la sexualité des mineurs," *Libération*, 26 January 1977. "A propos d'un procès," *Le Monde*, 26 January 1977. Sirinelli, *Intellectuels et passions françaises*, 437–9. Gabriel Matzneff had plaintively called for a petition in November 1976 when he had been brought up on charges for remarks made on the television show *Apostrophes*. Matzneff, "L'Amour est-il un crime?" *Le Monde*, 7–8 November 1976. Before the 1992 reform of the entire penal code, French criminal law distinguished among "outrage against public morals" [*l'outrage aux bonnes moeurs*], usually related to publications and the press, "public indecency" [*l'outrage public à la pudeur*], "indecent assault," either with or without violence [*les attentats à la pudeur*], and "attacks on morals," "debauchery," and "corruption of minors" [*les attentats aux moeurs, la débauche, la corruption des mineurs*].

5 P. Verdon, "Procès Dejager: les familles rassurées," *Rouge*, 31 January 1977. Pierre Georges, "L'Enfant, l'amour, l'adulte," *Le Monde*, 29 January 1977.

6 Sirinelli, *Intellectuels et passions françaises*, 439–41. Sirinelli sees these two petitions as symptoms of a certain "airiness" among French intellectuals in the late 1970s.

7 The PCF announcement came as a surprise during a film festival (22–26 April) sponsored by the Groupe de libération homosexuel (politique et quotidien). There were also heated debates around the festival's final program, "Pederasty and the Sexuality of Children." Michèle Solat, "Une 'Semaine homosexuelle' à Paris," *Le Monde*, 22 April 1977. Suzette Triton, "Le PCF déclare officiellement qu'il ne soutient pas l'homosexualité mais condamne toute répression contre elle," *Rouge*, 25 April 1977. C.S., "Ce soir à la semaine GLH-PQ: 'Pédérastie et sexualité des enfants,'" *Rouge*, 26 April 1977. Denise Avenas, "La Pédérastie: un débat qui bouscule nos édifices moraux," *Rouge*, 28 April 1977. Claire Devarrieux, "Débats sur l'homosexualité," *Le Monde*, 2 May 1977.

8 Commission de révision du Code pénal, *Avant-projet définitif de code pénal (avril 1978).*

9 The best critical discussion of some of these figures is Lapouge and Pinard-Legry, *L'Enfant et le pédéraste.*

10 Daniel Guérin, "Pour le droit d'aimer un mineur," *Marge* 2 (July–August 1974). Cf. Guérin, *Son Testament*. René Schérer, "Pédophilie: notes de lecture," *Homosexualités–Marginalités*, Special Issue of *Marge* 11 (October–November 1976).

11 *Enfances*, Special Issue of *Sexpol* 9 (October 1976). The journal's title was a homage to Wilhelm Reich. On parents, children, and sex, see Guereau, *L'Enfant et son désir d'aimer* and Hanry, *Les Enfants, le sexe et nous.*

12 Hocquenghem, *Homosexual Desire*, 141. Duvert, *Le Bon sexe illustré.* Matzneff, *Les Passions schismatiques*, 139, 147. Matzneff, *Les Moins de seize ans*, 38, 41. Hocquenghem, "L'Enfance d'un sexe," *Normalisation de l'école–Scolarisation de la société*, Special Issue of *Les Temps modernes* 340 (November 1974); repr. in *Le Dérive homosexuelle*, 114. Michel Foucault, David Cooper, Jean-Pierre Faye, Marie-Odile Faye, and Marine Zecca, "Confinement, Psychiatry, Prison" [12 May 1977], in Foucault, *Politics, Philosophy, Culture*, 204–5; orginally "Enfermement, psychiatrie, prison," *Change* 32–3 (1977).

13 Hocquenghem, *Homosexual Desire*, 141. Schérer, "A propos de Fourier: lutte de classes et lutte de civilisations," foreword to Fourier, *L'Ordre subversif*, 26–8, 36–40. Published the same month as Deleuze and Guattari's *Anti-Oedipus*, Schérer's volume was part of a more extensive Fourier revival in the early 1970s. See Emile Lehouck, "La Parole à Charles Fourier," *La Quinzaine littéraire* 149 (1 October 1972) and Daniel Guérin, *Charles Fourier.* Matzneff, *Les Moins de seize ans*, 38, 30, 42, 91–8, and *Les Passions schismatiques*, 131–3, 140, 130.

14 [Jules Selma], "Jean-Pierre 9 ans: 'je voudrais embrasser une fille sur le cul,'" *Tout!* 8 (1 February 1971).

15 *Trois milliards de pervers*. The petition, "Sale race! Sale pédé!" was signed by Daniel Ben-Saïd, François Châtelet, Deleuze, Guattari, Hocquenghem, Lapassade, Jean-François Lyotard, Schérer, and Henri Weber, among others.

16 Hocquenghem and Schérer, *Co-ire: album systématique de l'enfance*, Special Issue of *Recherches* 22 (May 1976; 2nd ed. April 1977).

17 Schérer, "Post-face," in Hocquenghem, *L'Amphitéâtre des morts*. Interview with René Schérer (May 1999).

18 Hocquenghem, "L'Enfance d'un sexe," 109–21. Schérer, *Emile perverti.* Duvert, *Le Bon sexe illustré.*

19 Schérer used this Foucauldian language a year before *Discipline and Punish* (1975) was published. Schérer himself notes this in "Les Droits des enfants," in Lapassade and Schérer, *Le Corps interdit*, 87. Rather than see Schérer et al. as repeating or applying Foucault's insights (and they certainly borrowed from him), it is worth seeing Foucault himself as operating within an ambience from

which he borrowed and to which he contributed. Though he had little to say about Schérer, Foucault remarked in 1981: "With Hocquenghem one encounters many interesting questions, and I have the impression that on certain points we are in agreement." J. François and J. de Wit, "Interview met Michel Foucault" (22 May 1981), *Krisis: Tijdschrift voor filosofie* (March 1984), in Foucault, *Dits et écrits*, 4:663.

20 Schérer, *Une Erotique puérile*, 15–16 and *L'Emprise des enfants entre nous*.

21 Schérer, *Une Erotique puérile*, 9–12, 185, and *L'Emprise*, 233–7.

22 Schérer, *Une Erotique puérile*, 17–22, 182–5, and *L'Emprise*, 234–7. In *L'Emprise* (235), Schérer gives a more balanced view to the extent that, in trying to let children speak for themselves, he admits that among themselves children can be as phallic and repressive as any group of adults.

23 Schérer, *Une Erotique puérile*, 25–6, 182–3, and "A propos de Fourier," 43. The term "topological justice" is Jean-François Lyotard's in his *Duchamp's Trans/formers*.

24 Matzneff, *Les Passions schismatiques*, 121, 123–5, 132, 137, and *Les Moins de seize ans*, 30–1, 41, 45, 59–60, 67, 140. On sexualized incarnationism, see *Les Passions schismatiques*, 151. Matzneff was Eastern Orthodox, and his journals from the 1960s and 1970s show doubt mixed with erotic fixation in megalomaniacally "Christian" proportions. The term "pedophile," he said, stinks of "camphor and bromide." Adult lovers of children are the "Carbonari of love," in reference to the generally anti-absolutist but otherwise vague secret political societies of the early nineteenth century. Ibid., 121, 145.

25 Ibid., 124, 125–6, 140–3, 145. *Les Moins de seize ans*, 73–6.

26 Foucault, *Résumé des cours*, 76–80. Now see Foucault, *Abnormal*.

27 Foucault, *The History of Sexuality*, 104.

28 Foucault, *The Use of Pleasure*, 221–4, 253, and *The Care of the Self*, 198.

29 Foucault et al., "Confinement, Psychiatry, Prison," 206, 200–1. Compare Gisèle Halimi: "A sexual choice has nothing to do with the law. It's nobody's business. With one limit. Violence. And that is why children must be protected." Interview with Halimi (March 2001).

30 Foucault et al., "Confinement, Psychiatry, Prison," 202, 204–5, 209. Foucault, *Dits et écrits*, 3:355.

31 Foucault, Hocquenghem, and Jean Danet, "Sexual Morality and the Law," in Foucault, *Politics, Philosophy, Culture*; orginally "La Loi de la pudeur," *Recherches* 37 (April 1979).

32 Association Choisir/La Cause des femmes, *Viol*. "La Prostitution des enfants," *Rouge*, 1–2 April 1978. Marco, "Après l'émission 'Aujourd'hui madame' sur la prostitution des enfants: un point de vue," *Rouge*, 3 April 1978. "La Prosti-

tution des enfants en France," *Le Quotidien de Paris*, 12 April 1978. "Les Enfants qui se prostituent: I. la misère à vendre," *Le Matin*, 21 April 1978.

33 Foucault et al., "Sexual Morality and the Law," 272–3, 275, 277.

34 Ibid., 276–7, 280–1.

35 Ibid., 283–4.

36 Ibid., 285.

CHAPTER NINETEEN

1 Gauthier-Hamon and Teboul, *Entre père et fils*, 112–15. On the Coral Affair, see Martel, *The Pink and the Black*, 142–6.

2 Mossuz-Lavau, *Les Lois de l'amour*. Tissot, *La Liberté sexuelle et la loi*. Copley, *Sexual Moralities in France*.

3 Falconnet and Lefaucheur, *La Fabrication des mâles*. Laurent, *Féminin-masculin*. Finkielkraut and Bruckner, *Le Nouveau désordre amoureux*. Gill Allwood has demonstrated how French masculinity studies since the 1970s have been "thinner" in France than in the United Kingdom and the United States. Allwood, *French Feminisms*. The work of Daniel Welzer-Lang did much for masculinity studies in France during the 1990s. See also Nye, *Masculinity and Male Codes of Honor in Modern France*.

4 Topp, *Those Without a Country*, 18–24, 135–73.

5 Elisabeth Badinter voices a common French view that "the problem of masculinity is less acute in France than elsewhere." Badinter, *XY*, 5. Cf. the comment of Alain Touraine: "In the United States, men and women hate each other. In France, they love each other." Interview with Touraine (April 1999). Pierre Bourdieu ultimately set "masculine domination" within the problematic of social and symbolic domination in general. Bourdieu, *Masculine Domination*.

6 The crime was excused if "immediately provoked." Before the abolition of the death penalty in 1981, if the male victim died within a fittingly biblical "forty days," the penalty was death. If the victim did not die, those convicted of "unprovoked" castration were automatically sentenced to life in prison. *Code Pénal*, Art. 316 and 325. The statute was repealed in 1992.

7 The entire episode is recounted by Liliane Kandel, "Sous la plage, les medias," *Est-ce ainsi que les hommes jugent?* Special Issue of *Les Temps modernes* 391 (February 1979).

8 Ibid., 1168.

9 Serge July, "Il est interdit d'interdire, y compris pour les femmes," *Libération*, 6 December 1978.

10 Bruno Frappat, "Féminisme et répression," *Le Monde*, 6 December 1978.

11 Interview with Gisèle Halimi (March 2001).
12 Interview with Françoise Picq (June 1999).
13 Numerous works on "moral panic" have been written between Cohen, *Folk Devils and Moral Panics* and Sonya O. Rose, "Cultural Analysis and Moral Discourses: Episodes, Continuities, and Transformations," in Bonnell and Hunt, eds., *Beyond the Cultural Turn*. Contrast the discussions of transgression by Martin Jay, "The Limits of Limit-Experience: Bataille and Foucault," in Jay, *Cultural Semantics*, and by Stallybrass and White, *The Politics and Poetics of Transgression*.
14 Interview with Cathy Bernheim (March 2001).
15 Domenach, *Une Morale sans moralisme*.
16 Foucault, "Sexual Act, Sexual Choice" (Interview with James O'Higgins) [fall 1982–winter 1983], in Foucault, *Ethics*.

CHAPTER TWENTY

1 Pierre de Boisdeffre, "La Revue littéraire (les nouveaux philosophes)," *Revue des deux mondes* (August 1977).
2 Bernard-Henri Lévy, "Les Nouveaux philosophes," *Les Nouvelles littéraires* (10 June 1976). Paul Guilbert, "Naissance d'une philosophie 'multinationale,'" *Nouveaux philosophes ou nouvelle philosophie*, Special Issue of *La Nef* 66 (January–April 1978). "Les Nouveaux philosophes et leur éditeur," *Informations Hachette* (August–September 1977).
3 Biographical details from Boggio, *Bernard-Henri Lévy*. Publication under Lévy's wing did not necessarily qualify one as a New Philosopher, since Lévy also published Catherine Clément, Christian Delacampagne, Dominique Lecourt, and Michel Serres, who were never counted within the New Philosophers' circle. Jean-Luc Marion, who published with Lévy, was sometimes included. Gerard Petitjean, "Les Nouveaux gourous," *Le Nouvel Observateur* (7 July 1976), added Jean Baudrillard, Guy Hocquenghem, and Nikos Poulantzas to his list of "children of '68." Paugam, *Génération perdue*, added Michel Butor, Antoine de Gaudemar, Jean-Edern Hallier, Marek Halter, and Bernard Kouchner.
4 Interview with Jean-Paul Dollé (June 1999).
5 Soljénitsyne [Solzhenitsyn], *L'Archipel du Goulag*. The Russian original was published in Paris in December 1973, and the French translation followed in June 1974. For his French reception preceding the publication of *The Gulag Archipelago*, see *Soljénitsyne: le colloque du Cerisy* (8–12 June 1973), published in April 1974, esp. "Ethique et esthétique, le rapport à l'Occident," 165–210. The bulk of the Gulag debate occurred before the French translation

was published. Jean-Paul Sartre was defending Solzhenitsyn as early as 1969; with Elisa Triolet, Louis Aragon, Jean-Louis Bory, Vercors, Christine Rochefort, and others, he signed a petition of the Comité national des écrivains français. See "L'Exclusion de Soljénitsyne est une erreur monumentale," *Le Monde*, 19 November 1969. For the Gulag affair, see Hourmant, *Le Désenchantement des clercs*, 57–88, and Christofferson, *French Intellectuals Against the Left*, ch. 2. Glucksmann, *La Cuisinière et le mangeur d'hommes*. Lefort, *Un Homme en trop*.

6 Glucksmann, *The Master Thinkers*. Lévy, *Barbarism with a Human Face*.

7 See Dosse, *History of Structuralism*, 2:282. In what follows, the term *metaphysics* refers to ultimate foundations and principles behind or beyond the realm of ordinary contingent experience.

8 Benoist, *Marx est mort*. Dollé, *Le Désir de révolution*. Lardreau, *Le Singe d'or*.

9 Dollé, *Voie d'accès au plaisir*. Nemo, *L'Homme structural*. Benoist, *Tyrannie du Logos* and *La Révolution structurale*. Guérin, *Nietzsche, Socrate héroique*. Susong, *La Politique d'Orphée*. Clavel, *Ce que je crois*. Jambet and Lardreau, *Ontologie de la Révolution*, vol. 1, *L'Ange*. Clavel, *Dieu est Dieu, nom de Dieu*.

10 Hourmant, *Le Désenchantement des clercs*, 99–102.

11 Jambet, *L'Apologie de Platon*. Benoist, *Pavane pour une Europe défunte*. Dollé, *Haine de la pensée*. Paul-Lévy, *Karl Marx, histoire d'un bourgeois allemand*.

12 See Bouscasse and Bourgeois, eds., *Faut-il brûler les nouveaux philosophes?* 53–4, on the Théâtre Oblique debate; Paugam, *Génération perdue*.

13 Bouscasse and Bourgeois, eds., *Faut-il brûler les nouveaux philosophes?* 54–9. Participants at the "Representation and Power" meeting included Christian Jambet, Philippe Sollers, Jacques Attali, Pierre Legendre, Julia Kristeva, Jean-Paul Aron, Nikos Poulantzas, and Michel Guérin. "Desire and the Law" placed Maurice Clavel, Jean-Toussaint Desanti, André Glucksmann, and Bernard-Henri Lévy in conversation. "The Reason of the State and the Rights of Man" saw diverse panels that included the likes of Jean-Marie Benoist, Michel Butel, Marek Halter, Bernard Kouchner, and Mario Bettati. Members of the group Marge, claiming the part of Gilles Deleuze and Félix Guattari, disrupted at least one meeting.

14 Max Gallo, "An Interview with André Glucksmann," *Telos* 33 (fall 1977): 96.

15 Also published that year were Clavel, *Nous l'avons tous tué ou "Ce juif de Socrate!..."*; Clavel and Sollers's dialogue *Délivrance*; Dollé, *L'Odeur de la France*.

16 Gilles Deleuze, "A propos des nouveaux philosophes et d'un problème plus général," *Supplément* to *Minuit* 24 (May 1977); repr. "Gilles Deleuze contre

les 'nouveaux philosophes,'" *Le Monde*, 19–20 June 1977, and in Bouscasse and Bourgeois, eds., *Faut-il brûler les nouveaux philosophes?*; "On the New Philosophers and a More General Problem," *Discourse* 20, no. 3 (fall 1998): 37–43; also trans. "On the New Philosophers (Plus a More General Problem)," in Deleuze, *Two Regimes and Madness*. Lyotard, *Instructions païennes*. Macciocchi, *De la France*, 380. Cornelius Castoriadis, "Les Divertisseurs," *Le Nouvel Observateur* (20 June 1977); repr. in Bouscasse and Bourgeois, eds., *Faut-il brûler les nouveaux philosophes?*; "The Diversionists," *Telos* 33 (fall 1977): 102–6. Régis Debray, "Les Pleureuses du printemps," *Le Nouvel Observateur* (13 June 1977); repr. in Bouscasse and Bourgeois, eds., *Faut-il brûler les nouveaux philosophes?*; "Springtime Weepers," *Telos* 33 (fall 1977): 111. Jacques Rancière, "Portrait du vieil intellectual en jeune dissident," *Le Nouvel Observateur* (25 July 1977); repr. in Bouscasse and Bourgeois, eds., *Faut-il brûler les nouveaux philosophes?*; "Reply to Lévy," *Telos* 33 (fall 1977): 122. Henri Lefebvre, "Le Grand désarroi," *Libération*, 30 June 1977. Catherine B. Clément, "Philippulus le prophète," *Le Matin*, 27 May 1977. Nikos Poulantzas at the Beaubourg "Representation and Power" meeting (28 March 1977), cited by Nicolas Prayssac, "Un Concept moucheté," *L'Humanité*, 30 March 1977; repr. in Bouscasse and Bourgeois, eds., *Faut-il brûler les nouveaux philosophes?* 58–9. René Schérer, "Une Résistance ambiguë," *Le Monde*, 3 June 1977. Blandine Barret-Kriegel, "Chatterton au Sheraton ou les méthodes de travail du nouveau philosophe," *Le Matin*, 27 June 1977. Daniel Lindenberg, "Maurice Barrès (1862–1923), nouveau philosophe," *Le Matin*, 28 July 1977. Jean-Marie Vincent, "Du Goulag à l'abbaye de Vézelay," *Rouge*, 6 July 1977. Michel de Certeau cited by Bernard Weisz, "Le Nouveau bla-bla-bla," *L'Humanité*, 11 November 1977. Aubral and Delcourt, *Contre la nouvelle philosophie*, 13–32. Quaduppani, *Catalogue du prêt à penser français depuis 1968*. Cf. Jean Cau, "Les 'Nouveaux philosophes': la pensée encore à gauche, la plume déjà à droite," [*Le Figaro-Dimanche*], [n.d.]. Hirsch, *The French New Left*, 200–1. Reader, *Intellectuals and the Left in France since 1968*, 108.

17 Roger-Pol Droit, "Les Lanciers de la métaphysique," *Le Monde*, 27 May 1977.

18 Among the first analyses of French intellectuals in the new media climate were Debray, *Le Pouvoir intellectuel en France*; and Hamon and Rotman, *Les Intellocrates*.

19 Dollé cited in Paugam, *Génération perdue*, 41. Dollé, "Il n'y a pas de gourous," *Le Monde*, 27 May 1977. Guérin, "Une Lettre de Michel Guérin," *Le Monde*, 3 June 1977.

20 *Apostrophes* (27 May 1977), TF1, Archives Institut National d'Audiovisuel. Cf. Gallo, "An Interview with André Glucksmann," 96.

21 Lévy, "La Nouvelle philosophie n'existe pas," and Jambet and Lardreau, "Une Dernière fois contre la 'nouvelle philosophie,'" *La Nef* 66 (January–April 1978), citation from 39.
22 Françoise Verny, cited in Le Goff, *Mai '68*, 419.
23 Interview with Jean-Paul Dollé (June 1999).
24 Schiwy, *Les Nouveaux philosophes*, 12–49.
25 Foucault, "La Grande colère des faits" [Review of Glucksmann, *The Master Thinkers*], *Le Nouvel Observateur* (9 May 1977); repr. in Foucault, *Dits et écrits* (1994), 3:277–81. Philippe Sollers, "La Révolution impossible," *Le Monde*, 13 May 1977; repr. in Bouscasse and Bourgeois, eds., *Faut-il brûler les nouveaux philosophes?* 82–8. Roland Barthes, "Lettre à Bernard-Henri Lévy," *Les Nouvelles littéraires* (26 May 1977); repr. in Bouscasse and Bourgeois, eds., *Faut-il brûler les nouveaux philosophes?* 89–95. Sollers and Barthes appreciated Lévy's rhetoric. Droit, "Les Lanciers de la métaphysique," noted that, alongside Lacanianism, the other principal unifying theme was the rejection of Marxism (except for Benoist, for whom such a rejection was nothing new).
26 Touraine, *Return of the Actor*.
27 It is also worth pondering an overall parallel when one considers the foreign reception of French theory. While fashionableness immediately appeared as grounds to belittle and discredit New Philosophy, such criticisms did not halt the massive onslaught of French theory in Anglo-American lands. It would be a good exercise for an Anglo-American poststructuralist to read the New Philosophers and explain how his or her premises differ significantly. True, Anglo-American adepts of French theory made sophistication a virtue, whereas New Philosophy tended toward the sound bite, and the return to metaphysical absolutism and humanism by the latter would have made any self-respecting deconstructionist cringe. However, New Philosophy's historical pessimism and attention to language, desire, power, and ethics uncannily forecasted many terms of Anglo-American debates in the 1980s and 1990s. It may be that the eventual emergence of the couple "French-theory-and-ethics" amounted in part to a belated digestion of themes addressed earlier, if superficially, by the New Philosophers.
28 Interview with Roger-Pol Droit (July 2003).
29 Foucault, interview with Lévy, "The End of the Monarchy of Sex," in Lotringer, ed., *Foucault Live*.
30 Jérôme Bindé, "L'Internationale des nouveaux philosophes," *Le Quotidien de Paris*, 26 September 1977.
31 Jean-Jacques Brochier, "Les Philosophes contre la liberté," *Le Magazine littéraire* (May 1977).

32 The one notable exception was his unfortunately charitable assessment of the Iranian Revolution of 1979. See Afary and Anderson, *Foucault and the Iranian Revolution.*

33 Schiwy, *Les Nouveaux philosophes*, 10.

34 Domenach, *Enquête sur les idées contemporaines*, 55–6.

35 Foucault and Glucksmann on the television show *La Part de la vérité* (4 July 1977), TF1, Archives Institut National d'Audiovisuel.

36 Camus, *The Rebel.*

37 In a vast literature, see the excellent work by Falk, *The Dilemmas of Dissidence in East-Central Europe.*

38 Chiama and Soulet, *Histoire de la dissidence*, 8.

39 Christofferson, *Intellectuals Against the Left*, ch. 4.

40 See Julia Kristeva, "Un Nouveau type d'intellectuel: le dissident," *Tel quel* 74 (winter 1977); "A New Type of Intellectual: The Dissident," in *The Kristeva Reader*, and the discussions in Marx-Scouras, *The Cultural Politics of Tel Quel*, and ffrench, *The Time of Theory*. Foucault's talk of "resistance" at this time certainly resonated with this current and had the added virtue of evoking the French Resistance. The trend was not without criticism. See, for example, Lecourt, *Dissidence ou révolution?*; "Dissidence or Revolution?" in *The Mediocracy.*

41 Dominique Grisoni, "Crépuscule du monde, aurore de la pensée?" *Le Magazine littéraire* (June 1977). On New Philosophy as anarchistic, see Gayatri Spivak and Michael Ryan, "Anarchism Revisited: A New Philosophy," *Diacritics* 8, no. 2 (summer 1978).

42 Bouscasse and Bourgeois, eds., *Faut-il brûler les nouveaux philosophes?* 257.

43 Le Goff, *Mai '68*, 414.

44 Patrick Pharo, "Ethique et politique ou les intellectuels dans l'histoire," *L'Année sociologique* 3rd. ser., vol. 30 (1979–80).

45 Ibid., 132–3, 136–7, 146–7, 158–60.

CHAPTER TWENTY-ONE

1 Jean-Denis Bredin, "Un Rôle immense et minuscule," *Nouveaux philosophes ou nouvelle philosophie*, Special Issue of *La Nef* 66 (January–April 1978): 62.

2 Christofferson, *Intellectuals Against the Left*, ch. 5. Cf. Hourmant, *Le Désenchantement des clercs.*

3 The idea of Gulags in 1970s France seems silly in retrospect, and even if the PCF built a reputation of opposition to civil liberties, during these years it also took steps toward moderation and liberalization. Such actions were, as Christofferson rightly notes, too little, too late. Yet he takes his notion of a

fear factor at face value, leaving it largely unthematized. Were such fears founded? If not, how did they play the role they are alleged to have played? Why? By surviving May 1968 intact, the Fifth Republic proved its endurance, and insecurity was thus a reflux. Although exaggeration may be real, it needs to be explained. My argument, in contrast, is that no political project could fulfill anticipations born in 1968, since many of those anticipations were not primarily political.

4 Pierre Viansson-Ponté, "Acrobates ou penseurs?" *La Nef* 66 (January–April 1978): 26. Paul Guilbert, "Naissance d'une philosophie 'multinationale,'" *La Nef* 66 (January–April 1978): 20. Claude Mauriac, "Il ne faut pas tuer l'espérance," *Le Monde*, 6 June 1977; repr. in Bouscasse and Bourgeois, eds., *Faut-il brûler les nouveaux philosophes?* 210–14. "Un Entretien avec David Rousset," *Le Quotidien de Paris*, 29 November 1977. Diane Ribardière, "Ils nous font la leçon," *Courrier de parlement*, [n.d.]. René Pascal, "Sommes-nous donc en 1905?" *La Croix*, 2 July 1977.

5 See my "The Red Guards of Paris."

6 Jambet and Lardreau, "Une Dernière fois contre la 'nouvelle philosophie,'" *La Nef* 66 (January–April 1978), 37.

7 Glucksmann, *La Cuisinière et le mangeur d'hommes*, 11–12.

8 Alain Peyrefitte, "Une Nouvelle philosophie bien française," *La Nef* 66 (January–April 1978): 52.

9 The Parti socialiste was created in 1969 from the dissolved Section française de l'Internationale ouvrière (1905–69). Unless otherwise noted, what follows is summarized from Derbyshire, *Politics in France*, and Wright, *France in Modern Times*.

10 *Programme commun de gouvernement du Parti communiste français et du Parti socialiste (27 juin 1972)*, 49–50. A valuable study would be to compare the details of the *Programme commun* with *Changer la vie* (1972), the program the Socialist Party accepted prior to the Common Program, and also with the version of the *Programme commun* (1978) the PS trumpeted after the Union of the Left collapsed in 1977.

11 Giscard d'Estaing, *Towards a New Democracy*. The charge that some New Philosophers were Giscardians also found its substance here.

12 For the PCF version, which gives transcripts of meetings between Marchais and Mitterrand and traces the collapse of the Union from March to September 1977, see Juquin, *Programme commun* (1977). While each major party blamed the other for the collapse, it is hard to avoid the judgment that the PCF preferred the familiar position of certain electoral defeat to playing the junior partner in a ruling coalition with the PS. Even with the Left bickering within itself, its performance in the March 1978 legislative election was impressive.

On the first ballot, the Left won 49.3% against the Right's 46%. The second ballot, clearly reflecting anxieties over PCF influence, which Chirac had drummed up, pushed the Right to a 50.5% majority. The PS had for the first time since 1936 won more votes than the PCF, sending the latter into terminal decline, as confirmed when Mitterrand took the Elysée in 1981.

13 Denis Roche, "Les Philosophes du fesse-à-fesse," *Libération*, 10 June 1977.

14 Lévy cited in Paugam, *Génération perdue*, 179. Jambet cited in ibid, 60. Jambet and Lardreau, "Le Goulag spirituel est déjà là," *Le Monde*, 27 May 1977. Glucksmann, *The Master Thinkers*, 205; translation modified.

15 Bernard Pingaud, "La Tentation d'irresponsibilité," *Le Matin*, 14 June 1977; repr. in Bouscasse and Bourgeois, eds., *Faut-il brûler les nouveaux philosophes?* 144–7. Catherine Kintzler, letter to *L'Humanité*, 7 July 1977. A revised version of a similar letter published in *Le Matin*, 4 June 1977. Glucksmann cited in Boggio, *Bernard-Henri Lévy*, 151. Cf. ibid., 151–3. J.-M. Jeng, "Les Nouveaux chiens de garde," *L'Humanité*, 13 June 1977. Jeng refers to Nizan, *The Watchdogs*. Nicolas Prayssac, "Gare aux gourous," *L'Humanité*, 17 June 1977; repr. in Bouscasse and Bourgeois, eds., *Faut-il brûler les nouveaux philosophes?* 107–8. Pierre Juquin, "La Liberté parlons-en," *L'Humanité-Dimanche*, 8 July 1977; repr. in Bouscasse and Bourgeois, eds., *Faut-il brûler les nouveaux philosophes?* 147–8. L.B., [Review of *La Barbarie à visage humain*], *Mouvement des radicaux de gauche* (September 1977).

16 Philippe Buchon, "Les Penseurs de l'après-Mai," *Le Spectacle du Monde* (June 1977).

17 Maurice Duverger, "Les Iconoclastes!" *Le Monde*, 10 June 1977.

18 Jean Creiser, "Bernard-Henri Lévy, démolisseur d'idoles," *Le Figaro*, (fall 1977).

19 Jules Roy, "Disciples de Camus?" *La Nef* 66 (January–April 1978). Etienne Borne, "Ces garçons qui font scandale," *La Croix*, 10 June 1977. "Pleine page sur Bernard-Henri Lévy: contre la barbarie à visage humain," *La Voix du Nord*, 29 October 1977. Jean-Paul Dollé celebrated Heidegger and Hölderlin, although Claude Prévost's suggestion that Heidegger was the "*cellule-mère*" of the New Philosophers was certainly exaggerated. Prévost, "Poser les questions, oui! Mais comment?" *France nouvelle*, 24 July 1977. J.-P. M., "La Fin d'une parade," *Le Matin*, 27 May 1977 and 28 July 1977. Olivier Cohen, "La Génération perdante," *Libération*, 27 May 1977.

20 Tony Judt has suggested a parallel between Pascal and Camus. Given the importance of Camus for some of the New Philosophers, the suggestion adds to our sketch. Judt, *The Burden of Responsibility*, 135. For another linkage of cultural Jansenism and a very different French intellectual, see Kolakowski,

"Georges Sorel: A Jansenist Marxist," in *Main Currents of Marxism*, vol. 2, *The Golden Age*.

21 Sedgwick, *Jansenism in Seventeenth-Century France*. Kolakowski, *God Owes Us Nothing*. Goldmann, *The Hidden God*. Van Kley, *The Religious Origins of the French Revolution*.

22 On tragedy, see Goldmann, *The Hidden God*, 11, 33, 62; on the "hidden God," 36, 38; on "extreme" and "moderate" Jansenism, 53; on "in the world but not of it," 50, 160, 199, 219, 283. Goldmann's notion that Jansenist "tragedy" embodied the dialectic *in utero* remains suggestive (59, 174); however, his linkage of the Jansenist mentality to the frustrated ambitions of a Third Estate increasingly disenfranchised by absolutism was forced (100–41).

23 Van Kley, *The Religious Origins of the French Revolution*, 13. The technical theological difference between Jansenism and Calvinism, according to Van Kley, turned on the role of the Fall: for Jansenists, Adam got Man into trouble; for Calvinists, God had predestined the elect from the start. Thus there was nothing "irresistible" about Jansenist grace – God could take it away whenever He wanted. Ibid., 61–3. Cf. Kolakowski, *God Owes Us Nothing*, 115–16, and Goldmann, *The Hidden God*, 8.

24 Ibid., 275, 282. Sedgwick, *Jansenism in Seventeenth-Century France*, 198. Van Kley, *The Religious Origins of the French Revolution*, 63.

CHAPTER TWENTY-TWO

1 Clavel, *Ce que je crois*.

2 Mikro, "La Véhémence et la pudeur," *Réforme*, 7 July 1975. Michel Le Bris, "Contre l'ordre, la puissance de l'esprit," *Le Monde*, [n.d.]. Robert Kanters, "Maurice Clavel: à la trace de Dieu," *Le Figaro*, 24–5 May 1975. Also, Michel Puech, "Clavel en modulation de fréquence," *Libération*, 3 February 1975. Mauriac, *Et comme l'espérance est violente*. Cf. Bel, *Maurice Clavel*, 201.

3 Jean de Fabrègues, "Un Raisonable 'fou de Dieu' parmi nous," *France Catholique*, 30 May 1975.

4 André Glucksmann, *La Part de la vérité* (4 July 1977), TF2, Archives Institut National d'Audiovisuel. Cf. Glucksmann, *The Master Thinkers*, 205–6. Clavel and Sollers, *Délivrance*, 86. Foucault, cited in Clavel, *Ce que je crois*, 139. Foucault, "Vivre autrement le temps," *Le Nouvel Observateur* (30 April 1979), cited in Eribon, *Michel Foucault*, 255. Bel, *Maurice Clavel*, 335–7. Jean-Marie Domenach, "Le Grande polémique," *Le Dieu de Clavel*, Special Dossier in *Esprit* (July–August 1976): 117. Jean Daniel cited in Bel, *Maurice Clavel*, 354. Cf. Daniel, "Préface," *La Suite appartient à d'autres*, where he calls Clavel "one of the freest, truest, and savory beings in the great tradition

of the political pamphleteers – or, as [Clavel] said, of the *transcendental journalists*" (11). Clavel is buried in the church cemetery at Vézelay about twenty feet from Georges Bataille.

5 Domenach, *Enquête sur les idées contemporaines*, 60.

6 Hourmant, *Le Désenchantement des clercs*, 101.

7 The following account is indebted to Gachoud, *Maurice Clavel.*

8 Clavel and Sollers, *Délivrance*, 31.

9 Clavel, *Critique de Kant.*

10 Clavel, *Ce que je crois*, 251, 264. Clavel and Sollers, *Délivrance*, 45. Bel, *Maurice Clavel*, 314.

11 Ibid., 206.

12 Clavel, *Ce que je crois*, 133.

13 Clavel and Sollers, *Délivrance*, 93.

14 Clavel, *Ce que je crois*, 18, 28, 116, 183. Clavel and Sollers, *Délivrance*, 63, 77–8, 114. Jacqueline Piatier, "La Divine subversion," *Le Monde*, 29 May 1975.

15 Clavel, *Ce que je crois*, 140, 198, 255. Bel, *Maurice Clavel*, 239. Schiwy, *Les Nouveaux philosophes*, 84. Clavel and Sollers, *Délivrance*, 19, 53–4. Clavel, *Qui est aliéné?*

16 Bel, *Maurice Clavel*, 202, 251, 266.

17 There was more coherence than one might think between Clavel's Resistance-inspired Gaullism and his friendship with the Maoists. One might bear in mind that the Resistance and left-wing Gaullists had seen the war as an occasion for the emancipatory reinvention of "man," even if de Gaulle himself and his main supporters were obviously less ambitious. For Clavel, who identified himself as a partisan of "Gaullo-gauchisme," de Gaulle had ultimately betrayed the Resistance emancipatory project; thus Clavel's curious claim during the Ben Barka Affair that he wanted to save Gaullism from de Gaulle. Cf. Clavel and Sollers, *Délivrance*, 152.

18 "Maurice Clavel et nous," *Supplément* to *Royaliste* [1979?], 57.

19 Clavel, *Ce que je crois*, 25.

20 Anonymous, "Ce que je crois" (Excerpts), *Panorama d'Aujourd'hui* (February 1975), 64. Kanters, "Maurice Clavel." Piatier, "La Divine subversion."

21 At times Clavel disavowed his debt to Pascal, whom he found, like Kierkegaard, still too philosophical. Others, though, insisted on the connection. Alain Arnaud wrote that "one sees Clavel taking a little Pascal (abbreviated), a lot of Kant (poorly read), in order to arrive at Léon Bloy." Arnaud, "Le Grand bond en arrière," *Esprit* (July–August 1976). See Clavel and Sollers, *Délivrance*, 26, 28, 44–5, 150, 224. Clavel, *Ce que je crois*, 18, 23, 66, 192–3, 222–3. "Maurice Clavel répond à François Biot," *Témoignage chrétien*, 12 June 1975.

22 Luce Giard, "La Grande parade," *Le Dieu de Clavel*, Special Dossier in *Esprit* (July–August 1976): 112. Clavel, *Ce que je crois*, 22.
23 Clavel, *Nous l'avons tous tué ou "Ce juif de Socrate!..."*.
24 Ibid., 16, 26.
25 Ibid., 10–24. Bel, *Maurice Clavel*, 326–7.
26 Guérin, *Nietzsche, Socrate héroique*. Jambet, *Apologie de Platon*.
27 Michel Grandjean, "Emmanuel Levinas: Alterité, Exil et Parole," BDIC: F Δ Rés. 576/8.
28 See Clavel's open letter to Glucksmann entitled *Deux siècles chez Lucifer*.
29 Clavel, "L'Ange exterminateur," *Le Nouvel Observateur* (22 March 1976), 60; repr. in Bouscasse and Bourgeois, eds., *Faut-il brûler les nouveaux philosophes?* 22–6. Cf. Bel, *Maurice Clavel*, 318–19.
30 Clavel, *Dieu est Dieu*, 71.
31 Clavel and Sollers, *Délivrance*, 152.
32 Jean-Jacques Brochier, "Naissance d'une pensée," *Le Magazine littéraire* (September 1976).

CHAPTER TWENTY-THREE

1 Jambet and Lardreau, *Ontologie de la* révolution, vol. 1, *L'Ange*; part. trans. "The French New Philosophers," *The Chicago Review* 32, no. 3 (winter 1981). The authors wrote different parts of their collectively credited works.
2 Jambet and Lardreau, *Le Monde*.
3 Anonymous, "L'Ange," *Le Nouvel Observateur* (8 March 1976). Roger-Pol Droit, "L'Ange de la révolution culturelle: des érmites aux Gardes Rouges," *Le Monde*, 11 March 1976. Marcel Neusch, "Une Philosophie de la 'révolution culturelle': L'Ange," *La Croix*, 31 July 1976. Bertrand Poirot-Delpech, "Maitres à dé-penser," *Le Monde*, 29 April 1976. Michel Field, "L'Ange," *Rouge*, 17 June 1976. Gilles Hertzog, "L'Ange entre Mao et Jésus," *Le Magazine littéraire* (May 1976). Claude Mauriac, "La Lutte avec l'ange," *Le Figaro*, 20–1 March 1976.
4 Jambet and Lardreau, *L'Ange*, 10.
5 Ibid., 22, 33–6.
6 Ibid., 56, 58, 60–1, 67.
7 Philippe Nemo, "Le Maître et le Rebelle," *Les Nouvelles littéraires* (1 April 1976). Neusch, "Une Philosophie de la 'révolution culturelle': L'Ange." François Ewald, *"Le Maître est un tigre de papier," Le Quotidien de Paris* [1976]. Hertzog, "L'Ange entre Mao et Jésus." Jambet and Lardreau, *Le Monde*, 18–19.
8 Lévy, *The Testament of God*.

9 Jambet and Lardreau, *Le Monde*, 9–10, 12, 18, 20.
10 Ibid., 12, 15, 23–4.
11 Recalling the Lacanian view of desire as empty lack, Lardreau suggested that desire shared with Kantian morality the impossibility of actualization. In a sense, desire, like the moral ideal, was noumenal: intelligible but non-phenomenological and at the limit between the possible and the impossible. Ibid., 32, 35, 37, 39, 43.
12 Compare Foucault's 1976 Collège de France course "*Society Must Be Defended*," which focuses on war.
13 Jambet and Lardreau, *Le Monde*, 42–3, 57–8, 99–100.
14 The notion of human non-relation built on Lacan's assertion that "there are no sexual relations" – meaning in part that all attempts at sexual fulfillment were haunted by the impossibility of fulfillment. Ibid., 60.
15 Ibid., 79, 83. Cf. 85, 94.
16 Ibid., 95–102.
17 Ibid., 102–4.
18 Ibid., 106–8.
19 Starr, *Logics of Failed Revolt*. In one of the few English-language analyses of *L'Ange*, Starr argues that Jambet and Lardreau backed away from Lacanian insights in a fit of castration anxiety. Reducing a desire to move past Lacan to the structures of Lacanianism, however, somewhat misses the point.
20 Jean-Marie Benoist, "Les Nouveaux philosophes: le temps des 'possédés,'" *Paradoxes* (June 1977).

CHAPTER TWENTY-FOUR

1 Glucksmann, *The Master Thinkers*, 112, 181–2, 248.
2 Ibid., 11–23.
3 Ibid., 37–41, 60, 62–5, 100, 131–3, 177, 219–22, 237–40.
4 See esp. ibid., 47–65.
5 Ibid., 51, 60, 248.
6 See ibid., 20, 58–9, 96, 189–90, 217–19. One might say that Glucksmann went some distance in applying Foucault's institutional analysis to the field of political theory, an enterprise Foucault himself had undertaken in his 1976 Collège de France course "*Society Must Be Defended*," esp., 106–18, 161.
7 Glucksmann, *The Master Thinkers*, 58.
8 Ibid., 36, 38, 47, 49–50, 56–7, 61.
9 Ibid., 53, 68–70, 74–85.
10 Ibid., 72, 95–100, 114–15.
11 Ibid., 86, 159, 164, 171, 202, 219–22.

12 Ibid., 179, 195–6, 249–52, 257–9.

13 Lévy, *Barbarism with a Human Face*, 4, 9. "Were it not for *L'Ange* I probably would not have risked this book." Ibid., xii.

14 Ibid., 15–17, 42. Legendre, *L'Amour du censeur*.

15 Ibid., xi.

16 Ibid., xi, 37, 63, 89, 130, 189. References to the intolerable and insupportable appear on 19, 20, 35, 92, 125, 195.

17 Ibid., 192–3.

18 Ibid., 193–7.

19 Ibid., 65, 77–8, 103, 133, 135, 176, 183, 193, 197.

20 Goldmann, *Immanuel Kant*.

21 Rousseau, though less important for Goldmann, was certainly important for Kant, and only the inclusion of Freud and Lacan pulls the New Philosophers fully away from the philosophical ground Goldmann analysed.

22 Domenach, *Enquête sur les idées contemporaines*, 58. Cf. Jambet and Lardreau, "Une Dernière fois contre la 'nouvelle philosophie,'" 36.

23 Pharo, "Ethique et politique," 160.

24 Le Goff, *Mai '68*, 413.

25 Alain Peyrefitte, "Une Nouvelle philosophie bien française," *La Nef* 66 (January–April 1978): 53–4. *Antigone* was the subject of Lacan's 1959–60 seminar on the "Ethics of Psychoanalysis." See Lacan, *The Ethics of Psychoanalysis*.

CHAPTER TWENTY-FIVE

1 Mongin, *Face au scepticisme*.

2 See, for instance, Schwartz, *A Mathematician Grappling with His Century*, 429–90. On Poland and political ethics see Michnik, *Penser la Pologne*, and Tischner, *Ethique de Solidarité*.

3 Baudrillard, *La Gauche divine*, 124.

4 I twist his meaning slightly. Stanley Hoffmann et al., *In Search of France*, 50, cited in Wright, *France in Modern Times*, 411.

5 Verstraeten, *Violence et éthique*. Axelos, *Pour une éthique problématique*. "Manifeste pour la vérité et la moralité en politique," *Le Monde*, 4 July 1973. Vidal-Naquet, *Mémoires*, 2:362. Schwartz, *A Mathematician Grappling with His Century*, 91. Bouveresse, *Wittgenstein*. Centre d'études et de recherche marxistes, *Morale et société*. Lionel Jospin's contribution to the proceedings bears rereading. Souriau, *La Couronne d'herbes*. Audry, *Les Militants et leurs morales*. Gorz, *Fondements pour une morale*. *Une Morale pour demain?* Special Issue of *La Nef* 67 (1978). Langlois, *Et vous êtes de gauche*, 12, 14.

6 Serge Audier, *Tocqueville retrouvé*.

7 Noted voices in this lively energizing of historical scholarship, which Olivier Mongin wryly commented had occurred at the very moment that History as a collective project seemed to be emptying out, included: Maurice Agulhon, Michel de Certeau, Georges Duby, Jacques Le Goff, Emmanuel Le Roy Ladurie, Pierre Nora, Michelle Perrot, Jacques Revel, Michel Vovelle, and Paul Veyne. Mongin, *Face au scepticisme*. Domenach, *Enquête sur les idées contemporaines*. Dosse, *New History in France*. Burke, *The French Historical Revolution*.

8 Igounet, *Histoire du négationnisme en France*. Wood, "French Thought under Mitterrand." As noted on 375n8, the controversy revolved around Farías, *Heidegger and Nazism*.

9 Dosse, *History of Structuralism*, 2:282.

10 Mongin, *Face au scepticisme*, 336. Cf. 79 where Mongin mentions the "latent and rarely formulated opposition" between Ricoeur and Levinas.

11 Dosse, *Paul Ricoeur*. See also Ricoeur's article on ethics in Kritzman, ed., *The Columbia History of Twentieth-Century French Thought*.

12 Ricoeur, *Oneself as Another* and *History and Truth*.

13 Madison, ed., *Sens et existence*. Cohen and Marsh, eds., *Ricoeur as Another*. Wall, Schweiker, and Hall, eds., *Paul Ricoeur and Contemporary Moral Thought*. The last volume focuses on Ricoeur's notion of "human capability."

14 Interview with Marcel Gauchet (June 1999). Gauchet sees ethics as having figured implicitly throughout the 1970s; only in the late 1970s did the theme become explicit.

15 Friedlander, *Vilna on the Seine*, 188.

16 "Excerpts from the Philosophy of Vladimir Jankélévitch," Special Dossier in *Critical Inquiry* 22, no. 3 (spring 1996). In his introduction, Arnold Davidson writes: "I hope that his publication in these pages will be but the beginning of his English-speaking life." Now see Jankélévitch, *Music and the Ineffable* and *Forgiveness*.

17 "Entretien," *Vladimir Jankélévitch*, Special Issue of *L'Arc* 75 (1979): 7.

18 Dosse, *History of Structuralism*, 2:284.

19 Basset et al., *Ecrits pour Jankélévitch*. *Vladimir Jankélévitch*, Special Issue of *L'Arc* 75 (1979).

20 Robert Maggiori, "Le Vagabond de l'entre-deux," *Libération*, 19 March 1978. "'Holocauste': la haine devant le miroir" (Interview with Jean-Paul Enthoven), *Le Nouvel Observateur* (19 February 1979). [Interview with Christian Delacampagne and Robert Maggiori], *Le Monde*, 4 November 1979; repr. in *Entretiens avec Le Monde*, vol. 1, *Philosophes*. "La Vérité par hasard," *Le Nouvel Observateur* (14 January 1980). *Le Monde*, 18 December 1981.

21 Lescourret, *Emmanuel Levinas*.

22 Jay, *Downcast Eyes*, 560, citing *Le Monde*, 23 November 1984.
23 Lévy, *The Testament of God*.
24 Lévy, *L'Idéologie française*. See the dossier in *Esprit* (May 1981), which assesses the general uproar the book caused.
25 Friedlander, *Vilna on the Seine*. Auron, *Les Juifs d'extrême-gauche en mai 68*.
26 Finkielkraut, *The Imaginary Jew*.
27 Benny Lévy's participation in the important transitional Cercle socratique was briefly evoked in chapter 22. Friedlander, *Vilna on the Seine*, 92–106, 124–39.
28 De Beauvoir, *Adieux*. Cohen-Solal, *Sartre*, 510–13. Friedlander, *Vilna on the Seine*, 135–8.
29 For a balanced assessment of the relationship see Ronald Aronson, "Introduction: Sartre's Last Words," in Sartre and Lévy, *Hope Now*.
30 Cohen-Solal, *Sartre*, 67, 75–6, 83, 92–3, 103, 142, 162–3, 268, 270, 277, 287–8, 333–4, 339, 435. De Beauvoir, *The Ethics of Ambiguity*. Jeanson, *Sartre and the Problem of Morality*. See also, Gorz, *La Morale de l'histoire*.
31 Anderson, *Sartre's Two Ethics*, ch. 7.
32 Ibid., 112, 186 n6. Sartre, "Rome lecture," cited in Anderson, ibid., 112–13.
33 Anderson, ibid., 114.
34 Sartre, ibid., 115.
35 Anderson, citing Sartre, ibid., 117.
36 See the discussion in Arthur, "Unfinished Projects."
37 Anderson, *Sartre's Two Ethics*, 117.
38 Ibid., 120, 123–4.
39 Fanon, *The Wretched of the Earth*.
40 Sartre in Anderson, *Sartre's Two Ethics*, 127–8.
41 Cohen-Solal, *Sartre*, 476.
42 See also his remarks on *la morale* in the 1977 documentary *Sartre par lui-même*. The documentary was filmed in February–March 1972, in other words, immediately following the Toul press conference discussed in chapter 2. *Sartre by Himself*, 77–81. In a 1978 interview he commented: "I was drawn to the moral conception of action and human relationships. That's what the Maoists were for me." Cohen-Solal, *Sartre*, 484–5.
43 Sartre and Lévy, *Hope Now*, 70–2.
44 Ibid., 91, 93, 80, 106–8. See also Lévy's reading of Sartre in light of Jewish messianism, *Le Nom de l'homme*.
45 Sartre, *Notebooks for an Ethics*. Raymond Aron, cited in Winock, *Le Siècle des intellectuels*, 756.
46 Foucault, "Power, Moral Values, and the Intellectual" (Interview with Michael Bess), San Francisco (3 November 1980), Audio version, IMEC: D384.

47 Paul Rabinow, "Introduction: The History of Systems of Thought," in Foucault, *Ethics*, xxvi.
48 Armstrong, ed., *Michel Foucault Philosopher*. Smart, ed., *Michel Foucault*, vol. 3. Gutting, ed., *The Cambridge Companion to Foucault*. O'Leary, *Foucault*. Rabinow, "Introduction."
49 Foucault, *Dits et écrits*, 1:91–2, 237–8, 556, 616, 655, 789, 792; 2:87, 122, 381, 531–3. *The Order of Things* referred to by Rabinow, "Introduction," xxvi.
50 Foucault, *Dits et écrits*, 3:21, 41, 252, 277, 560, 565, 794.
51 Foucault, *Ethics*, 130, 132, 137–8, 146, 154–5, 157–63, 170–1, 182–3, 194–5, 223, 228, 256.
52 Foucault, *Dits et écrits*, 4:414.
53 Foucault, *Ethics*, 253–80, and "Politics and Ethics: An Interview," in *The Foucault Reader*, 373–80.
54 Foucault, *Ethics*, 255–6, 258–66.
55 Foucault, "Politics and Ethics," 375.
56 Foucault, *Dits et écrits*, 4:505–7.
57 Foucault, *Ethics*, 284–8, 291, 300.
58 Foucault, *Dits et écrits*, 4:731–2.
59 Foucault, *Politics, Philosophy, Culture*, 262–3, 265.
60 Foucault, *Ethics*, 111, 114–17. A point he repeats in "What is Enlightenment?" Ibid., 318.
61 Foucault, *Politics, Philosophy, Culture*, 243, 253–4.
62 Foucault, *Dits et écrits*, 4:696.
63 Foucault, *Ethics*, 292–3, 296, 298–9.
64 Ibid., 262.
65 Sartre, "Existentialism is a Humanism" [1946], in Kaufmann, ed., *Existentialism*, 364.
66 Perelman, *Introduction historique à la philosophie morale*. Grosser, *Au nom de quoi* and *Le Sel de la terre*. Jankélévitch, *Le Paradoxe de la morale*. Levinas, *Ethique et infini*. Conche, *Le Fondement de la morale*. Jacob, *Cheminements*. Kremer-Marietti, *La Morale*. Sartre, *Notebooks for an Ethics*. Nancy, *L'Impératif catégorique*. Lévy, *Questions de principe*. Misrahi, *Ethique, politique et bonheur*. Lyotard, *The Differend*. Jankélévitch, *L'Irréversible et la nostalgie*. Irigaray, *An Ethics of Sexual Difference*. Finkielkraut, *La Sagesse de l'amour*. Comte-Sponville, *Le Mythe d'Icare*. Morin, "Une Prise de conscience inconsciente: le pacifisme européen," in *Le Rose et le noir*. Joffrin, *Un Coup de jeune*. Dray, *La Guerre qu'il ne fallait pas faire*. Keitenbach, *Tartuffe aux affaires*.
67 De Beauvoir, *The Ethics of Ambiguity*, 156.

68 Deleuze and Guattari, *Anti-Oedipus*, 112. Guattari, "Tombeau pour l'Oedipe" (22 August 1971), Félix Guattari Archives, IMEC: ET01–38. Matzneff, *Les Passions schismatiques*, 57. Lévy, *Barbarism with a Human Face*, 20. Jambet and Lardreau, *Le Monde*, 79–97. Pompidou, *Entretiens et discours*, vol. 1, *1968–1974*, 152.

CONCLUSION

1 Sartre, *Critique de la raison dialectique*, 9. Hazel Barnes's different translation conveys the sense but not the tightness of the original. Sartre, *Search for a Method*, xxxiv.

2 Sophie Dufau, "Vivre éthique: la philosophie sort du boudoir," *Libération*, 16 December 2000.

3 Roger-Pol Droit, "Ethique en stock," *Le Monde*, 11 May 2001.

4 Canto-Sperber, *L'Inquiétude morale et la vie humaine*. "Pour la philosophie morale," *Le Débat* (November–December 1992). Canto-Sperber ed., *Dictionnaire d'éthique et de philosophie morale*. "Les Nouvelles morales: éthique et philosophie," Special Issue of *Le Magazine littéraire* 361 (January 1998).

5 Eric Dupin, "Recherche morale sociale désespérément," *Libération*, 22 February 2001.

6 Badiou, *Ethics*. Lecourt, *The Mediocracy*, 138; see also his *Contre la peur* and *Prométhée, Faust, Frankenstein*. Comte-Sponville, *A Small Treatise on the Great Virtues*. Baudrillard, *La Transparence du mal*. Boltanski, *Distant Suffering*. Debray, *I.F., suite et fin*. Domenach, *Une Morale sans moralisme*. Ferry, *Le Nouvel ordre écologique*. Finkielkraut, *L'Humanité perdue*. Levinas, *Entre nous* and various republications of earlier works. Lipovetsky, *Le Crépuscle du devoir*. Lyotard, *Moralités postmodernes*. Misrahi, *La Signification de l'éthique* and *Qu'est-ce que l'éthique?* Ricoeur, *Oneself as Another* and *The Just*. Sève, *Pour une critique de la raison bioéthique*. Todorov, *The Morals of History*, *Facing the Extreme*, and *Hope and Memory*.

7 Arendt, *The Origins of Totalitarianism*, 460–6.

8 Deleuze, *Nietzsche and Philosophy*, 44.

9 Jean Ayme, "Essai sur l'histoire de la psychothérapie institutionnelle," in Delion, ed., *Actualité de la psychothérapie institutionnelle*, 34.

10 See, for example, René Lourau's contrast of "instituted forms" and "instituting actions" and of "*social norms*" and "*social relations*." Lourau, *Analyse institutionnelle et pédagogie*. Castoriadis, *The Imaginary Institution of Society*.

11 Debbasch and Bourdon, *Les Associations*. Pellissier, *À but non lucratif*. Belorgey, *Cent ans de vie associative*. More generally, see Hirst, *Associative Democracy*.

12 Rosanvallon, *Le Modèle politique français*, 428. Debbasch and Bourdon, *Les Associations*, 5. Belorgey, *Cent ans de vie associative*, 23, 27.

13 One symptom was the emergence of the history *of* associations. See Agulhon, *Le Cercle dans la France bourgeoise* and "Vers une histoire des associations," *Esprit* 6 (1978).

14 Sheri Berman has suggested that associational democracy fed the weakness of the Weimar Republic and contributed to the rise of Hitlerism. Berman, "Civil Society and the Collapse of the Weimar Republic." Cf. her "Civil Society and Political Institutionalization," and Stefan-Ludwig Hoffman's thorough survey "Democracy and Associations in the Long Nineteenth Century."

15 Saint-Just, "Fragments sur les institutions républicaines," 142.

16 The comparison is an exercise in imagination and not homologous to the British/French divide: Thomas Hobbes was against the vacuum and Pascal for it.

17 Badiou, *Ethics*. Lecourt, *The Mediocracy*. Jameson, *A Singular Modernity*, 2, calls ethics one of philosophy's "hoariest subfields" and its revival a sign of the "regressions of the current age." Debray, *I.F., suite et fin*, 95–106, has condemned contemporary "moral narcissism."

Bibliography

ARCHIVES

Bibliothèque de documentation internationale contemporaine (University of Paris-X) (BDIC)
Daniel Guérin Archives
Gauche prolétarienne Archives
Bibliothèque Marguerite Durand
Bibliothèque nationale de France
Centre du documentation of the Mouvement français pour le planning familial
Editions Grasset
Institut National d'Audiovisuel
Institut Mémoires de l'édition contemporaine (IMEC)
Michel Foucault Archives (including Groupe d'information sur les prisons (GIP) Archives)
Félix Guattari Archives
Personal papers of Lianne Mozère

PERIODICALS

Actuel Marx
American Behavioral Scientist
American Historical Review
Anaïs portugéses de psichuiatria
Annals of the American Academy of Political and Social Science
Année sociologique
APL *Dossier*
APL *Informations*

L'Arc
Behavioral Science
Bulletin JR Jeunesse révolutionnaire
Bulletin Législatif Dalloz
Cahiers de la Gauche prolétarienne
Cahiers prolétariens
Canadian Review of Comparative Literature
La Cause du peuple
La Cause du peuple–J'Accuse
Change
Combat
Le Comité d'action des prisonniers: journal des prisonniers
Communications
Contemporary French Civilization
Courrier de parlement
Critical Inquiry
Critique
La Croix
Cultures et conflits
Le Débat
Défense Active
Diacritics
Discourse
Encyclopaedie Universalis
Esprit
L'Express
Le Figaro
Le Figaro-Dimanche
France catholique
France nouvelle
Frankfurter Rundschau
French Historical Studies
The Gay & Lesbian Review
L'Histoire
L'Humanité
L'Humanité-Dimanche
L'Information psychiatrique
Informations Hachette
International Journal of Cultural Studies
J'Accuse

Journal de Genève
The Journal of Modern History
Journal officiel de la République Française
Journal of Politics
Krisis: Tijdschrift voor filosofie
Leftwright Intervention
Lettre internationale
Libération
Libre
Lutte Ouvrière
Le Magazine littéraire
Marge
Le Matin
Minuit
Le Monde
Mouvement des radicaux de gauche
La Nef
Négation
New Left Review
The New York Times
Le Nouvel Observateur
Les Nouvelles littéraires
Panorama d'Aujourd'hui
Paradoxes
Partisans
Politique-hebdo
Pouvoirs
La Presse de Tunisie
Psychiatrie française
Psychothérapie institutionnelle
La Quinzaine littéraire
Le Quotidien de Paris
Recherches
Recherches universitaires
Réforme
Revue des deux mondes
Revue française de science politique
Rouge
Royaliste
Salmagundi

Secours rouge: journal du Secours rouge
Semiotext(e)
Sexpol
Le Spectacle du Monde
Studies
Tages Anzeiger Magazin
Tel Quel
Telos
Témoignage chrétien
Tempi moderni
Les Temps modernes
Theory, Culture & Society
Thesis Eleven
Tout!
L'Unité
La Voix du Nord
World Politics

BOOKS AND ARTICLES

Abraham, Henry J. *The Judicial Process: An Introductory Analysis of the Courts of the United States, England, and France*. 6th ed. New York: Oxford University Press, 1993.

Afary, Janet, and Kevin B. Anderson. *Foucault and the Iranian Revolution: Gender and the Seducations of Islam*. Chicago: University of Chicago Press, 2005.

Agulhon, Maurice. *Le Cercle dans la France bourgeoise, 1810–1848*. Paris: Armand Colin, 1977.

– "Vers une histoire des associations." *Esprit* 6 (1978).

Allwood, Gill. *French Feminisms: Gender and Violence in Contemporary Theory*. London: UCL Press, 1998.

Althusser, Louis. *The Future Lasts Forever*. Trans. Richard Veasey. New York: New Press, 1993. Originally *L'Avenir dure longtemps, suivi de Les Faits* (Paris: Stock/IMEC, 1992).

Anderson, Perry. *The Origins of Postmodernity*. London: Verso, 1998. Reprint, 2002.

Anderson, Thomas C. *Sartre's Two Ethics: From Authenticity to Integral Humanity*. Chicago: Open Court, 1993.

L'Antipsychiatrie. Special Issue of *La Nef* 42 (January–May 1971).

Arendt, Hannah. *The Origins of Totalitarianism*. New York: Harcourt, 1951; new ed., 1973.

– *On Violence*. New York: Harcourt, 1970.

Armstong, Timothy, J., ed. *Michel Foucault, Philosopher*. Trans. Timothy J. Armstrong. Intro. Georges Canguilhem. New York: Routledge, 1992. Originally *Michel Foucault, philosophe*, ed. François Ewald (Paris: Seuil, 1989).

Aron, Raymond. *The Elusive Revolution: Anatomy of a Student Revolt*. Trans. Gordon Clough. New York: Praeger, 1969. Originally *La Révolution introuvable* (Paris: Fayard, 1968).

Arthur, Susan Paige. "Unfinished Projects: Decolonization and the Philosophy of Jean-Paul Sartre, 1945–1980." PhD diss., University of California, Berkeley, 2004.

Artières, Philippe, Laurent Quéro, and Michelle Zancarini-Fournel, eds. *Le Groupe d'information sur les prisons: archives d'une lutte, 1970–1972*. Postface Daniel Defert. Paris: Institut Mémoires de l'édition contemporaine, 2003.

Association Choisir/La Cause des femmes. *Viol: le procès d'Aix*. Paris: Gallimard, 1978.

Association la Griffonne [Martine Bosshart, et al.]. *Douze ans de femmes au quotidien: douze ans de luttes féministes en France, 1970–1981*. Paris: La Griffonne, 1981.

Aubral, François, and Xavier Delcourt. *Contre la nouvelle philosophie*. Paris: Gallimard, 1977.

Audier, Serge. *Tocqueville retrouvé: genèse et enjeux du renouveau tocquevillien français*. Paris: Librairie Philosophique J. Vrin, 2004.

Audry, Colette. *Les Militants et leurs morales*. Paris: Flammarion, 1976.

Auron, Yaïr. *Les Juifs d'extrême-gauche en mai 68: une génération révolutionnaire marquée par la Shoah*. Paris: Albin Michel, 1998.

Axelos, Kostas. *Pour une éthique problématique*. Paris: Minuit, 1972.

Badinter, Elisabeth. *XY: On Masculine Identity*. Trans. Lynda Davis. New York: Columbia University Press, 1995. Originally *XY: de l'identité masculine* (Paris: Odile Jacob, 1992).

Badiou, Alain. *Ethics: An Essay on the Understanding of Evil*. Trans. Peter Hallward. London: Verso, 2001. Originally *L'Ethique: essai sur la conscience du Mal* (Paris: Hatier, 1993).

Baker, Peter. *Deconstruction and the Ethical Turn*. Gainesville, Florida: University Press of Florida, 1995.

Barthes, Roland. "Writing the Event." In *The Rustle of Language*. Trans. Richard Howard. New York: Hill and Wang, 1986. Originally "L'Ecriture de l'événement," in *Mai 68: la prise de la parole*, Special Issue of *Communications* (1968). Reprint, in *Le Bruissement de la langue* (Paris: Seuil, 1984).

Barton, Russell. *Institutional Neurosis*. Bristol: John Wright and Sons, 1959.

Basaglia, Franco. *L'Institution en négation: rapport sur l'hôpital psychiatrique de Gorizia*. Trans. Louis Bonalumi. Paris: Seuil, 1970. Originally *L'istituzione negata* (Turin: G. Einaudi, 1968).

Basset, Monique, Anne-Elisabeth Bertheau, Catherine Clément, and Elisabeth de Fontenay, et al. *Ecrits pour Jankélévitch*. Paris: Flammarion, 1978.

Bataille, Georges. *The Accursed Share: An Essay on General Economy*. Trans. Robert Hurley. 2 vols. New York: Zone, 1988–91. Originally *La Part maudite: essai d'économie générale*. vol. 1, *La Consumation* (Paris: Minuit, 1949). Reprint, with *La Notion de dépense*, 1967.

Bateson, Gregory, et al. "Toward a Theory of Schizophrenia." *Behavioral Science* 1, no. 3 (October 1956).

Baudrillard, Jean. *La Gauche divine: chroniques des années 1977–1984*. Paris: Grasset, 1985.

– *La Transparence du mal: essai sur les phénomènes extrêmes*. Paris: Galilée, 1990.

Bauman, Zygmunt. *Postmodern Ethics*. Oxford: Blackwell, 1993.

– *Life in Fragments: Essays in Postmodern Morality*. Oxford: Blackwell, 1995.

Beaumont, Gustave de, and Alexis de Tocqueville. *On the Penitentiary System in the United States and its Application in France*. Trans. and Intro. Francis Lieber. New York: A.M. Kelley, 1833; 1970. Originally *Du système pénitentiaire aux Etats-Unis et de son application en France, suivi d'un appendice sur les colonies pénales et de notes statistiques* (Paris: H. Fournier jeune, 1833).

Beauvoir, Simone de. *Adieux: A Farewell to Sartre*. Trans. Patrick O'Brien. New York: Pantheon, 1984. Originally *La Cérémonie des adieux* (Paris: Gallimard, 1981).

– *All Said and Done*. Trans. Patrick O'Brien. New York: Putnam, 1974. Originally *Tout compte fait* (Paris: Gallimard, 1972).

– *The Ethics of Ambiguity*. Trans. Bernard Frechtman. New York: Carol Publishing Group, 1994. Originally *Pour une morale de l'ambiguïté* (Paris: Gallimard, 1947).

Behnke, Kerstin. "Fragments, Not Wholes: Antinomian Thoughts in 'Literary Studies.'" *Canadian Review of Comparative Literature* 26, no. 3 (2001).

Bel, Monique. *Maurice Clavel*. Paris: Bayard, 1992.

Bell, Daniel. *The Cultural Contradictions of Capitalism*. New York: Basic Books, 1976.

Belorgey, Jean-Michel. *Cent ans de vie associative*. Paris: Presses de Sciences Politiques, 2000.

Bénéton, Philippe, and Jean Touchard. "Les Interprétations de la crise de mai-juin 1968." *Revue française de science politique* 20, no. 3 (June 1970).

Benoist, Jean-Marie. *Marx est mort*. Paris: Gallimard, 1970.

– *La Révolution structurale*. Paris: Grasset, 1975.
– *Tyrannie du Logos*. Paris: Minuit, 1975.
– *Pavane pour une Europe défunte*. Paris: Hallier, 1976.
Bensaïd, Daniel, and Henri Weber. *Mai 1968: une répétition générale*. Paris: Maspero, 1968.
Beran, David. *Early British Romanticism, the Frankfurt School, and French Post-Structuralism: In the Wake of Failed Revolution*. New York: P. Lang, 2001.
Berman, Art. *From the New Criticism to Deconstruction: The Reception of Structuralism and Post-Structuralism*. Urbana, Illinois: University of Illinois Press, 1988.
Berman, Marshall. *All That Is Solid Melts into Air: The Experience of Modernity*. New York: Simon & Schuster, 1982.
Berman, Paul. *A Tale of Two Utopias: The Political Journey of the Generation of 1968*. New York: Norton, 1996.
Berman, Sheri. "Civil Society and the Collapse of the Weimar Republic." *World Politics* 49, no. 3 (April 1997).
– "Civil Society and Political Institutionalization." *American Behavioral Scientist* 40, no. 5 (1997).
Besançon, Julien, ed. *"Les Murs ont la parole": journal mural, Mai 68: Sorbonne, Odéon, Nanterre, etc*. Paris: Claude Tchou, 1968.
Bibliothèque de documentation internationale contemporaine. *Mémoires de 68: guide des sources d'une histoire à faire*. Foreword Michelle Perrot. Paris: BDIC/Verdier, 1993.
Blond, Georges. "L'Antipsychiatrie, le réel, l'imaginaire et le symbolique." Thèse de médecine, Université de Paris–VI, 1973.
Boggio, Philippe. *Bernard-Henri Lévy: une vie*. Paris: Table Ronde, 2005.
Bogue, Ronald. *Deleuze and Guattari*. London: Routledge, 1989.
Boltanski, Luc. *Distant Suffering: Morality, Media, Politics*. Trans. Graham Burchell. Cambridge: Cambridge University Press, 1999. Originally *La Souffrance à distance: morale humanitaire, médias et politique* (Paris: Métailié, 1993).
Bonnell, Victoria E., and Lynn Hunt, eds. *Beyond the Cultural Turn*. Berkeley: University of California Press, 1999.
Bonnemaison, Gilbert. *La Modernisation du service public pénitentiaire: rapport au Premier Ministre et au Garde des Sceaux, Ministre de la Justice*. Paris: Ministère de la Justice, 1989.
Bouillon, Martine. *Viol d'anges: pédophilie: un magistrat contre la loi de silence*. Paris: Calmann-Lévy, 1997.
Boukhari, Ahmed. *Le Secret: Ben Barka et le Maroc: un ancien agent des services spéciaux parle*. Neuilly-sur-Seine: Lafon, 2002.

Boullant, François. *Michel Foucault et les prisons*. Paris: Presses universitaires de France, 2003.

– "1974: 'l'affaire Mirval.'" In *Prison et résistances politiques: le grondement de la bataille*. Special Issue of *Cultures et conflits* 55 (2004).

Bourdieu, Pierre. *Masculine Domination*. Trans. Richard Nice. Stanford: Stanford University Press, 2001. Originally *La Domination masculine* (Paris: Seuil, 1998).

Bourg, Julian. "Hello to All That: Rescuing May 1968." *French Cultural Studies* 14, no. 1 (February 2002).

– "Les Contributions accidentelles du marxisme au renouveau des droits de l'homme en France dans les années 1970." In *Les Libéralismes au regard de l'histoire*. Special Issue of *Actuel Marx* 32 (September 2002).

– ed. *After the Deluge: New Perspectives on the Intellectual and Cultural History of Postwar France* (Lanham, Maryland: Lexington, 2004).

– "The Red Guards of Paris: French Student Maoism of the 1960s." *History of European Ideas* 31, no. 4 (2005).

Bourges, Hervé, et al. *The Student Revolt: The Activists Speak*. Trans. B.R. Brewster. London: Panther, 1968. Originally *La Révolte étudiante: les animateurs parlent* (Paris: Seuil, 1968).

Bourseiller, Christophe. *Les Maoïstes: la folle histoire des grades rouges français*. Paris: Plon, 1996.

Bouscasse, Sylvie, and Denis Bourgeois, eds. *Faut-il brûler les nouveaux philosophes? le dossier du "procès."* Paris: Nouvelles Editions Oswald, 1978.

Bouveresse, Jacques. *Wittgenstein: la rime et la raison: science, éthique et esthétique*. Paris: Minuit, 1973.

Brownmiller, Susan. *Le Viol*. Foreword Benoîte Groult. Trans. Anne Villelaur. Paris: Stock, 1976. Originally *Against Our Will: Men, Women, and Rape* (New York: Simon & Schuster, 1975).

Buck-Morss, Susan. *The Dialectics of Seeing: Walter Benjamin and the Arcades Project*. Cambridge, Massachusetts: MIT Press, 1989.

Burke, Peter. *The French Historical Revolution: The Annales School, 1929–1989*. Stanford: Stanford University Press, 1991.

Camus, Albert. *The Rebel: An Essay on Man in Revolt*. Trans. Anthony Bower. New York: Knopf, 1984. Originally *L'Homme révolté* (Paris: Gallimard, 1951).

Canguilhem, Georges. *The Normal and the Pathological*. Trans. Carolyn R. Fawcett. Intro. Michel Foucault. New York: Zone, 1989. Originally "Essai sur quelques problèmes concernant le normal et le pathologique," Thèse de médecine, Université de Strasbourg (Clermont-Ferrand: La Montagne, 1943). Reprint, with additions, *Le Normal et le pathologique* (Paris: Presses universitaires de France, 1966).

Canto-Sperber, Monique. "Pour la philosophie morale." *Le Débat* 72 (November–December 1992).
– *L'Inquiétude morale et la vie humaine*. Paris: Presses universitaires de France, 2001.
– ed. *Dictionnaire d'éthique et de philosophie morale*. 3rd ed. Paris: Presses universitaires de France, 2001.
Capdevielle, Jacques, and René Mouriaux. *Mai 68: l'entre-deux de la modernité: histoire de trente ans*. Paris: Presses de la Fondation nationale des sciences politiques, 1988.
Cariou, Marie. *Freud et le désir*. Paris: Presses universitaires de France, 1973.
Casamayor [Serge Fuster]. *Où sont les coupables?* Paris: Seuil, 1953.
– *Les Juges*. Paris: Seuil, 1956.
– *Combats pour la justice*. Paris: Seuil, 1968.
– *La Justice pour tous*. Paris: Flammarion, 1969.
– *La Police*. Paris: Gallimard, 1973.
Castel, Robert. *Le Psychanalysme*. Paris: Maspero, 1973.
– *La Gestion des risques: de l'anti-psychiatrie à l'après-psychanalyse*. Paris: Minuit, 1981.
Castoriadis, Cornelius. "The Diversionists." Trans. Dorothy Gehrke. *Telos* 33 (fall 1977). Originally published in *Le Nouvel Observateur* (20 June 1977).
– *The Imaginary Institution of Society*. Trans. Kathleen Blamey. Cambridge, Massachusetts: MIT Press, 1987. Reprint, 1998. Originally *L'Institution imaginaire de la société* (Paris: Seuil, 1975).
– "The Ethicists' New Clothes." In *World in Fragments: Writings on Politics, Society, Psychoanalysis, and the Imagination*. Ed. and trans. David Ames Curtis. Stanford: Stanford University Press, 1997. Originally "Le Cache-misère de l'éthique," *Lettre internationale* 37 (summer 1993). Reprint, in *Les Carrefours du labyrinthe*. vol. 4, *La Montée de l'insignifiance* (Paris: Seuil, 1996).
Cauchard, Paul. *Force et sagesse du désir: une analyse de l'éros*. Paris: Fayard, 1972.
Centre d'études et de recherches marxistes. *Morale et société: semaine de la pensée marxiste, 16–22 janvier 1974*. Paris: Editions sociales, 1974.
Centre d'étude, de recherche et de formation institutionnelle. *L'Institutionalisation des collectifs de travail: monographie sur la clinique de La Borde*. vol. 1, *Présentation générale de la recherche*. Paris: CERFI, 1974.
Certeau, Michel de. *The Capture of Speech and Other Political Writings*. Ed. Luce Giard. Trans. Tom Conley. Minneapolis: University of Minnesota Press, 1997. Originally *La Prise de parole: pour une nouvelle culture* (Paris: Desclée de Brouwer, 1968). Reprint, *La Prise de parole, et autres écrits politiques*. Ed. Luce Giard (Paris: Seuil, 1994).

C'est demain la veille: entretiens [de journalistes d'Actuel] avec Michel Foucault, Herbert Marcuse, et al. Paris: Seuil, 1973.

Changer la vie: programme de gouvernement du Parti Socialiste. Foreword François Mitterrand. Paris: Flammarion, 1972.

Chanoit, Pierre F. *La Psychothérapie institutionnelle.* Paris: Presses universitaires de France, 1995.

Charrière, Henri. *Papillon.* Paris: Robert Laffont, 1969.

Chasseguet-Smirgel, Janine, ed. *Les Chemins de l'anti-Oedipe.* Paris: Bibliothèque de Psychologie Clinique, 1974.

Châtelet, François, ed. *Histoire de la philosophie.* 8 vols. Paris: Hachette, 1972–73.

Chauvin, Remy. *Ethology: The Biological Study of Animal Behavior.* Trans. Joyce Diamanti. New York: International Universities Press, 1977. Originally *L'Ethologie: étude biologique du comportement animal* (Paris: Presses universitaires de France, 1975).

Chiama, Jean, and Jean-François Soulet. *Histoire de la dissidence: opposition et révolte en URSS et dans les démocraties populaires de la mort de Staline à nos jours.* Paris: Seuil, 1982.

Christofferson, Michael Scott. *French Intellectuals Against the Left: The Anti-Totalitarian Moment of the 1970s in French Intellectual Politics.* New York: Berghahn, 2004.

Cinquante ans d'organisation des institutions psychiatriques. Special Issue of *Psychiatrie française* 28, no. 1 (March 1997).

Clavel, Maurice. *Qui est aliéné?* Paris: Flammarion, 1970.

– *Ce que je crois.* Paris: Grasset, 1975.

– *Dieu est Dieu, nom de Dieu.* Paris: Grasset, 1976.

– *Nous l'avons tous tué ou "Ce juif de Socrate!..".* Paris: Seuil, 1977.

– *Deux siècles chez Lucifer.* Paris: Seuil, 1978.

– *Critique de Kant.* Intro. Jean-Toussaint Desanti. Paris: Flammarion, 1980.

Clavel, Maurice, and Philippe Sollers. *Délivrance: entretiens recueillis par Jacques Paugam dans le cadre de son émission "Parti pris" sur France-Culture.* Paris: Seuil, 1977.

Clouscard, Michel. *Néo-fascisme et idéologie du désir: les tartuffes de la révolution.* Paris: Denoël, 1973. Reprint, *Néo-fascisme et idéologie du désir: genèse du libéralisme liberataire.* Bordeaux: Castor Astral, 1999.

Code Pénal. Paris: Dalloz, 1967–68.

Cohen, Richard A., and James L. Marsh, eds. *Ricoeur as Another: The Ethics of Subjectivity.* Albany, New York: State University of New York Press, 2002.

Cohen, Stanley. *Folk Devils and Moral Panics: The Creation of the Mods and Rockers.* London: MacGibbon and Kee, 1972.

Cohen-Solal, Annie. *Sartre: A Life*. Ed. Norman MacAfee. Trans. Anna Cancogni. New York: Pantheon, 1987. Originally *Sartre* (Paris: Gallimard, 1985).

Coldrey, Barry M. "The Sexual Abuse of Children: The Historical Perspective." *Studies* 85, no. 340 (winter 1996).

Colebrook, Claire. *Ethics and Representation: From Kant to Post-Structuralism*. Edinburgh: Edinburgh University Press, 1999.

Comité d'action santé. *Médecine*. Paris: Maspero, 1968.

Comité de soutien aux détenus (Bordeaux) and Comité pour la liberté et contre la répression (Paris). *Huit détenus politiques de Bordeaux déclarent, Prison de la Santé, 27 mai 1969*. Bordeaux: Comité de soutien aux détenus (Bordeaux) and Comité pour la liberté et contre la répression (Paris), 1969.

Comité pour la vérité sur l'affaire Ben Barka. *L'Affaire Ben Barka*. Postface Maurice Clavel. Paris: [Témoignage chrétien], 1966.

– *Enseignements et lacunes du premier procès*. Paris: [Témoignage chrétien], 1967.

– *La Mort de Mehdi Ben Barka: un dossier à rouvrir*. Paris: Le Comité pour la vérité sur l'affaire Ben Barka, 1973.

Comité vérité Toul. *La Révolte de la Centrale Ney, 5–13 décembre 1971*. Paris: Gallimard, 1973.

Commission de révision du Code pénal. *Avant-projet définitif de code pénal (avril 1978)*. Paris: Documentation française, 1978.

Comte-Sponville, André. *Le Mythe d'Icare: traité du désespoir et de la béatitude*. Paris: Presses universitaires de France, 1984.

Conche, Marcel. *Le Fondement de la morale*. Villers-sur-Mer: De Mégare, 1982.

Cooper, David. *Psychiatrie et antipsychiatrie*. Trans. Michel Braudeau. Paris: Seuil, 1970. Originally *Psychiatry and Anti-Psychiatry* (London: Tavistock, 1967).

– *Mort de la famille*. Trans. Ferial Drosso-Bellivier. Paris: Seuil, 1972. Originally *The Death of the Family* (New York: Pantheon, 1970).

Copley, Antony. *Sexual Moralities in France, 1780–1980: New Ideas on the Family, Divorce, and Homosexuality*. New York: Routledge, 1989.

Cressole, Michel. *Deleuze*. Paris: Editions universitaires, 1973.

Critchley, Simon. *The Ethics of Deconstruction: Derrida and Levinas*. Oxford: Blackwell, 1992.

– *Ethics, Politics, Subjectivity: Essays on Derrida, Levinas, and Contemporary French Thought*. London: Verso, 1999.

Cuau, Bernard. *L'Affaire Mirval ou Comment le récit abolit le crime*. Forewords Michel Foucault and Pierre Vidal-Naquet. Paris: Presses d'Aujourd'hui, 1976.

Cummins, Eric. *The Rise and Fall of California's Radical Prison Movement*. Stanford: Stanford University Press, 1994.

Dansette, Adrien. *Mai 1968*. Paris: Plon, 1971.

Daniel, Jean. *La Suite appartient à d'autres*. Paris: Stock, 1979.

Daumézon, Georges, and Philippe Koechlin. "La Psychothérapie institutionnelle française contemporaine." *Anaïs portugéses de psichuiatria* 4, no. 4 (1952).

Davis, Todd F., and Kenneth Womack, eds. *Mapping the Ethical Turn: A Reader in Ethics, Culture, and Literary Theory*. Charlottesville, Virginia: University Press of Virginia, 2001.

Debbasch, Charles, and Jacques Bourdon. *Les Associations*. 3rd ed. Paris: Presses universitaires de France, 1990.

Debray, Régis. "Springtime Weepers." Trans. Dorothy Gehrke. *Telos* 33 (fall 1977). Originally "Les Pleureuses du printemps," *Le Nouvel Observateur* (13 June 1977).

– "A Modest Contribution to the Rites and Ceremonies of the Tenth Anniversary." Trans. John Howe. *New Left Review* 115 (May–June 1979). Originally published in *Modeste contribution aux discours et cérémonies officielles du dixième anniversaire* (Paris: Maspero, 1978).

– *Teachers, Writers, Celebrities: The Intellectuals of Modern France*. Intro. Francis Mulhern. Trans. David Macey. London: NLB, 1981. Originally *Le Pouvoir intellectuel en France* (Paris: Ramsay, 1979).

– *I.F., suite et fin*. Paris: Gallimard, 2000.

Dedijer, Vladimir, and Arlette Elkaïm-Sartre, eds. *Tribunal Russell: le jugement de Stockholm*. Paris: Gallimard, 1967.

Defert, Daniel, and Jaques Donzelot. "La Charnière des prisons." *Le Magazine littéraire* 112–13 (May 1976).

Delacampagne, Christian. *L'Antipsychiatrie: les voies du sacré*. Paris: Grasset, 1974.

Deleuze, Gilles. "The Schizophrenic and Language: Surface and Depth in Lewis Carroll and Antoine Artaud." In Josué Harari, ed., *Textual Strategies: Perspectives in Poststructuralist Criticism*. Ithaca, New York: Cornell University Press, 1979. Originally "Le Schizophrène et le mot," *Critique* 255–6 (August–September 1968).

– *Nietzsche and Philosophy*. Trans. Hugh Tomlinson. New York: Columbia University Press, 1983. Originally *Nietzsche et la philosophie* (Paris: Presses universitaires de France, 1962).

– *Kant's Critical Philosophy: The Doctrine of the Faculties*. Trans. Hugh Tomlinson and Barbara Habberjam. Minneapolis: University of Minnesota Press, 1984. Originally *La Philosophie critique de Kant: doctrine des facultés* (Paris: Presses universitaires de France, 1963).

– "The Intellectual and Politics: Foucault and the Prison." Interview by Paul Rabinow and Keith Gandal. *History of the Present* 2 (spring 1986). Reprint, "Foucault and Prison," in Deleuze, *Two Regimes of Madness*.

– *Bergsonism*. Trans. Hugh Tomlinson and Barbara Habberjam. New York: Zone, 1988. Originally *Le Bergsonisme* (Paris: Presses universitaires de France, 1966).
– *Périclès et Verdi: la philosophie de François Châtelet*. Paris: Minuit, 1988.
– *Spinoza: Practical Philosophy*. Trans. Robert Hurley. San Francisco: City Lights, 1988. Originally *Spinoza: philosophie pratique* (Paris: Minuit, 1981). Adapted from *Spinoza: textes choisis* (Paris: Presses universitaires de France, 1970).
– *Expressionism in Philosophy: Spinoza*. Trans. Martin Joughin. New York: Zone, 1990. Originally *Spinoza et le problème de l'expression* (Paris: Minuit, 1968).
– *The Logic of Sense*. Ed. Constantin Boundas. Trans. Mark Lester and Charles Stivale. New York: Columbia University Press, 1990. Originally *Logique du sens* (Paris: Minuit, 1969).
– "Lettre-préface." Foreword to *Sahara: l'esthétique de Gilles Deleuze*, by Mireille Buydens. Paris: Librairie Philosophique J. Vrin, 1990.
– *Empiricism and Subjectivity: An Essay on Hume's Theory of Human Nature*. Trans. Constantin V. Boundas. New York: Columbia University Press, 1991. Originally *Empirisme et subjectivité: essai sur la Nature humaine selon Hume* (Paris: Presses universitaires de France, 1953).
– *The Deleuze Reader*. Ed. and Intro. Constantin V. Boundas. New York: Columbia University Press, 1993.
– *Difference and Repetition*. New York: Columbia University Press, 1994. Trans. Paul Patton. Originally *Différence et répétition* (Paris: Presses universitaires de France, 1968).
– *Negotiations, 1972–1990*. Trans. Martin Joughin. New York: Columbia University Press, 1995. Originally *Pourparlers, 1972–1990* (Paris: Minuit, 1972).
– *Essays Critical and Clinical*. Intro. Daniel W. Smith. Trans. Daniel W. Smith and Michael A. Greco. Minneapolis: University of Minnesota Press, 1996. Originally *Critique et clinique* (Paris: Minuit, 1993).
– "On the New Philosophers and a More General Problem." Trans. Bertrand Augst. *Discourse* 20, no. 3 (fall 1998). Originally "A propos des nouveaux philosophes et d'un problème plus général," *Supplément* to *Minuit* 24 (May 1977).
– *Proust and Signs: The Complete Text*. Trans. Richard Howard. Minneapolis: University of Minnesota Press, 2000. Originally *Marcel Proust et les signes* (Paris: Presses universitaires de France, 1964; 2nd rev. ed. 1970; 3rd rev. ed. 1976).
– *Desert Islands and Other Texts 1953–1974*. Ed. David Lapoujade. Trans. Michael Taormina, et al. Los Angeles: Semiotext(e), 2004. Originally *L'Ile désert et autres textes: textes et entretiens 1953–1974* (Paris: Minuit, 2002).

– *Two Regimes of Madness: Texts and Interviews 1975–1995*. Ed. David Lapoujade. Trans. Ames Hodges and Michael Taormina. Los Angeles: Semiotext(e), 2006. Originally *Deux régimes de fous: textes et entretiens 1975–1995* (Paris: Minuit, 2003).

Deleuze, Gilles, and Gérard Fromanger. *Fromanger: le peintre et le modèle*. Paris: Baudard Alvarez, 1973.

Deleuze, Gilles, and Félix Guattari. "Le Synthèse disjunctive." In *Klossowski*. Special Issue of *L'Arc* 43 (1970).

– *Anti-Oedipus: Capitalism and Schizophrenia*. Trans. Robert Hurley, Mark Seem, and Helen R. Lane. Foreword Michel Foucault. New York: Viking, 1977. Originally *Capitalisme et schizophrénie*. vol. 1, *L'Anti-Oedipe* (Paris: Minuit, 1972; 2nd ed. 1973).

– *Kafka: Toward a Minor Literature*. Foreword Réda Bensmaïa. Trans. Dana Polan. Minneapolis: University of Minnesota Press, 1986. Originally *Kafka: pour une littérature mineure* (Paris: Minuit, 1975).

– *A Thousand Plateaus: Capitalism and Schizophrenia*. Trans. Brian Massumi. Minneapolis: University of Minnesota Press, 1987. Originally *Capitalisme et schizophrénie*. vol. 2, *Mille plateaux* (Paris: Minuit, 1980).

– *What Is Philosophy?* Trans. Hugh Tomlinson and Graham Burchell. New York: Columbia University Press, 1994. Originally *Qu'est-ce que la philosophie?* (Paris: Minuit, 1991).

Deleuze, Gilles, and Claire Parnet. *Dialogues*. Trans. Hugh Tomlinson and Barbara Habberjam. New York: Columbia University Press, 1987. Originally *Dialogues* (Paris: Flammarion, 1977).

Deleuze, Gilles, and Léopold Sacher-Masoch. *Masochism*. Trans. Jean McNeil. New York: George Braziller, 1971. Originally *Présentation de Sacher-Masoch* (Paris: Minuit, 1967; reprint, Paris: 10/18, 1974).

Delion, Pierre, ed. *Actualité de la psychothérapie institutionnelle*. Vigneux: Matrice, 1994.

Derbyshire, Ian. *Politics in France: From Giscard to Mitterrand*. Cambridge: Chambers, 1987.

Descombes, Vincent. *Modern French Philosophy*. Trans. L. Scott-Fox and J.M. Harding. Cambridge: Cambridge University Press, 1980. Originally *Le Même et l'autre: quarante-cinq ans de philosophie française (1933–1978)* (Paris: Minuit, 1979).

Dews, Peter. *Logics of Disintegration: Post-Structuralist Theory and the Claims of Critical Theory*. London: Verso, 1987.

Dollé, Jean-Paul. *Le Désir de la révolution*. Paris: Grasset, 1972.

– *Voie d'accès au plaisir: la métaphysique*. Paris: Grasset, 1974.

– *Haïne de la pensée*. Paris: Hallier, 1976.

– *L'Odeur de la France*. Paris: Grasset, 1977.

Domenach, Jean-Marie. "Le Grande polémique." In *Le Dieu de Clavel*. Special Dossier in *Esprit* (July–August 1976).

– *Enquête sur les idées contemporaines*. Paris: Seuil, 1981.

– *Une Morale sans moralisme*. Paris: Flammarion, 1992.

Dosse, François. *New History in France: The Triumph of the Annales*. Trans. Peter V. Conroy, Jr. Urbana, Illinois: University of Illinois Press, 1994. Originally *L'Histoire en miettes: des "Annales" à la "nouvelle histoire"* (Paris: La Découverte, 1997).

– *History of Structuralism*. vol. 1, *The Rising Sign*. vol. 2, *The Sign Sets, 1967–Present*. Trans. Deborah Glassman. Minneapolis: University of Minnesota Press, 1997. Originally *Histoire du structuralisme*. vol. 1, *Le Champ du signe*, and vol. 2, *Le Chant du cygne, de 1967 à nos jours* (Paris: La Découverte, 1991–92).

– *Paul Ricoeur: les sens d'une vie*. Paris: La Découverte, 1997.

Dray, Julien. *La Guerre qu'il ne fallait pas faire: la génération morale se rebiffe*. Paris: Albin Michel, 1991.

Dreyfus-Armand, Geneviève, Robert Frank, Marie-Françoise Lévy, and Michelle Zancarini-Fournel, eds. *Les Années 68: le temps de la contestation*. Bruxelles: Complexe, 2000.

Duchen, Claire. *Feminism in France: From May '68 to Mitterrand*. London: Routledge, 1986.

Dumas, Alexandre. *The Count of Monte Cristo*. New York: Modern Library, 1996. Originally *Le Comte de Monte-Cristo* (Paris: Pétion, 1845).

Duvert, Tony. *Le Bon sexe illustré*. Paris: Robert Laffont, 1974.

– *L'Enfant au masculin*. Paris: Minuit, 1980.

Eisenstadt, S.N. "Generational Conflict and Intellectual Antinomianism." *Annals of the American Academy of Political and Social Science* 395 (May 1971).

Elkaïm, Mony. *Réseau alternative à la psychiatrie: collectif international: textes*. Paris: Union générale d'éditions, 1977.

Enfances. Special Issue of *Sexpol* 9 (October 1976).

Entretiens avec Le Monde. vol. 1, *Philosophies*. Intro. Christian Delacampagne. Paris: La Découverte/Le Monde, 1984.

Epistémon [Dider Anzieu]. *Ces idées qui ont ébranlé la France*. Paris: Fayard, 1968.

Eribon, Didier. *Michel Foucault*. Trans. Betsy Wing. Cambridge, Massachussetts: Harvard University Press, 1991. Originally *Michel Foucault* (Paris: Flammarion, 1989).

– ed. *L'Infréquentable Michel Foucault: renouveaux de la pensée critique: actes du colloque Centre Georges Pompidou 21–22 juin 2000*. Paris: EPEL, 2001.

Executive Committee of the IRA [International Red Aid]. *Ten Years of International Red Aid in Resolutions and Documents, 1922–1932*. n.d.: n.p.

Falconnet, Georges, and Nadine Lefaucheur. *La Fabrication des mâles*. Paris: Seuil, 1975.

Falk, Barbara J. *The Dilemmas of Dissidence in East-Central Europe: Citizen Intellectuals and Philosopher Kings*. Budapest: Central European University Press, 2003.

Falque, Edith. *Sortie de prison*. Paris: Editions et publications premières, 1971.

Fanon, Frantz. *The Wretched of the Earth*. Trans. Constance Farrington. Foreword Jean-Paul Sartre. New York: Grove Weidenfeld, 1991. Originally *Les Damnés de la terre* (Paris: Maspero, 1968).

Fargier, Marie-Odile. *Le Viol*. Paris: Grasset, 1976.

Farías, Víctor. *Heidegger and Nazism*. Eds. and foreword Joseph Margolis and Tom Rockmore. Trans. Paul Burrell, with Dominic Di Bernardi, and Gabriel R. Ricci. Philadelphia: Temple University Press, 1989. Originally *Heidegger et le nazisme* (Paris: Verdier, 1987).

Favard, Jean. *Les Prisons*. Paris: Gallimard, 1987.

Feenberg, Andrew, and Jim Freedman. *When Poetry Ruled the Streets: The French May Events of 1968*. Albany, New York: State University of New York Press, 2001.

Fehér, Ferenc, ed. *The French Revolution and the Birth of Modernity*. Berkeley: University of California Press, 1990.

Les Femmes s'entêtent. Special Issue of *Les Temps modernes* 333–4 (April–May 1974).

Ferinot, Jean. *8 h 15: de De Gaulle à Pompidou*. Paris: Plon, 1972.

Ferry, Luc. *Le Nouvel ordre écologique: l'arbre, l'animal et l'homme*. Paris: Grasset, 1992.

Ferry, Luc, and Alain Renault. *French Philosophy of the Sixties: An Essay on Antihumanism*. Trans. Mary Schnackenberg Cattani. Amherst: University of Massachusetts Press, 1990. Originally *La Pensée 68: essai sur l'anti-humanisme contemporain* (Paris: Gallimard, 1985).

ffrench, Patrick. *The Time of Theory: A History of* Tel Quel *(1960–1983)*. Oxford: Clarendon Press; New York: Oxford University Press, 1995.

Fields, A. Belden. *Trotskyism and Maoism: Theory and Practice in France and the United States*. New York: Autonomedia, 1988.

Finkielkraut, Alain. *La Sagesse de l'amour*. Paris: Gallimard, 1984.

– *The Imaginary Jew*. Trans. Kevin O'Neill and David Suchoff. Lincoln: University of Nebraska Press, 1994. Originally *Le Juif imaginaire* (Paris: Seuil, 1980).

– *L'Humanité perdue: essai sur le e siècle*. Paris: Seuil, 1996.

Finkielkraut, Alain, and Pascal Bruckner. *Le Nouveau désordre amoureux*. Paris: Seuil, 1977.

Fize, Michel. *Une Prison dans la ville...: histoire de la "prison-modèle" de la Santé: 2ème époque: 1914–1983*. Paris: Ministère de la Justice, 1983.

Flood, Christopher, and Nick Hewlett, eds. *Currents in Contemporary French Intellectual Life*. New York: St Martin's Press, 2000.

Folie pour folie. Special Issue of *Partisans* 62–3 (November–December 1972).

Foucault, Michel. *The Archaeology of Knowledge*. Trans. A.M. Sheridan Smith. New York: Pantheon, 1972. Originally *L'Archéologie du Savoir* (Paris: Gallimard, 1969).

– *Discipline and Punish: The Birth of the Prison*. Trans. Alan Sheridan and Allen Lane. London: Penguin, 1977. Originally *Surveiller et punir* (Paris: Gallimard, 1975).

– *The History of Sexuality, Volume 1: An Introduction*. Trans. Robert Hurley. New York: Pantheon, 1978. Originally *La Volonté de savoir* (Paris: Gallimard, 1976).

– "On Popular Justice: A Discussion with Maoists." In Foucault, *Power/Knowledge: Selected Interviews and Other Writings, 1972–1977*. Ed. Colin Gordon. Brighton, England: Harvester Press, 1980. Originally "Sur la justice populaire: débat avec les maos," *Les Temps modernes* 310 bis. (1972).

– *The Foucault Reader*. Ed. Paul Rabinow. New York: Pantheon, 1984.

– *The Use of Pleasure*. Volume 2 of *The History of Sexuality*. Trans. Robert Hurley. New York: Pantheon, 1985. Originally *L'Usage des plaisirs* (Paris: Gallimard, 1984).

– *The Care of the Self*. Volume 3 of *The History of Sexuality*. Trans. Robert Hurley. New York: Pantheon, 1986. Originally *Le Souci de soi* (Paris: Gallimard, 1984).

– *Madness and Civilization: A History of Insanity in the Age of Reason*. Part. trans. Richard Howard. New York: Random House, 1965; 1988. Originally *Folie et déraison: histoire de la folie à l'âge classique* (Paris: Plon, 1961).

– *Politics, Philosophy, Culture: Interviews and Other Writings, 1977–1984*. Ed. Lawrence D. Kritzman. Trans. Alan Sheridan, et al. New York: Routledge, 1988.

– *Foucault Live: Collected Interviews, 1961–1984*. Ed. Sylvère Lotringer. Trans. Lysa Hochroth and John Johnston. New York: Semiotext(e), 1989; 1996.

– *Résumé des cours, 1970–1982*. Paris: Julliard, 1989.

– *Dits et écrits*. Eds. Daniel Defert and François Ewald. 4 vols. Paris: Gallimard, 1994. Reprint, 2 vols. 2001.

– *Ethics: Subjectivity and Truth: The Essential Works of Michel Foucault, 1954–1984: Volume 1*. Ed. Paul Rabinow. Trans. Robert Hurley et al. New York: New Press, 1997. Originally published in *Dits et écrits*.

– *"Society Must Be Defended": Lectures at the Collège de France, 1975–1976.* Eds. Mauro Bertani and Alessandro Fontana. Trans. David Macey. New York: Picador, 2002. Originally *"Il faut défendre la société": cours au Collège de France, 1975–1976* (Paris: Gallimard/Seuil, 1997).

– *Abnormal: Lectures at the Collège de France, 1974–1975.* Eds. Valerio Marchetti and Antonella Salomani. Trans. Graham Burchell. New York: Picador, 2003. Originally *Les Anormaux: cours au Collège de France, 1974–1975* (Paris: Seuil/Gallimard, 1999).

Foucault, Michel, and Gilles Deleuze. "Intellectuals and Power." In Foucault, *Language, Counter-Memory, Practice: Selected Essays and Interviews.* Ed. and Intro. Donald F. Bouchard. Trans. Donald F. Bouchard and Sherry Simon. Ithaca, New York: Cornell University Press, 1977. Originally "Les Intellectuals et le pouvoir," in *Gilles Deleuze*, Special Issue of *L'Arc* 49 (1972).

Foucault, Michel, and the members of GIS. "Médecine et lutte de classes." *La Nef* 49 (October–December 1972).

Fourastié, Jean. *Les Trente glorieuses, ou la révolution invisible de 1946 à 1975.* Paris: Fayard, 1979.

Fourquet, François, and Lion Murard, eds. *Histoire de la psychiatrie de secteur, ou le secteur impossible?* Special Issue of *Recherches* 17 (1975; 2nd rev. ed. 1980).

Friedlander, Judith. *Vilna on the Seine: Jewish Intellectuals in France since 1968.* New Haven: Yale University Press, 1990.

Froment, Jean-Charles. *La République des surveillants de prison: ambiguïtés et paradoxes d'une politique pénitentiaire en France (1958–1998).* Paris: LGDJ, 1998.

Front homosexuel d'action révolutionnaire. *Rapport contre la normalité.* Paris: Champ Libre, 1971.

Furet, François. *Interpreting the French Revolution.* Trans. Elborg Forster. Cambridge: Cambridge University Press; Paris: Maison des sciences de l'homme, 1981. Originally *Penser la Révolution française* (Paris: Gallimard, 1978).

Furet, François, Antoine Liniers [Olivier Rolin], and Philippe Raynaud. *Terrorisme et démocratie.* Paris: Fayard, 1985.

Furet, François, and Mona Ozouf, eds. *A Critical Dictionary of the French Revolution.* Cambridge, Massachusetts: Harvard University Press, 1989. Originally *Dictionnaire critique de la Révolution française* (Paris: Flammarion, 1988).

Gachoud, François. *Maurice Clavel: du glaive à la foi.* Paris: Presses universitaires de France, 1982.

Gagey, Roland. *La Révolution sexuelle.* Paris: L.D., 1968.

Gallo, Max. "An Interview with André Glucksmann." Trans. Dorothy Gehrke. *Telos* 33 (fall 1977). Originally published in *L'Express* (18–24 July 1977).

Gallop, Jane. *Feminist Accused of Sexual Harassment*. Durham, North Carolina: Duke University Press, 1997.

Gannett, Lewis. "The Closet's Final Frontier." *The Gay & Lesbian Review* 7, no. 1 (31 January 2000).

Garber, Marjorie, Beatrice Hanssen, and Rebecca L. Walkowitz, eds. *The Turn to Ethics*. New York: Routledge, 2000.

Gauchet, Marcel. "Les Droits de l'homme n'est pas une politique." *Le Débat* 3 (July–August 1980).

Gauthier-Hamon, Corinne, and Roger Teboul. *Entre père et fils: la prostitution homosexuelle des garçons*. Paris: Presses universitaires de France, 1988.

Gavi, Philippe, Jean-Paul Sartre, and Pierre Victor [Benny Lévy]. *On a raison de se révolter*. Paris: Gallimard, 1974.

Gay, Peter. *Weimar Culture: The Outsider as Insider*. New York: Harper & Row, 1968.

Geismar, Alain, *Déclaration d'Alain Geismar: pourquoi nous combattons*. Paris: Maspero, 1970.

Geismar, Alain, Serge July, and Erlyn Morane. *Vers la guerre civile*. Paris: Editions et publications premières, 1969.

Genosko, Gary, ed. *Deleuze and Guattari: Critical Assessments of Leading Philosophers*. 3 vols. London: Routledge, 2001.

– *Félix Guattari: An Aberrant Introduction*. London: Continuum, 2002.

Geraci, Joseph, ed. *Dares to Speak: Historical and Contemporary Perspectives on Boy-Love*. Swaffham, Norfolk: The Gay Men's Press, 1997.

Gide, André. *Retour de l* . Paris: Gallimard, 1936.

Girard, Jacques. *Le Mouvement homosexuel en France, 1945–1980*. Paris: Syros, 1981.

Girard, René. *Critique dans un souterrain*. Lausanne: Editions l'Age, 1976.

– *Violence and the Sacred*. Trans. Patrick Gregory. Baltimore: Johns Hopkins University Press, 1977. Originally *La Violence et le sacré* (Paris: Grasset, 1972).

– *"To Double Business Bound": Essays on Literature, Mimesis, and Anthropology*. Baltimore: Johns Hopkins University Press, 1978.

Giscard d'Estaing, Valéry. *Towards a New Democracy*. Trans. Vincent Cronin. London: Collins, 1977. Originally *La Démocratie française* (Paris: Fayard, 1976).

Glucksmann, André. *Stratégie et révolution en France 1968*. Paris: Christian Bourgeois, 1968.

– *La Cuisinière et le mangeur d'hommes: essai sur l'Etat, le marxisme, les camps de concentration*. Paris: Seuil, 1975.

– *The Master Thinkers*. Trans. Brian Pearce. New York: Harper & Row, 1980. Originally *Les Maîtres penseurs* (Paris: Grasset, 1977).

Goldman, Pierre. *Dim Memories of a Polish Jew Born in France*. Trans. Joan Pinkham. New York: Viking, 1977. Originally *Souvenirs obscurs d'un juif polonais né en France* (Paris: Seuil, 1975).

Goldmann, Lucien. *The Hidden God: A Study of Tragic Vision in the* Pensées *of Pascal and the Tragedies of Racine*. Trans. Philip Thody. London: Routledge & Kegan Paul; New York: Humanities Press, 1964. Originally *Le Dieu caché: étude sur la vision tragique dans les* Pensées *de Pascal et dans le théâtre de Racine* (Paris: Gallimard, 1955).

– *Immanuel Kant*. Trans. Robert Black. London: NLB, 1971. Originally *Mensch, Gemeinschaft, und Welt in der Philosophie Immanuel Kants: Studien zur Geschichte der Dialektik* (Zürich: Europa Verlag, 1945). In French as *La Communauté humaine et l'univers chez Kant* (Paris: Presses universitaires de France, 1948). Rev. ed. *Introduction à la philosophie de Kant* (Paris: Gallimard, 1967).

Goldschmidt, Victor. *Le Système stoïcien et l'idée de temps*. Paris: Librairie Philosophique J. Vrin, 1953.

Gombin, Richard. *Le Projet révolutionnaire: éléments d'une sociologie des événements de mai–juin 1968*. Paris: Mouton, 1969.

Gorz, André. *La Morale de l'histoire*. Paris: Seuil, 1959.

– *Fondements pour une morale*. Paris: Galilée, 1977.

Grosser, Alfred. *Au nom de quoi: fondements d'une morale politique*. Paris: Seuil, 1969.

– *Le Sel de la terre: pour l'engagement moral*. Paris: Seuil, 1981.

Groupe d'information sur les prisons. *Intolérable les prisons: le enquête dans vingt prisons*. Paris: GIP, 1971.

– *Intolérable les prisons 2: le enquête dans une prison modèle: Fleury-Mérogis*. Paris: GIP, 1971.

– *L'Assassinat de George Jackson*. Foreword Jean Genet. Paris: GIP, 1971.

– *Intolérable 4: Suicides de prison (1972)*. Paris: GIP, 1973.

Groupe d'information sur la répression. *Lutte de classes à Dunkerque: les morts, les mots, les appareils d'état*. Paris: Galilée, 1973.

Groupe information santé. *Oui nous avortons!* Paris: Editions Gît-le-coeur, 1973.

– *La Médecine désordonnée: d'une pratique de l'avortement à la lutte pour la santé*. Paris: GIS, 1974.

Groupe d'information et de soutien des travailleurs immigrés (GISTI), and Collectif d'alphabétisation. *Le Petit livre juridique des travailleurs immigrés: conditions de séjour et de travail*. Paris: Maspero, 1974.

Groupe d'information des travailleurs sociaux. *Le Travail social contre qui?* Paris: GITS, 1974.

Guattari, Félix. *Psychanalyse et transversalité.* Foreword Gilles Deleuze. Paris: Maspero, 1972.

– *Molecular Revolution: Psychiatry and Politics.* Trans. Rosemary Sheed. Intro. David Cooper. Hardmondsworth: Penguin, 1984. Essays originally published in *Psychanalyse et transversalité* (Paris: Maspero, 1972) and *La Révolution moléculaire* (Fontenay-sous-Bois: Recherches, 1977).

– *Chaosophy.* Ed. Sylvère Lotringer. New York: Semiotext(e), 1995.

– *Chaosmosis: An Ethico-Aesthetic Paradigm.* Trans. Paul Bains and Julian Pefanis. Bloomington: Indiana University Press, 1995. Originally *Chaosmose* (Paris: Galilée, 1992).

– *Soft Subversions.* Ed. Sylvère Lotringer. New York: Semiotext(e), 1996.

– *The Guattari Reader.* Ed. Gary Genosko. Oxford: Blackwell, 1996.

– *The Three Ecologies.* Trans. Ian Pindar and Paul Sutton. New Brunswick, New Jersey: Athlone Press, 2000. Originally *Les Trois écologies* (Paris: Galilée, 1989).

– *The Anti-Oedipus Papers.* Trans. Kélina Gotman. Los Angeles: Semiotext(e), 2006. Originally *Ecrits pour l'Anti-Oedipe*, ed. Stéphane Nadaud (Paris: Lignes et Manifestes, 2004).

[Guattari, Félix, et al.] *Neuf thèses de l'opposition gauche.* Paris: Nouvelles éditions sociales et internationales, 1966.

Gueneau, Monique. *L'Enfant et son désir d'aimer: les parents devant la sexualité de leurs enfants.* Paris: Centurion, 1971.

Guérin, Daniel. *Charles Fourier: vers la liberté en amour.* Paris: Gallimard, 1975.

– *Les Assassins de Ben Barka: dix ans d'enquête.* Paris: Guy Authier, 1975.

– *Son testament.* Paris: Encre, 1979.

Guérin, Michel. *Nietzsche, Socrate héroique.* Paris: Grasset, 1975.

Gueroult, Martial. *Spinoza.* vol. 1, *Dieu.* vol. 2, *L'Ame.* Paris: Aubier Montaigne, 1968–1974.

Gutting, Gary, ed. *The Cambridge Companion to Foucault.* Cambridge: Cambridge University Press, 1994.

Habermas, Jürgen. *Knowledge and Human Interests.* Trans. Jeremy J. Shapiro. Boston: Beacon, 1971. Originally *Erkenntnis und Interesse* (Frankfurt am Main: Suhrkamp, 1968).

– *Legitimation Crisis.* Trans. Thomas McCarthy. Boston: Beacon, 1975. Originally *Legitimationsprobleme im Spätkapitalismus* (Frankfurt am Main: Suhrkamp, 1973).

– *The Philosophical Discourse of Modernity: Twelve Lectures*. Trans. Frederick Lawrence. Cambridge, Massachusetts: MIT Press, 1987. Originally *Der philosophische Diskurs der Moderne* (Frankfurt am Main: Suhrkamp, 1985).

Halimi, Gisèle. *Le Procès de Burgos*. Foreword Jean-Paul Sartre. Paris: Gallimard, 1971.

– *The Right to Choose*. Trans. Rosemary Morgan. St Lucia, Australia: University of Queensland Press, 1977. Originally *La Cause des femmes* (Paris: Grasset, 1973).

Hamon, Hervé, and Patrick Rotman. *Les Intellocrates: expédition en haute intelligentsia*. Paris: Ramsay, 1981.

– *Génération*. vol. 1, *Les Années de rêve*. vol. 2, *Les Années de poudre*. Paris: Seuil, 1987–88.

Hanry, Pierre. *Les Enfants, le sexe et nous: l'adulte et l'excédante enfance de la sexualité*. Toulouse: Privat, 1977.

Hardt, Michael, and Antonio Negri. *Empire*. Cambridge, Massachusetts: Harvard University Press, 2000.

– *Multitude: War and Democracy in the Age of the Empire*. New York: Penguin, 2004.

Heidegger, Martin. *Pathmarks*. Ed. William McNeill. Trans. Frank A. Capuzzi. Cambridge: Cambridge University Press, 1998. Originally *Wegmarken* (Frankfurt am Main: Klostermann, 1976).

Hess, Remi. *Les Maoïstes français: une dérive institutionnelle*. Paris: Anthropos, 1974.

Hirsch, Arthur. *The French New Left: An Intellectual History from Sartre to Gorz*. Boston: South End Press, 1981.

Hirst, Paul. *Associative Democracy: New Forms of Economic and Social Governance*. Cambridge: Polity Press, 1994.

Himmelfarb, Gertrude. *On Looking into the Abyss: Untimely Thoughts on Culture and Society*. New York: Knopf, 1994.

Histoires de La Borde: dix ans de psychothérapie institutionnelle à la clinique de Cour-Cheverney (1953–1963). Special Issue of *Recherches* 21 (March–April 1976).

Hochmann, Jacques. *Pour une psychiatrie communautaire: thèses pour une psychiatrie des ensembles*. Foreword Georges Daumézon. Paris: Seuil, 1971.

– and A. Andre. "La Comtesse du regard, essais de 'familialisme' appliqué." In *La Mort d'Oedipe et l'anti-psychanalyse*. Special Dossier in *Esprit* 40, no. 12 (1972).

Hocquenghem, Guy. *L'Après-mai des faunes: volutions*. Paris: Grasset, 1974.

– "L'Enfance d'un sexe." In *Normalisation de l'école–Scolarisation de la société*. Special Issue of *Les Temps modernes* 340 (November 1974).

– *La Dérive homosexuelle*. Paris: Editions universitaires, 1977.

– *Homosexual Desire*. Trans. Daniella Dangoor. Intro. Michael Moon. Foreword Jeffrey Weeks. Durham, North Carolina: Duke University Press, 1993. Originally *Le Désir homosexuel* (Paris: Editions universitaires, 1972).

– "Towards an Irrecuperable Pederasty." In Jonathan Goldberg, ed., *Reclaiming Sodom*. Trans. Chris Fox. New York: Routledge, 1994. Originally "Aux pédérastes incompréhensibles," *Partisans* (July 1972). Reprint, in *La Dérive Homosexuelle*.

– *L'Amphithéâtre des morts: mémoires anticipées*. Foreword Roland Surzur. Postface René Schérer. Paris: Gallimard, 1994.

Hocquenghem, Guy, and René Schérer. *Co-ire: album systématique de l'enfance*. Special Issue of *Recherches* 22 (May 1976; 2nd. ed. April 1977).

Hoffman, Stefan-Ludwig. "Democracy and Associations in the Long Nineteenth Century: Toward a Transnational Perspective." *The Journal of Modern History* 75 (June 2003).

Hoffmann, Gerhard, and Alfred Hornung, eds. *Ethics and Aesthetics: The Moral Turn of Postmodernism*. Heidelberg: C. Winter, 1996.

Hoffmann, Stanley, et al. *In Search of France*. Cambridge, Massachusetts: Harvard University Press, 1963.

Holland, Eugene W. *Deleuze and Guattari's* Anti-Oedipus*: Introduction to Schizoanalysis*. London: Routledge, 1999.

Houellebecq, Michel. *The Elementary Particles*. Trans. Frank Wynne. New York: Knopf, 2000. Originally *Les Particules élémentaires* (Paris: Flammarion, 1998).

Hourmant, François. *Le Désenchantement des clercs: figures de l'intellectuel dans l'après-Mai 68*. Rennes: Presses universitaires de Rennes, 1997.

Houziaux, Alain. *Le Désir, l'arbitraire et le consentement: pour une éthique du tragique*. Foreword André Dumas. Paris: Aubier Montaigne, 1973.

Hughes, H. Stuart. *Consciousness and Society: The Reorientation of European Social Thought, 1890–1930*. New York: Vintage, 1958.

– *Sophisticated Rebels: The Political Culture of European Dissent, 1968–1987*. Cambridge, Massachusetts: Harvard University Press, 1988.

Igounet, Valérie. *Histoire du négationnisme en France*. Paris: Le Grand livre du mois, 2000.

Illich, Ivan. *Tools for Conviviality*. New York: Harper & Row, 1973.

Ingraham, Barton L. *Political Crime in Europe: A Comparative Study of France, Germany, and England*. Berkeley: University of California Press, 1979.

Irigaray, Luce. *An Ethics of Sexual Difference*. Trans. Carolyn Burke and Gillian C. Gill. Ithaca, New York: Cornell University Press, 1993. Originally *Ethique de la différence sexuelle* (Paris: Minuit, 1984).

Jaccard, Roland. *L'Exil intérieur: schizoïdie et civilisation*. Paris: Presses universitaires de France, 1975.

Jacob, André. *Cheminements: de la dialectique à l'éthique*. Paris: Anthropos, 1982.

Jambet, Christian. *L'Apologie de Platon*. Paris: Grasset, 1976.

Jambet, Christian, and Guy Lardreau. *Ontologie de la révolution*. vol. 1, *L'Ange*. Paris: Grasset, 1976.

– *Le Monde: réponse à la question: qu'est-ce que les droits de l'homme?* Paris: Grasset, 1978.

– "The French New Philosophers." *The Chicago Review* 32, no. 3 (winter 1981). Partially translated from *Ontologie de la revolution*. vol. 1, *L'Ange* (Paris: Grasset, 1976).

Jameson, Fredric. *The Political Unconscious: Narrative as Socially Symbolic Act*. Ithaca, New York: Cornell University Press, 1981.

– *Postmodernism, or The Cultural Logic of Late Capitalism*. Durham, North Carolina: Duke University Press, 1991.

– *A Singular Modernity: Essay on the Ontology of the Present*. London: Verso, 2002.

Jankélévitch, Vladimir. "Entretien." In *Vladimir Jankélévitch*. Special Issue of *L'Arc* 75 (1979).

– *Le Paradoxe de la morale*. Paris: Seuil, 1981.

– *L'Irréversible et la nostalgie*. Paris: Seuil, 1983.

– *Music and the Ineffable*. Foreword Arnold I. Davidon. Trans. Carolyn Abbate. Princeton: Princeton University Press, 2003. Originally *La Musique et l'ineffable* (Paris: Armand Colin, 1961).

– *Forgiveness*. Trans. Andrew Kelley. Chicago: University of Chicago Press, 2005. Originally *Le Pardon* (Paris: Aubier-Montaigne, 1967).

Jarrel, Marc. *Eléments pour une histoire de l'ex-gauche prolétarienne: cinq ans d'intervention en milieu ouvrier*. Paris: NBE, 1974.

Jaspers, Karl. *Strindberg and Van Gogh: An Attempt of a Pathographic Analysis with Reference to Parallel Cases of Swedenborg and Hölderlin*. Trans. Oskar Grunow and David Woloshin. Tucson: University of Arizona Press, 1977. Published in French as *Strindberg et Van Gogh, Swedenborg–Hölderlin: étude psychiatrique comparative*. Foreword Maurice Blanchot. Paris: Minuit, 1953; 2nd ed. 1970. Originally *Strindberg und van Gogh: versuch ainer pathographischen Analyse unter vergleichender Heranziehung von Swedenborg und Hölderlin* (Bern: E. Bircher, 1922).

Jaubert, Alain, and Philippe Artières. *Michel Foucault, une journée particulière*. Photographs Elie Kagan. Lyon: Ædelsa, 2004.

Jay, Martin. *Marxism and Totality: The Adventures of a Concept from Lukács to Habermas*. Berkeley: University of California Press, 1984.

– *Downcast Eyes: The Denigration of Vision in Twentieth-Century French Thought*. Berkeley: University of California Press, 1993.

– *Cultural Semantics: Keywords of Our Time*. Amherst: University of Massachusetts Press, 1998.

Jeanson, Francis. *Sartre and the Problem of Morality*. Trans. Robert Stone. Bloomington: University of Indiana Press, 1980. Originally *Le Problème moral et la pensée de Sartre*, foreword Jean-Paul Sartre (Paris: Myrte, 1943).

Joffrin, Laurent. *Un Coup de jeune: portrait d'une génération morale*. Paris: Arléa-Librairie les Fruits du Congo, 1987.

– *Mai 68: histoire des événements*. Paris: Seuil, 1988; 2nd ed. 1998.

Judt, Tony. "Review of Jacques Capdevielle and René Mouriaux, *Mai 68: l'entre-deux de la modernité: histoire de trente ans*." *American Historical Review* 95, no. 3 (June 1990).

– *Past Imperfect: French Intellectuals, 1944–1956*. Berkeley: University of California Press, 1992.

– *The Burden of Responsibility: Blum, Camus, Aron, and the French Twentieth Century*. Chicago: University of Chicago Press, 1998.

Juquin, Pierre. *Programme commun: l'actualisation à dossiers ouverts*. Paris: Editions Sociales, 1977.

Kaltenbach, Pierre-Patrick. *Tartuffe aux affaires: génération morale et horreur politique, 1980–2000*. Paris: Editions de Paris, 2001.

Kandel, Liliane. "Sous la plage, les medias." In *Est-ce ainsi que les hommes jugent?* Special Issue of *Les Temps modernes* 391 (February 1979).

Kaplan, Roger F.S. *The Decline of Radicalism and the Triumph of the Left in France*. New Brunswick, New Jersey: Transaction Publishers, 2003.

Kaufman, Eleanor, and Kevin Jon Heller, eds. *Deleuze and Guattari: New Mappings in Politics, Philosophy, and Culture*. Minneapolis: University of Minnesota Press, 1998.

Kaufmann, Walter, ed. *Existentialism: From Dostoevsky to Sartre*. Intro. and trans. Walter Kaufmann. New York: The World Publishing Company, 1956.

– *Nietzsche: Philosopher, Psychologist, Anarchist*. 4th ed. Princeton: Princeton University Press, 1974.

Kessel, Patrick. *Le Mouvement "maoïste" en France*. 2 vols. Paris: 10/18, 1972.

Khalfa, Jean, ed. *Introduction to the Philosophy of Gilles Deleuze*. London: Continuum, 2002.

Khilnani, Sunil. *Arguing Revolution: The Intellectual Left in Postwar France*. New Haven: Yale University Press, 1994.

Kimbro, Stephanie L. "*Les Lieux de Mémoire*: French Collective Memory of World War II in the Events of May 1968." Master's thesis, Miami University, 2000.

Koestler, Arthur. *Le Zéro et l'infini*. Trans. Daphne Hardy. Paris: Calmann-Lévy, 1945. Originally *Darkness at Noon* (London: J. Cape, 1940).

Kolakowski, Leszek. *Main Currents of Marxism*. vol. 2, *The Golden Age*. Trans. P.S. Falla. Oxford: Clarendon, 1978. Originally *Główne nurty marksizmu*, 3 vols. (Paryz [Paris]: Instytut Literacki, 1976–78).

– *God Owes Us Nothing: A Brief Remark on Pascal's Religion and on the Spirit of Jansenism*. Chicago: University of Chicago Press, 1992.

Koupernik, Cyrille. *L'Antipsychiatrie: sens ou non-sens?* Paris: Presses universitaires de France, 1974.

Kremer-Marietti, Angèle. *La Morale*. Paris: Presses universitaires de France, 1982.

Kritzman, Lawrence D., ed. *The Columbia History of Twentieth-Century French Thought*. New York: Columbia University Press, 2006.

Kristeva, Julia. "A New Type of Intellectual: The Dissident." In *The Kristeva Reader*. Ed. Toril Moi. New York: Columbia, 1986. Originally "Un Nouveau type d'intellectuel: le dissident," *Tel quel* 74 (winter 1977).

– *Revolt, She Said: An Interview with Philippe Petit*. Ed. Sylvère Lotringer. Trans. Brian O'Keeffe. Los Angeles: Semiotext(e), 2002. Originally *Contre la dépression nationale: entretien avec Philippe Petit* (Paris: Textuel, 1998).

Kurlansky, Mark. *1968: The Year that Rocked the World*. New York: Ballantine, 2004.

La Boétie, Etienne de. *Le Discours de la servitude volontaire* [1552–53]. Ed. Miguel Abensour. Intro. Miguel Abensour and Marcel Gauchet, with commentaries by Pierre Clastres, Claude Lefort, et al. Paris: Payot, 1976. Reprint, 1993.

Labro, Philippe, et al. *This Is Only a Beginning*. Trans. Charles Lam Marlmann. New York: Funk and Wagnalls, 1969. Originally *Ce n'est qu'un début* (Paris: Editions et publications premières, 1968).

Lacan, Jacques. "Seminar on 'The Purloined Letter.'" Trans. Jeffrey Mehlman. In *French Freud*. Special Issue of *Yale French Studies* 48 (1972). Originally "La Lettre volée" [1955], *La Psychanalyse* 2 (1957). Reprint, in Lacan, *Ecrits*.

– *Ecrits: A Selection*. Trans. Alan Sheridan. New York: Norton, 1977. Originally *Ecrits*, 2 vols. (Paris: Seuil, 1966).

– *The Ethics of Psychoanalysis, 1959–1960*. Trans. Dennis Porter. New York: Norton, 1992. Originally *L'Ethique de la psychanalyse: 1959–60*. Ed. Jacques-Alain Miller (Paris: Seuil, 1986).

Lacroix, Jean. *Le Désir et les désirs*. Paris: Presses universitaires de France, 1975.

Lafont, Max. *L'Extermination douce: la mort de 40,000 malades mentales dans les hôpitaux psychiatriques en France sous le régime de Vichy*. Foreword Lucien Bonnafé. Ligné, France: L'Arefppi, 1987. Reprint, Latresne, France: Bord de l'eau, 2000.

LaFountain, Marc J., ed. *Postmodern Ethics*. Carrollton, Georgia: West Georgia College, 1995.

Laing, Ronald David. *La Politique de l'expérience: essai sur l'aliénation, et L'Oiseau de paradis*. Trans. Claude Elsen. Paris: Stock, 1969. Originally *The Politics of Experience, and The Bird of Paradise* (Harmondsworth: Penguin, 1967).

– *Le Moi divisé: de la santé mentale à la folie: essai*. Trans. Claude Elsen. Paris: Stock, 1970. Originally *The Divided Self: An Existential Study in Sanity and Madness* (Baltimore: Penguin, 1959).

– *Noeuds*. Trans. Claude Elsen. Paris: Stock, 1971. Originally *Knots* (Harmondsworth: Penguin, 1970).

– *Soi et les autres*. Trans. Gilberte Lambrichs. Paris: Gallimard, 1971. Originally *The Self and Others: Further Studies in Sanity and Madness* (London: Tavistock, 1961).

Laing, Ronald David, and Aron Esterson. *L'Equilibre mental, la folie et la famille*. Trans. Micheline Laguilhommie. Paris: Maspero, 1971. Originally *Sanity, Madness, and the Family* (London: Tavistock, 1964).

Lambert, Benjamin. *Défense d'interdire: almanach nostalgique de mai 1968*. Paris: Méréal, 1997.

Langlois, Denis. *Les Dossiers noirs de la police française*. Paris: Seuil, 1971.

– *Guide du militant*. Paris: Seuil, 1972.

– *Et vous êtes de gauche*. Paris: Galilée, 1979.

Lapassade, Georges, and René Schérer. *Le Corps interdit: essais sur l'éducation négative*. Paris: ESF, 1976.

Lapouge, Benoît, and Jean-Luc Pinard-Legry. *L'Enfant et le pédéraste*. Paris: Seuil, 1980.

Lardreau, Guy. *Le Singe d'or: essai sur le concept d'étape du marxisme*. Foreword François Châtelet. Paris: Mercure de France, 1973.

Lasch, Christopher. *The Culture of Narcissism: American Life in an Age of Diminishing Expectations*. New York: Norton, 1978.

Laurent, Alain. *Féminin-masculin: le nouvel équilibre*. Paris: Seuil, 1975.

Le Bris, Michel. *L'Homme aux semelles de vent*. Paris: Grasset, 1977.

Lecourt, Dominique. *Contre la peur: de la science à l'éthique, une aventure infinie*. Paris: Hachette, 1990.

– *Prométhée, Faust, Frankenstein: fondements imaginaires de l'éthique*. Le Plessis-Robinson: Synthélabo, 1996.

– *The Mediocracy: French Philosophy Since the Mid-1970s*. Trans. Gregory Elliott. London: Verso, 2002. Originally *Les Piètres penseurs* (Paris: Flammarion, 1999) and *Dissidence ou révolution?* (Paris: Maspero, 1978).

Le Dantec, Jean-Pierre. *Les Dangers du soleil*. Paris: Presses d'Aujourd'hui, 1978.

Lefebvre, Henri. *The Explosion: Marxism and the French Revolution*. Trans. Alfred Ehrenfeld. New York: Monthly Review Press, 1969. Originally *L'Irruption de Nanterre au sommet* (Paris: Syllepse, 1998).

Lefort, Claude. *Un Homme en trop: réflexions sur "L'Archipel du Goulag."* Paris: Seuil, 1976.

– *The Political Forms of Modern Society: Bureaucracy, Democracy, Totalitarianism*. Ed. and Intro. John B. Thompson. Trans. John B. Thompson, Alan Sheridan, and Terry Karten. Cambridge, Massachusetts: MIT Press, 1986.

Legendre, Pierre. *L'Amour du censeur*. Paris: Seuil, 1974.

Le Goff, Jean-Pierre. *Mai 68: l'héritage impossible*. Foreword François Gèze. Paris: La Découverte, 1998; rev. ed. 2002.

Lemonnier, Augustin-Michel, ed. *Lumière sur l'échafaud: lettres de prison de Jacques Fesch, guillotiné le 1er octobre 1957 à 27 ans*. Paris: Editions Ouvrières, 1971.

Lescourret, Marie-Anne. *Emmanuel Levinas*. Paris: Flammarion, 1994.

Levinas, Emmanuel. *Ethics and Infinity: Conversations with Philippe Nemo*. Trans. Richard A. Cohen. Pittsburgh: Duquesne University Press, 1985. Originally *Ethique et infini: dialogues avec Philippe Nemo* (Paris: Fayard, 1982).

– *Entre nous: On Thinking-of-the-Other*. Trans. Michael B. Smith and Barbara Harshav. New York: Columbia University Press, 1998. Originally *Entre nous: essais sur le penser-à-l'autre* (Paris: Grasset, 1991).

Levine, Michel. *Affaires non classées: enquêtes et dossiers de la Ligue des droits de l'homme*. Foreword Daniel Mayer. Paris: Fayard, 1973.

Lévy, Benny. *Le Nom de l'homme: dialogue avec Sartre*. Paris: Verdier, 1984.

Lévy, Bernard-Henri. *Barbarism with a Human Face*. Trans. George Holoch. New York: Harper & Row, 1979. Originally *La Barbarie à visage humain* (Paris: Grasset, 1977).

– *The Testament of God*. Trans. George Holoch. New York: Harper & Row, 1980. Originally *Le Testament de Dieu* (Paris: Grasset, 1979).

– *L'Idéologie française*. Paris: Grasset, 1981.

– *Questions de principe*. Paris: Denoël, 1983.

Libération des femmes: année zéro. Special Issue of *Partisans* 54–5 (July–October 1970).

Lilla, Mark, ed. *New French Thought: Political Philosophy*. Princeton: Princeton University Press, 1994.

– *The Reckless Mind: Intellectuals in Politics*. New York: The New York Review of Books, 2001.

Limqueco, Peter, and Peter Weiss, eds. *Prevent the Crime of Silence: Reports from the Sessions of the International War Crimes Tribunal founded by Bertrand Russell: London, Stockholm, Roskilde*. Foreword Noam Chomsky. New York: Bertrand Russell Peace Foundation, 1971.

Lindenberg, Daniel. *Le Rappel à l'ordre: enquête sur les nouveaux réactionnaires*. Paris: Seuil, 2002.

Lipovetsky, Gilles. *L'Ere du vide: essais sur l'individualisme contemporain*. Paris: Gallimard, 1983.
– *Le Crépuscle du devoir: l'éthique indolore des nouveaux temps démocratiques*. Paris: Gallimard, 1992.
Livrozet, Serge. *De la prison à la révolte: essai-témoignage*. Foreword Michel Foucault. Paris: Mercure de France, 1973.
– *Aujourd'hui, la prison*. Paris: Hachette, 1976.
Lourau, René. *Analyse institutionnelle et pédagogie*. Paris: Epi, 1971.
Lorenz, Konrad. *The Foundations of Ethology: The Principal Ideas and Discoveries in Animal Behavior*. Trans. Konrad Lorenz and Robert Warren Kickert. New York: Simon & Schuster, 1982. Originally *Vergleichende Verhaltensforschung: Grundlagan der Ethologie* (Vienna: Springer, 1978).
Lotringer, Sylvère, and Sande Cohen, eds. *French Theory in America*. New York: Routledge, 2001.
Lyotard, Jean-François. *Instructions païennes*. Paris: Galilée, 1977.
– *The Differend: Phrases in Dispute*. Trans. Georges Van Den Abbeele. Minneapolis: University of Minnesota Press, 1988. Originally *Le Différend* (Paris: Minuit, 1983).
– *Duchamp's Trans/formers*. Trans. Ian McLeod. Venice, California: Lapis Press, 1990. Originally *Les Transformateurs Duchamp* (Paris: Galilée, 1977).
– *Libidinal Economy*. Trans. Iain Hamilton Grant. Bloomington: Indiana University Press, 1993. Originally *Economie libidinale* (Paris: Minuit, 1974).
Macciocchi, Maria-Antonietta. *De la France*. Paris: Seuil, 1977.
Macey, David. *The Lives of Michel Foucault: A Biography*. New York: Vintage, 1995.
– *Frantz Fanon*. New York: Picador, 2000.
Madison, Gary Brent, ed. *Sens et existence: en hommage à Paul Ricoeur: receuil*. Paris: Seuil, 1975.
Madison, Gary Brent, and Marty Fairbairn, eds. *The Ethics of Postmodernity: Current Trends in Continental Thought*. Evanston, Illinois: Northwestern University Press, 1999.
Manceaux, Michèle. *Les Maos en France*. Foreword Jean-Paul Sartre. Paris: Gallimard, 1972.
Manfred, Frank. *What Is Neostructuralism?* Trans. Sabine Wilke and Richard Gray. Foreword Martin Schwab. Minneapolis: University of Minnesota Press, 1989. Originally *Was ist Neostrukturalismus?* (Frankfurt am Main: Suhrkamp, 1983).
Mannheim, Karl. "Conservative Thought." Trans. Karl Mannheim and Paul Kecskemeti. In *From Karl Mannheim*. Ed. Kurt H. Wolff. New York: Oxford University Press, 1971. Originally "Das konservative Denken: Soziologische Beiträge zum Werden des politisch-historischen Denkens in Deutschland," *Archiv für Sozialwissenschaft und Sozialpolitik* 57, no. 1 (1927).

Mannoni, Maud. *Le Psychiatre, son "fou" et la psychanalyse*. Paris: Seuil, 1970.

Marcellin, Raymond. *L'Ordre public et les groupes révolutionnaires*. Paris: Plon, 1969.

– *L'Importune vérité*. Paris: Plon, 1978.

Marchitello, Howard, ed. *What Happens to History? The Renewal of Ethics in Contemporary Thought*. London: Routledge, 2001.

Marshall, Bill. *Guy Hocquenghem: Beyond Gay Identity*. Durham, North Carolina: Duke University Press, 1996.

Martel, Frédéric. *The Pink and the Black: Homosexuals in France since 1968*. Trans. Jane Marie Todd. Stanford: Stanford University Press, 1999. Originally *Le Rose et le noir: les homosexuels en France depuis 1968* (Paris: Seuil, 1996; rev. ed. 2000).

Martin, Patrick, ed. *Pratiques institutionnelles et théorie des psychoses: actualité de la psychothérapie institutionnelle*. Paris: Harmattan, 1995.

Martineau, Christine, and Jean-Pierre Carasso. *Le Travail dans les prisons*. Paris: Champ libre, 1972.

Marwick, Arthur. *The Sixties: Cultural Revolution in Britain, France, Italy, and the United States, c. 1958–c. 1974*. Oxford: Oxford University Press, 1998.

Marx-Scouras, Danielle. *The Cultural Politics of* Tel Quel*: Literature and the Left in the Wake of Engagement*. University Park, Pennsylvania: Pennsylvania State University Press, 1996.

Massumi, Brian. *A User's Guide to Capitalism and Schizophrenia: Deviations from Deleuze and Guattari*. Cambridge, Massachusetts: MIT Press, 1992.

Matheron, Alexandre. *Individu et communauté chez Spinoza*. Paris: Minuit, 1969.

Matzneff, Gabriel. *Les Moins de seize ans*. Paris: Julliard, 1974.

– *Les Passions schismatiques*. Paris: Stock, 1977.

Mauriac, Claude. *Le Temps immobile*. vol. 3, *Et comme l'espérance est violente*. Paris: Livre de poche, 1986.

May, Todd. *The Moral Theory of Poststructuralism*. University Park, Pennsylvania: Pennsylvania State University Press, 1995.

– *Gilles Deleuze: An Introduction*. Cambridge: Cambridge University Press, 2005.

Merleau-Ponty, Maurice. *Humanism and Terror: An Essay on the Communist Problem*. Trans. John O'Neill. Boston: Beacon, 1969. Originally *Humanisme et terreur: essai sur le problème communiste* (Paris: Gallimard, 1947).

Merquior, J.G. *From Prague to Paris: A Critique of Structuralist and Post-Structuralist Thought*. London: Verso, 1986.

Michnik, Adam. *Penser la Pologne: morale et politique de la résistance*. Foreword Leszek Kolakowski. Paris: La Découverte/Maspero, 1983.

Mill, John Stuart. *A System of Logic, Ratiocinative and Inductive: Being a Connected View of the Principles of Evidence and the Methods of Scientific Investigation*. London: J.W. Parker, 1843.

Miller, James. *The Passion of Michel Foucault*. New York: Simon & Schuster, 1993.

Ministère de la Justice. *Régime pénitentiaire spécial: textes, rapports et documents de référence*. Paris: Documentation Française, 1971.

Minutes du procès d'Alain Geismar. Foreword Jean-Paul Sartre. Paris: Documentation Française, 1970.

Misrahi, Robert. *Le Désir et la réflexion dans la philosophie de Spinoza*. Paris: Gordon & Breach, 1972.

– *Ethique, politique et bonheur*. Paris: Seuil, 1983.

– *La Signification de l'éthique: pour l'application de l'éthique aux problèmes de la vie et de la santé*. Le Plessis-Robinson: Synthélabo, 1995.

– *Qu'est-ce que l'éthique? l'éthique et le bonheur*. Paris: Armand Colin, 1997.

Mongin, Olivier. *Face au scepticisme: les mutations du paysage intellectuel*. Paris: Hachette, 1994; 2nd ed. 1998.

Montag, Warren, and Ted Stolze, eds. *The New Spinoza*. Minneapolis: University of Minnesota Press, 1997.

Une Morale pour demain? Special Issue of *La Nef* 67 (1978).

Morford, Janet H. "Histoires du CERFI: la trajectoire d'un collectif de recherche sociale." DEA thesis, Ecole des Hautes Etudes en Sciences Sociales, Paris, 1985.

Morin, Edgar. *Le Rose et le noir*. Paris: Galilée, 1984.

Morin, Edgar, and Marek Halter. *Mais*. Paris: Nouvelles Editions Oswald, 1978.

Morin, Edgar, Claude Lefort, and Jean-Marc Coudray [Cornelius Castoriadis]. *Mai 1968: La Brèche: premières réflexions sur les événements*. Paris: Fayard, 1968; rev. ed. 1988.

Mossuz-Lavau, Janine. *Les Lois de l'amour*. Paris: Payot, 1991.

Mouvement français pour le planning familial. *D'une révolte à une lutte: 25 ans d'histoire du planning familial*. Paris: Tierce, 1982.

Moyn, Samuel. *Origins of the Other: Emmanuel Levinas Between Revelation and Ethics*. Ithaca, New York: Cornell University Press, 2005.

Mozère, Liane. *Le Printemps des crèches: histoire et analyse d'un mouvement*. Paris: Harmattan, 1992.

Muraz, Roland. *La Parole aux Français: cinq ans de sondages*. Paris: Dunod, 1977.

Nancy, Jean-Luc. *L'Impératif catégorique*. Paris: Flammarion, 1983.

Negri, Antonio. *The Savage Anomaly: The Power of Spinoza's Metaphysics and Politics*. Trans. Michael Hardt. Minneapolis: University of Minnesota Press,

1990. Originally *L'anomalia salvaggia: saggio su potere e potenza in Baruch Spinoza* (Milan: Feltrinelli, 1981).

Nemo, Philippe. *L'Homme structural.* Paris: Grasset, 1975.

Niel, Mathilde. *Le Mouvement étudiant ou la révolution en marche: signification du mouvement étudiant contemporaine.* Paris: Courrier du livre, 1968.

Nietzsche, Friedrich. *The Will to Power.* Ed. Walter Kaufmann. Trans. Walter Kaufmann and R.J. Hollingdale. New York: Random House, 1968. Originally *Der Wille zur Macht: Versuch einer Umwerthung aller Werthe (Studien und Fragmente)*, vol. 15 of *Nachgelassene Werke*, eds. Peter Gast, Ernst Horneffer, and August Horneffer, foreword Elisabeth Förster-Nietzsche (Leipzig: C.G. Neumann Verlag, 1901).

Nizan, Paul. *The Watchdogs: Philosophers and the Established Order.* Trans. Paul Fittingoff. New York: Monthly Review Press, 1971. Originally *Les Chiens de garde* (Paris: Rieder, 1932).

Norris, Christopher. *Spinoza and the Origins of Modern Critical Theory.* Oxford: Blackwell, 1991.

Nouveau fascisme, nouvelle démocratie. Special Issue of *Les Temps modernes* 310 bis. (May 1972).

Nouveaux philosophes ou nouvelle philosophie. Special Issue of *La Nef* 66 (January–April 1978).

Les Nouvelles morales: éthique et philosophie. Special Issue of *Le Magazine littéraire* 361 (January 1998).

Nye, Robert A. *Masculinity and Male Codes of Honor in Modern France.* New York: Oxford University Press, 1993.

O'Leary, Timothy. *Foucault: The Art of Ethics.* London: Continuum, 2001.

Ory, Pascal. *L'Entre-deux-mai: histoire culturelle de la France, mai 1968–mai 1981.* Paris: Seuil, 1983.

Oury, Ferdinand, and Aida Vasquez. *Vers une pédagogie institutionnelle.* Foreword Françoise Dolto. Paris: Maspero, 1967.

– *De la classe coopérative à la pédagogie institutionnelle.* Foreword Jean Oury. Paris: Maspero, 1971.

Oury, Jean. *Psychiatrie et psychothérapie institutionnelle.* Foreword François Tosquelles. Paris: Payot, 1976.

– *Il, donc.* Paris: Union générale d'éditions, 1978.

Oury, Jean, Félix Guattari, and François Tosquelles. *Pratique de l'institutionnel et politique.* Vigneux: Matrice, 1985.

Pascal, Blaise. *Pensées* [1670]. Intro. Léon Brunschvicg. Paris: Garnier-Flammarion, 1972.

Passerini, Luisa. *Autobiography of a Generation: Italy, 1968.* Trans. Lisa Erdberg. Foreword Joan Wallach Scott. Hanover, New Hampshire: University

Press of New England, 1996. Originally *Autoritratto di gruppo* (Florence: Giunti, 1988).

Patton, Paul, ed. *Deleuze: A Critical Reader*. Oxford: Blackwell Publishing, 1996.

Paugam, Jacques. *Génération perdue: ceux qui avaient vingt ans en 1968? Ceux qui avaient vingt ans à la fin de la guerre d'Algérie? Ou ni les uns ni les autres?* Paris: Robert Laffont, 1977.

Paul-Lévy, Françoise. *Karl Marx, histoire d'un bourgeois allemand*. Paris: Grasset, 1976.

Pavel, Thomas G. *The Feud of Language: A History of Structuralist Thought*. English version Thomas G. Pavel, with Linda Jordan. Oxford: Blackwell, 1989. Originally *Le Mirage linguistique: essai sur la modernisation intellectuelle* (Paris: Minuit, 1988).

Pellissier, Jérôme. *À but non lucratif: 1901–2001: cent ans de liberté d'association*. Foreword Henri Leclerc. Paris: Fischbacher, 2001.

Perelman, Chaïm. *Introduction historique à la philosophie morale*. Bruxelles: Editions de l'Université de Bruxelles, 1980.

Perry, Wendy Ellen. "Remembering Dreyfus: The 'Ligue des Droits de l'Homme' and the Making of the Modern French Human Rights Movement." PhD diss., University of North Carolina, Chapel Hill, 1998.

Pharo, Patrick. "Ethique et politique ou les intellectuels dans l'histoire." In *L'Année sociologique*. 3rd ser. vol. 30. Paris: Presses universitaires de France, 1982.

Picq, Françoise. *Libération des femmes: les années-mouvement*. Paris: Seuil, 1993.

Pisan, Annie de, and Anne Tristan. *Histoires du* . Paris: Calmann-Lévy, 1977.

Poel, Ieme van der. *Une Révolution de la pensée: maoïsme et féminisme à travers* Tel Quel, Les Temps modernes *et* Esprit. Amsterdam: Rodopi, 1992.

Polack, Jean-Claude, and Danielle Sabourin. *La Borde ou le droit à la folie*. Paris: Calmann-Lévy, 1976.

Pompidou, Georges. *Entretiens et discours*. vol. 1, *1968–1974*. Paris: Plon, 1975.

Posner, Charles, ed. *Reflections on the Revolution in France: 1968*. Harmondsworth: Penguin, 1970.

Postel, Jacques, and David F. Allen. "History and Anti-Psychiatry in France." In Mark S. Micale and Roy Porter, eds., *Discovering the History of Psychiatry*. Oxford: Oxford University Press, 1994.

Les Prisonniers politiques parlent: le combat des détenus politiques, grève de la faim, procès des diffuseurs de "La Cause du people." Paris: Maspero, 1970.

Le Programme commun de gouvernement de la gauche: propositions socialistes pour l'actualisation. Foreword François Mitterrand. Paris: Flammarion, 1978.

Le Programme commun de gouvernement du Parti communiste français et du Parti socialiste (27 juin 1972). Foreword Georges Marchais. Paris: Editions Sociales, 1972.

Prost, Antoine. "Les Grèves de mai–juin 1968." *L'Histoire* 110 (April 1988).

Quaduppani, Serge. *Catalogue du prêt à penser français depuis 1968*. Paris: Balland, 1983.

Qu'est-ce que le Secours Rouge International? Paris: Editions du Secours Rouge International, 1924.

Racamier, Paul-Claude, et al. *Le Psychanalyste sans divan: la psychanalyse et les institutions de soins psychiatriques*. Paris: Payot, 1970.

Rajchman, John. *Truth and Eros: Foucault, Lacan, and the Question of Ethics*. New York: Routledge, 1991.

Rajsfus, Maurice. *Mai 68: sous les pavés, la répression, mai 1968–mars 1974*. Paris: Le Cherche-midi, 1998.

Rancière, Jacques. "Reply to Lévy." *Telos* 33 (fall 1977). Trans. Maryska Suda. Originally published in *Le Nouvel Observateur* (31 July 1977).

Reader, Keith A. *Intellectuals and the Left in France since 1968*. London: Macmillan, 1987.

Reader, Keith, with Khursheed Wadia. *The May 1968 Events in France: Reproductions and Interpretations*. New York: St Martin's Press, 1993.

Reich, Wilhelm. *The Mass Psychology of Fascism*. Eds. Mary Higgins and Chester M. Raphael. Trans. Vincent R. Carfagno. New York: Farrar, Straus, and Giroux, 1970. Originally *Massenpsychologie des Faschismus: zur Sexualökonomie der politischen Reaktion und zur proletarischen Sexualpolitik* (Copenhagen: Verlag für Sexualpolitik, 1933).

—*L'Irruption de la morale sexuelle*. Trans. Pierre Kamnitzer. Paris: Payot, 1972. Originally *Der Einbruch der Sexualmoral: zur Geschichte der sexuellen Ökonomie* (Berlin: Verlag für Sexualpolitik, 1932).

Reinach, Joseph. *Vers la justice par la vérité*. Paris: P.V. Stock, 1898.

Rémy, Monique. *De l'utopie à l'intégration: histoire des mouvements de femmes*. Paris: Harmattan, 1990.

Renan, Ernest. *Drames Philosophiques*. Paris: Calmann-Lévy, 1888; 1949.

La Révolte de la prison de Toul: délinquance sociale et justice gauchiste. Special Issue of *Négation* avant-premier numéro (1971).

Ricoeur, Paul. *History and Truth*. Trans. and Intro. Charles A. Kelbley. Evanston, Illinois: Northwestern University Press, 1965. Originally *Histoire et vérité* (Paris: Seuil, 1955).

– *Oneself as Another*. Trans. Kathleen Blamey. Chicago: University of Chicago Press, 1992. Originally *Soi-même comme un autre* (Paris: Seuil, 1990).

– *The Just*. Trans. David Pellauer. Chicago: University of Chicago Press, 2000. Originally *Le Juste* (Paris: Esprit, 1995).

Robert, Brigitte. "Les Luttes autour des prisons 1971–1972: le Groupe d'information sur les prisons et la naissance du CAP." DEA thesis, Institut d'Etudes Politiques, Paris, 1981.

Rochefort, Christiane. *Les Enfants d'abord*. Paris: Grasset, 1976.

Rojek, Chris. "Stuart Hall and the Antinomian Tradition." *International Journal of Cultural Studies* 1, no. 1 (1998).

Ropartz, Philippe. *Qu'est-ce que l'éthologie?: histoire, orientations actuelles*. Strasbourg: Université Louis Pasteur, 1975.

Rosanvallon, Pierre. *Le Modèle politique français: la société civile contre le jacobinisme de 1789 à nos jours*. Paris: Seuil, 2004.

Rose, Sonya O. "Cultural Analysis of Moral Discourses: Episodes, Continuities, and Tranformations." In Victoria E. Bonnell and Lynn Hunt, eds. *Beyond the Cultural Turn*. Berkeley: University of California Press, 1999.

Ross, Kristin. *May '68 and Its Afterlives*. Chicago: University of Chicago Press, 2002.

Rousseau, Jean-Jacques. *Discourse on the Origin and the Foundation of Inequality among Mankind* [1755]. Ed. and Intro. Lester G. Crocker. New York: B. Franklin, 1971.

Ruwet, Jean-Claude. *Introduction to Ethology: The Biology of Behavior*. Trans. Joyce Diamanti. New York: International Universities Press, 1972. Originally *Ethologie: biologie du comportement* (Bruxelles: C. Dessart, 1969).

Saint-Alban: mythes et histoire: les premières rencontres de Saint-Alban (juin 1986). Special Dossier in *Information psychiatrique* 63 (October 1987).

Saint-Just. "Fragments sur les institutions républicaines" [1793–1794]. *L'Esprit de la Révolution, suivi de Fragments sur les institutions républicaines*. Paris: Union générale d'éditions, 1963.

Salas, Denis, and Emmanuelle Verleyn. "Casamayor l'insoumis." In *Résister à l'impuissance démocratique*. Special Issue of *Esprit* (October 2002).

Santoni, Ronald E. *Sartre on Violence – Curiously Ambivalent*. University Park, Pennsylvania: Pennsylvania State University Press, 2003.

Sartre, Jean-Paul. *Being and Nothingness: An Essay on Phenomenological Ontology*. Trans. Hazel E. Barnes. New York: Philosophical Library, 1956. Originally *L'Etre et le néant: essai d'ontologie phénoménologique* (Paris: Gallimard, 1943).

– *Search for a Method*. Trans. and Intro. Hazel E. Barnes. New York: Knopf, 1963. Originally *Critique de la raison dialectique, précédé de Question de méthode*, vol. 1, *Théorie des ensembles politiques* (Paris: Gallimard, 1960).

– *Life/Situations: Essays Spoken and Written*. Trans. Paul Auster and Lydia Davis. New York: Pantheon, 1977. Originally *Situations X, politique et autobiographie* (Paris: Gallimard, 1976).

– *Sartre by Himself: A Film Directed by Alexandre Astruc and Michel Contat with the participation of Simone de Beauvoir, Jacques-Larent Bost, Andre Gorz, Jean Pouillon*. Trans. Richard Seaver. New York: Urizen, 1978. Originally *Sartre: un film* (Paris: Gallimard, 1977).

– *Critique of Dialectical Reason*. Ed. Jonathan Rée. Trans. Alan Sheridan-Smith. 2 vols. London: Verso, 1982–90. Originally *Critique de la raison dialectique* (Paris: Gallimard, 1960).

– *Notebooks for an Ethics*. Trans. David Pellauer. Chicago: University of Chicago Press, 1992. Originally *Cahiers pour une morale* (Paris: Gallimard, 1983).

Sartre, Jean-Paul, and Arlette Elkaïm-Sartre, eds. *Tribunal Russell II: le jugement final*. Paris: Gallimard, 1968.

Sartre, Jean-Paul, and Benny Lévy. *Hope Now: The 1980 Interviews*. Trans. Adrian van den Hoven. Chicago: University of Chicago Press, 1996. Originally *L'Espoir maintenant: les entretiens de 1980* (Paris: Verdier, 1991).

Schérer, René. "A Propos de Fourier: lutte de classes et lutte de civilisations." Foreword to *L'Ordre subversif: trois textes sur la civilisation*, by Charles Fourier. Paris: Aubier Montaigne, 1972.

– *Emile perverti, ou des rapports entre l'éducation et la sexualité*. Paris: Robert Laffont, 1974.

– "Pédophilie: notes de lecture." In *Homosexualités–Marginalités*. Special Issue of *Marge* 11 (October–November 1976).

– *Une Erotique puérile*. Paris: Galilée, 1978.

– *L'Emprise des enfants entre nous*. Paris: Hachette, 1979.

Schiwy, Günther. *Les Nouveaux philosophes*. Paris: Denoël/Gonthier, 1979.

Schnapp, Alain, and Vidal-Naquet. *The French Student Uprising, November 1967–June 1968*. Trans. Maria Jolas. Boston: Beacon, 1971. Originally *Journal de la commune étudiante, texte et documents, novembre 1967–juin 1968* (Paris: Seuil, 1969).

Schorske, Carl E. *Fin-de-siècle Vienna: Politics and Culture*. New York: Knopf, 1979.

Schrift, Alan D. *Twentieth-Century French Philosophy: Key Themes and Thinkers*. Oxford: Blackwell, 2006.

Schwartz, Laurent. *Le Problème de la torture dans la France d'aujourd'hui, 1954–1961*. Paris: Cahiers de la République, 1961.

– *A Mathematician Grappling with His Century*. Trans. Leila Schneps. Basel: Birkhäuser, 2001. Originally *Mathématicien aux prises avec le siècle* (Paris: Odile Jacob, 1997).

Scott, Joan Wallach. *Only Paradoxes to Offer: French Feminism and the Rights of Man*. Cambridge, Massachusetts: Harvard University Press, 1996.

Seal, Patrick, and Maureen McConville. *Red Flag/Black Flag: French Revolution 1968*. New York: G.P. Putnam's Sons, 1968.

Sebbar, Leïla. *Le Pédophile et la maman: l'amour des enfants*. Paris: Stock, 1980.

Sedgwick, Alexander. *Jansenism in Seventeenth-Century France: Voices from the Wilderness*. Charlottesville, Virginia: University Press of Virginia, 1977.

Sedgwick, Peter. *Psycho Politics: Laing, Foucault, Goffman, Szasz, and the Future of Mass Psychiatry*. New York: Harper & Row, 1982.

Seidman, Michael. *The Imaginary Revolution: Parisian Students and Workers in 1968*. New York: Berghahn, 2004.

Sève, Lucien. *Pour une critique de la raison bioéthique*. Paris: Odile Jacob, 1994.

Shaw, George Bernard. *Imprisonment*. New York: Brentano, 1924.

Silverman, Hugh J., ed. *Philosophy and Desire*. New York: Routledge, 2000.

Sirinelli, Jean-François. *Intellectuels et passions françaises: manifestes et pétitions au e siècle*. Paris: Gallimard, 1990.

Smart, Barry, ed. *Michel Foucault: Critical Assessments*. 7 vols. London: Routledge, 1994–95.

Société d'histoire du droit. *Justice populaire: actes des journées de la Société d'histoire du droit, tenues à Lille, 25–28 mai 1989*. Hellemmens: Ester, 1992.

'68 dans l'histoire et dans la culture politique européenne. Conference held at the Université de Paris–IV (Sorbonne), February 1999.

Sokal, Alan D., and Jean Bricmont. *Fashionable Nonsense: Postmodern Intellectuals' Abuse of Science*. New York: Picador, 1999.

Soljénitsyne: le colloque du Cerisy. Paris: Union générale d'éditions, 1974.

Solzhenitsyn, Alexandr. *The Gulag Archipelago, 1918–1956: An Experiment in Literary Investigation*. 3 vols. Trans. Thomas P. Whitney and H. Willetts. New York: Harper & Row, 1978. Published in French as *L'Archipel du Goulag, 1918–1945: essai d'investigation littéraire*, 3 vols. (Paris: Seuil, 1974–76). Originally *Arkhipelag gulag: 1918–1956: opyt khudozhestvennogo issledovaniia*, 3 vols. ([Paris]: YMCA-Press, 1973–75).

Sommier, Isabelle. *La Violence politique et son deuil: l'après-68 en France et en Italie*. Rennes: Presses universitaires de Rennes, 1998.

Souriau, Etienne. *La Couronne d'herbes: esquisse d'une morale des bases purement esthétiques*. Paris: Union générale d'éditions, 1975.

Spinoza, Benedict de. *Works of Spinoza*. 2 vols. Trans. R.H.M. Elwes. New York: Dover, 1955.

Spivak, Gayatri, and Michael Ryan. "Anarchism Revisited: A New Philosophy." *Diacritics* 8, no. 2 (summer 1978).

Stallybrass, Peter, and Allon White. *The Politics and Poetics of Transgression*. Ithaca, New York: Cornell University Press, 1986.

Starobinski, Jean. *Jean-Jacques Rousseau: Transparency and Obstruction*. Intro. Robert J. Morrissey. Trans. Arthur Goldhammer. Chicago: University of Chicago Press, 1988. Originally *Jean-Jacques Rousseau, la transparence et l'obstacle* (Paris: Plon, 1957). Reprint, with *Sept essais sur Rousseau* (Paris: Gallimard, 1971).

Starr, Peter. *Logics of Failed Revolt: French Theory after May '68*. Stanford: Stanford University Press, 1995.

Stephens, Julie. *Anti-Disciplinary Protest: Sixties Radicalism and Postmodernism*. Cambridge: Cambridge University Press, 1998.

Stivale, Charles J. *The Two-Fold Thought of Deleuze and Guattari: Intersections and Animations*. New York: Guilford Press, 1998.

– ed. *Gilles Deleuze: Key Concepts*. Montreal: McGill-Queen's University Press, 2005.

Sturrock, John, ed. *Structuralism and Since: From Lévi-Strauss to Derrida*. Intro. John Sturrock. Oxford: Oxford University Press, 1979.

Suri, Jeremi. *Power and Protest: Global Revolution and the Rise of Detente*. Cambridge, Massachusetts: Harvard University Press, 2003.

Susong, Gilles. *La Politique d'Orphée*. Paris: Grasset, 1975.

Theweleit, Klaus. *Male Fantasies*. vol. 1, *Women, Floods, Bodies, History*. Foreword Barbara Ehrenreich. vol. 2, *Male Bodies: Psychoanalyzing the White Terror*. Foreword Anson Rabinbach and Jessica Benjamin. Trans. Stephen Conway, with Erica Carter and Chris Turner. Minneapolis: University of Minnesota Press, 1987–89. Originally *Männerphantasien*, 2 vols. (Frankfurt: Verlag Roter Stern, 1977–78).

Tilkin, Françoise. *Quand la folie se racontait: récit et antipsychiatrie*. Amsterdam: Rodopi, 1990.

Tischner, Jozef. *Ethique de Solidarité*. Limoges: Droguet-Ardant, 1983.

Tissot, Olivier de. *La Liberté sexuelle et la loi*. [Paris]: Balland, 1984.

Todorov, Tzvetan. *The Morals of History*. Trans. Alyson Waters. Minneapolis: University of Minnesota Press, 1995. Originally *Les Morales de l'histoire* (Paris: Grasset, 1991).

– *Facing the Extreme: Moral Life in the Concentration Camps*. Trans. Arthur Denner and Abigail Pollak. New York: Henry Holt, 1996. Originally *Face à l'extrême* (Paris: Seuil, 1991).

– *Hope and Memory: Lessons from the Twentieth Century*. Trans. David Bellos. Princeton: Princeton University Press, 2003. Originally *Mémoire du mal: tentation du bien: enquête sur le siècle* (Paris: Robert Laffont, 2000).

Topp, Michael Miller. *Those Without a Country: The Political Culture of Italian American Syndicalists*. Minneapolis: University of Minnesota Press, 2001.

Touraine, Alain. *The May Movement: Revolt and Reform: May 1968 – The Student Rebellion and Workers' Strikes – The Birth of a Social Movement*. Trans. Leonard F.X. Mayhew. New York: Random House, 1971. Originally *Le Mouvement de mai ou le communisme utopique* (Paris: Seuil, 1968; rev. ed. 1972).

– ed. *Mouvements sociaux d'aujourd'hui: acteurs et analystes*. Paris: Editions Ouvrières, 1979.

– *Return of the Actor*. Trans. Myrna Godzich. Minneapolis: University of Minnesota Press, 1988. Originally *Le Retour de l'acteur: essai de sociologie* (Paris: Fayard, 1984).

Trois milliards de pervers: grande encylopédie des homosexualités. Special Issue of *Recherches* 12 (March 1973).

Tsang, Daniel, ed. *The Age Taboo: Gay Male Sexuality, Power, and Consent*. Boston: Alyson Publications, 1981.

Tse-tung, Mao. *Selected Works of Mao Tsetung*. 5 vols. Peking: Foreign Languages Press, 1965.

– *Selected Readings from the Works of Mao Tsetung*. Peking: Foreign Languages Press, 1971.

Turkle, Sherry. *Psychoanalytic Politics: Jacques Lacan and Freud's French Revolution*. London: Free Association Books, 1978; 2nd ed. 1992.

– "French Anti-Psychiatry." In David Ingleby, ed., *Critical Psychiatry: The Politics of Mental Health*. New York: Pantheon, 1980.

Van Kley, Dale K. *The Religious Origins of the French Revolution: From Calvin to the Civil Constitution, 1560–1791*. New Haven: Yale University Press, 1996.

Verdiglione, Armando, ed. *Psicanalisi e politica: Atti del Convegno di studi tenuto a Milano l'8–9 maggio* 1973. Milano: Feltrinelli, 1973.

Verstraeten, Pierre. *Violence et éthique: esquisse d'une critique de la morale dialectique à partir du théâtre politique du Sartre*. Paris: Gallimard, 1972.

Vidal-Naquet, Pierre. *L'Affaire Audin, 1957–1978*. Paris: Minuit, 1958; 2nd rev. ed. 1989.

– *Mémoires*. vol. 2, *Le Trouble et la lumière, 1955–1998*. Paris: Seuil, 1998.

Vigarello, Georges. *A History of Rape: Sexual Violence in France from the Sixteenth to the Twentieth Century*. Trans. Jean Birrell. Cambridge: Polity Press, 2001. Originally *Histoire du viol: e– e siècle* (Paris: Seuil, 1998).

Vimont, Jean-Claude. *La Prison politique en France: genèse d'un monde d'incarcération spécifique e– e siècles*. Paris: Economica, 1993.

Violet, Bernard. *L'Affaire Ben Barka*. Paris: Fayard, 1991.

Vive la révolution! *Changer la vie: document politique*. Kremlin-Bicêtre: 1970, n.p.

Vladimir Jankélévitch. Special Issue of *L'Arc* 75 (1979).

von Tangen Page, Michael. *Prisons, Peace, and Terrorism: Penal Policy in the Reduction of Political Violence in Northern Ireland, Italy, and the Spanish Basque Country, 1968–97*. New York: St Martin's Press, 1998.

Wall, John, William Schweiker, and W. David Hall, eds. *Paul Ricoeur and Contemoprary Moral Thought*. New York: Routledge, 2002.

Weber, Henri. "Reply to Debray." *New Left Review* 115 (May–June 1979).

– *Que reste-t-il de mai 68? essai sur les interprétations des "Evénements."* Paris: Seuil, 1988; 2nd ed. 1998.

Weeks, Jeffrey. *Sexuality and Its Discontents: Meanings, Myths, and Modern Sexualities*. London: Routledge and Kegan Paul, 1985.

White, Edmund. *Genet: A Biography*. New York: Knopf, 1993.

Willhoite, Fred. "Ethology and the Tradition of Political Thought." *Journal of Politics* 33 (1971).

Winock, Michel. *Le Siècle des intellectuels*. Paris: Seuil, 1997; rev. ed. 1999.

Wolfson, Louis. *Le Schizo et les langues*. Foreword Gilles Deleuze. Paris: Gallimard, 1970.

Wood, Philip R. "French Thought under Mitterrand: the Social, Economic and Political Context for the Return of the Subject and Ethics, for the Heidegger Scandal, and for the Demise of the Critical Intellectual." In *Mitterrand II*. Special Issue of *Contemporary French Civilization* 15, no. 2 (summer/fall 1991).

Wormser, Gérard, ed. *Jean-Paul Sartre, violence et éthique*. Lyon: Sens Public, 2005.

Wright, Gordon. *France in Modern Times*. 5th ed. New York: Norton, 1995.

Zola, Emile. *Humanité-vérité-justice: L'Affaire Dreyfus: lettre à la jeunesse*. Paris: Fasquelle, 1897.

Index

Abraham, Henry J., 62
Actes (publication), 69
Adler, Alfred, 135, 372n29
Agence de presse libération (APL), 45, 48–9, 88, 232, 261, 269, 355n2
Agulhon, Maurice, 403n7
AIDS, 17, 219, 304
Algerian War, 25, 62–5, 70, 76, 80–1, 96–7, 101, 140–1, 184, 308, 318, 359n26
Alinsky, Saul, 285
Althusser, Louis, 11, 31, 52–4, 98, 146, 206, 231, 237–8; Althusserianism, 58, 232
anarchism, 26, 29, 53–4, 72, 117, 135, 143, 207, 244, 299
anarchy, 23–4, 182
Anderson, Thomas, 316–18
L'Ange (Jambet and Lardreau), 233, 273, 275–82, 287, 296, 401n19, 402n13; angelism, 246, 259, 277–82, 287, 298
Annales school, 310
antiauthoritarianism, 7–8, 15, 17, 26–7, 29, 31, 36, 53–4, 60, 106, 108, 120, 123, 171, 338–9
Antigone, 301, 402n25
antinomianism, 6–8, 13–15, 17, 36, 106–7, 111, 120, 139, 158, 163–4, 168, 170–3, 222, 228–9, 238–9, 286, 292, 296, 340–2, 350n9, 380n28
Anti-Oedipus (Deleuze and Guattari), 15, 106–7, 110–25, 137–9, 142–3, 145–6, 149, 152–5, 157–172, 174–5, 188, 190, 207, 215, 234, 280, 322, 333, 341; desiring machines in, 106, 112–16, 120–1, 154, 157, 160, 165, 167, 171, 188–9, 210, 228, 341, 346, 368n4; de-territorialization in, 115–16, 122, 165, 167, 267; and ethics, 120–4, 170–3; materialist psychiatry in, 114, 118, 122, 161, 169; reception of, 117–20; schizoanalysis, 15, 116, 121, 123, 161–2, 166, 188; schizzes, 113–16, 140, 165–7, 267
Anti-Oedipalism, 15, 106–7, 111–13, 117–18, 120–3, 125, 137–8, 143, 153, 162, 164, 168–75, 188, 228, 238
anti-psychiatry, 15, 102, 106–11, 123, 128, 131, 136–7, 162, 164, 175, 303, 371n10
anti-Semitism, 293, 310, 314
anti-totalitarianism, 170, 249–52, 274, 307, 352n26
Antoine, Monique, 196–7
Anzieu, Didier, 129
APL. *See* Agence de presse libération
Aragon, Louis, 205, 392n5
Aron, Raymond, 29–30, 32–3, 35–8, 41, 227, 232, 280, 309, 314, 316, 321, 345
Aron, Jean-Paul, 206, 392n13
Artaud, Antonin, 118, 152, 162–4, 166
Association of Families of Prisoners, 83
associations, 17, 32, 39, 62, 69–71, 83, 96, 100, 142, 243, 303, 331, 343–5, 364n70, 381n8, 384n1, 407n13, 407n14
Atelier Populaire, 22
Attali, Jacques, 324, 392n13
Attica, 68, 87
Aubral, François, 234–5, 255
Audin, Maurice, 70, 80; Audin Committee, 70
Audry, Colette, 308

Auger, Colette, 196–7
Augustine, 112; Augustinianism, 257
autonomy, 85, 95, 130, 145, 182, 189, 212, 267, 276, 278, 327, 330, 345, 351n20, 382n7; and universality, 280–7, 315
Avril, Pierre, 29
Axelos, Kostas, 118, 308
Ayme, Jean, 127, 344

Baader-Meinhof group, 99, 319; *See also* terrorism
Bachelard, Gaston, 129
Baden-Baden, 24
Badinter, Elisabeth, 390n5
Badinter, Robert, 69
Badiou, Alain, 146, 336
Balibar, Etienne, 146
Balvet, Paul, 126
barbarism, 235, 238, 244, 252, 255, 281, 283–7, 297–8, 300, 364n4
Barrès, Maurice, 257
Barret-Kriegel, Blandine, 234
Barthes, Roland, 11–12, 205, 237, 394n25
Basaglia, Franco, 108
Baudrillard, Jean, 11, 255, 307, 336, 391n3
Beauvoir, Simone de, 51, 58, 66, 70, 72–3, 205, 314–16, 332, 345
Beckett, Samuel, 163
Belgium, 194–5, 204, 331
Ben Barka, Mehdi, 70, 80, 264, 269
Bénéton, Philippe, 28, 31, 35
Benoist, Alain de, 235
Benoist, Jean-Marie, 231, 233, 235, 288, 392n13, 394n25
Bensaïd, Daniel, 388n15
Bergson, Henri, 114, 144, 154, 160, 257, 311, 376n38, 379n11
Berman, Paul, 26, 51
Berman, Sheri, 407n14
Bernanos, Georges, 257, 264, 270
Bernheim, Cathy, 187, 191, 222–3
Bettati, Mario, 392n13
Bindé, Jérôme, 239
Binswanger, Ludwig, 322
Björk, 114
Black Panthers, 68
Blanchot, Maurice, 163, 262
Blondel, Maurice, 379n11
Bloy, Léon, 399n21
Boltanski, Luc, 336
Bonnafé, Lucien, 127
Bory, Jean-Louis, 205, 392n5
Boudon, Raymond, 29
Boundas, Constantin, 156
Bourdieu, Pierre, 29, 33, 339, 390n5
bourgeoisie, 6, 9, 25, 45–6, 52, 54, 58, 74, 76, 83–4, 90, 99, 102, 179–80, 182, 186, 222, 265, 322, 340, 382n19; family, 6, 83, 112, 114–16, 118, 120, 168, 188, 190, 338, 395; petit-bourgeois, 55, 381n17; *see also* justice
Bourgeois, Denis, 244
Bourseiller, Christophe, 51, 56
Bouscasse, Sylvie, 244
Bouveresse, Jacques, 308–9
Braudel, Fernand, 310
Bredin, Jean-Denis, 247
Brezhnev, Leonid, 77
Brochier, Jean-Jacques, 239, 275
Brover, Maurice, 53
Brownmiller, Susan, 194
Bruay-en-Artois, 99, 273
Buchon, Philippe, 256
Butel, Michel, 231, 392n13
Butler, Judith, 146
Butor, Michel, 3, 391n3

Cahiers de la Gauche prolétarienne (publication), 54, 56
Cahiers prolétariens (publication), 73
Caldaguès, Michel, 184
Calvinism, 258, 398n23
Camus, Albert, 242, 257, 277, 285, 298, 316, 397n20
Canguilhem, Georges, 127
Canto-Sperber, Monique, 335
capitalism, 13, 20, 26, 31–2, 36, 39, 112, 115–16, 143, 166–7, 174, 182, 188, 256, 268, 291, 297–8, 310, 317–18, 341, 268n5, 373n7, 383n7; anti-capitalism, 64
CAPS. *See* Comité d'action des prisonniers
Carroll, Lewis, 152, 162–3
Cartry, Michel, 135
Casamayor (pseud. Serge Fuster), 80
Cassandras (the), 197–8
Cassin, René, 81
Cassou, Jean, 58
Castel, Robert, 84, 109, 138
Castoriadis, Cornelius, 5, 26, 29, 31–2, 35, 39, 234, 344
Castro, Gilbert, 79
Castro, Roland, 68, 182–3, 306
Castroism, 26, 61

Catholicism, 9, 80, 83–4, 90, 109, 204, 257, 259, 264–5, 270, 379n11; Social Catholicism, 14, 80; *see also* Maurice Clavel; *see also* Jansenism
Cavaignac, Louis Eugène, 64
censorship, 9, 47, 65–6, 86, 192, 214, 220, 235, 343, 383n13
Centre Beaubourg, 233–4, 392n13
Centre d'étude, de recherche et de formation institutionnelle (CERFI), 130–2, 134, 142–3, 159, 167, 370n9, 374n20
Cercle socratique, 274, 404n27
CERFI. *See* Centre d'étude, de recherche et de formation institutionnelle
Certeau, Michel de, 7, 28, 35, 234, 403n7
Chaban-Delmas, Jacques, 88, 253
Chaigneau, Hélène, 127
Champ Libre, 85–6
Chanoit, Pierre, 128
Chapelle St Bernard, 81
Châtelet, François, 118–19, 169, 205, 388n15
Chiama, Jean, 243
children, 40, 118, 143, 251, 341; 68-ers as, 27, 29, 295, 333, 391n3; and sexuality, 180, 190, 204–17, 220, 321, 330, 333, 388n11, 389n22, 389n24, 289n29; and violence, 16, 205, 208, 212, 214–15, 217–18, 289n20
China, 52, 91, 251, 358n7; *see also* Maoism
Chirac, Jacques, 61, 198, 253–4, 305, 397n12
Choisir, 197, 345, 384n1
Christianity, 7, 71, 126, 171, 212, 235, 255, 261–2, 270–2, 276–8, 323–4, 328, 338, 379n11, 289n24
Christofferson, Michael Scott, 243, 249–51, 307, 352n26, 395–6n3
Cité Universitaire, 74
civil liberties, 14, 39, 59, 67–8, 78, 101, 395n3
citizenship, 10, 23–4, 33, 35, 39, 41, 46, 63, 72, 92–4, 101–2, 108–10, 179, 252, 285, 294, 303, 333, 337, 343–4, 347, 358n7
Cixous, Hélène, 56, 84, 88
class; children as, 207, 211; exploited, 86, 91, 94; interclass, 84; perverts as, 216; surpassing category of, 84, 120, 182, 228, 255, 343; revolution or conflict, 6, 22, 27, 29, 46, 49, 52–5, 60, 69, 72–4, 78, 86–7, 90–1, 99, 182, 196, 200, 228, 291, 302, 318, 340–1; *see also* bourgeoisie; *see also* working class
Clastres, Pierre, 135
Claudel, Paul, 264
Clavel, Maurice, 16, 29, 51, 58, 81, 88, 232–4, 237, 239, 245–6, 257–9, 261–75, 277, 287–8, 292–4, 297–8, 313, 321, 355n2, 358n6, 358n12, 392n13, 399n4, 399n17, 399n21
Clément, Catherine, 234, 391n3
Clévenot, Michel, 270
Cohen, Olivier, 257
Cohen-Solal, Annie, 318
Cohn-Bendit, Daniel, 3, 20–1, 25, 63, 181, 204
Cold War, 243, 249, 316
Collectif juridique de défense des femmes, 197
Collège de France, 47, 79, 213, 273, 401n6, 401n12
Collomb, Albert, 87
colonialism, 317; anti-colonialism, 317–18, 320
Combes, Émile, 288
Comité d'action pédérastique révolutionnaire, 182
Comité d'action des prisonniers (CAP), 95, 98, 364n70
Comité des intellectuels pour l'Europe des libertés, 307
Comité internationale des mathématiciens, 243
Comité national des écrivains français, 392n5
Comité du 5 janvier pour une Tchécoslovaquie libre et socialiste, 243
Comité de vérité et justice, 273
Comité de vérité de Toul, 46, 49, 88
Comité pour la vérité sur l'affaire Ben Barka, 70
Commentaire (publication), 309
Commission de révision du Code pénal, 206, 214
Committee for Public Safety, 70
Common Program, 253–55, 299, 396n10; *see also* Union of the Left
communism, 9, 12, 24–5, 54–5, 57, 70–1, 75, 126, 130, 135, 140, 170, 231, 243, 249, 254, 292, 315–16, 340; non-communist, 68, 140, 231, 249; *see also* Karl Marx; *see also* Marxism
Communist Party; Czechoslovakian, 360n33; Italian, 316; French. *See* Parti communiste français

Compagnies républicaines de sécurité (CRS), 21, 65, 89
Comte, Auguste, 368n4
Comte-Sponville, André, 331, 336
Conche, Marcel, 331
Confédération française démocratique du travail, 326
Confédération générale du travail, 55
Conseil constitutionnel, 345, 382n19
Conseil national de la vie associative, 345
Conseil d'ordres des médecins, 355n5
conservativism, 9, 120, 180, 219, 258, 269, 334
consumer society, 6, 25, 302
Cooper, David, 108, 174, 214
Copi, 205
Cousin, Victor, 257
Creiser, Jean, 256
Creon, 301
Cressole, Michel, 205
CRS. *See* Compagnies républicaines de sécurité

Dadoun, Roger, 120
Danet, Jean, 206, 214–17
Danton, Georges, 70, 358n7
Daumézon, Georges, 125, 127
Davezies, Robert, 273
Davis, Angela, 68
Le Débat (publication), 309
Debray, Régis, 31–3, 36, 38, 68, 231, 234, 306, 336
Debord, Guy, 11
Debussy, Claude, 312
Défense Active, 69, 358n6
Défense Active (publication), 269
Défense Collective, 358n6
Defert, Daniel, 79–80, 82, 84–5, 90–2, 95, 361n11, 363n51
Dejager Affair, 205–6
Delcourt, Xavier, 234–5, 255
Deleuze, Fanny, 191, 205
Deleuze, Gilles, 191, 205, 362n35, 369n13, 374n1, 376n26, 376n38, 377n1, 379n11, 383n8, 388n15; and Maurice Clavel, 262, 267; as counter-revolutionary, 280; Deleuzean, 296, 368n1; on desire, 106–7, 110–17, 119–23, 150–1, 154, 157–8, 160–3, 165, 167–72, 174–6; on ethics, 106–7, 111–12, 121–4, 145, 149–50, 152–8, 160–2, 171–2, 175, 376n33; on events, 152, 155–6, 158, 160, 162; and fascism, 116, 122, 157, 161, 168–75; and Michel Foucault, 94–5, 240, 322, 368n58, 368n1; and French theory, 11–12, 238, 341; and the GIP, 84, 88, 91–2, 94–5, 122, 365n3; and Félix Guattari, 15, 106–7, 110–25, 138, 140, 144, 153–4, 157–72, 174–6, 179, 188–9, 191, 205, 209–10, 228, 234, 267, 278, 286, 291, 295, 322, 333, 341, 346, 368n1, 368n7, 377n5, 388n13, 392n13; and the Jaubert Commission, 87; and Bernard-Henri Lévy, 295–6, 298; and Maoism, 51; on New Philosophy, 234; on schizophrenia, 15, 106–7, 111–12, 115–24, 152, 157–8, 160–3, 165–8, 170–5; on the "specific intellectual," 48, 84; on Benedict de Spinoza, 15, 107, 114, 123, 145–6, 148–54, 157–8, 160, 165, 240, 367n19; and the Toul prison revolts, 48; and Vincennes, 56, 110, 122, 188; on vitalism, 100, 114, 123, 153–8, 160, 163, 165, 171–2, 175; *see also Anti-Oedipus*; *see also* ethology
democracy, 4, 6, 12, 31–2, 34–6, 39–40, 42, 59, 61, 67, 69, 71–2, 80, 92–3, 95–6, 99–100, 135, 142, 228–9, 253, 255, 294, 333, 345–7; anti-democratic, 34; associational, 71, 345, 407n14; direct, 7, 27, 48–9, 85, 106, 228, 230, 249–50, 294; ethics of, 12, 95; liberal, 39–40, 292; non-democratic, 92; people's, 60, 69, 341, 352n26; self-representation, 7, 15, 83, 85–6, 102
depoliticization, 36–9, 230, 237, 256, 302–3
deradicalization, 9–10, 14, 194, 229–30, 270, 313–14
Derrida, Jacques, 11–12, 33, 206, 313
Desanti, Jean-Toussaint, 392n13
Descartes, René, 149, 295, 298, 346
Descombes, Vincent, 121, 172
Deshayes, Richard, 75, 269
desire, 5, 10, 33, 108, 122, 207, 237, 242, 281, 284–5, 297, 307, 333; and children, 183, 207; ethics of, 16, 175, 222; and fascism, 122, 157, 169–72; and feminism, 200, 220, 238, 278, 283, 287; Foucault on, 122, 207, 323, 325–6; and French theory, 11, 238, 309, 394n27; homosexuality, 188–92, 283; and Institutional Psychotherapy, 130, 132–3, 136–7, 139–41, 143, 341; and law, 113, 234, 277–8;

party of (*désirants*), 34, 107, 109–10, 229, 239–40, 296, 354n27; liberation of, 14–15, 107, 120, 122, 137, 162, 171, 179–82, 207, 220, 222, 240, 267, 278, 287, 323, 326; limits on, 16, 180–1, 222–3, 229, 238, 341; philosophy of, 15–17, 102, 106–7, 109–11, 114, 117, 120, 123, 137, 147, 160, 174, 176, 179, 207, 237–9, 267, 270, 272, 274, 276, 278, 280, 283, 286–7, 295–6, 299; and psychoanalysis, 112–17, 119, 121–22, 161, 168, 188–9, 276–8, 282, 285, 401n11; and schizoanalysis, 15, 111–17, 121–23, 160–5, 167–8, 175–6, 378n9; sexual, 15, 109, 181, 201, 222, 287, 337, 342; Spinoza on, 146–7, 150–1, 154; *see also Anti-Oedipus*
Détective (publication), 220–1; *Détective* Affair, 220–1
Dhavernas, Odile, 201
dialectics, 18, 42, 49, 129, 200, 221, 230, 274, 288, 299, 311, 315, 325, 331, 398n22
dialectical thought, 91, 145, 230, 259, 292, 299
difference; and Gilles Deleuze, 144, 151; French theory, 11, 123; gender and sex, 180–1, 204, 287; Guy Lardreau on, 282–3, 285–7; and liberalism, 298; right to, 35, 282, 286–7
Dionysus, 145, 274, 340
discourse, 49, 69, 135, 142, 198, 202–3, 210–11, 215, 217, 222, 239, 272, 277–8, 287, 322; anti-totalitarian, 249–50; of political criminality, 198, 385n17; ethical, 11, 237; and French theory, 11, 237; of mastery, 256, 277–8; and New Philosophy, 235, 237, 242; pedophiliac, 180, 205–8, 214, 219–20; public, 16, 85, 94, 99, 194, 202, 243; and psychoanalysis, 133, 299, 371n18; revolutionary, 69, 93, 256, 268; of rights, 71, 93, 210, 286; *see also* language; *see also* linguistics
dissidence, 14, 68, 122, 137, 232, 243–4, 249, 252, 256, 259, 285–6, 303, 342; in the Soviet bloc, 16, 143, 233, 243–4, 250, 252, 292, 294, 307
Doctors Without Borders, 12, 303
Dollé, Jean-Paul, 110, 231, 233, 236, 300
Dolto, Françoise, 206
Domenach, Jean-Marie, 4, 7, 9, 29, 80–1, 87, 119, 223, 240–1, 262–3, 300, 336
Donati, Arlette, 111, 159
Donzelot, Jacques, 82, 84, 92, 120, 175, 361n11
Dosse, François, 310–12
Dreyfus Affair, 14, 70–1, 80, 329
Droit, Roger-Pol, 235, 237, 239, 276, 335
Duby, Georges, 403n7
Duchamp, Marcel, 114
Dufau, Sophie, 335
Duméry, Henry, 379n11
Dumont, Louis, 309
Dupin, Eric, 336
Duprat, François, 29
Durkheim, Emile, 344
Dutroux, Marc, 204
Duverger, Maurice, 256
Duvert, Tony, 206–7, 209–10, 387n3

Ecole des Beaux-Arts, 22, 187
Ecole freudienne de Paris, 159, 371n18, 377n1
Ecole normale supérieure, 51, 53, 75, 187, 231, 261, 357n18
Editions Grasset, 231–3, 236
elections, 6, 37–9, 64, 99, 102, 250, 256, 299, 337; legislative, 16, 31, 252–5, 305, 307, 331; and 1968, 3–4, 24–5; presidential, 253; of François Mitterrand (1981), 4, 36, 38, 98, 219, 221, 229, 248, 300, 304–8, 307, 332, 397n12
Elkaïm, Mony, 138
Elkaïm-Sartre, Arlette, 315
Enlightenment, 282, 288, 293, 296, 363n47
enquête. See investigation
épanouissement (opening, flowering), 7, 13, 100, 182–3
epistemology, 33, 112, 237, 240–1, 244, 299, 321, 339; *episteme*, 265–6
eroticism, 109, 133, 171, 174, 184, 190, 207–11, 218, 389n24
ersatz contestation, 6, 10, 38, 59–60, 75, 92, 102, 228–9, 296, 336–7, 346
Eshak, Youri, 195–8, 200–1
Esprit (publication), 4, 80, 84, 90, 262, 309, 311
ethical fascination, 5–7, 10, 17, 107, 231, 245, 301, 308, 331–2, 334, 336, 340, 346
ethical turn, 4–18, 32–4, 37–42, 106–8, 111, 122, 137–8, 145, 153, 155, 158, 170, 228, 230, 233, 237, 244–6, 249, 256, 270, 279–80, 295, 301, 303–5, 310, 321, 330, 335–8, 345–7, 349n1, 349n5, 352n26

ethics, 4–18, 36–40, 50, 60, 71, 102, 106–7, 137, 175–6, 222–3, 228–31, 241, 248–9, 274–5, 300–1, 303–6, 308–15, 331–43, 345–7, 351n20, 352n29, 377n48, 394n27, 403n14, 407n16; and *Anti-Oedipus*, 107, 111–12, 120–5, 137–8, 145, 157, 161–2, 164, 171–2, 175, 238; and Maurice Clavel, 263, 273; and Gilles Deleuze, 94, 123, 145, 149–58, 160, 171, 175–6, 376n33; and Michel Foucault, 94, 107, 111, 121–2, 137, 157, 161, 164, 171–2, 216, 239, 321–30; and André Glucksmann, 289; and the Groupe d'information sur les prisons, 86, 92, 94–5, 102; implicit and explicit, 5–6, 8–11, 16–17, 36, 40, 89–90, 94, 106–7, 112, 137, 172, 222–3, 230–1, 236–7, 240–1, 245, 258–9, 263, 280, 295, 300, 303, 308–9, 314, 321, 323, 330, 337–8, 340–1, 403n14; and Institutional Psychotherapy, 123, 125–6, 131, 136–8, 171, 175, 371n18; and Christian Jambet and Guy Lardreau, 276, 279–81, 285, 287; and Jansenism, 259, 263, 273, 277, 300; and Bernard-Henri Lévy, 295–8; of liberation, 6–8, 10, 34, 36, 340; and New Philosophy, 137, 230–1, 233, 237–8, 240–2, 244–6, 247–8, 252, 257, 263, 299–301, 394n27; political, 9, 12, 32–4, 40, 95, 223, 228–9, 244, 280, 309, 336, 346; and Jean-Paul Sartre, 315–21, 329–30; sexual; 219, 222–3, 304, 324; and Benedict de Spinoza, 146–7, 149–50, 152–5, 157–8, 175–6
ethology, 123, 153, 155–8, 160, 163, 172, 340–2, 377n48
ethos, 50, 60, 137, 139, 146, 228, 238, 247, 329, 352n28, 352n29; antiauthoritarian, 53, 341; antinomian, 7, 14–15, 158, 168, 171–3, 222, 286, 341–2; Foucault on, 325–7; and law, 6–7, 13–17, 106, 111, 120–1, 137, 158, 171, 221, 229, 286, 290–1, 339–42, 352n29; of life, 149, 155–8; of 1968, 17, 27, 39, 53–4, 61, 93, 95, 105, 107, 137, 168, 171, 181, 222, 228–30, 286, 304, 307, 309, 340–2
evil, 145, 151, 185, 240, 245, 259, 281, 284, 297–8, 300, 312, 376n26
Ewald, François, 273, 279, 327, 363n51
existentialism, 46, 117, 127, 135–6, 139, 231, 235, 276, 312–13, 315, 317, 319, 327, 372n33
Ey, Henri, 127

familialism, 15, 106, 112, 114–16, 164, 170–2, 189, 209–10, 212, 215, 366n7
Fanon, Frantz, 127, 318
Fargier, Marie-Odile, 194–6
far left, 14, 25, 34, 45, 49, 57, 64–5, 68–9, 71–2, 78, 95, 97–9, 102, 105, 108, 111, 140, 159, 171, 179–80, 182, 184–5, 193–5, 198–9, 206, 221–2, 227–30, 256, 259, 269–70, 286, 337, 343, 382n21; Italian, 57
fascism, 30, 46, 59, 62, 64, 67, 69, 77, 116, 122, 157, 159, 161, 168–74, 249, 292, 295; anti-fascism, 15, 122, 175; "leftist," 64, 185
Faure, Edgar, 29
Fauré, Gabriel, 312
Faurisson, Robert, 310
Faye, Jean-Pierre, 205, 214
Faye, Marie-Odile, 214–15
Fédération des groupes d'études et de recherches institutionnelles (FGERI), 142
feminism, 15–16, 40, 107, 179–80, 183, 185, 187, 190–204, 206, 212, 214, 216–17, 219–23, 229, 234, 238–9, 278, 280, 287, 338, 341–2, 382n21, 383n16, 384n1, 384n5, 385n16, 386n28; anti-feminism, 193, 200, 221–2, 287; *see also* Mouvement de libération des femmes
Femmes en lutte, 384n5
Ferinot, Jean, 41
Ferry, Luc, 32–3, 35–6, 38, 336
FGERI. *See* Fédération des groupes d'études et de recherches institutionnelles
FHAR. *See* Front homosexuel d'action révolutionnaire
Fichte, Johann Gottlieb, 289–91, 293–5
Fifth Republic. *See* French Republic
Finkielkraut, Alain, 51, 314, 336
First International Congress on Group Therapy, 139
Flins, 56
FLN. *See* Front de libération nationale
Forbidden to forbid. *See* "It is forbidden to forbid"
Foucault, Michel, 11–12, 33, 56, 100, 105, 159, 191, 206, 223, 232, 269, 273, 278, 309, 342, 351n20, 355n5, 360n2, 361n21, 362n39, 363n47, 363n56, 364n65, 368n1, 374n1, 383n8, 388–9n19, 395n40, 401n6; on

Anti-Oedipus, 15, 107, 111, 121–2, 137, 157, 161, 164, 171–2, 174; and Maurice Clavel, 262–3, 265–7, 270–1, 274; *Discipline and Punish*, 84, 96, 239–40, 291, 329, 388n19; and ethics, 5, 17, 304, 321–30, 332; and the Groupe d'information sur les prisons, 14, 46–50, 79–84, 86–94, 96, 98; *The History of Sexuality*, 213–14, 278, 321–3, 329; intergenerational sexuality, 206–7, 210, 213–17, 219; as moralist, 321; and New Philosophy, 237–41, 291, 294, 298; and the "specific intellectual," 48, 84, 94, 102, 328
Fouquet, Pierre, 127
Fouquières-les-Lens. *See* Lens tribunal
Fourier, Charles, 190, 207, 210–211, 388n13
Fourth Republic. *See* French Republic
Franco, Francisco, 77, 127
Frappat, Bruno, 221
freedom, 9, 15, 20, 34, 72, 77, 93, 100, 153, 183, 207, 211, 221, 250, 282, 292, 303, 313, 338; Raymond Aron on, 30, 32; Simone de Beauvoir on, 332; Michel Foucault on, 5, 321, 324, 326–7, 330, 332; liberal-democratic, 20, 36, 39, 59, 64, 66–7, 72, 74, 96, 99, 183; and prison, 91–2, 98; Jean-Paul Sartre on, 46, 184, 315–19, 332; and 1968, 7, 13; and Benedict de Spinoza, 145, 147–8, 153
French Communist Party. *See* Parti communiste français
French Republic, 27, 30, 37–8, 69, 74, 80, 89, 92, 232, 269; Fifth, 7, 14, 29, 36, 41, 60, 62–4, 97, 99, 101–2, 105, 137, 227, 229, 244, 252–3, 296, 337, 396n3; Fourth, 41, 96, 127; Third, 70; *see also* Republicanism
French Revolution, 8, 31, 34, 70, 89, 96, 213, 248–9, 258, 290–1, 295, 309, 320, 332, 344, 349n2, 352n27, 358n7, 363n54, 363n56
French theory, 11–13, 33, 112, 162, 211, 233, 237–8, 240, 244, 256, 265, 274, 281, 286, 312–13, 341, 350n17, 350n18, 351n21, 394n27
Freud, Sigmund, 112–15, 217, 131, 189, 268, 280–3, 309, 333, 402n21; Freudianism, 54, 113–14, 136, 159, 161, 169, 209, 282; post-Freudian, 169
Freudo-Marxism, 126, 136, 181, 241
Friedlander, Judith, 312
Friends of *La Cause du peuple* (The), 66, 71, 78–9, 345
Fromanger, Gérard, 160, 377n5
Front de libération nationale (FLN), 62–3, 71, 76, 140
Front homosexual d'action révolutionnaire (FHAR), 183–4, 186–8, 190–1, 206, 209, 222
Furet, François, 309–10
Furtos, Jean, 120
Fuster, Serge. *See* Casamayor

Gallimard, Robert, 66, 345
Garaudy, Roger, 270
Garde des Sceaux. *See* Minister of Justice
Gargantua, 290–2
Gauche prolétarienne (GP), 14, 45–6, 51, 53–9, 64–7, 71–3, 75, 79–80, 82–3, 85, 87–8, 90–2, 99, 228, 231–2, 269, 273–4, 277, 295, 314, 345, 363n58
Gauchet, Marcel, 37, 309, 311, 403n15
Gaudemar, Antoine de, 391n3
Gaulle, Charles de, 3–4, 21, 23–4, 27, 29, 41, 63–4, 66, 97, 102, 227, 252, 261, 264, 300, 304, 306–7, 399n17; Gaullism, 9, 142, 229, 253, 261, 264–5, 268, 358n21, 399n17; post-Gaullism, 41, 102, 251
Gavi, Philippe, 205, 318
gay liberation. *See* liberation
Geismar, Alain, 53–4, 66, 76, 273, 357n21
gender, 5, 9–10, 15–16, 19–20, 40, 45, 68, 70, 109, 116, 132, 170, 179–223, 230, 253, 283, 286–7, 306, 317, 333, 337, 341–2, 358n6, 381n8, 381n17, 382n21, 384n1, 384n5, 385n16, 390n5
Genet, Jean, 68, 84, 184, 189, 191, 381n13
Gentis, Roger, 127
Germany, 3, 22, 24–5, 57, 168–9, 211, 251, 289–91, 293, 295, 311, 313, 343, 359n13
Giard, Luce, 273
GIP. *See* Groupe d'information sur les prisons
Girard, René, 110, 119, 172, 280, 380n28
GIS. *See* Groupe d'information de santé
Giscard d'Estaing, Valéry, 98, 235, 251, 253–4, 269, 298–300, 304–6, 314, 396n11
GITS. *See* Groupe d'information des travailleurs sociaux
Glucksmann, André, 16, 51, 58, 87, 90–1, 205, 232, 234, 236–7, 239, 241, 245–6,

250, 252, 254–5, 259–60, 262, 273–5, 289–95, 297–8, 313, 392n13, 401n6; *The Master Thinkers*, 232, 234, 260, 289–95
God, 16, 147–8, 150, 152, 154, 158, 258, 261, 265–6, 268–73, 275, 279, 288, 295, 398n23
Goldman, Pierre, 198, 200–1, 310, 385n18
Goldmann, Lucien, 258, 272, 299, 398n22, 402n21
Goodchild, Philip, 157–8, 377n48
Gorz, André, 308
GP. *See* Gauche prolétarienne
Gramsci, Antonio, 247
Grandjean, Michel, 275
Grasset, J.-B., 274
Green, André, 117, 119
Grenelle accords, 23
Grisoni, Dominique, 244
Grosser, Alfred, 331
Groupe d'information sur les asiles, 100
Groupe d'information sur la répression, 100
Groupe d'information de santé (GIS), 100
Groupe d'information et de soutien des travailleurs immigrés, 365n8
Groupe d'information des travailleurs sociaux (GITS), 100–1
Groupe d'information sur les prisons (GIP), 14–15, 46–9, 52, 79–96, 98, 100–2, 105, 122, 228, 230, 239, 281, 294–5, 297, 326, 329, 360n2, 362n39, 363n51, 364n70, 365n8, 365n3, 385n17; formation of, 79–82; investigations of, 81–6; vision of, 89–95
Groupe de libération homosexuel (politique et quotidien), 387n7
Groupe de travail sur la psychothérapie et sociothérapie institutionnelle (GTPSI), 139–40
groupuscules (small groups), 25, 109, 227
Grumbach, Tiennot, 69, 182
GTPSI. *See* Groupe de travail sur la psychothérapie et sociothérapie institutionnelle
Guattari, Félix, 11–12, 138–43, 191, 205, 208, 219, 238, 255, 273, 298, 333, 358n6, 366n7, 367n19, 371n16, 373n7, 383n8, 388n15; and Gilles Deleuze, 15, 106–7, 110–25, 138, 140, 144, 153–4, 157–72, 174–6, 179, 188–9, 209–10, 228, 234, 267, 278, 286, 291, 295, 322, 333, 341, 346, 368n1, 368n7, 377n5, 388n13, 392n13; and Institutional Psychotherapy, 15, 107, 111, 120, 123, 125, 127, 129–31, 138–40, 143, 171, 174–5, 341
Guérin, Daniel, 191, 205–6
Guérin, Michel, 231, 233, 236, 274, 292, 392n13
Gueroult, Martial, 146, 375n11
Guevara, Ernesto Che, 31
Guichard, Jacques, 270
Gulag, 16, 238–9, 249–52, 255, 289, 391n5, 395n3

Habermas, Jürgen, 7
Halbwachs, Maurice, 81
Halbwachs, Pierre, 81, 88
Halimi, Gisèle, 70, 221, 306, 384n1, 389n29
Halter, Marek, 392n13
Hayden, Tom, 306
hedonism, 13, 32, 34, 36–7, 338
Hegel, G.W.F., 148, 150, 154, 171, 289–95, 299; anti-Hegelianism, 145; Hegelianism, 145–6
Heidegger, Martin, 145–6, 310, 332, 352n29, 397n19
Helsinki Accords, 243
Hennig, Jean-Luc, 205
Hertzog, Gilles, 277, 280
heterosexuality, 184, 188–9, 206, 214, 383n8
history; laws of, 7, 13, 228, 340–1; philosophy of, 60, 171, 228–30, 241–2, 286, 307
Hitler, Adolf, 20, 168, 170, 287, 291–2; Hitlerism, 122, 290, 407n14
Hobbes, Thomas, 151, 283, 286, 407n15
Hocquenghem, Guy, 15, 110, 187–93, 198–9, 205–10, 213–18, 222, 283, 286, 383n8, 383n16, 385n17, 388n15, 389n19, 391n3
Hölderlin, Friedrich, 397n19
Holocaust, 17, 289, 310–11, 314
homosexuality, 15, 45, 109–10, 116, 143, 170, 179–92, 199–200, 204–6, 208–9, 215, 219–21, 283, 286–7, 323, 346, 383n8, 383n9, 385n17; dark homosexuality, 15, 187, 189–90, 286;
homophobia, 217; *see also* sex; *see also* sexual; *see also* sexuality
hors la loi. *See* outside the law
Houellebecq, Michel, 333
Hughes, H. Stuart, 26
human (the), 7, 93, 119, 135, 162, 164, 166, 186, 223, 241, 244, 248, 257–9,

265–8, 271–3, 291, 333, 337, 342, 345, 347, 403n13; experience, 284, 291, 317, 321, 333, 343; Guy Lardreau on, 281, 283–4, 286, 401n14; Jean-Paul Sartre on, 317–18, 320–1, 404n42; sciences, 237, 241, 265, 274, 311; Benedict de Spinoza on, 148–50; *see also* rights
humanism, 10, 36, 48, 98, 108–9, 188, 191, 238, 244, 262, 265–6, 268, 309, 315, 317–18, 342, 394n27; anti-humanism, 10, 33, 48, 191, 262–3, 265–6, 288
humanitarianism, 12, 14, 16–17, 38, 71, 230, 303, 306, 334
L'Humanité (publication), 255
humanity, 10, 17, 39, 242, 245, 272, 316, 318, 331, 337, 341–3
Hume, David, 144, 267
hunger strikes, 75–8, 81, 87–8, 98, 360n27
Husak, Gustav, 77, 360n33

idealization, 33, 59, 85, 89, 161, 172, 209, 243, 282, 293, 315–18, 337–8, 347, 373n7, 401n11
immigrants, 45, 54, 56–7, 59–60, 71, 105, 182, 196, 199, 202, 314, 358n6, 365n8
imperialism, 64, 199
individualism, 10, 17, 30–7, 39, 113, 116, 130, 132–3, 140–1, 146–7, 151, 161, 216, 244–5, 264, 266, 271, 283–5, 293, 297, 302–3, 308, 317, 331–3, 343, 346, 381n17; *see also* self; *see also* subjectivity
Ingraham, Barton, 65
Institutional Analysis, 344
Institutional Pedagogy, 344
Institutional Psychotherapy (IP), 15, 107, 111, 120, 123, 125, 128, 130–2, 136–40, 143, 166, 171, 175, 303, 341, 344, 371n10; and Félix Guattari, 129–30; history of, 125–8; and Jean Oury, 127–30, 174–5; and La Borde, 129–37; and liberation, 126, 132, 135–7; and Saint-Alban, 126–7
institutions, 5, 10, 12, 14, 17, 26, 37, 39, 70, 86, 91, 102, 106, 108, 110, 165–6, 191, 200, 208, 219, 228, 291, 330–1, 337, 340, 342–3; and desire, 33, 107, 139, 189, 341; and ethics, 12, 123, 131, 136–8; family as, 114–15; Michel Foucault on, 47, 49, 291, 324, 329–30, 401n6; French meaning of, 17, 303, 343–6; GIP on, 90, 95; Félix Guattari on, 130, 139–43, 160, 164, 172; intermediary, 30, 32, 36, 41, 345; judicial, 60, 70–1, 74, 105, 197–8, 201, 203, 223; penal, 14, 17, 47, 49, 86, 102, 105, 110, 329, 337; political, 86, 99, 106, 221, 253; psychiatric, 15, 17, 80 102, 105, 107, 110, 126, 128, 130–7, 165, 174–5, 337, 341, 371n18; state, 14, 41, 61, 69, 105, 230
intellectual history, 35, 303
intellectual life, 11–13, 33, 37, 39–40, 117, 123, 127, 135–6, 140, 142, 145, 168, 230–1, 233, 235–7, 242, 247–8, 257, 276, 290, 304, 306, 308–12, 328, 332, 335, 342
intellectual politics. *See* politics
intellectuals, 5, 10, 12, 26, 28, 48–9, 51, 66, 69, 73–4, 79, 82, 84–7, 89, 94–5, 99, 140, 236, 243, 245, 249, 254, 264, 269, 298, 301, 307, 318, 324, 328, 337, 350n9, 387n6, 393n18, 397n20; "specific," 48, 84, 94, 102, 328
Interdit d'interdire. *See* "It is forbidden to forbid"
intergenerational relations, 16, 180, 182, 191, 204–9, 212–14, 216–20, 222, 229, 287, 389n24; *see also* sex
International Tribunal of Crimes against Women, 194
intolerable, 14, 17, 49, 86, 89, 93–4, 102, 106, 180, 244, 281, 287, 295, 297, 303, 307, 321, 326, 329, 333, 341, 402n16
investigation (*enquête*), 14, 47–8, 52–3, 70–1, 75, 79, 82, 85–8, 90, 99, 142, 255
IP. *See* Institutional Psychotherapy
Irigaray, Luce, 11, 146, 313, 331
Israel, 66, 315
"It is forbidden to forbid" (*Interdit d'interdire*), 5, 8, 13, 22, 33, 36, 40, 158, 180, 210, 221–2, 290
Italy, 57, 59, 108, 128, 138, 146, 165, 168, 251, 316, 363n47

Jacob, André, 331
J'Accuse (publication), 90
Jaccard, Roland, 117, 368n9
Jackson, George, 68, 86
jails. *See* prisons
Jambet, Christian, 87, 231–3, 236–7, 239, 245–6, 251, 254, 258–9, 273–81, 285–9, 292, 294, 296–7, 299, 313, 392n13, 401n19; *see also L'Ange*; *see also Le Monde*

Jameson, Fredric, 166, 173, 407n16
Jankélévitch, Vladimir, 17, 58, 81, 240–1, 304, 309–13, 331–2, 403n16
Jansenism, 16, 225, 237, 245, 248, 257–9, 263, 270, 272–3, 277, 288, 300, 397–8n20, 398n22, 398n23
Jarry, Alfred, 163
Jaspers, Karl, 166
Jaubert, Alain, 87–90, 93, 269; Jaubert Commission, 87
Jervis, Giovanni, 108, 138
Joffrin, Laurent, 31, 34–6, 39
Jones, Maxwell, 127
jouissance (pleasure, enjoyment), 182, 185, 201, 280
Joyce, James, 163
Judaism, 22, 30, 80–1, 146, 292–4, 311–15, 320, 353n17, 404n44; philo-Semitism, 315
judicial system, 7, 34, 49, 60, 63–4, 67, 69–75, 78, 90–3, 96–7, 99, 101, 105, 120–1, 189, 193–4, 196–7, 199–202, 205, 210, 213, 216, 220, 222–3, 229, 253, 278, 341, 363n51, 36n33; *casier judiciaire*, 47, 87; Cour d'Assises, 194–5, 197, 199, 202, 345; Supreme Court of Appeals (Cour de Cassation), 62, 77; Court of State Security (Cour de Sûreté de l'Etat), 62–3, 66, 73, 98, 305, 357n21; Tribunal correctionel, 194–5; *see also* justice; *see also* law
Judt, Tony, 12–13, 397n20
Julien, Michel, 77
July, Serge, 51, 53–4, 73, 221–2
Juquin, Pierre, 255
justice, 40, 46–50, 68–72, 78–80, 86, 92, 96, 269, 343; criminal system, 14, 47–8, 63, 69, 74–5, 78, 80, 91–2, 94, 99, 189, 193, 198–202, 223; bourgeois, 69, 71, 73, 91, 99, 182, 195–8, 206; class, 69, 74, 78; and feminism, 193–203; popular, 14, 69–75, 78, 90–2, 98–9, 295, 358n21, 358n7; revolutionary, 49–50, 68–70; savage, 69, 195, 198, 385n16; Soviet, 243; "topological," 211, 389n23; *see also* judicial system; *see also* law; *see also* Popular Tribunals
Kafka, Franz, 119, 121, 155, 163, 169
Kant, Immanuel, 7, 144–5, 153, 176, 241, 257, 263, 265–7, 270, 277, 280–3, 285–6, 298–9, 315, 317, 332, 342, 350n9, 351n20, 399n21, 402n21; Kantianism, 33, 153, 266, 281–2, 336, 401n11
Kanters, Robert, 261
Khmer Rouge, 251, 307
Kiejman, Georges, 69, 88
Kierkegaard, Søren, 265–6, 268, 360n9, 372n33, 399n21
Kintzler, Catherine, 255
Klein, Melanie, 113, 127
Koechlin, Philippe, 125, 127
Koestler, Arthur, 251
Koskas, Roger, 195–6, 198, 201–2
Kouchner, Bernard, 205, 391n3, 392n13
Koupernik, Cyrille, 117–18
Kravchenko, Victor, 251
Kremer-Marietti, Angèle, 331
Kristeva, Julia, 11–12, 352n29, 392n13

La Boétie, Etienne de, 118, 169, 172, 292; *see also* voluntary servitude
La Borde clinic, 122–3, 125, 127, 129–40, 142–3, 160, 164, 174, 346, 374n20; and empty speech, 133–5; and ethics, 136–7; and *la grille*, 131–3; history of, 129–37; intellectual crossroads of, 135–6
La Cause du peuple (publication), 53, 65–6, 71, 76, 78–9, 87, 97, 345
Lacan, Jacques, 11, 33, 108, 112–15, 117, 121, 127, 129–30, 133–4, 139–40, 159, 161, 237–8, 267, 272, 277, 279, 282, 285, 351n20, 371n18, 401n14, 401n19, 402n21, 402n25; Lacanianism, 109, 111, 113, 121, 123, 125, 129–30, 132–33, 135, 161, 164, 188, 209, 239, 276, 278, 285–6, 296, 299, 394n25, 401n11, 401n19
Lacroix, Jean, 110
Ladurie, Emmanuel Le Roy, 403n7
Laing, Ronald David, 108, 166
Lang, Jack, 205, 219, 305
Langlois, Denis, 69, 87, 308
language, 74, 112, 119, 138, 160, 167, 170, 242, 259, 269, 295, 310, 345; of ethics, 6, 10, 308, 312, 323, 332–3; empty speech, 130, 133–4; and Foucault, 171, 240, 291, 388n19; opacity of, 11, 162, 172, 238, 297, 309; and New Philosophers, 238, 291, 297, 394n27; post-1968 alternative, 10, 111, 117, 230, 240, 301; and psychoanalysis, 115, 161, 209, 278; of revolution, 6, 15, 42, 67, 72, 93, 248, 299; of rights, 15, 93, 210–11; taking or

freeing up speech (*prendre la parole*), 22, 28, 86, 95, 142, 181–2, 302; *see also* discourse; *see also* linguistics
Lanzmann, Claude, 66
Lapassade, Georges, 191, 205–6, 210, 388n15
Lardreau, Guy, 231–3, 236–7, 239, 245–6, 251, 254, 258–9, 273–89, 294, 296–7, 299, 313, 333, 401n11, 401n19; *see also L'Ange*; *see also Le Monde*
Latin Quarter, 20–2, 42, 227
law, 5, 7–8, 10, 14–16, 36–7, 47, 49–50, 60, 62–3, 69, 71–2, 78, 122, 155, 189–90, 197–8, 201, 213–17, 222, 305, 337, 342, 344–5, 365n8, 383n1, 385n18; Simone de Beauvoir on, 332; bourgeois, 73, 90, 182, 193; criminal, 63, 73, 198, 201, 212–3, 387n4; critique of, 40, 64, 221, 223, 384n1; Michel Foucault on, 91, 223, 325; and feminists, 40, 192–4, 197, 200, 202–3, 221, 238, 384n1; André Glucksmann on, 290–5; group, 141, 382–3n7; "higher," 71, 238; of history, 7, 13, 228, 340–1; Guy Hocquenghem on, 188; and homosexuality, 199; illegality, 65, 74, 93, 345, 382n19; Immanuel Kant on, 145, 153; liberal, 39, 121; and limits, 180, 193, 205, 222; "local," 125, 133, 136–7; and justice, 71, 92, 198; martial, 307; and mastery, 278–9, 290–1, 296; and mores, 221; and nature, 32, 151; and order, 101; people's 73–4, 182; and psychoanalysis, 188–91, 201; reform, 39, 188–9, 206, 213, 215–16, 219; Republican, 16, 57, 62, 81, 137, 180, 189, 193, 213, 229, 234, 238, 333, 342; of revolution, 54; and rights, 39, 69; and sexual violence, 15–16, 180, 197; and sexuality, 204–6, 210, 214–20, 389n29; and state, 15, 17, 32, 54, 63–5, 69, 74, 81, 91, 137, 197–8, 200–1, 219, 221, 229–30, 238, 293, 295, 324, 340–1; subjects of, 210, 327, 329; *see also* antinomianism; *see also* desire; *see also* ethos; *see also* legislation; *see also* outside the law
Lawrence, D.H., 162
Le Bris, Michel, 66, 97, 231, 261, 273, 275, 300
Le Coral Affair, 219
Le Dantec, Jean-Pierre, 53, 65–6, 87, 97, 269, 273, 357n18
Le Goff, Jacques, 403n7
Le Goff, Jean-Pierre, 34–8, 236, 244, 300, 354n27
Le Guillant, Germaine, 127
Lecourt, Dominique, 9, 336, 391n3
Lefebvre, Henri, 26, 234
Lefort, Claude, 26, 29–32, 35, 37, 39–40, 232, 309
Left (the), 11, 16, 22–4, 31, 35, 52, 120, 180, 192, 195–7, 200–1, 219–22, 235–7, 244–5, 249–52, 254–6, 261, 264, 269, 288, 296, 299–300, 304–7, 312, 331, 336, 337–9, 346, 385n18, 396–7n12; ideal-typical, 17, 337–8; independent, 68, 98, 140, 205, 249, 306; intellectual-political, 9, 204, 206, 220, 236, 262, 307, 331, 333, 385n18; libidinal, 229, 267; New, 45, 72, 296, 343; *see also* far left; *see also* leftism
leftism, 4, 14, 20, 34, 47, 49, 55–7, 62, 64, 67–70, 72, 76–7, 98, 101–2, 108–9, 117, 120, 125, 157, 159, 179–81, 184–5, 188, 193–5, 198, 200–1, 205, 220–1, 235, 239, 245, 261, 269–70, 312, 314, 333, 341, 382n21; *see also* far left; *see also* Left
Legendre, Pierre, 296, 392n13
legislation, 40, 214–16, 306; against abortion (1920), 197; Algerian War era, 62–3; *Anti-Casseurs* Law (30 April 1970), 65–6, 69; *Law on Associations of 1901*, 62, 142, 344; Law of 10 January 1936 (against extremist violence), 62; *Law of 1 July 1972* (against hate crimes and racism), 345; mores statutes, 184, 191, 205–6, 217, 221, 303, 305, 387n4; on rape, 194, 202–3, 219; "Security and Liberty" Law (2 February 1981), 98; Veil Law (20 December 1974), 384n1; *see also* law
Leibniz, Gottfried Wilhelm, 149, 152
Leiris, Michel, 66, 205
Lenin, Vladimir Ilyich, 38, 101; Leninism, 182, 338; neo-Leninism, 34, 354n27; *see also* Marxism
Lens tribunal, 72–5, 78, 82, 91, 100
les années soixante-huit ('68 years), 4–5, 13, 17, 28, 35, 39–42, 45, 49, 51, 57–9, 61, 63, 65, 70, 85, 102, 105, 107, 109, 111, 131, 146, 174, 182, 194, 229–30, 242, 252, 259, 273, 306, 311, 318, 328, 332–3, 367n14
lesbianism, 184, 186–7, 191

Lettre ouverte pour la révision du Code pénal (Open Letter for the Revision of the Penal Code), 205–6, 216
Levinas, Emmanuel, 17, 240–1, 275, 304, 309–15, 329, 331–2, 336, 351n20, 403n10; Levinasianism, 319, 336
Levi-Strauss, Claude, 135
Lévy, Benny, 51, 53, 56, 66, 75, 79, 87, 90–1, 273–4, 294, 314–15, 318–21, 329, 404n27, 404n44
Lévy, Bernard-Henri, 16, 231–4, 236–7, 239, 242, 245–6, 250, 254–5, 259–60, 273, 275–6, 280, 289, 313–14, 331, 333, 391n3, 392n13, 394n25; *Barbarism with a Human Face*, 232, 234, 260, 295–6, 402n13
Lévy, Thierry, 201
Lévy, Tony, 53
Lewin, Kurt, 127
liberal professionals, 5, 10, 14, 48, 53–4, 69, 86, 99, 101
liberalism, 12–14, 32–42, 183, 216, 229, 254, 281, 298, 303, 332, 342; neo-liberalism, 12, 35; *see also* democracy
liberation, 8, 13–15, 17, 26–7, 34, 58, 60, 102, 106, 222–3, 240–2, 247, 252, 263, 271, 290, 297, 306, 322, 325–9, 332, 336–7; children, 204–7, 210–11, 220; gay, 109, 116, 170, 179–82, 187, 191, 206, 283, 287; of the mentally ill, 108, 175, 303; sexual, 17, 179–81, 187, 195, 205–7, 210; women's, 16, 109, 116, 170, 179–82, 184, 191, 203, 206, 382; *see also* desire; *see also* ethics; *see also* Institutional Psychotherapy
Liberation. *See* World War II
Libération (publication), 8, 126, 194–202, 205–6, 219–21, 254, 269, 323–4, 335, 355n2
liberty. *See* freedom
Ligue des droits des femmes, 197
Ligue des droits de l'homme et du citoyen, 70
Lindenberg, Daniel, 234, 353n18
linguistics, 127, 131–2, 135, 143, 237; linguistic turn, 162; *see also* language; *see also* discourse
Linhart, Nicole, 75
Linhart, Robert, 75, 87
Lip watch factory, 230
Lipovetsky, Gilles, 32–6, 38, 303, 336
Livrozet, Serge, 364n70, 385n17
Locke, John, 303, 346
Lorenz, Konrad, 155
Lucretius, 118
Lyon, 3, 87, 97–8, 274, 364n70, 385n17
Lyotard, François, 11, 56, 110, 119, 205, 211, 234, 238, 240, 255, 267, 304, 313, 331, 336, 389n23

Macciocchi, Maria-Antonietta, 234, 262
Macey, David, 48, 80
Macherey, Pierre, 146, 155
madness. *See* mental illness
Maggiori, Robert, 8
Maire, Edmond, 326
Malle, Louis, 66
Malraux, André, 29, 261
Manceaux, Michèle, 88, 318
Manent, Pierre, 309
Mannoni, Maud, 109
Marge (publication), 108, 175, 206, 392n13
Le Matin (publication), 202, 255
Mao Tse-tung, 52–3, 242, 251, 277, 286; Maoism, 14, 17, 26, 45–6, 49, 51–61, 66–9, 71–82, 84–5, 87, 90–1, 99, 170, 182, 206, 230–2, 250–1, 256–7, 259, 261, 269, 273, 275–7, 280, 286, 289, 294, 298, 314, 318, 329, 357n18, 361n6, 373n10, 385n17, 399n17, 404n42; and violence, 54–60; *see also* investigation
Marcellin, Raymond, 14, 29, 61–4, 72, 76, 88, 227, 345
March 22nd Movement, 20, 26, 53, 61, 109
Marchais, Georges, 253, 396n12
Marcuse, Herbert, 26, 109, 169, 181, 188, 367n14
Maritain, Jacques, 29
Marx, Karl, 60, 77, 93, 116, 167, 233, 249–50, 268, 280, 286, 289–91, 293–5, 299, 333
Marxism, 3, 6–10, 13, 16, 27, 51–5, 60, 91, 93, 132, 135, 146, 228, 231, 234–5, 237, 241, 247–52, 256–7, 262–3, 265, 268, 270, 280, 290, 294, 296, 298–9, 306, 309, 316–18, 320, 332, 334, 340–1, 343, 394n25; anti-Marxism, 231, 237, 247, 251–2, 276, 288, 298; and Christianity, 270, 272; existential, 135; Freudo-Marxism, 126, 181, 241; Marxism-Leninism, 26, 51, 79, 84, 93, 182–3, 341; Spinozist, 146; *see also* Maoism; *see also* Vladimir Ilyich Lenin
masculinity, 15, 185, 191, 200, 205, 220, 229, 390n3, 390n5; machoism, 187;

misogyny, 184, 192; phallocentrism, 217; phallocratism, 191
Maslow, Abraham, 318
mastery, 95, 148, 209, 235, 242, 254, 256, 266, 277–81, 283–6, 296–7; the Master, 277–9, 281, 284–6, 297; master thinkers, 290–1, 293–5, 304
Matheron, Alexandre, 146
Matzneff, Gabriel, 205–8, 210, 212–13, 220, 333, 387n4, 389n24
Mauriac, Claude, 84, 88–9, 233, 250, 261, 269, 277, 365n3
May 1968, events of, 3–10, 12–42, 45, 49, 51–6, 59, 61, 69, 76, 105–9, 116, 128, 138, 140, 144, 146, 158–60, 168–71, 174–5, 179–82, 188–9, 194, 197, 221–2, 227–32, 234–5, 238–42, 246–7, 249, 251–2, 259–61, 265, 267–9, 273, 277, 285–6, 290, 292, 294–5, 298–9, 301–3, 305–7, 309, 311, 314, 332–3, 336–8, 340–2, 345, 349n1, 349n2, 352n26, 352n29, 396n3; ethos of, 17, 39, 53, 93, 95, 105, 137, 168, 171, 181, 222, 228–9, 286, 307, 309, 342; spirit of 1968, 6, 8, 13, 22, 33, 39, 48–9, 53, 85–6, 106, 131, 158, 170, 194, 228, 238, 260, 332, 338, 340–1, 352n26
media, 3, 16, 35, 45, 66, 73, 86, 98, 118, 143, 194, 231–2, 234–5, 237, 239, 248, 250, 253–4, 259, 261, 263–5, 269, 274, 308, 328, 334, 337, 387n4, 393n18
Mendès-France, Pierre, 24, 69
mental illness, 10, 15, 17, 40, 79, 100, 106–11, 115–18, 122–3, 126–7, 132, 136–7, 140, 158, 162–7, 171, 175, 228, 261, 263, 265, 267–8, 272, 328, 337, 367n11, 371n18, 373n7; *see also* schizophrenia
Merleau-Ponty, Marianne, 88–9
Merleau-Ponty, Maurice, 129, 257, 298
metaphysics, 17, 29, 35, 147, 154, 212, 230, 233–5, 240–2, 247, 252, 260, 266–7, 269, 274, 276–7, 279, 288–9, 293–4, 296–7, 301, 310, 342, 392n7, 394n27
Meunier, Jean-Claude, 273
Mill, John Stuart, 155
Minister, 24, 69; of Culture, 305; of Education, 301; of Finance, 253; of the Interior, 14, 55, 61, 64, 88, 253; of Justice (Garde des Sceaux), 69, 76–7, 81, 87, 97, 102, 252, 335, 355n5; of Sports, 20, 181; Prime, 21, 24, 88, 254, 305
Ministry; of the Armed Forces, 65; of Health, 108, 127; of the Interior, 63, 65; of Justice, 89, 98, 102
Mirabeau, Honoré, 96, 364n1
Mirval, Patrick, 97
Misrahi, Robert, 146–7, 154, 158, 331, 336, 375n17
Missoffe, François, 20, 181
Mitterrand, François 4, 13, 16, 34–5, 69, 98, 219, 221, 229, 231, 248, 253–4, 278, 298, 300, 304–7, 324, 331–2, 350n14, 396–7n12; Mitterrandism, 307, 309, 331
MLF. *See* Mouvement de libération des femmes
modernity, 4, 7, 9–11, 19, 30–1, 39, 64, 76, 96, 99, 101, 115, 125, 146, 166, 168, 219, 229, 248, 257, 262, 265–8, 271, 273, 285, 289–91, 293–5, 298, 303, 321–2, 324, 332–3, 338–40, 351n20, 368n5; modernism, 9, 25, 31, 300, 303
"Mohamed," 185–6, 199–200
Le Monde (Jambet and Lardreau), 280–7
Le Monde (publication), 41, 48, 117–18, 169, 202, 205–6, 220–1, 233, 235, 256, 271, 313
Mongin, Oliver, 34, 311, 332, 342, 403n7, 403n10
Mont Valérin, 58, 269
Montaigne, Michel de, 331
Montand, Yves, 81
moral (the), 7, 9–12, 26–7, 30, 37, 69, 71–2, 80, 82, 93–4, 100, 102, 145, 147, 151, 180, 184, 191, 198, 223, 237, 279–80, 282, 300–1, 304, 306, 308, 315–16, 331–2, 337–8, 340, 344, 407n16; attitude, 281–7, 300, 333; or ethical, 8, 223, 244–5, 247, 308, 310, 339; Michel Foucault on, 321–5, 327–8; panic, 222, 239; philosophy, 145, 310–14, 331, 335–6; relativism, 11, 33, 40, 338; rigorism, 117, 338–9; Jean-Paul Sartre on, 279, 315–18, 321, 329–30, 404n42
moralism, 9, 16, 121, 172, 177, 180, 193–4, 204, 220–3, 288, 300, 315, 336, 338, 346
moralist, 16, 171, 223, 297–9, 301, 316, 321
morality, 6, 9, 16, 43, 150–1, 184, 190, 192, 222, 238, 279–80, 282, 295, 298–9, 308, 315, 318, 322, 327–9, 331, 338–40, 383n7, 401n11

Moreno, Jacob Levy, 127
mores, 9–10, 39, 42, 184, 186, 219, 221, 303, 337, 382n19
Morin, Edgar, 26, 29–32, 35, 39, 331
Morocco, 70, 264
Mounier, Emmanuel, 80
Moutet, Josyane, 196–8, 200
Mouvement d'action judiciaire, 69, 195, 201
Mouvement français pour le planning familial, 381n8
Mouvement démocratique féminin, 181
Mouvement de libération des femmes (MLF), 16, 54, 109, 116, 170, 179–81, 183, 185–7, 190–1, 193, 197, 201, 206, 221, 230, 283, 287, 342, 381n8; *see also* feminism; *see also* liberation
Mouvement jeune révolutionnaire, 181
Mouvement des radicaux de gauche, 253–5
Mozère, Liane, 126, 128
Muldworf, Bernard, 205
Münster, Arno, 164
Mussolini, Benito, 168
Mutualité (meeting hall), 49, 66, 87, 194–5
Mutuelle nationale des étudiants de France, 140

Nancy, Jean-Luc, 331
Napoleon Bonaparte, 290, 295, 349n2
National Assembly, 3, 24, 62, 184, 220, 254, 364n1
National Ethics Committee, 304
Nazism, 4, 21, 46, 48, 56, 126, 145, 157, 169, 250, 298, 332
Negri, Antonio, 138, 146
Nemo, Philippe, 231, 233, 245, 279, 331
neo-liberalism. *See* liberalism
Nerval, Gérard de, 257
New Philosophers, 16–17, 107, 122, 170, 231–42, 244–52, 254–61, 263, 270, 275, 277, 288–9, 295, 299–301, 304, 306–8, 310, 321, 342, 391n3, 394n27, 396n11, 397n19, 397n20, 402n21
New Philosophy, 117, 230, 232–8, 240–1, 244–5, 247–8, 250, 252, 254–7, 259–60, 262, 273, 276, 280, 289, 295, 300–1, 394n27
New Social Movements, 9, 29, 35, 37, 86, 182–3
Newton, Huey, 187, 306
Nietzsche, Friedrich, 120, 123, 144–6, 148, 153–4, 160, 166, 226, 289–91, 293, 295, 309, 330, 332, 341–2; Nietzscheanism, 120, 123, 145, 149, 154, 156–7, 175, 327, 380n28
nihilism, 11, 13, 30, 33–7, 39–40, 95, 222, 259, 265, 267, 288, 302, 321, 330, 332, 338
1968. *See* May 1968
1960s. *See* Sixties (the)
Nizan, Paul, 255
Nobel Prize; in Literature, 243; for Peace, 81, 243, 307
Nogrette, Robert, 98
Nora, Pierre, 403n7
norm, 6–8, 10, 33, 35–6, 106, 111, 156, 181, 188–9, 192, 210, 222, 227, 238, 317–18, 322, 338–40, 346, 406n10; normalcy, 106, 117, 127, 188–9, 207; normativity and normalization, 10, 14–15, 32–3, 36, 40, 92–3, 106, 116–17, 120–1, 137, 151, 165, 167, 172–3, 176, 181, 188–92, 207, 210, 214, 222, 237, 317, 322, 324, 36, 338–40, 351n23
Norris, Christopher, 146
Le Nouvel Observateur (publication), 233, 239, 261–5, 276
Nouvelle résistance populaire (NRP), 56, 58, 64, 72, 81, 98, 231, 357n21
NRP. *See* Nouvelle résistance populaire

OAS. *See* Organisation armée secrète
ontology, 5, 112, 157, 241, 276, 279, 313, 316–7, 322
OPP. *See* Organisation des prisonniers politiques
Oppenheimer, Robert, 94
Opposition gauche, 140, 159
Organisation armée secrète (OAS), 62, 76, 97
Organisation des prisonniers politiques (OPP), 67, 75–9, 82–4, 101
Ory, Pascal, 4
others, 10, 17, 22, 113, 146, 151, 170, 183, 223, 239, 278, 283–4, 286, 311, 313, 317, 319, 324–8, 330–2, 337, 340, 342–3; *see also* subjectivity
Oury, Fernand, 129
Oury, Jean, 127–31, 136, 139–40, 143, 163, 371n18, 372n33, 373n6; on *Anti-Oedipus*, 174–5
outside the law (*hors la loi*), 7, 16, 39, 47, 92, 193, 198, 200–1, 203, 213, 215, 341–2

Overney, Pierre, 98–9, 198

Pantagruel, 292
Panurge, 290, 292, 294
Parti communiste français (PCF), 20, 23–4, 26, 29, 31, 37, 52, 55–8, 71, 140, 206, 235, 237, 248–51, 253–6, 305, 316, 387n7, 395n3, 396–7n12
Parti socialiste (PS), 23–4, 31, 34, 37, 231, 237, 248, 250, 253–5, 296, 298, 305, 308, 396n9, 396n10, 396–7n12
Parti socialiste unifié, 23–4
Pascal, Blaise, 4, 257–8, 265–6, 270–3, 279, 286, 295, 299, 397n20, 399n21, 407n15; Pascalian, 259, 270, 272–3, 279, 285, 288, 299
Pascal, René, 251
Passeron, Jean-Claude, 29, 84
Patton, Paul, 156–8, 377n48
Paugam, Jacques, 233
Paul-Lévy, Françoise, 231, 233
PCF. *See* Parti communiste français
pedagogy, 129, 143, 204–5, 208–13, 344, 387n24
pederasty. *See* intergenerational relations
pedophilia. *See* intergenerational relations
penal system, 14, 47, 49, 63, 69, 88–9, 96–8, 189, 193, 197–8, 200, 206, 213–14, 216–17, 219, 303, 305, 329, 341, 387n4, 390n6; Penal Code, 63, 89, 198, 206, 213–14, 217, 219, 303, 387n4; *see also* prisons
Perelman, Chaïm, 331
Perrot, Michelle, 403n7
pessimism, 239–42, 247, 256–9, 271–3, 282, 288, 296–9, 306
petits commerçants (small business owners), 56, 66
Peyrefitte, Alain, 98, 252, 301
Pharo, Patrick, 244–5, 300
phenomenology, 32, 127, 313, 315, 329, 379n11, 401n11
Piao, Lin, 251
Picq, Françoise, 185–6, 193, 202, 221
Pingaud, Bernard, 255
Pivot, Bernard, 236
Plato, 112, 257, 274, 293; Platonism, 191, 211
pleb, 246, 289, 292, 294
Pleven, René, 76, 81, 87–9, 97, 361n11
Poe, Edgar Allan, 139
Polack, Jean-Claude, 126–7, 135
Poland, 17, 243, 307, 325–6; *see also* Solidarity movement
police, 14, 20–3, 27, 45, 49, 55–7, 59, 61–7, 69, 71–5, 78, 81, 87, 89, 92, 101, 105, 137, 167, 184, 187, 191, 200–1, 207–8, 230, 242, 253, 269, 294, 341, 343
political (the), 9, 17, 26, 38, 40, 54, 235, 245, 354, 256, 261, 281, 284–5, 307, 309, 331, 346–7; problematization of, 9, 38, 309
political regime (prisons), 63, 75–7, 81, 97, 268, 359n26, 361n11; *see also* prisoners
politics, 5, 6, 9, 12–17, 26, 28, 32–5, 37, 40, 55, 68, 72, 98, 109, 118, 120, 127, 129, 151, 166–70, 182–90, 196–201, 207, 211, 223–30, 234, 237–65, 272, 281–91, 298–346; electoral, 6, 37–8, 248, 250, 252, 256, 299, 307, 331, 337; intellectual, 10, 13, 118, 233–4, 245, 249, 263, 307, 332; progressive, 53, 75, 98, 118, 180, 193, 219, 221, 288, 297; revolutionary, 4, 6, 8–9, 12, 17, 26, 37–8, 40, 110, 167, 228, 235, 241, 245, 254, 256, 261, 281, 284–5, 307, 309, 331, 336, 346–7; *see also* depoliticization
Politzer, Georges, 257
Pompidou, Georges, 21, 24, 29, 63–5, 101, 227, 251–3, 269, 306, 333, 363n38
Poncin, Claude, 131
Popular Front, 62, 126, 129, 253, 305
popular justice. *See* justice; *see also* Popular Tribunals
Popular Tribunals, 70, 72–5, 78, 82, 90–1, 358n7, 359n13, 385n17
pornography, 180, 184, 201, 205, 217
Portuguese revolution (1975), 249, 251
postmodernism, 11, 17, 35, 267, 304, 350n17, 351n20
poststructuralism, 11, 144, 308, 351n20, 394n27
Poujadisme, 56, 298
Poulantzas, Nikos, 234, 391n3, 392n13
Prague, 68
Prévost, Claude, 387n19
prisons, 5, 10, 14–15, 17, 21–2, 45–50, 54, 59–60, 65–9, 72, 75–94, 96–102, 105, 110, 122, 180, 196–9, 202, 205, 228, 303, 319, 321, 329, 337, 341, 345–6, 357n20, 360n2, 362n39, 363n47, 385n17, 385n18, 390n6; Bastille, 76, 96, 105; Fleury-Mérogis, 86, 88, 97; La Santé, 81, 83, 97, 102, 357n18, 361n21;

Toul, 45–9, 84, 87–8, 97, 102, 105, 355n5, 404n42
prisoners, 14, 22, 40, 45–50, 59–60, 63, 68–9, 71–2, 75–9, 81–99, 102, 228, 286, 297, 341, 358n6, 359n26, 363n56; common law, 75–7, 79, 82–3, 91, 363n56; political, 63, 75–9, 81–2, 359n26, 361n11
proletariat, 31, 54–5, 77, 90, 99, 101, 227, 280, 287, 296, 322, 340; lumpenproletariat, 77, 91, 294
Proust, Marcel, 144, 162
PS. *See* Parti socialiste
psychiatry, 5, 10, 15, 17, 48, 83–4, 86, 88, 100–2, 105–11, 114, 117–20, 122, 125–30, 134–9, 141–3, 161–2, 165–9, 189, 214, 216, 228, 243, 264, 303, 337, 341, 344–6; *see also* anti-psychiatry
psychoanalysis, 15, 106, 108–14, 116–20, 123, 125–6, 129–36, 139, 141, 143, 146, 159–62, 166–71, 188–9, 210, 239, 277, 282, 284, 286, 296, 299, 341, 352n29, 402n25; critique of, 109, 113, 159, 239, 296, 341, 378n8; Oedipal complex, 112, 114–15, 145, 165, 170, 188–92, 207, 341, 366n7; *see also* familialism
public sphere, 9, 67, 84, 188, 229, 337

Quaduppani, Serge, 235
Querrien, Anne, 205, 358n6

Rabelais, François, 290
Rabinow, Paul, 94, 328
race, 9, 166, 184–5, 195–6, 199–200, 382n21; racism, 166, 185, 199, 345
radicalism, 4, 9, 16, 23–5, 27, 32, 34–5, 39–40, 46, 49, 52, 55, 59, 65, 67–9, 71–2, 75, 84–6, 91–3, 95–6, 102, 105–7, 123, 135, 157, 179, 182, 185, 198, 220–2, 244, 247–50, 264, 268–9, 273, 278, 294, 302, 306–7, 327, 336, 341, 346, 350n14, 383n16, 384n1, 385n16; *see also* deradicalization
Raguenes, Jean, 273
Rajsfus, Maurice, 64
Rancière, Danielle, 80–5, 87, 90, 93
Rancière, Jacques, 79, 84, 146, 234
rape, 99, 183, 193–203, 206–8, 212–17, 219–21, 223, 239, 287, 291, 345; Aix-en-Provence trial (1978), 194, 202–3, 215; *see also* sexual violence
"Rape" Commission of the 18th Arrondissement, 197
Rassemblement pour la République, 254
Reagan, Ronald, 219, 306
rebellion, 14, 29, 35, 45, 51, 62, 64, 77, 87, 106, 121–2, 137, 190, 199, 235, 237–9, 241–4, 252, 256, 259–60, 276–80, 285–6, 289, 296–8, 307, 338; ethics of, 280, 297; the Rebel, 277–9, 281, 285–6
recuperation, 8, 159, 181, 190, 194, 200, 221, 229, 242, 276, 278, 296
reformism, 4, 6, 17, 23, 27, 29, 31, 37, 39, 42, 61, 65, 84–5, 89–90, 94–8, 102, 105, 108, 118, 126, 159, 180, 188–91, 194, 197, 204–6, 212–17, 229, 243, 247–8, 296, 299, 302–3, 305, 307, 343, 363n47, 381n8, 387n4
Reich, Wilhelm, 109, 122, 169, 172, 181, 195, 367n14, 388n11
religion, 6, 9–11, 16, 26, 80, 118–19, 152, 179, 213, 222, 240, 243, 246, 248, 259, 262, 266–7, 270, 272, 274, 279, 298–9, 301, 310, 313–14, 324, 331–2, 334, 338, 340, 342, 355n5
Renault factory, 23, 99
Renault, Alain, 32–3, 35–6, 38
Republic. *See* French Republic
Républicains indépendants, 253–4
Republicanism, 8, 10, 16, 26, 38, 57, 61–2, 80, 96, 189, 193, 195, 213, 229–30, 234, 238, 303, 307, 309–10, 333, 342; anti-Republicanism, 64
Réseau alternative – la psychiatrie, 138
resistance, 17, 46, 56, 58–60, 69, 72, 77, 120, 126, 131–3, 238–9, 244, 252, 258–9, 264, 277, 281, 285, 287, 289–90, 292, 294–5, 297–8, 315, 341, 395n40
Resistance (French). *See* World War II
Revel, Jacques, 403n7
revolt, 3–4, 6, 15, 17, 23, 26, 29–31, 35–7, 45–9, 85–9, 91, 94, 97–8, 105–6, 108–9, 111, 120, 123, 139, 168, 182, 186, 242, 245, 272, 279 287, 290, 294, 312, 340–1, 385n17
revolution, 4, 6–10, 12–17, 22–3, 25–8, 30–2, 34–42, 45, 48, 51, 53–61, 63–72, 74, 76, 83–5, 89–91, 93–4, 96, 99, 101, 105–6, 108–12, 116–17, 121, 135, 142, 147, 159, 161, 163–71, 179–83, 185, 187–8, 191, 193–4, 197, 199, 206, 211, 213, 220, 222, 227–30, 237, 240–2, 244–8, 256, 258–9, 261–2, 267–9,

271–4, 276–7, 279–81, 286, 289–91, 294–6, 299, 302, 305, 307, 309, 316, 318, 320–1, 323, 329, 332–3, 336–7, 340–6, 382n19, 383n7, 384n1, 385n17, 395n32; *see also* French Revolution
revolutionary justice. *See* justice
Ribaillier, Brigitte, 195–6, 200–2
Ribardière, Diane, 250–1
Ricoeur, Paul, 17, 241, 304, 309–11, 332, 336, 403n10, 403n11, 403n13
Right (the), 11, 17, 20, 25, 55–6, 62, 96–7, 180, 198, 231, 235, 249–50, 253–5, 269, 299, 305, 337–9, 359n26, 397n12; New Right, 235
rights; and children, 210–11; Declaration of the Rights of Man and Citizen, 93, 352n27, 364n65; democratic, 96; to difference, 35, 282, 286–7; divine, 344; equality of, 34; of excluded, 271; and feminism, 193; foreigners', 345; Michel Foucault on, 323, 328; human, 5, 17, 35, 38, 40, 71, 81, 99, 234, 238, 243–4, 246, 250, 286, 300, 306–7, 309, 332, 334, 342–3; Kantian, 286, 336; to know, 81, 92–3; language of, 15, 93, 210–11, 286; and law, 47, 69, 71, 92; liberal; 32, 38–9, 65, 72; of man, 93, 234, 245–6, 276–7, 280–2, 286; natural, 151; and popular justice, 74; and power, 151; of prisoners, 47–8, 76–7, 86–7, 92–3, 97; to repress, 170; reproductive, 100, 183, 193, 219, 221, 383n1; Republican, 96; and revolution, 15, 72, 93; to speak, 52, 221; student; 181; and sexuality, 183, 185, 187; United Nations Declaration on Human Rights, 81
Rimbaud, Arthur, 182
Ringart, Nadja, 185–6
Riss, Christian, 269, 274
Robbe-Grillet, Alain, 206
Roche, Denis, 254
Rochefort, Christiane, 205, 392n5
Rolin, Olivier, 53, 56, 274, 356n16
Rosanvallon, Pierre, 37, 309
Rose, Edith, 48, 84, 88, 94, 105, 355n5, 363n50
Ross, Kristin, 12–13
Rousseau, Jean-Jacques, 209, 280, 284, 296, 299, 333, 402n21; Rousseauean, 63, 211, 286
Rousset, David, 250
Roussillon, René, 120
Roussopoulos, Paul, 200–1
Royer, Jean, 184, 253, 269
rue d'Ulm. *See* Ecole normale supérieure
Russell, Bertrand, 70–1
Russell International War Crimes Tribunal, 70, 73, 359n13

Sabourin, Danielle, 126–7, 135
Sacher-Masoch, Leopold von, 144, 162
sadism, 157, 208, 212; sado-masochism, 191–2
Saint Francis de Sales, 172
Saint-Alban clinic, 126–8
Saint-Just, Louis de, 344, 346
Sakharov, Andrei, 243, 307
Salvaresi, Elisabeth, 200
Sarraute, Nathalie, 3
Sartre, Jean-Paul, 191, 205, 279, 308, 334, 382n19, 392n5; and ethics, 5, 17, 315–21, 328–32; and Michel Foucault, 46, 48–50, 74, 80, 88–9, 94, 304, 309, 325, 328–30, 332; and Félix Guattari, 129, 136, 139, 142; and Emmanuel Levinas, 313–14; and Benny Lévy, 273, 314–15; and Maoism, 51, 56, 58, 66, 68, 71, 73, 80, 184, 269, 345; and 1968, 26, 32; and popular justice, 71, 73–4; and prisons, 46, 48–50, 76, 88–9, 356–7n20, 404n42; and Russell Tribunal, 70–1, 73; and Secours rouge, 71; violence, 99–100, 308, 318–21, 329, 356n19
Saumery clinic, 128–9
Savio, Mario, 242
Schelling, F.W.J., 311
Schérer, René, 189, 205–11, 213, 219–20, 234, 388n13, 388n15, 388–9n20, 389n22
Schiavo, Jean, 53, 274
schizoanalysis. *See Anti-Oedipus*
schizophrenia, 106–7, 111–12, 115–18, 120, 122–4, 137, 140, 142, 152, 157–8, 160–8, 170–5, 190, 267, 280, 303, 341, 373n7
Schleiermacher, Friedrich, 264
Schmelck, Robert, 88; Schmelck Commission, 88
Schopenhauer, Arthur, 343
Schrift, Alan D., 146
Schwartz, Laurent, 70, 308
Sebag, Lucien, 135
Secours populaire, 71
Secours rouge (publication), 269
Secours rouge (SR), 67, 71–6, 78–9, 81–4, 87, 92, 101, 269

Secours rouge international, 71
self, 10, 17, 172, 238, 282–3, 285, 311, 313, 319, 324–8, 330, 337, 342–3; *see also* individualism; *see also*, subjectivity
self-criticism (*autocritique*), 53, 55, 75
self-management (*autogestion*), 7, 37, 85, 131, 135, 231
self-representation. *See* direct democracy
Serge, Victor, 251
Serres, Michel, 56, 391n3
Setti, Lakdhadar, 202–3
Sève, Lucien, 336
sexual liberation. *See* liberation
sex, 5, 10, 174, 180–2, 187, 189–91, 205–10, 213–16, 219, 229, 251, 267, 278, 334, 337; and children, 16, 180, 182–4, 187, 190, 204–14, 216–20, 222, 229, 287, 321, 330, 386n1, 389n22, 389n24, 389n29; *see also* intergenerational relations
sexual; ethics, 219, 222, 304, 324; liberation, 17, 179–81, 187, 195, 205–7, 210; misery, 195–6, 223; politics, 179–80, 204, 207, 213, 221, 223, 228, 234, 238, 305; relations, 16, 114, 116, 180, 204, 208, 278, 287, 401n14; revolution, 15, 109, 179–82, 185, 188, 191, 222, 267, 342; violence, 15–16, 180, 195–6, 198, 200–2, 206, 214–15, 220, 222, 229, 234, 238, 278, 287; *see also* rape; *see also* liberation
sexuality, 9, 15–16, 20, 40, 172, 179–84, 190–2, 194, 204, 206–9, 216, 219, 278, 287, 202, 321–2, 327–8, 338, 342, 381n8, 382n21; history of, 213–14, 278, 321, 323, 326, 329; and law, 214–16, 219, 289n21; reproductive, 15, 100, 183, 189, 193, 207, 214, 383n8; *see also* homosexuality
Shaw, George Bernard, 98
Signoret, Simone, 81
Situationist International, 26, 109
Sixties (the), 10, 12–13, 17, 26, 28, 33, 38, 40, 109, 242, 309, 336–9, 345, 349n1, 350n9
Smith, Daniel, 153
Socialisme ou Barbarie, 26, 29, 257
socialism, 24, 31, 235, 250, 297–8, 305, 316, 331, 373n7; *see also* Parti socialiste
Société des gens de lettres de France, 3
Société de psychothérapie institutionnelle (SPI), 139–40, 159
Socrates, 94, 176, 209, 212, 272, 274–5, 292–4; inscientia, 274, 292–3
Solat, Michèle, 197
Solidarity movement (Poland), 17, 304, 307, 325
Sollers, Philippe, 205, 237, 262, 264, 267–8, 270, 272, 274, 392n13, 394n25
Solzhenitsyn, Alexandr, 16, 232, 243, 249–52, 257, 270, 392n5
Sommier, Isabelle, 57–60, 65, 99
Sorbonne, 13, 19–22, 27, 63, 81, 129, 140, 146, 182, 227, 311, 448n16; *see also* universities
SOS Femmes, 197
SOS Racisme, 331
Soulet, Jean-François, 243
Souriau, Etienne, 308
Soviet Union, 16, 68, 70–1, 233, 238, 243, 247, 249–51, 292, 294, 307, 316
SPI. *See* Société de psychothérapie institutionnelle
Spinoza, Benedict de, 15, 107, 124, 144–54, 157–8, 160, 170, 240, 257, 283, 346, 367n19, 374n1, 374n4, 375n6; revival, 146–8; Spinozism, 114, 123, 145–50, 149, 152–5, 157–8, 160 165, 171, 175–6, 299, 375n11, 375n17; Spinozist Marxism, 146
special regime (prisons). *See* political regime
SR. *See* Secours rouge
Stalin, Joseph, 243, 250, 287, 289, 292; Stalinism, 26, 170, 243, 251, 257, 298, 316; anti-Stalinism, 251
statism, 64, 245, 257, 299, 342; anti-statism, 257, 293, 299–300, 303; extra- or supra-statism, 14, 70–1, 230, 238, 303, 342
Steinem, Gloria, 306
Stéphane, André, 29
Stoicism, 123, 152, 324, 376n33
Storti, Martine, 202, 205
Strasbourg, 26
structuralism, 11–12, 127, 135–6, 139, 235, 237, 240–1, 274, 281, 308, 310–11, 332
students, 3–4, 19–27, 29, 31, 35, 41, 45, 51–6, 61, 63, 65, 68, 70, 101, 118, 128–9, 140–1, 146, 158, 181, 195, 209, 227, 232, 237, 268–9, 286, 306, 311–12
subjectivity, 109, 113, 120, 143; decentred, 303, 342; Michel Foucault on, 322–9; group, 139, 141–2, 189; humanist, 244; intersubjectivity, 14, 34, 106, 133, 137,

157, 164, 284, 319; legal-juridical, 210, 286, 291, 329; Emmanuel Levinas on, 313; and literature, 162; and mastery, 284–6; modern rational, 266–7; nomadic, 116, 120; and psychoanalysis, 113, 133, 165; religious, 264, 266; Jean-Jacques Rousseau on, 284; and structuralism, 237, 332; *see also* individualism; *see also* self
Susong, Gilles, 231, 233
Syndicat de la magistrature, 69
Syndicat des médecins des hôpitaux psychiatriques, 127
Szasz, Thomas, 108

Talmudic, 313–4
Tanguely, Jean, 165
Tautin, Gilles, 56
Témoignage chrétien (publication), 72
terrorism, 30, 57, 59, 62–3, 99, 227, 249, 251, 269, 318, 320, 334; the Terror, 70
Thatcher, Margaret, 219
Théâtre de l'Odéon, 22, 27
Thélème abbey, 290–2, 294
theocentrism, 264
Third Republic. *See* French Republic
tiers-mondisme (Third World-ism), 25, 231
Tocqueville, Alexis de, 29, 38, 96, 303, 333, 347; Tocquevillean moment, 38, 209
Todorov, Tzvetan, 336
toleration, 190, 213, 215, 338
Tosquelles, François, 127–8, 130
totalitarianism, 37, 64, 170, 223, 231, 238, 247, 249–50, 262, 292, 297–8, 309; anti-totalitarianism, 170, 249–52, 274, 307, 352n26
Touchard, Jean, 28, 31, 35
Toul prison. *See* prisons
Touraine, Alain, 29, 86, 182, 238, 390n5
Tournier, Michel, 162
Tours, 184, 269
Tout! (publication), 183–7, 191, 199, 206, 208, 381n17
Tramoni, Jean-Antoine, 198
transversality, 139–43, 159–60, 163–4, 209
Trente glorieuses, 25
Trilling, Lionel, 7
Trotskyism, 26, 34, 57, 61, 72, 129–30, 135 140–1, 187, 205, 251, 373n10
Truffaut, François, 66
Truth and Justice Commissions, 70
Turkle, Sherry, 108, 111, 175

UJC(ml). *See* Union des jeunesses communistes marxistes-léninistes
Union des démocrates pour la République, 253
Union des étudiants communistes, 140, 373n10
Union des jeunesses communistes marxistes-léninistes (UJC(ml)), 51–3, 55, 58, 373n10
Union of the Left, 31, 37, 237, 248, 250, 252–6, 296, 299, 305, 396n10, 396n12; *see also* Common Program
unions, 4, 21–6, 30, 45, 53, 55, 59, 69, 127, 140, 182, 255, 305, 322, 326, 344–5
United States, 25, 27–8, 37, 68, 70, 81, 87, 96, 108, 127, 180, 194, 204, 242, 292, 311, 334, 337, 343–5, 354n27, 362n39, 390n3, 390n5
universalism, 11, 39, 80, 152, 180, 210, 230, 238, 252, 280–7, 312, 315, 323, 329, 337, 342, 368n1, 384n1
universities, 3, 5, 20–1, 25–6, 29–30, 35, 54, 61–2, 86, 105, 144, 146, 181, 227, 255; of Antony, 352n1; of California at Berkeley, 242; of Nanterre, 19–20, 26, 28, 53, 181, 311; of Paris, 19–20, 110; of Vincennes, 49, 56, 78, 118, 122, 188, 195, 208–9; of Zagreb, 129; *See also* Sorbonne
utopianism, 7–8, 10, 27–8, 89, 181, 183, 211, 222, 282, 290, 299, 302, 306; non-utopianism, 126, 136

vacuole, 125, 134, 136–7, 141
Van Kley, Dale K., 258, 398n23
Vercors, 392n5
Verdun, 293
Vernier, Jean-Claude, 53
Verny, Françoise, 231, 236
Verstraeten, Pierre, 308
Veyne, Paul, 403n7
Vézelay, 273–5, 399n4
Viansson-Ponté, Pierre, 41, 250
Vichy, 26, 80, 126, 168, 311; *see also* World War II
Vidal-Naquet, Pierre, 80–1, 308, 361n6
Vietnam War, 20, 25, 27, 52, 61–2, 70–1, 251, 289, 292, 294
Vietnamese "boat people," 307
Vilna, 313
Vincent, Jean-Marie, 205, 234

violence, 3, 5, 10, 14–17, 21, 23, 26, 30, 38, 45, 47, 49–51, 54–62, 64–5, 68, 70, 78, 87, 91–2, 96–7, 99, 105, 156, 180, 194–8, 200, 202, 205–6, 208, 212, 214–15, 217–18, 220, 222–3, 227–9, 234, 238, 252, 269, 278, 283, 287, 289, 308, 310, 318–21, 329, 337, 340, 356n19, 385n16, 387n4, 389n29; *see also* sexual violence
vitalism, 114, 123, 153–8, 160, 163, 165, 171–2, 175
Vive la révolution (VLR), 182, 185, 187
VLR. *See* Vive la révolution
Voie communiste, 140
Voltaire, 66, 299
voluntary servitude, 118, 122, 169–70, 285, 292, 307
Von Trier, Lars, 114
Vovelle, Michel, 403n7

Weber, Henri, 34, 36, 39, 388n15
Weber, Max, 64
Weil, Simone, 264
Weimar Republic, 407n14
Weisz, Bernard, 235
Wittgenstein, Ludwig, 112, 308
Wolfson, Louis, 162–3
Wolin, Richard, 175
women's liberation movement. *See* Mouvement de libération des femmes; *see* liberation
workerism, 6, 27, 53, 296, 341
working class, 20, 24, 27, 58–9, 294, 317, 322
World War I, 293, 349n2
World War II, 9, 76, 108, 126, 168–9, 189, 249, 264, 311, 315, 349n2, 358n8; Occupation, 4, 56, 64–5, 81, 125; Liberation, 26, 70, 169; Resistance, 58, 64, 71, 76, 80, 126–7, 249, 261, 269, 311, 395n40, 399n17; *see also* Vichy

Zancarini, Jean-Claude, 53
Zecca, Marine, 214
Zourabichvili, François, 155–6